"Brexit is not only a matter involving the United Kingdom and the European Union. It also has far reaching external implications which this timely collection explores. The Handbook is a welcome contribution to the study of the multifaceted consequences of a state's withdrawal from the EU."

Christophe Hillion, *University of Oslo, Norway, and Leiden University, the Netherlands*

"This research handbook offers the most comprehensive overview to date of the legal implications of Brexit from the perspective of EU external relations law and international law. While much has been written on the internal consequences of Brexit, for the UK and the EU – and as the parties engage in complex negotiations on the framework of their future relations – this edited collection sheds light on the effects that Brexit poses for international treaties and international organizations, identifying the challenges and the options ahead."

Federico Fabbrini, *Founding Director of the Brexit Institute, Dublin City University, Ireland*

"Now that the United Kingdom has exited the European Union, its relations with many of its trading partners will be regulated by an unfamiliar mix of Union and international law. This timely volume seeks to bring some order into what might otherwise look like chaos, learning the lessons of the withdrawal procedure itself and identifying a variety of topics that will require the urgent attention of politicians and lawyers in the coming years. It is a must for any Brexit library."

Kieran Bradley, *Former Special Brexit Adviser to the EU Court of Justice*

The Routledge Handbook on the International Dimension of Brexit

This handbook provides comprehensive and expert analysis of the impact of the Brexit process and the withdrawal of the United Kingdom from the European Union on existing and future EU–UK relations within the context of both EU and international law.

Examining the wider international law implications, it additionally assesses the complex legal consequences of Brexit for both the EU and the UK in their dealings with third states and other international organizations. With contributions from renowned specialists in the field of EU external action, each chapter will analyse specific policy areas to address key challenges arising from the Brexit process for the EU and the UK and propose solutions to overcome these problems. The handbook aims to fill a gap in research by assessing the consequences of Brexit under EU external relations law and international law. As such, it is hoped it will set the research agenda for coming years on the international dimension of Brexit.

The Routledge Handbook on the International Dimension of Brexit is an authoritative and essential reference text for scholars and students of international and European/EU law and policy, EU politics, and British politics and Brexit, as well as of key relevance to legal practitioners involved in Brexit, governments, policy-makers, civil society organizations, think tanks, practitioners, national parliaments and the Court of Justice.

Juan Santos Vara is Professor of Public International Law and European Law, Jean Monnet Chair in EU External Action, and Coordinator of the European Joint Master's in Strategic Border Management (Frontex) at the University of Salamanca, Spain.

Ramses A. Wessel is Professor of European Law at the University of Groningen, the Netherlands. He is also Vice-President of the European Society of International Law (ESIL) and co-founder of the Centre for the Law of EU External Relations (CLEER) in The Hague.

Polly R. Polak is PhD candidate in EU law funded by the Regional Government of Castille and Leon, University of Salamanca, Spain, where she also lectures in EU Law and International Relations and coordinates the Master's degree in EU Studies.

Routledge International Handbooks

Routledge Handbook of Street Culture
Edited by Jeffrey Ian Ross

The Routledge International Handbook of Simmel Studies
Edited by Gregor Fitzi

Routledge Handbook of Counter-Narratives
Edited by Klarissa Lueg and Marianne Wolff Lundholt

Routledge Handbook of Art, Science, and Technology Studies
Edited by Hannah Star Rogers, Megan K. Halpern, Kathryn de Ridder-Vignone, and Dehlia Hannah

Routledge Handbook of Bounded Rationality
Edited by Riccardo Viale

Routledge International Handbook of Charisma
Edited by José Pedro Zúquete

Routledge International Handbook of Working-Class Studies
Edited by Michele Fazio, Christie Launius, and Tim Strangleman

Routledge Handbook of Digital Media and Communication
Edited by Leah A. Lievrouw and Brian D. Loader

Routledge International Handbook of Religion in Global Society
Edited by Jayeel Cornelio, François Gauthier, Tuomas Martikainen and Linda Woodhead

The Routledge Handbook on the International Dimension of Brexit
Edited by Juan Santos Vara and Ramses A. Wessel; Associate Editor, Polly R. Polak

The Routledge Handbook of Critical Finance Studies
Edited by Christian Borch and Robert Wosnitzer

For more information about this series, please visit: www.routledge.com/Routledge-International-Handbooks/book-series/RIHAND

The Routledge Handbook on the International Dimension of Brexit

Edited by Juan Santos Vara and Ramses A. Wessel

ASSOCIATE EDITOR
POLLY R. POLAK

Routledge
Taylor & Francis Group
LONDON AND NEW YORK

First published 2021
by Routledge
2 Park Square, Milton Park, Abingdon, Oxon OX14 4RN

and by Routledge
52 Vanderbilt Avenue, New York, NY 10017

Routledge is an imprint of the Taylor & Francis Group, an informa business

British Library Cataloguing-in-Publication Data
A catalogue record for this book is available from the British Library

Library of Congress Cataloging-in-Publication Data
Names: Santos Vara, Juan, editor. | Wessel, Ramses A., editor. |
Polak, Polly R., editor.
Title: The Routledge handbook on the international dimension of Brexit /
edited by Juan Santos Vara and Ramses A. Wessel ; assistant editor,
Polly R. Polak.
Other titles: Handbook on the international dimension of Brexit
Description: Abingdon, Oxon ; New York, NY : Routledge, 2021. |
Series: Routledge international handbooks | Includes bibliographical references
and index.
Identifiers: LCCN 2020024096 (print) | LCCN 2020024097 (ebook) |
ISBN 9780367434069 (hardback) | ISBN 9781003002970 (ebook)
Subjects: LCSH: European Union–Great Britain. | Great Britain–Foreign
economic relations–European Union countries. | European Union
countries–Foreign economic relations–Great Britain. | Great Britain–Foreign relations–
European Union countries. | European Union countries–Foreign relations–
Great Britain. | European cooperation.
Classification: LCC HC240.25.G7 R679 2021 (print) | LCC HC240.25.G7
(ebook) | DDC 341.242/20941–dc23
LC record available at https://lccn.loc.gov/2020024096
LC ebook record available at https://lccn.loc.gov/2020024097

ISBN: 978-0-367-43406-9 (hbk)
ISBN: 978-1-003-00297-0 (ebk)

Typeset in Bembo
by Wearset Ltd, Boldon, Tyne and Wear

Contents

Contributors

Chloé Brière is Professor of European Law and Post-Doctoral Researcher funded by the Belgian National Fund for Research (FRS-FNRS) at the Université libre de Bruxelles. Her PhD obtained in 2016 addressed the external dimension of the EU's policy against trafficking in human beings. She now conducts research on the EU's external relations law, including in criminal matters. Her research interests also include EU criminal law and free movement of persons. Her recent publications include an article on the primacy of EU law as a source of the EU's duty to respect human rights abroad (in CLEER Paper 2020/1 with A. Navarsatian), or a contribution on the cooperation of Europol and Eurojust with external partners (in H. Hofmann, E. Vos, and M. Chamon (eds), *The External Dimension of EU Agencies and Bodies*, Edward Elgar 2019).

Fernando Castillo de la Torre is Director-Principal Legal Adviser in the Legal Service of the European Commission, where he has been working since 1996 in the teams for internal market, competition, external relations and currently heads the team for agriculture, fisheries and animal and plant health. He studied both law and political science in Madrid (Spain), graduating in 1989 and 1990 respectively. He subsequently undertook postgraduate studies at the College of Europe in Bruges (Belgium). He worked in the chambers of the President of the European Court of Justice between 1997 and 2002. He has been agent for the European Commission in more than 450 cases in the European Court of Justice. He has given numerous lectures and has published widely on the relationship between legal orders (international, EU and national), the external relations of the EU, judicial review and litigation before EU Courts, competition law and the internal market.

Adam Cygan is a Professor of EU law at the University of Leicester and currently a principal investigator on an ESRC Brexit Priority Grant "Parties, Parliament and the Brexit Process". His research looks at the work of national parliaments in EU law and in particular how the UK Parliament has interacted with the EU legislative process. His current ESRC research is examining the implementation of Brexit by the UK Parliament and how the UK Parliament is adapting to its future relationship with the EU as a third country. Central to this research is looking at how Parliament will address questions of regulatory governance after Brexit, especially in the field of trade policy.

Wybe Th. Douma is senior legal adviser at the Dutch Ministry of Social Affairs and Employment, voluntary researcher at the Department of European, Public and International Law, Ghent University and independent legal expert at EU Legal. He is co-founder and board member of the Centre for the Law of EU External Relations (CLEER), co-founder and editor of the European Environmental Law website, contributor to various legal journals and fellow at the Centre for International Legal Cooperation (CILC). He frequently publishes and teaches on international trade law, various aspects of EU law and environmental law. Recent publications include "Investor–State Dispute Settlement in EU Trade Agreements in the Light of EU Policy and Law" in M. Andenas, L. Pantaleo, M. Happold and C. Contartese (eds), *EU External Action in International Economic Law* (Asser Press 2020) and "The Limits to Precaution in International Trade Law: From WTO Law to EU Trade Agreements" in L. Squintani, J. Darpö, L. Lavrysen and P.-T. Stoll (eds), *Managing Facts and Feelings in Environmental Governance* (Edward Elgar 2019).

Peter Van Elsuwege is Professor of EU law and Jean Monnet Chair at Ghent University, where he is co-director of the Ghent European Law Institute (GELI). He is also visiting professor at the College of Europe (Natolin Campus) and board member of the Centre for the Law of EU External Relations (CLEER) at the Asser Institute in The Hague. His research activities essentially focus on the law of EU external relations, with a particular interest in the legal framework of the relations between the EU and its East European neighbours. He is, amongst others, the author of *From Soviet Republics to EU Member States: A Legal and Political Assessment of the Baltic States' Accession to the EU* (Brill 2008) and the editor (together with R. Petrov) of the books *Legislative Approximation and Application of EU Law in the Eastern Neighbourhood of the European Union: Towards a Common Regulatory Space?* (Routledge 2014) and *Post-Soviet Constitutions and Challenges of Regional Integration* (Routledge 2018). In addition, he has published extensively in leading law journals such as *Common Market Law Review*, *European Law Review*, *European Constitutional Law Review* and others.

Elaine Fahey is Jean Monnet Chair of Law and Transatlantic Relations and Professor of Law at the Institute for the Study of European Law (ISEL), the City Law School, City, University of London. In 2020, she was a Visiting Fellow at the Department of Law, EUI, Florence (sabbatical leave). She was an Emile Noël Fellow at New York University (NYU) Law School and a visiting professor at Keio University Law School, Tokyo, Japan in 2017–2018. She is an editor of the Routledge UACES series. Her publications include a monograph, *The Global Reach of EU Law* (Routledge 2016) and the edited volumes *Framing Convergence with the Global Legal Order: The EU and the World* (Hart 2020), *On Brexit: Law, Justices and Injustices* (Edward Elgar 2019), *Framing the Subjects and Objects of EU law* (Edward Elgar 2017), *The Actors of Postnational Rule-Making: Conceptual Challenges of European and International Law* (Routledge 2015), *A Transatlantic Community of Law* (Cambridge University Press 2014), *Institutionalisation Beyond the Nation State* (Springer 2018) and the textbook, *An Introduction to Law & Global Governance* (Edward Elgar 2018).

Teresa Fajardo is Associate Professor in the Department of International Law and International Relations in Granada University where she teaches Public International Law at the Faculty of Law and International and European Environmental Law at the Science Faculty. She read law at Granada and Poitiers Universities and the Licence Spéciale en Droit Européen at the Institut d'Etudes Européennes at the Université Libre de Bruxelles. In her thesis, she explored the EU External Action in the field of Environmental Protection. She has spent stages at the Legal Service of the European Commission and has been a visiting researcher at the universities of Brussels, Geneva, King's College London and Cambridge. Her research fields are international and European environmental law, EU migration law and policy, and soft law. She is engaged in several inter-university and EU projects and initiatives relating to international and European environmental law.

Paula García Andrade is Associate Professor of Public International law and European Union law of the Faculty of Law (ICADE) of the Universidad Pontificia Comillas, Madrid. Her research activities focus on EU external relations law, particularly regarding questions of competence and institutional balance, as well as on the external dimension of EU immigration and asylum law. Her recent publications include "The EU Accession to the Geneva Convention Relating to the Status of Refugees: Legal Feasibility and Added Value" (2019) 23 *SYbIL*; "EU External Competences on Migration: Which Role for Mixed Agreements" in S. Carrera, J. Santos Vara and T. Strik (eds), *Constitutionalising the External Dimensions of EU Migration Policies in Times of Crisis Legality, Rule of Law and Fundamental Rights Reconsidered* (Edward Elgar Publishing 2019); and "EU External Competences on Migration: How to Act Externally When Thinking Internally" (2018) 55(1) *Common Market Law Review*. She regularly collaborates with the teaching and research activities of the Odysseus academic network for legal studies on immigration and asylum. She is Associate Editor of *European Papers* and member of the Editorial Board of the *Revista de Derecho Comunitario Europeo*.

Mauro Gatti is Assistant Professor of EU Law at the University of Bologna. Formerly lecturer at The Hague University of Applied Sciences, postdoc at the University of Luxembourg, and visiting lecturer at the University of Verona and the European Law and Governance School (Athens). His areas of interest include EU foreign affairs law, human rights law and disaster response law. Publications include *European External Action Service* (Brill/Nijhoff 2016) and *Constitutional Issues of EU External Relations Law* (Nomos 2018, with Eleftheria Neframi).

Panos Koutrakos is Professor of EU Law and Jean Monnet Professor of EU Law at City, University of London. He is the author of, amongst others, *EU International Relations Law*, 2nd edition (Hart Publishing 2015) and *The EU Common Security and Defence Policy* (Oxford University Press 2013). He has edited various collections of essays (his latest is *Research Handbook on the Common Foreign and Security Policy of the European Union* (with S. Blockmans) (Edward Elgar Publishing 2018). He is the joint editor of *European Law Review*.

Adam Łazowski is a Professor of EU law at the Westminster Law School, University of Westminster. His research focuses on EU pre-accession policy, EU external relations, internal market, EU criminal law as well as withdrawal from the EU. On the latter topic he has published extensively in academic journals (*European Law Review*, *Common Market Law Review*, *Public Law*, *Journal of European Public Policy*) and edited volumes (Oxford University Press and Cambridge University Press). His monograph on legal parameters of EU exit is forthcoming in 2020 (Edward Elgar Publishing). He serves in editorial boards of *New Journal of European Criminal Law*, *European Papers* and *Croatian Yearbook of European Law and Policy*. In November 2012, he provided oral and written evidence to the House of Lords EU Select Committee (enquiry into the EU Enlargements) and, in December 2015, provided oral and written evidence to the Scottish Parliament (enquiry into withdrawal from the EU).

Tobias Lock is Professor of Law at the National University of Ireland, Maynooth. He has published widely on Brexit and is the EU constitutional law adviser to the Culture, Tourism, Europe and External Relations Committee of the Scottish Parliament. He received a British Academy Rising Star Engagement Award in 2018 for his Brexit work. He also works on EU fundamental rights law and served as a member of the Scottish First Minister's Advisory Group on Human Rights Leadership. He is a contributor – mainly on fundamental rights – to the *The EU Treaties and the Charter of Fundamental Rights*, M. Kellerbauer, M. Klamert and J. Tomkin (eds) (Oxford University Press 2019) and recently published an article in the *Common Market Law Review* on rights and principles in the EU Charter

Scarlett McArdle is a Senior Lecturer in Law at the University of Lincoln. Her research interests lie in the field of international responsibility, EU external relations, common security and defence policy, and international institutions. A recent publication is "CSDP and the Development of the 'Global EU': The Progress of EU in the Shadow of Brexit" (2020) 4(1) *Europe in the World.*

Gregory Messenger is Senior Lecturer in Law at the University of Liverpool, UK where he teaches world trade law and constitutional law. He is a trade law and policy specialist with research interests principally in world trade law (multilateral and regional) and its interface with key policy areas including public health, sustainable development, industrial strategy and dispute settlement. Since October 2018 he has been a UK Research Council (AHRC/ESRC) funded Knowledge Exchange Fellow in the Foreign and Commonwealth Office working on trade issues. Prior to joining the University of Liverpool, he was a Junior Research Fellow at Queen's College, University of Oxford where he also completed his doctoral studies. He is a Member (British Branch) of the International Law Association Committee on Sustainable Development and the Green Economy in International Trade Law, and has published widely on trade law, including his book *The Development of World Trade Organization Law: Examining Change in International Law* (Oxford University Press 2016).

Jed Odermatt is a lecturer at the City Law School, City, University of London where he is convenor of the International Law and Affairs Group (ILAG) and member of the Institute for the Study of European Laws (ISEL). His research interests include public international law, the law of international organizations and the law of EU external relations. His recent work has focused on the international law dimension of Brexit. He is the editor (with R.A. Wessel) of *Research Handbook on the European Union and International Organizations* (Edward Elgar 2019).

Andrea Ott is a Professor of EU External Relations Law at the Law Faculty of Maastricht University. Since 2011 she has held a Jean Monnet Chair in EU law and is member of the CLEER board at the Asser Institute in The Hague. She is a member of the Editorial Board of the CLEER Papers series and the *Maastricht Journal of European and Comparative Law.* Her research and publications focus on EU external relations issues and differentiated integration in the EU.

Polly R. Polak is a PhD candidate in EU law funded by the Regional Government of Castille and Leon at the University of Salamanca (Spain) where she also lectures in EU Law and International Relations and coordinates the Master's Degree in European Union Studies. Her thesis concerns the legal regime of withdrawal from the EU in light of Brexit and will be defended in 2021. She has carried out a three-month research stay at Queen Mary University of London under a SRUK/CERU mobility grant. She also received a Yuste Charles V Award grant. A recent publication is "Brexit and the Balance of Free Movement and Social Justice" in E. Fahey and T. Ahmed (eds), *On Brexit: Law, Justices and Injustices* (Edward Elgar 2019) and previous experience includes an internship with Spanish Advocate General Manuel Campos at the Court of Justice of the EU and Research Assistant to Philippe De Bruycker at the Odysseus academic network for legal studies on immigration and asylum (ULB).

Sara Poli is full Professor of European Law at the University of Pisa (Italy). Previously, she worked at the Universities of Rome "Tor Vergata", of Trieste and of Southampton. She has taught at the College of Europe (Bruges) where she also received the Diploma of the Master of Legal Studies. She obtained her PhD at the Scuola Superiore di Studi Universitari and perfezionamento S. Anna (Pisa) where she also did her undergraduate studies. She has received a number of grants such as the DAAD short term research grants, the Jean Monnet Chair, the Marie Curie Fellowship, the Fulbright–Schuman fellowship, the Vlac fellowship of the Royal academy of Belgium for science and the arts, the Robert Schuman fellowship (European University Institute) and a three-year grant from the Italian Ministry of University and the University of Trieste. She has published on different areas of EU law in national and international journals; in recent years, she has focused her research on EU external relations. Her latest book is dedicated to the EU autonomous restrictive measures (2019).

Juan Santos Vara is Professor of Public International Law and European Law, Jean Monnet Chair in EU External Action, Coordinator of the European Joint Master's in Strategic Border Management (Frontex) at the University of Salamanca. He is co-editor and one of the founders of *European Papers: a Journal on Law and Integration*. He has recently co-edited the following books: *The Democratization of EU International Relations Trough EU Law* (Routledge 2019) and *Constitutionalising the External Dimensions of EU Migration Policies in Times of Crisis: Legality, Rule of Law* and *Fundamental Rights Reconsidered* (Edward Elgar Publishing 2019). His research activities focus on the law of EU external relations and migration, asylum and border management policies.

Agnieszka Stobiecka-Kuik is a member of the Legal Service of the European Commission since 2003 (State Aid Team, Anti-dumping/Anti-Subsidy Team and for the past three years coordinates LS MARE Team). She is currently contributing to the internal and interinstitutional consultation process on various legislative proposals related mainly to fisheries, regularly deals with questions concerning international negotiations in this field as well as acts as an agent for the Commission in over 140 court cases in a variety of sectors, ranging from agriculture, asylum to Art. 19 TEU. She obtained a law degree from the University of Poznan, and is a Cambridge British Law Centre alumni. She served as a President of the International Board of ELSA, holds an LLM degree from KU Leuven, was a trainee in the Court of First Instance as well as a Fulbright research scholar at Columbia University. She is a speaker and lecturer on EU law at conferences and summer schools, and has published a number of articles related to her field of expertise. She is active in the Commission's Citizens dialog, Back to school and Back to university initiatives in her home country, Poland.

Viktor Szép is Junior Research Fellow at the Institute for Legal Studies, Centre for Social Sciences, MTA Centre of Excellence and Assistant Lecturer at the Faculty of Social Sciences, Eötvös Lorand University (ELTE). He is also a PhD candidate in EU law. His thesis focuses the EU's sanctions imposed against Russia. A recent publication is "New Intergovernmentalism Meets EU Sanctions Policy: The European Council Orchestrates the Restrictive Measures Imposed Against Russia" (2019) *Journal of European Integration*.

Allan F. Tatham, called as a barrister (Gray's Inn) in 1992, was invited to Hungary and lectured at the law faculties of ELTE University and later of Péter Pázmány Catholic University, subsequently becoming an adjunct professor. In addition, he worked at the Hungarian Constitutional Court and later as legal adviser at the Delegation of the European Commission to Hungary in the lead up to accession. He has lectured widely on EU law for over 25 years, particularly in Central and Eastern Europe and published extensively on EU enlargement and law harmonization as well as, more recently, on withdrawal from the Union. Since 2011, he has been lecturing in EU law, international law and international relations at the Faculty of Law, Universidad CEU San Pablo, Madrid, where he currently researches into international and regional courts.

Ramses A. Wessel is Professor of European Law at the University of Groningen, the Netherlands. He is Vice-President of the European Society of International Law (ESIL) and co-founder of the Centre for the Law of EU External Relations (CLEER) in The Hague. He is editor-in-chief and founder of the *International Organizations Law Review* and of the *Netherlands Yearbook of International Law*; editor of *European Papers* and of *Nijhoff Studies in European Union Law* and member of the Editorial Board of the *CLEER Papers* series and of *Europe and the World*. He has published widely on issues of international and European institutional law. Recent books include *EU External Relations Law: Text, Cases and Materials* (Hart 2020); and *Research Handbook on the European Union in International Organizations* (Edward Elgar 2019).

Jan Wouters is Full Professor of International Law and International Organizations, Jean Monnet Chair ad personam European Union and Global Governance, Director of the Institute for International Law and of the Leuven Centre for Global Governance Studies (both a Jean Monnet Centre of Excellence and a University Centre of Excellence) at KU Leuven, and President of the University's Board for International Policy. He is Adjunct Professor at Columbia University (New York) and Visiting Professor at Sciences Po (Paris), LUISS (Rome) and the College of Europe (Bruges). A Member of the Belgian Royal Academy and Of Counsel at Linklaters, Brussels, he has published widely on international and EU law, international organizations and global governance, and corporate and financial law, including more than 70 books, 150 journal articles and 240 chapters in international books. He is Coordinator of a large Horizon 2020 Project, RECONNECT (Reconnecting Europe with its Citizens through Democracy and Rule of Law). He advises and regularly trains international organizations and governments, and is often asked to comment on international events in the media. In 2020 he was Visiting Professor at Université Paris2, Paris, and at Queen Mary University, London.

Ewa Żelazna is a lecturer at the University of Leicester's Law School. She was a visiting research fellow at the Max Planck Institute for Comparative Public Law and International Law in Heidelberg and the Asser Institute in The Hague. She worked at the Investment Treaty Forum of the British Institute of International and Comparative Law and completed an internship at the CJEU, with Judge Christopher Vajda. Her main research interests are in the fields of EU constitutional law, EU external relations and international investment law. In 2018, she has completed a PhD entitled "The EU Investment Policy after the Treaty Lisbon 2009: An Institutional Perspective".

Acknowledgements

This book was conceived in the framework of the Jean Monnet Chair in EU External Action at the University of Salamanca (574677-EPP-1-2016-1-ES-EPPJMO-CHAIR).

With the support of the
Erasmus+ Programme
of the European Union

1

The implications of Brexit for EU and UK external relations

An introduction

Juan Santos Vara, Ramses A. Wessel and Polly R. Polak

1.1 Introduction

This handbook comes at a crucial moment in time. It was finalized on Europe Day, exactly 70 years after Robert Schuman underlined the need for 'a united Europe'.[1] At the same time, that same Europe is confronted with the withdrawal of one of its Member States. Schuman argued that 'Europe will not be made all at once, or according to a single plan. It will be built through concrete achievements which first create a de facto solidarity.' These days, European solidarity is challenged and, indeed, has not proven capable of keeping all Member States on board. With his 'realisation of the first concrete foundation of a European federation indispensable to the preservation of peace', Schuman could not have predicted some Member States would end up seeing close European cooperation as something standing in the way of their own national and global ambitions.[2]

At the time of writing, no decisions have been taken on the final shape and form of the agreement (or agreements) governing the future relationship between the EU and the UK. The Withdrawal Agreement (WA), that established the terms of the UK's orderly withdrawal from the EU, entered into force on 1 February 2020.[3] The WA regulates the transition period, keeping the UK outside the EU institutional framework, while still fully applying EU law. The end of the transition is foreseen on 31 December 2020, with a possibility of a single extension, either for one or two years. The UK and the EU have also adopted the Revised Political Declaration of 17 October 2019 setting out the framework for the future relationship between the EU and the UK.[4] Both parties committed to establishing an ambitious partnership that reflects the political and geographical proximity and economic inter-dependence between the EU and the UK. The Political Declaration should serve as a point of departure of the negotiations, but it does not predict with any certainty, let alone reveal, the outcome of the negotiation process.

Negotiations between both parties started in March 2020 and are today ongoing, thus they cannot serve either to fully anticipate the future relations between the EU and the UK. The EU has always expressed its willingness to maintain close ties and develop a comprehensive framework for the future relationship.[5] This position is reflected in the 'Draft text of the Agreement on the New Partnership with the United Kingdom' of March 2020 published by the Commission at the beginning of the negotiations. It covers all areas of the negotiations including trade and economic cooperation, law enforcement and judicial cooperation in criminal matters, participation in Union programmes and other thematic areas of cooperation.[6] However, the UK does not seem to share this position. The UK Government considers that the negotiations should be focused on reaching a trade agreement following the Canada-style free trade agreement (FTA) and that cooperation in areas beyond trade should be covered in separate agreements.[7]

The implications of the future arrangements reach beyond the relationship between the EU and the UK and have a clear international dimension. The EU's external relations have developed over time and EU competences in this area have not only increased in number but also in nature and scope. In many areas the EU has been in the lead in international negotiations and conclusion of international agreements, either because of an existing exclusive competence (e.g. in trade) or because of existing expertise and the wish to act as a cohesive force (e.g. climate). This has obvious consequences not only for the EU but for the UK now it is no longer a Member State. Brexit implies that the international legal position of the UK will have to be reset and certain dimensions of its statehood will have to be reactivated. In practical terms, it will no longer be able to rely on the EU's expertise in international trade (including in the World Trade Organization, WTO) and it will have to seriously upgrade its own delegations in international organizations in which it was mainly active as an EU member.[8] In other words, in many international settings the UK will have to face the reality of a major shift, that is, the transition from an EU to a non-EU state. This, *inter alia*, entails that the UK has to negotiate a large number of international agreements, including – or perhaps above all – the so-called 'EU only' agreements to which the Member States are not a party in their own right. The EU treaty database currently lists over 1100 international agreements concluded by the EU and/or Euratom with countries around the world, ranging from trade and economic issues to human rights and the environment.[9] As shown in some contributions to this book, simply 'rolling over' these agreements is not always possible, for instance because third states may aim for a better deal than the one they had with the EU.[10]

Apart from the new international relations the UK will have to enter into and certain adaptations the EU will have to make in some of its current relations with third states and international organizations, the relationship between the EU and the UK will also be governed by international law. Indeed, while one could argue that the origin of the WA is to be found in EU law – as it was concluded between the EU and a (leaving) Member State – any future arrangement finds its basis in international (treaty) law. Brexit thus became a question of international law when the UK became a third state. As such, the former member is no longer part of defining the EU's external relations but has turned into a target of this policy. Whatever the scope and depths of the new relationship, it will be international in nature while EU law will continue to apply to the UK only on the basis of its voluntary acceptance.

1.2 Aim of the book

The international dimension of Brexit runs the risk of being overshadowed by assessing the new EU–UK relations from the perspective of EU law only. This book aims at filling a gap in the literature by performing a comprehensive assessment of the consequences of Brexit under EU external relations law and international law. As indicated above, Brexit is not only relevant for internal EU policies, but also has important implications for the relationship between the EU and the UK with other states and international organizations. The objective of this book is to analyse the applicable rules of both EU and international law in relation to the withdrawal of the UK from the EU. EU and international law not only framed the withdrawal itself, but will also regulate the future relations between the EU and the UK. Rather than looking back on the process, this volume takes a future perspective and addresses key challenges arising from the Brexit process for the EU and the UK.

Ever since the notification of the UK's intention to withdraw from the EU, legal scholarship has pointed to a variety of complex legal problems. While the focus has clearly been on the ways in which the UK could remain connected to the EU, the consequences for the EU's (and the UK's) external relations regime are equally complex. Both EU external relations law and international law have something to say about the problems that still need to be solved and the ones that can be expected on the basis of the new arrangements.

Our aim is to examine different scenarios and offer new avenues to develop the relations between the EU and the UK and with regards to other international actors. This book thus intends to make a substantial contribution to the academic state of the art on the future relationship between both parties as well as assess the legal consequences of Brexit for them in their dealings with third states and other international organizations. Its future oriented perspective allows the book to be relevant for the post-Brexit period, offering guidance and proposing solutions to the future challenges that are now emerging alongside the formation of the future relationship between the EU and the UK.

1.3 Structure of the book

The following 22 chapters of this volume provide a comprehensive study of Brexit focusing on the future relationship between the EU and UK and the wider international law implications. This introduction does not aim to summarize all of them. It has a more modest ambition of presenting the major objectives of the different contributions. The handbook presents novel perspectives on the future relationship between the EU and UK and on the impact Brexit will have on the international relations of both parties through the contributions of a number of legal scholars of different levels of seniority as well as legal experts of the European Commission who are all researching and working in this field.[11]

The volume is formally structured around the international law implications of Brexit in six areas that were identified as key themes worth tackling for a comprehensive analysis: 'The framework for the future relationship between the EU and the UK (Part I); 'Brexit and existing EU international agreements' (Part II); 'International organizations and EU diplomacy after Brexit' (Part III); 'Common Foreign, Security and Defence Policy after Brexit' (Part IV); 'Brexit and specific international arrangements' (Part V); and 'Contested and external effects of Brexit' (Part VI).

Part I aims to present the *framework for the future relationship between the EU and the United Kingdom*. For this purpose, attention is devoted to the implications of the withdrawal procedure itself laid down in Article 50 TEU and the various EU official documents that have supplemented the scant withdrawal clause by including additional requirements set out, in particular, in the Union's Guidelines[12] and the Negotiating Directives.[13] In this sense, even though Article 50 TEU does not provide for a transition period, it was perceived from the beginning of the Brexit negotiations that it would be necessary in order to avoid a legal void while negotiating the future relationship between both parties. As explained above, the current transition period facilitates the negotiation of a future treaty or treaties governing the new relationship. Since the UK is no longer a member of the EU, during the transition period the parties' relations are ruled by an international treaty, namely, the WA.

In Chapter 2, *Allan F. Tatham* conducts a comprehensive analysis of the values and principles underlying EU withdrawal and their application in future contexts. He considers that a stark dichotomy lies in the fact that withdrawal, even though it represents the most fundamental form of rejection of the Union and its law, must nevertheless occur according to the relevant EU rules and principles. Tatham argues that, as happened with the accession process under Article 49 TEU, the EU institutions have developed the provisions of Article 50 TEU on withdrawal by complementing its terms with various official documentation. Taken together, they have given birth to the withdrawal or 'Brussels criteria' that govern this and any future secession of an EU Member State.

Tobias Lock, in Chapter 3, provides a closer examination of the UK's peculiar position during the transition period and shows that the transition period does not represent a mere continuation of the status quo. During the transition period the UK will be in a twilight zone between EU membership and third country status. He argues that already during transition the UK has completed the move from being a subject of EU law to the status of object of EU law. This is due to the fact that its relations with the EU are now defined by an international agreement rather than by EU law proper. Lock explores the implications of the key provisions on transition in the WA and the imbalance between the UK and the EU during transition.

Adam Cygan and Ewa Żelazna evaluate in Chapter 4 the positions of parliaments in the process that governs the conclusion of the framework for future relations between the EU and the UK and discuss challenges that these parliaments face in ensuring democratic legitimacy of the agreement. They consider that, due to their consent powers and considerable experience in international negotiations, parliaments in the EU are in a better position to scrutinize the treaty-making process than the UK Parliament. The impact that the future agreement will have on individual Member States and its political importance provide a rationale for incorporating the voice of national parliaments.

Chapter 5, by *Polly R. Polak*, focuses on the significant gap-filling operation carried out by the European institutions in order to cope with the extremely complex process of withdrawal on the basis of the very scant regulation of Article 50 TEU. During the Brexit negotiations, sometimes legal voids have simply been filled by extending EU rules on international treaty-making to the withdrawal process despite the clause only referring to paragraph 3 of Article 218. In other cases, separate Treaty principles have applied, notably, the principle of sincere cooperation due to the status of Member and not of third country of the withdrawing state. Finally, other specific withdrawal rules have emerged anew from the practice. All of this has allowed the process to be designed by the EU in its interests while at the same time favouring the emergence of a heavily conditioned legal procedure of EU withdrawal that is different both from withdrawal mechanisms in ordinary international organizations and also in comparison to other EU external action.

Part II focuses on *the impact of Brexit on existing EU international agreements*, particularly in the context of the negotiation of future agreements between the EU and the UK. In this regard, it offers a detailed picture of the implications of Brexit for key policy areas, such as trade, air navigation and the Area of Freedom, Security and Justice (AFSJ). It intends to capture the complexities that Brexit has for EU and UK external relations in light of the WA and, in general, international law.

In Chapter 6, *Panos Koutrakos* highlights how Brexit was advocated as the great disruptor which would unshackle the UK from the heavy-handed and inflexible trade policy imposed by the EU while in fact a lot of time and energy has been spent seeking to ensure continuity of the EU's trade agreements. His chapter unpacks the relationship between the rhetoric of rupture and the practice of continuity. It does so by focusing on the effect of international trade agreements that were binding on the UK pursuant to its EU membership and by analysing how they were approached by both the British and the EU authorities and how they have been managed under the UK–EU WA and UK law.

The contribution by *Wybe Th. Douma*, in Chapter 7, looks into the implications of Brexit for aviation. To avoid serious disruptions in air transport services, temporary contingency measures were adopted during the withdrawal negotiations and which might still be used in case the negotiations on the future EU–UK do not succeed. In any case, the positions put forward by the Member States and the Commission on external competences issues during those original debates form the prelude to the manner in which the air traffic relations between the EU, its Member States and the UK will be negotiated for the period after 2020. Douma also explores the possible costs for the UK of exiting the single aviation market, notably for its aviation industry and national Civil Aviation Authority. Paradoxically, the discontinuation of the UK's membership of the European Aviation Safety Agency could reduce the UK's influence on the shaping of global aviation standards. Furthermore, the measures that several UK airlines took in order to meet the EU ownership and control rules are examined. Finally, some of the prospects of concluding new EU–UK aviation agreements before the end of 2020 are touched upon.

Paula García Andrade analyses, in Chapter 8, the effects of the withdrawal of the UK from the EU on external action in the AFSJ, in which the UK enjoyed a particular derogation regime. She examines, from the perspective of both EU and international law, the legal consequences that Brexit has on international agreements concluded by the EU in the exercise of its competences under Title V of the TFEU, distinguishing between those agreements which did not bind the UK on the basis of its opt-out regime of the AFSJ and those agreements to which the UK opted-in in accordance with Protocols 21 and 19. The different situation of EU-only agreements and mixed agreements is addressed, paying also particular attention to the special nature of association agreements, normally concluded in a mixed form.

The contribution by *Adam Łazowski*, in Chapter 9, looks into one of the arguments repeated ad nauseum by supporters of Brexit: that once the UK leaves the EU it will embark on a Global Britain project and, free of the shackles of EU membership, will negotiate trade agreements with countries around the world. The author proves that the early steps taken by the authorities in London have focused merely on rolling-over pre-Brexit agreements. The analysis of 20 agreements concluded thus far proves that EU agreements have not only served as a point of departure for post-Brexit deals, they have been either directly or indirectly copy–pasted into UK agreements with third countries.

As explained at the beginning of this introduction, Brexit has important implications for the relationship between the EU and the UK with other states and international organizations. Part III of the handbook aims to explore the impact of the withdrawal of the UK from the EU *on the participation of these actors in other international organizations and in EU diplomacy itself.*

Gregory Messenger analyses in Chapter 10 the relationship between the UK and the EU at the WTO. In identifying the core legal questions arising from UK withdrawal from the EU for trade relations at the WTO, Messenger looks to possible areas of cooperation and disagreement for both parties, challenging expectations that they will fall into either a dynamic of confrontation or subservience. Instead, he argues that the experience thus far, and the priorities for the future, set the ground for a relationship built on constructive creative competition.

In Chapter 11, *Jan Wouters* focuses on the implications of Brexit for the functioning of the United Nations Security Council (UNSC) from the perspective of the EU. He outlines the importance of the UK's permanent seat in the context of the Brexit debate, both from the viewpoint of the UK and from the EU and its 27 Member States. Wouters explores what as of now has been agreed about the UK and EU's future relationship within the UNSC, in particular in the 'Political Declaration setting out the framework for the future relationship between the European Union and the United Kingdom'. He revisits the current EU Treaty mechanisms for

EU 'actorness' in the UNSC and highlights recent dynamics in the practices of EU Member States sitting on the UNSC.

Mauro Gatti argues in Chapter 12 that withdrawal of the UK may weaken the EU diplomatic network, since few Member States have a diplomatic network comparable to the UK. Brexit might also complicate the provision of consular protection to unrepresented EU citizens in third countries and increase the workload of other Member States' diplomatic and consular missions. To address these problems, the Member States may strengthen diplomatic coordination and increase the responsibilities of EU delegations in the sensitive area of consular protection. Gatti holds that an important precedent in this respect might be set by the new EU delegation in the UK, which should ensure the implementation of the UK's WA and, consequently, the protection of EU nationals in the UK.

In Chapter 13, *Fernando Castillo de la Torre* and *Agnieszka Stobiecka-Kuik* give an overview of the impact of Brexit in the area of external fisheries policy. They examine the WA, but also the possible consequences of a 'hard' Brexit and the alternative measures proposed or examined so far in order to mitigate it. The examination of the situation which would have resulted in a 'no deal' scenario may still be interesting in the case of absence of an agreement or arrangement covering fisheries after the end of the transition period. The authors also analyse more specifically the impact of Brexit on each category of international agreements, namely multilateral agreements, Regional Fisheries Management Organisations and bilateral agreements. They make specific remarks on the future agreement covering fisheries that the EU and the UK undertook to make best endeavours to conclude by 1 July 2020.

Part IV focuses on the *Common Foreign, Security and Defence Policy (CFSP) after Brexit*. It has been understood from the beginning of the Brexit negotiations that the UK will probably remain committed to the objectives of the CFSP after Brexit. This may be due to the more intergovernmental nature of the EU competence in this area with respect to other EU policies. After triggering Article 50 TEU, the UK has continuously argued that there is a common interest in developing a close cooperation in foreign, security and defence policies in the future. This part not only provides a detailed examination of the provisions of the WA that specifically apply to the CFSP field during the implementation period, but with a cross-cutting approach also looks into how the UK and the EU may shape their cooperation in the CFSP after the expiry of the implementation period. In particular, it identifies areas in which there will probably be convergence between the UK and EU approaches, such as with sanction policies.

The UK has frequently indicated that Brexit should not lead to a complete detachment from the EU's CFSP, but that in this area EU membership should be replaced by a new security partnership. In Chapter 14, *Ramses A. Wessel* maps the legal institutional obstacles and possibilities for the UK to continue participating in CFSP by analysing both the WA and, in particular, the existing rules on participation of third states in the CFSP and Common Security and Defence Policy (CSDP) framework. In doing so he draws on current examples of third state participation in EU foreign and security policy.

Sara Poli examines in Chapter 15 the way the UK sanctions policy is likely to be shaped during the implementation period and after its expiry. The most important elements of the Sanction Act and Money Laundering Act (SAMLA) will be highlighted. It will be shown how in the post-Brexit era the UK will be able to set out its own autonomous restrictive measures. The UK sanctions policy is likely to align with that of the EU, although the UK may wish in some cases to go beyond the sanctions regimes adopted by the EU. Finally, the chapter sketches reasons for concern linked to due process rights and to the protection of the right to an effective judicial protection that arise out of the SAMLA; the implications of the regained sovereignty for the addressees of sanctions will also be assessed.

In Chapter 16, *Viktor Szép* and *Peter Van Elsuwege* examine whether the EU and the UK are clearly committed towards further cooperation in sanctions policies and how this may materialise in practice. They address this question from the alignment experience of other third countries. Based upon a legal and statistical analysis of existing models and taking into account relevant UK and EU policy documents and political declarations, Szép and Van Elsuwege establish different scenarios for future cooperation in the field of sanctions. They argue that, in contrast to the experience of other neighbouring countries, cooperation between the EU and the UK will most likely be a more open format for consultation and cooperation rather than a one-way alignment with the EU's sanctions regimes.

Scarlett McArdle focuses, in Chapter 17, on the cooperation between the EU and the UK in crisis management operations in the future. Indications are that the UK will continue to engage with crisis management, with both sides agreed from the outset on the need for continued cooperation in the area of security and defence. With the UK seeking a partnership deeper than any previously envisaged, the potential exists for significant lack of clarity on where responsibility may lie for breaches of international law committed by personnel in crisis management operations in which the UK is involved in the future.

Part V of the volume aims to exemplify *the broad implications of Brexit for a wide spectrum of policy areas*. This part is devoted to some of those policies whose specific features justify the interest in dedicating special chapters to each of them.

Chapter 18 by *Andrea Ott* assesses to what extent the UK can opt-in to EU agencies. It analyses the framework and conditions of third-country participation by emphasizing that agencies serve EU policies and that third countries have committed to applying certain EU policies or participating in the EU internal market. Consequently, participation in EU agencies by outsiders is classified into four categories (*sui generis* participation under international law, semi-membership of Schengen third countries, European Economic Area (EEA) members without voting rights and observers). It will be assessed what conditions are connected to this participation and to what extent the UK fits in any of these categories.

In Chapter 19, *Teresa Fajardo* underscores the many challenges arising from disentangling the UK from international environmental agreements ratified as part of the EU and its Member States. After Brexit, the UK will have to determine the way it will be bound both by international environmental agreements and *soft law*, according to the general requirements that have been agreed upon in the WA and the Political Declaration. International environmental agreements and soft law also play an important role in the first draft legal agreement for the future EU–UK Partnership presented by the EU as they serve to set out the bases for a common level playing field for the protection of the environment.

Chapter 20 by *Chloé Brière* conducts an analysis of the future of judicial cooperation in criminal matters between the EU and the UK. The definition of new modalities of cooperation during the transition period and beyond does not occur in a legal vacuum. With the globalization of crime and the necessity to investigate the multilateral dimension of criminal cases, the EU has developed a diversity of cooperation mechanisms with third countries, including through Eurojust, its specialized judicial cooperation agency. Brière explores how Brexit impacts on such precedents of cooperation, in particular in the context of the negotiations on the future relationship between both parties.

As a last element, Part VI focuses on the *contested and external effects of Brexit*. It looks at this issue from both the perspectives of EU and UK external relations and international law. Brexit will have important implications for different policy areas and territories and there will be a need to find practical solutions to develop the future relationship between the EU and the UK, as well as to assess the implications for various areas of contested sovereignty. The Protocol on

Gibraltar, as well as the Protocol on Ireland/Northern Ireland and the Protocol on the Sovereign Bases Areas in Cyprus, form an integral part of the WA (Art. 182 WA). In addition, Brexit will arguably become an important focal point of the reach of EU law and of a high level of regulatory alignment – as a starting point – unlike that of any other third country before.

Juan Santos Vara (Chapter 21) looks into the implications of the WA for Gibraltar. The Protocol on Gibraltar and the Memoranda of Understanding agreed between Spain and the UK in November 2018 will not allow Spain to assert its sovereignty in relation to Gibraltar, but they have given Spain an excellent opportunity to 'take back control' over many issues of serious concern to Spain. He argues that even though the Memoranda are not legally binding instruments, the Brexit negotiations allowed Spain to gain leverage in the dispute while postponing a direct push for sovereignty. Failure to find solutions to the issues that concern Spain with respect to Gibraltar will have an impact on the negotiations between the EU and UK. Santos Vara considers that a compromise between both countries may be included in a future framework agreement negotiated between the EU and the UK, following the precedent of the Protocol on Gibraltar.

Jed Odermatt explores in Chapter 22 how the UK's withdrawal from the Union has also uncovered sovereignty questions for the UK's international relations. It discusses the UK's relationship with Palestine, Cyprus (Sovereign Base Areas and Northern Cyprus) and Western Sahara, as examples of how sovereignty questions arise through Brexit. He shows how the Brexit process is not only related to internal sovereignty, but also reveals the UK's conception of international legal sovereignty. Odermatt argues that the UK will have to decide whether to align its foreign policy in relation to such territories with that of the EU, especially in relation to the jurisprudence of the Court of Justice.

A final chapter by *Elaine Fahey* (Chapter 23) focuses specifically on the cross-channel reach of EU Law in the UK post-Brexit. The UK will form a unique case study of the global reach of EU law where the depth of alignment will require careful sectoral examination and specific temporal delineation. Fahey's contribution is not fixated upon an outcome at the time of writing and explores the longer-term trends on the application of EU rules outside trade agreements, the exportation of EU rules in trade agreements and the interpretation of EU rules post-exit in UK law. She considers global governance perspectives, EU law and EU international relations and the reach of EU law, political economy and regulatory alignment with the EU, EU law and international agreements on human rights and values regression and conditionality and domestic UK provisions on EU law post-exit on the retention of EU law.

Notes

1 Schuman Declaration (9 May 1950) www.robert-schuman.eu/en/declaration-of-9-may-1950 accessed 9 May 2020.

2 In the words of British prime minister Boris Johnson: 'We are big enough to do amazing things'. Speech at the Conservative Party Conference (3 October 2017) https://blogs.spectator.co.uk/2017/10/boris-johnsons-conservative-conference-speech-full-text/ accessed 1 May 2020.

3 Agreement on the withdrawal of the United Kingdom of Great Britain and Northern Ireland from the European Union and the European Atomic Energy Community [2020] OJ L29/7.

4 Political Declaration setting out the framework for the future relationship between the European Union and the United Kingdom, OJ [2020] C34/12 (PD).

5 European Council (Art 50) Guidelines (Brussels, 23 March 2018) EUCO XT 20001/18.

6 Draft Text of the Agreement on the New Partnership with the United Kingdom (Brussels, 18 March 2020).

7 HM Government, 'The Future Relationship with the EU: The UK's Approach to Negotiations' (Policy Paper, 2020); Draft Text of the Agreement on the New Partnership with the United Kingdom (Brussels, 18 March 2020).

8 See Ramses A Wessel and Jed Odermatt (eds), *Research Handbook on the European Union and International Organisations* (Edward Elgar Publishing 2019).
9 See http://ec.europa.eu/world/agreements/default.home.do accessed 1 May 2020. The database allows one to search for bilateral or multilateral agreements in relation to the specific activities of the Union.
10 See also Joris Larik, 'EU External Relations Law and Brexit: "When Pluto was a planet"' (2020) 4 Europe and the World: A Law Review 1.
11 It is based on the papers presented at the workshop on 'EU External Relations after Brexit – Implications under EU and International Law', organized by Juan Santos Vara and Ramses Wessel at the University of Salamanca on the 7 and 8 March 2019 in cooperation with the Centre for the Law of EU External Relations (CLEER). The contributions to the volume benefited from further reflection and the discussions that took place at and after the workshop. The works were tested against the views of practitioners from the legal services of the Commission and some Member States that attended the workshop.
12 European Council (Art 50) Guidelines (n 3).
13 Council of the European Union, 'Directives for the negotiation of an agreement with the United Kingdom of Great Britain and Northern Ireland setting out the arrangements for its withdrawal from the European Union' (Brussels, 22 May 2017).

Part I

The framework for the future relationship between the EU and the UK

2

Towards the formulation of the 'Brussels criteria'

The values and principles underlying EU withdrawal and their application in future contexts

Allan F. Tatham

2.1 Introduction

The United Kingdom (UK) is the first Member State to make use of its right to withdraw from the European Union (EU). In the absence of direct precedents,[1] it is no simple matter to try to determine the main points of the 'Brussels criteria' for EU withdrawal, so called as a counterweight to the 'Copenhagen criteria' for EU accession.[2] Moreover, from the three pivotal issues framing the recent withdrawal negotiations and final agreement (citizens' rights, divorce bill and Ireland), it will not be possible to extrapolate directly the conditionality surrounding a future withdrawal – particularly given the unique challenges facing UK–Ireland relations post-Brexit.

Despite these limitations bounded by a solitary precedent, it will be argued that some withdrawal conditionality has already emerged. In fact, the institutional and procedural conservatism of the Union, as evidenced in its adaptation of the accession process and instruments and their application to its neighbourhood policy,[3] can be usefully deployed in the present context. Consequently, while the basic terms of the withdrawal procedure[4] are set out in Article 50 TEU, as has happened with its counterpart[5] Article 49 TEU on enlargement, these provisions have been supplemented by requirements set out in various EU official documentation created during the negotiations for the UK's departure. The most important of these are the Union's Guidelines[6] and Negotiating Directives,[7] the 2019 Withdrawal Agreement,[8] the linked EU–UK Political Declaration on the framework of their future relationship[9] and the ruling of the Court of Justice of the European Union (CJEU) in the *Wightman* case.[10]

Unlike the established practices surrounding EU enlargement that are underpinned by Article 49 TEU,[11] the novelty of the withdrawal process necessarily called for rapid innovation that needed to acknowledge the UK's continuing membership of the Union while simultaneously preparing for it to become a third country. As earlier contended,[12] the CJEU confirmed in *Wightman*[13] that the common values set out under Article 2 TEU formed part of the foundations of the EU legal order[14] and thus mattered as much in the manner of a Member State's withdrawal as in its accession.[15] This Article provides:

> The Union is founded on the values of respect for human dignity, freedom, democracy, equality, the rule of law and respect for human rights, including the rights of persons belonging to minorities. These values are common to the Member States in a society in which pluralism, non-discrimination, tolerance, justice, solidarity and equality between women and men prevail.

This chapter accordingly seeks to detail the main components of the 'Brussels criteria' for EU withdrawal and the values underlying them. It will do this by identifying and briefly analysing, in turn: (i) the foundational principle underlying the whole process, namely the concept of an orderly withdrawal; (ii) the criteria for the withdrawal decision; (iii) the main negotiating principles; and (iv) the main criteria as distilled from the Withdrawal Agreement. Lastly, the conclusion will take the Brexit experience and suggest to what extent aspects of the Brussels criteria might be potentially incorporated into the Union's future negotiating processes. Such incorporation would thereby allow for the concomitant inclusion of the relevant values that underpinned the Brexit negotiating process.

2.2 An 'orderly withdrawal': the foundational concept

Underlying the whole departure process, from the decision to withdraw from the EU to the actual leaving and beyond, is the concept of an 'orderly withdrawal'.[16] It entails a commitment to a negotiated settlement between the parties under the terms of Article 50(2) and (3) TEU that, as emphasised in *Wightman*,[17] establish a procedure to enable a withdrawal to take place 'in an orderly fashion'. This was actually expressed at the start of the negotiations, with the EU giving priority to an orderly withdrawal in its Guidelines[18] and both parties later confirmed that their objective in agreeing to the Withdrawal Agreement[19] was 'to ensure an orderly withdrawal'.

In the present situation, an orderly withdrawal occurs according to the democratic process and under the rule of law. It aims[20] at promoting legal certainty for citizens, businesses and other stakeholders and, to the extent possible, minimising disruption caused by the process. Such withdrawal also emphasises the importance that the EU attaches to an institutionally logical and sequential procedure as it has already managed to create with respect to the accession process.[21]

The EU's preference for an orderly withdrawal nevertheless does not prevent a Member State from leaving without an agreement (the so-called 'no-deal' scenario), if the negotiations were to fail or the withdrawing state were to be unable to ratify the Withdrawal Agreement. Such withdrawal would necessarily be subject to all the attendant consequences,[22] for example, immediate trading on terms of the World Trade Organization (WTO) (without any transitional period to adapt to life outside the Union) and the threat to the status and well-being of EU citizens in the withdrawing state and the latter's nationals in the Union.

2.3 Decision to withdraw

2.3.1 Geographical criterion

The whole process for withdrawal commences when a Member State intimates its desire to leave the Union in accordance with Article 50 TEU. Similar to Article 49 TEU under which only a European *state* can apply for membership of the Union, under Article 50(1) TEU only an EU Member *State* can withdraw from the Union. It thus underlines the continuing sovereignty of and equality between the Member States as well as the voluntary nature of their belonging to that Union.[23] The wording of Article 50 TEU consequently cannot of itself form the legal basis for the secession of part of an EU Member State. Rather, a combination of national, EU and international law and principles would arguably govern such process of secession.[24]

2.3.2 National constitutional criterion

Article 50 TEU provides further that a Member State can decide to withdraw from the Union 'according to its own constitutional arrangements' and 'shall notify the European Council of its intention'.

Respect for the principle of subsidiarity lies at the very foundation of this criterion. After all, under Article 5(3) TEU, subsidiarity is meant to protect the autonomy of Member States from unnecessary Union action. Played out within the context of withdrawal, the right to leave the Union under Article 50 TEU supports[25] the 'procedural operationalization of the principle of subsidiarity' and so delegates responsibility for determining continued membership to the state itself.

In withdrawing, a state remains bound by EU values that include democracy and the rule of law. In seeking to comply with them, the withdrawing state might be constitutionally required under its domestic laws to gain the support of its population directly through a popular referendum, before commencing the withdrawal procedure.[26] Alternatively, a parliamentary vote on the issue might suffice, especially where the government is elected on a promise to withdraw.[27]

Having held the 2016 referendum,[28] the UK Supreme Court ruled in the first *Miller* case[29] that – due to the profound effect on domestic legal rights and on the constitution that would occur on leaving the Union – a parliamentary vote would still be needed to approve the government's notification of withdrawal. Only once that parliamentary approval was forthcoming in March 2017 could the UK officially notify the European Council of its intention to withdraw, according to 'its own constitutional arrangements'.

On the basis of subsidiarity and the voluntary nature of EU membership, the CJEU subsequently held in *Wightman* that Member States also retain the power to revoke the notification of the withdrawal unilaterally. Such revocation would need to be done[30] 'in an unequivocal and unconditional manner, by a notice addressed to the European Council in writing, after the Member State concerned has taken the revocation decision in accordance with its constitutional requirements'. The purpose of that revocation would be twofold: first, to confirm the state's unchanged and continuing status as an EU Member State; and, second, to terminate definitively the withdrawal procedure. If this had been applied to the UK, then it would have needed to revoke its decision to withdraw probably by holding another referendum or popular vote, possibly confirmed by statute or parliamentary vote.

2.4 Principles of negotiations

2.4.1 Sincere co-operation

Both the UK's formal notification of withdrawal[31] and the Guidelines[32] referred to being bound by the principle of sincere co-operation, acknowledged as a 'fundamental general principle of the EU legal order'[33] and enshrined in Article 4(3) TEU. Under that provision, the EU and its Member States assist each other in full mutual respect when carrying out tasks flowing from the Treaties, the Brexit negotiations being such a task.[34]

The European Council further explained the practicalities of sincere co-operation in the context of the withdrawal negotiations,[35] underlining the point that the UK was bound by that principle while it was still a Member State. It drew a line between, on the one hand, the UK's continuing involvement in ongoing Union business as well as its refraining from interfering with progress in driving forward the Union's priorities; and, on the other hand, the expectation that the UK would recognise the need of the EU27 to meet and discuss matters related to the post-Brexit situation, without the presence of the UK. Thus, unlike an acceding state that is allowed to attend EU meetings as an observer in preparation for its eventual accession, the withdrawing state is not permitted to be present at meetings dealing with its departure. The reason is quite simple: as the EU27 did not wish the UK delegation to benefit from first-hand experience of any dissent between the remaining Member States and so capitalise on such knowledge in the negotiations.[36]

2.4.2 Transparency

Transparency is a general principle of EU law,[37] set out variously in primary law,[38] the 2001 Regulation on public access to those documents[39] and the CJEU case law decided under it.[40] It enables citizens to participate more closely in the decision-making process[41] and to guarantee that the administration is more accountable to the citizen. Transparency thereby contributes to strengthening the principles of democracy and respect for fundamental rights under Article 2 TEU and in the EU Charter of Fundamental Rights (CFR). The Union legal framework on transparency aimed at creating a definite shift in attitude, namely, that EU legislative work could no longer be understood as a traditional, secretive diplomatic process[42] beyond public scrutiny.

This heightened regard for transparency and openness in 'internal' EU law-making clashes with the 'wall-of-secrecy model' that characterises external relations. In this respect,[43] the Union institutions can refuse access to a document where disclosure would undermine the protection of the public interest as regards international relations.

Nevertheless, the CJEU in its rulings[44] and the European Commission in its practice forged during the Transatlantic Trade and Investment Partnership (TTIP) negotiations[45] have each sought to reduce the ambit of this exception on the one hand, while reforming the existing information sharing systems in order to increase transparency in international trade negotiations on the other. Within this context, the European Parliament (EP) – in promoting its increasing role and oversight in EU external relations – has been a chief protagonist in pushing for greater transparency.[46]

The Brexit negotiations bestrode this traditional 'internal'/'external' binary classification in policy brief, charting as it did the metamorphosis from the status of Member State to third country for the withdrawing state (a reversal of the situation in the accession process). These negotiations presented the EU institutions with an opportunity to learn from the rulings of the CJEU as well as from their mistakes in the TTIP scenario in order to develop a policy of disclosure based on transparency.

The EU underlined the need to conduct the Brexit negotiations in a transparent manner.[47] Due to the obvious heightened interest and scrutiny generated by them, the Council issued its own Guiding Principles for Transparency[48] that sought to balance openness with the necessary secrecy of proceedings in order to secure confidence between the negotiating parties. As the Guiding Principles stated:[49] 'These principles aim at facilitating effective public scrutiny and providing a steady flow of public information throughout the negotiations whilst preserving the space to form EU positions and negotiate with the UK'. In short, EU legal rules on transparency ensured[50] 'timely and directly accessible information to the public in particular around negotiation rounds'.

The EP – which institution did not participate in the negotiations per se – was nevertheless a privileged partner in them, with the Union negotiator required to keep it 'closely and regularly informed throughout the negotiations' and by maintaining regular contacts with the Council. The Guiding Principles annexed[51] a useful table, laying down a clear typology of documents used in the negotiations and the different transparency regimes applicable to them – whether they originated from the Council, the Commission, the EU27 Member States or the UK – as well as indicating the intended recipients of such documents and their method of disclosure.

The Guiding Principles consequently opened up the negotiations to greater public scrutiny than any before, thereby allowing citizens, businesses and other stakeholders to be regularly appraised of the conduct of negotiations, either through the Commission website[52] or through meetings with or access to Michel Barnier, the EU chief negotiator.[53]

2.4.3 Criteria for extending negotiations

The two-year negotiation period under Article 50(3) is extremely short[54] considering the complexity of the withdrawal process and the need to indicate the future form of close partnership between the EU and the withdrawing state. Consequently, Article 50(3) TEU further provides the European Council, acting unanimously and in agreement with the withdrawing state, with the power to extend such period. From experiences in respect of the UK's withdrawal as well as contemporary political and academic opinion, it would be safe to say that the European Council will only support an extension in three particular circumstances, namely, in order to allow time: (i) to ratify the Withdrawal Agreement as happened during the Brexit negotiations[55] with the result that the original withdrawal date (31 March 2019) was set back beyond the two years from the UK's notification to leave and finally occurred on 31 January 2020; (ii) to prepare for a 'no-deal' exit;[56] or (iii) to hold a general election or another referendum.[57]

2.5 Withdrawal Agreement

2.5.1 Good neighbourly relations

The principle of maintaining good neighbourly relations already arose in the context of the accession process, most particularly in respect of relations with the Western Balkan states *inter se*.[58] More recently, the Lisbon Treaty added Article 8 TEU that introduced specific requirements for the EU in respect of neighbouring countries by which the Union is to develop a special relationship with them, 'aiming to establish an area of prosperity and good neighbourliness, founded on the values of the Union and characterised by close and peaceful relations based on cooperation'. While these intentions are primarily directed at states to the East and the South of the Union,[59] they apply no less to the non-EU states covered by the European Economic Area (EEA) Agreement as well as Switzerland and the post-Brexit UK. Article 8 TEU thus makes it clear that these relations are based inter alia on respect for the EU's values and norms.[60]

Against this background, the Guidelines and related documents also put great store on the UK's post-withdrawal relations with the EU.[61] While the Union wanted to ensure that the UK should remain its close partner, this was not an open-ended promise. For the UK to enjoy good neighbourly relations, several matters needed to be resolved including the problem of a new external (EU) border being created between the UK and EU27 and the nature of the future trading terms between the parties, together with consideration of a (possible) limited temporal extension of EU rules pending final determination of that trading relation which will be addressed first.

2.5.1.1 Transitional period

Given the brief timescale under Article 50 TEU, the Guidelines further allowed for transitional arrangements to be determined, as long as they were in the interests of the Union and provided[62] for 'bridges' towards the foreseeable framework for the future relationship between the EU27 and the UK. The principles underlying such a smooth or orderly transition required it to be 'clearly defined, limited in time, and subject to effective enforcement measures'. A time-limited prolongation of Union rules was subsequently provided for in the Withdrawal Agreement,[63] so that the UK would have to apply the existing EU regulatory, budgetary, supervisory, judicial, and enforcement instruments and structures after its withdrawal, until 31 December 2020. In this twilight period, the UK would no longer be represented or vote in the EU institutions but would still bound by (new) EU law and (new) CJEU rulings, a norm-taker rather than part of a norm-maker.

2.5.1.2 Issues concerning land borders

On land borders, EU Member States have used interstate solidarity in Article 3 TEU as the underlying value by which they have largely[64] eliminated disputes on border demarcations *inter se*. These include the need to resolve outstanding disputes before acceding to the Union[65] or by easing border tensions within the EU for which the improved relations between Ireland and the UK and the context of the Good Friday Agreement are obvious examples.[66]

With the departure of the UK, three borders changed from being internal to external EU borders between: (i) the UK and Ireland; (ii) the UK Sovereign Bases and Cyprus; and (iii) the UK Overseas Territory of Gibraltar and Spain.[67] Identified in the Guidelines,[68] the EU maintained its initial position of interstate solidarity throughout the negotiations. As a result, the Withdrawal Agreement provides each border issue with its own annexe[69] that provides an individual specialised committee (under the umbrella EU–UK Joint Committee) to supervise issues arising from the provisions governing them.[70]

The most intractable issue in the negotiations proved to be the need to maintain a 'frictionless border' between Northern Ireland and the Republic. The parties were taxed by the need to balance preservation of the 1998 Good Friday (Belfast) Agreement (co-sponsored by the EU) that had brought peace to the North; the longstanding Common Travel Area between the UK and the Republic; and the requirements of the indivisibility of the EU's single market.[71] The solution in the 2019 Withdrawal Agreement amounted to a 'trade-off', effectively requiring maintenance of full regulatory alignment between Northern Ireland and the EU in customs matters and related areas of the single market, subject to approval by the Northern Irish Assembly after four or eight years.[72] Following the 2020 transition period, this solution will create, in effect, a customs boundary down the Irish Sea between the islands of Great Britain and Ireland, thereby severing the UK's own internal market.

2.5.1.3 Future trading terms

As for post-exit trading relations, this would depend on the attitude of the withdrawing Member State and the reasons for its departure.[73] Consequently, it might seek the possibility of 'remaining' in the EEA (via European Free Trade Area (EFTA))[74] or of establishing bilateral trading relations similar to Switzerland,[75] Turkey[76] or Ukraine.[77] Nevertheless, the premise of all these agreements is to deepen integration with the EU and in particular its internal market, to varying, progressive degrees. These agreements remain models but it is questionable whether they would be useful for a state going in the opposite direction.

Instead, the withdrawing state might seek to negotiate a free trade agreement (FTA) or an FTA with enhanced features to reflect its erstwhile (deep trading) relationship with the EU.[78] Based on Article 50(2) TEU,[79] negotiating and ratifying the post-exit trading relationship would be governed by either Article 207 and/or Article 217 TFEU (together with the procedure set out under Article 218 TFEU). Article 207 TFEU concerns FTAs between the EU and a third country when the EU acts within the framework of its common commercial policy. A comparatively short transition period (as in the post-Brexit context) militates against conclusion of an FTA like the Comprehensive Economic and Trade Agreement (CETA) between the EU and Canada.[80] Due to its mixed nature,[81] covering competences of both the EU and the Member States, the necessary national parliamentary ratifications greatly extended the timescale for CETA's entry into force. A simple FTA, falling within the Union's exclusive competences,[82] might therefore be preferable given the brief timescale.

Article 217 TFEU concerns the conclusion of association agreements with third countries that involve reciprocal rights and obligations as well as common actions. They accordingly represent deeper and closer long-term arrangements between the parties. In the Brexit context, the objectives for such future trading and other relations were set out in the Guidelines[83] and were given clearer expression in the Political Declaration.[84] Since the parties wished to have a future relationship that was highly ambitious as regards its scope and depth,[85] Article 217 TFEU might be chosen by the EU as the Treaty basis for the trade and other agreements with the UK. In general terms, the EU and the UK agreed that their economic partnership would be 'ambitious, wide-ranging and balanced' but could not amount to participation in (parts of) the single market and customs union since this would undermine its integrity and proper functioning. Such partnership would preserve 'a level playing field' between them ensuring open and fair competition,[86] together with respecting their individual regulatory and supervisory regime and standards and their application.[87]

Beyond trade, the parties are also seeking to negotiate (in parallel) a series of partnerships in other fields, especially concerning the fight against terrorism and international crime, as well as security, defence and foreign policy.[88] As regards the negotiations for these partnerships,[89] both parties are to 'use their best endeavours, in good faith and in full respect of their respective legal orders' to negotiate them expeditiously as well as ratify or conclude them in order to ensure, as far as possible, that they will apply from the end of the transition period.

Given the UK government's determination[90] to complete these negotiations within the transition period without any extension,[91] the parties are now more likely to pursue a 'bare-bones' FTA under Article 207 TFEU, within the exclusive competences of the Union. This would allow the Commission to negotiate and the Council to adopt the FTA (with the consent of the EP) and so avoid complex negotiations, exclude national parliamentary ratification and considerably expedite the process. However, if the transition period were to be extended, it might then be possible to conclude such FTA as an association agreement under Article 217 TFEU[92] that would allow for further 'add-ons,' for example, in the way that the EEC–Turkey Association Agreement 1963 was subsequently complemented by the 1995 Customs Union,[93] or as the centrepiece of a package of parallel partnerships in line with the terms of the Political Declaration.

2.5.2 *Social criteria: citizens' rights*

As part of its objectives under Article 3 TEU, the Union is to promote 'the well being of its peoples' and, in its external relations, to contribute 'to the protection of its citizens'. In this respect, one of the obvious consequences of EU withdrawal is a loss of or change to an individual's status as an EU citizen. According to Article 50(3) TEU, on withdrawal 'the Treaties shall cease to apply' including those that confer EU citizenship on nationals of Member States and determine their rights: withdrawing state nationals thereby lose their EU citizenship and concomitant rights on their country's departure from the Union.[94] By the same token, on withdrawal EU citizens in the withdrawing state also lose their rights under the Treaties.

Both the British[95] and Union sides recognised such problems before the start of negotiations. The Guidelines,[96] for example, noted the fundamental nature of EU citizenship and recognised, as the first negotiating priority, the need to agree reciprocal guarantees to safeguard the status and rights derived from EU law upon Brexit for both EU citizens in the UK and UK nationals in the EU27 as well as their families. Such guarantees had to be 'effective, enforceable, non-discriminatory and comprehensive' and to include the right to acquire permanent residency after five years. In this matter, then, several values underlie the social criteria in the withdrawal context, namely, democracy, solidarity, equality or non-discrimination, and legal certainty.

2.5.2.1 Democracy

Democracy plays an important role in the withdrawal process in respect of EU citizens. Apart from the need for the EP to give its consent under Article 50(2) TEU to any withdrawal agreement, that provision is silent as to the role and status of Members of the European Parliament (MEPs) from the withdrawing state. According to Article 10(2) TEU, the EP is to directly represent citizens at the Union level so that 'directly elected MEPs represent the collective interests of Union citizens rather than the parochial interests of the withdrawing state'.[97] Such approach arguably permits citizens of other EU Member States residing in the withdrawing state to have a certain degree of representation in the political process of withdrawal.[98] The inverse might also be said in relation to the withdrawing state's nationals in the remaining EU Member States.

The EP confirmed its pivotal role in representing the interests of all (pre-withdrawal) EU citizens in the context of the negotiations when it set up an ad hoc six-member, cross-party Brexit Steering Group (that excluded MEPs from Eurosceptic parties in the EP). It also appointed as its Brexit co-ordinator and main interlocutor with the other EU institutions, Guy Verhofstadt, former Belgian Prime Minister and the then Chair of ALDE (Group of the Alliance of Liberals and Democrats for Europe) in the EP.[99] In this capacity, he regularly championed the protection of rights for both groups of citizens affected by the UK withdrawal, while the EP itself was at pains to remind the negotiators that it had a veto over any final withdrawal agreement that properly failed to respect citizens' rights.[100]

2.5.2.2 Solidarity

Social solidarity under Article 3 TEU can be understood as requiring the Union to ensure its own citizens, post withdrawal, are properly protected and their rights guaranteed in the withdrawing state. Yet there might also be an argument made that social solidarity in some ways extends to the ex-EU citizens of the withdrawing state on the territory of the Union.[101] Reading the Preamble to the Treaties ('an ever closer union of the peoples of Europe') and Article 3(5)

TEU on solidarity with people outside the Union, it could be said that the Union should maintain its solidarity with those UK nationals who have already exercised their right to move and reside in the EU27. Indeed, the Commission's position paper on citizens' rights appeared to support this social solidarity contention since – among the general principles that should apply to the Withdrawal Agreement – was one that provided[102] for the 'same level of protection as set out in Union law at the date of withdrawal of EU27 citizens in the UK and UK nationals in the EU27'.

2.5.2.3 Equality or non-discrimination

Another value linked to social solidarity is equality or non-discrimination.[103] In the Negotiating Directives,[104] the Union sought to safeguard the status and rights derived from EU law post Brexit not only those to be enjoyed subsequent to the UK leaving (e.g. rights related to old age pensions) but also those that were in the process of being obtained, including the possibility to acquire them under current conditions after Brexit (e.g. the right of permanent residence after a continuous period of five years which residence had already started before the withdrawal date).

The Commission's position paper on citizens' rights reiterated this requirement for equal treatment[105] 'in the UK of EU27 citizens as compared to UK nationals, and in EU27 of UK nationals as compared to EU27 citizens, in accordance with Union law' as well as 'amongst EU27 citizens by and in the UK in all matters covered by the Withdrawal Agreement'. Consequently, the Withdrawal Agreement ensured that such rights were to be enforceable and based on the principle of non-discrimination[106] which latter principle was expressly confirmed by a prohibition of any discrimination on grounds of nationality with respect to citizens' rights.[107]

2.5.2.4 Legal certainty

The application of legal certainty to the rights of EU citizens in the withdrawal process is also vital,[108] more especially as a means to protect legitimate expectations as well as acquired (vested) rights. On the one hand, the protection of legitimate expectations provides[109] that 'those who act reasonably and in good faith on the basis of the law as it is or at least seems to be should not suffer from disappointment of those expectations'. On the other hand, a legal right, once acquired, should not be withdrawn.[110]

Protection of acquired rights in an EU withdrawal context had been provided in the Treaty allowing Greenland to leave the then EEC:[111] 'The Commission shall make proposals to the Council … for the transitional measures which it considers necessary … with regard to the maintenance of rights acquired by natural or legal persons during the period when Greenland was part of the Community'.

In the case of Brexit, by emphasising the two elements of legal certainty, the negotiating parties expressly agreed that their overall objective, through the Withdrawal Agreement, was to provide reciprocal protection for EU27 and UK citizens in order to let them effectively exercise their rights under EU law (acquired rights) and based on previous life choices (legitimate expectations) where they had exercised their rights of free movement by the time of Brexit.[112]

Moreover, in order to protect citizens' rights under the Withdrawal Agreement as directly enforceable rights for the lifetime of those covered[113] and to give those citizens legal certainty, the parties agreed that it was in their best interest to guarantee a consistent interpretation and application of those rights and so set up the appropriate mechanisms to ensure this.[114] Rights under the Withdrawal Agreement[115] are therefore subject to ultimate enforcement through an

Article 267 TFEU reference to the CJEU or through an analogous procedure for UK courts post Brexit (although this is limited to eight years from entry into force of that Agreement).[116]

2.5.3 *Financial criterion: settling the divorce bill*

The withdrawing state needs to reach a final settlement with the Union on its future budgetary contributions as well as the return of the state's assets deposited in various Union institutions, for example, paid-in subscribed capital held by the European Investment Bank or paid-in capital held by the European Central Bank. Agreement must further be made on financial contributions for its nationals who were former EU civil servants (e.g. on pensions).

Consequently, as an integral part of an orderly withdrawal and in the interests of interstate solidarity, the UK was required to settle the details of its outstanding Brexit divorce bill and ensure that its financial obligations to the Union would be met in full. Under the Withdrawal Agreement,[117] both parties agreed to honour the mutual commitments undertaken while the UK had been a member of the Union through 'a single financial settlement'. In that respect, the Agreement sets out the provisions of such settlement extensively,[118] starting with the UK's contribution to and participation in the implementation of the Union budgets for 2019 and 2020.[119] It further intimates that the monies due under the single financial settlement will be paid out over a number of years, thereby spreading the burden of costs over a longer period of time.

2.5.4 *Legal criterion: requirement to maintain the* **acquis**

The withdrawing state will have been harmonising its legal rules to those of the EU since well before the date of its accession as happened with the Central and Eastern Europe countries.[120] During membership, the creation and application of a considerable body of EU law and related case law as well as practice would have been built up. It would therefore be inconceivable that – during the two-year negotiation period under Article 50 TEU or even with post-withdrawal transitional arrangements in place – the withdrawing state would be in a position to replace wholesale the entire accumulated EU *acquis* with new domestic rules.

In that overall context, the UK's maintenance of the specific *acquis* under the Withdrawal Agreement, both during and (to some extent) after the transition period, also became a requirement of the withdrawal criteria. By underlining legal certainty for individuals and companies as well as states through a transition period, the Withdrawal Agreement attempted to reassure those affected that there would be no sudden rupture in the legislative regimes between the two parties.[121]

Using the principles of sincere co-operation and good faith in the Agreement, the EU has attempted to create unique solutions to a (hitherto) unique situation. Whereas the principles of direct effect and primacy do not bind accession countries before they join the Union,[122] those two principles will (in some way) bind UK courts and the administration well into the future. Thus the provisions of the Withdrawal Agreement are to produce in the UK the same legal effects as those which they produce in the EU and its Member States. In particular, legal or natural persons will be able to rely directly on the provisions of the Agreement that meet the conditions for direct effect under EU law;[123] and the UK courts and administration will be required to disapply legal provisions incompatible with the Withdrawal Agreement.[124]

Further, British judicial and administrative authorities must interpret and apply those Articles of the Withdrawal Agreement that refer to EU law, its concepts or provisions in accordance with the methods and general principles of Union law[125] as well as CJEU case law. Relevant CJEU cases delivered before the end of the transition period[126] are binding on those domestic authorities while they are only required to 'have due regard to' such case law handed down post transition.[127] These provisions mirror those provided for in the 1994 EEA Agreement according to which CJEU cases were to have similar effects, depending on whether they were made before or after signature of that Agreement.[128] In its practice, however, the EFTA Court has not distinguished between pre- and post-EEA Agreement CJEU case law, thereby respecting it in its entirety and applying it directly without temporal discrimination in cases before it.[129] If UK courts were to follow this line of reasoning, it would then mean that they would in effect be binding themselves to future CJEU decisions in interpreting the Withdrawal Agreement and the EU law related to it, irrespective of the date of their being made.

Lastly, while British courts can make references under Article 267 TFEU until the end of the transition period under any area of EU law,[130] they retain that right in respect of citizens' rights until eight years after the end of that period.[131] Under the Withdrawal Agreement, this effectively keeps in place the *acquis* of Directive 2004/38/EC[132] and its related EU legal provisions, as interpreted by CJEU case law, at least until the end of 2028.

2.5.5 *Institutional and administrative criteria*

The Withdrawal Agreement[133] made it clear that on Brexit the UK would be excluded from the nomination, appointment or election of members of the institutions, bodies, offices and agencies of the Union, as well as from participation in their decision-making and attendance at their meetings. Moreover,[134] the entry into force of that Agreement brought to an end the mandates of all members of institutions, bodies and agencies of the Union nominated, appointed or elected in relation to UK membership of the EU. This meant of course that UK nationals in the institutions, for example, MEPs, the European Commissioner and the judges at the CJEU, all had to step down.[135] UK withdrawal also required the relocation of two of the Union's agencies situated in London, the European Medicines Agency and the European Banking Authority, ultimately to Amsterdam and Paris respectively.[136]

2.6 Conclusion

This chapter has shown that, as happened with the accession process under Article 49 TEU, the EU institutions have developed the provisions of Article 50 TEU on withdrawal by complementing its terms with various official documentation.[137] Taken together, they have given birth to the withdrawal or Brussels criteria that govern this and any future secession of an EU Member State. In identifying those criteria, it has been possible to look at how the Union's values have underlain them in the present withdrawal process.

In organisational terms, the EU has definitely strengthened its internal (inter-institutional) coherence during the Brexit negotiations and external unity vis-à-vis third countries. It has also reinforced observance of the values of legal certainty, solidarity (both social solidarity in respect of EU citizens as well as inter-state solidarity) and non-discrimination. This reinforced coherence bodes well for the future conduct of negotiations with third countries – whether for accession, broad comprehensive or free trade agreements.

While the manner of the EP's involvement in the withdrawal negotiations has reinforced this unified approach, at the same time, it has also allowed the EP to enhance its own role. Viewed merely from the express Treaty terms, the EP's powers in the process appear limited to a passive right to information: the provisions of Article 208(10) TFEU merely require that the EP is to be 'immediately and fully informed at all stages' of the negotiations. However, given the manner in which the EP had amplified its part in the TTIP negotiations, it sought to build on that prior experience in the Brexit negotiations. Consequently, although not part of the EU negotiating side, it appointed its own Brexit co-ordinator early on in order to better organise and present its position. As the only popularly and directly elected EU institution, the EP leveraged this position to champion the interests of its constituency, namely EU citizens (and UK nationals). It has accordingly underscored its legitimate concerns in that field by ensuring respect for democracy, the rule of law and social solidarity.

Given its experience during the Brexit negotiations, the EP will probably continue to enhance its role in the next round of negotiations with the UK. Such development opens up an increasing opportunity to deepen its involvement and scrutiny of subsequent treaty negotiations with third countries.

In terms of the application of the Union's values in the future, several points may be made. First, according to Article 3(5) TEU, in its external relations, the Union is to uphold and promote its values. Moreover these values have long formed part of the conditionality for entering into accession negotiations, continuing those negotiations and ultimately of acceding to the Union.[138] Although the CJEU confirmed prior academic opinion[139] in its reasoning in the *Wightman* case,[140] namely that Article 2 TEU values were equally applicable to withdrawal as they were to accession, a future Intergovernmental Conference might decide to incorporate Article 2 by express reference into Article 50 TEU.

Second, the need to observe the principle of sincere co-operation during negotiations guided the parties – despite the vagaries of the process – to an acceptable solution, especially taking into account the particular concerns on Northern Ireland. However, sincere co-operation (as developed by the CJEU) will continue to guide the EU as well as the UK in the future execution of the provisions of the 2019 Withdrawal Agreement.[141]

Lastly, the most notable progress has been made with transparency, the application of which to the withdrawal negotiations assisted the EU in keeping the various stakeholders – Member States, businesses and citizens – firmly on side compared to previous sets of negotiations. In this sense, the hope would be that the EU institutions continue to be as parsimonious in future negotiations with their use of the 2001 Regulation (to prevent disclosure of documents related to external relations) as they have already been in those culminating in the 2019 Withdrawal Agreement.

It appears then that the EU institutions clearly learned their lesson from the debacle over the TTIP and ensured an open and transparent manner to sharing information with the public on the progress towards a negotiated Withdrawal Agreement with the UK. This is a positive indication for the future rounds of the post-Brexit negotiations on the various bilateral partnerships as well as those concerned with third-country trade agreements or even accession.

Notes

1 For example, three entities have previously seceded from the Union: Algeria in 1962 (on independence from France); Greenland in 1985 (while remaining a self-governing part of the Kingdom of Denmark); and Saint Barthélemy in 2012 (on changing it status from an outermost region of the EU to an overseas country or territory associated with it).

2 Allan F Tatham, *Enlargement of the European Union* (Kluwer Law International 2009) 206–231.

3 For a discussion on this process, Allan F Tatham, 'Ampliación y Política europea de Vecindad de la UE' in José María Beneyto (ed), *Acción exterior de la UE*, Vol IX, *Tratado de Derecho y Políticas de la Unión Europea* (IDEE and Thomson Reuters Aranzadi 2017) ch 9, 501, 562–566.

4 Case C-327/18 PPU *RO* EU:C:2018:733, para 46; Case C-621/18 *Wightman v. Secretary of State for Exiting the European Union* EU:C:2018:999, paras 50–51.

5 *Wightman* (n 4) para 63.

6 European Council (Art 50) Guidelines (Brussels, 29 April 2017) 1 www.consilium.europa.eu/media/21763/29-euco-art50-guidelinesen.pdf accessed 7 April 2020 (Guidelines).
7 Council of the European Union, Directives for the negotiation of an agreement with the United Kingdom of Great Britain and Northern Ireland setting out the arrangements for its withdrawal from the European Union (Brussels, 22 May 2017) www.consilium.europa.eu/media/21766/directives-for-the-negotiation-xt21016-ad01re02en17.pdf accessed 7 April 2020 (Negotiating Directives).
8 Council of the European Union, Agreement on the withdrawal of the United Kingdom of Great Britain and Northern Ireland from the European Union and the European Atomic Energy Community [2019] OJ C384 I/1 (Withdrawal Agreement, WA).
9 Council of the European Union, Political declaration setting out the framework for the future relationship between the European Union and the United Kingdom [2019] OJ C384 I/178 (Political Declaration).
10 *Wightman* (n 4).
11 Tatham (n 2) 130–134.
12 Allan F Tatham, '"Don't Mention Divorce at the Wedding, Darling"! EU Accession and Withdrawal after Lisbon' in Piet Eeckhout, Andrea Biondi and Stefanie Ripley (eds), *European Union Law after the Lisbon Treaty* (Oxford University Press 2012) ch 6, 128, 148–149; and Piet Eeckhout and Eleni Frantziou, 'Brexit and Article 50 TEU: A Constitutionalist Reading' (2017) 54 Common Market Law Review 695, 696–697.
13 *Wightman* (n 4) paras 62–63.
14 *Wightman* (n 4) para 62.
15 Tatham (n 12) 148–149.
16 The concept has more than a dose of irony about it, considering its military and security overtones within the context of a retreat or the political overtones of a colonial power leaving a particular territory: Christopher Bellamy, 'Hong Kong Forces Withdrawal Outlined' *Independent* (London, 19 July 1993) www.independent.co.uk/news/uk/politics/hong-kong-forces-withdrawal-outlined-1485942.html accessed 7 April 2020.
17 *Wightman* (n 4) para 56.
18 Guidelines (n 6) 1.
19 Recital 5, Preamble, WA.
20 Guidelines (n 6) 1 and 3–7.
21 Tatham (n 2) 239–269.
22 Tatham (n 12) 152.
23 *Wightman* (n 4) para 63.
24 Jean-Claude Piris, 'Political and Legal Aspects of Recent Regional Secessionist Trends in some EU Member States (II)' in Carlos Closa (ed), *Secession from a Member State and Withdrawal from the European Union: Troubled Membership* (Cambridge University Press 2017) ch 6, 88, 88–93.
25 Viktor Vanberg, 'Bürgersouveränität und wettbewerblicher Föderalismus: Das Beispiel der EU' in Wolf Schäfer (ed), *Zukunftsprobleme der europäischen Wirtschaftsverfassung* (Duncker & Humblot 2004) 51, 82–84.
26 Tatham (n 12) 149.
27 The UK Labour Party had promised, in 1981, that if it were elected then Britain would withdraw from the EEC without holding any referendum: 'European Community: We'll Love You and Leave You' *The Economist* (London, 25 July 1981) 53.
28 Allan F Tatham, 'The Constitutional Challenges that the Brexit Negotiations have Created in the United Kingdom: An overview' (2018) 59 RDCE 263–302.
29 *R (on the application of Miller) v Secretary of State for Exiting the European Union (Miller I)* [2017] UKSC 5, [2017] 2 WLR 583.
30 *Wightman* (n 4) para 75.
31 Theresa May, 'Prime Minister's Letter to Donald Tusk Triggering Article 50' (London, 29 March 2017) www.gov.uk/government/uploads/system/uploads/attachment_data/file/604079/Prime_Ministers_letter_to_European_Council_President_Donald_Tusk.pdf accessed 7 April 2020.
32 Guidelines (n 6) paras 25–27.
33 Thomas Streinz, 'Editorial – Cooperative Brexit: Giving Back Control Over Trade Policy' (2017) 15 ICON 271, 277.
34 Streinz (n 33) 278.
35 Guidelines (n 6) paras 25–27.

36 The continuing centrality of sincere co-operation in post-Brexit relations between the UK and the EU is underscored by the fact that its core elements were incorporated into Art 5 WA.
37 Koen Lenaerts, '"In the Union we Trust": Trust Enhancing Principles of Community Law' (2004) 41 Common Market Law Review 317, 321.
38 For example, Arts 10, 11, 15 and 16 TEU and Art 42 CFR.
39 Regulation 1049/2001/EC of the European Parliament and of the Council of 30 May 2001 regarding public access to European Parliament, Council and Commission documents [2001] OJ L145/43.
40 Paul P Craig and Grainne de Búrca, *EU Law: Text, Cases and Materials* (6th edn, Oxford University Press 2015) 570–574.
41 Recital 2, Preamble, Reg 1049/2001/EC.
42 Martin Westlake and David Galloway, *The Council of the European Union* (John Harper Publishing 2004) 372–373.
43 Art 4(1)(a), Reg 1049/2001/EC.
44 Craig and de Búrca (n 40).
45 Evelyn Coremans, 'From Access to Documents to Consumption of Information: The European Commission Transparency Policy for the TTIP Negotiations' (2017) 5(3) *Politics and Governance* 29–39.
46 Vigjilenca Abazi and Johan Adriaensen, 'Allies in Transparency? Parliamentary, Judicial and Administrative Interplays in the EU's International Negotiations' (2017) 5(3) *Politics and Governance* 75, 76.
47 Guidelines (n 6) para 2.
48 General Secretariat of the Council, Guiding principles for transparency in negotiations under Article 50 TEU (Brussels, 22 May 2017) https://docplayer.net/48366469-Council-of-the-european-union-brussels-22-may-2017-or-en.html accessed 7 April 2020 (Guiding Principles).
49 Guiding Principles (n 48) 2.
50 Guiding Principles (n 48) 2.
51 Guiding Principles (n 48) 6–7.
52 See European Commission, Brexit negotiations: information on the United Kingdom's withdrawal and its future relationship with the European Union https://ec.europa.eu/commission/brexit-negotiations_en accessed 7 April 2020.
53 European Commission, Meetings of Chief Negotiator Michel Barnier with organisations and self-employed individuals http://ec.europa.eu/transparencyinitiative/meetings/meeting.do?host=fa02e4e1-d738-413e-8b4e-ed8381a90e86 accessed 7 April 2020.
54 Jochen Herbst, 'Observations on the Right to Withdraw from the European Union: Who are the "Masters of the Treaty"?' (2005) 6 German LJ 1755, 1757–1758.
55 For example, European Council Decision (EU) 2019/476 taken in agreement with the United Kingdom of 22 March 2019 extending the period under Article 50(3) TEU [2019] OJ L 80 I/1.
56 Stefano Fella, 'Extending Article 50: Could Brexit be Delayed?' House of Commons Library Briefing Paper CBP 8496 (London, 21 March 2019) 37 https://researchbriefings.parliament.uk/ResearchBriefing/Summary/CBP-8496 accessed 7 April 2020.
57 Fella (n 56) 38–41.
58 Tatham (n 2) 218–224.
59 Tatham (n 3) 534–566.
60 Although Article 3(5) TEU already provides that the Union shall uphold and promote its values and interests in relations with the wider world.
61 Guidelines (n 6) para 1; and Political Declaration (n 9) para 3.
62 Guidelines (n 6) para 6.
63 Arts 126–132 WA.
64 But see the continuing division of Cyprus, post accession: Tatham (n 2) 132–139.
65 Tatham (n 2) 221–222.
66 Tatham (n 28) 290–293.
67 On these issues, see Juan Santos Vara (Chapter 21) and Jed Odermatt (Chapter 22) in this handbook.
68 Guidelines (n 6) paras 11–12 and 24.
69 Protocol on Ireland/Northern Ireland [2019] OJ C384 I/92; Protocol relating to the Sovereign Bases of the United Kingdom of Great Britain and Northern Ireland in Cyprus [2019] OJ C384 I/136; and Protocol on Gibraltar [2019] OJ C384 I/143.
70 Arts 164–165 WA.

71 Tatham (n 28) 292–295.
72 Allan F Tatham, 'El largo y sinuoso camino: un análisis de la negociación del Brexit desde la perspectiva británica' (2020) 84–85 *El Cronista del Estado social y democrático de derecho* 28, 37–39.
73 Juha Raitio and Helena Raulus, 'The UK EU Referendum and the Move Towards Brexit' (2017) 24(1) MJ 25, 37–42.
74 Adam Łazowski, 'EEA Countries (Iceland, Liechtenstein and Norway)' in Steve Blockmans and Adam Łazowski (eds), *The European Union and Its Neighbours* (TMC Asser Press 2006) ch 4, 95, 108–137.
75 Christa Tobler and Jacques Beglinger, *Grundzuege des bilateralen (Wirtschafts-) Rechts: Systematische Darstellung in Text und Tafeln* (Dike Verlag 2013).
76 Tatham (n 2) 142–153.
77 Tatham (n 3) 548–549.
78 Political Declaration (n 9) paras 5 and 16.
79 Eeckhout and Frantziou (n 12) 716–717.
80 Comprehensive Economic and Trade Agreement (CETA) between Canada, of the one part, and the European Union and its Member States, of the other part [2017] OJ L11/23.
81 Christophe Hillion and Panos Koutrakos (eds), *Mixed Agreements in EU Law Revisited: The EU and its Member States in the World* (Hart Publishing 2010).
82 Art 3(1)(e) TFEU. On relevant competences to conclude FTAs, see the CJEU in Opinion 2/15 *Free Trade Agreement with Singapore* EU:C:2017:376.
83 Guidelines (n 6) paras 20–22.
84 Political Declaration (n 9) para 17.
85 Political Declaration (n 9) para 5.
86 Political Declaration (n 9) paras 17 and 77.
87 Political Declaration (n 9) paras 17–18.
88 Political Declaration (n 9) paras 3 and 80–117.
89 Art 184 WA.
90 As set out in UK law in European Union (Withdrawal) Act 2018, s 15A, as inserted by European Union (Withdrawal Agreement) Act 2020, s 33.
91 The alternative – where no trade deal is eventually concluded or where the withdrawing state leaves the Union without even a transitional period under a ratified withdrawal agreement – would be to trade on WTO terms with the EU.
92 European Parliament, Resolution on the framework of the future EU–UK relationship (Strasbourg, 14 March 2018) para 5 www.europarl.europa.eu/doceo/document/TA-8-2018-0069_EN.html accessed 7 April 2020.
93 Tatham (n 2) 141–148.
94 Case C-135/08 *Rottmann v. Freistaat Bayern* EU:C:2009:588, Opinion of AG Maduro, para 23; cf Clemens M Rieder, 'The Withdrawal Clause of the Lisbon Treaty in the Light of EU Citizenship: Between Disintegration and Integration' (2013) 37 Fordham International Law Journal 147, 168–172.
95 May (n 31).
96 Guidelines (n 6) para 8.
97 Michael Dougan, 'The Convention's Draft Constitutional Treaty: A "Tidying-Up Exercise" that needs Some Tidying-Up of Its Own' (2003) 27 *Federal Trust Constitutional Online Paper Series* 1, 8 https://papers.ssrn.com/sol3/papers.cfm?abstract_id=507782 accessed 7 April 2020.
98 Rieder (n 94) 159.
99 European Parliament, 'Parliament appoints Guy Verhofstadt as representative on Brexit matters' *Press Release* 41661 (Brussels, 8 September 2016) www.europarl.europa.eu/news/en/press-room/20160908IPR41661/parliament-appoints-guy-verhofstadt-as-representative-on-brexit-matters accessed 7 April 2020.
100 Shehab Khan, '"Brexit Deal will be Vetoed if Citizens' Rights are not Protected," President of European Parliament Says' *Independent* (London, 20 April 2017) www.independent.co.uk/news/uk/politics/brexit-veto-eu-citizens-rights-not-protected-antonio-tajani-says-a7694036.html accessed 7 April 2020.
101 Eleanor Spaventa, 'Mice or Horses? British Citizens in the EU 27 after Brexit as "Former EU Citizens"' (2019) 44 European Law Review 589–604.
102 European Commission, Position paper on 'Essential Principles on Citizens' Rights' (Brussels, 12 June 2017) para I(1) https://ec.europa.eu/commission/sites/beta-political/files/essential-principles-citizens-rights_en_3.pdf accessed 7 April 2020 (Citizens' Rights).

103 Allan F Tatham, *EC Law in Practice: A Case-Study Approach* (Hvg-Orac 2006) 32–36. Now also found in Article 21 CFR as well as in secondary legislation enacted under Article 19(1) TFEU.
104 Negotiating Directives (n 7) para 20.
105 Citizens' Rights (n 102) para I(2)–(3).
106 Recital 6, Preamble, WA.
107 Art 12 WA.
108 Jérémie Van Meerbeeck, 'The Principle of Legal Certainty in the Case-Law of the European Court of Justice: From Certainty to Trust' (2016) 41 European Law Review 275, 275.
109 Juha Raitio, 'Legal Certainty, Non-Retroactivity and Periods of Limitation in EU Law' (2008) 2 Legisprudence 1, 3.
110 Case C-309/89 *Codorníu SA v. Council of the European Union* EU:C:1994:197.
111 Treaty amending, with regard to Greenland, the Treaties establishing the European Communities, Protocol on special arrangements for Greenland [1985] OJ L29/1, Art 2.
112 Michel Barnier and David Davis, Joint Report from the negotiators of the European Union and the United Kingdom Government on progress during phase 1 of negotiations under Article 50 TEU on the United Kingdom's orderly withdrawal from the European Union (Brussels, 8 December 2017) para 6 https://ec.europa.eu/commission/sites/beta-political/files/joint_report.pdf accessed 7 April 2020 (Joint Report).
113 Negotiating Directives (n 7) para 20. The Commission reiterates this as a general principle too: Citizens' Rights (n 102) para I(5).
114 Joint Report (n 112) paras 37–41.
115 Citizens' Rights (n 102) para IV(1)–(2).
116 Art 158(1) WA.
117 Recital 10, Preamble, WA.
118 Arts 135–157 WA.
119 Art 135 WA.
120 Tatham (n 2) 355–374.
121 Recital 8, Preamble, WA.
122 Allan F Tatham, 'Constitutional Judiciary in Central Europe and the Europe Agreement: Decision 30/1998 (VI.25) AB of the Hungarian Constitutional Court' (1999) 48 International & Comparative Law Quarterly 913.
123 Art 4(1) WA.
124 Art 4(1) WA.
125 Art 4(3) WA.
126 Art 4(4) WA.
127 Art 4(5) WA.
128 Agreement on the European Economic Area (EEA) ([1994] OJ L1/3) Art 6; read with Agreement between the EFTA States on the Establishment of a Surveillance Authority and a Court of Justice ([1994] OJ L344/3) Art 3(2).
129 Allan F Tatham, 'Where Culture, Language and Politics Meet: Is There Any Place for National Identity in the EEA Legal System?' (2016) 2(2) *UNIO – EU Law Journal* 108, 115.
130 Art 86(2) WA.
131 Art 158 WA. This would also include any extension to that transition period made by the Joint Committee under Art 132(1) WA.
132 Directive 2004/38/EC of 29 April 2004 on the right of citizens of the Union and their family members to move and reside freely within the territory of the Member States [2004] OJ L158/77.
133 Art 7 WA.
134 Recital 8, Preamble, WA.
135 For British nationals working in EU institutions as officials or agents, certain possibilities existed for their continued employment but no general right: Herwig C H Hofmann, *The Impact of Brexit on the Legal Status of European Union Officials and Other Servants of British Nationality*, Study for JURI Committee of the European Parliament (Brussels, November 2017) www.europarl.europa.eu/RegData/etudes/STUD/2017/596837/IPOL_STU(2017)596837_EN.pdf accessed 7 April 2020.
136 Procedure leading up to a decision on the relocation of the European Medicines Agency and the European Banking Authority in the context of the United Kingdom's withdrawal from the Union (Brussels, 22 June 2017) www.consilium.europa.eu/media/21503/22-euco-conclusions-agencies-relocation.pdf accessed 7 April 2020.

137 Polly R Polak (Chapter 5) in this handbook.
138 Tatham (n 2) 193–237.
139 Tatham (n 12); and Eeckhout and Frantziou (n 12).
140 *Wightman* (n 4).
141 Art 5 WA.

3
In the twilight zone
The transition period in the Withdrawal Agreement

Tobias Lock

3.1 Introduction

An agreement on the United Kingdom's (UK) withdrawal from the European Union (EU) was finally ratified by the House of Commons in the UK by way of the EU (Withdrawal Agreement) Act 2020 and by the Council of the EU and the European Parliament in January 2020. It allowed the UK to leave the EU 'with a deal' at midnight on 31 January 2020.

The Withdrawal Agreement (WA) deals with five key substantive issues: citizens' rights; the financial settlement; separation provisions concerning ongoing procedures, goods on the market, etc.; a Protocol on Ireland/Northern Ireland, which aims to ensure that the land border on the island of Ireland can be kept free from border infrastructure; and the transition period, which forms the subject of this chapter.

The necessity of a transition period stems from the two-step process presupposed by Article 50 TEU: in a first step, Article 50 TEU provides for a WA taking account of the future relationship (in a political declaration) to be negotiated; and, in a second step, negotiations on the future relationship itself can commence. Importantly, Article 50 TEU does not provide an appropriate legal basis for the conclusion of an agreement on the future relationship and neither does it provide for a transition period.[1]

The EU Commission has always argued that the two steps could not happen simultaneously because the EU could only conduct treaty negotiations with third countries and that the UK would only be a third country once the WA is in force, i.e. as soon as it had formally ceased to be a Member State.[2]

A transition period – or in UK parlance implementation period – was therefore needed to buy extra time for the negotiation of a future relationship agreement. Otherwise, both sides would face a gap in their legal relations during which trade and other forms of cooperation would happen on the basis of general international law. This would not only be economically costly, but also highly impractical as it would require two adjustments: first from EU membership to general international law – i.e. World Trade Organization (WTO)-based trade and security cooperation on the basis of older treaties, such as the Council of Europe's Convention on Extradition – and then another adjustment back to a closer relationship with a comprehensive free trade agreement and a deep security partnership.

During the transition period – initially lasting until the end of 2020, but extendable once by either one or two years – most provisions of EU law continue to apply to the UK – technically a third country – as if it were a Member State with the main exception being the UK's exclusion from the EU's institutions and decision-making processes during that period. At the same time, a number of other provisions in the WA – in particular those on citizens' rights and on ongoing procedures, goods in transit, etc. – will not become operational until the transition period has ended.[3]

There are good reasons to suggest that Article 50 TEU provided the appropriate legal basis for the transition period despite the fact that it is not expressly mentioned in the provision. Article 50 TEU is a unique provision amongst the Union's external competences in that it is not defined thematically or in policy terms, but in terms of its purpose: to come to an agreement setting out the arrangements for the withdrawal of a Member State. It presupposes a 'winding up' element, which is one of the reasons why it cannot be the basis for the future relationship. As explained, the transition period facilitates an orderly withdrawal from the EU, in particular if one accepts the European Commission's argument that a future relationship treaty cannot even be negotiated – let alone concluded – while a state is still a member of the EU.[4] The winding up purpose of Article 50 TEU means however that it must be strictly time-limited and that any possibility of extending the transition period cannot lead to that period becoming of indefinite duration.

The following pages provide a closer examination of the UK's peculiar position during the transition period and show that the transition period does not represent a mere continuation of the status quo.[5] During the transition period the UK will be in a twilight zone between EU membership and third country status. It will be shown that already during transition the UK has completed the move from being a subject of EU law to the status of object of EU law. This is due to the fact that its relations with the EU are now defined by an international agreement rather than by EU law proper. While the transition period largely masks this fundamental change there are a number of instances where the new relationship between the EU and the UK is already obvious. This chapter commences with a brief introduction of the dichotomy between subjects and objects of EU law and a discussion of the key provisions on transition in the WA. It then explores the imbalance between the UK and the EU during transition; followed by a discussion on whether the transition period is compliant with the right to participate in elections guaranteed by the European Convention on Human Rights (ECHR); the final part of the chapter addresses the practical and legal difficulties associated with securing an extension to the transition period, after the deadline for requesting such an extension has expired.

3.2 From subject to object: a status quo transition?

At the most basic level, Brexit results in a change of status for the UK vis-à-vis the EU: it moves from being a Member State to being a non-Member State.[6] From the perspective of EU law this means that – at least after the transition period has ended – the UK is no longer a subject of EU law, but merely an object.[7] For the purposes of this contribution, the subjects of EU law are understood in the traditional sense as bearers of rights and obligations.[8] According to the European Court of Justice's (CJEU) seminal decision in *van Gend en Loos* the subjects of EU law 'comprise not only member states but also their nationals'.[9] By contrast to those bearing rights under EU law and thus being given an opportunity to actively participate in its making, the objects of EU law are whatever is regulated by it.[10] This includes third countries. In a similar vein, UK nationals are no longer EU citizens and thus no longer subjects of EU law. Their status is now defined by the WA – namely by international law – and EU legislation and may be further defined by the agreement on a future relationship.

This change in status to becoming an object of EU law is also signified by a change in the law governing EU–UK relations: a shift from an EU law relationship to one that is governed by public international law.

The transition period masks this to a certain extent by including the following basic rule governing transition in Article 127 (1) WA. It says that unless 'otherwise provided in this Agreement, Union law shall be applicable to and in the United Kingdom during the transition period'. The stated aim is to conserve the status quo as far as possible in order to cause the least possible amount of rupture on Brexit day.

According to Article 4 WA 'the provisions of this Agreement and the provisions of Union law made applicable to it shall produce in respect of and in the United Kingdom the same legal effects as those which they produce within the Union and its Member States'. This is reiterated by Article 127 (3) WA, which therefore confirms that the provisions of the WA – and in particular those concerning the transition period – are capable of having direct effect and that they must take primacy over conflicting national law.

According to long-standing CJEU case law, provisions in EU agreements are capable of being directly effective if two conditions are fulfilled: first, the nature and structure of the agreement must not prevent an individual from relying on its provisions;[11] second, the individual provision must contain 'a clear and precise obligation which is not subject, in its implementation or effects, to the adoption of any subsequent measure'.[12] The above quote from Article 4 WA strongly suggests that the drafters of the WA envisaged the agreement being capable of producing such effects. This is reinforced by the next sentence in Article 4 (1) WA which says that '[a] ccordingly, legal or natural persons shall in particular be able to rely directly on the provision contained or referred to in this Agreement which meet the conditions for direct effect under Union law'. While both sentences address the effects in the UK, their wording presupposes that the WA produces equivalent effects in the EU legal order and in that of the Member States.

Article 4 WA means that during the transition period, EU law will continue to be capable of producing direct effects in the UK. What is unprecedented about the transition period is that these effects do not result from membership in a supranational organisation, but that they are the result of an agreement concluded under 'ordinary' international law.

3.3 In the twilight zone: exploring the difference

The following analysis will demonstrate that the UK has already made its move from subject to object of EU law during the transition period. This conclusion is reached despite the fact that aspects of EU membership will be preserved during the transition period. The most apparent difference between the UK's status as a Member State and that during the transition period concerns its lack of representation at the EU level since 31 January 2020. But there are further differences that lead to an imbalance in the rights and obligations between the UK and the EU Member States.

3.3.1 Lack of representation

While the UK is (largely) subject to EU law as if it continued to be a Member State, transition will result in one crucial change to the status quo: the UK will not be represented in the EU's institutions. Articles 7 and 128 (1) WA make it clear that the UK is not considered a Member State for the 'nomination, appointment or election of members of the institutions, bodies, offices and agencies of the Union' as well as 'the participation in the decision-making and the attendance in the meetings of the institutions'. And the UK no longer participates in the decision-making of bodies, offices and agencies of the Union. Moreover, UK citizens are no longer able to elect members of the European Parliament.[13] The UK is therefore bound by EU law without having a say in the adoption of new legislation.

During transition, the Union's enforcement mechanisms remain operational, i.e. in particular public enforcement by the European Commission. Moreover, private enforcement of EU law through domestic courts and the preliminary reference procedure remains possible as the CJEU will continue to have the same jurisdiction as provided for in the Treaties.[14]

The basic feature of the transition period is therefore that the UK continues to be bound by EU law – on the basis of an international law treaty – and subject to its enforcement mechanisms, but without being represented. This is a key difference to membership. It marks the change from subject to object of EU law. This becomes most apparent in the UK's and its nationals' lack of representation at the EU level, which has always been crucial for their subjectivity under EU law. The centrality of representation to the status as a subject of EU law was pointed out by the CJEU in *van Gend en Loos*, 'the nationals of the States brought together in the Community are called upon to cooperate in the functioning of this Community through the intermediary of the European Parliament and the Economic and Social Committee'.[15] In addition to this lack of representation, there are other imbalances hidden in the WA to support this conclusion further.

3.3.2 Sources of the law and equality

There is an imbalance inherent in the transition rules contained in the WA. This imbalance results from the legal status that the rules governing the transition period have under EU law. The doctrine of primacy serves as an example where one can – at least in theory – observe a lack of equivalence.

Article 4 (2) WA places the UK under an obligation to grant the requisite powers to its judicial and administrative authorities to disapply inconsistent or incompatible domestic provisions, through domestic primary legislation. The reason for a lack of equivalence here stems from the fact that the legal basis for the applicability of EU law to and in the UK is the WA and no longer the EU Treaties. From a (dualist) UK perspective, this makes no difference: domestic legislation is needed to give effect to international obligations whether these stem directly from the EU Treaties or from a different treaty, namely, the WA.

From the EU's perspective – and also from that of its Member States – the situation differs, however. The rights of a UK trader during the transition period, for instance, are no longer sourced directly in the EU Treaties, but only indirectly with the WA being the actual source of the rights. Like every international agreement concluded by the Union, the WA ranks below the Treaties but above secondary EU law in the EU's hierarchy of norms.[16] This means that in theory at least the provisions of the WA – including the EU primary and secondary law made applicable by it – are subject to review in the Court of Justice as to their compatibility with EU primary law; by contrast, no such review can occur if a case is brought in a UK court.

This difference in the sources for rights and obligations has implications for the principle of equality of the Member States. According to Article 4 (2) TEU the Union shall respect the equality of Member States before the Treaties, which is a fundamental concept of EU law.

It is axiomatic that since 31 January 2020 the UK is no longer a Member State. At the same time during the transition period according to Article 7 (1) WA 'any reference to Member States ... shall be understood as including the United Kingdom' unless otherwise provided in the WA. Does this mean that the exclusion of the UK from decision-making procedures during transition is in violation of Article 4 (2) TEU given that the WA decrees that the reference to the Member States in that provision must be understood to include the UK?

Such a conclusion would seem to be wrong, however. The UK is no longer a Member State as defined in the EU Treaties so that the Treaties themselves do not require the UK to be treated equally to continuing Member States. That duty only results from the WA. The restrictions on the UK's voting rights and participation in the EU institutions also flow from the WA; so that the resulting restrictions on the principle of equality originate from the same legal source. This means that due to the differently sourced rights and obligations during the transition phase the WA does not contradict Article 4 (2) TEU.

The consequences of Article 7 (1) WA that EU law is supposed to largely apply to and in the UK as if it were a Member State are relatively straightforward in many cases, for example, agricultural subsidies. What the discussion of Article 4 (2) TEU suggests, however, is that the UK's position vis-à-vis the EU is weaker during transition than that of the remaining Member States. In other words, it is no longer a subject of EU law with equal rights to the Member States, but its object with only those rights given to it by way of agreement of the EU institutions.

As the following discussion will show, the UK is in a different position also when it comes to the continued application of certain foundational principles that provide much of the glue that keeps EU law together. While many of these principles have their basis in Treaty provisions, their content has often been significantly shaped by the CJEU's case law.

3.3.3 Mutual trust

What implications does this have for other constitutional principles, such as mutual trust? Can these key principles be applied to third states? Mutual trust underpins the Area of Freedom, Security and Justice (AFSJ). According to the CJEU 'the principle of mutual trust between the Member States is of fundamental importance in EU law, given that it allows an area without internal borders to be created and maintained'.[17]

While mutual recognition is mentioned in a number of competence clauses,[18] mutual trust is not mentioned in the Treaties. It is suggested here that mutual trust as the basis for mutual recognition is not based on the actual psychological mindset of the Member States and their representatives, but rather is legal fiction. The case law of the CJEU suggests that the Member States are obliged by EU law to trust each other and recognise each other's standards, procedures, etc., because of the legal and institutional framework provided for or underpinned by EU law. In *RO* the CJEU pointed out that EU law was

> based on the fundamental premise that each Member State shares with all the other Member States, and recognises that they share with it, a set of common values on which the European Union is founded. That premise implies and justifies the existence of mutual trust between the Member States that those values will be recognised, and therefore, that EU law implementing them will be respected.[19]

It follows in particular, that all Member States be considered 'to be complying with EU law and particularly with the fundamental rights recognised by EU law'.[20]

Only in exceptional circumstances, notably where there is reliable evidence of a real risk of inhuman and degrading treatment in the issuing Member State,[21] is it permissible to not consider that Member State to be compliant with fundamental rights, so that mutual trust cannot be assumed.

How far does the UK's third country status during transition affect the operability of the principle of mutual trust? As argued above, the principle is first and foremost a legal concept and not an empirical one. This means the existence of actual trust is not a prerequisite. Instead, mutual trust is a legal fiction based on a common framework of rules and in particular fundamental rights. Whether this changes during the transition period is an open question. On the one hand, the mere fact that the UK is no longer a Member State might mean that the basis for mutual trust has been eroded. Since the UK is no longer a Member State, references to the shared values of EU Member States seem to no longer apply. One can find some evidence for this in Article 185 WA. Despite the fact that according to Article 62 (1) (b) WA the Framework Decision on the European Arrest warrant continues to apply, Article 185 WA allows Member States to refuse execution of European Arrest Warrants issued by the UK against their own nationals. This is because some national constitutions – for example, Germany's – prohibit the extradition of their own nationals to non-EU states.[22]

On the other hand, the case law of the Court of Justice on mutual trust and Brexit can be understood to suggest that the principle of mutual trust continues to apply where the UK is concerned. One can see an indication of this in the *RO* case already. Asked whether the UK's notification of its intention to leave the EU according to Article 50 TEU meant that a Member State no longer had to execute European Arrest Warrants issued by the UK, the Court responded that this did not constitute an exceptional circumstance that would warrant refusal to execute a warrant. Asked further whether the fact that the person whose surrender had been requested might be imprisoned in the UK until after the UK had left the EU – so that the EU Charter of Fundamental Rights would no longer apply – the CJEU held that the UK would continue to be a party to the ECHR even after Brexit, so that fundamental rights, in particular the prohibition on torture, inhuman and degrading treatment and punishment in Article 3 ECHR, would continue to operate.[23]

Given that during the transition period the UK even remains bound by the Charter and that the UK's legal order continues to be underpinned by the EU's legal and institutional framework, there are therefore some reasons to suggest that the principle of mutual trust continues to apply as previously, though some question marks remain.

3.3.4 Duty of loyalty

Much like mutual trust, the duty of loyalty appears to be based on a special bond between the Union and its Member States.[24] It performs a central role in the interpretation of EU law and has taken on particular salience when it comes to the transposition of directives and in EU external relations law. It finds manifestation in Article 4 (3) TEU as the principle of sincere cooperation.

The reference in the WA to the applicability of EU law in and to the UK during transition includes Article 4 (3) TEU. This suggests that in most cases there is no basis for deviating from this duty, neither to the benefit of the UK nor to that of the EU. One can, however, question whether the duty of loyalty continues to apply in the same way in the field of EU external relations. In external relations law the duty of loyalty restricts the Member States' room for manoeuvre in two main fields: mixed agreements and situations in which the EU is unable to conclude an agreement in a field of its competence and must consequently do so 'through the medium of the Member States'.[25] The duty of loyalty serves the purpose of ensuring 'the unity in the international representation of the Union and its Member States' and thus strengthens their negotiating power.[26] It prohibits the Member States from preventing the Union from carrying out the tasks entrusted to it by the Treaties[27] and places upon them special duties of action and abstention.[28]

During the transition period, the UK remains bound by the international agreements concluded by the Union or by the Member States on behalf of the Union and by mixed agreements.[29] Consequently, one would expect the duty of loyal cooperation to continue to apply to the UK in the same way as it applied during its membership. And, indeed, Article 129 (3) WA expressly mentions the principle of sincere cooperation and prohibits the UK from acting in a way that is likely to be prejudicial to the Union's interest.

However, the UK is in a peculiar position in this regard. While it remains bound by EU obligations arising from treaties concluded by the Union, by the Member States on behalf of the Union and from mixed agreements, it is not automatically entitled to rights under those agreements as it is no longer a Member State. This is obvious where EU-only agreements are concerned. In the case of mixed agreements or indeed agreements concluded by the Member States on behalf of the EU, the situation is less straightforward. In some cases, the agreement may be of an essentially bilateral nature – for example, the European Economic Area Agreement – so that it cannot automatically entitle the UK as a non-Member State. In other cases, especially a multilateral setting, the mixed agreement or an agreement concluded by the Member States on behalf of the EU might be operational by itself after Brexit. At the same time, the UK is no longer able to participate in the work of any bodies set up by EU international agreements.[30]

What does this mean for the duty of loyalty? In one sense, during transition the UK is under an aggravated duty of loyalty. If one conceives of EU membership as a pooling of sovereignty, the duty of loyalty in the external relations context is acceptable because each Member State has a voice in the process of negotiating, ratifying and implementing the agreement. While usually conducted by the European Commission, EU treaty negotiations require authorisation by the Council and must be conducted in accordance with its negotiating directives.[31] Ratification happens by way of a Council decision and in some cases the European Parliament's consent is additionally required.[32] And implementation may at times require the adoption of EU legislation. Hence there are numerous ways in which the duty of loyalty is counterbalanced by opportunities to participate.

Because the UK is excluded from this form of representation during transition, this counterbalance is missing. Hence one can argue that the duty of loyalty weighs more heavily on the UK during transition. On the other hand, the UK is partly relieved from the duty of loyalty during the transition period. As the *Inland Waterways* decisions showed, once the Council has given the Commission a mandate to negotiate an agreement, the Member States are under a duty of close cooperation with the Union institutions in order to facilitate the achievement of the Union's tasks and to ensure the coherence and consistency of action in its international representation.[33] This is regardless of the type of competence upon which the Union is acting.

During the transition period, the UK is, however, expressly allowed to

> negotiate, sign and ratify international agreements entered into in its own capacity in the areas of exclusive competence of the Union, provided those agreements do not enter into force or apply during the transition period, unless so authorised by the Union.[34]

This would suggest that the duty of loyalty does not apply to the UK in a situation envisaged in the *Inland Waterways* cases. Even if the Commission has obtained a mandate to negotiate an agreement with a third country, the UK would be in a position to simultaneously negotiate its own agreement with that same country.

Two questions remain, however: first, whether there are any other restraints on the UK, for example, a duty to not frustrate the EU's negotiating efforts, for instance; and, second, what the impact of the limitation to the Union's exclusive competences in Article 129 (4) WA is. On the first question, it would seem reasonable to suggest that during transition the UK remains bound by a general duty of sincere cooperation. Hence the exception made in Article 129 (4) WA should not release the UK from an obligation to conduct its own negotiations in a manner that would not frustrate the Union's own efforts. On the second question, the limitation to EU exclusive competences seems odd in light of the broad *Inland Waterways* case law. Why should the UK be allowed to negotiate within the EU's exclusive competence – which no Member State would ever be allowed to do without the EU's permission – but not in an area of shared competence? It is suggested here that the provision should be read down in this sense and that the limitation to exclusive competences should not be understood as an exclusion of shared competence but rather mean that 'even in areas of exclusive competence' the UK may negotiate, sign and ratify international agreements.

3.3.5 The status of UK citizens during transition: fundamental still?

There are also question marks over the status of UK citizens during the transition period. Do they – as third country nationals – enjoy rights similar to those of EU citizens? According to Articles 9 TEU and 20 TFEU, EU citizenship is premised on Member State nationality. Since 31 January 2020 UK citizens therefore no longer qualify as EU citizens under the Treaties. At the same time, according to Article 127 (1) WA during the transition period, EU law continues to apply to and in the UK as before; and pursuant to Article 127 (6) WA references to the Member States are to be understood as including the UK.

Does this mean that UK citizens continue to be EU citizens during transition? The WA is not explicit about this, but there are good reasons to suggest that they are not, even though they continue to enjoy many of the rights of EU citizens. One could of course advance the argument that if any reference to the Member States must be understood to include the UK, then the reference to 'nationals of the Member States' in Article 20 TFEU includes nationals of the UK. This view, it is submitted, encounters a number of legal and conceptual difficulties.

First, it would ignore the fact that according to the WA certain citizenship rights have been expressly excluded. While this means *e contrario* that the drafters of the WA envisaged the other citizens' rights to operate as normal, it results in UK citizens to not be able to avail of the full panoply of citizens' rights during transition. According to Article 127 (1) (b) WA these are the right to participate in citizens' initiatives in Articles 11 (4) TEU and 24 (1) TFEU and acts adopted on their basis; the right to vote and stand in European Parliament and municipal elections in their Member State of residence under the same conditions as nationals (Articles 20 (2) (b) and 22 TFEU and 39 and 40 CFR and acts adopted on their basis). This leaves UK citizens with the same free movement rights, rights to diplomatic protection and rights to petition as EU citizens. Yet they no longer possess crucial participatory rights appearing in the *van Gend en Loos* quote above, which suggests that they have now lost their status as subjects of EU law.

Second, it would be problematic from a constitutional law point of view given that the Treaties convey the status of EU citizen on citizens of the Member States, which in the words of the CJEU was destined to be their 'fundamental status' under EU law.[35] Under the hierarchy of norms in EU law it would be problematic if such a fundamental status could be granted by a mere international agreement concluded between the Union and a third country, which procedurally could be seen to circumvent the Treaty amendment process.

Third, it is also questionable in how far EU citizens' rights that have been largely stripped of their participatory component – in particular the right to vote – can still be considered the fundamental status of UK citizens during transition. This is particularly so with democracy forming one of the Union's founding values.[36] For these reasons, UK citizens can no longer be considered the equivalent to EU citizens during the transition period even though they continue to enjoy the same free movement rights.[37]

In the context of participatory rights, one can observe an interesting lack of a parallel between EU citizens resident in the UK and UK citizens resident in the EU. While the latter are now excluded from participating in European Parliament elections, the former might still be able to do so, provided their Member State allows them as non-residents to register and vote by post or proxy. Furthermore, all EU citizens – whether resident in the EU or not – may sign a citizens' initiative.

As far as the 'fundamental status' is concerned, the question arises whether – if the argument advanced here is correct – this might make a difference to the substance of the rights enjoyed by UK citizens during transition. For instance, the CJEU employed the 'fundamental status' in the *Ruiz Zambrano* case, which extended the reach of EU citizenship rights.[38] It followed from this fundamental status that Article 20 TFEU stood in the way of national measures that would deprive EU citizens 'of the genuine enjoyment of the substance of the rights conferred'.[39] This meant that the third country national carer of an EU citizen who is a minor must be given a right of residence even in the EU Member State of which the EU citizen is a national although normally EU citizen rights only operate where there is a cross-border element to the case.

It is an open question whether the Court – if faced with a case from the UK during the transition period raising similar difficulties – would decide in a comparably progressive fashion by making recourse to the concepts of 'fundamental status' and 'genuine enjoyment'. Given UK nationals' lack of subjectivity under EU law, there are good reasons to suggest that it would not.

3.4 Legality: the right to vote

The transition period raises questions of legality where the exclusion of UK citizens from the right to vote in European Parliament elections is concerned. As discussed above, during the transition period, the UK is no longer represented in the EU's institutions and decision-making processes. Therefore, if a piece of EU legislation is adopted during the transition period and also enters into force during that period, the UK will be bound by it without having had a say in it. It is recalled in this context that from the point of view of EU law this exclusion of UK citizens is laid down in an international agreement that must be compliant with EU primary law. The exclusion raises questions both regarding its compliance with the ECHR and with EU law. These will be addressed in turn.

In the well-known *Matthews* case, the European Court of Human Rights (ECtHR) found a violation of Article 3 Protocol 1 as residents of Gibraltar had been excluded from participation in elections to the European Parliament.[40] Article 3 Protocol 1 ECHR provides as follows: 'The High Contracting Parties undertake to hold free elections at reasonable intervals by secret ballot, under conditions which will ensure the free expression of the opinion of the people in the choice of the legislature.' In *Matthews* the ECtHR established that the European Parliament was a 'legislature' in this sense. The key question for the purposes of this contribution is then whether during the transition period the European Parliament will have the characteristics of a legislature in the UK even though by virtue of Article 127 (1) (b) WA the UK electorate is excluded from European Parliament elections. If new EU legislation is passed during the transition period, the UK is automatically bound by it as if it were a Member State. In case of a regulation, it will be directly applicable in the UK from its entry into force; in case of a directive, it may have direct effect once the transposition period is over.

It would therefore seem that the findings of the ECtHR made in *Matthews* with regard to Gibraltar would equally apply to the UK during the transition period.[41] The ECtHR pointed in particular to the co-decision procedure – which has since been extended and is now the ordinary legislative procedure – and to the European Parliament's role in the appointment and supervision of the European Commission – also since strengthened – as well as in the budgetary process. All of these are relevant to the UK during transition. Hence it is difficult to see how Article 3 Protocol 1 ECHR is not engaged here.

However, the right to vote is not absolute, but is subject to implied limitations.[42] As far as the transition period is concerned, the answer as to whether the UK and the EU might have overstepped their margin of appreciation in this regard is not straightforward. On the one hand, one could argue that the wholesale exclusion of the UK electorate goes to the essence of the right to free elections and is therefore outside the margin of appreciation. On the other hand, the transition period is strictly time-limited at two years and 11 months at the most; the number of new pieces of legislation will probably be rather limited; and the UK will be in a position to abandon all of them once the transition period is over. Moreover, the UK Parliament has ratified the WA and thus given its consent to the transition period with all its consequences as a legislature. Arguably there is thus little difference to the transfer of legislative powers to the executive (so-called Henry VIII powers), which are rather common.

If one arrived at the conclusion that the WA violated Article 3 Protocol 1 ECHR, there would be no doubt that a UK citizen (or indeed an EU citizen living in the UK) could bring a case against the UK before the ECtHR claiming such a violation.[43] The next question would be whether this would also constitute a violation of EU primary law and how this could be reviewed. It should first be noted that there is no fully equivalent provision to Article 3 Protocol 1 ECHR in the EU Charter of Fundamental Rights. Article 39 (1) of the Charter replicates Article 22 (1) TFEU, but it is merely an equality provision ensuring equal treatment of EU citizens with nationals of the EU Member State in which they reside. Article 39 (2) CFR – which corresponds to Article 14 (3) TEU – enshrines a right to vote, but it is confined to EU citizens.[44] Since Brexit, UK citizens are no longer EU citizens; and indeed, Article 127 (1) (b) WA expressly says that Article 39 of the Charter is not applicable Union law during the transition period.[45]

Hence one needs to ask whether there is a right akin to Article 3 Protocol 1 ECHR that forms part of the general principles of EU law, which continue to be a source of fundamental rights.[46] While not directly binding on the EU, the ECHR provides the most important source of inspiration for EU fundamental rights recognised as general principles of EU law. One can therefore argue that a broader right to vote – not strictly limited to EU citizens – is part of the general principles of EU law. While there is no direct confirmation of this view in the CJEU's case law, the case of *Spain v UK* implicitly recognises such a right. The case arose in the aftermath of the *Matthews* judgment with Spain arguing that changes to UK electoral law to allow the electorate of Gibraltar to participate in European Parliament elections was incompatible with the Treaty. In dismissing Spain's case, the CJEU referenced the *Matthews* case on a number of occasions. It noted in particular:

> In the light of that caselaw of the European Court of Human Rights and the fact that that Court has declared the failure to hold elections to the European Parliament in Gibraltar to be contrary to Article 3 of Protocol No 1 to the Convention in that it denied 'the applicant, as a resident of Gibraltar' any opportunity to express her opinion on the choice of the members of the European Parliament, the United Kingdom cannot be criticised for adopting the legislation necessary for the holding of such elections under conditions equivalent, with the necessary changes, to those laid down by the legislation applicable in the United Kingdom.[47]

There are thus good reasons to suggest that the CJEU considers the right to vote as guaranteed by Article 3 Protocol 1 ECHR to be a general principle of EU law, so that the WA would need to comply with it in order to be valid.

3.5 Transition extension

Due to the delays in the ratification of the WA and the consequently delayed exit date, the transition period is due to last only 11 months. The resulting time-pressure – exacerbated by the break in negotiations during the Covid-19 lockdowns in early 2020 – may make an extension of the transition period practically necessary.

3.5.1 Extension under the WA

Article 132 WA allows the Joint Committee to decide on an extension of the transition period. This decision can only be taken once and may extend the transition period for either one year or two, i.e. either until the end of 2021 or the end of 2022. The Joint Committee – composed of representatives from the EU and the UK – decides by mutual consent.[48] During an extended transition period, EU law would remain applicable to and in the UK much like during the original transition period. The UK would, in important areas, move further away from the status quo, however. It would not automatically take part in EU programmes and activities but would be fully considered a third country. This means in particular that the UK would not be taking part in the Common Agricultural Policy or the EU's research programmes.

According to Article 132 WA the extension decision has to be taken 'before 1 July 2020'. Past experience with extensions under Article 50 TEU where extension decisions were made only days before the expiry of the negotiation period strongly suggest that this constitutes an unrealistically early deadline. In addition, UK legislation contains an express prohibition on the UK Government to agree an extension.[49] There is therefore little prospect of the transition period being extended according to Article 132 WA. And even if an extension does happen, it may turn out to be too short. The question is what solutions – if any – could be adopted if there was a political need to extend the transition period (again) after 1 July 2020. Two solutions come to mind. The first consists in an amendment of the WA allowing for the extension decision to be taken at a later stage. The second solution would try to circumvent the limitations contained in the WA in its entirety by agreeing a new transitional settlement separately. Both bring with them advantages and drawbacks.

3.5.2 Amending the WA

The first option to get around the time-limit of having to request an extension before 1 July 2020 would be to amend Article 132 WA accordingly. Under international law, treaties are generally open to amendments provided that the parties agree.[50] Unless the treaty itself provides for a specific procedure – as the WA does for an extension under Article 132 WA – a treaty amendment is effected by concluding another treaty. Hence under the principle of conferred powers the EU must possess the requisite competence that covers the amendment in substantive terms. In most cases of historic treaty amendments – typically by way of a protocol to the original treaty[51] – this requirement did not pose particular problems: after all, the Union will have had competence to conclude the original treaty, say on trade in goods. Usually amendments will concern the same subject matter so that the same external competence can be used.

Where the WA is concerned, there is some uncertainty over this approach as it is unclear whether the original basis for concluding the agreement – Article 50 TEU – can also be used to amend it after the WA has entered into force. The wording of Article 50 (2) TEU says that a

> Member State which decides to withdraw shall notify the European Council of its intention. In the light of the guidelines provided by the European Council, the Union shall negotiate and conclude an agreement with that State, setting out the arrangements for its withdrawal, taking account of the framework for its future relationship with the Union.

The question is whether this means that Article 50 TEU can only be used as a legal basis so long as the withdrawing Member State still is a Member State of the EU, i.e. until either the entry into force of the WA or the withdrawing Member State's exit without an agreement by lapse of time. The wording of Article 50 TEU is not conclusive. It only deals with the conclusion of the WA as such, but not with its amendment.

One can find arguments in favour of a broad understanding of Article 50 TEU. Its overall purpose is to facilitate an orderly withdrawal from the EU. While it acknowledges the possibility of a disorderly exit without an agreement, the preference for an orderly withdrawal is clear from its wording ('failing that') and also from its drafting history.[52] The question is whether this overall purpose of Article 50 TEU suffices to read into it a competence to amend the WA after its entry into force. A counter-argument would be that Article 50 TEU itself shows that while an orderly withdrawal is desirable, the Member States were not willing to give the EU competence to comprehensively deal with all the consequences of withdrawal. It is clear from Article 50 TEU that the EU's standard – and limited – competences must be used in two types of cases: first, in the event that a Member State leaves without an agreement by lapse of time, any mitigation measures agreed between the former Member State and the EU cannot be based on Article 50 TEU. Second, Article 50 TEU is clear that the future relationship agreement cannot be based on it.

On a strict reading therefore, an amendment to the WA would not be covered by Article 50 TEU. After all, the withdrawing Member State is no longer a Member State so that Article 50 TEU can no longer be used for any treaty concluded with it. This reading finds support in the exceptional nature of Article 50 TEU as a competence clause. EU competences typically relate to substantive law areas. For instance, the exclusive external competence found in Article 207 TFEU inter alia empowers the EU to conclude 'tariff and trade agreements relating to trade in goods and services'. By contrast, Article 50 TEU cuts across all policy areas and gives the EU an exclusive and broad competence to conclude a WA. Despite its breadth, it is procedurally relatively light-touch in that it only requires a qualified majority in the Council and approval by the European Parliament. The exceptional nature of Article 50 TEU would suggest that it cannot be used as a competence base for agreeing an amendment to the WA given the maxim that exceptions should be interpreted narrowly.

This suggests that the change in status from Member State to non-Member State is key for the availability of Article 50 TEU as a competence base. The momentous nature of this change in status – or from subject to object of EU law – has been demonstrated above. One can additionally point to the CJEU's pronouncements on the nature of the withdrawal process. In *RO* the Court reiterated that EU law 'continues in full force and effect in that State until the time of its actual withdrawal from the European Union'.[53] And in *Wightman* the Court highlighted that for as long as a Member State is a Member State, it enjoys the full privileges of being a Member State which means that it cannot be forced out of the EU against its will even if it has already handed in its notification to withdrawal according to Article 50 TEU.[54] Yet this implies that the second a Member State is out of the EU, everything has changed. Consequently, the better arguments are in favour of considering Article 50 TEU to not be available as a legal basis for amending the WA after withdrawal.

It follows that any amendment to the WA would need to be based on a specific competence clause found in the Treaties. Where the transition period is concerned, a single competence clause cannot be found as the transition period covers all subject matters including immigration, foreign and security policy, etc.

On the part of the EU a mixed agreement would therefore be necessary to amend Article 132 WA and thereby extend the transition period after 30 June 2020. This makes the ratification of any such agreement on the EU side highly complex.

3.6 Conclusion

The transition period marks a twilight zone in the exiting Member State's journey from subject to object of EU law and a shift from EU law to international law as the legal regime governing the relationship. While EU law applies to and in the UK largely in the same manner as it did before Brexit, there are crucial exceptions, which make the status of the UK as a former Member State transitioning to a third country unique. The UK and its citizens must now be considered objects of EU law in that they no longer have a right to participate in EU decision-making while being subject to the full enforcement of EU law. During transition, certain foundational principles – equality, mutual trust, loyalty and citizens' rights – apply in a modified manner. While this is compliant with the demands of EU primary law, which remains the ultimate yardstick for the validity of the withdrawal agreement, it requires a bigger justificatory effort when it comes to the disenfranchisement of UK citizens, which is only acceptable because the transition period is strictly time-limited. The transition period also raises important questions as far as the possibility of extending it is concerned. As soon as the deadline for agreeing an extension has passed, the EU and the UK will face high legal and practical hurdles to recreate the effects of an extended transition period.

Notes

1 Piet Eeckhout and Eleni Frantziou, 'Brexit and Article 50 TEU: A Constitutionalist Reading' (2017) 54 Common Market Law Review 695, 715–716.
2 This view is not entirely convincing: while it is clear that no agreement between the EU and the UK could enter into force before the UK has ceased to be a Member State, there is no reason why it should not be possible to negotiate it; see also ibid, 716–717.
3 See Council of the European Union, Agreement on the withdrawal of the United Kingdom of Great Britain and Northern Ireland from the European Union and the European Atomic Energy Community [2019] OJ C384 I/1 art 185 (WA).
4 Of course, if one does not share this view, a transition period could be avoided by negotiating the WA and the future relationship agreement in parallel; if time runs out, both sides could agree to extend the negotiating period in accordance with Article 50 (3) TEU and thus avoid a 'cliff edge' exit.
5 As, for example, claimed by the then UK Chancellor of the Exchequer Philip Hammond quoted in the *Financial Times* (16 December 2017) www.ft.com/content/97ed6a98-e17a-11e7-a8a4-0a1e63a52f9c accessed 27 March 2020.
6 For a view of the status of a Member State during its withdrawal negotiations see the chapter by Polly R Polak in this volume.
7 The author would like to thank Elaine Fahey for pointing this out.
8 A broader exploration of the subjects and objects of EU law can be found in Samo Badutzky and Elaine Fahey (eds), *Framing the Subjects and Objects of Contemporary EU Law* (Edward Elgar Publishing 2017).
9 Case 26/62 *van Gend en Loos* ECLI:EU:C:1963:1.

10 See Samo Badutzky and Elaine Fahey, 'The Subjects and Objects of EU Law: Exploring a Research Platform', in Badutzky and Fahey (n 8) 16.
11 See, for example, Case 149/96 *Portugal v Council* EU:C:1999:574, para 47.
12 Case 12/86 *Demirel* Opinion of AG Darmon EU:C:1987:232, para 14.
13 More on this at section 3.4.
14 See WA, art 131.
15 *Van Gend en Loos* (n 9); of course, this representation was – and remains – limited, see Joseph H H Weiler, '*Van Gend en Loos*: The Individual as Subject and Object and the Dilemma of European Legitimacy' (2014) 12 International Constitutional Law 94.
16 See, for example, Friedrich Erlbacher, 'Article 216 TFEU' in Marcus Klamert, Manuel Kellerbauer and Jonathan Tomkin (eds), *The EU Treaties and the Charter of Fundamental Rights* (Oxford University Press 2019), para 11.
17 Opinion 2/13 *Accession of the European Union to the European Convention for the Protection of Human Rights and Fundamental Freedoms* EU:C:2014:2454, para 191.
18 TFEU arts 53(1), 67(3) and (4), 70, 81(1) and (2) (a), 82(1) and (2).
19 Case 327/18 PPU *RO* EU:C:2018:733, para 34.
20 Ibid, para 35.
21 Case 404/15 *Aranyosi and Căldăraru* EU:C:2016:198, paras 88–89.
22 See Article 16 (2) of the Basic Law.
23 *RO* (n 19) para 52.
24 A parallel concept – *Bundestreue*, lit federal loyalty – is present in German constitutional law and appears to have served as a role model for the duty of loyalty under EU law, see Klamert (n 22) para 26.
25 Opinion 2/91 *ILO* EU:C:1993:106, para 37.
26 Case 246/07 *Commission v Sweden* EU:C:2010:203, para 104.
27 Joined Cases 3, 4 and 6/76 *Kramer* [1976] ECR 1279, paras 44–45.
28 Case 804/79 *Commission v United Kingdom* EU:C:1981:93, para 28.
29 See WA, art 129 (1).
30 WA, art 129 (2).
31 TFEU art 218 (2).
32 TFEU art 218 (6).
33 Case 266/03 *Commission v Luxembourg* EU:C:2005:341, para 60; Case 433/03 *Commission v Germany* EU:C:2005:462, para 66.
34 WA, art 229 (4).
35 Case 184/99 *Grzelczyk* EU:C:2001:458, para 31.
36 TEU, art 2.
37 And largely thereafter provided they have made use of them (with the exception of a right to onward movement), see Part 2 of the WA on citizens' rights.
38 Case 34/09 *Ruiz Zambrano* EU:C:2011:124, para 41.
39 Ibid, para 42.
40 *Matthews v United Kingdom* ECHR 1999-I.
41 On the implications of Brexit for Gibraltar, see Juan Santos Vara, Chapter 21 in this volume.
42 *Hirst v United Kingdom (No 2)* ECHR 2005-IX, para 60.
43 This is argued by George Peretz, 'The Brexit Withdrawal Agreement may Violate the European Convention on Human Rights' (*Prospect Magazine*, 11 October 2018) www.prospectmagazine.co.uk/politics/the-brexit-withdrawal-agreement-may-violate-the-european-convention-on-human-rights accessed 27 March 2020.
44 To that effect see Case 650/13 *Delvigne* EU:C:2015:648.
45 Interestingly, Article 14 (3) TEU is not excluded.
46 See TEU, art 6 (3).
47 Case C-145/04 *Spain v United Kingdom* ECLI:EU:C:2006:543, para 96.
48 Article 166 (3) WA.
49 See s 33 of the European Union (Withdrawal Agreement) Act 2020.
50 This is reflected in Article 39 of the Vienna Convention on the Law of Treaties.
51 For example, The Protocol to the Framework Agreement between the European Union and its Member States, on the one part, and the Republic of Korea, on the other part, to take account of the accession of the Republic of Croatia to the European Union [2018] OJ L 161/3 (based on Articles 207 and 212 TFEU) or the Amending Protocol to the Agreement between the European Community and

the Swiss Confederation providing for measures equivalent to those laid down in Council Directive 2003/48/EC on taxation of savings income in the form of interest payments [205] OJ L 333/12 (based on Article 115, in conjunction with Article 218(6)(b) and the second subparagraph of Article 218(8) TFEU).

52 See CONV 648/03, Annex II, p 9, where it says that

> while it is desirable that an agreement should be concluded between the Union and the withdrawing State on the arrangements for withdrawal and on their future relationship, it was felt that such an agreement should not constitute a condition for withdrawal so as not to void the concept of voluntary withdrawal of its substance.

53 *RO* (n 19) para 45.

54 Case 621/18 *Wightman* EU:C:2018:999, para 65.

4 Parliamentary involvement in the negotiations on the EU–UK trade agreement

Adam Cygan and Ewa Żelazna

4.1 Introduction

The period of the UK's membership in the EU has led to the development of a strong interdependence between the two economies. EU law has permeated a vast majority of legislative spheres in the UK, affecting lives of citizens. Businesses have grown accustomed to complying with EU regulatory standards and participation in the single market has facilitated the establishment of complex, 'just-in-time' supply chains.[1] The existing procedural and regulatory interdependence makes the costs of the UK's withdrawal from the Union high and the negative impact of the decision to leave could be minimised by preserving, so far as possible, the common legal framework. A close regulatory alignment between the two economies is also desirable because of their geographical proximity, shared interests, history and values. While these aspects had been taken into consideration in the UK's 2018 White Paper,[2] the government, which came to power in December 2019, has adopted a different position at the start of negotiations on the future relationship, calling for a Canada-style free trade agreement (FTA).[3]

A standard FTA will afford the UK a relatively high level of legislative sovereignty, when compared to the existing arrangements, but will come at the expense of market access. Furthermore, the EU's FTAs negotiated since 2006 are characterised by their comprehensive and evolving nature. In addition to cross-border trade in goods and services, these treaties establish standards in a broad range of other areas, such as consumer and data protection, environmental and labour standards, intellectual property, competition and state aid.[4] The new generation FTAs affect the legislative activity 'behind the border' to a greater extent than earlier treaties, which aimed only to lower tariffs and quotas.[5] In the light of this, a framework for future cooperation between the EU and the UK will most probably have a considerable impact upon lives of citizens, whatever its form. This provides a strong justification for a robust parliamentary scrutiny of the EU–UK agreement.

Against this background, this chapter evaluates positions of parliaments in the process that governs the conclusion of the framework for future relations between the EU and the UK and discusses challenges that these parliaments face in ensuring democratic legitimacy of the agreement. The next section of the chapter discusses the scope of and the form that the future cooperation is likely to take, which will determine the level of parliamentary involvement in the EU (4.2). The chapter then examines powers of the European Parliament and national parliaments and the role that they can play in the negotiations on the future agreement (4.3 and 4.4). The final section evaluates competences of the UK Parliament (4.5).

4.2 A comprehensive framework for EU–UK relations or a standard trade agreement?

In the EU, the extent of parliamentary involvement in the treaty-making process is determined by the scope of international commitments. Agreements that encompass areas falling within EU shared competences can be subjected to double parliamentary scrutiny at both supranational and national levels.[6] Since the commencement of negotiations on the UK's withdrawal from the Union, the EU has consistently proposed maintaining close ties and developing a comprehensive framework for a future relationship.[7] This position is reflected in the text tabled at the outset of negotiations by the EU, which covers economy and trade, security partnership, as well as participation in the Union's various programmes.[8] Such an agreement would require involvement of Member States in the ratification process and, as a 'mixed agreement', it would need to be signed and concluded by the Member States, on the basis of an approval from their parliaments.[9]

The UK mandate considers cooperation in areas beyond trade, such as, for example, law enforcement and judicial cooperation in criminal matters or asylum and illegal migration but implies that such matters could be covered in a separate agreement.[10] It stresses that a comprehensive FTA should be at the core of future cooperation between the UK and the EU.[11] The EU possesses exclusive competence to conclude trade agreements without the Member States.[12] In such a case, an agreement would require a decision of the Council taken by a qualified majority vote and the consent of the European Parliament.[13] However, the framework of bilateral treaties that has governed the relationship between the EU and Switzerland has become difficult to manage, in the course of time.[14] Based on this experience, the EU has expressed a preference for a comprehensive treaty with the UK.[15]

Notwithstanding the EU's position, since *Opinion 2/15* the Commission has avoided mixity when concluding agreements that fall within the scope of the common commercial policy.[16] The ratification process of comprehensive FTAs with involvement of the Member States have become more politicised in recent years, which can be exemplified with the debates surrounding the signature of the Comprehensive Economic and Trade Agreement (CETA) with Canada.[17] The new generation FTAs negotiated since 2006 address broad issues regulating market access and have had a much broader impact upon EU citizens and national interest of the Member States. They have, however, been one of the means through which the Commission has sought to unlock the potential for economic growth and, in the aftermath of the economic crisis, their swift conclusion has become a priority. In the light of this, the Commission's strategy has sought to reduce the risk of a single Member State blocking the entry into force of a trade agreement.[18]

Opinion 2/15 provided what may be termed a 'legal blueprint' for negotiations and conclusion of EU FTAs and equipped the Commission with appropriate tools to achieve its aims.[19] The judgment clarifies the scope of exclusive competence in common commercial policy and confirms that only non-direct investment and aspects of investor–state dispute resolution fall outside its scope.[20] As a consequence, the Commission has decided to decouple the investment protection chapters from comprehensive FTAs and conclude them as stand-alone, mixed agreements.[21] This allowed for the exclusion of Member States from the ratification of FTAs and improvements in efficiency have become immediately apparent. For example, the trade agreement with Japan, which was signed in July 2018, entered into force in five months.[22] This can be contrasted with the EU–South Korea FTA,[23] which took five years to be ratified by all Member States, or the agreement with Central America, and Columbia and Peru FTAs that were signed in 2012, but have not yet entered into force.[24] While the adopted practice improves the effectiveness of the EU as an international actor, it eschews a possibility of engaging national parliaments in a meaningful way in the treaty-making process, which in the light of the increasing depth and breadth of trade agreements could undermine their legitimacy and create tension between the Union and its Member States.[25]

Nonetheless, the flexibility provided by the established practice may prove useful in the context of the EU–UK negotiations, which are being conducted amidst the global pandemic of COVID-19 and to a challenging deadline, with the transition period expiring by the end of 2020.[26] The Commission's initial recommendation has left room for manoeuvre in this regard, by specifying that a substantive legal basis for the conclusion of the agreement could be changed at the end of the negotiations, when the full extent of the commitments can be accurately evaluated.[27] Furthermore, the Council's mandate acknowledges difficulties posed by the short timeframe and provides that the Commission should aim to achieve as much as possible during the transition period but be prepared to continue negotiations on outstanding issues after its expiry.[28] The European Parliament envisages that future cooperation will rest on three pillars, one of which is the economic partnership.[29] While it identifies Article 217 TFEU on association agreements as a possible legal basis, it also acknowledges the relevance of Article 207 TFEU on the common commercial policy, which could provide an avenue for a swift conclusion of a trade component, as an EU-only agreement.[30] In such a scenario the democratic legitimacy of the EU–UK trade agreement will be ensured solely by the European Parliament.[31]

4.3 The position of the European Parliament

Notwithstanding the procedural arrangements for the conclusion of the EU–UK agreement, the European Parliament will have the primary responsibility of ensuring the Commission's accountability in the course of negotiations. While the scrutiny conducted by national parliaments would, from the perspective of ensuring high levels of democratic legitimacy, be a valuable addition to the process, it occurs only after an international agreement has been signed, whereas the consolidated procedure in Article 218 TFEU envisages a role for the European Parliament in the negotiating process.[32] Since the entry into force of the Treaty of Lisbon, the Parliament has developed a robust constitutional practice that ensures its meaningful participation and enables it to influence the negotiating agenda.[33]

In this context, the Parliament has utilised particularly well its right to be immediately and fully informed throughout the treaty-making process.[34] In relation to agreements that fall within the scope of the common commercial policy, the obligation is further reinforced by Article 207(3) TFEU, which requires the Commission to report regularly to the European Parliament on the progress of negotiations. The aim of these provisions is to enable the Parliament to exercise democratic control over EU external action and contribute towards ensuring its coherence and consistency.[35] Their importance has been stressed by the Court of Justice, which held that the duty to keep the Parliament informed about EU foreign relations is an expression of the democratic principle upon which the Union is founded that people should participate in the exercise of power through a representative assembly.[36]

The Commission and the Parliament have given effect to the provisions of the Treaty in a so-called Framework Agreement.[37] Although it has a non-binding status, the experience of negotiations on new generation FTAs has proven the Commission's willingness to adhere to it in practice. This has led to the development of a good working relationship between the two institutions in external economic relations.[38] The Framework Agreement obliges the Commission to inform the Parliament about its intentions to propose the start of negotiations and forward a proposal for a mandate at the same time as this information is transmitted to the Council.[39] In negotiations on the new generation FTAs, the Parliament has used these arrangements to assert a strong position from the beginning of the treaty-making process. While only the Council has the authority to open negotiations, the Parliament's consent powers provide it with considerable leverage to ensure that its voice is heard by other institutions. Parliament's opposition to a treaty expressed in the early stages of negotiations would 'cast a shadow' over its successful conclusion and significantly undermine the EU's position.[40]

In the context of the framework for cooperation between the EU and the UK, the Parliament stated its views soon after the Commission published a proposal for negotiating guidelines.[41] In a non-legislative resolution, the Parliament has supported a close regulatory alignment, maintenance of existing employment and mobility rights for citizens, high standards for data protection, food safety and animal health, as well as ambitious commitments to combating climate change.[42] This position can be contrasted with the UK government endorsing merely boiler plate arrangements for sustainability that have been incorporated in the EU's agreements with countries such as Canada, Japan and South Korea.[43] These provisions have a limited capability of addressing challenges that arise in the unique context of the EU–UK negotiations due to inter alia geographical proximity. The non-legislative resolution of the European Parliament highlights, for example, that, as a large number of species migrates between the UK and the EU, lowering of environmental protection and animal health standards could result in a loss of biodiversity and increase the risk of transmission of zoonotic diseases.[44] Such a contribution of the Parliament in the early stages in negotiations could strengthen the position of the Commission on matters such as trade and sustainable development; after all, the conclusion of any agreement depends on the parliamentary approval. Furthermore, it improves the democratic legitimacy of the agreement by encouraging a broad debate about its impact on the welfare of citizens.

Throughout the negotiating process, the Parliament is supposed to be provided with the same information as the Council and guaranteed sufficient time to formulate opinions.[45] Provisions of the Framework Agreement oblige the Commission to take the Parliament's suggestions into account and explain whether they were incorporated in the text of the negotiated agreement.[46] This can take place during parliamentary committee meetings or plenary sessions, which are frequently attended by Commission officials in order to discharge their reporting duties.[47] In the context of the new generation FTAs, the European Parliament has issued non-legislative resolutions virtually at all stages, expressing its views about the Commission's proposed negotiating mandate, progress of negotiations and upon providing its consent to conclusion of an international treaty, in order to outline priorities for future cooperation between the EU and a third country partner. While the primary responsibility for scrutinising international negotiations is vested in a responsible committee, Members of the European Parliament frequently pose written questions to the Commission and the Council.[48] This demonstrates their commitment towards actively representing EU citizens in international negotiations. The proactive role that the Parliament has adopted in past negotiations has highlighted its capability to provide effective scrutiny of international treaty negotiations, as well as its influence to shape the final outcome.

In general, in the context of trade negotiations, the Parliament has emerged as the guardian of human rights, sustainability, transparency and other values that the EU's external action is required to promote.[49] The Parliament has made the effort to influence the EU's negotiating agenda and its contribution facilitated a deepening of commitments to environmental and labour protection in the EU's new generation FTAs. For example, it has been reported that the Parliament was able to impact on the content of the agreement with South Korea with regards to labour standards, which provided a template for EU FTA negotiations.[50] The European Parliament has been actively shaping the evolution of the EU's new generation FTAs. In a recent non-legislative resolution passed upon the conclusion of the EU–Vietnam FTA, the Parliament has called on the Commission to strengthen the environmental commitments with a sanctions-based enforcement mechanism.[51] This can be contrasted with the UK's negotiating mandate, which stipulates that the dispute resolution mechanism should not be applicable to trade and sustainable development aspects of the agreement.[52] While the UK's position could prove problematic in concluding the EU–UK agreement, in the past the European Parliament has made a visible effort not to unduly burden FTA negotiations with non-trade related elements, recognising that their primary aim is market liberalisation.[53]

4.4 Provisional application, conclusion and the role of national parliaments

A comprehensive framework for cooperation that encompasses a broad range of areas will likely require provisional application.[54] This tool is frequently used by the EU to mitigate negative effects of a long period required for all Member States to complete their ratification procedures.[55] In the past, it has been used for economic agreements with countries such as South Korea,[56] Columbia and Peru,[57] Ecuador,[58] Central America[59] and Canada.[60] Given the constraints imposed on the negotiating timeframe by the expiry of the transition period, a provisional application of an EU–UK agreement will be essential to ensure continuity of cross-border activity and will help to minimise disruption to business. However, if the negotiating parties decide to conclude the trade component separately, the speedy ratification process of EU-only agreements, which requires only the consent of the European Parliament, will render provisional application unnecessary, as demonstrated by the recent conclusion of FTAs with Japan[61] and Vietnam.[62]

Formal arrangements governing the provisional application put the European Parliament in a relatively weak position as the Treaty vests the decision-making powers at this stage solely in the Council.[63] While the Framework Agreement requires the Commission to inform the European Parliament of its intentions to propose provisional application, it allows for a derogation from this obligation in urgent cases.[64] Nonetheless, the constitutional practice that has emerged since the entry into force of the Treaty of Lisbon has mitigated to some extent the negative effects of a decision on provisional application on the democratic legitimacy of EU international agreements. The experience in the area of external trade demonstrates that a large number of agreements do not become effective until the Parliament has expressed its consent, albeit that in the absence of formal requirements the practice is not always followed.[65]

The European Parliament does not reject international agreements lightly and since the entry into force of the Treaty of Lisbon it has approved all comprehensive economic agreements with a large majority. Notwithstanding, in the past, it withheld its consent to the Terrorist Finance Tracking Programme Agreement with the US,[66] objected to the conclusion of the Anti-Counterfeiting Trade Agreement[67] and postponed a vote on the EU–US Passenger Name Record (PNR) Agreement[68] due to concerns over data protection. The Parliament also requested an Opinion on the compatibility of the EU–Canada PNR Agreement with Article 16 TFEU on protection of personal data and the provisions of the Charter.[69] High standards in data protection have been one of the priorities of the European Parliament and have been mentioned in its initial resolution on the EU–UK agreement, where reservations were expressed about the

UK legislation in this area.[70] This could prove to be a stumbling block in obtaining the European Parliament's approval. It could also prompt the Parliament to refer the agreement for review by the Court of Justice,[71] which would delay the consent procedure until an Opinion is delivered.[72] In case of an incompatibility, the agreement would be precluded from entering into force.[73]

If a comprehensive framework for cooperation between the EU and the UK is concluded as a mixed agreement (or several mixed agreements) it will be subjected to additional scrutiny by national parliaments after its signature. While the procedure may deliver a higher level of democratic legitimacy, the procedural arrangements put national parliaments in a weak position. The current Treaty framework and a lack of established cooperation with the European Parliament preclude the possibility of engaging national parliaments during the course of negotiations, which renders them merely veto players, rather than agenda setters. Nevertheless, in the past, some national parliaments managed to make their voice heard during the conclusion of international agreements and caused uncertainty over and delays to the ratification procedure. Some notable examples include opposition to the signature of CETA in Belgium, or to the EU–Ukraine Association Agreement in the Netherlands.[74] Article 9 of Protocol No 1 annexed to the Treaty of Lisbon could provide an avenue for developing closer cooperation between the European Parliament and national parliaments in external relations that could be undertaken within the framework of the Conference of Parliamentary Committees for Union Affairs of Parliaments of the European Union (COSAC).[75] However, circumstances surrounding negotiations on the EU–UK agreement, specifically challenges created by the global pandemic of COVID-19, do not provide favourable conditions to develop innovative solutions for cooperation between the European Parliament and national parliaments on this occasion.

4.5 The position of the UK Parliament in negotiations on the EU–UK agreement

On the other side of the negotiating table, the pandemic of COVID-19 also presents unique challenges to the UK Parliament as it seeks to hold the government to account and scrutinise the negotiations with the EU. The challenge has been exacerbated by the government's persistent refusal to extend the transition period and recently passed legislation, which permit Parliament to have only a minor role in the conclusion of the EU–UK agreement.

In this regard, the provision of the EU (Withdrawal) Act 2018 that enabled active involvement of the Parliament in the Brexit process,[76] has been repealed.[77] Section 13 of the Act required Parliament's consent to the conclusion of the Withdrawal Agreement, as well as the Political Declaration and, in case of rejection, an approval of the government's proposed course of action. In the UK constitutional tradition, which has maintained executive dominance in foreign relations, this was an unprecedented arrangement.[78] Nonetheless, Parliament's participation in the Brexit process created momentum for a broader reform in UK treaty-making practice. This was demonstrated by the first version of the EU (Withdrawal Agreement) Bill, which provided the institutional framework for the implementation of the Withdrawal Agreement and for the conclusion of the EU–UK agreement on the future relationship.[79] Provisions of the original Bill further strengthened the position of Parliament by requiring the government to obtain its approval of the negotiating mandate, submit quarterly reports on the progress of negotiations and secure its consent for the agreement's entry into force.[80] The arrangements have been visibly inspired by the EU process for conclusion of international treaties, though they put the UK Parliament in a better position at the start of negotiations in comparison to the European Parliament.

However, the Bill fell as a result of the 12 December 2019 General Election, in which the Conservative government secured a working majority. The final version of the EU (Withdrawal Agreement) Act, which received Royal Assent on 23 January 2020, significantly reduced the role of Parliament by returning to the ordinary framework that has governed the conclusion of international treaties prior to Brexit.[81] Thus, in accordance with long-established practice, the EU–UK framework agreement will be negotiated, signed and ratified using the Royal Prerogative power. The Constitutional Reform and Governance Act 2010 (CRAGA), which applies in this context, does not facilitate active involvement of Parliament.[82]

The Act requires that an agreement, after its signature, be laid before Parliament for 21 sitting days before its ratification.[83] Within this period either House has an opportunity to express its objections in the form of a resolution.[84] If Parliament opposes a treaty, a responsible minister has to present a statement justifying why the treaty should nevertheless be ratified and afford to the House of Commons another 21-day period to raise any objections.[85] As the process can be repeated an unlimited number of times by the House of Commons, in theory, Parliament could block conclusion of an international treaty indefinitely. However, such a situation has never occurred in practice and, in fact, Parliament has not objected to the conclusion of an international treaty since the CRAGA process was established.[86] Another weakness of the existing framework is that it does not provide a mechanism to ensure that a debate and a vote on a treaty take place and leaves an option for the government to block time for debate.[87] Evidence presented to the House of Lords Select Committee on the Constitution has highlighted that the Parliament did not have an opportunity to debate on CETA until the treaty was concluded despite requesting a debate for over 12 months.[88]

As the UK is a dualist system, international agreements require implementation through a legislative act. Therefore, at this stage, Parliament has the power to preclude an agreement signed by the government from entering into force by refusing to enact necessary legislation. However, as pointed out in Theresa May's White Paper on the Future Relationship between the EU and the UK, such a decision would risk the UK breaking its international obligations, jeopardising market access and undermining cooperation.[89] Furthermore, a currently large Conservative majority in the Commons is another aspect which makes it unlikely that Parliament would undermine the government's negotiating efforts by refusing to enact requisite legislation. Thus, in the overall assessment, the UK Parliament lacks adequate leverage to exert real influence in the treaty-making process, which puts it in a much weaker position when compared to the European Parliament or even parliaments of the EU Member States.[90]

Notwithstanding this inadequacy of the current framework for ensuring meaningful involvement of Parliament in negotiations on the future relationship between the EU and the UK, effective scrutiny is not impossible. Based on experience with the Withdrawal Agreement negotiations, parliamentary committees will play a key role in holding the government to account. Select committees in the UK Parliament operate on a cross-party, consensus-seeking basis.[91] As found in a paper by Lynch and Whitaker, the committees had some influence over the government during the Brexit process, albeit the committees' chairs criticised the government for not engaging with their reports. This issue could be more prevalent in negotiations on the EU–UK future agreement given the short timeframe set for their completion. Nonetheless, the committees were able to shape the debates, highlight major concerns and bring them to the attention of the public.[92] Their capacity and capability to conduct scrutiny of international treaty negotiations in the Brexit process is demonstrated by 66 Brexit-related inquiries conducted in 2017–19.[93]

The House of Commons Committee on Exiting the European Union set up in autumn 2016 had taken the lead in scrutinising the withdrawal process.[94] It examined the government's Brexit negotiating directives, reported regularly on progress of negotiations and evaluated the legislative path to the implementation of the Withdrawal Agreement. The Committee made a positive contribution by shedding light on the process and choices presented to the UK in negotiations.[95] A key area of the Committee's interests was the rights of citizens. One of its reports concluded that the government should not use citizens' rights as a bargaining chip in negotiations with the EU and demanded stronger legal guarantees to those living both in the UK and the EU.[96] Throughout the course of negotiations, Parliament has consistently pressed the government for more clarity, certainty and transparency which, in the view of the Committee on Exiting the European Union, ultimately were not achieved and resulted in the Withdrawal Agreement being repeatedly rejected by the House of Commons.[97] This experience highlights the scale of the challenge before the UK Parliament in trying to influence the government during international treaty negotiations.

With the end of negotiations on the Withdrawal Agreement, the Committee for Exiting the European Union has been replaced with the Committee on the Future Relationship with the European Union. Its mandate is to examine matters relating to the negotiations on the future relationship with the EU. Building on the practice established during the Brexit process, facilitated through the election of Hilary Benn as the chair, the Committee has been closely following negotiations, conducting hearings of government ministers and publishing reports on the progress of the agreement. In addition, the existing EU committees of the House of Lords and Commons have contributed to the scrutiny of the negotiating mandate.

The EU Select Committee of the House of Lords demonstrated considerable creativity in using section 29 of the EU (Withdrawal Agreement) Act 2020 in order to evaluate negotiating directives and question relevant ministers.[98] The provision was intended to allow debates on changes to EU legislation which may raise matters of national interest for the UK in the transition period. It gives powers to EU committees of both Houses to prepare reports on such issues and requires that a debate take place within 14 days of publication.[99] The House of Lords EU Committee's report on the EU–UK agreement, has highlighted a significant gap between the position of the UK government at the start of negotiations and the intentions it expressed in the Political Declaration.[100] The Committee expressed concerns that due to this change, the positions of the EU and the UK significantly diverge and in some areas are completely incompatible.[101] This proactive attitude demonstrated by the House of Lords EU Committee has facilitated an open parliamentary and public debate on the future agreement which was missing at the start of negotiations. In a similar vein, the European Scrutiny Select Committee of the House of Commons has considered preparing a response on negotiating mandates that incorporates views of all select committees, which may have an interest. Given the broad nature of the negotiations this would certainly improve the quality of parliamentary scrutiny. However, the fast pace of negotiations makes it difficult to deliver such a coordinated response in a timely manner.

4.6 Conclusions

As the EU trade agreement affects all sectors of the economy and lives of citizens in the EU and the UK, the involvement of parliaments in the process that leads to its conclusion is essential to ensure democratic legitimacy. The analysis in this chapter demonstrated that, due to their consent powers and considerable experience in international negotiations, parliaments in the EU are in a better position to scrutinise the treaty-making process than the UK Parliament. The impact that the future agreement will have on individual Member States and its political importance provide a rationale for incorporating the voice of national parliaments.

However, the circumstances surrounding the negotiations, specifically the challenging deadline and the outbreak of COVID-19, create a risk that national assemblies could be sidelined in the conclusion of the comprehensive economic trade agreement that will settle the future relationship between the EU and the UK. Nonetheless, the established constitutional practice for international treaty-making in the area of common commercial policy and the proactive attitude of the European Parliament in negotiations provide good guarantees of democratic legitimacy. In the UK, select committees play a key role in holding the government into account. However, the current legal framework consisting of the EU (Withdrawal Agreement) Act 2020 and the Constitutional and Governance Act 2010 do not facilitate active involvement of the Parliament in negotiations. While the committees have used their best endeavours to scrutinise how the government conducts negotiations and provide a forum for open parliamentary and public debates, they face a difficult task in trying to exert real influence over the government

Notes

1 Adam Cygan, Philip Lynch and Richard Whitaker, 'UK Parliamentary Scrutiny of EU Political and Legal Space after Brexit' (forthcoming 2020) *Journal of Common Market Studies*.
2 HM Government, 'The Future Relationship between the United Kingdom and the European Union' (Policy Paper, 2018).
3 HM Government, 'The Future Relationship with the EU: The UK's Approach to Negotiations' (Policy Paper, 2020); Draft Text of the Agreement on the New Partnership with the United Kingdom (Brussels, 18 March 2020).
4 Commission (EU), 'Report from the Commission to the European Parliament, the Council, the European Economic and Social Committee and the Committee of Regions on Implementation of EU Free Trade Agreements: 1 January–31 December 2017' COM(2018)728 final, 12.
5 Isabella Mancini, 'Fundamental Rights in the EU's External Trade Relations: From Promotion "Through" Trade Agreements to Protection "in" Trade Agreements' in Eva Kassoti and Ramses Wessel (eds) *EU Trade Agreements and the Duty to Respect Human Rights Abroad* (CLEER Papers 2020).
6 Art 3 TFEU; C-600/14 *Germany v Council* EU:C:2017:935, paras 67–68; Opinion 2/15 *Free Trade Agreement between the European Union and the Republic of Singapore* EU:C:2017:376, para 244.
7 European Council (Art 50) Guidelines (Brussels, 23 March 2018) EUCO XT 20001/18; Political Declaration setting out the framework for the future relationship between the European Union and the United Kingdom, OJ [2020] C34/12 (PD).
8 Draft Text of the Agreement on the New Partnership with the United Kingdom (Brussels, 18 March 2020).
9 Marc Maresceau, 'A Typology of Mixed Bilateral Agreements' in Christophe Hillion and Panos Koutrakos (eds), *Mixed Agreements Revisited: The EU and Its Member States in the World* (Hart 2010).
10 HM Government (n 3) paras 27–57.
11 Ibid, para 6.
12 TFEU, arts 3(1)(e), 207.
13 TFEU, arts 207 and 218.
14 Council Conclusions (EU), On EU Relations with EFTA Countries, 3060th General Affairs Council Meeting (Brussels, 14 December 2010), para 48; Christine Kaddous, 'Switzerland and the EU: Current Issues and New Challenges under the Draft Institutional Framework Agreement' in Sieglinde Gstöhl and David Phinnemoren (eds), *The Proliferation of Privileged Partnerships between the European Union and Its Neighbours* (Routledge 2019) 68.
15 European Parliament, 'Resolution on the Proposed Mandate for Negotiations for a New Partnership with the United Kingdom' (Strasbourg, 12 February 2020) para 3; Draft Text of the Agreement on the New Partnership with the United Kingdom (Brussels, 18 March 2020).
16 Opinion 2/15 (n 6).

17 Guillaume Van der Loo, 'CETA's Signature: 38 Statements, a Joint Interpretative Instrument and an Uncertain Future' (CEPS Commentary, 31 October 2016).
18 Guillaume Van der Loo and Ramses Wessel, 'The Non-Ratification of Mixed Agreements: Legal Consequences and Solutions' (2017) 54 Common Market Law Review 735.
19 Opinion 2/15 (n 6).
20 Ibid.
21 European Commission, Proposal for a Council Decision on the conclusion of the Free Trade Agreement between the European Union and the Republic of Singapore, COM(2018) 196 final.
22 Council Decision (EU) 2018/966 on the signing, on behalf of the European Union, of the Agreement between the European Union and Japan for an Economic Partnership [2018] OJ L 174/1; Council Decision (EU) 2018/1907 on the conclusion of the Agreement between the European Union and Japan for an Economic Partnership [2018] OJ L 330.
23 Council Decision (EU) 2011/265 on the signing, on behalf of the European Union and Provisional Application of the Free Trade Agreement between the European Union and its Member States of the one part, and the Republic of Korea, of the other Part [2011] OJ L 127/1; Council Decision (EU) 2015/2169 on the conclusion of the Free Trade Agreement between the European Union and its Member States, of the one part, and the Republic of Korea, of the other part [2015] OJ L 307/2.
24 Council Decision (EU) 2012/734 on the signing on behalf of the European Union, of the Agreement Establishing an Association between the European Union and its Member States, on the one hand, and Central America on the other, and provisional application of Part IV thereof concerning trade matters [2012] OJ L 346/1; Council Decision (EU) 2012/735 on the signing, on behalf of the Union and Provisional Application of Trade Agreement between the European Union and Its Member States, of the one part, and Columbia and Peru, of the other part [2012] OJ L 354/1.
25 Namur Declaration (5 December 2016); Brussels Declaration, 'Trading Together: For Strong and Democratically Legitimised International Agreements' (27 January 2017); Jan Wouters and Kolja Raube, 'Rebels with a Cause? Parliaments and EU Trade Policy After the Treaty of Lisbon' in Juan Santos Vara and Soledad Rodríguez Sánchez-Tabernerro, *The Democratisation of EU International Relations Through EU Law* (Routledge 2018) 69.
26 Agreement on the withdrawal of the United Kingdom of Great Britain and Northern Ireland from the European Union and the European Atomic Energy Community [2020] OJ L 29/7, art 126; European Union (Withdrawal Agreement) Act 2020, s 33.
27 European Commission, Recommendation for a Council Decision authorising the opening of negotiations for a new partnership with the United Kingdom of Great Britain and Northern Ireland, COM(2020) 35 final, 3.
28 Council (EU), Annex to Council Decision 2020/266/EU authorising the opening of negotiations with the United Kingdom of Great Britain and Northern Ireland for a new partnership agreement [2020] OJ L58/53, para 9.
29 European Parliament (n 15) paras 2, 3, 5.
30 Ibid.
31 TFEU, arts 207, 218.
32 TFEU, art 218(10).
33 Bjorn Kleizen, 'Mapping the Involvement of the European Parliament in EU External Relations: A Legal and Empirical Analysis' (CLEER Working Papers, 2016) 21; Ariadna Ripoll Servent, 'The Role of the European Parliament in International Negotiations After Lisbon' (2014) 21 Journal of European Public Policy 568; Katharina Meissner, 'Democratizing EU External Relations: The European Parliament's Informal Role in SWIFT, ACTA and TTIP (2016) 21 European Foreign Affairs Review 269.
34 TFEU, art 218(10). For a view of the European Parliament's role during the negotiation of the UK's Withdrawal Agreement see Polly R Polak's chapter in this volume.
35 It is also an essential procedural requirement within the meaning of Art 263 and its violation is a ground for annulment of an EU act, see: Case C-658/11 *Parliament v Commission (Mauritius)* EU:C:2014:2025, para 80.
36 Case C-658/11 (n 35); Case C-263/14 *Parliament v Council (Tanzania)* EU:C:2016:435, para 70.
37 Framework Agreement on relations between the European Parliament and the European Commission (2010) OJ L 304/47, para 23.
38 Youri Devuyst, 'European Union Law and Practice in the Negotiation and Conclusion of International Trade Agreements' (2013) 12 Journal of International Business & Law 259.

39 Framework Agreement (n 37) Annex III, paras 1–2.
40 Ripoll Servent (n 33) 561; Ariadna Ripoll Servent and Alex MacKenzie, 'The European Parliament as a "Norm Taker"? EU–US Relations after SWIFT Agreement' (2012) 17 European Foreign Affairs Review 71.
41 European Parliament (n 15).
42 Ibid.
43 HM Government (n 3) 74–77.
44 European Parliament (n 15) paras 36, 47.
45 Framework Agreement (n 37) art 24, Annex III para 3.
46 Ibid, Annex III paras 4 and 5.
47 Devuyst (n 38) 300.
48 See, for example: European Parliament, Written questions by Members of the European Parliament and their answers given by a European Union institution [2014] OJ C 273/1; European Parliament, Written questions with answer: written questions by Members of the European Parliament and their answers given by a European Union institution [2014] OJ C 288/1. EU–Vietnam trade agreement: European Parliament, Written questions by Members of the European Parliament and their answers given by the European Union institutions [2013] OJ C 248E/1; CETA: European Parliament, Written questions by Members of the European Parliament and their answers given by a European Union institutions [2013] OJ C 321 E/1; EU–Japan: European Parliament, Written questions by Member States and their answers given by European Union institutions [2013] OJ C 321 E/1.
49 TEU, art 21; Laura Feliu and Francesc Serra, 'The European Union as a "Normative Power" and the Normative Voice of the European Parliament' in Stelios Stavridis and Daniela Irrera (eds), *The European Parliament and its International Relations* (Routledge 2015); Juan Santos Vara, 'The European Parliament in the Conclusion of International Agreements Post-Lisbon: Entrenched between Values and Prerogatives' in Juan Santos Vara and Soledad Rodríguez Sánchez-Tabernerro, *The Democratisation of EU International Relations Through EU Law* (Routledge 2018), 69.
50 Devuyst (n 38) 297–298.
51 European Parliament, Non-legislative resolution on the draft Council Decision on the conclusion of the Free Trade Agreement between the European Union and the Socialist Republic of Viet Nam (Strasbourg, 12 February 2020), para 20.
52 HM Government (n 3) 74–77.
53 Tobias Leeg, 'Normative Power Europe? The European Union in the Negotiations on a Free Trade Agreement with India' (2014) 19 European Foreign Affairs Review 335.
54 TFEU, art 218(5).
55 Mauro Gatti, 'Provisional Application of EU Trade and Investment Agreements: A Pragmatic Solution to Mixity Issue' in Katia Fach Gómez (ed), *La Política de la Unión Europea en Materia de Derecho de las Inversiones Internacionales* (JB Bosch Editor 2017).
56 Council (n 23).
57 Council (n 24).
58 Council (EU) Decision 2016/2369 on the signing, on behalf of the Union, and provisional application of the Protocol of Accession to the Trade Agreement between the European Union and its Member States, of the one part, and Colombia and Peru, of the other part, to take account of the accession of Ecuador [2016] OJ L 356.
59 Council (n 24).
60 Council (EU) Decision 2017/38 on the Provisional Application of the Comprehensive Economic and Trade Agreement (CETA) between Canada on the one Part and the European Union and its Member States, of the other Part [2017] OJ L 11/1080.
61 Council (n 22).
62 Council Decision (EU) 2019/1121 on the signing, on behalf of the European Union of the Free Trade Agreement between the European Union and the Socialist Republic of Viet Nam [2019] L177/1; European Parliament, Legislative resolution on the draft Council Decision on the conclusion of the Free Trade Agreement between the European Union and the Socialist Republic of Viet Nam, (Strasbourg, 12 February 2020).
63 TFEU, art 218(5).
64 Framework Agreement (n 37) Annex III, para 7.
65 Santos Vara (n 49) 68.

66 European Parliament, Legislative resolution on the Proposal for a Council Decision on the conclusion of the agreement between the European Union and the United States of America on the processing and transfer of financial messaging data from the European Union to the United States for purposes of the Terrorist Finance Tracking Program [2010] C 341 E/100; Elaine Fahey, 'Law and Governance as Checks and Balances in Transatlantic Security: Rights, Redress, and Remedies in EU–US Passenger Name Records and the Terrorist Finance Tracking Programme' (2013) 32 Yearbook of European Law 368.
67 European Parliament, Legislative resolution on the draft Council Decision on the conclusion of the Anti-Counterfeiting Trade Agreement [2013] C 349 E/552, para 7. Juan Santos Vara (n 49), 70.
68 European Parliament, Resolution on the launch of negotiations for Passenger Name Record (PNR) agreements with the United States, Australia and Canada [2011] C 81 E/74; Juan Santos Vara, 'Transatlantic Counter-Terrorism Cooperation Agreements on the Transfer of Personal Data: A Test for Democratic Accountability in the EU' in Elaine Fahey and Deirdre Curtin (eds), *A Transatlantic Community of Law: Legal Perspectives on the Relationship between the EU and US Legal Orders* (Cambridge University Press 2014) 237–245.
69 Opinion 1/15 *Agreement between EU and Canada on the Transfer of Passenger Name Record* EU:C:2016:656.
70 European Parliament (n 15) paras 32–34.
71 TFEU, art 218(11).
72 European Parliament, Rules of Procedure 9th Parliamentary Term (2019–2024), December 2019, Rule 114.
73 TFEU, art 218(11).
74 Van der Loo (n 17).
75 Ricardo Passos, 'Mixed Agreement from the Perspective of the European Parliament' in Hillion and Koutrakos (n 9) 291.
76 Philip Lunch, Richard Whitaker and Adam Cygan, 'Brexit and the UK Parliament: Challenges and Opportunities' in Thomas Christiansen and Diane Fromage (eds), *Brexit and Democracy: The Role of Parliaments in the UK and the European Union* (Palgrave Macmillan 2019).
77 European Union (Withdrawal Agreement) Act 2020, s 31.
78 Anthony Aust, *Modern Treaty Law and Practice* (3rd edn, Cambridge University Press 2013).
79 European Union (Withdrawal Agreement) HC Bill 2019 (2019–20) [7], s 31.
80 Ibid, 31.
81 European Union (Withdrawal Agreement) Act 2020, ss 31, 32.
82 Constitutional Reform and Governance Act 2010, s 20.
83 Ibid, s 20(1).
84 Ibid, 20(4)(a).
85 Ibid, 20(4)(b).
86 Select Committee on the Constitution, *Parliamentary Scrutiny of Treaties*, (HL 2017–19, 345) para 17.
87 Jill Barrett, 'Treaties Beyond the EU' in Adam Cygan and Meg Russell (eds) *Parliament and Brexit* (UK in the Changing Europe, 2020).
88 Select Committee on the Constitution (n 86) para 26.
89 HM Government (n 3), para 54.
90 Monika Brusenbauch Meislova, 'The European Parliament in the Brexit Process: Leading Role, Supporting Role or Just a Small Cameo?' in Christiansen and Fromage (n 76) 254.
91 Philip Lynch and Richard Whitaker, 'Select Committees and Brexit: Parliamentary Influence in a Decisive Policy Area' (2019) 72 Parliamentary Affairs 923, 941.
92 Ibid.
93 Ibid, 924.
94 For an assessment of the Committee's work by its Chair, Hilary Benn, see: Hilary Benn, 'The Exiting the European Union Committee' in Cygan and Russell (n 87).
95 Ibid.
96 Exiting the European Union Committee, 'The Progress of the UK's Negotiations on EU Withdrawal' (HC 2017–19, 372), paras 1–13.
97 Benn (n 94); Exiting the European Union Committee, 'The Progress of the UK's Negotiations on EU Withdrawal: The Withdrawal Agreement and Political Declaration' (HC 2017–2019 1778).

98 European Union Committee, Report pursuant to Section 29 of the European Union (Withdrawal Agreement) Act 2020: Council Decision authorising the opening of negotiations with the United Kingdom of Great Britain and Northern Ireland for a new partnership agreement (HL 2019–21, 32).
99 European Union (Withdrawal Agreement) Act 2020, s 29.
100 Ibid, paras 15–29.
101 Ibid, para 144.

5 EU withdrawal law after Brexit

The emergence of a unique legal procedure

Polly R. Polak

5.1 Introduction

The process of withdrawal from the European Union (EU) initiated by the United Kingdom (UK) when it triggered the hitherto unused Article 50 TEU on 29 March 2017 and which finalised on 1 February 2020 with the entry into force of its Withdrawal Agreement, is a unique legal procedure. It is true that the EU's withdrawal clause presents major differences from standard withdrawal mechanisms in ordinary international organisations which generally consist of a mere duty for the departing state to notify the other parties, within a certain time before leaving, but do not set up full-blown procedures aimed at securing a negotiated and orderly withdrawal.[1] Article 50, on the other hand, establishes a set of procedural rules regulating the modus operandi for withdrawal, albeit in a rudimentary fashion. Another important difference with normal exit provisions is that Member State withdrawal from the Union is not a negotiation carried out between the parties to the EU Treaties but between the withdrawing state and the European institutions, and the result is an EU international agreement following Article 218 TFEU.[2] However, this chapter focuses on how EU withdrawal is a unique legal procedure also in comparison to other EU external action.

Brexit has set precedent for any future Member State withdrawal from the EU in view of the fact that from the UK's withdrawal process a new EU withdrawal law has emerged filling in the legal gaps left by Article 50 TEU.[3] In effect, as Allan F. Tatham already pointed out:

> for Article 50, a rather bare skeleton exists and while academic discourse attempts to add substance to the body, it would probably take the actual use or threat to use the provision which would stimulate the EU institutions to outline their understanding of its operation.[4]

Now, the parties to the Brexit negotiations have offered us that unprecedented look into the workings of Article 50 TEU which this chapter divides in two. First, it will establish the European institutions' interpretation of the EU's exit clause which has evolved through their heavy involvement in the Brexit process (section 5.2) and, second, it will deal with the special status of the UK as a Member State that triggered Article 50 and with it a two-year process of negotiations to which it was party not as a third country but as a full(ish) EU Member that continued to be bound by the Treaties (5.3). What we will discover is that during the Brexit negotiations there has been a significant gap-filling operation in order to cope with an extremely complex process on the basis of a very scant regulation. In some cases, those legal voids have been filled simply by extending EU rules on international treaty-making to the withdrawal process despite Article 50 only referring to paragraph 3 of Article 218. In other cases, separate Treaty principles have applied. Finally, other specific withdrawal rules have emerged anew from the practice. From all of this two conclusions are forthcoming: that the EU withdrawal process has been designed by the institutions in favour of the Union while imposing a heavily conditioned legal regime on the withdrawing state, and that EU withdrawal is a unique legal procedure with special qualities that distinguish it not only from standard international withdrawal law but also from other EU external action (5.4).

5.2 The role of the European institutions and their impact on the withdrawal process

Article 50(2) TEU makes it clear that, on the Union side, the process is driven by its institutions and not by the Member States. Likewise, the ensuing divorce deal is not an interstate agreement but an EU treaty 'negotiated in accordance with Article 218(3) of the Treaty on the Functioning of the European Union'.[5] However, the provision fails to address many other key issues that necessarily arose during the UK's withdrawal. This made gap-filling via legal interpretation essential and, one might even say, the magic formula that allowed the EU to govern the withdrawal process pursuant to its own interests. In the first place, due to the withdrawal agreement envisaged by Article 50 being concluded 'on behalf of the Union by the Council, acting by a qualified majority, after obtaining the consent of the European Parliament',[6] it could have been understood that either its content had to be limited to areas of EU exclusive powers or that, despite no mention of the Member States, these would have had to ratify the withdrawal agreement as a mixed treaty if it had fallen outside those competences.[7] The EU nonetheless bypassed these limitations by taking the view that Article 50 TEU conferred on it 'an exceptional horizontal competence' to cover in the withdrawal agreement all matters necessary to arrange the withdrawal. In other words, the EU could conclude a withdrawal agreement on the basis of Article 50 TEU even if it covered areas beyond the scope of its exclusive competence.[8] This institutional reading of the incomplete exit clause has allowed the EU to exploit the classic logic of EU exclusivity in international negotiations, that is, to undisputedly reinforce its unified position and defend its interests during the process. In the same vein, it has taken advantage of other external action provisos that have served the same purpose even though Article 50 only refers to paragraph 3 of Article 218 TFEU. Finally, it has unilaterally designed the missing pieces of the procedure also in its favour and compelled the withdrawing state to negotiate its exit in a newly emerging legal and procedural labyrinth which has now set precedent for a heavily conditioned process of EU withdrawal.

5.2.1 The European Council

Admittedly, one of the most important rules that has dealt the EU the upper hand is enshrined in Article 50 and that is the leading role it grants the European Council. It is to this institution that the notification of the intention of withdrawal must be sent in order to activate the process and it also decides by unanimity whether the two-year negotiating period can be extended.[9] Once the European Council has been notified, it establishes the guidelines to be followed during the negotiations of the withdrawal agreement.[10] This privilege has proven crucial to the development of the Brexit process; it granted the EU the power to successfully impose the structure and timetable on the negotiations that suited its purposes. What is more, it was able to organise the procedure with considerable freedom for there were few established rules and no precedent. Indeed, regarding the structure and content of the talks, that is, what a withdrawal process under Article 50 actually entails, its paragraph 2 simply states that

> *In the light of the guidelines provided by the European Council*, the Union shall negotiate and conclude an agreement with that State, setting out the arrangements for its withdrawal, taking account of the framework for its future relationship with the Union.
>
> *(emphasis added)*

The second part of paragraph 2 of Article 50 TEU was not initially interpreted by the parties in the same way. From the very beginning, the UK's interests in the negotiations were not so much the 'arrangements for its withdrawal' but to discuss the future EU–UK relationship.[11] In this sense, what the British Government expected from its withdrawal negotiations was 'to have reached an agreement about our future partnership by the time the two year Article 50 process has concluded'.[12] This overlapping of the withdrawal and the future relationship negotiations to be carried out in parallel and in under two years might seem over-ambitious, but it was a fair reading of Article 50(2).[13] The EU, on the other hand, did not accept the UK's intention of negotiating the future relationship within the withdrawal agreement under Article 50 TEU. On the contrary, the European Council (Article 50) Guidelines understood that Article 50 talks were to be aimed solely at concluding an agreement on matters necessary to ensure an orderly withdrawal.[14] The future relationship, on the other hand, could only be dealt with as a preliminary and preparatory framework which had to materialise fully in a new set of negotiations with the UK once it had become a third country, i.e. once its Article 50 withdrawal agreement had entered into force. Likewise, the EU decided on the material issues that, although not determined either by the exit clause, were to be included in the withdrawal agreement: citizens' rights, a financial settlement and a solution to avoiding a border on the island of Ireland.[15] Furthermore, these were to be dealt with in a first phase of talks which would not progress on to a second phase dealing with the framework for the future relationship until the EU27 was satisfied with those initial three pillars.[16] It is interesting to understand how crucial the ordering of the negotiations – either in parallel or in phases – was for the balance of power within them. Both the selection of the three specific issues to be considered 'arrangements for withdrawal' and the phased approach acted in the Union's interests. It is no secret that the UK strongly favoured parallelism because it would have enabled it to engage in trade-offs between the terms of withdrawal and the terms of the future relationship. This would have given it a stronger negotiating hand because it would have included talks on security cooperation and international affairs, areas in which the UK is undoubtedly a strong player.[17] The EU, on the other hand, strengthened its negotiating position by adopting a phased approach and refusing to discuss future relations until it had secured an acceptable withdrawal deal.[18] This formula introduced a sequencing and conditionality that is not specified in the letter of Article 50, increasing even more EU leverage in the negotiations and enhancing the probability of the resulting agreement being in line with the Union's interests.[19] Indeed, the concept of 'sufficient progress' was vague enough to allow the EU27 to freely decide when such progress had been achieved. Given the tight Article 50 negotiating schedule of two years (and extension requiring European Council unanimity)[20] as well as the importance for the withdrawing state to move on to phase two talks to at least frame the future relationship and offer some certainty to markets and businesses back home, concessions on the UK's side became unavoidable.[21]

5.2.2 The European Commission

In this procedural set-up designed by the European Council, the roles of the remaining European institutions during the withdrawal process – which are not described in detail in the Treaties either – have also been decisive. The Council of the European Union, by remission of Article 50 TEU to Article 218(3) TFEU, is entrusted with the double task of authorising the opening of withdrawal negotiations and nominating the negotiator for the EU.[22] True to form, there is no Article 50 rule on who should negotiate on the EU's behalf, the Council or the Commission. However, even before the UK's notification had been sent, the remaining Heads of State and Government – despite their reluctance to give up control over the process[23] – decided they were not the best placed to conduct the Brexit talks and invited the Council to nominate the European Commission.[24] Michel Barnier and his Article 50 Task Force (TF50) were put in charge of Brexit. This has given the EU an especially united front and a powerful negotiating position which it has strategically exploited, as well as prevented the UK from capitalising on divergent national interests. There is little doubt that after decades of experience negotiating trade agreements, the Commission was at an advantage from the outset and more than prepared to bring out its arsenal of well-tested negotiating tactics which it generally deploys as the stronger party in any international negotiation. The European Commission has in this sense played a bigger role in the withdrawal process than originally prescribed by Article 50 TEU. This, in turn, has bolstered further the importance of process and rules during EU withdrawal, as negotiating with the Commission is a typically rigid and rule-based procedure. In this vein, and as Oliver Patel observes,

> there is no legal reason why TF50 alone [i.e. the Commission] should negotiate with the UK. Rather, the EU designed the process in this way because it was in its interest for everything to go through a single, inflexible channel.[25]

Additionally, the Commission's renowned forte as a united bloc was skilfully preserved by limiting the divorce negotiations to matters in which it was much easier for all EU countries to have perfectly aligned interests. All of them of course wanted the UK to protect the rights of their citizens residing there, to pay the divorce bill and to let the Republic of Ireland solve the problem of its border.[26]

5.2.3 The Council of the European Union

The participation of the Council of Ministers and the European Parliament (EP) has relied on paragraphs of Article 218 other than paragraph 3 when convenient.[27] The Council, for example, was tasked with adopting a detailed mandate – the negotiating directives – for the talks between Mr Barnier and the UK executive. This is an extension of the EU's rules on international treaty-making to the withdrawal process that is not initially foreseen by Article 50 which only refers to the third paragraph. Council negotiating directives, on the other hand, are envisaged in 218(2): 'The Council shall authorise the opening of negotiations, adopt negotiating directives, authorise the signing of agreements and conclude them.' Still, it is also true that this extended role of the Council was reduced to endorsing the directives for the negotiations that had previously been drafted by the European Commission and presented as an annex to its Recommendation for a Council Decision authorising it to begin the Brexit talks.[28] However, by having the directives approved by the Council, chief negotiator Barnier has been bound by a strict mandate which has also played to the EU's advantage. In this sense, the UK was unable to extract concessions from the EU because the EU negotiator had a mandate from which it could not stray. In effect, the only way for the European Commission to have deviated would have been to go back to the Member States to obtain authorisation, stalling further the negotiations that the UK so critically needed to get on with in the strict timeframe of Article 50.[29] In other words, there was only one realistic way to get the EU to talk about the future relationship, and that was by getting the European Council to decide that sufficient progress had been made on the three issues prioritised by the 27. The Council also established its own separate Brexit working group made up of representatives of the 27 Heads of State or Government (a.k.a. Sherpas) called the Ad hoc Working Party on Article 50, to which Mr Barnier would report back on the progress of the Brexit talks.[30] This is another improvised application, this time of paragraph 4, of Article 218 TFEU: 'The Council may address directives to the negotiator and designate a special committee in consultation with which the negotiations must be conducted.' However, the European Council December Statement[31] also required the Commissions' team integrate a representative of the Presidency of the Council and of the European Council to participate in all negotiation sessions. This, on the contrary, is an innovation to the usual approach to treaty negotiations under Article 218 TFEU[32] and injects a special degree of intergovernmentalism into an otherwise highly supranational withdrawal process. There has indeed been a sustained flow of information between the Commission negotiator and the Member States who have been able to raise their concerns about the direction of the negotiations during the entire process.[33]

5.2.4 The European Parliament

Finally, the EP, according to Article 50(2) TEU, is only required to consent to the conclusion of the withdrawal agreement. Following the Treaties to the letter, the role of the EP in Member State withdrawal appears to be limited to intervening at the very end of the process. However, this veto power has instilled this institution with significant influence also during the negotiations even when it does not formally participate in them. Because its approval was crucial to the success of the negotiations or, more specifically, to their final outcome,[34] the EP has been immediately and fully informed at all stages – in the manner of Article 218(10) TFEU – of the Brexit procedure in order to reduce the risk of it denying ratification of a text about which it had not previously been consulted.[35] In this sense, the first official document to be approved by a European institution after the UK's Article 50 notification was none other than a European Parliament Resolution of 5 April 2017. The resolution indicated what the EP position was and that the forthcoming European Council Guidelines had to take it into account as it was to 'form the basis of Parliament's assessment of the negotiation process'. It also stated that full involvement of the EP was 'a necessary precondition for it to give its consent to any agreement reached between the European Union and the United Kingdom'.[36] All later negotiating documents by the other institutions have welcomed and given due regard to this and other EP resolutions, primarily by prioritising EU citizens' rights during withdrawal which are accordingly protected in the Withdrawal Agreement.[37]

5.3 The legal status of a withdrawing Member State

For any Member State wishing to leave the EU after the Lisbon Treaty and despite what certain actors might have stated during the UK referendum campaign,[38] the Article 50 TEU procedure is the only legal route to withdrawal.[39] In effect, the EU's withdrawal clause as *lex specialis* displaces public international law[40] and postpones a Member State's effective departure until after a minimum of two years has elapsed since sending its notification of intention of withdrawal.

This immediately raises the question of whether the legal status of that Member remains the same or is altered in any sense during that period.[41] A first readjustment to a withdrawing state's membership after activating the procedure is laid out in Article 50(4):

> For the purposes of paragraphs 2 and 3, the member of the European Council or of the Council representing the withdrawing Member State shall not participate in the discussions of the European Council or Council or in decisions concerning it.

This is a very circumscribed shift in a withdrawing member's status which affects its decision-making rights only in the European Council and Council of the EU and only in relation to discussions and decisions in the framework of Article 50 TEU, that is, relating to its withdrawal.[42] In this sense, for some authors a legal fiction is created by which a Member State, while negotiating its withdrawal, becomes 'like' a third country[43] whereas all other rights and obligations in these two institutions plus all participation in every other EU body remains the same until withdrawal is effective.[44] Concerning the Brexit process, the most legally notable consequence of this paragraph 4 rule was the UK's removal from the list of presidencies of the Council of the European Union where it had been assigned the second half of 2017.[45] Curiously, the Decision was actually approved after the UK 'announced' that it was leaving, even though it had not yet formally triggered Article 50 TEU. Thus, practice has shed further light on the 'special' legal status of a Member State in the process of withdrawing from the EU. First, that certain changes are already effected before the official notification is sent and, second, that despite a withdrawing state being likened to a third country it is still bound by most of its obligations under the EU Treaties even while negotiating its withdrawal.[46]

5.3.1 Pre-notification status

Regarding pre-notification withdrawal effects, we find that the European Council that was held a few days after the referendum, on 28 and 29 June 2016, was only attended by the UK Head of Government David Cameron on the first day where he explained the situation in the UK after the vote.[47] The following day, however, was used for an informal meeting with a new EU27 format where the remaining Heads of State or Government discussed the implications of Brexit without the British Prime Minister. All European Council meetings held after the UK made it known publicly that it would be withdrawing from the Union but still before it sent its official notification dedicated either a day or half a day to the EU27 format excluding the UK.[48] More importantly, the EU27 would use those meetings to establish what we might call certain 'pre-notification principles'. The first was that, although it was up to the British Government to notify the European Council of the UK's intention to withdraw from the Union, it should be done 'as quickly as possible'. The second, complementing the first, was that '[t]here can be no negotiations of any kind before this notification has taken place'.[49]

Once again, we find a lack of prevision on the part of the Article 50's drafters who seem to have left more things to be determined in the course of its application than in its words.[50] Indeed, nothing is prescribed as to when a Member State should notify the European Council of its intention to make use of the withdrawal clause so, at first sight, it might appear that the state enjoys unfettered discretion in relation to the timing of its notification. However, it has been suggested that a public announcement of a decision to withdraw from the EU creates such uncertainty for the remaining members that an unjustified and long delay until official notification would go against the principle of loyal cooperation.[51] Nonetheless, others have correctly pointed out that it would also be very difficult to specify an appropriate timeframe.[52] One must take into consideration that by effect of Article 50 TEU, once its notification is sent, a state has only a guarantee of two years to carry out extremely complex divorce negotiations and to prepare itself for the tremendous reality of converting from member to third country. Indeed, the principle of loyal cooperation which also binds the Union to its Members must allow for the multiplex preparations of the state wishing to withdraw.[53]

These pre-negotiation preparations have to be carried out by the outgoing state on its own. Indeed, the second pre-notification principle established by the EU27 was 'no negotiations before notification' although there is nothing in the withdrawal clause banning informal discussions before notice.[54] Without this second rule, which the Union and all its Member States have taken very seriously during the Brexit process, a withdrawing country might seek certain advantages in its right to delay notification. This it could do by trying to conduct informal pre-negotiations with the EU and de facto extending the short two-year negotiation period. The EU27 have not allowed this because Article 50's strict schedule is generally considered an ally of the EU and a pressure on the withdrawing state which will inevitably cave to the former's demands before its negotiating time is up.[55] A withdrawing state might also abuse its right to delay notification by opening negotiations with other members individually and undermine the Union's negotiating strength as a bloc.[56] This too was avoided by the Union's determination to remain united, quite to the surprise of many in London.[57]

5.3.2 The withdrawing state as a full(ish) Member State

The next question concerns a Member State's obligations regarding its withdrawal once it has notified its intention to withdraw. In this respect, there are two different views: the first argues that an existing state can simply notify and then sit out the two-year wait, making no attempt to negotiate or seek an agreed withdrawal before leaving with no deal.[58] This is the result, it is argued, of the possibility envisaged by Article 50 TEU of a departure without a withdrawal agreement or, in other words, of the unilateral character of the right to withdraw.[59] The alternative view, however, believes the exit clause does not operate in a legal vacuum and assesses withdrawal in light of the Treaties that continue to bind the Member State until its effective departure, particularly bearing in mind the principle of loyal cooperation enshrined in Article 4(3) TEU.[60] In this view, what is certain is that the European institutions have a clear obligation to negotiate and conclude a withdrawal agreement pursuant to the second sentence of paragraph 2 of Article 50 TEU: 'In the light of the guidelines provided by the European Council, the Union *shall* negotiate and conclude an agreement with that State' (emphasis added). This is a direct command that means the notification triggers an obligation addressed to the Union to negotiate a withdrawal agreement. If, however, we take into account the principle of loyal cooperation during withdrawal,[61] the duty to negotiate a deal must also include the withdrawing Member State as it is still bound by Article 4(3) TEU and is thus under an obligation to assist the Union in carrying out that task of agreeing a withdrawal treaty.[62] In this sense, John Weerts talks about how the principle of loyal cooperation might 'temper' the right to withdraw: 'Il n'est pas inutile de souligner l'influence du principe de coopération loyale sur la conduite des négociations, tempérant le caractère *ad nutum* du droit de retrait.'[63] Takis Tridimas also puts it quite simply:

> Both parties have an obligation to conduct negotiations in good faith and in a spirit of cooperation. This duty derives from international law and also the duty of loyal cooperation provided by Article 4(3) TEU, which continues to bind the withdrawing Member State until it leaves the EU.[64]

In any event, it is only an obligation of conduct to negotiate in good faith a withdrawal agreement during the two-year period established in the Treaty but, to borrow the expression used in Article 50(3), 'failing that' the Member State is free to leave without any deal in place.

The notion that the EU withdrawal clause should be applied in the spirit of the Treaties and in compliance with their principles has become clear during the Brexit process where the principle of loyal cooperation has significantly received the most attention. The UK's notification of its intention to withdraw, which came in the form of a letter by the then UK Prime Minister Theresa May addressed to the then President of the European Council Donald Tusk, proposed as its first principle to help shape the negotiations that the parties 'engage with one another constructively and respectfully, in a spirit of sincere cooperation'.[65] Thus, this first understanding by a Member State of Article 50 TEU corroborates the idea that the obligations of loyalty deriving from the principle of sincere cooperation should be given due regard during withdrawal and that the natural result of sending the notification envisaged in Article 50(2) is to follow it with two years of negotiations as subsequently set out in the remainder of the provision. In response to the country's notification, the European Council's (Article 50) Guidelines highlighted the two core principles of the Union's position for the negotiations. The first consisted of the two-phased approach to the negotiations which would give priority to an orderly withdrawal. The second was the principle of sincere cooperation. This was specifically due to the fact that until the official leave date, the United Kingdom remained a full Member of the EU, subject to all rights and obligations set out in the Treaties and under EU law.[66] Likewise, the European Parliament Resolution reads:

> whereas until it leaves the European Union the United Kingdom must enjoy all the rights and fulfil all the obligations deriving from the Treaties, including the principle of sincere cooperation laid down in Article 4(3) of the Treaty on European Union.[67]

Finally, as it is well known, the UK had to request a total of three extensions of its Article 50 talks with a view to finalising the ratification of its Withdrawal Agreement. The second European Council Decision extending the negotiating period[68] was graver than the first[69] and included a paragraph which is also worth reproducing in part:

> The European Council takes note of the commitment by the United Kingdom to act in a constructive and responsible manner throughout the extension period in accordance with the duty of sincere cooperation, and expects the United Kingdom to fulfil this commitment and Treaty obligation in a manner that reflects its situation as a withdrawing Member State. To this effect, the United Kingdom shall facilitate the achievement of the Union's tasks and shall refrain from any measure which could jeopardise the attainment of the Union's objectives, in particular when participating in the decision-making processes of the Union.

The message is clear: although the two-year negotiating period stipulated in Article 50 TEU had come and gone, during the extension the same set of principles now consolidated as part of the EU withdrawal process proceeded to apply. The departing state continued to have Member State status in the terms set out above, i.e. it remained bound by EU law in general and by the EU withdrawal law that was emerging through this unprecedented practice. The Decision also highlights the significance the principle of sincere cooperation has gained in the process, so much so that the withdrawing country was specifically reminded that it must remain loyal also during any extension periods. Thus, it should carry on striving in good faith towards a consensual and orderly withdrawal.

That the other party negotiating its withdrawal treaty is bound by the principle of loyal cooperation is another anomaly in EU external action. Indeed, a Member State with a bona fide obligation to seek a divorce deal with the EU in under two years does not have the most basic bargaining tool in international negotiations, that is, the ability to credibly threaten to walk away from them. This is an even more important tactic for a weak negotiating party that has very little leverage for other reasons, such as its smaller and more trade-dependent economy.[70] Of course, the threat of walking away if the terms are unacceptable is only standard practice in difficult negotiations because the result of failing to reach an agreement is to simply revert back to the status quo. EU withdrawal negotiations are different because they can result in a no deal exit by default if the Article 50 TEU process is not extended or detained and an agreement has not been achieved in time. As it is difficult to imagine that such a cliff-edge scenario could ever be in the Union's interests – to which the withdrawing Member State is required to remain loyal – this is another reason they both have an obligation to negotiate a consensual departure pursuant to EU law. Hence, threatening to leave the negotiating table during the first two years (plus any extensions) is not only unrealistic in economic and political terms but neither is it possible under the Treaties to which a departing Member continues to be bound during its withdrawal process. The British Government's early declarations[71] assuring that no deal was better than a bad deal for the UK and its apparent readiness to walk away from negotiations if they were not heading towards a satisfactory outcome, were not present in Theresa May's Article 50 letter. On the contrary, it asserted that the process was to be made smooth and successful by a constructive and respectful engagement in spirit of sincere cooperation and emphasised the need to avoid a no deal scenario.[72] It is likely a no deal Brexit had such a high profile in UK media and political debate more as a bluff to fool domestic audiences than the other party to the withdrawal negotiations.[73]

5.4 Conclusions

This chapter has established the legal regime of EU withdrawal that has emerged from the Brexit practice and, ultimately, through the important gap-filling exercise carried out by the European institutions to complete the unfinished work of the drafters of Article 50 TEU.[74] We have seen how the Union's official position and agenda-setting for these and probably any possible future withdrawal negotiations have been formulated through a complex interaction between the European Council, the European Commission, the Council of the EU, the EP and all the preparatory bodies and task forces of these forums. Likewise, the rules they have followed have not only stemmed from Article 50 TEU but also from Article 218 TFEU despite sole remission to paragraph 3, while new norms specific to the withdrawal process have also been created.

We have also noted that the exiting state, due to its necessary engagement in its divorce talks while remaining a Member State, is compelled to act like one during its departure process. Thus, although on the basis of Article 50(4) a withdrawing party is in a sense likened to a third country when it comes to negotiating its exit, the UK's negotiations have been structured around its obligations arising from the Treaties and especially from the duty of loyal cooperation in Article 4(3) TEU. The significance is that this obligation, which has long been recognised as a general principle which applies in all constellations under Union law, has now been established as a fundamental and structural principle underpinning the procedure of withdrawal too.

This newly emerged EU withdrawal process is a hybrid between inter-state negotiations among the parties to an international agreement and the much more *sui generis* act of withdrawing from a supranational entity. The special involvement of the institutions has allowed the EU to strategically exploit its 'exclusive' competence to negotiate and conclude the withdrawal agreement while at the same time allowing for Member State participation without weakening its unity. A process that is distinct in many ways from other EU external action, both the special status of the withdrawing state and the fact that the Brexit process has been designed pursuant to the Union's interests have left behind a new legal and procedural regime which has set precedent for a unique but also heavily conditioned process of withdrawal from the EU.

Notes

1 This contribution has been written within the framework of the research project EUMABEXT, funded by the Spanish Government (RTI2018-099097-B-I00). The author would like to thank Ramses A Wessel and Juan Santos Vara for their comments on an earlier draft of this chapter. Christoph Hillion, 'Withdrawal Under Article 50 TEU: An Integration-Friendly Process' (2018) 55 Common Market Law Review 29, 3. As examples, he refers to Article 56 of the Vienna Convention, Article 7 of the Statute of the Council of Europe, Article 56 of the EFTA Convention and Article 127 of the EEA Agreement.

2 Henry G Schermers and Niels M Blokker, *International Institutional Law* (6th edn, Martinus Nijhoff 2018). See also: Ramses A Wessel, 'You Can Check Out Any Time You Like, But Can You Really Leave? On "Brexit" and Leaving International Organizations' (2016) 13 International Organizations Law Review 197; Catherine M Brölmann, Richard Collins, Sufyan Droubi and Ramses A Wessel, 'Exiting International Organizations: A Brief Introduction' (2018) 15 International Organizations Law Review 243.

3 As Hillion stated before the referendum, the EU withdrawal procedure, clearly incomplete, would need to be supplemented by ad hoc arrangements the way the Article 49 TEU accession process has been elaborated by its many uses: Christoph Hillion, 'Accession and Withdrawal in the Law of the European Union' in Damian Chalmers and Anthony Arnull (eds), *The Oxford Handbook of European Union Law* (Oxford University Press 2015).

4 Allan F Tatham, '"Don't Mention Divorce at the Wedding, Darling!": EU Accession and Withdrawal after Lisbon' in Andrea Biondi, Piet Eeckhout and Stefanie Ripley (eds), *EU Law after Lisbon* (Oxford University Press 2012) 154.

5 TEU, art 50(2):

> A Member State which decides to withdraw shall notify the European Council of its intention. In the light of the guidelines provided by the European Council, the Union shall negotiate and conclude an agreement with that State, setting out the arrangements for its withdrawal, taking account of the framework for its future relationship with the Union. That agreement shall be negotiated in accordance with Article 218(3) of the Treaty on the Functioning of the European Union. It shall be concluded on behalf of the Union by the Council, acting by a qualified majority, after obtaining the consent of the European Parliament.

6 Ibid.

7 Andrew Duff, 'Brexit: What Next?' (Statement to the Constitutional Affairs Committee of the European Parliament, 8 November 2016).

8 Annex to the European Commission Recommendation for a Council Decision authorising the Commission to open negotiations on an agreement with the United Kingdom of Great Britain and Northern Ireland setting out the arrangements for its withdrawal from the European Union (Brussels, 3 May 2017) COM(2017) 218 final; later endorsed by the Council of the EU in its negotiating directives.

9 TEU, art 50(3):

> The Treaties shall cease to apply to the State in question from the date of entry into force of the withdrawal agreement or, failing that, two years after the notification referred to in paragraph 2, unless the European Council, in agreement with the Member State concerned, unanimously decides to extend this period.

10 TEU, art 50(2) (n 5).

11 So much so that the UK's initial negotiating position set out twelve principles that the UK wished would guide its withdrawal process from the EU and only the last entitled 'Delivering a smooth, orderly exit from the EU', dealt with the actual exit while the remaining eleven were dedicated to the

'new partnership' (UK Government, 'The United Kingdom's exit from and new partnership with the European Union White Paper' (Policy Paper, 2 February 2017)).

12 Ibid. For more on the UK's February White Paper see: Polly R Polak, 'Brexit: Theresa May's Red Lines Get Tangled up in Her Red Tape. A Commentary on the White Paper' (2017) 2 European Papers 403; Michael Emerson, 'After the UK's Brexit White Paper: What's the Next Move Towards a CFTA?' (CEPS Policy Insights, 2017).

13 This reading can be found in the doctrine, for example, Valentin Kreilinger, Sophie Wolfstädter and Laura Maria, 'Brexit Negotiation Phases and Scenarios of a Drama in Three Acts' (Jacques Delors Institut Policy Paper, 2017) 9; Adam Łazowski, 'Withdrawal from the European Union and Alternatives to Membership' (2012) 37 European Law Review 523.

14 These other arguments in favour of a narrower role for the withdrawal agreement can be found, inter alia, in Jens Dammann, 'A Little Bit Brexit? An Analysis of the Rules Governing Post-Withdrawal Treaties' (2018) 53 Texas International Law Journal 153.

15 Vaughne Miller, Arabella Lang and Jack Simson-Caird, 'Brexit: How Does the Article 50 Process Work?' (House of Commons Briefing Paper, 2017), 22–26.

16 European Council Article 50 guidelines for Brexit negotiations (Brussels, 29 April 2017) EUCO XT 20004/17.

17 Charles Grant, 'Mrs May's Emerging Deal on Brexit: Not Just Hard, but also Difficult' (Centre for European Reform Policy Paper, 2017).

18 Paul Craig, 'The Process: Brexit and the Anatomy of Article 50' in Federico Fabbrini (ed), *The Law and Politics of Brexit* (Oxford University Press 2017).

19 Emily Jones, 'The Negotiations: Hampered by the UK's Weak Strategy' (2019) European Journal of Legal Studies 23, 33:

> Crucially, the EU also insisted on a two-phase approach to the negotiations, structuring discussions to its advantage by frontloading the issues on which it wanted to secure commitments from the UK, including on citizens' rights, the financial settlement, and the Northern Ireland border, before it would negotiate on the future trading relationship, which was of particular interest to the UK.

20 TEU, art 50(3) (n 9).

21 David A Green, 'Brexit Diary: What does Donald Tusk mean by "Realism"?' (Jack of Kent, 2017).

22 TFEU, art 218(3):

> The Commission, or the High Representative of the Union for Foreign Affairs and Security Policy where the agreement envisaged relates exclusively or principally to the common foreign and security policy, shall submit recommendations to the Council, which shall adopt a decision authorising the opening of negotiations and, depending on the subject of the agreement envisaged, nominating the Union negotiator or the head of the Union's negotiating team.

23 European Parliament, 'Questions to the European Commission concerning the nomination of Michel Barnier as the Commission's chief Brexit negotiator' (1 August 2016).

24 Informal meeting of the Heads of State or Government of 27 Member States, as well as the Presidents of the European Council and the European Commission (Brussels, 15 December 2016).

25 Oliver Patel, 'The EU and the Brexit Negotiations: Institutions, Strategies and Objectives' (UCL Brexit Insight, 2018).

26 Whereas opinions are more likely to differ regarding international trade or migration (John Springford, Sam Lowe and Beth Oppenheim, 'Will the Unity of the 27 Crack?' (Centre for European Reform Policy Brief, 2018)).

27 It is interesting to consider whether other paragraphs in Article 218 TFEU which were not deployed during Brexit might also be applicable to the withdrawal process, such as 218(11), i.e. the possibility of seeking an Opinion from the Court of Justice of the European Union on whether the Withdrawal Agreement is compatible with the Treaties. See: Polly R Polak, 'The UK Withdrawal Agreement as a Sui Generis EU International Treaty and its Admissibility to the CJEU's Opinion Procedure' in José Martín y Pérez de Nanclares and Daniel González Herrera (eds), *El diálogo judicial internacional en la protección de los derechos fundamentals* (Tirant lo Blanch 2019).

28 Council of the European Union Directives for the negotiation of an agreement with the United Kingdom of Great Britain and Northern Ireland setting out the arrangements for its withdrawal from the European Union (Brussels, 22 May 2017) XT 2016/17.

29 Jones (n 19) 33.
30 Council Decision (EU) 2017/900 concerning the establishment of the ad hoc Working Party on Article 50 TEU chaired by the General Secretariat of the Council.
31 Informal meeting (n 24).
32 Steve Peers, 'Guide to the Brexit Negotiations' (EU Law Analysis, 2017).
33 Agata Gostynska-Jakubowska, 'Brexit Maze: The Role of EU Institutions in the Negotiations' (Centre for European Reform Policy Brief, 2017).
34 Jesús Carmona, Carmen-Cristina Cîrlig and Gianluca Sgueo, 'UK Withdrawal from the European Union: Legal and Procedural Issues' (European Parliament Research Service, 2017) 16.
35 For the EP's enhanced role in other consent procedures and a comparison with Member State withdrawal, read: Edoardo Bressanelli, Nicola Chelotti and Wilhelm Lehmann, 'Negotiating Brexit: The European Parliament Between Participation and Influence' (2019) 42 Journal of European Integration 347. See also: Juan Santos Vara and Soledad Rodríguez Sánchez-Tabernero, *The Democratisation of EU International Relations Through EU Law* (Routledge 2019).
36 European Parliament Resolution on negotiations with the United Kingdom following its notification that it intends to withdraw from the European Union, 2017/2593(RSP).
37 For an interesting account of the role of the EP as well as national parliaments during the negotiations towards the future EU–UK trade deal see Adam Cygan and Ewa Żelazna's chapter in this volume.
38 The Vote Leave campaign published a framework for establishing a new UK–EU deal after the referendum on the 15 June 2016 which deceitfully stated that:

> Article 50 is not the sole lawful means of leaving the EU. If this were the case, Greenland could not have left the EU in 1985, but it did. Greenland left under what is now the 'ordinary revision procedure', or article 48 of the Treaty on European Union (TEU) .... Under international law, it is also possible to leave the EU under article 54 of the 1969 Vienna Convention on the Law of Treaties.
>
> *(www.voteleavetakecontrol.org/a_framework_for_taking_back_control_and_establishing_a_new_uk_eu_deal_after_23_june.html accessed 9 April 2020)*

39 Jean-Claude Piris, 'If the UK Votes to Leave: The Seven Alternatives to EU Membership' (CER Policy Brief, 2016); Vernon Bogdanor, 'Brexit, the Constitution and the Alternatives' (2016) 27 Kings Law Journal 314, 315. See also: Kenneth Armstrong, 'The Vote Leave Framework for a New UK–EU Deal: Analysis' (CELS Working Paper, 2016); Thomas Streinz, 'Cooperative Brexit: Giving Back Control over Trade Policy' (2017) 15 International Journal of Constitutional Law 271, 274.
40 VCLT, art 54:

> The termination of a treaty or the withdrawal of a party may take place: (a) In conformity with the provisions of the treaty; or (b) At any time by consent of all the parties after consultation with the other contracting States.

41 It is also interesting to question the status of a state once it has withdrawn but remains bound by EU law during a transition period (see the chapter by Tobias Lock in this volume).
42 It is also noteworthy that Article 50 TEU does not include any status change regarding a withdrawing Member State's participation in the EP. This seems reasonable given that directly elected MEPs represent the collective interests of Union citizens, not the parochial interests of the withdrawing state. Given the impact Member State withdrawal has on European rights and the fact that British MEPs do not represent the British Government but, on the contrary, have an independent mandate and represent the citizens of the EU, the MEPs elected by the citizens of the withdrawing state continued to fully participate in the EP's activities and even maintained their full role in the ratification of their country's withdrawal agreement. See: Michael Dougan, 'The Convention's Draft Constitutional Treaty: A "Tidying-up Exercise" that Needs Some Tidying-up of its Own' (Federal Trust for Education and Research 2003) 8; Peter-Tobias Stoll, 'The Role and Powers of the European Parliament in the Brexit Process' (In-Depth Analysis for the EP IMCO Committee, 2017) 16.
43 Araceli Mangas Martín, 'Retirada de un Estado de una Organización Internacional: los procesos del Brexit' (Anales de la Real Academia de Ciencias Morales y Políticas, 2017) 308.
44 Christophe Hillion, 'Article 50 TUE: analyse juridique' [2016] Revue trimestrielle de droit européen 719, 726.

45 Council Decision 2016/1316 amending Decision 2009/908/EU, laying down measures for the implementation of the European Council Decision on the exercise of the Presidency of the Council, and on the chairmanship of preparatory bodies of the Council.

46 The message that membership rights and obligations remain the same until effective departure was repeated by the institutions from the very beginning. See: Press statement by President Donald Tusk on the outcome of the referendum in the UK, 24 June 2016: 'Until the United Kingdom formally leaves the European Union, EU law will continue to apply to and within the UK. And by this I mean rights and obligations.' This was followed on the same day by another from the rest of the European institution's presidents and with the same reassurance: 'According to the Treaties which the United Kingdom has ratified, EU law continues to apply to the full to and in the United Kingdom until it is no longer a Member' (Statement by the EU leaders and the Netherlands Presidency on the outcome of the UK referendum, 24 June 2016) See also: Informal meeting at 27 Statement, 29 June 2016.

47 European Council Conclusions (Brussels, 28 June 2016) EUCO 26/16.

48 After the referendum but before the UK sent its withdrawal letter to the European Council on the 29 of March 2017, the EU27 met informally on several occasions, including on 16 September 2016 in Bratislava, on 15 December 2016 in Brussels, on 3 February 2017 in Malta and on 10 March 2017 in Brussels, to discuss the implications of Brexit and the future of the EU without the UK.

49 Informal meeting (n 24).

50 Although this might be a good place to recall that one of the authors of Article 50 TEU, Giuliano Amato, admitted in a conference at Rome on 21 July 2016 that it was designed as a classic safety valve and not actually to be used.

51 Mauro Gatti, 'Article 50 TEU: A Well-Designed Secession Clause' (2017) 2 European Papers 159.

52 Araceli Mangas Martín, 'Cuestiones jurídicas en torno al Brexit: notificación, plazos, formación de la voluntad, orientaciones y revocación' (2018) 34 Anuario Español de Derecho Internacional 813, 820.

53 TEU, art 4(3):

> Pursuant to the principle of sincere cooperation, the Union and the Member States shall, in full mutual respect, assist each other in carrying out tasks which flow from the Treaties. The Member States shall take any appropriate measure, general or particular, to ensure fulfilment of the obligations arising out of the Treaties or resulting from the acts of the institutions of the Union. The Member States shall facilitate the achievement of the Union's tasks and refrain from any measure which could jeopardise the attainment of the Union's objectives.

54 Holger Hestermeyer, 'How Brexit Will Happen: A Brief Premier on EU Law and Constitutional Law Questions Raised by Brexit' (2016) 33 Journal of International Arbitration (2016) 429.

55 Gatti (n 51); Tim Oliver, 'Europe's Brexit Headache: Critical Reflections on the EU's Approach to Brexit' (Clingendael Spectator, 2018); Frances Coppola, 'Playing the Unplayable Game: The Impossible Reality of Brexit. What Problems Lie Ahead for the UK Government as it takes on the Brexit Negotiations?' (2017) 24 IPPR Progressive Review 25, 27.

56 Charles Grant, 'Why the 27 are taking a Hard Line on Brexit' (Centre for European Reform Insight 2016) 1:

> The British government knows that the Article 50 exit procedure was designed to put the country leaving the EU at a disadvantage. So, prior to invoking the article, its envoys have been urging other EU governments to give some indication of which demands would be acceptable to them; they don't want their opening bids to be shot down as soon as the procedure starts. But the 27 – fearing that British diplomacy may sow divisions among them – have refused any 'pre-negotiation'.

57 Hussein Kassim, 'The EU Institutions' in Anan Menon (ed), *Article 50 One Year On* (UK in a Changing Europe, 2018) 31.

58 Gavin Phillipson, 'A Dive into Deep Constitutional Waters: Article 50, the Prerogative and Parliament' (2016) 79 Modern Law Review 1064, 1067.

59 Alberto López Basaguren, 'Brexit: la secesión de la Unión Europea. Entre teoría y realidad' (2017) 40 UNED. Teoría y Realidad Constitucional 111, 117.

60 Streinz (n 39) 272: 'While the now-famous article 50 of the Treaty on European Union (TEU) sets up a rudimentary structure for the withdrawal process, general principles of EU law fill the gaps. One of them is the principle of sincere cooperation.'; Adam Łazowski, 'Exercises in Legal Acrobatics: The Brexit Transitional Arrangements' (2017) 2 European Papers 845, 848.

61 Jean-Victor Louis, 'Le droit de retrait de l'Union Européenne' (2006) 42 Cahiers de droit européen 293, 307; who refers not only to respecting the principle of loyalty but also the principle of solidarity during the exercise of the right to withdraw from the EU.
62 TEU, art 4(3) (n 53).
63 John Weerts, 'L'évolution du droit de retrait de l'union européenne et sa résonance sur l'intégration européenne' (2012) 48 Cahiers de droit européen 345, 393.
64 Takis Tridimas, 'Article 50: An Endgame Without an End?' (2016) 27 King's Law Journal 297, 306.
65 The United Kingdom Prime Minister's letter to Donald Tusk triggering Article 50, 29 March 2017.
66 European Council Article 50 guidelines (n 16).
67 European Parliament Resolution (n 36).
68 European Council Decision taken in agreement with the United Kingdom extending the period under Article 50(3) TEU (Brussels, 11 April 2019) EUCO XT 20013/19.
69 European Council Decision taken in agreement with the United Kingdom, extending the period under Article 50(3) TEU (Brussels, 22 March 2019) EUCO XT 20006/19.
70 Cecilia Albin, *Justice and Fairness in International Negotiation* (Cambridge University Press 2001) 1–23.
71 UK Government, Theresa May's Lancaster Speech on the Government's negotiating objectives for exiting the EU (17 January 2017).
72 The United Kingdom Prime Minister's letter (n 65).
73 Sunder Katwala, 'The Brexit Negotiations: What do the British Want?' (FES Perspective, 2017) 1–2. See also: 'Britain's Diplomatic Delusions' *The Economist* (London, 23 August 2018).
74 With a view to understanding how EU values have underlain the legal regime of EU withdrawal see Allan F Tatham's chapter in this volume.

Part II

Brexit and existing EU international agreements

6
Managing Brexit
Trade agreements binding on the UK pursuant to its EU membership

Panos Koutrakos

6.1 Introduction

Trade agreements do not normally set the pulse racing. They come about following a process that takes time and energy, and involves painstaking negotiations about technical and complex issues most of which are rarely known to audiences other than the industries affected by them. Brexit, however, has brought trade agreements to the centre of public discourse. This is partly due to a narrative that dominated both the campaign that led to the referendum of 23 June 2016 and the post-referendum period. This narrative centred on the international stature of the UK, the constraints imposed by EU membership and the potential that Brexit would unleash and would allow the country to negotiate ambitious trade deals with many third countries.

This narrative became all the more pronounced soon after the Brexit referendum. The Department for International Trade was established and the project 'Global Britain' became the hallmark of the difference that, according to the British Government, Brexit would make. Quite what this difference would entail has not yet become clearer by the triteness which the Government of the day heaped upon it. The then Prime Minister Theresa May stated that Brexit 'should make us think of global Britain, a country with the self-confidence and the freedom to look beyond the continent of Europe and to the economic and diplomatic opportunities of the wider world'.[1] The then Foreign Secretary, and current Prime Minister, Boris Johnson said that 'whether we like it or not we are not some bit part or spear carrier on the world stage. We are a protagonist – a global Britain running a truly global foreign policy.'[2] As time went by, the Government's explanations were not burdened by any further clarity. While he was still Foreign Secretary, Boris Johnson declared:

> We are big enough to do amazing things. We have the ability to project force 7,000 miles, to use our permanent membership of the UN security council to mobilise a collective response to the crisis in North Korea. We contribute 25 per cent of European aid spending and yet no one seriously complains that we have a sinister national agenda and that is why the phrase global Britain makes sense because if you said Global China or Global Russia or even alas Global America it would not have quite the same flavour.[3]

With delicious succinctness, the House of Commons Foreign Affairs concluded its inquiry into Global Britain by stating that '[n]o minister during our inquiry was able to give the Committee a definitive explanation of "Global Britain"'.[4]

The vacuous concept of Global Britain notwithstanding, there was no doubt even early on that negotiating trade agreements would be a significant part of the UK's post-Brexit foreign policy. In 2017, the then Secretary of State for International Trade, Liam Fox, said that

> [t]he UK government's ambition is to build a Global Britain – a nation that is outward-looking and internationalist, rejecting insularity and continuing to play a prominent role in global affairs. Trade is central to this ambition. We want Britain to become a global champion of free trade, a nation at the heart of world commerce, working with our international allies and partners to remove barriers and liberalise trading practices.[5]

Brexit, therefore, was advocated as the great disruptor which would unshackle the United Kingdom from the heavy-handed and inflexible trade policy imposed by the European Union. And yet, a lot of time and energy has been spent seeking to ensure continuity of the EU's trade agreements. This chapter will unpack the relationship between the rhetoric of rupture and the practice of continuity by focusing on the effect of international trade agreements that were binding on the UK pursuant to its EU membership. It will analyse how they were approached by both the British and the EU authorities and how they have been managed under both the UK–EU Withdrawal Agreement (WA)[6] and UK law.[7]

6.2 The status of the EU's trade agreements and Brexit

Trade agreements have been at the centre of the rhetoric about the UK's global role since the start of the referendum campaign. Before, however, the British Government had to decide formally how to approach the trade agreements that were binding on the UK pursuant to its EU membership, the rhetoric from the Brexiter side was characterised by only variable levels of absurdity: originally, it was argued that withdrawal from the EU would not change the application of the existing trade agreements as the latter would apply automatically post-Brexit; this position then morphed into the argument that the UK would be in a position to renegotiate all existing agreements or at least to have them all replicated automatically. Whether ignorant, delusional or disingenuous, this approach to the post-Brexit status of the EU's trade agreements did not cease to be bombastic well after the referendum. In a Conservative Party fringe event in 2017, the then International Trade Secretary, Liam Fox, stated that '[w]e're going to replicate the 40 EU free trade agreements that exist before we leave the European Union so we've got no disruption of trade'.[8] He added, 'I hear people saying "oh we won't have any [free trade agreements] before we leave". Well believe me we'll have up to 40 ready for one second after midnight in March 2019.'[9] This was entirely consistent with the tone of the broader narrative about the negotiating power of the UK, as the following infamous statement by the then International Trade Secretary bears out: 'the free trade agreement that we will have to do with the European Union should be one of the easiest in human history'.[10]

It was in that deeply toxic political environment that the EU's trade agreements and their post-Brexit implications for the UK attracted attention. The trade relations between the UK and third countries whilst the former was an EU member were governed by two types of international agreements. The first consisted of agreements concluded by the EU alone the content of which falls within the EU's exclusive competence.[11] These agreements only bound the UK as a matter of EU law pursuant to Article 216(2) TFEU and, therefore, would not be applicable once EU law ceased to be the law of the land in the UK. The second category covered trade agreements which were mixed, concluded by both the EU and the UK (along with the other Member States) and a third country, given that parts of them fall within the scope of national competence.[12] Such trade agreements are, in essence, of a bilateral character. They are concluded 'of the one part' by the EU and its Member States and, 'of the other part', by the third country and refer to the UK in its status as a Member State of the EU. The Free Trade Agreement with South Korea, for instance, defines the parties to it in Article 1(2) as 'the European Union or the Member States or the European Union and the Member States'.[13] This is further borne out by the wording of these agreements, as reference is made to Member States as 'Contracting Parties to the Treaty on the European Union and the Treaty on the Functioning of the European Union, hereinafter referred to as the "Member States of the European Union"'. This is in contrast to other agreements with groups of countries where each country is referred to separately. For instance, the Association Agreement between the EU and Central American States defines its parties as 'the Republics of Costa Rica, El Salvador, Guatemala, Honduras, Nicaragua and Panama, referred to as the "Republics of the Central American Party"'.[14]

It follows from the above that, once the UK left the EU and lost its status as a Member State, it would also cease to be a party to such Agreements,[15] unless a legal formula were agreed upon about the extension of their application. This conclusion is also borne out by a clause in a large number of mixed agreements on their territorial application. The EU–Central America Association Agreement, for instance, makes it clear that it applies only, as far as the EU is concerned, 'to the territories in which the Treaty on the European Union and the Treaty on the Functioning of the European Union are applied and under the conditions laid down in those Treaties'.[16] In any case, the requirement that such mixed agreements be renegotiated would follow from their context. These are package deals, and part of the package is the status of the UK as a Member State of the EU. Third contracting States may well argue that the withdrawal of the UK would amount to a fundamental change of circumstances pursuant to Article 62 of the Vienna Convention on the Law of Treaties.

Things are different when it comes to the UK's participation in mixed agreements of a multilateral nature in the context of which continuity is easier to achieve. A case in point are multilateral environmental agreements (MEAs)[17] which, according to the British Government, will continue to bind the UK after its withdrawal from the EU.[18] One would need to enquire whether the agreement in question pursues certain common objectives without striking a bargain of the type we find in bilateral trade agreements. In other words, when it comes to agreements which do not impose a collective set of obligations on the EU and its Member States and which would not require the consent of the parties in order to achieve the disentanglement of the EU's from the UK's obligations, there is no legal and policy interest in whether this objective is carried out on the basis of the UK as part of the EU or on its own. It follows that Brexit has not affected the status of the UK as a party to such agreements. It would, then, be a question of the legal formula that would clarify this state of continuity. For instance, a declaration could be adopted which would notify the other contracting parties of the separation of the UK from the EU as far as the aspects of the agreements that fall within the EU's competence are concerned and the UK would, then, be ensuring compliance with the agreement pursuant to domestic legislation. In this case, it would be difficult to envisage a situation where the EU's interlocutors would be able to invoke a fundamental change of circumstances.

Given the range of mixed agreements of a multilateral nature, the above may entail an adjustment the scope of which would vary. For instance, in the context of the Paris Agreement on climate change,[19] the UK has submitted a joint Nationally Determined Contribution together with other EU Member States, whilst post-Brexit it needs to submit its own.[20] Once we step away from the MEAs context, the adjustment that is required is of a more serious and complex nature. In relation to the World Trade Organization (WTO) Agreements,[21] the adjustment of the UK's membership has not been uncontroversial, as illustrated by the apportionment of tariff rate quotas on agricultural products proposed jointly by the EU and the UK and the strong objections of third countries.[22] It becomes apparent, therefore, that even in the context of agreements to which the UK is a party in its own right, the transition to the post-Brexit state may require negotiation, and that no negotiation is without its complexities or surprises. This is all the more so in the case of package deals such as the one underpinning the WTO Agreements.

In the light of the analysis in this section, two questions arise. The first is about the UK–EU WA and how it has dealt with the effect of the EU's trade agreements following the UK's withdrawal from the EU. The second is about the UK's approach to these agreements given the country's imminent and much sought after freedom to negotiate trade agreements. The following sections will address these questions in turn.

6.3 The status of the existing trade agreements under the Withdrawal Agreement

The WA provides in Article 126 for a transitional period that will last until 31 December 2020 (unless it is extended by 30 June for a maximum of two more years). During this period, the WA introduces, for all intents and purposes, the principle of continuity regarding the application of EU law in the UK legal order and UK–EU relations. This principle applies to international agreements too, as the WA confirms that the term EU law covers the international agreements to which the Union is a party and the international agreements concluded by the Member States acting on behalf of the Union.[23]

This principle is further elaborated upon in Article 129 of the Agreement. Entitled 'Specific arrangements relating to the Union's external action', it provides as follows in its first paragraph:[24]

> Without prejudice to Article 127(2), during the transition period, the United Kingdom shall be bound by the obligations stemming from the international agreements concluded by the Union, by Member States acting on its behalf, or by the Union and its Member States acting jointly, as referred to in point (a)(iv) of Article 2.

The underlying rationale for the principle of continuity is spelled out in the preamble to the Agreement:

> [I]t is in the interest of both the Union and the United Kingdom to determine a transition or implementation period during which – notwithstanding all consequences of the United Kingdom's withdrawal from the Union as regards the United Kingdom's participation in the institutions, bodies, offices and agencies of the Union, in particular the end, on the date of entry into force of this Agreement, of the mandates of all members of institutions, bodies and agencies of the Union nominated, appointed or elected in relation to the United Kingdom's membership of the Union – Union law, including international agreements, should be applicable to and in the United Kingdom, and, as a general rule, with the same effect as regards the Member States, in order to avoid disruption in the period during which the agreement(s) on the future relationship will be negotiated.[25]

The main objective of ensuring the continuity of trade relations with third countries did not emerge in the WA in a policy vacuum. In fact, it had been set out by the EU early on. In its Article 50 Negotiating Guidelines of April 2017, the European Council pointed out that it

> expects the United Kingdom to honour its share of all international commitments contracted in the context of its EU membership. In such instances, a constructive dialogue with the United Kingdom on a possible common approach towards third country partners, international organisations and conventions concerned should be engaged.[26]

This point was taken up by the Council which, in its May 2017 negotiating directives, stated the following:

> in line with the European Council guidelines, a constructive dialogue should be engaged as early as practicable with the United Kingdom during the first phase of the negotiation on a possible common approach towards third country partners, international organisations and conventions in relation to the international commitments contracted before the withdrawal date, by which the United Kingdom remains bound, as well as on the method to ensure that the United Kingdom honours these commitments.[27]

This theme of continuity was carried over in the second round of negotiations, about the transitional period. In its Article 50 Guidelines of December 2017, the European Council stated that, given the British position to leave the customs union, it would

> calibrate its approach as regards trade and economic cooperation in the light of this position so as to ensure a balance of rights and obligations, preserve a level playing field, *avoid upsetting existing relations with other third countries*, and to respect all other principles set out in its guidelines of 29 April 2017, in particular the need to preserve the integrity and proper functioning of the Single Market.[28]

It was in the light of the above that the Council's Negotiating Directives of January 2018 also provided for the continuing application of existing international agreements concluded by the EU.[29]

Continuity as a matter of international law, however, is not a unilateral issue. This dimension is acknowledged in the WA itself, as Article 129(1) WA is accompanied by an asterisked footnote which provides as follows: 'The Union will notify the other parties to these agreements that during the transition period the United Kingdom is to be treated as a Member State for the purposes of these agreements.'

From a policy point of view, given the scope and depth of the WA, it may be difficult to envisage third States raising obstacles to this course of action. Two main reasons support this view. First, the WA is of such broad scope that it may be argued that, in functional terms, and the UK's formal withdrawal from the EU notwithstanding, nothing will change during the transition period as far as the application of EU law to the UK is concerned. Given that EU law covers international agreements binding on the EU, including the UK,[30] it would be reasonable to assume that the continuing application of international agreements would not raise policy concerns for the EU's contracting parties. Second, the transition period is of limited duration and, therefore, any concerns that the EU's interlocutors may have about the unfolding uncertainty regarding their post-Brexit trade relations with the UK would be bound to be time-limited.

From a legal point of view, however, the arrangement envisaged in Article 129 WA requires the consent of the third parties which are the Union's interlocutors in the context of each and every agreement concluded under Article 218 TFEU. To that effect, in January 2020, the Member States, including the UK, endorsed a note verbale which will be sent by the relevant

Head of Mission to the EU's partners.[31] This short document sets out the WA arrangements and provides that the EU and Euratom 'notify' the contracting parties of agreements referred to in Article 129(1) WA that 'the United Kingdom is treated as a Member State of the Union and of Euratom for the purposes of these international agreements'.[32] The above document refers to how the UK is treated by the EU under the WA agreements, as the Union does not have the power to state how third countries would treat the UK under international law. In this vein, the note verbale does not suggest that the EU's and UK's contracting parties act in a specific manner in response. It merely informs them of the internal EU arrangement which is about 'business as usual' for a limited period of time.

The remainder of Article 129 WA sets out the main parameters within which the UK would be deemed to be a party to EU agreements whilst not an EU Member State.[33] In particular, it is about three issues. The first may be summarised as the 'present but not really' principle: the continuing binding effect of international agreements on the UK notwithstanding, no UK representatives would be present at meetings of bodies set up under such agreement during the transition period, unless the UK participates in its own right (that is, not pursuant to its prior EU membership) or it is invited by the EU to attend as part of the EU's delegation on an ad hoc basis required, in particular, for the effective implementation of the WA.[34]

The second issue is about the duty of cooperation. This hallmark of the EU's legal order[35] in general and EU external relations law in particular[36] is adjusted to the specific context set out by the WA. On the one hand, in order to reflect the principle of continuity, the duty of cooperation applies during the transition period and imposes a duty on the UK 'to refrain from any action or initiative which is likely to be prejudicial to the Union's interests, in particular in the framework of any international organisation, agency, conference or forum of which the United Kingdom is a party in its own right'.[37] On the other hand, the application of the duty is not extended in an uncompromising manner. It reflects, instead, the transitional nature of the time-limited period set out in the WA by enabling the UK to

> negotiate, sign and ratify international agreements entered into in its own capacity in the areas of exclusive competence of the Union, provided those agreements do not enter into force or apply during the transition period, unless so authorised by the Union.[38]

The third issue, finally, is the provision of ad hoc cooperation 'whenever there is a need for coordination, the United Kingdom may be consulted, on a case-by-case basis'.[39]

6.4 Rollover agreements: carrying over the theme of continuity (or what to do until we have decided what to do)

As was mentioned above, the narrative during the referendum campaign and in the early months after June 2016 about the application of existing trade agreements was unencumbered by either logic or legal and policy concerns. Considerable energy was, then, spent on ensuring that the trade agreements with third countries that bound the UK pursuant to its EU membership would continue to apply either in the event of a no-deal Brexit or following the expiry of the transition period that would be provided for in the UK–EU WA. This was in order both to avoid sudden disruption in legal relationships and to give the UK time to form its own trade policy and, then, to pursue it.

It became apparent quite early on that the process of rolling over the existing trade agreements would be neither automatic nor easy. After all, trade treaties are the outcome of long and complex negotiations and of package deals and compromises reached in a very specific policy context. Once the UK relied on the goodwill of a third country to extend these deals in a completely new context, it could not be certain that the latter party would resist the temptation to unravel specific aspects of the deal. Even if third countries felt no need to amend the substantive provisions of an existing agreement, the UK would be asking, in effect, to be bound by obligations previously negotiated by the EU in a completely different policy context.

The process of rolling over prior to the formal withdrawal of the UK from the EU has led to the negotiation of agreements with the following countries:

- Andean Countries (Colombia, Ecuador, Peru);[40]
- Cariforum;[41]
- Central America (Costa Rica, El Salvador, Guatemala, Honduras, Nicaragua, Panama);[42]
- Chile;[43]
- Eastern and Southern Africa (ESA) (Madagascar, Mauritius, Seychelles, Zimbabwe) Economic Partnership Agreement;[44]
- Faroe Islands;[45]
- Georgia;[46]
- Norway and Iceland on trade in goods;[47]
- Israel (Trade and Partnership Agreement);[48]
- Jordan establishing an association;[49]
- Kosovo (Partnership, Trade and Cooperation Agreement);[50]
- Lebanon (Association Agreement);[51]
- Liechtenstein (Additional Agreement extending to Liechtenstein certain provisions of the UK–Switzerland Trade Agreement);[52]
- Morocco (Association);[53]
- Pacific States (Fiji, Papua New Guinea) Economic Partnership Agreement;[54]
- Palestinian Authority (Political, Trade and Partnership Agreement);[55]
- Southern African Customs Union (Botswana, Eswatini, Lesotho, Namibia, South Africa) and Mozambique Economic Partnership Agreement;[56]
- South Korea;[57]
- Switzerland;[58]
- Tunisia.[59]

As the above agreements were negotiated by the UK at a time when it was still a Member State, the question may be raised whether the British authorities had acted in accordance with their EU law duty of sincere cooperation.[60] After all, not only does the power to negotiate and conclude agreements with third countries in broad areas of economic activity fall with the EU's exclusive competence, but even in areas of shared competence the power of Member States to act on their own is constrained considerably.[61] It would be unduly formalistic, however, to construe the duty of sincere cooperation so broadly as to prevent the UK from preparing in any way for its post-Brexit relations. The logic of the rollover agreements was about extending the status quo. As the latter had been secured pursuant to EU law, and given that the theme of continuity regarding international agreements emerges in the Union's own Article 50 TEU negotiating documents, seeking to extend the application of existing agreements was not problematic in terms of EU law. On the one hand, extending the status quo did not have the potential of undermining either the EU's negotiating position or the effectiveness of the relevant agreements. This would not be the case if the British Government had sought to negotiate new agreements with third countries whilst the UK was still a Member State. On the other hand, the duty of sincere cooperation also binds the EU which should not be in a position to raise obstacles to prudent action aiming to prepare a Member State for an event envisaged in the Treaties, that is, withdrawal from the EU, without interfering with EU policies. In this respect, it is worth considering that Article 129(4) WA itself provides for a flexible reading of the duty of sincere cooperation during the transition period: as the UK may conclude new trade agreements with third countries during that period, it is by no means apparent why it should not be free, whilst a Member State, to negotiate the extension of existing agreements.

The number of agreements negotiated by the UK at the time of writing is not inconsiderable. The overall assessment of their negotiation confirms, nonetheless, the point made above in this chapter about the lack of realism that underpinned the British approach to international trade after the 2016 referendum. This is the case on various grounds. The first is about policy. Not only do the agreements not cover all those binding the UK pursuant to its EU membership (and, after 1 February 2020, pursuant to Article 129(1) WA), but also large and important trading partners are missing from the list. The UK, for instance, has not concluded rollover agreements with Japan, Canada or Turkey. This was not due to lack of effort on the British part. The former International Trade Secretary, Liam Fox, blamed third countries for this omission: he stated that '[w]e're ready and we've put all our proposals forward ... a number of countries ... are unwilling to put the preparations in for no-deal'.[62] And yet, whilst striking given the much-touted ambition expressed by the British Government, this absence is hardly surprising. Japan, for instance, made it clear that the regulation of its trade relations with the UK post-Brexit is intrinsically linked to the trade relationship between the latter and the EU. It is eminently sensible that the UK's interlocutors would wish to wait and see what type of relationship the UK would develop with the EU first. What was not sensible was the effort of the Secretary for International Trade to exercise pressure on Japan to speed up negotiations, a move that is reported to have won no sympathy for the British trade policy.[63] Another example of how the policy of rollover agreements did not take sufficient account of the broader trade policy reality is illustrated by the absence of an agreement with Canada. The publication by the British Government on 13 March 2019 of its temporary tariff rates policy, according to which 87 per cent of imports by value would be eligible for tariff free treatment,[64] removed any incentive for Canada to extend automatically the post-Brexit application of the Comprehensive Economic and Trade Agreement (CETA) to the UK.

The second reason that underlines the somewhat limited impact of the rollover agreements is about their substantive content. These agreements were presented as duplicating the existing agreements between the EU and its trading partners. A closer look, however, reveals a more nuanced picture. A case in point is the Agreement with Switzerland. The EU–Switzerland Mutual Recognition Agreement applies to twenty sectors.[65] The rolled-over Agreement between UK and Switzerland, however, applies only to three sectors (motor vehicles; good laboratory practice; medical products, good manufacturing practice inspection and batch inspection), whereas the remaining (including medical devices and construction materials) are not covered. The reason given in the UK–Switzerland Agreement has to do with the 'interdependencies with EU laws and systems'.[66] In other words, as Switzerland is committed to legislative equivalence with the EU, it cannot simultaneously commit to mutual recognition of UK practices, unless the latter also conform to the EU rules. The ensuing gap would entail additional cost, due to further testing and certification requirements, for exporters, unless a decision was taken by the Joint Committee[67] to apply the Agreement to the additional product sectors. Such a decision would follow an assessment of the level of divergence or alignment of the applicable technical regulations between Switzerland and the UK which, given the harmonisation between the EU and Swiss technical regulations, would be based on an assessment of the alignment between the UK and EU rules over the product sectors currently not covered by the

UK–Switzerland Agreement. This is a tangible, and by no means isolated, example of how intrinsically linked the negotiations between the UK and third countries are with the negotiations between the UK and the EU.

There are other examples of the differing scope between the rollover agreements and the existing agreements that the EU has concluded and which the former were designed to replicate. Consider, for instance, the context of customs, as the UK Authorised Economic Operators will no longer qualify for expedited treatment on the Swiss border, until the UK has adopted a scheme considered equivalent by the EU to its own scheme. The field of agriculture further illustrates the point. The UK–Switzerland Trade Agreement is designed to extend the application of, amongst others, the EU–Switzerland Agreement on trade in agricultural products.[68] A range of areas, however, which is covered by the latter (organic products regarding certification, labelling, and sale of products as organic, sanitary and phytosanitary measures in relation to plant health, animal feed, seeds, and animal health and trade in animals and animal products) are excluded from the former. In practical terms, this suggests that the Swiss authorities would only be able to accept imports of animals and animal products from the UK once the UK was listed by the European Commission as a third country for animal health purposes.[69]

The third reason which explains the somewhat limited impact of the existing rollover agreements has to do with the weaker negotiating position of the UK. Consider, for instance, the example of an area where the UK has negotiated successfully, namely the principle of bilateral cumulation of origin: rollover agreements provide that EU inputs would continue to be accounted for as being from the UK, and vice versa, for the purpose of meeting the local content requirements necessary to qualify for the zero tariff treatment. On the one hand, this is an example of an approach that provides UK companies with time to adjust their supply chains until the UK has negotiated without having to draw on the EU's trade policy. On the other hand, the application of the principle of cumulation is not uniform. The UK–South Korea Agreement, for instance, limits this rule to three years after the entry into force of the Agreement,[70] hence providing companies just enough time to adjust their supply chains in the post-Brexit environment. Compared to the other countries with which the UK has negotiated a trade agreement, South Korea is the most important economy and had, therefore, the weight to negotiate with the UK the narrower application of the rules laid down in its original agreement with the EU.

In addition to the above policy, substantive and practical factors in the light of which the rollover agreements ought to be assessed, there are two broader points that their negotiation process has revealed. The first is about the confusion regarding the UK's own policy. Rollover agreements are not only intended to prevent UK business from the shock of the abrupt removal of the protection afforded to them by existing trade agreements. They are also designed to give the UK time to develop its own trade policy. After all, for all its bluster about the need to unshackle itself from what the Union has been doing as a world trade actor, the UK has not been in a position to develop a clear sense of direction for its own trade policy. This is not only because of legal constraints, such as the EU's competence and the strict implications of the duty of sincere cooperation, or the all-consuming negotiation of the WA which left little time and energy for other policy-making for three-and-a-half years after the Brexit referendum. It is also because of an absence of consensus as to what the objectives of the UK's trade policy should be, a point illustrated clearly by the well-reported tension within the previous British Government as to whether tariffs should be eliminated in order to open up competition or set high in order to protect domestic industries.[71]

The second remarkable feature of the rollover agreements is the lack of transparency that characterised their negotiation. This was a point that was picked up quite early on in Parliament.

For instance, the Chairman of the House of Lords EU Committee wrote to the Brexit Secretary of State for Exiting the EU enquiring about various aspects of these agreements: what were the criteria for including certain agreements but not others? What was the rationale for the sequencing of the Government's programme of rollover agreements?[72] These were in addition to questions about some broad statements the Government had made regarding the continuing application of some agreements or the possibility that some agreements might not be laid in Parliament for ratification.[73] The British Government was also criticised in Parliament for lack of or insufficient consultation with the devolved administration.[74] The lack of consultation was not confined to public authorities but was extended to industry.[75] Given the constant criticism levelled against the EU for its lack of transparency in its trade negotiations, the shadow in which the rollover agreements were approached by the British Government was nothing short of staggering. This is particularly so given the considerable progress that the EU has made over the last few years in negotiating in a more transparent manner.[76]

6.5 Conclusion

Negotiating trade agreements is a long and complex process at the best of times. And this is not the best of times. First, the UK has not negotiated trade agreements for over forty years, given the transfer of competence in the area to the EU. Whilst there is no doubt about the skills of the British civil service, to negotiate trade agreements is a muscle that they have not flexed for a long time.[77] Second, there is an increasing tendency in international treaty-making for big package deals. In the case of the EU, this is illustrated by the Deep and Comprehensive Free Trade Agreements that the Commission has been advocating since the mid 2000s[78] and the ambitious trade deals that it has been negotiating since then, including with South Korea[79] and Canada.[80] The UK market is not inconsiderable but cannot be compared to a market of 500 million people. Third, such agreements take longer to negotiate. A case in point is CETA: negotiations started in 2009 and the agreement is not yet in force. Long negotiations, however, are by no means confined to the EU: the trade agreement between Canada and South Korea, for instance, took fourteen rounds of negotiations over nine years to conclude. This point is borne out by an intervention by eight former US Treasury Secretaries: '[A]s our experience in the United States with trade negotiations shows it is a difficult environment to negotiate and approve agreements and the risk of accidents is real'.[81] Fourth, for all its enthusiasm for trade negotiations with parties other than the EU, the UK is limited in what it can do in the immediate future, given that the complex negotiations with the EU are bound to become an all-consuming affair for the British civil service.

It is in the light of the above that the lightness with which Brexiters approached trade negotiations both before and after the 2016 referendum is breathtaking. And, in their approach, as in so many things about Brexit, rupture and continuity seem to coexist. This chapter showed how, in the area of international agreements concluded by the EU and binding on the UK pursuant to its EU membership and, during the transition period, pursuant to the WA, the rhetoric of rupture was replaced, or at least supplanted temporarily, by the practice of continuity. Ensuring continuity and managing its implications in the area of international trade is no mean feat, not least given the formidable challenges and open questions that this analysis examined. British policy-makers may think that they have already learnt this lesson. In fact, they have only caught a glimpse of what is to come.

Notes

1 Speech at the Conservative Party Conference, 2 October 2016, www.politicshome.com/news/uk/political-parties/conservative-party/news/79517/read-full-theresa-mays-conservative accessed 5 March 2020.
2 Speech at Chatham House, 2 December 2016, www.gov.uk/government/speeches/beyond-brexit-a-global-britain accessed 5 March 2020.
3 Speech at the Conservative Party Conference, 3 October 2017, https://blogs.spectator.co.uk/2017/10/boris-johnsons-conservative-conference-speech-full-text/ accessed 5 March 2020.
4 Foreign Affairs Committee, 'Global Britain' (HC 2017–9, 780) para 5.
5 Speech in Malaysia, 6 April 2017, www.gov.uk/government/speeches/malaysia-and-britain-partners-in-a-post-brexit-world accessed 5 March 2020.
6 Agreement on the withdrawal of the United Kingdom of Great Britain and Northern Ireland from the European Union and the European Atomic Energy Community [2020] OJ L 29/7.
7 See also Adam Łazowski and Ramses Wessel, 'The External Dimension of Withdrawal from the European Union' [2016] Revue des affaires européennes 623; G Van der Loo and S Blockmans, 'The Impact of Brexit on the EU's International Agreements' (CEPS Commentary, 2016) www.ceps.eu/publications/impact-brexit-eu%E2%80%99s-international-agreements accessed 5 March 2020; Marise Cremona, 'UK Trade Policy' in M Dougan (ed), *The UK After Brexit: Legal and Policy Challenges* (Intersentia 2017) 247; Jed Odermatt, 'Brexit and International Law: Disentangling Legal Orders' (2017) 31 Emory International Law Review 1051; Ramses Wessel, 'Consequences of Brexit for International Agreements Concluded by the EU its Member States' (2018) 55 Common Market Law Review 101; Marise Cremona, 'The Withdrawal Agreement and the EU's International Agreements' (2020) 45 European Law Review 237.
8 www.businessinsider.com/liam-fox-promises-to-sign-40-free-trade-deals-the-second-after-brexit-2017-10?r=UK accessed 5 March 2020.
9 Ibid.
10 He said that in a radio interview in July 2017, www.theguardian.com/politics/2017/jul/20/liam-fox-uk-eu-trade-deal-after-brexit-easiest-human-history?CMP=aff_1432&utm_content=ESI+Media+-+The+Independent&awc=5795_1551746545_44ca227b447fddf3cc411cf20b5cb513 accessed 5 March 2020.
11 See, for instance, the EU–South Africa Agreement on trade in wine [2002] OJ L 28/4.
12 See, for instance, the Free Trade Agreement with South Korea [2011] OJ L 127/6. On mixed agreements, see Christoph Hillion and Panos Koutrakos, *Mixed Agreements Revisited: The EU and its Member States in the World* (Hart Publishing 2010).
13 [2011] OJ L 127/6.
14 [2012] OJ L 346/3, art 352.
15 Cremona suggests that the UK would need to withdraw formally from the agreement in question or renegotiate its participation pursuant to an amending protocol: Cremona (n 7) 000.
16 Ibid, art 360.
17 See UK Environmental Law Association, 'Brexit and Environmental Law: The UK and International Environmental Law After Brexit' (UKELA Report, 2017) www.ukela.org/common/Uploaded%20files/brexit%20docs/international%20env%20law%202017.pdf accessed 5 March 2020.
18 See, for instance, Written statement to the House of Commons by Thérèse Coffey, Parliamentary Under Secretary of State for the Department for Environment, Food and Rural Affairs, 18 September 2017 in response to written questions from Caroline Lucas, MP:

> The UK will continue to be bound by international Multilateral Environmental Agreements (MEAs) to which it is party. We are committed to upholding our international obligations under these agreements and will continue to play an active role internationally following our departure from the EU. We will give due consideration to the ratification of MEAs in the future to which the UK is not currently party in its own right, (recognising that some risks have no relevance to the UK).

19 Paris Agreement adopted under the United Nations Framework Convention on Climate Change [2016] OJ L 282/4.
20 The EU may conclude a fulfilment agreement with a third country: see Agreement between the European Union and its Member States, of the one part, and Iceland, of the other part, concerning Iceland's

participation in the joint fulfilment of the commitments of the European Union, its Member States and Iceland for the second commitment period of the Kyoto Protocol to the United Nations Framework Convention on Climate Change [2015] OJ L 207/17. Such an agreement between the EU and the UK would be necessary if the latter remained part of the EU Emissions Trading System after the end of transition period laid down in the WA.

21 Council Decision 94/800/EC concerning the conclusion on behalf of the European Community, as regards matters within its competence, of the agreements reached in the Uruguay Round multilateral negotiations (1986–1994) [1994] OJ L 336/1.

22 See the letter of 11 October 2017 of the EU Permanent Representative to the WTO and the UK Permanent Representative to the international organisations in Geneva, https://tradebetablog.files.wordpress.com/2017/10/letter_from_eu_and_uk_permanent_representatives.pdf accessed 5 March 2020 and the position of 26 September 2017 by the representatives of a number of countries including the USA, New Zealand, Canada, Brazil and Argentina, https://tradebetablog.files.wordpress.com/2017/10/us-et-al-letter-on-trqs.pdf accessed 5 March 2020. For the EU's unilateral apportionment, see Regulation (EU) 2019/216 of the European Parliament and of the Council of 30 January 2019 on the apportionment of tariff rate quotas included in the WTO schedule of the Union following the withdrawal of the United Kingdom from the Union, and amending Council Regulation (EC) No 32/2000 [2019] OJ L 38/1. For the UK's position, see UK Government, Communication to WTO members following the UK's withdrawal from the EU (1 February 2020) https://assets.publishing.service.gov.uk/government/uploads/system/uploads/attachment_data/file/862657/200131_GC_statement_pdf.pdf accessed 5 March 2020.

23 WA, art 2(a)(iv).

24 The reference to Article 127(2) in Article 129(1) of the Agreement is about the EU's Common Foreign and Security Policy (CFSP). The former provision reads as follows:

> In the event that the Union and the United Kingdom reach an agreement governing their future relationship in the areas of the Common Foreign and Security Policy and the Common Security and Defence Policy which becomes applicable during the transition period, Chapter 2 of Title V of the TEU and the acts adopted on the basis of those provisions shall cease to apply to the United Kingdom from the date of application of that agreement.

25 WA, 8th recital.

26 European Council Article 50 guidelines for Brexit negotiations (Brussels, 29 April 2017), para 13.

27 Council 21009/17 BXT 16 ADD Directives for the negotiation of an agreement with the United Kingdom of Great Britain and Northern Ireland setting out the arrangements for its withdrawal from the European Union (Brussels, 22 May 2017), para 18.

28 European Council Article 50 guidelines (Brussels, 15 December 2017), para 4 (emphasis added).

29 Council Supplementary directives for the negotiation of an agreement with the United Kingdom of Great Britain and Northern Ireland setting out the arrangements for its withdrawal from the European Union (Brussels, 29 January 2018), para 15.

30 TFEU, art 216(2); Case 181/73 *Haegeman v Belgium* EU:C:1974:41, para 5. More on this, see Panos Koutrakos, *EU International Relations Law* (2nd edn, Hart Publishing 2015) 209 ff.

31 Cover letter and Note verbale on the Agreement on the Withdrawal of the United Kingdom of Great Britain and Northern Ireland from the European Union and the European Atomic Energy Community, COM(2018) 841 final, 5 December 2018.

32 Ibid, para 5.

33 There are also some CFSP-specific provisions in Article 129(6)–(7):

> 6. Following a decision of the Council falling under Chapter 2 of Title V TEU, the United Kingdom may make a formal declaration to the High Representative of the Union for Foreign Affairs and Security Policy, indicating that, for vital and stated reasons of national policy, in those exceptional cases it will not apply the decision. In a spirit of mutual solidarity, the United Kingdom shall refrain from any action likely to conflict with or impede Union action based on that decision, and the Member States shall respect the position of the United Kingdom.
>
> 7. During the transition period, the United Kingdom shall not provide commanders of civilian operations, heads of mission, operation commanders or force commanders for missions or operations conducted under Articles 42, 43 and 44 TEU, nor shall it provide the operational headquarters for such missions or operations, or serve as framework nation for Union battlegroups. During the

transition period, the United Kingdom shall not provide the head of any operational actions under Article 28 TEU.

34 WA, art 129(2).

35 TEU, art 4(3).

36 See amongst others Case C-266/03 *Commission v Luxembourg* EU:C:2005:341; Case C-459/03 *Commission v Ireland (re: MOX Plant)* EU:C:2006:345; Case C-247/07 *Commission v Sweden (PFOs)* EU:C:2010:203. See also M Cremona, 'Defending the Community Interest: The Duties of Cooperation and Compliance' in Marise Cremona and Bruno De Witte (eds), *EU Foreign Relations Law* (Hart Publishing 2008) 125; Christophe Hillion, 'Mixity and Coherence in EU External Relations: The Significance of the "Duty of Cooperation"' in Christophe Hillion and Panos Koutrakos (eds), *Mixed Agreements Revisited: The EU and its Member States in the World* (Hart Publishing 2010) 87, and Eleftheria Neframi, 'The Duty of Loyalty: Rethinking its Scope Through its Application in the Field of EU External Relations' (2010) 47 Common Market Law Review 323.

37 WA, art 129(3).

38 WA, art 129(4).

39 WA, art 129(5). This provision is without prejudice to Article 127(2) WA which reads as follows:

> In the event that the Union and the United Kingdom reach an agreement governing their future relationship in the areas of the Common Foreign and Security Policy and the Common Security and Defence Policy which becomes applicable during the transition period, Chapter 2 of Title V of the TEU and the acts adopted on the basis of those provisions shall cease to apply to the United Kingdom from the date of application of that agreement.

40 https://assets.publishing.service.gov.uk/government/uploads/system/uploads/attachment_data/file/808914/MS_22.2019_Andean_Trade.pdf accessed 5 March 2020.

41 Cariforum comprises Antigua and Barbuda, Barbados, Belize, the Bahamas, Dominica, the Dominican Republic, Grenada, Guyana, Jamaica, Saint Christopher and Nevis, Saint Lucia, Saint Vincent and the Grenadines, Trinidad and Tobago, https://assets.publishing.service.gov.uk/government/uploads/system/uploads/attachment_data/file/803413/1._CARIFORUM_Command_Paper_Part_One.pdf accessed 5 March 2020.

42 https://assets.publishing.service.gov.uk/government/uploads/system/uploads/attachment_data/file/823557/MS_32.2019_Agreement_establishing_an_association_between_the_UK_and_Central_America.pdf accessed 5 March 2020.

43 https://assets.publishing.service.gov.uk/government/uploads/system/uploads/attachment_data/file/776912/CS_Chile_2.2019_Association.pdf accessed 5 March 2020.

44 www.gov.uk/government/publications/ms-no42019-agreement-establishing-an-economic-partnership-agreement-between-the-eastern-and-southern-africa-states-and-the-uk accessed 5 March 2020.

45 https://assets.publishing.service.gov.uk/government/uploads/system/uploads/attachment_data/file/780113/CS_Denmark_1.2019_FTA.pdf accessed 5 March 2020.

46 https://assets.publishing.service.gov.uk/government/uploads/system/uploads/attachment_data/file/844167/CS_Georgia_1.2019_UK_Georgia_Strategic_Partnership_and_Cooperation_Agreement.pdf accessed 5 March 2020.

47 https://assets.publishing.service.gov.uk/government/uploads/system/uploads/attachment_data/file/795291/MS_17.2019_Iceland_Norway_Trade.pdf accessed 5 March 2020.

48 https://assets.publishing.service.gov.uk/government/uploads/system/uploads/attachment_data/file/781440/CS_Israel_1.2019_Trade.pdf accessed 5 March 2020.

49 https://assets.publishing.service.gov.uk/government/uploads/system/uploads/attachment_data/file/854391/CS_Jordan_1.2019_UK_Jordan_Agreement_establishing_an_Association.pdf accessed 5 March 2020.

50 https://assets.publishing.service.gov.uk/government/uploads/system/uploads/attachment_data/file/854384/CS_Kosovo_1.2019_UK_Kosovo_Partnership__Trade_and_Cooperation_Agreement.pdf accessed 5 March 2020.

51 https://assets.publishing.service.gov.uk/government/uploads/system/uploads/attachment_data/file/840961/CS_Lebanon_1.2019_Agreement_establishing_an_Association_between_the_United_Kingdom_of_Great_Britain_and_Northern_Ireland_and_the_Republic_of_Lebanon.pdf accessed 5 March 2020.

52 https://assets.publishing.service.gov.uk/government/uploads/system/uploads/attachment_data/file/782493/CS_Liechtenstein_1.2019_Trade.pdf accessed 5 March 2020.

53 https://assets.publishing.service.gov.uk/government/uploads/system/uploads/attachment_data/file/854581/CS_Morocco_2.2019_UK_Morocco_Agreement_establishing_an_Association.pdf accessed 5 March 2020.

54 www.gov.uk/government/publications/ms-no152019-interim-economic-partnership-agreement-between-the-united-kingdom-of-great-britain-and-northern-ireland-and-the-pacific-states accessed 5 March 2020.

55 https://assets.publishing.service.gov.uk/government/uploads/system/uploads/attachment_data/file/781389/MS_14.2019_IPTP_PLO.pdf accessed 5 March 2020.

56 www.gov.uk/government/publications/uksacu-and-mozambique-economic-partnership-agreement-ms-no342019 accessed 5 March 2020.

57 www.gov.uk/government/publications/ukkorea-free-trade-agreement-with-exchange-of-notes-cs-korea-no12019 accessed 5 March 2020.

58 https://assets.publishing.service.gov.uk/government/uploads/system/uploads/attachment_data/file/780200/CS_Swiss_4.2019_FTA.pdf accessed 5 March 2020.

59 https://assets.publishing.service.gov.uk/government/uploads/system/uploads/attachment_data/file/842050/CS_Tunisia_1.2019_UK_Tunisia_Agreement_establishing_an_Association.pdf accessed 5 March 2020.

60 The duty of cooperation may appear pertinent in other pre-Brexit contexts too: for instance, an informal British–Australian working group was meeting since mid-2017 to prepare for a possible trade deal (*Financial Times*, 26 July 2019 'Australia Aims for Rapid Post-Brexit Trade Deal with Britain'). Similarly, a UK–US Trade and Investment Working Group was launched in July 2017 (UK Department for International Trade, 25 July 2017, www.gov.uk/government/news/us-uk-trade-working-group-lays-groundwork-for-potential-future-free-trade-agreement accessed 5 March 2020).

61 For a strict view on the implications of the duty of cooperation following notification and prior to withdrawal, see Wessel (n 7) at 108 *et seq*.

62 Jim Pickard 'UK Signs Biggest Trade Deal since Brexit Vote with Switzerland' *Financial Times* (London, 11 February 2019). On the negotiations with countries with which no rollover agreement has been concluded, such as Japan, Singapore, Mexico, Turkey, Ukraine, Egypt, Colombia, Ecuador and Peru, see Letter by Secretary of State for Exiting the EU (25 January 2019, to House of Commons Foreign Affairs Committee) www.parliament.uk/documents/commons-committees/foreign-affairs/Correspondence/2017-19/Secretary-State-Tom-Tugendhat-dexeu-17-19.pdf accessed 5 March 2020.

63 Henry Mance 'UK–Japan Trade Talks Sour after Letter from Hunt and Fox' *Financial Times* (London, 17 February 2019).

64 https://assets.publishing.service.gov.uk/government/uploads/system/uploads/attachment_data/file/785554/Tariff_Reference_Document_12_March_2019.pdf accessed 5 March 2020.

65 [2002] OJ L 114/369.

66 Department for International Trade, 'Continuing the United Kingdom's Trade Relationship with the Swiss Confederation' (February 2019), para 96, https://assets.publishing.service.gov.uk/government/uploads/system/uploads/attachment_data/file/830644/Continuing-the-UKs-trade-relationship-with-the-Swiss-Confederation-parliamentary-report__4___1_.pdf accessed 5 March 2020.

67 In accordance with Article 1(2)(b) of the UK–Switzerland Agreement.

68 [2002] OJ L 114/132.

69 Swiss Federal Department of Foreign Affairs, www.eda.admin.ch/dea/en/home/verhandlungen-offene-themen/offene-themen/brexit.html accessed 5 March 2020.

70 See UK–Korea FTA, Protocol Concerning the Definition of 'Originating Products' and Methods of Administrative Cooperation, footnote to Article 3.1 which also provides for a review of the principle by the Parties to begin no later than two years after the entry into force of the Agreement.

71 See, for instance, James Blitz, 'The Big Cabinet Row Over No Deal Tariffs' *Financial Times* (London, 20 February 2019).

72 Letter of 6 February, www.parliament.uk/documents/lords-committees/eu-select/scrutiny-brexit-related-treaties/treaty-scrutiny-letter-6Feb.pdf accessed 5 March 2020.

73 Ibid.

74 See European Union Committee, 'Scrutiny of International Agreements: Treaties Considered on 12 February 2019' (HL 2017–19, 287), paras 5–6. See also International Trade Committee, 'UK Trade Policy: Transparency and Scrutiny' (HC 2017–19, 1043), https://publications.parliament.uk/pa/

cm201719/cmselect/cmintrade/1043/1043.pdf. For an official response to the latter, see UK Trade Policy: Transparency and Scrutiny: Government Response of the Committee's Sixth Report (Sixth Special Report of Session 2017/19, HC 2027). See, more generally, B A Melo Araujo, 'UK Post-Brexit Trade Agreements and Devolution' (2019) Legal Studies 555.

75 See, for instance, Sarah Gordon 'Business Expresses Fury at UK Failure to Roll Over EU Trade Deals' *Financial Times* (London, 6 February 2019).

76 See, for instance, the recent practice of publishing the negotiating directives adopted by the Council. See European Commission, 'Factsheet on the Transparency Policy in EU Trade', https://trade.ec.europa.eu/doclib/docs/2018/november/tradoc_157486.pdf accessed 5 March 2020. For a challenging account, see Eugénia C. Heldt, 'Contested EU Trade Governance: Transparency Conundrums in TTIP Negotiations' (2019) Comparative European Politics 000.

77 See Foreign Affairs Committee, 'Delivering Global Britain: FCO Skills' (HC 2017–19, 1254) paras 32 *et seq.*, https://publications.parliament.uk/pa/cm201719/cmselect/cmfaff/1254/1254.pdf.

78 COM(2006) 567 fin 'Global Europe – Competing in the World – A Contribution to the EU's Growth and Jobs Strategy' (Brussels, 4 October 2006). See Billy A Melo Araujo, *The EU Deep Trade Agenda: Law and Policy* (Oxford University Press 2016).

79 [2011] OJ L 127/6.

80 [2017] OJ L 11/23.

81 Letter in *The Times*, 20 April 2016, 9.

7 Come fly with me?

Brexit and air transport

Wybe Th. Douma

7.1 Introduction

The regulation of transport between the European Union and the United Kingdom forms an interesting example of the various challenges that Brexit brings about.[1] At times, these challenges force the EU Member States and the EU's institutions to reconsider external competences questions in various areas. Air transport forms a case in point, as will be set out in this chapter.

The stakes are high. The UK has the largest aviation industry in Europe[2] and over 160 million airline passengers were transported between the EU and the UK in 2018.[3] The World Trade Organization (WTO) fall-back position would not offer a solution for air traffic. New agreements will need to be concluded between the EU and the UK in order to avoid serious disruptions. While it might seem straightforward that both sides would benefit from the conclusion of such new agreements, in practice many hurdles appear.

One of these hurdles is the division of competences between the EU and its Member States to conclude agreements with third countries in the area of air transport. While the question of the division of external competences between the EU Member States and the EU forms a familiar topic for those dealing with the law of EU external relations,[4] the discussions surrounding the proposed contingency measures aimed at a continuation of air transport in case of a failure of the negotiations on a Withdrawal Agreement brought some peculiarities to the fore worth taking a closer look at. Have the EU Member States retained their competence to agree on air traffic rights with third countries, and would this allow individual Member States to conclude bilateral agreements on the issue with third countries? Or would that be contrary to EU primary law obligations or EU secondary law?[5] And could air transport agreements between the UK and individual EU Member States that pre-date the UK's EU membership 'revive' in case no new arrangement is being concluded? The European Commission claims this is not the case, but the argument can be made that such agreements could play a role again.

The contingency measures were designed at a time when it was still uncertain whether the parties would be able to conclude a Withdrawal Agreement. The measures did not enter into force because a Withdrawal Agreement was agreed upon,[6] which continues the pre-Brexit situation until the end of 2020. Ideally, the EU, its Member States and the UK will manage to conclude new agreements on air transport and air safety and in this manner ensure the continuation of flights between the EU and the UK from 2021 onwards.

This chapter will demonstrate that Brexit and air traffic forms a multifaceted challenge both for the EU and its Member States on the one hand and for the United Kingdom on the other hand. First of all, in section 7.2 some of the issues at stake are discussed. After sketching the manner in which air transport relationships are shaped, the ownership and control rules are turned to. They are the reason several aviation companies adopted measures aimed at securing their rights to operate in the Union. Furthermore, the discontinuation of the UK's membership of the European Aviation Safety Agency (EASA) – to the distress of the UK aviation industry as well as the responsible UK agency – is discussed. After that, attention turns to the opposing views on the division of competences between the EU and its Member States in the air transport area (section 7.3), and the role these views played in shaping the contingency measures (section 7.4). Together, these aspects highlight the multifaceted challenges both for the EU and its Member States (notably in terms of the division of competences) and for the UK in terms of some of the choices that the country needs to make in shaping its future relationship with the EU, and what 'taking back control' can mean in practice. The last part of this chapter will look back at the main lessons learned, and some of the prospects of concluding new EU–UK aviation agreements before the end of 2020. Could the contingency measures, designed to enter into force if no Withdrawal Agreement could be reached in time, play a role if the 2020 negotiations do not fly?

7.2 Issues at stake

7.2.1 Lack of a WTO fall-back for air transport

Having left the EU on 1 February 2020, after the transition period is over, the operating licences granted to airlines by the United Kingdom Civil Aviation Authority (CAA) will no longer be valid in the EU.[7] As a consequence, UK carriers will no longer enjoy the right to provide air services to and inside the EU. Vice versa, the same will hold true for EU carriers. The WTO fall-back position that exists for the trade in goods offers no solution for air traffic. While a GATS Annex on Air Transport Services exists, the Agreement does not apply to traffic rights and related services.

Furthermore, the UK will cease to be covered by air transport agreements that the Union has concluded with third countries (for example the Air Transport Agreement with Switzerland)[8] or those that were concluded by the EU and its Member States acting jointly (like the Open Skies Agreement with the USA).[9] To avoid disruptions in this respect, the UK secured new air transport agreements with the USA and Canada,[10] as well as with a dozen smaller countries.[11] The challenge ahead is securing such agreements with the EU and its Member States as well.

Because it remained uncertain whether a Withdrawal Agreement could be reached and approved by all parties involved, the EU adopted air traffic contingency measures with basic connectivity rules[12] and safety aspects[13] aimed at avoiding interruption of air traffic. These ensured a legal basis for the provision of air services between the UK and the EU Member States by the respective carriers in case of a 'hard Brexit', subject to the UK conferring equivalent rights to EU air carriers. The measures did not replicate the advantages of membership of the Single European Sky and the European Common Aviation Area (ECAA):[14] they only encompassed basic 'point to point' connectivity for a limited period of time. Contrary to the pre-Brexit period, under the contingency measures intra-EU27 flights would not be allowed any more for British companies and, vice versa, intra-UK flights would not be allowed for EU27 companies, i.e. companies with an EU operating licence.

7.2.2 Ownership and control challenges

In order to be allowed to operate on intra-EU27 routes, companies need an EU operating licence. The main conditions for such a licence are laid down in Regulation 1008/2008.[15] First of all, the airline's principal place of business needs to be located in a Member State. Furthermore, Member States and/or nationals of Member States need to own more than 50 per cent of the undertaking and effectively control it, except as provided for in an agreement with a third country to which the Community is a party.[16] The contingency measure sets out that if an air carrier holding an EU27 operating licence ceases to comply with these requirements due to Brexit, such a company has to remedy this situation within six months.[17] A new agreement on air traffic between the EU, its Member States and the UK for the post-2020 situation might also include such a provision.

Under the regular rules, Aer Lingus and Iberia, both with International Airlines Group (IAG) as their parent company, might not have been permitted to fly within Ireland and Spain or to any other EU airport after Brexit.[18] While IAG is registered in Spain, it could nonetheless be considered a non-EU entity after Brexit if the share of non-EU (including British) shareholders exceeds 50 per cent.[19] AIG thus needed to shift its shareholding to above 50 per cent EU ownership.[20] The holding company had argued that the local ownership of voting rights already ensured EU control and ownership, regardless of the ownership of the economic rights. To be safe, however, IAG chose to limit non-European ownership to 47.5 per cent. The company announced that national regulators in Spain, Ireland, France and Austria have all confirmed that the plans on ownership and control for the individual airlines would satisfy EU rules.[21]

Other airlines took similar steps. UK-based easyJet established separate operating units in Austria and Switzerland, and re-registered 130 of its aircraft in Austria. Furthermore, it has been working on ensuring that the airline is majority-owned by EU shareholders. In March 2020, the airline had succeeded in ensuring that 49.9 per cent of its shareholders were from the European Economic Area (EEA), so only marginally below the required level. By adding the remaining EEA shareholders it could ensure the right to keep on servicing intra-Union flights. In the unlikely event that this turns out to be impossible, the airline has announced it will activate its EU ownership contingency plan of suspending shareholders' voting rights in respect of a small number of shares of non-EU nationals to ensure that the company complies with the EU ownership requirement. If need be, easyJet expects that it will in due course set a permitted maximum of non-EU ownership. The permitted maximum is expected to be set such that the contingency plan would take effect if EU ownership were below 50.5 per cent.[22]

As a last example, Ireland-based Ryanair has applied for and secured a UK air operator's certificate in addition to its Irish one, to ensure that it can continue to operate within the UK after Brexit. The company also announced that it will limit the voting rights of British shareholders in case of a no-deal Brexit. At the end of 2018, 49 per cent of its shares were held by EU shareholders, not including the UK.[23] In order to ensure reaching the 50 per cent threshold, the company decided that while UK shareholders may continue to hold shares post Brexit, these shares might lose their voting rights. Furthermore, when a UK shareholder decides to sell, they might only be permitted to sell to an EU national. These two restrictions should ensure that Ryanair can continue to be majority EU owned and controlled.[24]

7.2.3 Safety aspects

EU Member States are members of EASA while several third countries are associate members.[25] This agency is responsible for civil aviation safety, and carries out certification, regulation and standardisation tasks. It collects and analyses safety data, drafts and advises on safety legislation, and coordinates with similar organisations in other parts of the world. EASA aims at ensuring not just an EU, but a pan-European facilitation of the improvement of civil aviation safety. European countries like Iceland, Norway and Switzerland that have concluded agreements with the Union to adopt and apply relevant parts of the *acquis* are associated with its work, in accordance with the conditions of those agreements.[26] These non-EU associate members do not have voting rights in the board, but in practice they can influence the outcome of decision making, which takes place by consensus. They also benefit from the agreements that exist between the EU and third countries that enable them to sell products and provide services without the need for extra certificates. Last but not least, in practice EASA and the US Federal Aviation Authority (FAA) are the main norm setting bodies in the world.

Initially, the advantages of continuing its association with EASA prevailed in British politics. The terms on which the UK could remain part of EASA were explored. While this would mean abiding by the rules of this agency, associate membership was described by Prime Minister May as 'the only way to meet our objective of ensuring that these products only need to undergo one series of approvals, in one country'.[27] A Committee of the House of Commons also concluded:

> The evidence we have received from aerospace businesses, unions and academia is unanimous in support of the EU [*sic*] continuing its membership of EASA. Close global regulatory alignment in aerospace has resulted in benefits in terms of safety, the ease of global trade and efficiency, while it is unclear that there are any benefits from divergence at this time. Accordingly, the Committee notes and welcomes the Prime Minister's statement.[28]

The UK's Royal Aeronautical Society noted that the jurisdiction of the Court of Justice of the European Union (CJEU) over decisions taken by EASA effectively means that the CJEU can rule that an EASA decision is inapplicable or has to be modified; EASA would then change the decision and associated third countries would need to respect such a decision.[29] The UK's Civil Aviation Authority (CAA) itself decided not to plan for a new independent aviation safety system in the UK because 'it would be misleading to suggest that [this is] a viable option'. It was added that 'it makes no sense to recreate a national regulator. At best, you replicate the vast majority of European regulation, and you'd have to do it over an extended period of time. At worst, you create unnecessary barriers.'[30] The British aviation sector was also clearly in favour of associate membership.[31]

However, when push came to shove, in spite of the overwhelming amount of evidence and support in the UK for associate membership of EASA, this was considered incompatible with the UK having 'genuine economic and political independence'. Instead of following in the footsteps of countries like Iceland, Norway and Switzerland who opted to become associate EASA members, the UK decided to put the CAA in charge of issues like certifying the airworthiness of planes. In turn, this implies that a Bilateral Air Safety Agreement (BASA) with the EU will need to be concluded, as well as with other countries. On the basis of the Withdrawal Agreement, the UK has until the end of 2020 to revamp the CAA and conclude such agreements. During the transition period the UK continues to participate in the EASA system, without voting rights.

7.3 Air transport competences

7.3.1 Air traffic rights

In order for civil aviation companies to operate internationally, countries involved need to agree on the rights that these companies are granted and various obligations they need to observe, for instance regarding safety and consumer protection. Air transport agreements thus cover a multitude of topics. Because states are sovereign where their airspace is concerned,[32] the so-called air traffic rights are of primary importance. They grant airlines of a country the right to enter another country's airspace and land in its territory. Air traffic rights can encompass the permitting of the types of international services between two or more countries shown in Table 7.1.

The first two freedoms are known as transit rights and are widely accepted around the world. The freedoms with the highest numbers are rarely a part of air transport agreements. The ECAA[33] between the EU, its Member States and a number of third countries (but excluding the UK) covers all nine freedoms.[34]

7.3.2 Emergence of EU air transport policy

Following aviation reforms introduced in the USA in the late 1970s and influenced by the neo-liberal politics of the Thatcher government in the UK, the European Community (EC) set out to reform the aviation sector in three stages between 1987 and 1992. As of 1 April 1997, an internal market for air transport was in place in the Community in which a licensed airline from any Member State was allowed to provide commercial air transportation services anywhere within the EC.[35] Discrimination on the basis of nationality was no longer allowed where EC carriers were concerned.[36] Still, Member States continued to conclude air transport agreements with third states allowing only their airlines to fly to the third state, in violation of Community law. Under these circumstances, the external aspects of air transport formed a major challenge at the start of the 1990s.

The Commission wanted the Community to tackle this challenge. In 1992, it claimed that

> [o]n the basis of the Treaty and of the case law of the Court of Justice the Community has in any case exclusive competence for concluding bilateral air services agreements dealing in particular with market access, capacity, tariffs and related matters.[37]

On the basis of former art. 113 EC (now art. 207 TFEU) on common commercial policy, where the Community has exclusive competences, it requested the general authority to negotiate air transport agreements on behalf of the whole Community with third states. The proposal

Table 7.1 Air traffic rights

First freedom	Flying over a foreign country without landing (overflight).
Second freedom	Refuel or carry out maintenance in a foreign country without embarking or disembarking passengers or cargo (non-commercial landing).
Third freedom	Fly from the home country and land in a foreign country.
Fourth freedom	Fly from a foreign country and land in the home country.
Fifth freedom	Fly from the home country to a foreign country, stopping in another foreign country on the way.
Sixth freedom	Fly from a foreign country to another foreign country, stopping in the home country on the way.
Seventh freedom	Fly from a foreign country to another foreign country, without stopping in the home country.
Eighth freedom	Fly from the home country to a foreign country, then on to another destination within the same foreign country (consecutive cabotage).
Ninth freedom	Fly internally within a foreign country ('stand-alone' cabotage).

was never adopted. Member States were probably hesitant to relinquish their jurisdiction to enter into their own individual agreements with third countries to protect their own markets and national carriers.[38] The Council stressed that art. 84(2) EC constituted the proper legal basis for an operational development in the external aviation sector, and that the Member States retained their full powers in relations with third countries in the aviation sector, subject to measures already adopted or to be adopted by the Council in that domain. In this regard, it was emphasised, however, that in the course of bilateral negotiations the Member States concerned should take due account of their obligations imposed by Community law and should keep themselves informed of the interests of the other Member States.[39] The Council was right to object to the proposed legal basis. In *Opinion 1/94*, the Court held that international transport agreements did not fall within the ambit of art. 113 EC.[40] That left former art. 84(2) EC (now: art. 100(2) TFEU) on air transport as a legal basis, which forms a shared competence.

The wording of that provision was aptly described as 'decidedly infelicitous'.[41] Subsequent Treaty changes only partially remedied this.[42] Art. 100 TFEU as it stands now still distinguishes between transport by rail, road and inland waterway on the one hand, to which the provisions of the TFEU transport title apply, and sea and air transport on the other hand, where the EU legislature 'may lay down appropriate provisions'. This indicates a discretion to act, and leaves open the possibility for individual Member States to conclude agreements with third countries, in as far as the Union has not acted and in line with EU law.

Confronted with several Member States that concluded aviation agreements with the US, in December 1998 the Commission instigated the '*Open Skies*' cases,[43] essentially arguing that EC aviation law had developed in such a manner that the Community had attained exclusive competence to conclude aviation agreements with third countries. Thus, Member States entering into bilateral aviation agreements with the USA were acting contrary to EC law, the Commission claimed, referring inter alia to the *ERTA* jurisprudence[44] and *Opinion 1/94*.[45] The ECJ disagreed. With regard to art. 84(2) EC it stressed that 'so long as the Council has not, by an express decision based on that provision, created a Community competence to negotiate air transport agreements with non-member countries, Member States retain their competence to enter into bilateral commitments'.[46] It added that a situation in which an internal competence could effectively be exercised only at the same time as an external competence did not exist. Thus, an exclusive external competence to conclude an air transport agreement with the USA, within the meaning of *Opinion 1/76*, was lacking.[47] The fact that the Community does have exclusive competences regarding various specific aspects of such agreements, for instance computer reservation systems (CRS) and slots, did not change this conclusion that was reached on 5 November 2002.

As a result of the confirmation that the subject-matter of a future aviation agreement falls partly within the competence of the Union and partly within that of its Member States, Regulation (EC) No 847/2004 on the negotiation and implementation of air service agreements between Member States and third countries was adopted.[48] It sets out that Member States can conclude new air traffic agreements or amend existing ones, under certain conditions and following specific procedures. In line with the loyalty principle, such agreements may not harm the object and purpose of the Community common transport policy.[49]

As far as the US is concerned, eventually a mandate was issued to set up an agreement, resulting in the 2007 Open Skies agreement[50] of which '[i]t is evident that certain aspects of the agreement are within Community competences while others are not; moreover, there is no clear hierarchy of objectives. All this explains and justifies the mixed character of the agreement.'[51]

7.3.3 *Brexit and air transport competences*

So, what does this imply in the context of Brexit? Any agreement that the Union wants to conclude with the UK will need a mandate from the side of the EU Member States. If such a Union-wide agreement is not achieved, individual Member States could conclude their own bilateral agreements with the UK, provided they follow the rules and procedures set out in Regulation (EC) No 847/2004. As for existing agreements between Member States and the UK, the Commission claims that such agreements cannot be 'revived' after the transition period, but some are of a different opinion.[52]

Could art. 351 TFEU be of relevance here? It specifies that the rights and obligations arising from agreements concluded before 1 January 1958 between a Member State and a third country shall not be affected by the provisions of the Treaties, while calling upon the Member State to eliminate incompatibilities. The provision applied to the 1946 aviation agreement between the Netherlands and the UK[53] while the UK was still a third state. Now that the UK has left the Union, the argument can be made that art. 351 TFEU is applicable again.

The Dutch Ministry of Infrastructure and Waterworks is of the opinion that its agreement with the UK could be reconfirmed by the conclusion of a Memorandum of Understanding. On the side of the UK CAA, it has been made known that 'a single bilateral agreement with the EU as a whole' would be preferable. Another option, in the view of the CAA, would be the negotiation of bilateral agreements with individual EU Member States that wish to or find the EU-led process too slow. It is acknowledged that any EU Member State that wanted to go down that route would have to notify the EU and negotiate in a way that is compatible with EU law.[54] Where the issues for which the Union is exclusively competent are concerned, the Member States are not allowed to conclude their own agreements, unless they are explicitly mandated to do so by the Union.

7.4 Contingency measures related to air transport

7.4.1 *Commission proposals*

On 19 December 2018, the Commission presented two proposals regarding air transport: one on basic connectivity rules,[55] the other on safety.[56] Both have art. 100(2) TFEU as a legal basis. In spite of the urgency of adopting the proposed regulations, their adoption did not get off to a flying start due to disagreement over competences issues.

The Commission's proposal encompasses a traffic rights provision that provides UK air carriers the temporary right to perform scheduled and non-scheduled international air transport services between any pair of points situated one in the territory of the UK and the other in the territory of the EU, provided equivalent rights are granted by the UK to EU carriers.[57] The same proposed provision also warns the Member States to 'neither negotiate nor enter into any bilateral agreements or arrangements with the United Kingdom on matters falling within the scope of this Regulation' and not to 'otherwise grant UK air carriers, in connection with air transport, any rights other than those granted by this Regulation'.[58]

7.4.2 *Council amendments and Member States call for future mixed agreement*

After examining the Commission's proposal, the Council demanded that a new provision be added to explain that the exercise of Union competence pursuant to the Regulation was limited to the period of its application. After the end of that period, the Union would immediately cease to exercise that competence and the Member States would again exercise their competences in accordance with art. 2(2) TFEU.[59] The Council also proposed adding that the exercise of Union competence pursuant to the Regulation be without prejudice to the competence of the Member States concerning traffic rights in any ongoing or future negotiations, signature or conclusion of international agreements related to air services with any other third country, and with the United Kingdom with respect to the period after the Regulation ceased to apply.[60]

Supported by eleven other Member States, Germany has declared that fast negotiations for a new comprehensive air transport agreement with the UK are desirable. It stressed that the mandate decision requires a detailed examination of the Commission proposal for such a mandate. The importance of this is that the mandate will provide for a mixed agreement of the Union and the Member States.

7.4.3 Reactions

In a reaction to the Council's proposed amendments, the Commission concurred with the statements on the effects of the Regulation on the division of competences between the Union and the Member States in accordance with art. 2(2) TFEU. It recalled that that division is exhaustively dealt with in the Treaties, both for usual and exceptional circumstances. Against this background, it considers that the proposed Regulation does not prejudge the nature of the future relationship with the UK in the area of aviation and that the exercise of competence in its proposal is temporary and strictly limited to its period of validity.

The Commission added that it was for the Council to establish the terms of any decision authorising the opening of negotiations for a future relationship in accordance with art. 218(3) and (4) TFEU and generally with Union law, and in full respect of the division of competences between the Union and the Member States. The institution furthermore recalled the European Council Guidelines of 23 March 2018 on the future relation with the UK, established with a view to the opening of negotiations on the overall understanding of the framework for the future relationship. According to point 11 of those Guidelines, in the area of aviation the aim should be to ensure continued connectivity between the UK and the EU after the former's withdrawal from the Union. This could be achieved, inter alia, through an air transport agreement, combined with aviation safety and security agreements, while ensuring a strong level playing field (an issue that will be returned to in the last paragraph of this chapter). Having regard to those Guidelines, the Commission 'intends to submit the relevant recommendation to the Council as soon as possible in due time'.[61]

In the final Political Declaration it was set out that 'the Parties should ensure passenger and cargo air connectivity through a Comprehensive Air Transport Agreement (CATA)', covering 'market access and investment, aviation safety and security, air traffic management, and provisions to ensure open and fair competition, including appropriate and relevant consumer protection requirements and social standards'. Furthermore, they should make 'further arrangements to enable cooperation with a view to high standards of aviation safety and security, including through close cooperation between EASA and the United Kingdom's Civil Aviation Authority (CAA)'.[62]

7.4.4 The adopted contingency measures

Regulation (EU) 2019/502 on common rules ensuring basic air connectivity with regard to the withdrawal of the UK was adopted on 25 March 2019. Most of the objections raised from the side of the Council, notably those regarding competences, were taken on board, both in the preamble and in the body of the regulation. The following differences between the proposal and the adopted text can be noted.

Point 7 of the preamble spells out in detail that the Union is only temporarily exercising the relevant shared competence in view of the exceptional and unique circumstances; any effect of the regulation on the division of competences between the Union and the Member States should be strictly limited in time. As soon as the regulation ceases to apply, the shared competence will also cease to be exercised, and in accordance with art. 2(2) TFEU Member States will again exercise their competence as of that moment. It is also recalled that the scope of the exercise of the Union competence only covers the elements governed by the regulation 'and does not cover the whole area'. Furthermore, it is underlined that the respective competences of the Union and of the Member States with respect to the conclusion of international air transport agreements are to be determined in accordance with the Treaties and taking into account relevant Union legislation.

Art. 2 stresses that

> [t]he exercise of Union competence pursuant to this Regulation shall be without prejudice to the competence of the Member States concerning traffic rights in any ongoing or future negotiations, signature, or conclusion of international agreements related to air services with any other third country, and with the United Kingdom with respect to the period after this Regulation has ceased to apply.

In art. 4(3), references to the period during which the regulation applies were added:

> The Member States shall neither negotiate nor enter into any bilateral agreements or arrangements with the United Kingdom on matters falling within the scope of this Regulation *with respect to the period during which this Regulation applies. With respect to that period,* they shall not otherwise grant UK air carriers, in connection with air transport, any rights other than those granted by this Regulation.
>
> *(emphasis added)*

In this manner, it is again underlined that the Member States can resume interacting with the UK in the area of air transport once the regulation ceases to apply.

These rules would have allowed basic air traffic to continue as usual until 24 October 2020.[63] However, art. 16 para 3 of Regulation 2019/502 stipulates that it shall not apply if a withdrawal agreement concluded with the UK in accordance with art. 50(2) TEU has entered into force from the day following that on which Union law ceases to apply to the UK pursuant to art. 50(3) TEU. Hence, the contingency measures did not apply. The reason that they were described here is that they exemplify the lengths to which EU Member States need to go to preserve their prerogatives in EU external relations, on the one hand, and because the outcome of the discussions on air traffic competences are relevant for the negotiations of the post-2020 relationship with the UK.

7.5 Concluding remarks

7.5.1 Looking back: lessons learned

Faced with the disruptions that Brexit can cause in the area of air transport, the European Commission and the EU Member States agreed on a temporary solution in the form of two

Regulations, one on basic connectivity and one on safety aspects. At the request of the Council, amendments were introduced underlining that a future EU–UK air transport deal will take the form of a mixed agreement. The Commission responded positively to these concerns. In this manner, a turf war was avoided and a temporary solution was proposed to and accepted by the UK that would have ensured basic point-to-point connectivity. Due to the adoption of the Withdrawal Agreement, the contingency measures did not come to use. The measures were worth a closer look nevertheless, as they exemplify how EU external relations law at times can be first and foremost about the division of competences between the EU and the Member States.

Given the reasoned objections on the side of the industry, experts and the UK CAA against leaving EASA, it almost seems as if 'taking back control' at any cost was all that mattered here. The result of the decision not to become an associate member of EASA means that yet another agreement will need to be concluded with the EU, while the country in all likelihood will be losing out on the possibility to influence the shaping of global standards. This sure resembles a case of feeling like you win when you lose, in other words.

The question whether the EU Member States are still in control of aspects of air transport agreements with third countries (notably traffic rights) has also been examined. It became apparent that from the early 1990s onwards, the European Commission claimed that the Union was exclusively competent on such matters, yet the Council saw things differently. In the *Open Skies* cases the CJEU agreed that aspects of external aviation policy are retained as Member State competence. Effectively, that means that the Member States need to agree to a new EU–UK aviation agreement. If no such agreement can be reached, they might 'revive' existing bilateral agreements or conclude new ones, as long as they observe the conditions that EU law sets out.

7.5.2 Looking ahead: prospects for new EU–UK agreements

The competences questions in the area of air traffic remain relevant in 2020, when the EU, the Member States and the UK are to reach agreement over a new Comprehensive Air Transport Agreement (CATA) that would cover aviation rights as well as safety aspects. It is clear that such an agreement will be a mixed agreement. Will it be possible to reach such an agreement, considering the EU and UK positions on some of the topics that will need to be tackled in such a short timeframe?

Looking at the initial positions regarding the future EU–UK relationship on air transport and safety, several differences are apparent. The EU stresses that the envisaged partnership must ensure open and fair competition, encompassing robust commitments to ensure a level playing field in areas like state aid, competition, environmental standards, social and employment standards.[64] The UK mentions some of these topics, such as environmental protection, but not social and employment standards. The country only wants to commit to not weakening or reducing the level of protection of labourers in order to encourage trade or investment.[65] Violations of such a soft norm are nearly impossible to prove,[66] and even if they could be, the UK opposes the possibility of sanctions, citing precedents such as CETA, EU–Japan and EU–Korea.

Where safety is concerned, the UK proposes mutual acceptance of certification processes,[67] while the EU stresses that nothing in the envisaged partnership should entail reciprocal acceptance of the standards and technical regulations of the Parties.[68] There is work to be done by the negotiators, in other words. Time is not on their hands. Without an EU–UK partnership in aviation, and in the absence of contingency measures, after the end of the transition period no flights will be able to take place between the UK and the EU. An agreement should be achieved as soon as possible in order for airlines to schedule their routes and sell tickets in advance. If that would turn out to be impossible, reviving the air traffic contingency measures might form an option.

As aviation is not the only topic that needs to be agreed upon between the EU and the UK in a short period of time, and considering the coronavirus crisis that erupted shortly after the UK withdrew from the Union, an extension of the transition period would have been the wisest course of action. The UK would have had to revoke the provisions which ruled out such an extension.[69] It had until 1 July 2020[70] to straighten up and fly right. As we know by now, that ship has sailed.[71]

Notes

1 'Come Fly with Me' is an album and song by American singer Frank Sinatra, released in 1958. Parts of this contribution are based on Wybe Th Douma, Onur Güven, Luca Pantaleo, Karolien Pieters and Steffen van der Velde, 'Second opinion bij de Brexit-luchtvaartnota van het Ministerie van Infrastructuur en Waterstaat', (EU Legal, October 2018) www.rijksoverheid.nl/documenten/rapporten/2019/02/06/second-opinion-bij-de-brexit-luchtvaartnota-van-het-ministerie-van-infrastructuur-en-waterstaat accessed 29 March 2020.

2 Taylor Airey, 'A Study of the Effects of the United Kingdom Leaving the European Union on Airlines Flying To and From the UK' (Industry Affairs Committee of the International Air Transport Association (IATA), October 2018).

3 Charles Alcock, 'UK Air Transport Braces for No Deal Brexit Consequences' (AINonline, 12 September 2019).

4 Ramses Wessel and Joris Larik (eds), *EU External Relations Law: Text, Cases and Materials* (Hart Publishing 2020) and Pieter Jan Kuijper, Jan Wouters, Frank Hoffmeister, Geert de Baere and Thomas Ramopoulos, *The Law of EU External Relations: Cases, Materials and Commentary on the EU as an International Legal Actor* (Oxford University Press 2015).

5 Andrew Haines, the former chief executive of the UK CAA is quoted as suggesting concluding bilateral agreements. See: Institute for Government, 'UK–EU Future Relationship: Aviation' (24 February 2020). The paper itself notes that it is unclear whether it is consistent with EU law to negotiate individual agreements with ECAA member states if a deal with the EU as a whole cannot be reached.

6 Agreement on the withdrawal of the United Kingdom of Great Britain and Northern Ireland from the European Union and the European Atomic Energy Community [2020] OJ L 29/7 (Withdrawal Agreement).

7 European Commission, 'Notice to Stakeholders: Withdrawal of the United Kingdom and EU Rules in the Field of Air Transport' (Brussels, 19 January 2018). See also European Commission, 'Notice to Stakeholders: Withdrawal of the United Kingdom and EU Aviation Safety Rules' Rev 1 (Brussels, 18 January 2019).

8 Agreement between the European Community and the Swiss Confederation on Air Transport [2002] OJ L114/73.

9 Air Transport Agreement between the European Community and its Member States, on the one hand, and the United States of America, on the other hand [2007] OJ L134/4 (Air Transport Agreement).

10 Cathy Buyck, 'UK and U.S. Reach Post-Brexit Open Skies Deal' (AIN Online, 28 November 2018) Transport Canada press release, 'Canada, UK Conclude New Air Transport Agreement' (Skiesmag, 3 December 2018).

11 Albania, Georgia, Iceland, Israel, Jordan, Kosovo, Moldova, Montenegro, Morocco, North Macedonia, Norway and Switzerland. UK Government, 'Aviation Guidance' (5 November 2019).

12 Regulation (EU) 2019/502 on common rules ensuring basic air connectivity with regard to the withdrawal of the United Kingdom of Great Britain and Northern Ireland from the Union [2019] OJ L85 I/49.

13 Regulation (EU) 2019/494 on certain aspects of aviation safety with regard to the withdrawal of the United Kingdom of Great Britain and Northern Ireland from the Union [2019] OJ L85 I/11.

14 Multilateral Agreement on the establishment of a European Common Aviation Area [2006] OJ L 285/1 (ECAA).

15 Regulation (EC) No 1008/2008 on common rules for the operation of air services in the Community [2008] OJ L293/3.

16 Ibid, art 4, 8.
17 Regulation (EU) 2019/502 on common rules ensuring basic air connectivity with regard to the withdrawal of the United Kingdom of Great Britain and Northern Ireland from the Union [2019] OJ L85 I/49, art 7.
18 Jorge Valero, 'Brussels Cuts Iberia and Aer Lingus's Wings to Fly in EU After Brexit' (EurActiv, 19 December 2019).
19 'IAG's Post-Brexit EU Access in Doubt' (Ch-aviation, 10 January 2019).
20 Alan Dron, 'IAG Faces Brexit Conundrum' (Airways Magazine, 11 August 2017). Also see Irene Garica Perez and Lyubov Pronina, 'Half of Spanish Internal Flights at Stake in Hard Brexit', *Bloomberg* (New York, 9 January 2019).
21 IAG, 'H1 Earnings' (2 August 2019) 9.
22 EasyJet, 'EU Share Ownership: Implications of Brexit for UK and Non-EU Shareholders' (24 March 2020) http://corporate.easyjet.com/investors/shareholder-services/eu-share-ownership accessed 4 April 2020.
23 'Easyjet will wegen EU-Lizens britische Aktionäre loswerden', *Die Zeit* (Hamburg, 22 January 2019).
24 Ryanair, 'Ryanair Board Passes Resolutions to Protect the Company's EU Airline Licences Post-Brexit' (11 March 2019) https://investor.ryanair.com/wp-content/uploads/2019/03/Ryanair-Brexit-March-2019.pdf accessed 4 April 2020.
25 On the UK's participation in EU agencies after Brexit, see Andrea Ott's chapter in this handbook.
26 Regulation (EC) No 216/2008 on common rules in the field of civil aviation and establishing a European Aviation Safety Agency [2008] OJ L79/1. Since 11 September 2018: Regulation (EU) 2018/1139 [2018] OJ L 212/1.
27 Prime Minister's Office, 'PM Speech on our Future Economic Partnership with the European Union' (2 March 2018).
28 Business, Energy and Industrial Strategy Committee, 'The Impact of Brexit on the Aerospace Sector: 3 Regulatory Alignment' (19 March 2018). Obviously, the Committee intended to highlight the support of the UK continuing its EASA membership rather than the EU. Similar conclusions were drawn by the European Scrutiny Committee, 'EU Aviation Safety Agency' (21 February 2018).
29 Royal Aeronautical Society, 'Civil Aviation Regulation: What Future after Brexit?' (September 2017) www.aerosociety.com/media/6797/raes_civil_aviation_regulation_-_what_future_after_brexit.pdf accessed 29 March 2020.
30 Andrew Haines, Chief Executive of the CAA (Speech of 5 September 2017) https://pdf4pro.com/view/uktie-brexit-and-aviation-speech-civil-aviation-42849.html accessed 29 March 2020.
31 British Airways owner IAG expressed it was 'disappointed' with the decision and said the British CAA 'does not have the expertise required to operate as a world class safety and technical regulator', while adding that the 'CAA will require fundamental restructuring from top to bottom which will take time. There is no way that it can be done by 31 December.' Similar concerns were raised by the trade body ADS, which represents more than 1,100 UK businesses in the aerospace, defence, security and space sectors ('UK will Leave EU Aviation Safety Regulator at End of 2020' *BBC News* (London, 7 March 2020)).
32 Convention on International Civil Aviation (Chicago Convention), 1944, art 1: 'The contracting States recognize that every State has complete and exclusive sovereignty over the airspace above its territory', while art 6 adds that 'No scheduled international air service may be operated over or into the territory of a contracting State, except with the special permission or other authorization of that State.' The EU is not a party to this Convention.
33 ECAA (n 14). It consists of the EU28, Norway, Iceland, Montenegro, Serbia, Croatia, North Macedonia, Albania, Bosnia and Herzegovina and Kosovo. The full application of ECAA is reached through gradual transitions where associated parties are concerned (see art 27 and Protocols to ECAA).
34 Brian F Havel and Gabriel S Sanchez, *The Principles and Practices of International Aviation Law* (Cambridge University Press 2014) 97.
35 By virtue of Regulation 2408/92, [1992] OJ L 240/8. Free access to international intra-Community routes was introduced as of 1 January 1993, whereas full cabotage rights were added on 1 April 1997.
36 Moreover, pressures for privatisation of state-owned carriers were created. As a result, British Airways, KLM and Sabena were wholly or partially privatised during the 1980s. Lufthansa was privatised by 1997, and Air France in 2002.
37 European Commission, COM(92)434, para 50. It encompassed a Proposal for a Council Decision on a consultation and authorisation procedure for agreements concerning commercial aviation relations between Member States and third countries.

38 Peter P C Haanappel, *The Law and Policy of Air Space and Outer Space: A Comparative Approach* (Kluwer Law International 2003) 141.
39 Council conclusions of 15 March 1993, quoted by the Court in Case 476/98 *Commission v Germany* EU:C:2002:631, para 18.
40 Opinion 1/94 EU:C:1994:384. Also see Joined Cases 94/93 and 95/93 EU:C:1993:657, paras 54 ff; in which the Commission had asked for the annulment of two Council decisions on the conclusion of international transport agreements based on art. 75 EC instead of art. 113 EC, subsequently withdrawn (see [1995] OJ C229/17).
41 Paul Joan G Kapteyn, Pieter VerLoren van Themaat and Laurence W Gormley, *Introduction to the Law of the European Communities* (3d edn, Kluwer Law International 1998) 1184.
42 Originally, the provision left it up to the Council to decide by unanimity whether, to what extent and by what procedure appropriate provisions will be laid down for sea and air transport. Later, qualified majority was introduced instead of unanimity, while 'by what procedure' stayed – in spite of the addition that the procedural provisions of Article 75(1) and (3) applied.
43 Cases 466/98 *Commission v UK* EU:C:2002:624; 471/98 *Commission v Belgium* EU:C:2002:628; 472/98 *Commission v Luxembourg* EU:C:2002:629; 475/98 *Commission v Austria* EU:C:2002:630; 476/98 (n 39).
44 Case 22/70 *ERTA* EU:C:1971:32.
45 Opinion 1/94 (n 40).
46 Case 476/98 (n 39), para 77.
47 Ibid, paras 70 ff.
48 Regulation (EC) 847/2004 on the negotiation and implementation of air service agreements between Member States and third countries [2004] OJ L157/7.
49 Art 4 para 3 TEU jo. Art 4 para 3 Regulation (EG) nr 847/2004.
50 Air Transport Agreement (n 9).
51 Marc Maresceau, 'A Typology of Mixed Bilateral Agreements' in Christoph Hillion and Panos Koutrakos (eds) *Mixed Agreements Revisited: The EU and its Member States in the World* (Bloomsbury 2010) 26.
52 See for instance Monitor Deloitte, SEO Economisch Onderzoek and P Mendes de Leon, 'Eindrapportage Brexit impact analyse en mogelijke maatregelen voor de Nederlandse luchtvaart' (2 November 2018) 8.
53 Agreement between the Government of the Netherlands and the Government of the United Kingdom for Certain Air Services (London, 13 August 1946).
54 Andrew Haines, 'The Future of Open Skies Post-Brexit' (Speech of 1 December 2016) 6. See also Baines Simmons, 'Brexit and Aviation' (24 July 2018) 5.
55 European Commission, Proposal for a Regulation of the European Parliament and of the Council on common rules ensuring basic air connectivity with regard to the withdrawal of the United Kingdom of Great Britain and Northern Ireland from the Union, COM (2018) 893 final.
56 European Commission, Proposal for a Regulation of the European Parliament and of the Council on certain aspects of aviation safety with regard to the withdrawal of the United Kingdom of Great Britain and Northern Ireland from the Union, COM (2018) 894 final.
57 COM (2018) 893 (n 55), art 3(1).
58 Ibid, art 3(2).
59 Council, Interinstitutional file 2018/0433(COD) (Brussels, 27 February 2019) art 1a(1).
60 Ibid, art 1a(2). The Dutch minister of Infrastructure and Water Management had also indicated (TK 2018–2019, 22 112) that the Netherlands wants to determine on its own which third country can fly to the Netherlands and vice versa. The Netherlands thus opposed the idea that the Union would structurally exercise shared competences where air traffic rights are concerned, and proposed to adapt the proposal in such a manner that it would become clear that it concerned a one-off and temporary solution for an extraordinary situation, without any prejudice to the competence of the Member States concerning traffic rights in any future negotiations, nr 2766.
61 European Commission, Statement regarding the Proposal for a Regulation of the European Parliament and of the Council on common rules ensuring basic air connectivity with regard to the withdrawal of the United Kingdom of Great Britain and Northern Ireland from the Union (Brussels, 27 February 2019) http://data.consilium.europa.eu/doc/document/ST-6922-2019-ADD-1/EN/pdf accessed 29 March 2020.
62 Political Declaration setting out the framework for the future relationship between the European Union and the United Kingdom, Part X sub A (Transport, Aviation), 19 October 2019, paras 58 and 59.

63 Regulation (EU) 2019/502 as amended by Regulation (EU) 2019/1795 amending Regulations (EU) 2019/501 and (EU) 2019/502 as regards their periods of application [2019] OJ L279 I/1. Originally, the contingency measures were scheduled to apply for one year after a hard Brexit, i.e. until 30 March 2020. The new date coincides with the last day of the IATA summer season of 2020.

64 European Commission, Recommendation for a Council decision authorising the opening of negotiations for a new partnership with the United Kingdom of Great Britain and Northern Ireland, COM (2020) 35 final, points 57 ff. The EU has several pieces of legislation in place that protect workers' health and safety in the European civil aviation sector. After Brexit, the UK could decide to lower such standards, and in that manner create a competitive advantage for UK carriers.

65 Prime Minister's Office, 'The Future Relationship with the EU: The UK Approach to Negotiations' (February 2020).

66 Dominican Republic – Central America – United States Free Trade Agreement, Arbitral Panel established pursuant to chapter 20 in the matter of Guatemala – Issues relating to obligations under art 16.2.1(a) of the CAFTA-DR (14 July 2018). See 'Trade Dispute Panel Issues Ruling in US–Guatemala Labour Law Case' (Bridges, 6 July 2017) www.ictsd.org/bridges-news/bridges/news/trade-dispute-panel-issues-ruling-in-us-guatemala-labour-law-case accessed 4 April 2020.

67 Prime Minister's Office (n 65), para 8 sub a.

68 European Commission (n 64), para 65.

69 These provisions violate the Withdrawal Agreement's good-faith requirements. See Piet Eeckhout, 'The EU should be Concerned about the UK's Plans to Rule Out an Extension to the Transition Period' (UCL Brexit Blog, 19 December 2019) https://ucl-brexit.blog/2019/12/19/the-eu-should-be-concerned-about-the-uks-plans-to-rule-out-an-extension-to-the-transition-period/ accessed 29 March 2020. See the contribution of Tobias Locke in this volume.

70 Art. 132(1) of the Withdrawal Agreement sets this deadline. A request would necessitate the EU's consent.

71 *Straighten Up and Fly Right* (Robbie Williams, 2001; originally King Cole Trio, 1943).

8

Outside the opt-out

Legal consequences of the UK's withdrawal from the EU for external action in the AFSJ

Paula García Andrade

8.1 Introduction

The withdrawal of the United Kingdom from the European Union, which took effect on 31 January 2020, has significant implications for the external action of both subjects, particularly as regards the international agreements concluded, prior to Brexit, by the Union, either as EU-only or mixed agreements. Legal scholarship and public attention have mainly been focusing on the effects of Brexit on trade agreements,[1] given the high number of agreements concluded by the EU in this field, their political and economic importance, as well as the exclusive nature of Union external competences under the common commercial policy. Nonetheless, the consequences of the UK's withdrawal for the EU external action in the Area of Freedom, Security and Justice (AFSJ) deserve special attention too, particularly because of the peculiar regime enjoyed by the UK with respect to the policies framed within this area.

Under the variable geometry that characterises the AFSJ, none of the provisions of Title V of Part Three of TFEU, no act adopted pursuant to that Title and no provision of any international agreement concluded by the Union under that Title was binding on the UK. The UK's opt-out regime, regulated in Protocols 19 and 21 to the Treaties, could a priori imply that the withdrawal of the UK from the EU bears no important consequences on the external dimension of the AFSJ. However, the UK has also made use of the opt-in mechanism provided in these Protocols in order to be bound by some of the agreements concluded by the Union, adding significant difficulties to the already complex exercise of the EU external competences in the fields of immigration, asylum, judicial cooperation in civil matters and police and judicial cooperation on criminal matters.[2]

Against this special background, does Brexit imply that EU international agreements to which the UK has opted in cease to immediately apply now that the withdrawal has taken effect? Does international law require any condition or formality to be met? Do the replies to these questions differ in the case of mixed agreements to which the UK is also bound under international law? Which are the effects of Brexit on EU association agreements, in which the UK usually participates as a party with regard to AFSJ-related commitments? And what about the UK's powers to prepare its future external action on AFSJ issues outside the EU? From what point is the UK allowed to exercise those powers to negotiate and conclude its own international agreements with third countries?

This contribution therefore delves into the legal effects of the withdrawal of the UK on the EU external action in the AFSJ, by attempting to tackle these questions from both EU and international law. Section 8.2 examines the legal consequences of Brexit on the international agreements concluded by the EU in the exercise of its competences under Title V of the TFEU, distinguishing between those agreements which did not bind the UK on the basis of its opt-out regime of the AFSJ and those agreements to which the UK opted in in accordance to Protocols 21 and 19. The different situation of EU-only agreements and mixed agreements is addressed, paying also particular attention to the special nature of association agreements, usually concluded in a mixed form. Section 8.3 analyses the external margin of manoeuvre the UK enjoys before the end of the transition period in order to prepare its external action as a state operating outside the EU framework. Each section starts by shortly explaining the contours and implications of the variable geometry characterising the AFSJ and analyses the applicable provisions of the Withdrawal Agreement (WA) concluded between the Union and the UK, which entered into force on 1 February 2020,[3] especially those related to the transition or implementation period in which Union law, including international agreements, continue to apply in and to the UK.[4]

8.2 Legal effects of Brexit on international agreements concluded by the EU in the AFSJ

8.2.1 International agreements not binding on the UK on the basis of the opt-out regime

According to the derogation regime provided by Protocol 21, no provision of any international agreement concluded by the Union under Title V Part Three TFEU was binding on the UK.[5] At the same time, Protocol 19 acknowledges the existence of an enhanced cooperation in the areas covered by the Schengen *acquis* among EU Member States, whose resulting measures also include international agreements which were not binding on the UK.[6] As a consequence, these Protocols not only affect the scope and modalities of the exercise by the Union of its external – explicit and implied – competences on immigration, asylum, civil judicial cooperation and police and judicial cooperation on criminal matters,[7] but they also alter other provisions of the Treaties. First, the opt-out regime modifies the definition of the voting method within the Council when this institution is to adopt decisions within the procedure to conclude international agreements by the EU under art. 218 TFEU, as the UK representatives were not allowed to participate in those decisions.[8] Second, the territorial scope of application of AFSJ legal bases is also altered. This means that the terms of art. 216(2) TFEU are reinterpreted in the sense that those agreements concluded by the Union in AFSJ fields are not binding upon *all* Member States.

Once the withdrawal of the UK from the EU has fully materialised, the legal effects of AFSJ agreements to which the UK has a derogation are obviously not altered: apart from the fact that the Commission only has to worry about the opt-out regime of two – not three – Member States when negotiating with third countries in AFSJ fields, the UK will continue not to be bound by international agreements concluded by the EU in those areas.

During the transition period provided by the WA,[9] 'Union law shall be applicable to and in the United Kingdom'; more particularly as regards EU external action, the UK shall be bound, during that period, 'by the obligations stemming from the international agreements concluded by the Union, by Member States acting on its behalf, or by the Union and its Member States acting jointly'.[10] Among the exceptions to these rules, we find an evident one regarding provisions of the Treaties and acts which, pursuant to the opt-out Protocols, were not binding on the UK before the entry into force of the WA, that is, in its previous quality as an EU Member State.

Apart from the agreements the UK did not want to opt-in under Protocol 21, this is also the scenario applicable to agreements in which the UK was not allowed to opt-in under Protocol 19, such as the agreements on visa facilitation and visa waiver agreements the EU has concluded in the exercise of its *ERTA* exclusive competence on Schengen visas. As the Visa List Regulation and these agreements are a development of a part of the Schengen *acquis* in which the UK did not participate under Protocol 19, the UK could not opt-in and was thus not bound by these agreements before Brexit.[11]

Some distortions between EU and international law might, however, exist. Since art. 261(2) TFEU and Protocol 21 only have internal effects within the EU legal order and treaties are presumed, according to art. 29 VCLT,[12] to be binding on the entire territory of each party, the Commission had to clearly indicate in the text of the AFSJ agreements that they were not binding on the UK. Otherwise, and despite the derogation regime under EU law, the UK would have been bound by those agreements under international law,[13] and would continue to be so after Brexit. This is precisely what happens, for instance, with the Agreements between the EU and the United States on mutual legal assistance, on the one hand, and on extradition, on the other.[14] These conventions applied to the UK under the former third pillar on police and judicial cooperation in criminal matters (PJCC), but the UK had used the new opt-out possibility conferred by Protocol 36 to get excluded from acts adopted under Title VI TEU prior to the entry into force of the Lisbon Treaty.[15] The UK notification made under art. 10(4) Protocol 36 included the Council decisions on the conclusions of these two agreements.[16] As their texts do not except the UK from their territorial scope of application as they should, these EU Agreements with the US on mutual legal assistance and on extradition still formally apply to the UK under international law.[17]

8.2.2 International agreements to which the UK opted in

8.2.2.1 EU-only agreements

Protocol 21 on the position of UK and Ireland with regard to the AFSJ allowed the UK to notify, both *ex ante* and *ex post*, its wish to take part in international agreements concluded by the EU under Title V TFEU.[18] This possibility has regularly been employed by the UK regarding certain agreements on judicial cooperation on civil matters,[19] on judicial cooperation on criminal matters,[20] as well as on migration issues. In the latter field, the UK has opted in to most EU readmission agreements (EURAs),[21] in spite of the fact that these agreements should be considered, in my view, as a development of the Schengen *acquis* in which the UK could not participate.[22] Indeed, applying the clarifications provided by the Court of Justice of the European Union (CJEU),[23] the opt-in mechanism of art. 3 of Protocol 21 applied to agreements which do not constitute a development of the Schengen *acquis*, allowing the UK to simply notify to the Council its wish to participate in those measures. However, Protocol 19 applied to agreements qualified as a development of Schengen,[24] to which the UK could only opt-in if it had been previously authorised to participate in the part of the Schengen *acquis* that the agreement developed.[25] This situation only covered agreements on the fight against irregular immigration and PJCC-related agreements.[26]

From a procedural perspective, the UK could notify its wish to opt-in separately regarding each of the acts to be adopted by the Council under the procedure regulated in art. 218 TFEU, that is, the decision to open negotiations or mandate, the decision of signature and the decision of conclusion of the agreement.[27] However, the UK's opt-in to the mandate created, in my view, an obligation to participate also in the Council decisions on signature and conclusion on the basis of the principle of sincere cooperation. Otherwise, possible dysfunctions between international law and EU law could appear once again. If the UK opted in to the mandate and not to the decisions of signature and conclusion, negotiations had to be reopened in order to exclude the UK from the territorial scope of the agreement, allowing the third country to impose new requirements. In the absence of amendment, the agreement would have bound the UK under international law and not under EU law.[28]

Turning to Brexit consequences, those international agreements concluded by the EU in which the UK has opted in on the basis of Protocols 19 and 21 will no longer bind the UK. The UK has not been a party in its own right to these agreements under international law, but it was bound by them as a member of the Union and thus under EU law. The UK before Brexit – and thus any other Member State – was qualified as a third State in an improper sense,[29] since it did not participate as a party to the agreement under international law,[30] but was bound by its provisions in its quality of member of the international organisation that concluded the agreement. At the end of the transition period, the UK will become a 'full' third State with regard to EU agreements in which it had opted in, as it will no longer be bound by them on the basis of art. 216(2) TFEU.[31]

International law appears to only require a notification to the other country of the fact that the agreement ceases to apply to the UK as part of the EU.[32] An amendment to the agreements will not be necessary to accommodate the UK's withdrawal from the EU, in light of the terms used in the AFSJ agreements. For instance, according to the 'territorial application' provision of the EURA with Turkey, the Agreement applies, as the EU is concerned, to the territories in which EU Treaties apply.[33] Therefore, once the UK abandons the EU and thus the EU Treaties cease to apply in the UK, the EURA with Turkey becomes automatically inapplicable to its territory. In any case, it is advisable for the EU to issue a formal letter to all its partners informing them about the new composition of the Union and its evident effects on the territorial application of any international commitment assumed by the EU, clarifying also the transition period and its effects. This is precisely the purpose of the Note Verbale issued by the EU to its international partners and adopted in compliance of art. 129(1) WA, by which third countries and international organisations are informed that Union law, including international agreements concluded by the Union, by Member States acting on behalf of the Union or by the Union and its Member States jointly, continue to apply in and to the UK during the transition period and that thus 'the United Kingdom is treated as a Member State of the Union and of Euratom for the purposes of these international agreements'.[34] The UK's interest in joining, after the transition period, multilateral agreements concluded by the EU alone should, of course, not be excluded, as is the case of the 2007 Lugano Convention on jurisdiction and the recognition and enforcement of judgments in civil and commercial matters, whose rules might however complicate the UK's accession in its own right.[35]

Finally, we may also refer to international soft law instruments adopted by the EU, since the Note Verbale referred to above specifies that the above principles also apply to 'international instruments and arrangements without legally binding force'.[36] Under the AFSJ and more specifically on migration policy, in which recourse to soft law is quite intense, this would be the case of Mobility Partnerships (MPs), Common Agendas on Migration and Mobility and also ad hoc instruments such as the Joint Way Forward on Migration with Afghanistan or – if considered an EU instrument – the EU–Turkey Statement. Although these international soft law measures are indeed AFSJ instruments to which the UK opt-out/opt-in regime were meant to apply, the fact that no Council decision pursuant to art. 218 TFEU is adopted with regard to non-legally binding instruments does not allow us to have certainty about the UK's effective involvement in them, apart from the evidence of the supportive UK's position towards the recourse to these voluntary and non-binding instruments.[37] In the case of MPs, the UK had participated, as a signatory, in those adopted with Georgia (2009), Morocco (2013) and Tunisia (2014), but there is no formal evidence of the UK's involvement in commitments assumed by the EU under these partnerships.[38] However, as these instruments allow for the voluntary participation of Member States, together with the Union, they should rather be qualified as 'informal partial mixed agreements' to which the following considerations would apply.

8.2.2.2 Mixed agreements

The Brexit effects on EU-only agreements indeed differ from the ones on mixed agreements. As the UK is a party to these international agreements, which are jointly concluded by the Union and its Member States with one or more third countries, it will continue to be bound to them under international law once the withdrawal from the EU takes full effect.[39] During the transition period, AFSJ-related mixed agreements in which the UK had opted in will continue to bind the latter under EU law too, as stated in art. 129.1 WA, which refers to agreements concluded 'by the Union and its Member States acting jointly'. Once the transition period elapses, the scope of the UK's international commitments will, however, be altered. If the UK is now bound under international law to the provisions of a mixed agreement which fall within Member States' competences and, under EU law, to those provisions related to EU competences,[40] Brexit implies that, after the transition period, the UK will assume and be responsible for the international commitments corresponding to the whole agreement if it decides to continue to be party therein. In that case, a notification to the other parties would be required and, most probably, a readjustment in some of the assumed commitments too, as well as the adoption of national implementation measures in the UK for those provisions under the scope of EU competences until now.[41]

This is clearly the scenario applicable to 'multilateral' mixed agreements, in which Member States also participate in their own right, as is the case, for instance, of the Statute of the Hague Conference on Private international law (HCCH), to which the EU acceded in 2007 once the Statute was amended in order to allow for Regional Economic Integration Organizations' (REIO) membership.[42] Although the UK is already a member of the HCCH since 1955, it opted into the Council decision providing for EU accession.[43] As the UK is committed to continue to be an active and supportive member of the HCCH,[44] the full materialisation of Brexit requires a notification to the Hague Conference and its members, providing also for a readjustment of the scope of application of its Statute to the EU and the UK, particularly of the declaration of competences the EU annexed to its accession, which includes explicit references to the UK.[45]

The 2000 Palermo Protocols against smuggling of migrants and trafficking of human beings are also examples of 'multilateral' mixed agreements within the AFSJ, in which the new legal status of the UK seems slightly different. As these protocols include commitments related to EU external competences on migration as well as on development cooperation and economic, financial and technical cooperation, the Council had to adopt two separate decisions of conclusion for each Protocol by reason of the variable geometry affecting the migration-related commitments only.[46] The UK, having opted out of the Council decisions based on former Title IV of the EC Treaty, was therefore not bound under EU law by the migration-related provisions of these instruments,[47] but as a party in its own right. This situation will not be altered after the transition period, but a readjustment will be necessary too, in this case regarding development cooperation provisions which have been binding the UK by virtue of the EU party status in the Protocols.

The legal consequences of the UK's withdrawal from the EU appear certainly different for 'bilateral' mixed agreements, in which the EU and its Member States form a block with regard to the third country, and normally the Member States, as parties to the agreements, are explicitly referred to as 'Member States of the EU' and are granted rights and obligations in that quality.[48] Consequently, the UK should cease to be a party to a 'bilateral' mixed agreement,[49] requiring its formal denunciation or termination by the UK or even an amendment to the treaty, to be consented by all of its parties, in case readjustments are needed.[50] The Union appears to have opted for this solution but just resorting to a notification, as inferred from the terms of the Note Verbale mentioned above.[51]

A paradigmatic example of 'bilateral' mixed agreement would be association agreements by which the EU – and usually its Member States – establish a privileged relationship with a third country and which very often include AFSJ-related clauses.[52] Regarding the UK's participation, Protocol no. 21 would not a priori affect the EU's external competence to conclude association agreements of art. 217 TFEU, which means that the UK was bound, under art. 216(2) TFEU, by every association agreement concluded by the EU. The CJEU has indeed indicated that Protocol 21 on the opt-out situation of the UK and Ireland is not applicable to association agreements and their developments because of the distortions this would create for the functioning of the association.[53] Nevertheless, this is legally dubious in my view. In *Demirel* the Court clarified that the explicit external competence of the association allows the Union to assume international commitments with third countries 'in all the fields covered by the Treaties',[54] excluding thus the need to resort to the various legal bases corresponding to the policy fields included in the agreement. In spite of the fact that AFSJ commitments of association agreements are not based therefore on Title V TFEU provisions, it is difficult to argue that the Union could bind, through art. 217 TFEU, Member States which enjoy a reservation in EU primary law with regard to certain policy fields.[55] Consequently, the UK could not be bound by the AFSJ provisions of an association agreement. This explains why association agreements, usually concluded in a mixed form, specifically indicate that provisions falling within the scope of Title V TFEU bound the UK as a separate contracting party and not as a Member State of the EU, unless it notified that it had become bound on the basis of Protocol 21.[56]

In spite of being a separate party to association agreements and, in that capacity, having assumed their AFSJ provisions, the UK cannot continue to be a party to this kind of mixed agreement from the end of the transition period.[57] Their text clearly shows that the aim of the agreement is to establish an association 'between the EU and its Member States, of the one part, and [the third country], of the other part',[58] and that their territorial scope extends to the territories in which the EU Treaties apply and to that of the associated country.[59] It appears therefore clear that each Member State is party to an association agreement in its quality of EU Member State, although each one has ratified the agreement in its own right. The spirit and context of association agreements also demonstrate their specific nature, aimed at establishing a privileged relationship which brings the third country closer to the EU and its policies.[60] Consequently, the withdrawal of the UK from the EU implies that association agreements, even if concluded in a mixed form, cease to apply to the UK from the end of the transition period.[61] As it is a party under international law, a formal denunciation from the UK is required.

8.3 The UK's external margin of manoeuvre before effective withdrawal from the EU

The situation of variable geometry characterising the AFSJ could create the impression that, irrespective of the nature of EU external competences in these fields, the UK had full powers, as a Member State, to conclude its own international agreements with third countries in the areas covered by Title V TFEU. However, this picture has to be nuanced. First, where the UK had decided to opt-in to the Council's mandate to negotiate an international agreement on an AFSJ field, that opt-in prevented the UK from leading its own bilateral negotiations with that third country on the same issues. The opt-in to the mandate engendered in the UK a duty of cooperation towards the EU, which can be equated to a duty of abstention following the 'mandate theory' established by the CJEU in the *Inland Waterway* cases.[62] Second, once the UK notified its opt-in to the Council decision to conclude an EU agreement in a field of concurrent competence, the principle of pre-emption prevented the UK, as the rest of Member States, from negotiating and concluding a new bilateral agreement with that same country addressing the issues already covered in the agreement concluded by the EU. Third, the opt-in into an EU internal act which contains the common internal rules which give rise to an *ERTA* exclusive competence at the external plane also prevented the UK from entering into bilateral agreements with third countries in that field, and simultaneously mandated the UK to opt-in to the acts by which the Union exercised that exclusive external competence.[63] Consequently, in all those cases, the UK, as a Member State, was clearly not free to develop an independent external action in the AFSJ, but it regains of course the whole set of its external powers after the transition period. Until then, however, EU Treaties and thus its constitutional principles continue to apply to and in the UK,[64] with certain nuances.

As the European Council recalled, 'until it leaves the European Union, the United Kingdom remains full Member of the European Union and subject to all the rights and obligations set out in the Treaties and under EU law, including the principle of since cooperation'.[65] However, the need to 'take into account the specificities of the United Kingdom as a withdrawing Member State' in the international context was also recognised. This meant implicitly accepting the possibility for the UK to engage in talks and negotiations on its future external action,[66] as long as loyalty obligations towards the EU were honoured.[67] In practice, it is clear that the UK government has been not just exploring, but negotiating and even signing and concluding bilateral agreements with third countries in order to bring them into force from exit day in case of a no-deal scenario or no implementation period.[68] This course of action appears evident regarding trade,[69] constituting thus – unless consented by the EU – a clear infringement of the exclusive EU competence in this field.[70] Regarding AFSJ issues, the UK has also taken steps to replace existing EU-only agreements in fields of shared powers and in which it had opted in. The UK negotiations before exit day on bilateral PNR agreements with the United States and Australia, or those aimed at transitioning EURAs into bilateral readmission agreements,[71] constitute examples of infringements to the principle of pre-emption and the exclusivity by exercise derived from the common rules of the EU agreements in which the UK opted in.

The UK also deposited, before exit day, its own instruments of accession to multilateral conventions on civil judicial cooperation on which the EU is exclusively competent, such as the 2007 Hague Convention on the International Recovery of Child Support and Other Forms of Family Maintenance and the 2005 Hague Convention on Choice of Court Agreements. These are EU-only agreements to which the UK continues to be bound under EU law until the transition period is over, because of the UK's opt-in into the 'common internal rules' leading to *ERTA* exclusivity in these fields.[72] The first notifications by the UK to the depositary of these conventions were issued before exit day, on 28 December 2018, and asked for the UK's accession to have effects in case of a no-deal Brexit.[73] The last declarations issued by the UK on 31 January 2020 withdraw the previous ratification instruments, as these conventions continue to bind the UK as an EU Member State until the end of the transition period.[74] Prior to that time, the UK will deposit new instruments of ratification as an independent party.

Interestingly, the UK has even signed before exit day its own association agreements with countries such as Jordan or Morocco,[75] the latter including provisions on social security of Moroccan migrant workers. The fact that these bilateral agreements also cover AFSJ matters does not however constitute an infringement of EU competences, since the UK, as explained above, is bound by AFSJ provisions of association agreements under international law only.[76] What it seems controversial is the negotiation and signature of these bilateral association agreements before exit day, taking into account the exclusivity of the EU association competence as regards, for the UK, the non-AFSJ provisions of the agreements.[77]

The legal situation is different during the transition period. The WA explicitly states that the principle of sincere cooperation continues to bind the UK and requires it to refrain from 'any action or initiative which is likely to be prejudicial to Union's interests'.[78] The same provision nonetheless authorises the UK to 'negotiate, sign and ratify' international agreements in its own capacity 'in the areas of exclusive competence of the Union',[79] allowing therefore for a suspension of the obligations imposed by exclusivity,[80] as well as – we infer – those required by the principle of pre-emption in those scenarios of pre-emptive exclusivity or exclusivity by exercise.[81] These UK agreements cannot enter into force before the transition period elapses unless so authorised by the Union itself.[82] Note however that art. 129 only refers to the transition period which started on exit day. Consequently, until 1 February 2020 any negotiating and signing of bilateral treaties as described above could not be undertaken by the UK.

The WA also refers to the opt-in capacities of the UK during the transition period. As a non-Member State of the EU, the UK will no longer be allowed to notify its wish to participate in new measures to be adopted during the transition period within the AFSJ, including thus any act related to the conclusion of an international agreement by the EU, but only in those modifying or replacing already existing agreements in which the UK had already made opt-in before the entry into force of the WA.[83] Nevertheless, the Union may invite the UK to cooperate in relation to new measures 'in order to support continuing cooperation between the Union and the United Kingdom, *under the conditions set out for cooperation with third countries in the relevant measures*'.[84] In the absence of practical examples, these terms might refer to the kind of cooperation the EU establishes with third countries on AFSJ fields in general, or could also be a reference to European Economic Area (EEA) States which are associated to the Schengen *acquis* and have a particular relationship with the EU through their rapprochement to its policies such as those on migration and borders, for instance. It does not seem however feasible having the UK willing to follow the latter path in light of its derogation regime to EU policies in the AFSJ.

8.4 Concluding remarks

The legal consequences of Brexit for the EU's and UK's external action in AFSJ fields are significant, in spite of the derogation regime the UK has benefited from during its membership of the Union. Apart from the agreements concluded by the EU in which the UK did not participate under Protocols 21 and 19, agreements to which it opted in still apply to and in the UK as EU law until the end of the transition period foreseen in the WA. A more complicated picture is that of mixed agreements concluded in AFSJ fields by the EU and its Member States, including the UK in case of an opt-in. Whilst the UK may generally continue to be a party to 'multilateral' mixed agreements, now with full rights and obligations for the whole set of commitments addressed therein, it would cease to be a party to 'bilateral' mixed agreements after the transition period, since the Union and its Member States form a block vis-à-vis the third country. This will undoubtedly be the case of mixed association agreements. Although it is argued that the UK has assumed the AFSJ provisions as a separate party and thus under international law only, the specific nature of association agreements aimed at establishing a privileged relationship which brings the third country closer to the EU forces the UK to denounce them.

Also, the substantial use of the opt-in mechanism by the UK during its EU membership was not without consequences for the development by the UK of an independent external action in the AFSJ. The mandate theory derived from the principle of sincere cooperation, the principle of pre-emption and even *ERTA* exclusivity have certainly imposed on it significant restrictions, the effects of which were to be respected before exit day and during the transition period as being part of Union law applicable to and in the UK. There are, however, examples in the AFSJ of these principles being infringed before exit day. The Union has nevertheless shown itself clearly permissive and generous in interpreting the UK's status as a withdrawing state, which simultaneously casts doubts on the importance that the EU institutions will accord to the limited restrictions imposed by WA provisions on external action during the transition period. These are additional, but probably this time understandable, concessions to a state which had always profited from differential treatment within the EU. Although it had already started well before exit day, very significant external activity on the truly sensitive political fields of justice and home affairs thus awaits British diplomats during and beyond the transition period, for which they have preserved, in spite of the UK's opt-ins to EU external action, some negotiating expertise.

In sum, if extracting oneself from a derogation regime was expected to be simple, the legal imbroglio[85] characterising variable geometry in the AFSJ, in combination with the traditional complexity of EU external relations law, clearly contradicts this.

Notes

1 See, among others, Marise Cremona, 'UK Trade Policy' in Michael Dougan (ed), *The UK After Brexit: Legal and Policy Challenges* (Intersentia 2017) 247–265; Friedemann Kainer and René Repasi (eds) *Trade Relations After Brexit* (Nomos 2019); Robert G Volterra, 'The Impact of Brexit on the UK's Trade with Non-EU Member States Under the EU's Mixed Free Trade Agreements' (May 2017) Brexit Negotiations Series, Oxford Business Law Blog, www.law.ox.ac.uk/business-law-blog/blog/2017/05/brexit-negotiations-series-impact-brexit-uk%E2%80%99s-trade-non-eu-member accessed 1 April 2020.

2 On this issue, see, among others, Bernd Martenczuk, 'Variable Geometry and the External Relations of the EU: The Experience of Justice and Home Affairs' in Bernd Martenczuk and Servaas Van Thiel (eds), *Justice, Liberty and Security: New Challenges for EU External Relations* (VUBPress 2008); Claudio Matera, 'Much Ado about Opt-Out? The Impact of Variable Geometry in the External Dimension of the AFSJ' in Steven Blockmans (ed), *Differentiated Integration in the EU: From the Inside Looking Out* (CEPS 2014); Paula García Andrade, 'La geometría variable y la dimensión exterior del espacio de libertad, seguridad y justicia' in José Martín y Pérez de Nanclares (ed), *La dimensión exterior del espacio de libertad, seguridad y justicia de la Unión Europea* (Iustel 2012).

3 Agreement on the withdrawal of the United Kingdom of Great Britain and Northern Ireland from the European Union and the European Atomic Energy Community [2020] OJ L 29/7.

4 According to art 126 WA, the transition period started on the date of entry into force of the WA (1 February 2020) and will end on 31 December 2020, unless the Joint Committee created by the agreement extends it for up to one or two years (art 132).

5 Art 2 of Protocol 21, annexed to the Treaties, on the Position of the United Kingdom and Ireland in respect of the Area of Freedom, Security and Justice. Protocol no 22 grants a similar derogation to Denmark in the fields covered by Title V TFEU.

6 Protocol 19, annexed to the Treaties, on the Schengen *acquis* integrated into the framework of the European Union. Ireland is subject to the same regime under this Protocol as the UK, while Denmark is bound to the Schengen *acquis* as international obligations, not under EU law.
7 See Eddy De Smijter, 'The External Relations of a Differentiated European Community' in Bruno de Witte, Dominik Hanf and Ellen Vos (eds), *The Many Faces of Differentiation in EU Law* (Intersentia 2001) 282.
8 Art 1 of Protocol 21. See Steve Peers, *EU Justice and Home Affairs Law* (3rd edn, Oxford University Press 2011).
9 Art 126 WA.
10 Art 129(1) WA.
11 See, for example, Council Decision 2010/622 on the signing, on behalf of the European Union, of the Agreement between the European Union and the Federative Republic of Brazil on short-stay visa waiver for holders of ordinary passports [2010] OJ L275/3, para 8 preamble.
12 Vienna Convention on the Law of Treaties between States and International Organizations or between International Organizations, done at Vienna on 21 March 1986 (not yet in force), which replicates to a great extent the Vienna Convention on the Law of Treaties between States of 1969.
13 See Martenczuk (n 2) 511.
14 Council Decision 2009/820/CFSP [2009] OJ L 291/40. See List of acts published in the [2014] OJ C 430/17.
15 This opt-out regime was, however, not applicable to those acts amended before the expiry of the five-year transition period. List of acts published in [2014] OJ C 430/23. See, for example, Council Decision 2008/651 on the signature of the PNR Agreement with Australia, superseded by Council Decision 2012/381 on the conclusion of that Agreement, to which the UK opted in.
16 Annexed to 'UK notification according to Article 10(4) of Protocol No 36 to TEU and TFEU', Council doc 12750/13, 26 July 2013.
17 Art 10(5) Protocol 36 allowed the UK, at any time after the notification of its opt-out to pre-Lisbon acts on criminal cooperation, to use the opt-in mechanism again. This re opt-in notification concerned 35 out of approximately 130 'ex-third pillar' measures, not including these two agreements: Council doc 15398/14, 20 November 2014. See Valsamis Mitsilegas, 'European Criminal Law After Brexit' (2017) 28 Criminal Law Forum.
18 Arts 3 and 4 of Protocol 21.
19 See, for example, Council Decision 2009/430 concerning the conclusion of the Lugano Convention on jurisdiction and the recognition and enforcement of judgments in civil and commercial matters [2009] OJ L 147/1 or Council Decision 2011/432 on the approval, on behalf of the European Union, of the Hague Convention of 23 November 2007 on the International Recovery of Child Support and Other Forms of Family Maintenance [2011] OJ L 192/39.
20 See, for example, Council Decision 2010/616 on the conclusion of the Agreement between the European Union and Japan on mutual legal assistance in criminal matters [2010] OJ L 271/3, or Council Decision of 2010/411 on the signing, on behalf of the Union, of the Agreement between the European Union and the United States of America on the processing and transfer of financial messaging data from the European Union to the United States for the purposes of the Terrorist Finance Tracking Program [2010] OJ L 195/1.
21 The UK has opted in to every EURA except for those with Armenia, Azerbaijan and Cape Verde.
22 Recall art 23 of the CSA on expulsion and return and the 1991 collective readmission agreement the Schengen States signed with Poland. In this sense, see Nils Coleman, *European Readmission Policy: Third Country Interests and Refugee Rights* (Martinus Nijhoff Publishers 2008) 53.
23 Case C-77/05 *United Kingdom v Council (Frontex)* EU:C:2007:803 and C-137/05 *United Kingdom v Council (Passports and travel documents)* EU:C:2007:805.
24 On these cases, see, among others, Jorrit Rijpma, 'Case C-77/05, United Kingdom v Council, Judgment of the Grand Chamber of 18 December 2007 and Case C-137, United Kingdom v Council, Judgment of the Grand Chamber of 18 December 2007' (2008) 45 Common Market Law Review 835.
25 Art 4 of Protocol 19.
26 And not Schengen-visa facilitation and waiver agreements, as mentioned above, or agreements on external border controls, as they constitute developments of the Schengen *acquis* in which the UK did not take part. See Council Decision 2000/365 concerning the request of the United Kingdom of Great Britain and Northern Ireland to take part in some of the provisions of the Schengen acquis [2000] OJ L 131/43.

27 As understood by the UK Government in 'Report to Parliament on the Application of Protocols 19 and 21 to the Treaty on European Union and the Treaty on the Functioning of the European Union ("the Treaties") in Relation to EU Justice and Home Affairs (JHA) Matters (1 December 2009–30 November 2010)' (January 2011) 3.
28 For a deeper analysis on these issues, see García Andrade (n 2).
29 See José Manuel Sobrino and Adela Rey Aneiros, 'Las relaciones entre los estados partes en un tratado celebrado por una organización internacional y los Estados miembros de ésta' in Fernando M Mariño Menéndez (ed), *El derecho internacional en los albores del siglo XXI: homenaje al profesor Juan Manuel Castro-Rial Canosa* (Trotta 2002).
30 According to art 34 VCLT, a treaty does not create rights or obligations for a third State without its consent.
31 See *a contrario* art 127(1)(a), and art 129(1) WA.
32 Ramses A Wessel, 'Consequences of Brexit for International Agreements Concluded by the EU and its Member States' (2018) 55 Common Market Law Review 116; Guillaume Van der Loo and Steven Blockmans, 'The Impact of Brexit on the EU's International Agreements' (CEPS Commentaries, July 2016) www.ceps.eu/ceps-publications/impact-brexit-eus-international-agreements/ accessed 1 April 2020; Jed Odermatt, 'Brexit and International law: Disentangling Legal Orders' (2017) 31 Emory International Law Review 1057.
33 Art 22 of Agreement between the European Union and the Republic of Turkey on the readmission of persons residing without authorisation [2014] OJ L 134/3. The second paragraph explicitly exempts Denmark from its scope of application.
34 Template of Note Verbale published by the Commission on 31 January 2020, https://ec.europa.eu/info/sites/info/files/model-note-verbale-international-partners_en.pdf accessed 1 April 2020.
35 According to art 70, the 2007 Lugano Convention is open to accession by Member States of the European Free Trade Area (EFTA) and to any other State, provided, in the latter case, that it follows the stringent procedure in art 72 of the Convention and obtains the unanimous agreement of the parties, the Union included. See Giesela Rühl, 'Judicial Cooperation in Civil and Commercial Matters After Brexit: Which Way Forward?' (2018) 67 International Comparative Law Quarterly, 125–127. Norway, Iceland and Switzerland have already issued statements of support for the UK's accession to this Convention: UK's Ministry of Justice, News Story, 28 January 2020, www.gov.uk/government/news/support-for-the-uks-intent-to-accede-to-the-lugano-convention-2007 accessed 1 April 2020.
36 Also to international agreements that are not yet in force but are provisionally applied.
37 See, for example, Letter from the Minister for Immigration to the Chairman of the European Union Committee of the House of Lords, 18 February 2013, www.parliament.uk/documents/lords-committees/eu-sub-com-f/GAMM/gammreportgovtresponse.pdf accessed 1 April 2020.
38 Since MPs include the Union commitment to negotiate a EURA, the UK's opt-in to the Council decision authorising negotiations of an EURA with Tunisia might serve as evidence of its involvement in the Union part of the MP with Tunisia (Council decision no 15141/14, 5 December 2014).
39 Wessel (n 32) 117; Adam Łazowski and Ramses A Wessel, 'The External Dimension of Withdrawal from the European Union' (2016) 4 Revue des Affaires Européennes 623–638. As argued by Volterra, the determination of what constitutes the 'parties' to a mixed agreement must be done on the basis of public international law (and thus to art 2.1.f and g of the VCLT) and not EU law: Volterra (n 1).
40 On the link between competence and international responsibility under mixed agreements, see Piet Eeckhout, *EU External Relations Law* (2nd edn, Oxford University Press 2011) 262–264.
41 Wessel (n 32) 121.
42 Council Decision 2006/719 on the accession of the Community to the Hague Conference on Private International Law [2006] OJ L 297/1.
43 Ibid, para 12 of the preamble.
44 UK Department for Exiting the European Union, 'Providing a Cross-Border Civil Judicial Cooperation Framework: A Future Partnership Paper' 22 August 2017, https://assets.publishing.service.gov.uk/government/uploads/system/uploads/attachment_data/file/639271/Providing_a_cross-border_civil_judicial_cooperation_framework.pdf accessed 1 April 2020.
45 See Annex II to Council Decision referred to above (n 42). The consequences will be similar to that of 'agreements concluded by the Member States acting on behalf of the Union', to which the WA and the Note Verbale sent to EU partners also refer. These are agreements ratified by Member States, including the UK in case of opt-in, in the exercise of a delegation of an EU exclusive competence the Union could not exercise generally because of external factors. As Wessel (n 32) argues, after the transition period, the

UK 'simply regains its status as a full party in any practical sense now that it becomes responsible again in substantive terms'. A notification to the other parties about the new status and most probably a readjustment of the commitments assumed by the UK now in its own right will be necessary. An AFSJ example would be that of the 1996 Hague Convention on Parental Responsibility and Protection of Children to be ratified by EU Member States 'in the interest of the EU' under Council decision 2008/431 [2008] OJ L 151/36, to which the UK was bound. Art 129(1) WA clarifies that these agreements are part of the EU legal order: in this regard see Allan Rosas, 'The Status in EU Law of International Agreements Concluded by EU Member States' 2011 Fordham International Law Journal 34, 1333–1334, and Marise Cremona, 'Member States as Trustees of the Community Interest: Participating in International Agreements on Behalf of the European Community' (2009) 17 EUI Working Papers.

46 All published in [2006] OJ L262/24.

47 At present, the provisions on cooperation in criminal matters in these Protocols correspond to EU competence since the entry into force of the Lisbon Treaty. However, this does not affect the UK, since Protocol 21 also applies to PJCC from that moment.

48 See Volterra (n 1), Wessel (n 32) 119 and Panos Koutrakos, 'What Does Brexit Mean for International Trade Agreements?' (6 July 2016) *Blog post in Monckton Chambers*, www.monckton.com/brexit-mean-international-trade-agreements/ accessed 1 April 2020.

49 This is confirmed by the UK government in the Letter from the UK Secretary of State for Exiting the European Union to the Chairman of the European Union Committee of the House of Lords, 28 February 2018.

50 Van der Loo and Blockmans (n 32); Wessel (n 32) 120–121.

51

> At the end of the transition period, the United Kingdom will no longer be covered by the international agreements referred to in points 4 and 6 above. This is without prejudice to the status of the United Kingdom in relation to *multilateral* agreements to which it is a party in its own right.
>
> *(Template Note Verbale, point 9, emphasis added)*

A contrario, 'bilateral' mixed agreements cease to apply to the UK after the transition period.

52 In an association agreement, we usually find commitments related to migration, asylum, fight against organised crime, corruption, illicit drugs, money laundering, fight against terrorism and judicial cooperation in civil matters.

53 Case C-431/11 *United Kingdom v Council* (*EEA social security coordination*) EU:C:2013:589. See also the Opinion of AG Kokott in Case 431/11, EU:C:2013:187, paras 71–77, and in Case C-81/13, EU:C:2014:2114, paras 114–120.

54 Case 12/86 *Demirel* EU:C:1987:400, para 9.

55 See Martenczuk (n 2) 518. For further analysis, see Paula García Andrade, 'EU External Competences in the Field of Migration: How to Act Externally When Thinking Internally' (2018) 55/1 Common Market Law Review.

56 See, for example, the Association Agreement between the European Union and the European Atomic Energy Community and their Member States, of the one part, and Georgia, of the other part, [2014] OJ L 261/4; or the Euro-Mediterranean Agreement establishing an Association between the European Community and its Member States, of the one part, and the People's Democratic Republic of Algeria, of the other part [2005] OJ L 265/2.

57 See Wessel (n 32) 120–121.

58 See, for example, art 1 of the Association Agreement with Georgia. The readmission clause in art 68 of the Euro-Mediterranean Association Agreement with Egypt, for example, confirms this scenario, as it constantly refers to EC Member States.

59 Art 429 of the AA with Georgia.

60 Case 12/86, point 9.

61 Guillaume Van der Loo and Ramses Wessel, 'The Non-Ratification of Mixed Agreements: Legal Consequences and Solutions' (2017) 54 Common Market Law Review 735, 741–742.

62 Case C-266/03 *Commission v Luxembourg* EU:C:2005:341, para 60 and Case C-433/03 *Commission v Germany* EU:C:2005:462, para 66. See Paula García Andrade, 'The Duty of Cooperation in the External Dimension of the EU Migration Policy' in Sergio Carrera, Leonhard den Hertog, Marion Panizzon and Dora Kostakopoulou (eds) *EU External Migration Policies in an Era of Global Mobilities: Intersecting Policy Universes* (Brill/Nijhoff 2018).

63 For a more detailed analysis, see García Andrade (n 2). In this sense, see Martenczuk (n 2) 514.

64 On the basis of art 50(3) TEU as regards the period before exit day, and of art 127(1) WA during the transition period.
65 Guidelines adopted by the European Council at the special meeting of 29 April 2017, doc EUCO XT 20004/17, para 25.
66 See Adam Łazowski, 'Withdrawal from the European Union and Alternatives to Membership' (2012) 37 European Law Review 523–540. Also Wessel (n 32) 116 and 118; Łazowski and Wessel (n 39).
67 European Council Guidelines, para 26.
68 UK Department for Exiting the European Union, 'Guidance: International Agreements if the UK Leaves the EU Without a Deal', www.gov.uk/government/publications/international-agreements-if-the-uk-leaves-the-eu-without-a-deal/international-agreements-if-the-uk-leaves-the-eu-without-a-deal accessed 1 April 2020. According to information updated in November 2019, some of the listed agreements were 'ready to enter into force', 'may have been initialled or agreed in principle' or discussions were 'ongoing with the third country'. For an overview, see also Stefano Fella, 'UK Replacement of the EU's External Agreements after Brexit' (House of Commons Briefing Paper, 2019) https://commonslibrary.parliament.uk/research-briefings/cbp-8370/ accessed 1 April 2020.
69 UK Department for International Trade, 'Existing Free Trade Agreements if There's No Brexit Deal' (updated 19 December 2018) www.gov.uk/government/publications/existing-free-trade-agreements-if-theres-no-brexit-deal/existing-free-trade-agreements-if-theres-no-brexit-deal accessed 1 April 2020. See the list of trade agreements signed (published at 29 January 2020 and last updated on 4 February 2020) www.gov.uk/guidance/uk-trade-agreements-with-non-eu-countries accessed 1 April 2020.
70 In this sense Joris Larik, 'Sincere Cooperation in the Common Commercial Policy: Lisbon, a "Joined-Up" Union, and "Brexit"' (2017) 8 European Yearbook of International Economic Law 103.
71 See UK Department for Exiting the European Union, 'Guidance: Justice & Home Affairs' (updated 5 November 2019) www.gov.uk/government/publications/international-agreements-if-the-uk-leaves-the-eu-without-a-deal/justice-home-affairs accessed 1 April 2020.
72 Regulation (EU) 4/2009 and Regulation (EU) 1215/2012, respectively.
73 Available at HCCH website, www.hcch.net/en/instruments/conventions/status-table/notifications/?csid=1255&disp=resdn; www.hcch.net/en/instruments/conventions/status-table/notifications/?csid=1318&disp=resdn accessed 1 April 2020.
74 According to art 59(3) of the Hague Convention on the International Recovery of Child Support and Other Forms of Family Maintenance, Member States of REIOs are bound by this Convention by virtue of the signature, acceptance, approval or accession of the Organisation.
75 European Union Committee Scrutiny of international agreements: treaties considered on 4 February 2020, 4th Report of Session 2019–21-HL Paper 14, https://publications.parliament.uk/pa/ld5801/ldselect/ldeucom/14/1405.htm#_idTextAnchor016 accessed 1 April 2020.
76 During the transition period, UK representatives will not take part in bodies set up by EU-only or mixed agreements unless they participate on behalf of the UK in its own right (art 129(2) WA). A priori it could be argued that UK representatives cannot continue to take part in Association Councils as they are usually composed of members of the Council and of the Commission. It seems however that the Council member for the UK within an Association Council acts as an UK representative when the Association Council deals with AFSJ issues, and thus may continue to participate in the work of these bodies during the transition period.
77 In this sense, Ian Macleod, Ian Hendry and Stephen Hyett, *The External Relations of the European Communities* (Oxford University Press 1998) 371.
78 Art 129(4) WA.
79 Art 129(4) WA.
80 This authorisation would find its legal basis in art 2.1 TFEU: 'if so empowered by the Union'.
81 In the absence of explicit references to the limitations derived from pre-emption and from the duty of cooperation, the principle *qui potest plus, potest minus* leads us to understand the terms in art 129(4) WA as waiving these restrictions too.
82 See art 3 Council Decision 2020/135 on the conclusion of the Agreement on the withdrawal of the United Kingdom of Great Britain and Northern Ireland from the European Union and the European Atomic Energy Community [2020] OJ L 29/1 for the procedural aspects and substantive conditions which apply to this authorisation.
83 Art 127(5) WA.
84 Ibid, emphasis added.
85 Term used by Hervé Bribosia, 'Liberté, sécurité et justice: l'imbroglio d'un nouvel espace' (1998) Revue du Marché Unique Européen 27, to describe the AFSJ.

9

Copy–pasting or negotiating?

Post-Brexit trade agreements between the UK and non-EU countries

Adam Łazowski

9.1 Introduction

For the United Kingdom one of the alleged benefits of Brexit is the newly re-acquired right to negotiate trade agreements with countries around the world.[1] To use the phraseology, ever so gladly employed by the supporters of withdrawal from the European Union, now that the shackles of the EU are gone, the UK is again a fully sovereign nation ready to embark on a journey to Global Britain. Alas, apart from such bombastic claims, and fact free statements of leading Brexiters, there is scarce evidence that these desiderata are turning into reality.[2] This is the case even despite the fact that the UK authorities had engaged in negotiations with third countries well before the actual withdrawal from the EU. Arguably, the results of negotiations conducted thus far are disappointing and prove that delivering Global Britain may prove to be way more difficult than anticipated by its proponents. As the analysis provided in this chapter demonstrates, in case of future agreements between the UK and the EU's neighbours, there is more copy–pasting or cross-referencing than negotiating. To put it differently, the existing EU agreements with these countries are being largely rolled over, and rubber stamped as UK post-Brexit agreements. In several cases, even the notion of 'association', a well-established concept in EU external relations, has also been rolled over to bilateral relations between the UK and its trading partners, even though it seems to be an alien concept for such constellations. Furthermore, the 'short form' drafting technique, employed in a majority of agreements is – contrary to the UK government's argumentation – legally dubious. To give these arguments merit, the analysis provided in this chapter proceeds in the following fashion. As a starting point, section 9.2 provides an overview of the state of affairs as it stood on the day of the UK's withdrawal from the EU. The centre of gravity is on the negotiations, which have been completed and, consequentially, the text of post-Brexit agreements is now done and dusted. This lays down the foundations for section 9.3, focusing on case studies covering the agreements between the UK and selected neighbours of the EU. The *raison d'être* is to elaborate further on the main arguments put forward above, and also to determine which aspects regulated in EU agreements with third countries are rolled over.

9.2 The big picture: where are we now?

9.2.1 Introduction

The UK commenced its journey towards Global Britain in the early stages of its withdrawal from the EU.[3] Although still a Member State, and thus fully bound by EU law, it started preliminary talks with several countries around the world.[4] This, as argued in the academic literature, was not permissible under relevant EU legislation[5] and no special status was granted to the withdrawing country by the EU.[6] Interestingly enough, the European Commission has largely ignored the legality of the advances made by Whitehall around the world and opted not to trigger infringement proceedings. In all fairness one needs to note that the authorities in London were limiting themselves to countries with which the EU already has agreements.[7] Furthermore, the activities focused on negotiations and signing post-Brexit agreements. An overview of the closing sections in each and every agreement proves that their entry into force has been inextricably linked to the expiry of the transitional period regulated in the EU–UK Withdrawal Agreement.[8] This may be read as evidence that the intention of the UK government was not to engage in legal vandalism, but rather to secure a smooth transition of regulatory regimes applicable to trade with countries around the world. Seen through a UK lens, to commence the negotiations before actual Brexit was a rational move, particularly as the spectre of a chaotic no deal departure from the EU was looming on the horizon. The economic fallout would have been further exacerbated if the UK simultaneously cut its legal ties with the EU and other trading partners. But the question remains as to how this task has been executed. As alluded to in the introduction to the present chapter, if one puts the post-Brexit agreements under the microscope, many doubts arise.

As is well known, the UK has a long history of being an active participant in international trade. Yet, for a number of reasons, it has started its post-Brexit drive to become a champion of free trade as a non-EU country with a pen and a blank sheet of paper. The easiness with which some of the political elites trumpeted the new golden era has proven to be a mistake, as the rolling over of EU agreements is a rather complicated affair. To begin with, the EU benefits from a complex web of international treaties with countries scattered all around the globe. In many agreements the centre of gravity is on provisions governing various aspects of trade.[9] At the same time, a plethora of agreements has a much wider scope, taking cooperation with third countries to completely new levels. A good example is the recently concluded comprehensive association agreements (AA) with Ukraine,[10] Georgia[11] and Moldova.[12] Furthermore, the EU and Euratom are parties to countless sectoral agreements covering such areas as aviation,[13] energy[14] or readmission.[15] So, one of the first questions that the authorities in London had to answer was which of the existing agreements it would seek to roll over and which ones should be given priority. One needs to remember that it is not a one-sided affair. While the wishes of the UK were of importance, it would have been a mistake to assume *ab initio* that the non-EU countries were ready to automatically entertain requests received from Whitehall. To put it differently, the rolling over of EU agreements was perceived by some as a good opportunity to renegotiate the terms laid down therein.[16] The UK also faced a major institutional challenge. Since the conclusion of trade agreements falls under EU exclusive competence, the Member States traditionally lose their institutional and human capacity in this regard. Consequentially, the UK government had to create new institutional structures and faced a shortage of experienced negotiators. As well documented in the academic literature, one of the major issues was the lack of vision as to future relations with the EU and the challenges faced by the government in achieving enough support in the House of Commons.[17] All of this created a very demanding environment in which an attempt at rolling over EU trade agreements was being pursued. As a result, on the day of Brexit, the UK concluded the negotiations of 20 agreements, while engagement with many other countries was on-going, or about to start.

9.2.2 Choice of trading partners

As a starting point, the government had to decide on the choice of trading partners it would wish to negotiate with and, as already mentioned, the selection of agreements for rolling over had to be made. In this respect, one would expect a decision to be made on robust and objective political, economic and legal criteria. For instance, priority could be given to the main trading partners or countries of strategic political importance. With this in mind, a mere look at the list of countries with which the agreements have been concluded, and which are still being negotiated, is rather surprising.[18] First, the focus was primarily on the countries with which the EU has free trade agreements; preferential trade agreements were not the target of the rolling-over exercise. Second, the countries with which, at the time, the EU was negotiating free trade agreements were treated selectively. Third, many post-Brexit agreements have been concluded with third countries with which the volume of trade is marginal. The only exceptions are agreements with South Korea[19] (the twenty-second largest UK trading partner),[20] South Africa[21] (the twenty-seventh largest UK trading partner)[22] and Israel[23] (the forty-sixth UK trading partner).[24] At the same time, a lengthy and comprehensive trade agreement has been signed with Georgia,[25] which is the UK's 139th largest trading partner with less than a 0.1 per cent share of total trade.[26] The UK Free Trade Agreement with Denmark,[27] applicable to trade with the Faroe Islands, looks even more symbolic.[28] With this in mind, one should not be blamed for putting forward an argument that some of these agreements were prioritised mainly for statistical purposes, and thus serving the mainstream political narrative. It is notable that out of the 20 concluded agreements only nine were actually signed before the original Brexit date (29 March 2019).[29] The remaining 11 agreements were signed during three successive extensions of the UK's membership in the EU. As things stood on 31 January 2020, the rolling over of 16 other free trade agreements was still in progress. This included the highly ambitious EU agreements with Singapore,[30] Canada[31] and the already mentioned AA with Ukraine. Furthermore, the negotiations with Japan, with which the EU has a free trade agreement[32] and with Turkey, which is partly integrated with the EU *qua* a customs union,[33] have not been advanced yet. At the same time, the negotiations of brand-new trade agreements with other trading partners have barely commenced. For instance, politically important, but deeply contentious, talks with the United States commenced in March 2020 and soon after were effectively put on hold by the coronavirus pandemic.[34] No talks were in place with Russia or, for that matter, any other post-Soviet country with a Partnership and Co-operation Agreement in place.[35] Last but not least, the negotiations were yet to start with Australia and New Zealand, both of which are currently engaged in negotiations of free trade agreements with the EU.[36] It remains to be seen how the situation will evolve in the rather limited time left before the expiry of the Brexit transitional period. If it ends, as currently planned, on 31 December 2020 and trade negotiations are not completed, the UK would face a snap downgrade of trade relations with several third countries. Effectively, this would amount to trade under the World Trade Organization (WTO) rules and, in many cases, the consequential creation of additional barriers to trade.[37] One should note that this would also be the case for relations with the UK's main trading partner – the EU – should the parties fail to seal and dust a trade agreement by the end of the transition.

9.2.3 Rolling over means copy–pasting or cross-referencing

It is not surprising that the initial focus of the UK government was on rolling over existing EU agreements. Although it clearly ran against the 'taking back control' desiderata preached by the Brexiters, it was – as argued earlier – justifiable on economic grounds. It was also politically defendable as it permitted the authorities to propel the statistics and argue that Global Britain was in the making. As argued in the present chapter, the existing EU agreements have proven to be much more than starting points for UK negotiations with third countries. All 20 agreements that have been rolled over thus far have been either copy-pasted with minor modifications or incorporated into post-Brexit agreements *qua* cross-references. They are referred to by the UK government, respectively, as 'long form' and 'short form' agreements. The former offered consolidated texts serving transparency and legal certainty, while the latter make the legal regime patchy and difficult to navigate. Both methods merit a closer look, which is provided in turn.

The government justified the use of the 'short form' method on several grounds. For instance, the choice of *modus* for the UK–Morocco AA was determined by three debatable prerequisites. First, it allegedly offered a degree of flexibility permitting accommodation of different scenarios of future UK–EU relations. Second, it also served clarity for businesses, consumers and investors. Third, such an approach facilitated 'a clear legal text, making rights and obligations unambiguous where they have, by necessity, changed'.[38] It is notable that such a justification was not put forward only in relation to the Agreement in question, but it was largely copy–pasted also in the remaining reports attached to the draft agreements, as they were submitted to the UK Parliament.[39] In terms of contents, the agreements themselves follow the same pattern. The opening provisions provide that the EU agreements are incorporated into the rolled over agreements, subject to remaining provisions, which list sections of the former that will not be incorporated into the post-Brexit agreements. This includes, for instance, law approximation clauses, which are redundant in the case of post-Brexit deals.[40] It is hard, if not impossible, to see how this technique serves the three prerequisites listed above. It neither increases flexibility, nor delivers clarity and transparency. For sure, it has served expediency, saved additional translation costs and helped the UK government to tick the boxes faster.

When it comes to 'long form' agreements it is striking that, statistically speaking, they are in a minority. Even more surprising is the fact that they are largely a patchwork of copy–pasted provisions from agreements concluded by the EU. Once again, expediency took the helm, while 'taking back control' has been reduced to a figure of speech. Furthermore, it is quite unclear for what reasons this methodology was opted for in agreements with CARIFORUM states,[41] eastern and southern African countries,[42] Georgia,[43] the Pacific states,[44] South Korea[45] as well as Southern African Customs Union countries (and Mozambique)[46] but not with the other trading partners. As already noted, the 'long form' agreements provide a codified text, which serves precisely the objectives that, at least formally, have been set for the 'short form' agreements. They increase flexibility and, by all means, facilitate legal certainty and clarity. Furthermore, no incorporation may potentially serve the policy objectives of the UK government. To put it differently, to an ordinary member of the public, a 'long form' agreement may be sold as an agreement negotiated by the UK as part of the Global Britain project. At the same time, the incorporation methodology, which is at the heart of 'short form' modus operandi, openly acknowledges the source of the legal regime.

The question remains how all of this can be married with the 'taking back control' desiderata. These post-Brexit agreements are nothing but a spill-over of the EU deep trade agenda.[47] It should be also noted that only the Agreement with the Pacific states is properly considered as an interim solution.[48] The remaining agreements are designed in a more permanent fashion and, thus, they are likely to stay untouched for years. This will be particularly relevant to agreements with countries with which the volumes of trade are symbolic.

9.2.4 Highlighters out: let's get rid of …

The analysis conducted thus far proves that despite the bold rhetoric, the founding blocks of Global Britain are the agreements previously negotiated and concluded by the EU. Furthermore, they are brought back into the UK legal orders through the kitchen door, having been merely stripped – overtly or covertly – of their EU provenance. With this in mind, it is interesting to take a closer look at the typology of provisions which were removed as part of this exercise. Not surprisingly, any references to the EU are either replaced with references to the UK ('long form' agreements) or will implicitly disappear in the *mutatis mutandis* application of incorporated EU agreements. The latter is a solution opted for in the case of 'short form' agreements. Furthermore, the law approximation clauses have been removed as no longer fit for purpose for bilateral relations between the UK and other countries.[49] In the same vein, some of the trade provisions have been tweaked to serve the post-Brexit reality. Interestingly enough, the bilateral institutional structures remain largely untacked with joint councils and committees at the heart of the institutional set-up. Furthermore, references to the euro as the relevant currency remain. It is not surprising that in the majority of rolled-over agreements the notion of association is dropped. The latter is one of the idiosyncrasies of the EU external relations framework, with roots in the law of international organisations and the concept of 'associated membership'.[50] It is hard to see how the concept could be applied *mutatis mutandis* to bilateral relations between states. Yet, for rather unclear reasons, post-Brexit Agreements negotiated with Jordan,[51] Lebanon,[52] Morocco,[53] as well as with Central American countries[54] and with Chile,[55] are formally branded as AAs.[56] Sadly, no explanation for this development is furnished in any of the accompanying documents produced by the Department for International Trade.

It should be noted that tailor-made solutions were opted for in cases of enhanced multilateralism and enhanced bilateralism, prevalent in EU relations with European Economic Area (EEA)–European Free Trade Area (EFTA) countries and with Switzerland.[57] When it comes to the first, as an initial step, an agreement on trade in goods was negotiated and signed.[58] The *raison d'être* was to provide a basic legal framework should the UK exit the EU without a deal. But, with the Withdrawal Agreement in place, and thus a unilateral Brexit confined to the history books, the agreement with Norway and Iceland was shelved to be eventually replaced by a proper separation treaty governing the UK's exit from the EEA.[59] Details of the post-Brexit trade regime were yet to emerge when the present chapter was completed. When it comes to the UK–Switzerland Trade Agreement the situation was technically a bit more demanding as the EU–Swiss legal framework has developed in a very incremental fashion.[60] Instead of a more general agreement, supplemented by sectoral arrangements, it is a patchwork of over 120 agreements covering, inter alia, trade in goods,[61] free movement of persons[62] as well as association with Schengen.[63] Consequentially, some elements of that patchwork have had to be reflected in the post-Brexit UK–Switzerland Trade Agreement, which has taken the shape of a 'short form' agreement.[64] Furthermore, the parties signed a Memorandum of Understanding aiming at the development of future relations.[65]

9.3 A closer look: post-Brexit agreements with Georgia and Kosovo

9.3.1 Introduction

Having provided the big picture, it is fitting to put under the microscope a representative sample of rolled-over agreements. This will allow deeper delving into some of the arguments made in previous sections of this chapter. For the purposes of this exercise, the analysis will concentrate on post-Brexit agreements with Georgia and Kosovo. The choice is not accidental as it offers a good example of 'long form' and 'short form' agreements reflecting different families of AAs concluded over the years by the EU.

9.3.2 The UK–Georgia Strategic Partnership and Cooperation Agreement

As already noted, the EU–Georgia AA belongs to the model of deep and comprehensive free trade agreements which have been recently concluded with some of the countries covered by the European Neighbourhood Policy.[66] It provides for a very complex legal framework based on the 'more for more' principle. In return for compliance with countless EU legal acts listed in the Agreement, it offers Georgia preferential access to certain aspects of the Internal Market.[67] The EU–Georgia AA was the first of this generation of EU AAs to be rolled over into a post-Brexit agreement with the UK. It was signed on 21 October 2019. Symbolically, the ceremony took place in London during bilateral UK–Georgia consultations in the framework of the Wardrop Strategic Dialogue.[68]

In the present chapter the new Agreement merits attention for several reasons. First, it is one of six 'long form' agreements concluded thus far. Second, it is interesting to verify the extent to which the two sides reworked the original AA. This leads to the question of whether we are dealing with a legal transplant or with a fully fledged new Agreement, even when modelled on its predecessor.[69]

To begin with, the UK and Georgia opted for a bespoke title for the post-Brexit agreement: the UK–Georgia Strategic Partnership and Cooperation Agreement (SPCA). This is not surprising bearing in mind that the EU–Georgia AA was tailored to serve as a vehicle for association, that is, the already mentioned privileged relationship between the parties. The title of the new Agreement comprises two important notions: 'strategic partnership' and 'cooperation'. In purely legal terms the titles of international agreements are of secondary importance. Yet, from the political point of view, they do carry considerable weight. Taking geo-politics into account, the choice of title in this case serves particularly Georgia and the main desiderata of its foreign policy.

As one would expect from a 'long form' agreement, it is rather a bulky document. However, a detailed analysis of its provisions proves that their prolific nature is not necessarily linked to the inventiveness of the drafters but rather it is consequential of the voluminous prototype. The 'Strategic Partnership and Cooperation Agreement' has primarily been a copy–paste exercise. Its structure, as well as the content of its provisions, strikingly mirrors the EU–Georgia AA. Overall, there is a handful of provisions which have been added or altered. At the same time, almost all references to the EU, or EU law, have been diligently deleted.

The Agreement, just like the AA, opens with a rich preamble. It confirms that the *raison d'être* of the Agreement is the creation of a deep and comprehensive free trade area. A few new additions and tweaks to the Preamble merit attention. While the Agreement follows its prototype in a reference to Georgia's European aspirations and its European choice, it also adds an important paragraph mentioning 'significant progress Georgia has made to date in reform in support of

Georgia's EU membership aspirations'. The preamble also includes a reference to Georgia's Euro-Atlantic choice. Furthermore, considerably more accurate, yet less diplomatic, language is employed to describe the continuous threats to Georgia's territorial integrity. The preamble openly refers to 'Russia's illegal military presence and steps towards de-facto annexation of the Georgian regions of Abkhazia and Tskhinvali region/South Ossetia'. These issues, which for reasons that deserve no explanation, are further regulated in new additions inserted into provisions on the aims of political dialogue (Article 3 SPCA) and Articles 5–6 SPCA governing, respectively, matters of foreign and security policy as well as peaceful conflict resolution.[70]

An interesting addition can be found in Article 15 SPCA, which is dedicated to cooperation on migration, asylum and border management. While the text is largely copy–pasted from Article 15 AA, the last paragraph is a novelty. It creates an unequivocally formulated prohibition of discrimination on grounds of nationality in relation to working conditions, remuneration and dismissal. Not surprisingly, it comes with a caveat which limits the application to persons who are legally employed in the UK or in Georgia. Without a doubt, the inclusion of such a provision in the SPCA is plausible and potentially may serve as a basis for submission of claims in national courts.

Analysis of the Agreement leads to an inevitable conclusion that the attention of negotiators focused primarily not on new additions but rather on the removal of undesirable solutions as well as the reformulation of provisions contained in the AA.[71] First and foremost, 'Europe' seems to be the hardest word. Wherever possible, references to the EU or EU legislation have been removed. Deletion of many law approximation clauses, as well as relevant annexes with lists of the EU *acquis*, is perfectly justified.[72] Such solutions are idiosyncratic and reserved for EU agreements with third countries, in particular with its neighbours, which express EU membership aspirations. Yet, in a few cases deletions seem to be rather overzealous. For instance, Article 14 SPCA sets the framework for cooperation on data protection, yet – as points of reference – it merely refers to the Council of Europe and international standards. This is also reflected in Annex I to the SPCA. References to EU law, which can be found in corresponding provisions of the AA have been completely removed. While Regulation 2016/679 on data protection may not be perfect, it certainly sets some universal standards that could serve at least as an example of common standards.[73] Another example may be found in Article 138 (6) SPCA dedicated to the award of public procurement contracts. For descriptions of the characteristics of the required work, the contracting authorities are expected to employ international or national standards. Again, when compared with its prototype in the AA, a reference to the 'European' equivalents is missing. A case of overzealous pruning is also visible in Article 217 SPCA governing regulatory quality and good administrative behaviour. While the provision itself reproduces verbatim Article 225 AA, a footnote reference to a Council of Europe Recommendation has been deleted.[74] This is debatable for at least three reasons. First, both the UK and Georgia remain members of the Council of Europe. Second, the Recommendation in question is non-binding and serves merely as a point of reference. Third, Article 217 SPCA is rather general and requires the parties to cooperate, while the importance of good administration principles is only recognised in the provision in question. Thus, it may be perceived as yet another example of the political Brexit dogma, and all that comes with it, translated into legal reality. In purely legal terms, such a move is difficult to justify.

As far as reformulation is concerned, several provisions and sections originating from the EU–Georgia AA have been tweaked and pruned. This includes, for instance, Articles 349–351 on financial assistance and anti-fraud. In this respect, most of the provisions provided in Articles 383–402 AA have not been rolled over. Another example is Article 144 SPCA, which confirms that each party is free to determine the regime applicable to the exhaustion of intellectual property rights, but, unlike Article 152 AA, it also adds that the domestic legislation needs to be subject to provisions of agreement on Trade-Related Aspects of Intellectual Property Rights (TRIPS). Interesting solutions have been found in relation to institutional arrangements. The core structure resembles the design known from the AA, although the Association Council is rebranded into the Strategic Partnership and Cooperation Forum and builds on the already mentioned Wardrop Strategic Dialogue. At the same time, the parliamentary dimension is almost gone, with no replacement to the Parliamentary Association Committee envisaged in Article 354 (6) SPCA.[75] Furthermore, the Civic Society Platform (Articles 412–413 AA) is not replaced by a post-Brexit equivalent, although Article 233 SPCA provides for a UK–Georgia Joint Civil Society Forum.[76]

Another matter that merits attention is a selection of provisions which have not been deleted. While in a great majority of cases the choices are perfectly sound, some – nevertheless – raise doubts. To the first belong comprehensive frameworks governing settlement of disputes related to the Deep and Comprehensive Free Trade Areas (DCFTA) part (Articles 236–261 SPCA) and to other parts of the Agreement (Articles 360–361 SPCA).[77] On the dubious side, Article 227 SPCA brings in a strictly written commitment to uphold levels of protection of labour law and environmental law standards.[78] This is surprising bearing in mind the tensions over the level playing field ever so present in negotiations between the EU and the UK of the post-Brexit agreement.[79]

Last but not least, the closing provisions of the UK–Georgia SPCA offer a few novelties. For instance, a tailor-made modus operandi for the revision of the SPCA is provided in Article 362; furthermore, Article 366 comprises a carefully crafted set of rules on the entry into force and provisional application of the Agreement.

9.3.3 The Partnership, Trade and Cooperation Agreement with Kosovo

The Partnership, Trade and Cooperation Agreement (PTCA) with Kosovo was signed on 3 December 2019, thus two months shy of Brexit. It rolls over the Stabilisation and Association Agreement (SAA) recently concluded between the EU and Kosovo.[80] It is also the first of this family of EU AAs to be developed into a post-Brexit agreement,[81] while the negotiations with the remaining non-EU countries of the Western Balkans were pending on 31 January 2020.

Three key points are worth being made at the outset. First, the EU–Kosovo SAA is a relatively short free trade agreement, providing a skeleton framework for bilateral relations. Second, as in the case with the other SAAs, the creation of the free trade area is an end in itself. However the Agreement serves also much broader and ambitious objectives. It was designed as a tool for the association of Kosovo with the EU and, at the same time, as an instrument for stabilisation in the Western Balkan region. Furthermore, in the long term, the SAA is the ultimate legal vehicle for the future accession of Kosovo to the EU. With this in mind, the roll-over of the SAA had to take into account a recalibration of objectives underpinning the legal framework. Third, UK–Kosovo trade amounts to symbolic volumes, to the point that the Foreign and Commonwealth Office, in its report to the Parliament, admitted that exact data are not available. It was added, however, that the total trade in 2018 was worth approximately £1 million.[82]

The pruned aims of the rolled-over Agreement are reflected in its title. The notions of 'stabilisation' and 'association' have been replaced with more suitable concepts for the post-Brexit reality: 'partnership', 'trade' and 'cooperation'. It is notable that in the case of this Agreement, the parties opted for the 'short form'. It is a bit surprising as its prototype is rather short and straightforward, hence good material for a copy–pasting exercise.

Unlike the UK–Georgia Agreement presented above, the UK–Kosovo PTCA has a very brief and unambitious preamble, merely restating the factors behind it: Brexit and the need for continuous cooperation. This is also reflected in Article 1 PTCA. Surprisingly enough, the aim is to establish not only a free trade area but also an association. As noted earlier, an association between states is a rather alien concept, not properly founded in contemporary international law. The *raison d'être* of this move is not clear and not elaborated upon in governmental documents submitted to the UK Parliament.

The main part of the UK–Kosovo PTCA is brief and comprises a handful of provisions. At the heart of it is Article 3 PTCA, which provides: 'The provisions of the EU-Kosovo Agreement in effect immediately before they cease to apply to the United Kingdom are incorporated into and made part of this Agreement, *mutatis mutandis*, subject to the provisions of this instrument.' By means of such a cross-reference the EU–Kosovo SAA is being turned into a post-Brexit UK–Kosovo Agreement. This, however, is subject to a lengthy list of SAA provisions which do not apply. It is provided in the Annexes forming an integral part of the PTCA. They merit a closer look at this stage of the analysis.

The opening provision of the EU–Kosovo SAA defines the aims of association. For the purposes of the PTCA, Article 1 is incorporated, *sans* reference to the 'approximation' of Kosovar law with the EU *acquis*. At the same time, the parties opted not to roll-over Article 2 EU–Kosovo SAA, which codifies a legal fiction that the conclusion of the SAA does not amount to recognition by the EU of Kosovo as an independent country.[83] Arguably, for UK–Kosovo relations it remains a non-issue as the UK was one of the first countries to formally recognise the independence of Kosovo in 2008. The list of other not incorporated, or modified, provisions is rather long and extends to all sections of the SAA. Not surprisingly, this covers references to EU legislation and concepts inextricably linked to EU relations with Kosovo. For instance, Article 74 EU–Kosovo SAA dealing with law approximation has not been rolled over. The same applies to Articles 122–125 EU–Kosovo SAA covering financial cooperation. At the same time, the bilateral institutional structures have been largely kept in place, the main exception being a joint parliamentary committee which has become an optional feature. Furthermore, a reworked Protocol on origin of products has also been inserted as Annex II to the PTCA.

The overall impression is that the UK–Kosovo PTCA is a patchwork built on the EU–Kosovo SAA. A 'short form' agreement was, perhaps, easier to draft but it certainly does not deliver the advantages argued by the UK government. It offers neither clarity, nor transparency.

9.4 Conclusions

In early 2020, after over three years of partisan politics, of the Conservative Party negotiating with itself and of tough negotiations with the EU, the UK left the EU. Thanks to the transitional period laid down in the Withdrawal Agreement, many things remain the same until the end of transition. In legal terms, the UK remains bound by the EU agreements with third countries, and one of the reasons for this interim arrangement is to allow the UK to kick-start its Global Britain project.[84] As mentioned earlier, the UK had already embarked on that journey way before it was formally permitted to do so. However, despite grandiose arguments made by the UK political elite, once again the reality has proven that – as the Italian proverb goes – 'tra il dire e il fare c'è di mezzo il mare' ('between saying and doing, there is an ocean'). The high expectations raised by the referendum debate were downplayed by the government soon after the vote, when the first priority to be identified in the realm of relations with non-EU countries was to attempt a rolling over of the existing EU agreements with selected countries around the world. As elaborated in the present chapter, such a desideratum, at least prima facie, sits rather uncomfortably with the referendum slogans, the permanent criticism of the EU and its actions, as well as with the promised land of milk and honey as the UK 'goes it alone'. The end result is that only a handful of EU agreements has been rolled over in time for the original Brexit date. The negotiations of many more were concluded in the course of three consecutive extensions of UK membership of the EU. The analysis conducted in this chapter demonstrates that while, in statistical terms, the UK has ticked several boxes, many of the rolled-over agreements have been signed with countries which are not, by any stretch of the imagination, leading UK trading partners. Thus, in many cases, the post-Brexit agreements are likely to stay untouched for years. Hence, contrary to the official rhetoric, many agreements will not be the starting, but rather the end point. By copy–pasting EU arrangements with countries in different corners of the planet, the UK has not exactly 'taken back control', which – as is well known – was the Brexiters' slogan parroted ad nauseam. As acutely observed by Simon Jenkins '[a] government that resorts to slogans has lost an argument'.[85] This, although argued in relation to the coronavirus pandemic, equally applies to many aspects of Brexit.

At the same time, it is interesting to look at the rolling-over exercise through the EU's lenses. Its results demonstrate the degree of flexibility that the EU agreements can offer. When stripped down of their EU paraphernalia and idiosyncratic concepts, the agreements in question may be recycled into free trade agreements concluded outside the EU's framework. This also includes the notion of 'association' which, as argued in the present chapter, is primarily an EU law concept. Looking at several post-Brexit agreements concluded between the UK and third countries, this notion is getting a new lease of life (for the right or wrong reasons) and proves that the EU is not only an exporter of its laws but also of forms of cooperation.[86] Last but not least, a true paradox emerges from this exercise. As discussed in the academic literature, the most recent EU trade agreements, including the discussed AAs with Ukraine, Georgia and Moldova, have been deprived of direct effect.[87] This is not only contrary to the jurisprudence of the Court of Justice but also to the logic of upgrading bilateral relations with the EU's closest neighbours.[88] Paradoxically, the post-Brexit agreements, when implemented into the UK legal orders as per the forthcoming Trade Act, may prove to be more enforceable than their prototypes. Arguably, this is just one of many paradoxes that may emerge from the rolling-over exercise. Should the EU and the UK fail to conclude a trade agreement by the end of the transitional period, the UK would have very ambitious free trade agreements with countries with which there is hardly any trade, but it would default to way less advantageous conditions in trade with the EU, its main trading partner. Inevitably, this would trigger a fundamental question: is the game worth the candle?

Notes

1 Department for International Trade, 'Preparing for Our Future UK Trade Policy' (Policy Paper, 2017).

2 David Davis, 'Trade Deals. Tax Cuts. And Taking Time Before Triggering Article 50: A Brexit Economic Strategy for Britain' (Conservative Home, 11 July 2016) www.conservativehome.com/platform/2016/07david-davis-trade-deals-tax-cuts-and-taking-time-before-triggering-article-50-a-brexit-economic-strategy-for-britain.html accessed 20 April 2020. For a comment see Tony Barber, 'Waiting for the Golden Age of Brexit Trade Deals' *Financial Times* (London, 3 March 2020). More examples of such statements bordering between hyper-optimism and detachment from reality in Panos Koutrakos, 'Managing Brexit: Trade Agreements Binding on the UK Pursuant to its EU Membership' in the present volume.

3 See International Trade Committee, 'Continuing Application of EU Trade Agreements after Brexit' (HC 2017–19, 520).

4 As acutely observed by the House of Commons, the initial steps were largely disappointing. See Foreign Affairs Committee, 'Global Britain' (HC 2017–19, 780).

5 Adam Łazowski and Ramses A Wessel, 'The External Dimension of Withdrawal from the European Union' (2016) 4 Revue des Affaires européennes 623; Ramses A Wessel, 'Consequences of Brexit for

International Agreements Concluded by the EU and its Member States' (2018) 55 Common Market Law Review 101.

6 As argued in Adam Łazowski, 'EU Withdrawal: Good Business for British Business?' (2016) 22 European Public Law 115.

7 Yet, fact finding preliminary talks were held with countries all around the world, including Australia, New Zealand, China and the USA.

8 Agreement on the withdrawal of the United Kingdom of Great Britain and Northern Ireland from the European Union and the European Atomic Energy Community [2020] OJ L29/7. See further on the transitional period Michael Dougan, 'An Airbag for the Crash Test Dummies? EU–UK Negotiations for a Post-Withdrawal "Status Quo" Transitional Regime under Article 50 TEU' (2018) 55 Common Market Law Review 57; Adam Łazowski, 'Exercises in Legal Acrobatics: Brexit Transitional Arrangements' (2017) 2 European Papers 845, www.europeanpapers.eu/en/e-journal/exercises-in-legal-acrobatics-brexit-transitional-arrangements accessed 20 April 2020; Kenneth A Armstrong, 'After EU Membership: The United Kingdom in Transition' (2019) European Journal of Legal Studies Special Issue 87, https://ejls.eui.eu/issues/brexit-negotiations-may-government-special-issue/ accessed 20 April 2020.

9 See, inter alia, Free trade agreement between the European Union and its Member States, of the one part, and the Republic of Korea, of the other part [2011] OJ L127/6.

10 Association Agreement between the European Union and the European Atomic Energy Community and its Member States, of the one part, and Ukraine, of the other part [2014] OJ L161/3. See further Michael Emerson and Veronika Movchan (eds), *Deepening EU–Ukrainian Relations: What, Why and How?* (2nd edn, CEPS 2018); Guillaume Van Der Loo, *The EU–Ukraine Association Agreement and Deep and Comprehensive Free Trade Area: A New Legal Instrument for EU Integration Without Membership* (Brill Publishing 2016).

11 Association Agreement between the European Union and the European Atomic Energy Community and their Member States, of the one part, and Georgia, of the other part [2014] OJ L261/4. See further Michael Emerson and Tamara Kovziridze, *Deepening EU–Georgia Relations: What, Why and How?* (2nd edn, CEPS 2018).

12 Association Agreement between the European Union and the European Atomic Energy Community and their Member States, of the one part, and the Republic of Moldova, of the other part [2014] OJ L260/4. See further Michael Emerson and Denis Cenus a, *Deepening EU–Moldovan Relations: What, Why and How?* (2nd edn, CEPS 2018).

13 See, *exempli gratia*, Agreement between the United States of America and the European Community on cooperation in the regulation of civil aviation safety [2011] OJ L 291/3.

14 See, *exempli gratia*, Agreement between the European Atomic Energy Community and the Cabinet of Ministers of Ukraine for Co-operation in the Peaceful Uses of Nuclear Energy [2006] L261/27.

15 See, *exempli gratia*, Agreement between the European Community and the Republic of Albania on the readmission of persons residing without authorisation [2005] OJ L 124/22.

16 See further Koutrakos (n 2).

17 Paul Craig, 'Brexit: A Drama in Six Acts' (2016) 41 European Law Review 447; Paul Craig, 'Brexit, A Drama: The Interregnum' (2017) 36 Yearbook of European Law 3; Paul Craig, 'Brexit a Drama: The Endgame – Part I' (2020) 45 European Law Review 163.

18 As of 31 January 2020, the Post-Brexit agreements have been concluded with: Andean countries (Colombia, Ecuador and Peru); the CARIFORUM trade bloc (Antigua and Barbuda, Barbados, Belize, the Commonwealth of the Bahamas, the Commonwealth of Dominica, the Dominican Republic, Grenada, the Republic of Guyana, Jamaica, Saint Christopher and Nevis, Saint Lucia, Saint Vincent and the Grenadines, the Republic of Trinidad and Tobago); Central America (Costa Rica, El Salvador, Guatemala, Honduras, Nicaragua, Panama); Chile; Eastern and Southern Africa (ESA) trade bloc (Madagascar, Mauritius, Seychelles, Zimbabwe); Faroe Islands; Georgia; Iceland and Norway; Israel; Jordan; Kosovo; Lebanon; Liechtenstein; Morocco; Pacific states (Fiji, Papua New Guinea); Palestinian Authority; South Korea; Southern Africa Customs Union and Mozambique (SACUM) trade bloc (Botswana, Eswatini, Lesotho, Namibia, South Africa, Mozambique); Switzerland; Tunisia. At the time of Brexit, the negotiations were pending with: Albania; Algeria; Bosnia and Herzegovina; Cameroon; Canada; Côte d'Ivoire; East African Community (Burundi, Kenya, Rwanda, South Sudan, Tanzania, Uganda); Egypt; Ghana; Mexico; Moldova; Montenegro; North Macedonia; Serbia; Singapore; Ukraine.

19 Foreign and Commonwealth Office, 'Free Trade Agreement between the United Kingdom of Great Britain and Northern Ireland and the Republic of Korea' (CP 167, 2019).

20 Department for International Trade, 'Continuing the United Kingdom's Trade Relationship with the Republic of Korea' (2019) 9.
21 Foreign and Commonwealth Office, Economic Partnership Agreement between the Southern African Customs Union Member States and Mozambique, of the one part, and the United Kingdom of Great Britain and Northern Ireland, of the other part (CP 192, 2019).
22 Department for International Trade, 'Continuing the United Kingdom's Trade Relationship with the Southern African Customs Union Member States and Mozambique' (2019).
23 Foreign and Commonwealth Office, Trade and Partnership Agreement between the Government of the United Kingdom of Great Britain and Northern Ireland and the Government of the State of Israel (CP 59, 2019).
24 Department for International Trade, 'Continuing the United Kingdom's Trade Relationship with Israel' (2019) 9.
25 Foreign and Commonwealth Office, Strategic Partnership and Cooperation Agreement between the United Kingdom of Great Britain and Northern Ireland and Georgia (CP 196, 2019).
26 Department for International Trade, 'Continuing the United Kingdom's Trade Relationship with Georgia' (2019) 9.
27 Department for International Trade, 'Continuing the United Kingdom's Trade Relationship with the Faroe Islands' (2019) 7.
28 Foreign and Commonwealth Office, Free Trade Agreement between the United Kingdom of Great Britain and Northern Ireland and the Kingdom of Denmark in respect of the Faroe Islands (CP 32, 2019).
29 Details available at www.gov.uk/guidance/uk-trade-agreements-with-non-eu-countries#trade-agreements-from-1-january-2021 accessed 20 April 2020.
30 Free trade Agreement between the European Union and the Republic of Singapore [2019] OJ L294/3.
31 Comprehensive Economic and Trade Agreement (CETA) between Canada, of the one part, and the European Union and its Member States, of the other part [2017] OJ L11/23.
32 Agreement between the European Union and Japan for an Economic Partnership [2018] OJ L 330/3.
33 Agreement creating an association between the European Economic Community and Turkey [1964] OJ 217/3687.
34 See, inter alia, Department for International Trade, 'UK–US Free Trade Agreement' (2020).
35 Partnership and Cooperation Agreements were concluded with selected former countries of the Soviet Union. Many of them remain in force. See, inter alia, Agreement on partnership and cooperation establishing a partnership between the European Communities and their Member States, of one part, and the Russian Federation, of the other part [1997] OJ L327/3; Partnership and Cooperation Agreement between the European Communities and their Member States, of the one part, and the Republic of Azerbaijan, of the other part [1999] OJ L246/3.
36 For an academic appraisal see, inter alia, Christian Riffel, 'Squaring the Circle: High-Quality, Deep FTAs with Australia and New Zealand Without the EU Member States' approval?' (2019) 44 European Law Review 694.
37 See further, inter alia, Freya Baetens, '"No Deal is Better than a Bad Deal"? The Fallacy of the WTO Fall-Back Option as a Post-Brexit Safety Net' (2019) 2 Common Market Law Review 133.
38 Department for International Trade, 'Continuing the United Kingdom's Trade Relationship with Morocco' (2019) 7.
39 See, for instance, Department for International Trade, 'Continuing the United Kingdom's Trade Relationship with Lebanon' (2019) 7; Department for International Trade, 'Continuing the United Kingdom's Trade Relationship with the Swiss Confederation' (2019) 7; Department for International Trade, 'Continuing the United Kingdom's Trade Relationship with Tunisia' (2019) 7.
40 For a comprehensive overview see, inter alia, Roman Petrov, *Exporting the Acquis Communautaire through European Union External Agreements* (Nomos Verlag 2011); Roman Petrov and Peter Van Elsuwege (eds), *The Application of EU Law in the Eastern Neighbourhood of the European Union: Towards a Common Regulatory Space?* (Routledge 2013).
41 Foreign and Commonwealth Office, Economic Partnership Agreement between the CARIFORUM States, of the one part, and the United Kingdom of Great Britain and Northern Ireland, of the other part (CP 103, 2019).
42 Foreign and Commonwealth Office, Agreement establishing an Economic Partnership Agreement between the Eastern and Southern Africa States and the United Kingdom of Great Britain and Northern Ireland (CP 31, 2019).

43 Foreign and Commonwealth Office, Strategic Partnership and Cooperation Agreement between the United Kingdom of Great Britain and Northern Ireland and Georgia (CP 196, 2019).
44 Foreign and Commonwealth Office, Interim Economic Partnership Agreement between the United Kingdom of Great Britain and Northern Ireland, of the one part, and the Pacific States, of the other part (CP 76, 2019).
45 Foreign and Commonwealth Office, Free Trade Agreement, between the United Kingdom of Great Britain and Northern Ireland and the Republic of Korea (CP 167, 2019).
46 Foreign and Commonwealth Office, Economic Partnership Agreement between the Southern African Customs Union Member States and Mozambique, of the one part, and the United Kingdom of Great Britain and Northern Ireland, of the other part (CP 193, 2019).
47 See further on the EU free trade agenda Billy A Melo Araujo, *The EU Deep Trade Agenda: Law and Policy* (Oxford University Press 2016).
48 Foreign and Commonwealth Office, Interim Economic Partnership Agreement between the United Kingdom of Great Britain and Northern Ireland, of the one part, and the Pacific States, of the other part (CP 76, 2019).
49 See, *exempli gratia*, Annex I, pt 3(d) of UK–Morocco Agreement (Foreign and Commonwealth Office, Agreement establishing an Association between the United Kingdom of Great Britain and Northern Ireland and the Kingdom of Morocco (CP 202, 2019).
50 See further, inter alia, see David Phinnemore, *Association: Stepping-Stone or Alternative to EU Membership?* (Sheffield Academic Press 1999); Henry G Schermers and Niels M Blokker, *International Institutional Law* (6th edn, Brill Nijhoff 2018) 135–137.
51 Foreign and Commonwealth Office, Agreement establishing an Association between the United Kingdom of Great Britain and Northern Ireland and the Hashemite Kingdom of Jordan (CP 204, 2019).
52 Foreign and Commonwealth Office, Agreement establishing an Association between the United Kingdom of Great Britain and Northern Ireland and the Republic of Lebanon (CP 183, 2019).
53 Foreign and Commonwealth Office, Agreement establishing an Association between the United Kingdom of Great Britain and Northern Ireland and the Kingdom of Morocco (CP 202, 2019).
54 Foreign and Commonwealth Office, Agreement Establishing an Association between the United Kingdom of Great Britain and Northern Ireland and Central America (CP 128, 2019).
55 Foreign and Commonwealth Office, Agreement establishing an Association between the United Kingdom of Great Britain and Northern Ireland and the Republic of Chile (CP 35, 2019).
56 The notion of 'association' is also employed in some other rolled-over agreements. See, for instance, Article 1(3) of UK–Kosovo Agreement (Foreign and Commonwealth Office, Partnership, Trade and Cooperation Agreement between the United Kingdom of Great Britain and Northern Ireland and the Republic of Kosovo (CP 201, 2019)).
57 See further, inter alia, Adam Łazowski 'Enhanced Bilateralism and Multilateralism: Integration without Membership' (2008) 45 Common Market Law Review 1433.
58 Foreign and Commonwealth Office, Agreement between the United Kingdom of Great Britain and Northern Ireland, Iceland and the Kingdom of Norway on Trade in Goods (CP 89, 2019).
59 Agreement on arrangements between Iceland, the Principality of Liechtenstein, the Kingdom of Norway and the United Kingdom of Great Britain and Northern Ireland following the withdrawal of the United Kingdom from the European Union, the EEA Agreement and other agreements applicable between the United Kingdom and the EEA EFTA States by virtue of the United Kingdom's membership of the European Union, www.efta.int/sites/default/files/documents/eea/eea/legal-texts/2020_01_28_UK-EEA-EFTA_separation_agreement.pdf.pdf accessed 20 April 2020. On exit from the EEA see further Ulrich Shroeter and Heinrich Nemeczek, 'The (Unclear) Impact of Brexit on the United Kingdom's Membership in the European Economic Area' (2016) 27 European Business Law Review 921; Dóra Sif Tynes and Elisabeth Lian Haugsdal, 'In, Out or In-Between? The UK as a Contracting Party to the Agreement on the European Economic Area' (2016) 41 European Law Review 753; Ch. Hillion, 'Brexit means Br(EEA)xit: The UK Withdrawal from the EU and its Implications for the EEA' (2018) 55 Common Market Law Review 135; Ch. Hillion, 'Commentary to Article 127 [Withdrawal from the EEA Agreement]' in Finn Arnesen, Halvard Haukeland Fredriksen, Hans Petter Graver, Ola Mestad and Christoph Vedder (eds), *Agreement on The European Economic Area: A Commentary* (CH Beck, Hart Publishing, Nomos Verlag 2018).
60 See further, inter alia, Sabine Jenni, *Switzerland's Differentiated European Integration: The Last Gallic Village?* (Palgrave Macmillan 2016); Matthias Oesch, *Switzerland and the European Union: General*

Framework. Bilateral Agreements. Autonomous Adaptation (Nomos 2018). See also Frank Emmert, 'Switzerland and the EU: Partners, for Better or for Worse' (1998) 3 European Foreign Affairs Review 367; Laurent Goetschel, 'Switzerland and European Integration: Change Through Distance' (2003) 8 European Foreign Affairs Review 313; Adam Łazowski, 'Switzerland' in Steven Blockmans and Adam Łazowski (eds), *The European Union and Its Neighbours: A Legal Appraisal of the EU's Policies of Stabilisation, Partnership and Integration* (TMC Asser Press 2006) 147.

61 Agreement between the European Economic Community and the Swiss Confederation [1972] OJ L300/191. See further, inter alia, Edmund Wellenstein, 'The Free Trade Agreements between the Enlarged European Communities and the EFTA Countries', (1973) 10 Common Market Law Review 137.

62 Agreement between the European Community and its Member States, of the one part, and the Swiss Confederation, of the other, on the free movement of persons [2002] OJ L114/6. See further on Bilateral I package, inter alia, Stephan Breitenmoser, 'Sectoral Agreements Between the EC and Switzerland: Contents and Context' (2003) 40 Common Market Law Review 1137.

63 Agreement between the European Union, the European Community and the Swiss Confederation on the Swiss Confederation's association with the implementation, application and development of the Schengen acquis [2008] OJ L53/52. See further Łazowski (n 60) 169–173.

64 It incorporates the following elements of the EU–Swiss framework: Agreement in the form of an Exchange of Letters of 21 July 1972 between the Swiss Confederation and the European Economic Community concerning certain agricultural and fishery products (as amended); Agreement between the European Economic Community and the Swiss Confederation [1972] OJ L300/191; Agreement between the European Community and the Swiss Confederation on trade in agricultural products [2002] OJ L114/132; Agreement between the European Community and the Swiss Confederation on mutual recognition in relation to conformity assessment [2002] OJ L114/369; Agreement between the European Community and the Swiss Confederation on certain aspects of government procurement [2002] OJ L114/430; Cooperation Agreement between the European Community and its Member States, of the one part, and the Swiss Confederation, of the other part, to combat fraud and any other illegal activity to the detriment of their financial interests [2009] L46/8; Agreement between the European Community and the Swiss Confederation on the simplification of inspections and formalities in respect of the carriage of goods and on customs security measures [2009] L199/24; Agreement in the form of an Exchange of Letters between the Community and each of the EFTA countries that grants tariff preferences under the GSP (Norway and Switzerland), providing that goods originating in Norway or Switzerland shall be treated on their arrival on the customs territory of the Community as goods with content of Community origin [2001] L38/25.

65 Text available at https://assets.publishing.service.gov.uk/government/uploads/system/uploads/attachment_data/file/803719/memorandum-of-understanding-between-the-uk-and-switzerland.pdf accessed 20 April 2020.

66 See further, inter alia, Richard G Whitman and Stefan Wolff (eds), *The European Neighbourhood Policy in Perspective: Context, Implementation and Impact* (Palgrave Macmillan 2010). For a critical appraisal see Steven Blockmans, *The Obsolescence of the European Neighbourhood Policy* (Rowman & Littlefield International 2017).

67 See further Emerson and Kovziridze (n 11).

68 Wardrop Strategic Dialogue is a political platform for UK–Georgia relations named after Sir Oliver Wardrop, who was a well-known and respected aficionado of Georgia, its language and culture. In 1919–1920 he served as the UK's first Chief Commissioner of the Transcaucasus in Tbilisi. Sir Oliver Wardrop wrote an English–Svanetian dictionary, Svanetian being a distinct language using the Georgian script (Oliver Wardrop 'English–Svanetian Dictionary' (1911) XVI Journal of the Royal Asiatic Society 589). His sister, Marjory, translated a famous Georgian medieval epic (*The Knight in the Panther's Skin*), which was written by the Georgian national poet Shota Rustaveli. For his observations about Georgia see Sir Oliver Wardrop, *The Kingdom of Georgia: Travel in a Land of Women, Wine and Song* (reprint, Luzac & Company Ltd 1977).

69 See further on the notion of legal transplants Helen Xanthaki, 'Legal Transplants in Legislation: Defusing the Trap' (2008) 57 International & Comparative Law Quarterly 659; Beata Kviatek, *Explaining Legal Transplants: Transplantation of EU Law into Central and Eastern Europe* (Wolf Publishers 2015).

70 Article 5(3) SPCA is noteworthy as it explicitly mentions the cooperation between the parties in reforms of the Georgian defence and security sectors. The provision in question openly refers to ambition of authorities in Tbilisi to join NATO.

71 It is notable that following the methodology employed by the EU in its external relations, air transport will be covered by a separate agreement (see Article 120 SPCA).

72 This includes, inter alia, Article 47 AA (approximation with technical regulations), Article 55 AA (gradual with sanitary and phytosanitary, animal welfare and other legislative measures), Article 75 AA (approximation with customs *acquis*), Article 103 AA (gradual approximation with services legislation), Article 113 AA (approximation with *acquis* on electronic communication), Article 122 AA (approximation in the area of financial services), Article 126 AA (approximation with transport legislation), Articles 141 (2), 145–146 AA (approximation with EU public procurement legislation), Articles 417–419 AA (dynamic approximation).

73 Regulation (EU) 2016/679 of the European Parliament and of the Council on the protection of natural persons with regard to the processing of personal data and on the free movement of such data, and repealing Directive 95/46/EC (General Data Protection Regulation) [2016] OJ L119/1. See further, *inter alia*, Christopher Kuner, Lee A Bygrave, Christopher Docksey and Laura Drechsler (eds), *The EU General Data Protection Regulation (GDPR): A Commentary* (Oxford University Press 2020).

74 Recommendation of the Committee of Ministers to Member States on good administration, CM/Rec(2007)7 of 20 June 2007. See further, inter alia, Jill Wakefield, *The Right to Good Administration* (Kluwer 2007).

75 The provision in question merely provides that SPCA does not restrict possibilities for cooperation between the UK and Georgian parliaments.

76 It is a copy–paste of Article 241 AA.

77 Not surprisingly Article 267 AA, which envisages the jurisdiction of the arbitration panel to send references for preliminary ruling to the Court of Justice has been committed in the Strategic Partnership and Cooperation Agreement.

78 'Article 227. Upholding levels of protection.

1 The Parties recognise that it is inappropriate to encourage trade or investment by lowering the levels of protection afforded in domestic environmental or labour law.
2 A Party shall not waive or derogate from, or offer to waive or derogate from, its environmental or labour law as an encouragement for trade or the establishment, the acquisition, the expansion or the retention of an investment of an investor in its territory.
3 A Party shall not, through a sustained or recurring course of action or inaction, fail to effectively enforce its environmental and labour law, as an encouragement for trade or investment.'

79 See further, inter alia, Adam Cygan 'De-Europeanisation of UK Regulatory Governance and the Future UK–EU Trade Relationship' (2020) 20 ERA Forum 509, 519–524.

80 Stabilisation and Association Agreement between the European Union and the European Atomic Energy Community, of the one part, and Kosovo, of the other part [2016] OJ L71/3. See further Peter Van Elsuwege, 'Legal Creativity in EU External Relations: The Stabilization and Association Agreement Between the EU and Kosovo' (2017) 22 European Foreign Affairs Review 393.

81 Stabilization and Association Agreement between the European Communities and their Member States, of the one part, and the Former Yugoslav Republic of Macedonia, of the other part OJ 2004 L84/1; Stabilization and Association Agreement between the European Communities and their Member States, of the one part, and the Republic of Albania, of the other part OJ 2009 L107/116; Stabilization and Association Agreement between the European Communities and their Member States, of the one part, and the Republic of Montenegro, of the other part OJ 2010 L108/3; Stabilization and Association Agreement between the European Communities and their Member States, of the one part, and the Republic of Serbia, of the other part OJ 2013 L278/14; Stabilisation and Association Agreement between the European Communities and their Member States, of the one part, and Bosnia and Herzegovina, of the other part, OJ 2015 L 164/2. See further on this family of association agreements, *inter alia*, David Phinnemore, 'Stabilisation and Association Agreements: Europe Agreements for the Western Balkans?' (2003) 8 European Foreign Affairs Review 77.

82 Foreign and Commonwealth Office, 'Continuing the United Kingdom' Trade Relationship with the Republic of Kosovo' (2019) 10.

83 It does not sit comfortably with the concept of de facto recognition, known from public international law. See further, inter alia, James Crawford, *The Creation of States in International Law* (2nd edn, Oxford University Press 2005).

84 See Article 129 EU–UK Withdrawal Agreement. See further Marise Cremona, 'The Withdrawal Agreement and the EU's International Agreements' (2020) 45 European Law Review 237, 246–249.

85 Simon Jenkins, 'No One is in Charge of the UK's Coronavirus Response: And It Shows' *Guardian* (London, 20 April 2020).

86 I am grateful to Professor Ramses Wessel for drawing my attention to this phenomenon.

87 See, inter alia, Narine Ghazaryan, 'Who are the "Gatekeepers"?: In Continuation of the Debate on the Direct Applicability and the Direct Effect of EU International Agreements' (2018) 37 Yearbook of European Law 27.

88 As per judgment of the Court of Justice in case *Simutenkov*, the Partnership and Cooperation Agreements with former Soviet Union countries could produce direct effect. This, however, is excluded in the case of the new generation of Association Agreements with Ukraine, Georgia and Moldova, which were supposed to upgrade bilateral relations. See further Case C-265/03 *Igor Simutenkov v Ministerio de Educación y Cultura and Real Federación Española de Fútbol* EU:C:2005:213.

Part III

International organizations and EU diplomacy after Brexit

10

EU–UK relations at the WTO

Towards constructive creative competition

Gregory Messenger

10.1 Introduction

The World Trade Organization (WTO) is the principal international organization covering global trade.[1] The WTO both incorporated and replaced its predecessor the General Agreement on Tariffs and Trade (GATT) which had been intended to constitute one part of a larger International Trade Organization that was negotiated during Bretton Woods but did not enter into force.[2] As a consequence, the GATT was provisionally applied from 1947 to 1994 during which an ad hoc institutional apparatus developed.[3] This also meant that the GATT's relationship with its contracting parties tracked the European Union's (and its predecessors') development into a confident and pre-eminent actor on the global trade stage. Today, the WTO provides a forum for trade negotiations, an institutional framework to oversee the operation of binding treaty commitments, and settles disputes. It covers trade in goods, services, and intellectual property – and in all these areas, the EU is an active voice.

Membership of the WTO is open to states and 'separate customs territory possessing full autonomy in the conduct of its external commercial relations'.[4] It is on this basis that the EU has been an independent member of the WTO since its creation in 1995.[5] As part of the common commercial policy (CCP), trade policy falls under exclusive EU competence, and as such it represents its Member States.[6] While the EU and each Member State hold votes, when voting the EU holds the number of votes equal to the number of Member States that are WTO members.[7] In practice this point is moot, as voting is largely unheard of within the WTO which has continued the GATT-era practice of decision-making by consensus.[8] The unusual nature of EU membership at the WTO has had two important consequences for determining future relations between the EU and the UK.

The first is in representation: in the early days, Member States represented their own interests in certain non-exclusive fields of activity such as areas of intellectual property or the territorial scope of their obligations as regards overseas territories.[9] Over the years, the scope of the CCP expanded, for example, recently with *Opinion 2/15* whereby a wide range of issues covered under trade agreements (goods, services, sustainable development elements of trade, elements of investment) now fall under the CCP and, therefore, the exclusive competence of the Union.[10] As such, while Member States may attend certain meetings in Geneva, in practice it is the Commission that represents EU interests at the WTO, a brief it guards aggressively.[11] Trade is a (if not *the*) core competence for the EU, bringing it to the very centre of EU external policy. The Commission (and in particular, DG Trade) has developed a high-quality cadre of officials, prioritising trade policy as the most effective tool of its wider foreign policy objectives. In parallel, in the run up and subsequent to the referendum in 2016, the UK has stressed that a priority for UK policy is pursuing an independent trade policy to create opportunities for British business and citizens.[12] Quite apart from the economic interrelationship between the UK and EU, the primacy of trade policy as part of the external/foreign affairs priorities of both makes it a key nexus for relations between the two.

Second, as an institution bound by its legal bases, the EU's ability to represent trade policy at the WTO is tied to its ability to accept legal obligations under WTO law. Thus, disaggregating intertwined legal obligations at the WTO presents challenges. For example, commitments made by the EU under its GATT schedules which set out the ceiling for tariffs and tariff rate quotas (TRQs) create – for the EU as a whole – challenges at the WTO vis-à-vis third parties.[13]

As a consequence of the close legal relations between the parties in terms of trade law and the primacy they both place on trade policy, their relationship at the WTO will be one of the defining features of UK–EU relations for the foreseeable future.

This chapter proceeds as follows: section 10.2 sets out the current status of UK–EU relations at the WTO, providing an analysis of the key features of legal challenges faced by both sides relating to UK withdrawal; section 10.3 identifies the key areas of potential tension for the UK and EU in relation to each other at the WTO but also vis-à-vis third parties who could be affected by the consequences of cross-Channel relations; section 10.4 concludes, drawing on the lessons of the experience of UK–EU relations at the WTO thus far and the nature of the future legal challenges, positing a new dynamic built on constructive creative competition.

10.2 The story so far

With the UK's withdrawal from the EU, the two parties have had to come to an agreement over how to disaggregate their respective rights and duties at the WTO. This process, largely complete, marks the first stage of the UK's 'return' to the WTO and the initiation of a new working relationship between the EU and the UK in Geneva.

The challenge of disentangling the UK and the EU's legal obligations at the WTO has been considerable. Nonetheless, the two parties have now (largely) completed the process of UK withdrawal at the WTO. The three core challenges have related to the acceptance of the UK and EU's schedules, the UK's accession to the Government Procurement Agreement (GPA), and confirming the status of UK representation at the WTO during the transition period.[14]

10.2.1 Schedules

All WTO members must maintain a schedule of commitments for goods and services. Their goods schedules, legally binding commitments under the GATT, set out specific commitments at a product level. The schedules include a member's bound tariff rates for goods. This acts as a cap – the highest level at which members are able to set tariffs (absent an exception such as the imposition of a trade remedy).[15] They also include details regarding TRQs (commonly in agricultural trade).[16] Members' schedules form the backbone of the specific commitments for WTO members, with other commitments being general – that is, the same obligations applying to all members equally, such as national treatment or most-favoured nation.[17]

Services schedules, under the General Agreement on Trade in Services (GATS) are 'lighter' in the sense that while the GATT covers all goods, the GATS only covers non-governmental services where members have made specific commitments (with the exception of limited cross-cutting obligations such as most-favoured nation).[18] These commitments set out the sector under which a member choses to liberalise. It also determines the extent of that liberalisation, including by how the service is provided (its 'mode'). For example, a member may choose to fully liberalise its hotel sector to investment from foreign service providers ('mode 3' – commercial presence). It may limit this by numbers of actors if it wishes (e.g. ten service suppliers), and may also limit other elements of the hotel service sector, for example, refusing to make any commitments for the temporary presence of natural persons such as waiters or cooks ('mode 4').[19]

In the case of both goods and services, the UK was previously covered by the EU's schedules as an EU Member State. As an independent WTO member, the UK now requires its own schedules. In keeping with its overarching policy objective of security continuity of membership vis-à-vis third parties, the UK mostly replicated the existing goods and services schedules as they applied to it. Members were provided with the UK draft schedules in July and December 2018 for goods and services respectively.[20] With the exception of issues arising from the apportionment of TRQs, this technical work is now largely completed and UK commitments are to enter into force at the end of the transition period.[21]

10.2.2 EU only agreements and commitments

While the EU is a member of the WTO alongside its Member States, there have been WTO agreements concluded since 1995 that have been concluded as EU-only (i.e. not mixed) agreements. The GPA is one such example. The GPA is a plurilateral agreement, meaning that it is not a necessary commitment for WTO members unlike, for example, the GATT or the Dispute Settlement Understanding.[22] Under the GPA, the parties to it agree to offer reciprocal access to their government procurement markets. The value of government procurement is considerable[23] and by offering non-discriminatory access to these markets, members encourage the development of cross-border procurement.[24]

By acceding to the GPA not as a mixed agreement but instead as an EU-only agreement, the UK could not maintain its membership as it has done at the WTO more widely. As a consequence, the UK has had to negotiate accession to the GPA, due to enter into force at the end of the transition period.[25] This necessarily involved detailed negotiations with a range of WTO members, and successfully amending the UK's documentation to reflect Australia's accession also, all of which the UK has managed deftly (somewhat counter to the customary narrative of the UK as a trade ingénue). There are other agreements which also fell under this category of WTO commitment: the Trade Facilitation Agreement, the Protocol Amending the TRIPS Agreement, the 2015 Protocol to the Agreement on Trade in Civil Aircraft, the Ministerial Declaration on Trade in Information Technology Products, and the Ministerial Declaration on the Expansion of Trade in Information Technology Products. In all of these cases the UK has confirmed its continued acceptance of these commitments and declarations at the end of the transition period.[26]

10.2.3 Representation

During the transition period, the UK remains covered by the EU's schedules and commitments at the WTO. The UK is also, via the EU, subject to a series of legal disputes.[27] On expiry of the transition period, it will be for the UK to represent itself in raising and responding to disputes directly.

Nonetheless, the UK has been an active participant at the WTO in the meantime. In some instances, this has focused on expressing interest and political will in supporting broad policy objectives, such as promoting the place of smaller members in the WTO system and the development opportunities of trade. In others it has been more specific, contributing to debates over pressing issues such as the current challenges facing WTO rules on the regulation of industrial subsidies and the weak response to forced technological transfers.[28]

The UK has also been involved in important 'leg-work' – the core role of members at the WTO contributing to the effective functioning of the WTO system. In the UK's case, this has already entailed the chairing of the Committee on Regional Trade Agreements, chairing the accession working party for the Bahamas, and, particularly since the UK's withdrawal from the EU, active engagement in the Committee on Trade and Development supporting 'aid for trade' and working with the 'Joint Statement Initiatives' on e-commerce and domestic regulation.[29] Otherwise seemingly simple, though for the UK new, procedures have also begun in earnest, such as lodging its first notifications to the Committee on Technical Barriers to Trade.[30]

While early in 2016 there was a discussion as to the extent of the UK's 'independent' voice at the WTO during the transition period and the extent to which *any* expression of independent views undermined the duty of sincere cooperation, what has emerged is instead a far more pragmatic approach where the two parties are acting independently but closely in areas of mutual importance and relevance such as disputes.[31] This is not to say that there will be no challenges, the next section examines some of the possible bumps in the road, but what it does show is that doctrinaire exigencies of either EU law or sovereigntists' fantasies do not withstand the practical work that must be done in the trade sphere.

10.3 Life at the WTO

The technical process of adjusting the schedules of the UK and EU and the preparation of the accession of the UK to the GPA demonstrate how the two parties are clearly capable of working successfully and constructively with each other. As the UK exits the transition period, the EU and UK will have to work together in matters of shared interest at the WTO, as well as respond to the outstanding legacies of their decades' legal relationship.

10.3.1 EU and UK relations with third countries

The UK has made it clear that it will use its independent trade policy to pursue not only new free trade agreements (FTAs) with partners but also to support the work of the WTO.[32] In this regard, the UK, which has long been an advocate of the rules-based international order, has made clear its desire to support institutional reform at the WTO, contribute to the fisheries subsidies talks and wider environmental agenda, as well as drive an important new liberalisation agenda in e-commerce, small and medium enterprises (SMEs), domestic regulation, and climate and trade.[33] These are issues which, at a general level, the EU is well-disposed to also. In this sense, the UK's relations with other WTO members are not likely to be of particular concern for the EU outside conflicting objectives that may arise from policy drift between the two. Subsequent FTA policy may well raise issues for the two, though this will be most keenly felt in their bilateral relationship.[34]

The withdrawal of the UK from the EU does, however, leave some possible extant challenges for the UK and EU at the WTO. The three key outstanding questions relate to the division of TRQs, the application of trade defence instruments, and the application of the Northern Ireland Protocol under the Withdrawal Agreement.

10.3.1.1 Tariff rate quotas

The first are the outstanding challenges to the UK and EU schedules at the WTO. While these are formally two separate issues, in fact they are intertwined.

The principal issue relates to the calculation of the UK's TRQs.[35] Under a TRQ, a member sets a graded tariff rate linked to quantitative criteria. For example, country X has a TRQ for chicken cuts whereby the first 5000 tons enter tariff free, thereafter the next 20,000 tons are subject to a 10 per cent ad valorem tariff, and imports entering after the 25,000 tons are subject to a 70 per cent tariff. These commitments are made legally binding by virtue of the member's schedules. The ordinary management of TRQs is complex: some are used on a first-come-first-served basis; some on historical patterns of trade (i.e. Y has exported 80 per cent of chicken to X for the past seven years and is allocated 80 per cent of the quotas on this basis); some are allocated to specific members (so-called CSQs, 'county specific quotas'); and others use a combination of all of these.

With the UK leaving the EU, the pre-existing EU-wide TRQs will be divided between the two (through a process of apportionment). This is a technical process taking export/import data over a period of years to calculate the most accurate picture of current trade that can then be used to ensure that the final situation does not negatively affect trading partners. Three challenges arise on this basis: first relating to level of commitments, second the adequacy of the data, and third the value of flexibilities.

With regard to the first (the level of commitments made to members), the EU is in a difficult position. WTO members' commitments can be adjusted upwards where they find their existing schedules unpalatable.[36] As it involves offering 'less' in one area, this process customarily entails offering additional concessions to affected members in other tariff lines by way of compensatory adjustment.[37] However, the EU is not offering substantive compensation to its trading partners, as it does not consider that it is required to offer the same level of market access as the EU27 as it did as the EU28 (not least given the size of the UK economy). This position has elicited harsh criticism in Geneva at the Council for Trade in Goods for seeking to reduce its 'offer'. For some members (most vocally, New Zealand and Brazil) this is unacceptable:

> One major concern for Brazil was the lack of any indication by the EU of proper compensatory adjustments. As New Zealand had pointed out, the EU intended to compensate Members through recourse to concessions to be taken up by a distinct Member, the United Kingdom. In Brazil's view, it was only fair to wonder what the legal basis for such a heterodox methodology might be.[38]

For the UK, its offer is based on the calculation of the appropriate division of TRQs between the EU and UK on the basis of historical data. Thus, the UK's position is open to criticism on the basis of the data (and, as we shall see, how the value of a concession is calculated). It is not open to the same criticism of the EU: that it is seeking to reduce its bound commitments without compensating affected parties. Unsurprisingly, from the EU's perspective to do so would give complaining members two bites of the apple: compensation for reduced access to the EU market and equivalent access to the UK as well.

Complicating matters is also the adequacy of the data provided as a basis for decision-making. As an advanced group of economies, the EU has access to high quality data on trade flows. However, the demands placed by the division of TRQs is somewhat distinct, as it requires specific data at a product-by-product level including the quota usage for each.[39] For some of these exporters, in particular in developing countries, their ability to provide comprehensive alternative data may be limited. And for those that are able to – they may find their data does not match, and in any event, consider that it is for the EU and UK to provide this information. As a result, while the calculation of new TRQs is a 'technical' exercise, some WTO members (including Brazil, New Zealand, and Russia) still consider that they are unfairly prejudiced by this process, with Brazil describing the data presented by the EU as 'insufficient and inadequate'.[40]

Such concerns are exacerbated by the size of the EU agricultural market: Argentina, Australia, Bolivia, Brazil, Canada, Chile, China, Guatemala, El Salvador, Honduras, Japan, Malaysia, Mexico, New Zealand, Singapore, the United States, and Uruguay have all signalled the 'systemic' importance of the apportionment of EU TRQs between the EU and the UK given the size of the EU agricultural market, constituting (in the words of the New Zealand representative) 'probably the largest modification of commitments ever undertaken at the WTO'.[41]

It is worth noting that, even where such concerns rise to the level of formal dispute after the mandated consultation and negotiation phases, remedies at the WTO take the form of 'suspension of concessions' – in nearly all cases the increase in tariffs on goods from the wrongful member to the wronged member – and are capped at the level of 'nullification or impairment'.[42] In this instance, were the complaining member to win – the countermeasures would be limited to the value of the missing benefit from the TRQ division.[43]

The third concern, relating to flexibility, is more difficult to quantify. Take the example of a member which has exported to the EU but principally to the UK *within* the EU, it is most interested in its access to in-quota rates for the UK. Assuming the technical process of dividing TRQs has been conducted properly and represents an accurate division of benefits: how are the benefits of a TRQ to be assessed? In the case of New Zealand's claims we note that it is not only the value of the TRQ that is of interest – it is also the benefit that New Zealand products enjoy where they are able to change direction, comparatively late in the day, to specific Member States within the EU when exporting. Whereas they were previously able to target exports to the UK or, for example, the Netherlands, depending on conditions under the same quota regime, they are now required to choose in advance. The benefit in this instance is considered especially relevant for Members given the uncertainty over the future UK–EU trading agreement: 'The flexibility currently available to Members to supply the UK or continental markets would be affected at exactly the time when uncertainty over future trading conditions would make that flexibility more valuable than ever.'[44]

10.3.1.2 Trade remedies

The second key challenge relates to the use of trade defence instruments (TDIs – also known as trade remedies). Under WTO law, members are entitled to introduce trade remedies that would otherwise violate their obligations under their schedules in three specific cases: to counteract certain types of subsidy through the use of countervailing duties (CVDs) which are intended to offset the 'harmful' element of the government support; to counteract the effect of 'dumping' (whereby goods are exported below their normal value) through the use of anti-dumping duties (ADs); and safeguard measures which are used to protect domestic industry from unforeseen import surges that would otherwise injure them.[45] Such measures could be misused to provide protection to domestic industry under the cover of a legitimate trade instrument. As such, WTO law requires members to follow a set of procedural and substantive steps to demonstrate that the necessary conditions are met for the introduction of these quasi self-help remedies.[46]

The EU, as many other WTO members, makes frequent use of trade remedies. While the precise requirements vary between TDIs, in all instances – whether safeguards, CVDs, or ADs – the investigating authority (in the case of the EU, the Commission) must identify the industry affected, the extent to which it is suffering injury (or threatened by injury), and the cause. This requires making calculations on the basis of a market. Therefore, safeguard investigations (for example) that were conducted on the basis of the EU plus UK may not have the same outcome as one conducted for the EU absent the UK.

An illustrative example is useful: a hypothetical petition from the ceramics industry for support from the Commission, seeking additional tariffs to be imposed on ceramic products entering the EU. It argues that there has been a sudden surge in imports, that this is the result of unforeseen developments, and that the EU ceramics industry is under threat of injury without temporary protection in the form of a safeguard measure. Let us say that 70 per cent of the ceramics industry at risk that produced the good that is flooding the EU market is based in the UK. Were the UK to be excluded from the investigation (as will happen now), the case to be made that there has been serious injury is harder to make than would be previously. As a consequence, the investigating authorities of the EU and UK (Commission and Trade Remedies Investigations Directorate respectively) need to ensure that existing TDIs that are to apply after the end of the transition period still meet WTO obligations.

For the UK this entails conducting 'transition reviews' of existing EU TDIs. These reviews ascertain whether the UK-only TDI continues to meet the necessary criteria to maintain the formerly EU-wide measure (and thereby protect domestic industry).[47] The UK has examined existing EU-wide TDIs, consulted on whether they should be maintained for the UK, and subsequently set out their review and/or whether they will be withdrawn.[48] Absent a review, there is a risk that either the trade remedy that is needed to protect an industry is removed (thereby potentially harming domestic interests) or that members whose goods are affected by a trade remedy raise a legal claim that the measure has not been subject to the appropriate investigation. It is worth noting that over half of formal legal disputes at the WTO now related to TDIs and (in most instances) challenge the national investigation underpinning the introduction of a trade remedy. It is, therefore, an area of considerable legal risk. While there is no formal provision in the agreements for transition reviews of trade remedies,[49] the approach taken appears to meet the requirements of the relevant agreements (Agreement on Safeguards (AoS), Agreement on Subsidies and Countervailing Measures (ASCM), and Antidumping Agreement (ADA)). It should be noted also that the structure of the WTO disciplines on trade remedies is such that it provides a demanding, but minimalist, framework for determining what members must do to ensure that their TDIs comply with WTO obligations. Some members may add additional steps (for example, a public interest or economic interest requirement to introduce TDIs) – these distinct requirements that do not undermine the core disciplines do not present a legal challenge for the member in question.[50] Whether affected members agree will be a matter more of politics than law – there is little to be lost in challenging new TDIs or having the opportunity to challenge one a second time. This does not mean that there is *necessarily* a strong legal claim to be made.

10.3.1.3 The Northern Ireland Protocol

Perhaps the greatest unknown in terms of the UK–EU relationship and its potential impact on third parties is the operation of the Northern Ireland Protocol under the Withdrawal Agreement. While questions have been raised as to its compliance of the Protocol with WTO law in general terms,[51] in practice it will be only once the detailed application of the scheme is set that any detailed analysis will be able to be presented.[52]

The protocol's provisions set out a superficially clear arrangement: it confirms that Northern Ireland is part of the UK's customs territory (Article 4), will form part of the UK for any future trade agreements the UK may conclude, and is part of the UK's WTO schedules also (Article 5). In order to secure the UK's commitments under the Belfast (Good Friday) Agreement, it also ensures that no infrastructure or checks will be needed at or near the border between the Republic of Ireland and Northern Ireland. Part of the process for doing so entails the application by the UK of certain specific EU rules to Northern Ireland with regard to customs, VAT, electricity, and technical barriers to trade (including those applicable to agri-foods – commonly referred to as sanitary and phytosanitary measures).[53]

To ensure that there are no border restrictions between the Republic of Ireland and Northern Ireland, while at the same time accepting that tariffs are not payable on goods between Northern Ireland and Great Britain (forming a single customs territory), the Protocol provides the outline of a system to square this circle and mitigate the risk of goods entering either the UK or EU market 'via the backdoor'.

The Protocol provides that those goods sent from Great Britain to Northern Ireland that are 'at risk' of entering the EU from Northern Ireland, are subject to the EU tariff (as they are intended for the EU market and thus should be subject to the EU's common external tariff). Similarly, goods entering Northern Ireland from another non-EU state are subject to the UK's tariffs unless the good is at risk of moving into the EU. It will be for the UK/EU Joint Committee to determine the detail of guidance on whether goods are at risk of entering the EU market or not.

While there are other dimensions to the Protocol system, it is in the detail of this determination that questions may arise: it will be necessary for criteria to be clear, and the operation of the scheme to be automatic and transparent to avoid questions arising from the 'uniform, impartial, and reasonable manner' of application of trade regulations.[54] While unlikely, given the unusual nature of the Northern Ireland Protocol and the imaginative solution that it applies to an otherwise intractable issue, one should expect much attention from trading partners on its operation and application. Given the EU and UK's joint interest in supporting Irish relations, insofar as this may present challenges, it will be in common cause rather than as against each other.

10.3.2 Relations with each other

It is unclear how the UK and EU will formalise their trading relations: the nature of their future FTA will, in a large part, determine the contours of their relationship at the WTO. Could a bilateral disagreement bleed over into the multilateral sphere?[55] Might this be a preference of one or both of the parties? This section suggests that in practice the expectation of UK–EU relations at the WTO is of a mutually constructive, though at times competitive, relationship. There is still a wide range of areas where coordination not dispute is likely to be the order of the day for the EU and UK.

First, the UK has incorporated (nearly all of) the EU *acquis* into its legal system under the European Union (Withdrawal) Act 2018.[56] Having been a Member State of the EU for 47 years, its regulatory system is aligned with the EU's and the two parties already share positions on the vast majority of technical barriers to trade, sanitary and phytosanitary measures, and so on. As such, any issues arising from, for example, the application of a technical regulation (that is, a document which lays down product characteristics or their related processes and production methods, including the applicable administrative provisions, with which compliance is mandatory),[57] are likely to be shared by both parties. To place this in context: to date some of the most contentious trade disputes at the WTO have centred on regulatory barriers to trade (for example, over bans on the use of beef hormones, restrictions on the authorisation of genetically modified organisms, labelling for 'dolphin friendly' tuna, or bans on seal fur products).[58]

Second, the UK's continuity of trade programme, whereby a range of prior EU FTAs (including association agreements and economic partnership agreements) were transitioned to UK agreements, did not seek to negotiate entirely different settlements with trading partners.[59] Rather, the UK negotiated with partners on the basis of the pre-existing EU agreement, making alterations only where necessary (for example, where the EU agreement included elements which were EU specific).[60] As a consequence, the UK's first 'independent' trade agreements are largely aligned with EU bilateral trade policy. Clearly, this will diverge over time as views over the most important priorities for FTA policy change in each polity, however, as things *currently* stand, there is an in-built alignment between the UK and EU for relations with the states covered by continuity agreements.

As such, the starting place is that both are in agreement with regard to their WTO obligations – both in regard to others, but also to each other. Indeed, if one steps back to examine the overarching policy priorities of the EU and the UK in trade, they share a similar space. While commentary on the UK–EU relationship has focused on disagreement or divergence, in terms of debates at the WTO, the UK and EU have already identified shared or at least similar interests whether on services liberalisation, commitment to sustainability, importance of disciplines on industrial subsidies, support for SMEs, priority to find agreement on prohibited subsidies that contribute to illegal, unreported and unregulated fishing, and so on.

Finally, the key variable relates to the institutional dynamics of the WTO itself. As a largely decentralised body without a strong executive or administrative arm ('member driven' in the argot), the WTO functions on the basis of a complex network of overlapping coalitions and interest groups. Neither the EU nor the UK are able to achieve their objectives at the WTO alone, and will need to continue to work with other members – and each other – to secure their interests at the multilateral or plurilateral level. Note, the earlier referenced speech of the UK International Trade Secretary at the General Council, specifically identifying the importance of rules on forced technology transfers and industrial subsidies.[61] This is a priority for the United States. It is also a priority for the EU. It is *also* a priority for Japan. Three of the most influential and powerful actors in the trade system – none of which is able to shape rules to counter China's industrial practice without support from each other – and, in practice, the wider membership also. The WTO is a forum for coalition building and alliances: even where they disagree, it seems unlikely and indeed undesirable in this context that either side would take a hostile position at the cost of their overarching multilateral objectives.

10.4 Conclusion

The UK and EU are, in some regards, travelling in different directions in trade. The UK has been clear that it sees developing and pursuing an independent trade policy as a clear benefit of withdrawal from the EU. This necessarily entails the possibility of differing approaches to a range of trade policy issues, substantively or procedurally, and at both the multilateral and bilateral levels.

At the same time, the EU is also reviewing its own trade policy, building on its 'Trade for All Agenda'[62] to a new 'European Green Deal'.[63] It has proposed sharpening its teeth (in part in the face of US hostility to the Appellate Body), creating a Chief Trade Enforcement Officer.[64] This official and their team will be empowered to examine compliance of trade partners and potentially introduce 'rebalancing measures'.[65] Further, increased calls have come from France, Germany, Poland, and Italy to revise EU competition policy, to develop one more supportive of national champions, taking into account global challengers from China and the United States, necessitating reform of EU industrial strategy.[66]

Here we have two large economies, economically intertwined, and potentially pulling in different directions. It is understandable that there is concern that this might spark disagreement. While the development of an independent UK trade policy, alongside changes to EU trade policy (possibly influenced by an internal shift with the departure of the UK) may lead to diverging paths and eventually dispute, we have seen how (at the multilateral level) working relations between the two have been constructive. They have had to work together to complete a legally and politically difficult process, disaggregating their respective commitments at the WTO, and finding an accommodation that both meets their own needs (whether on Northern Ireland or representation) as well as effectively communicating this to the rest of the WTO membership that has less understanding (or at times, interest) in the more arcane challenges that underpin the relationship between the EU and its (former) Member States.

We have also seen how the stated objectives of both the EU and the UK in core challenges facing the WTO are similar: support for the rules-based international system, support for reform of rules on industrial strategy, support for the relationship between trade and sustainable development, and indeed policies that meet the climate challenges of today. Their methods may well differ in the months and years to come, as may their priorities. This is to be expected – and they will no doubt seek to convince each other that their approach is the better one. This form of constructive competition is a hallmark of decision-making in trade policy, and indeed international relations as a whole.[67] In a multipolar global economy absent a dominant hegemon, cooperative competition is the order of the day.

Notes

1 By its own admission. See WTO, 'What is the WTO?' www.wto.org/english/thewto_e/whatis_e/whatis_e.htm accessed 15 April 2020.

2 For an engaging account, see Benn Steil, *The Battle of Bretton Woods* (Princeton University Press 2013).

3 For an overview of this period: John H Jackson, 'History' in Rüdiger Wolfrum, Peter T Stoll and Holger Hestermeyer (eds), *Max Planck Commentaries on World Trade Law: Vol 5* (Brill Nijhoff 2010).

4 Article XII, Agreement Establishing the World Trade Organization (15 April 1994) LT/UR/A/2 122, 150 ('WTO Agreement').

5 The WTO Agreement was signed on 15 April 1994 and entered into force 1 January 1995, bringing into creation the WTO and a range of treaties that bind all members and are subject to compulsory dispute settlement (the so-called 'covered agreements'). Other agreements that only bind some members (plurilateral agreements) were also concluded at the same time (for example, Agreement on Government Procurement (15 April 1994) LT/UR/A-4/PLURI/2 171). Subsequent other agreements have also been concluded (for example, the Agreement on Trade Facilitation, Ministerial Decision of 7 December 2013, WT/MIN(13)/38, WT/L/913 42).

6 The European Court of Justice (as it was then) held that the WTO agreements had to be concluded as mixed agreements as, while the Community had exclusive competence under the common commercial policy to conclude the WTO agreements on goods, Member States and the Community were jointly competent for the agreements covering trade in services and intellectual property (the General Agreement on Trade in Services (15 April 1994) LT/UR/A-1B/S/1 161, 181–4, 188 ('GATS') and Agreement on Trade-Related Aspects of Intellectual Property Rights (15 April 1994) LT/UR/A-1C/IP/1 49 ('TRIPs') respectively). See Opinion 1/94 *WTO* EU:C:1994:384.

7 Article IX.1 (fn 2) WTO Agreement. 'The number of votes of the European Communities and their Member States shall in no case exceed the number of the Member States of the European Communities.'

8 Members are specifically instructed under Article IX.1 WTO Agreement to 'continue the practice of decision-making by consensus followed under GATT 1947' where possible (with provision for voting where agreement cannot be reached in this manner).

9 See the extension of the application of the WTO Agreement to the Crown Dependency of the Isle of Man in 1997 by way of UK deposit at the WTO: Communication from the United Kingdom, 3

March 1997, WT/Let/154. On overseas territories at the WTO, see Matthew Kennedy, 'Overseas Territories in the WTO' (2016) 65 International & Comparative Law Quarterly 741.
10 Opinion 2/15 ECLI:EU:C:2017:376.
11 This can be seen most explicitly in the EU's internal structures for managing external trade policy. The two key institutions, the Trade Policy Committee (the Council committee intended to advise and assist the Commission on trade policy) and the European Parliament Committee on International Trade (which acts as a co-decider for CCP legislation and is intended to scrutinise EU trade policy) are both used more frequently to inform parliamentarians and Member States of the activities of the Commission and for participants to flag concerns. Absent outright rejection by the European Parliament or in Council of key trade decisions, such bodies are in effect a form of enhanced consultation rather than cooperative decision-making.
12 For example, the Conservative and Unionist Manifesto 2019, 57:

> Free trade has been proven time and again to be the best way to increase exports, cut prices for consumers, increase investment and create jobs right here in the UK. We believe we can use this historic opportunity to connect the UK to the world's fastest growing nations, create new export opportunities and enrich ourselves and our trading partners.
> *(https://assets-global.website-files.com/5da42e2cae7ebd3f8bde353c/5dda924905da587992a064ba_Conservative%202019%20Manifesto.pdf accessed 15 April 2020)*

13 This and other issues are discussed in sections 10.2 and 10.3.
14 For a general overview of the issues, see Gregory Messenger, 'Membership of the World Trade Organization' in Michael Dougan (ed), *The UK after Brexit: Legal and Policy Challenges* (Intersentia 2017).
15 See Section 10.3.1.2.
16 See Section 10.3.1.1.
17 Commonly referenced in Articles III and I GATT respectively, though these general obligations also manifest themselves in specific WTO agreements on services, technical barriers to trade, and sanitary and phytosanitary measures among others.
18 Services are defined as 'any service in any sector except services supplied in the exercise of governmental authority'. Article I.3(b), General Agreement on Trade in Services (15 April 1994) LT/UR/A-1B/S/1.
19 See Articles XVI and XX GATS.
20 G/MA/TAR/RS/570.
21 S/C/W/380 and S/C/W/381.
22 Understanding on Rules and Procedures Governing the Settlement of Disputes (15 April 1994) LT/UR/A-2/DS/U/1 ('DSU'). The DSU marks the WTO out from other (non-EU) international organisations in that it provides for compulsory dispute settlement between WTO members. It is the only such system to which the US is a member.
23 The Organisation for Economic Co-operation and Development (OECD) states spend, on average, 12 per cent of GDP on procurement. See: OECD, *Government at a Glance 2019* (14 November 2019) www.oecd-ilibrary.org/governance/government-at-a-glance-2019_8ccf5c38-en accessed 15 April 2020.
24 The actual practice of international procurement is quite different: feasibility, size of operator, and offer of operator all play an important role. While some companies offer end-to-end construction services, for example, others only provide a single specialised element. The former are more likely to be successful and active participants in international procurement than the latter.
25 The GPA applies to the UK for the duration of the transition period: Decision of the Committee on Government Procurement dated 27 February 2019, Document GPA/CD/2. Agreement in principle on the UK's market access offer was reached on 27 November 2018. See Report (2018) of the Committee on Government Procurement (29 November 2018) GPA/AR/1.
26 See para 2.5, Communication from the United Kingdom (1 February 2020) WT/GC/206.
27

> Consistent with the principles of the Withdrawal Agreement, for the duration of the transition period, the United Kingdom will also continue to be treated as a Member State of the European Union for the purpose of ongoing WTO disputes to which the European Union is a party.

Para 2.7, Communication from the United Kingdom (1 February 2020) WT/GC/206.
28 See UK Press Release, 'Britain is Back: Liz Truss Calls for New Rules at WTO to Tackle Unfair Trade Practices' (3 March 2020) www.gov.uk/government/news/britain-is-back-liz-truss-calls-for-new-rules-at-wto-to-tackle-unfair-trade-practices accessed 15 April 2020. This is an agenda currently led by the 'trilateral' group of EU–Japan–US seeking to manage the impact of China at the WTO which, as

a large non-market economy, is creating difficulties for a system (it is claimed) that was not designed to handle state capitalism of this kind.

29 Given the membership's inability to conclude a large round of negotiations since the creation of the WTO in 1995, alternative methods have developed. Currently, members are engaged with JSIs on a plurilateral basis in an attempt to move discussions forward on key topics and crystallise support around these issues.

30 G/TBT/2/Add.128.

31 A possibility foreshadowed in style if not substance in Thomas Streinz, 'Cooperative Brexit: Giving Back Control Over Trade Policy' (2017) 15 International Journal of Constitutional Law 271.

32 Illustratively, see the speech of the UK International Trade Secretary to the WTO General Council on 3 March 2020 setting out a 'vision is of a newly independent UK, championing the cause of free, fair, rules-based trade' www.gov.uk/government/speeches/elizabeth-truss-outlines-bold-new-era-for-trade accessed 15 April 2020.

33 Ibid.

34 On this point, see section 10.3.2.

35 For an accessible introductory explanation, see Peter Ungphakorn, 'A Real Beginners' Guide to Tariff-Rate Quotas (TRQs) and the WTO' (8 September 2018), https://tradebetablog.wordpress.com/2018/09/08/beginners-guide-tariff-quotas/ accessed 15 April 2020.

36 For an account in relation to the UK's position, see Lorand Bartels, 'The UK's Status in the WTO after Brexit' (23 September 2016), https://ssrn.com/abstract=2841747 accessed 15 April 2020.

37 Most notably Article XXVIII GATT.

38 Minutes of the Meeting of the Council for Trade in Goods, 12 and 13 November 2018 (17 April 2019) G/C/M/133, para 6.3.

39 This is exacerbated by the 'Rotterdam effect' whereby large quantities of goods travel to (and through) the Port of Rotterdam. Goods that appear that they are for the Netherlands may in fact by transiting through to another EU Member State, or, alternatively, out of the EU and to a third market via Rotterdam. The success of Rotterdam's port presents logistical challenges for a non-EU UK as its own port infrastructure is upgraded to allow for increased goods trade (something that has been underway for some time now). However, in this instance, it also makes it hard to clarify the final destination of goods within the EU from a non-EU exporter.

40 G/C/M/133, para 6.3.

41 G/C/M/133, para 6.4.

42 Article 22.4 DSU.

43 A point made clearly in Bartels (n 36).

44 G/C/M/133, para 6.4.

45 TDIs are regulated by Article VI and XIX GATT, the Agreement on Implementation of Article VI (Anti-dumping) (15 April 1994) LT/UR/A-1A/3 (AD Agreement), Agreement on Safeguards (15 April 1994) LT/URA-1A/8 (AoS), Agreement on Subsidies and Countervailing Measures (15 April 1994) LT/UR/A-1A/9 (SCM Agreement).

46 'Quasi', as they are subject to review, domestically and at the WTO by panels and ultimately the Appellate Body.

47 See ss 51 and 56, Taxation (Cross-Border Trade) Act 2018 and part 12 of the Trade Remedies (Dumping and Subsidisation) Regulations.

48 Information on the UK's approach to transition reviews is available at www.gov.uk/government/publications/the-uk-trade-remedies-investigations-process/how-we-carry-out-transition-reviews-into-eu-measures#our-transition-review-process accessed 15 April 2020.

49 Herbert Smith Freehills, 'UK Initiates its First "Transition Review" Trade Defence Investigation: Overview and Further Information on UK Transitioned Measures and Associated Reviews' (21 February 2020), https://hsfnotes.com/crt/2020/02/21/uk-initiates-its-first-transition-review-trade-defence-investigation-overview-and-further-information-on-uk-transitioned-measures-and-associated-reviews/ accessed 15 April 2020.

50 For example, Article 15(1) Regulation (EU) 2015/478 of the European Parliament and of the Council of 11 March 2015 on common rules for imports (27 March 2015) L83/16.

51 See the discussions in: Jayne McCormack, 'Brexit: Does NI Tariffs Plan Violate WTO Law?' *BBC News* (London, 14 March 2019); Michael Gasiorek, 'Better than the Status Quo for Northern Ireland? Not Quite so Simple' (24 October 2019), https://blogs.sussex.ac.uk/uktpo/2019/10/24/better-than-the-status-quo-for-northern-ireland-not-quite-so-simple/ accessed 15 April 2020.

52 General concerns lend themselves to general answers: that the NI Protocol may create a general Article I GATT violation has been countered by possible both established practice as a form of interpretative device (as many WTO members have differential regimes applying within their territory, such as enterprise zones or free ports), claims under Article V GATT or even Article XXI GATT. This chapter does not examine these concerns at this level of abstraction as, indicated in the following paragraphs, it is only in the detail of the practice of the arrangement that it will become clear as to whether there are substantive WTO issues.
53 See Articles 5–10 Northern Ireland Protocol, and Annex 2.
54 Article X GATT.
55 US–Mexico and US–Canada relations provide interesting counterpoints to this dynamic, where unresolved disputes within NAFTA (North American Free Trade Agreement) were also tested at the WTO. For example, see 'Mexico – Tax Measures on Soft Drinks and Other Beverages', WT/DS308 and the long-running softwood lumber disputes (for concise reporting, see ICTSD, 'Canada-US Softwood Lumber Row Escalates with Filing of NAFTA, WTO Cases' (7 December 2017) www.ictsd.org/bridges-news/bridges/news/canada-us-softwood-lumber-row-escalates-with-filing-of-nafta-wto-cases accessed 15 April 2020.
56 See principally ss 3, 20(1), and Schedule 6, European Union (Withdrawal) Act 2018.
57 Annex 1.1, Agreement on Technical Barriers to Trade (15 April 1994) LT/UR/A-1A/10.
58 WTO disputes DS26, DS291, DS381, and DS400 respectively.
59 An overview of these agreements is available at www.gov.uk/guidance/uk-trade-agreements-with-non-eu-countries accessed 15 April 2020.
60 The explanatory memoranda and accompanying parliamentary reports provided to Parliament by Her Majesty's Government as part of the scrutiny process of treaties are instructive in this regard. For those agreements transitioned from EU to UK agreements, they include explanations of changes made. See, for example, Explanatory Memorandum on the Agreement establishing an association between the United Kingdom of Great Britain and Northern Ireland and the Republic of Chile (6 February 2019) Command Paper No CP35 and its accompanying report available at www.gov.uk/government/publications/continuing-the-uks-trade-relationship-with-chile-parliamentary-report accessed 15 April 2020.
61 UK International Trade Secretary to the WTO General Council on 3 March 2020 (n 32) and accompanying text.
62 European Commission, 'Trade for All: Towards a More Responsible Trade and Investment Policy' (October 2015), https://trade.ec.europa.eu/doclib/docs/2015/october/tradoc_153846.pdf accessed 15 April 2020.
63 See Communication from the Commission to the European Parliament, the European Council, the Council, the European Economic and Social Committee and the Committee of the Regions, 'The European Green Deal' (11 December 2019) COM(2019) 640 final.
64 See Proposal for a Regulation of the European Parliament and of the Council amending Council Regulation (EC) No 1215/2009 introducing exceptional trade measures for countries and territories participating in or linked to the European Union's Stabilisation and Association process (3 April 2020) COM(2020)135/F1.
65 Something not dissimilar to a GATT-era practice of the US that the EU challenged in the early days of the WTO, see US–Section 301 Trade Act (WT/DS152/14).
66 See the reporting (and text) of a leaked letter from the four Member States to Commissioner Vestager on 4 February 2020, www.politico.eu/article/eu-big-four-france-germany-italy-poland-press-executive-vice-president-margrethe-vestager-to-clear-path-for-champions/ accessed 15 April 2020.
67 Indeed, it is noteworthy that even during the Uruguay Round (1986–1994), when trade governance was more tightly focused around the US–European dynamic with Japan and Canada closely involved (the 'quad'), the input of many members, not all global powers, were essential in coming to an agreement over the final package of the WTO agreements. In particular, New Zealand, Brazil, Republic of Korea, India, Australia, Mexico, and Norway all had an important role to play in the conclusion of the Round. For a detailed account of the Uruguay Round, see the multi-volume work of T Stewart (ed), *The GATT Uruguay Round: A Negotiating History* (Kluwer Law International published between 1993 and 1999).

11

Brexit and its implications for the EU in the UN Security Council

Jan Wouters

11.1 Introduction

When the United Kingdom (UK) left the European Union (EU or Union) on 31 January 2020, the EU did not only lose its second largest economy, one of its two nuclear powers, the Member State with the largest defence budget[1] and its greatest national development donor.[2] It also lost one of the two Member States that have the unique privilege of being a permanent member on the United Nations Security Council (UNSC). How can the EU and its remaining Member States make the most strategic and tactical use of their loss of the UK in the UNSC? This contribution focuses on the implications of Brexit for the functioning of the UNSC from an EU point of view.[3] First, it will outline the importance of the UK's permanent seat in the context of the Brexit debate, both from the viewpoint of the UK itself and from the EU and its 27 Member States (section 11.2). Second, we will explore what has as of now been agreed about the UK and EU's future relationship within the United Nations (UN) and the UNSC, in particular as part of the 'Political Declaration setting out the framework for the future relationship between the European Union and the United Kingdom' (Declaration) (section 11.3).[4] Third, we will revisit the current EU Treaty mechanisms for EU 'actorness' in the UNSC, notably the system of Article 34(2), second paragraph, of the Treaty on European Union (TEU) (section 11.4), and pay attention to recent interesting dynamics in the practices of EU Member States sitting on the UNSC (section 11.5). Last, but not least, we will ask ourselves the question about an 'EU permanent seat' (section 11.6). Some concluding reflections wrap up our findings (section 11.7).

11.2 The UK's permanent seat on the UNSC and why it matters in the post-Brexit debate

11.2.1 UK perspective

For the UK, having a permanent seat on the UNSC remains a form of recognition of great power status. Having achieved it when the UN was created in 1945, the UK has proudly continued to hold its seat over the past 75 years of the UN's existence, in spite of the loss of its colonial empire and relative decline of global power and influence. As a permanent member of the UNSC the UK – and for that matter, also France – has continued to punch above its weight in international politics. The aura that comes with permanent UNSC membership transcends the Security Council itself: thus, when a permanent member speaks in the UN General Assembly (UNGA) or in any other UN committee, it is heard.[5]

Being a permanent member of the UNSC carries with it a number of special privileges,[6] including the legendary veto right, which the UK has exercised 30 times until 2020.[7] It also entails special responsibilities under the UN Charter,[8] although these have never been clearly spelled out.[9] In her speech of 20 September 2017 to the UNGA, UK Prime Minister Theresa May acknowledged these special responsibilities of the UK as a permanent member of the UNSC,[10] without, however, elaborating on how they would be met once the UK would be outside the EU.[11]

It has been said that the UK seems to have less power nowadays in the UN and in the UNSC, and that this is at least in part due to Brexit. Three recent events are often mentioned to illustrate this point.

First, in May 2017 the UK candidate lost out in the election for the director-general of the World Health Organization, which was won with a large majority by the Ethiopian candidate, Dr Tedros Adhanom Ghebreyesus.[12]

Second, on 22 June 2017, the UNGA voted, on the request of Mauritius, to refer the status of the Chagos Islands (UK territory) for an advisory opinion to the International Court of Justice (ICJ) – against UK objections[13] – resulting in a 2019 ICJ advisory opinion that obliges the UK to decolonize the territory,[14] endorsed by an UNGA resolution of 22 May 2019.[15] While both UNGA resolutions saw a three-split vote of the other EU Member States, it should be noted that a much larger number of EU Member States voted in favour of the 2019 resolution – strongly objected to by the UK – than for the 2017 resolution, showing decreasing support for the UK.[16]

Third, on 20 November 2017 the UK failed in its campaign for the re-election of 'the British judge' in the ICJ, resulting in a situation where the ICJ has no UK judge for the first time since 1946.[17] This was equally perceived as indication of the UK's loss of influence within the UN.[18]

Gowan has rightly observed that the defeats in question 'stem more from developing countries' desire to have a greater say at the UN than dynamics specific to Brexit'.[19] Still, if anything, the Chagos Islands saga seems to illustrate both the UK's growing isolation and the decreasing support by EU Member States between 2017 and 2019.

Brexit has, at least for some time, also affected the focus of UK engagement in the UN. In September 2018, the *Guardian* reported on Theresa May's difficult stand in the UNSC meeting on Iran earlier that week in New York:

> [I]n truth, the British voice on everything else at the UN counts for less than it did under Tony Blair, Gordon Brown – or even David Cameron ... if May has any foreign policy theme, it is submerged by Brexit. Broadcasters accompanying her to New York were each allocated four questions – and each confined themselves to Brexit – as if Iran, the UK's aid budget, Myanmar, Yemen or even the UK military bombing of Syria were non-issues. Such monomania leaves the impression that the UK is a country apart, involved in its own conversation, and checked out from the world debates. That is not a true picture of British diplomatic effectiveness at the UN – but sometimes impressions become the reality. Even if all goes to plan with Brexit, next year's general assembly will be just as hard. For the first time in decades, Britain will find itself as a non European Union member, forced to justify its claim to be one of the five permanent members of the UN security council – and British leaders (whoever they may be) will have to work even harder just to be heard.[20]

Most observers agree that Brexit diminishes the UK's foreign policy.[21] A recent report on the UK and the UN highlights the potential decline of British influence in the UN, and more specifically in the UNSC. Its conclusion is:

> While the UK's permanent seat on the Security Council is safe in the sense that it would need to consent to its own removal, our conclusion is that Brexit exacerbates concerns about the legitimacy of that privilege. The status of the UK at the UN, and particularly the legitimacy of the UK's position as a permanent member of the Security Council, will therefore be weakened if the impact of Brexit is not offset by effective 'compensatory' strategies.[22]

This finding has been corroborated by other recent studies. Thus, it has been demonstrated that 'membership of the EU helped the UK to mobilize material resources to support the leadership positions its diplomats staked out at the Council'.[23] Researchers have concluded that this can only be compensated by an increased UK material commitment, which 'will have to go further if it is to correct the perception in the UN that the UK will now no longer be able to influence the material resources of the much larger EU'.[24] Researchers conclude that

> diplomatic activism is not the only criteria of a responsible permanent member. The willingness to back that up with material leadership or, failing that, a more inclusionary approach towards those states that are making significant material contributions, is also important.[25]

11.2.2 EU perspective

Having left the EU, the UK no longer participates in the Union's Common Foreign and Security Policy (CFSP) nor in its Common Security and Defence Policy (CSDP),[26] which implies that for these policies the EU has one 'representative' (and one veto) less in the UNSC. However, both the UK and the EU want to preserve a close relationship regarding their security and defence policy in the post-Brexit era.[27] This is also what French President Emmanuel Macron called for in his op-ed, which appeared in all 28 EU Member States on 4 March 2019, arguing for a new 'European Security Council':

> A treaty on defence and security should define our fundamental obligations in association with Nato and our European allies: increased defence spending, a truly operational mutual defence clause, and a European Security Council, with the UK on board, to prepare our collective decisions.[28]

However, the next day, the *Guardian* published an op-ed by Simon Tisdall, where a good dose of British pragmatism struck down the French president's grand vision:

> Questions of trustworthiness and competence shed doubt on another key Macron proposal: a mutual defence treaty, increased EU-wide defence spending, and a 'European security council'. Although he talks of a continuing association with Nato, this plan looks like a reincarnation of long-simmering, essentially anti-American, quasi-Gaullist ideas about an independent Europe freed from US 'hegemony'.[29]

However this may be, without the UK, the EU might consider that the time has come to take further steps towards a more deeply integrated CFSP/CSDP.[30] Such a perspective was inter alia raised in Commission President Jean-Claude Juncker's state of the union speech in September 2016,[31] in the Rome Declaration of 25 March 2017,[32] and in the European Commission's reflection paper on the future of European defence of June 2017.[33] It has meanwhile resulted in the first case of permanent structured cooperation (PESCO).[34] The new Von der Leyen

Commission has also put a stronger CFSP and CSDP high on its political agenda,[35] although finding support for it in the context of the negotiations for the EU's new multi-annual financial framework is proving to be arduous.

11.3 Treaty mechanisms for EU 'actorness' at the UNSC

As is known, the EU is strongly committed to the UN. The UN is mentioned at least 15 times in the EU Treaties, and the EU has expressed its commitment to go for 'multilateral solutions to common problems, in particular in the framework of the United Nations' in Article 21(1) TEU.[36] The 2016 Global Strategy reinstates the commitment that the EU 'will promote a rules-based global order with multilateralism as its key principle and the United Nations at its core'.[37]

One of the EU's major challenges concerns the issue of how to secure, or strengthen, a voice for the Union at the UNSC. Indeed, Article 34(1) TEU stipulates that 'Member States shall coordinate their action in international organisations and at international conferences. They shall uphold the Union's positions in such forums.' EU Member States must therefore strive to define a common position and defend it within international institutions. However, the text of Article 34(2), second paragraph, TEU makes clear that the UNSC constitutes a remarkable exception to this general principle. Contrary to the general rule of Article 34(1) TEU, EU Member States sitting on the UNSC do not have an EU Treaty obligation to coordinate within the EU context, just one of concertation between themselves, and one of information sharing with all the other EU Member States and the High Representative. The latter takes place in weekly meetings in New York, both at the level of Heads of Mission (typically on a Tuesday) and at the level of experts (formerly called 'Article 34' meetings).[38] Moreover, it adds that EU Member States sitting on the UNSC can deviate from EU positions if this is needed in light of 'their responsibilities under the provisions of the United Nations Charter'. The aforementioned provision of the TEU is confirmed and even a bit reinforced by Declarations No. 13 and 14 to the Lisbon Treaty. Especially the latter declaration is very explicit, as it stipulates that the innovations of the Lisbon Treaty with regard to the EU's common foreign and security policy,

> [W]ill not affect the existing legal basis, responsibilities and powers of each Member State in relation to the formulation and conduct of its foreign policy, its national diplomatic service, relations with third countries and participation in international organisations, including a Member State's membership of the Security Council of the United Nations.

Still, an interesting innovation of the Treaty of Lisbon with regard to the EU in the UNSC is Article 34(2), third paragraph TEU. According to this provision, when the EU has defined a position on a subject on the UNSC's agenda, those Member States that sit on the UNSC 'shall request that the High Representative be invited to present the Union's position'. In practice, it is the EU Ambassador to the UN in New York who presents such position – nowadays on average 30 to 35 times a year.[39] Nevertheless, it is important to note that such positions are only formulated during public sessions of the UNSC: in the 'real' UNSC-only meetings, the High Representative or the EU Ambassador is not invited.[40]

Until recently, the EU seems not to have developed much strategic thinking on its role in the UNSC.[41] The EU's 2016 Global Strategy mentions the UNSC only in one instance: 'A commitment to global governance must translate in the determination to reform the UN, including the Security Council, and the International Financial Institutions'.[42] It is remarkable that the Global Strategy does not speak about strengthening the EU's voice in the UNSC.

There is no common EU strategy on UNSC reform, given underlying differences of opinion and conflicting ambitions, notably between Germany and Italy.[43]

However, most EU Member States with the status of elected member of the UNSC seem convinced that '[w]hat counts is one voice, not one seat',[44] and therefore tend to emphasize the need for EU coordination. An interesting illustration thereof is the joint declaration which the Dutch and Italian Ministers of Foreign Affairs, Bert Koenders and Paolo Gentiloni, adopted on 21 September 2016 on cooperation in the UNSC in 2017–18, when each of them were on the Council for one year (they had split the two-year mandate). According to the press statement of the Dutch Foreign Ministry the day after, '[b]oth during that period and in the run-up to it, they will work as closely as possible with one another and with other European Union Member States on the Council'.[45]

Germany has also recently insisted on the importance of the EU in the UNSC. Towards the end of Germany's campaign for a 2019–20 term, Chancellor Angela Merkel declared:

> The CSDP is very important to me, because we – also the Germans – can only really represent our interests if we commonly appear as Europeans. That is why my proposal is that we consider our non-permanent seats … as European seats, that we act together, … that we have a European white book for security policy and challenges, that we also define the challenges together, that we work together in the field of defense, and especially in the field of development policy.[46]

Moreover, speaking in the German Bundestag, Merkel proposed 'that we treat our non-permanent seat in future as a European seat'.[47] However, Brexit does not appear to have transformed the German campaign for *its own* permanent seat in the UNSC to a campaign for an *EU* permanent seat:[48] a clear indication thereof is the Franco-German Aachen Treaty provision quoted below (section 11.6), in which France commits to supporting the German candidacy for a permanent seat on the UNSC.[49]

The question arises how far EU coordination can really go in the context of the UNSC. The information sharing, for example, is not that simple, and, for elected EU Member States, 'giving their membership [a European] dimension does not necessarily mean sharing all information with EU partners, even on the contrary'.[50] Indeed, EU Member States sitting on the UNSC should be aware of their UN obligations. As Ambassador Verbeke puts it:

> [O]ne cannot … expect the EU Security Council members to lay all their cards open on the table. However much they would like to be EU-loyal, they have loyalties, and perhaps obligations too, towards the other Security Council members that they must respect for the sake of being and continuing to be trusted fellows within that principal organ of the United Nations.[51]

Drieskens has made a similar remark, emphasizing that EU Member States that sit as elected members on the UNSC have to 'walk on eggshells' during their term, 'carefully balancing their regional and global roles and responsibilities, under the watchful eye of their colleagues who are serving on a permanent basis'.[52] Mayr-Harting has pointed to the paradoxical situation that the EU Delegation to the UN in New York sometimes has 'earlier access to draft Security Council documents through non-EU diplomatic or even media sources than through the channels established in accordance with Article 34 of the TEU'.[53]

Despite these challenges, EU Member States sitting in the UNSC, especially elected ones, are gradually deepening the European dimension of their term, as shown by recent practices, in particular the joint media stakeouts (see section 11.5).

11.4 The Political Declaration on the future relationship

The Political Declaration has undergone a number of changes between the versions of 25 November 2018 and the final version, as published in the Official Journal of the EU,[54] of 19 October 2019. In the area of foreign policy, though, the two versions are largely[55] the same. The Declaration does not mention the UNSC, but it refers to continuing cooperation between the UK and the EU in the context of the UN.

Thus, paragraph 90 of the Declaration stipulates:

> The Parties support ambitious, close and lasting cooperation on external action to protect citizens from external threats, including new emerging threats, prevent conflicts, strengthen international peace and security, including through the United Nations and NATO, and address the root causes of global challenges such as terrorism or illegal migration. They will champion a rules-based international order and project their common values worldwide.

Paragraph 96 adds to this:

> The Parties should seek to cooperate closely in third countries, including on security, consular provision and protection, and development projects, as well as in international organisations and fora, notably in the United Nations. This should allow the Parties, where relevant, to support each other's positions, deliver external action and manage global challenges in a coherent manner, including through agreed statements, demarches and shared positions.

This being said, the Declaration makes amply clear that after the UK's departure from the EU there will be different 'foreign policies',[56] that interests may differ and that the cooperation should be flexible and scalable. As paragraph 92 stipulates:

> The Parties will shape and pursue their foreign policies according to their respective strategic and security interests, and their respective legal orders. When and where these interests are shared, the Parties should cooperate closely at the bilateral level and within international organisations. The Parties should design flexible and scalable cooperation that would ensure that the United Kingdom can combine efforts with the Union to the greatest effect, including in times of crisis or when serious incidents occur.

This leaves a lot of leeway for future courses of action. The Political Declaration does definitely not guarantee a systematic alignment of positions between EU and UNSC members and the UK in the UNSC. The question arises whether specific additional arrangements on this will be concluded between the UK and the EU-27 in the future.

11.5 Recent dynamics of EU Member States' practice in the UNSC

A number of recent developments have made the Union more visible in the UNSC. First, the UNSC has held annual briefings on cooperation between the EU and the UN since 2010 (except in 2012 and 2018), a reflection of growing EU–UN cooperation. Thus, on 12 March 2019, the UNSC held its annual meeting on strengthening the partnership with the EU, under its agenda item on cooperation between the UN and regional and subregional organizations in maintaining international peace and security. Federica Mogherini, the EU High Representative for Foreign Affairs and Security Policy, briefed the UNSC, inter alia, on the Middle East peace process, the situation in Libya, the humanitarian situation in Iraq, cooperation with other regional organizations, transnational crime, climate change and sustainable development.[57] At the February 2020 annual meeting, High Representative Josep Borrell represented the EU.[58] In 2014, the UNSC endorsed the relationship by adopting an important Presidential Statement on EU–UN cooperation, in which 'the significant contribution that the European Union makes in support of the maintenance of international peace and security' was commended.[59]

Second, since 2013, members of the UNSC have met annually with members of the EU's Political and Security Committee (PSC).[60]

Third, an important recently emerged practice is that the EU Member States that sit on the UNSC, sometimes including incoming and recently departed members,[61] make joint statements at the UNSC media stakeout, presenting the EU position on specific issues on the UNSC agenda.[62] Interestingly, at least one of such media stakeouts has taken place since February 2020 together with the UK Ambassador as 'European Union and United Kingdom'.[63] The statements are being read by the 'briefer of the month', i.e. on a rotational basis, one of the EU Member States sitting on the Security Council.[64]

There are other noteworthy practices, in New York, Brussels and in national capitals. In New York, there are two one can mention, in addition to the monthly teleconferences to discuss the upcoming UNSC agenda of work between elected Member States sitting on the UNSC.[65] These are the quarterly luncheons hosted by the EU Ambassador[66] and the monthly lunch between the political coordinators of the Member States' permanent missions and of the EU Delegation to go over the programme of the coming month and discuss opportunities for joint initiatives.[67]

As for Brussels, one can mention for instance High Representative Mogherini's meeting with the foreign ministers of the EU Member States sitting on the UNSC on 28 January 2019, emphasizing the importance of bringing the EU's views on peace and security and on multilateralism to the UNSC. In September 2018, in its conclusions defining the priorities for EU–UN cooperation on security for 2019–21, the Council of the EU 'recognize[d] both the mutually beneficial nature of the longstanding UN–EU cooperation on peacekeeping and civilian, police and military crisis management and the importance of continuing the close European cooperation in the UN Security Council'.[68]

At the capital level of Member States sitting on the UNSC, one can refer to bi-annual meetings between Ministry of Foreign Affairs' Directors for EU and UNSC issues to facilitate dialogue on core objectives and current UNSC affairs.[69]

Interestingly, these practices and a number of additional developments and initiatives have been brought together in a document of 7 December 2018 established by the Netherlands, Poland and Sweden, based on their experience in the UNSC as elected EU members.[70] The document also contains a number of recommendations, including exploring the possibility of integrating more UNSC-related content into United Nations Working Party (CONUN) meetings in Brussels by providing regular briefings from EU UNSC members.[71] It is to be hoped that these practices will be continued and deepened by current and future elected EU Member States on the UNSC, including the EU's only remaining permanent member, France.

Finally, it is interesting from a post-Brexit perspective that France (UNSC president in March 2019) and Germany (UNSC president in April 2019) have held a 'twin presidency' of the UNSC covering the months of March and April 2019.[72] Both countries' permanent representatives, François Delattre and Christoph Heusgen, took turns (in alphabetical order) presiding over the UNSC in these two months. During the two months, the French and German foreign ministers jointly attended specific UNSC meetings. As Ambassador Delattre observed: 'At the heart of these two months … we have placed our shared defense of multilateralism, the idea of global order based on law and strong international institutions that can enforce these rules'.[73] While largely symbolical, this twin presidency can be seen as a creative way in which EU Member States link their priorities and promote the objectives and values that are central to the EU's external actions within the UNSC – ultimately helping the Union to make its policy preferences better heard within that UN body.

11.6 Towards an EU permanent seat?

For many years there has been a lingering debate about the desirability (or not) of a permanent seat for the EU as such in the UNSC.[74] While, as of yet, the debate has not flared up prominently at European level in the post-Brexit context, recent developments in Germany[75] indicate that Brexit may have given it a new lease of life. On 28 November 2018, the German Finance Minister and Deputy Chancellor Olaf Scholz (from the German socialist party), in a speech in Berlin, proposed turning the French permanent seat within the UNSC into an EU one, with a remarkable quid pro quo:

> In the medium term, France's seat on the Security Council could be converted into a seat for the EU. In return, France would then have the right to appoint the EU ambassador to the United Nations in perpetuity. It's clear to me that this might require a little persuasion work in Paris, but it is a bold and shrewd goal.[76]

As could be expected, France rejected the idea outright. The French ambassador to the United States, Gérard Araud, added that 'it's legally impossible because it would run counter to the Charter of the United Nations. Changing it would be politically impossible.'[77] France's full response during a Q&A Press Briefing reads as follows:

> France is a permanent member of the UN Security Council in accordance with the provisions of the United Nations Charter of 1945. We assume our full responsibilities as a permanent member of the UN Security Council. When defending our national positions, we take all European positions into consideration. We actively participate, together with Germany and all other Member States, in the coordination of the EU's position. We are actively campaigning for UN Security Council reform. France supports the expansion of the Security Council and a revision of the UN Charter in order to allow Germany, as well as Japan, Brazil, India and two African countries, to become permanent members. Germany was elected to the UN Security Council for the 2019–2020 biennium. We are willing to coordinate our positions with Germany, in the spirit of the French–German partnership, to which we are deeply attached and in accordance with the Charter.[78]

Still, the idea for a permanent EU seat on the UNSC is clearly alive in Germany, and not only among social democrats: it was also floated in an op-ed by Annegret Kramp-Karrenbauer, chair of the German Christian-Democrat Party, on 10 March 2019.[79]

Remarkably, in the same period, January 2019, France and Germany concluded the Aachen Treaty on Franco-German Cooperation and Integration, which contains noteworthy provisions on closer cooperation regarding UN, and notably UNSC, matters. Thus, Article 5 stipulates that '[t]hey will instate exchanges between their Permanent Missions to the United Nations in New York, in particular between Security Council Teams'.[80]

Article 8 of the Aachen Treaty makes clear that closer Franco-German cooperation will not only foster EU uniform positions in the UN and in the UNSC in particular, but also that France fully supports Germany's candidacy for a permanent seat as part of the ongoing UNSC reform talks:

> (1) The two countries will cooperate closely in all organs of the United Nations within the framework of the Charter of the United Nations. They will coordinate their positions closely, including as part of wider efforts to coordinate the positions of the Member States of the European Union that are also members of the United Nations Security Council and in accordance with the positions and interests of the European Union. They will work together within the United Nations to advance the European Union's positions and commitments with respect to global challenges and threats. They will do their utmost to ensure that the European Union adopts a uniform position in the relevant organs of the United Nations.
>
> (2) The two countries undertake to continue their efforts to conclude intergovernmental negotiations on the reform of the United Nations Security Council. The admission of the Federal Republic of Germany as a permanent member of the Security Council is a priority of Franco-German diplomacy.

The above shows an intriguing divide between individual statements by German politicians in favour of a permanent EU seat and Germany's continued search for its own permanent seat at the UNSC. It will be interesting to see how this issue evolves, especially now that Brexit has taken part of the criticism away that the EU was overrepresented with two veto-holding permanent members in the UNSC.[81] A possible synthesis may become that the search for a German permanent seat serves as the short-term ambition, whereas the substitution thereof by an EU permanent seat could be seen as the ultimate, long-term goal.[82] However this debate may evolve, independently of the hurdles to effectuate the idea of a permanent EU seat within the 'westphalian' context of the UN and given the constraints of the UN Charter,[83] it is clear that such a seat can only be given meaningful content if more use is made of majority voting under the CFSP.[84] Precisely this matter is now increasingly being discussed within the post-Brexit EU-27.[85]

11.7 Concluding remarks

This contribution focused on the implications of Brexit for the functioning of the UNSC from an EU perspective. While it is clear that maintaining its own permanent seat on the UNSC is of primordial importance for the UK, we have pointed at indications of a weakening influence of the UK in the UN and at the challenges that will come for the country if it is to 'deserve' to continue to be a permanent member. Furthermore, while it is as of yet not clear whether the post-Brexit UK will continue to closely align itself with EU positions in the UNSC, the most recent media stakeouts that the EU Member States sitting on the UNSC have made, indicate that the UK is not averse to this. Our analysis has also shown that, while the EU Treaties do not provide for a coordination duty for Member States that sit on the UNSC, the current dynamics between those Member States indicate that, in fact, we may be evolving incrementally in this direction. Still, in the long run there are two elephants in the room: the question of a permanent seat for the EU as such, and the question of how strongly Germany will continue to campaign for its own permanent seat. The recently concluded Aachen Treaty between France and Germany makes clear that this idea is still very much alive.

Notes

1 This budget is said to be £45 billion, or 2.15 per cent of British gross domestic product (GDP): Ronan Le Gleut and Hélène Conway-Mouret, 'European Defence: The Challenge of Strategic Autonomy' (French Senate Rapport d'information, 3 July 2019) 60.
2 The UK is the third-largest donor country, spending US$19.4 billion on official development assistance (ODA) in 2018. Net ODA increased by 2 per cent between 2017 and 2018. The UK has met the UN target of spending 0.7 per cent of gross national income (GNI) on ODA since 2013, https://donortracker.org/country/united-kingdom accessed 26 March 2020.
3 For other studies specifically focusing on the UK's post-Brexit position in the UNSC and the wider UN, see Megan Dee and Karen E Smith, 'UK Diplomacy at the UN after Brexit: Challenges and Opportunities' (2017) 19 British Journal of Politics and International Relations 527; Jess Gifkins, Samuel Jarvis and Jason Ralph, 'Brexit and the UN Security Council: Declining British Influence?' (2019) 95 International Affairs 1349; Jason Ralph, Jess Gifkins and Samuel Jarvis, 'The UK's Special Responsibilities at the United Nations: Diplomatic Practice in Normative Context' (2019) 21 British Journal of Politics and International Relations 1; Jess Gifkins, Samuel Jarvis and Jason Ralph, *Global Britain in the United Nations* (UNA-UK February 2019).
4 Political Declaration setting out the framework for the future relationship between the European Union and the United Kingdom, OJ [2020] C34/12 ('PD').
5 Jean-Marc de la Sablière, *Le Conseil de sécurité des Nations Unies* (2nd edn, Larcier 2015), 76.
6 This includes also a veto right on any amendment of the UN Charter. See Arts 108 and 109(2) UN Charter. See also, more theoretically, Art 47(2) UN Charter, pursuant to which the 'Military Staff Committee shall consist of the Chiefs of Staff of the permanent members of the Security Council or their representatives'; however, this committee has never seen the light of day. Pursuant to Art 110(3) UN Charter, the Charter could only enter into force upon the deposit of ratifications by the five permanent members 'and a majority of the other signatory states'. See also, among the transitional security arrangements, Art 106 UN Charter. Another 'privilege' is the fact that permanent members can veto the (re-)appointment of the UN Secretary General, which makes that Secretary Generals have always nurtured close working relations with the permanent members.
7 The first time the UK used the veto right was together with France in the Suez crisis of 1956. See Foreign and Commonwealth Office, 'Vetoed Draft Resolutions in the United Nations Security Council 1946–2012', 5, para 3, www.gov.uk/government/publications/vetoed-draft-resolutions-in-the-united-nations-security-council-1946-2012 accessed 26 March 2020.
8 This is also acknowledged in EU law: see Art 34(2), para 2 TEU, pursuant to which 'Member States which are members of the Security Council will, in the execution of their functions, defend the positions and the interests of the Union, without prejudice to their responsibilities under the provisions of the United Nations Charter.' From the Treaty of Maastricht until the Treaty of Lisbon, this provision only applied for 'Member States which are permanent members of the Security Council' (Art J.5(4), para 2 TEU, version Treaty of Maastricht; Art 19(2), para 2 TEU, versions Treaty of Amsterdam and Treaty of Nice).
9 See Kishore Mahbubani, 'The Permanent and Elected Council Members' in David M Malone (ed), *The UN Security Council: From the Cold War to the 21st Century* (Lynne Rienner 2004) 256. Recently, it has been argued that the P5 have a duty to prevent genocide in light of conventional, customary and peremptory international law: John Heieck, *Duty to Prevent Genocide: Due Diligence Obligations among the P5* (Edward Elgar Publishing 2018); John Heieck, 'The Responsibility Not to Veto Revisited: How the Duty to Prevent Genocide as a Jus Cogens Norm Imposes a Legal Duty Not to Veto on the Five Permanent Members of the Security Council' in Richard Barnes and Vassilis P Tzevelekos (eds), *Beyond Responsibility to Protect: Generating Change in International Law* (Intersentia 2016).
10 www.gov.uk/government/speeches/theresa-mays-speech-to-the-un-general-assembly-2017 accessed 26 March 2020.
11 Ibid. Theresa May did say, however, in her speech that

> as one of these five members, the United Kingdom takes our special responsibility seriously. So I am proud that we have used the full weight of our diplomacy to ensure that we have not had to exercise our veto in a generation. Seeking to foster international cooperation, not frustrated.

12 See Sarah Boseley, 'WHO Elects First Ever African Director-General After Tense Vote', *Guardian* (London, 23 May 2017); Stephanie Nebehay and Tom Miles, 'Ethiopia's Tedros Wins WHO Race, First African to get Top Job', *Reuters* (Toronto, 23 May 2017).

13 UNGA Resolution 71/73, Request for an advisory opinion of the International Court of Justice on the legal consequences of the separation of the Chagos Archipelago from Mauritius in 1965 (15 June 2017). The resolution was adopted with 94 votes to 15, with 65 abstentions.

14 ICJ, Advisory Opinion of 25 February 2019, Legal consequences of the separation of the Chagos Archipelago from Mauritius in 1965, para 177, 183 in which the Court ruled (with 13 judges against one) that the UK's 'continued administration of the Chagos Archipelago constitutes a wrongful act entailing the international responsibility of that State' and that the UK is under an obligation to bring to an end its administration of the Chagos Archipelago as rapidly as possible, www.icj-cij.org/files/case-related/169/169-20190225-01-00-EN.pdf accessed 26 March 2020. See, for first comments, Marko Milanovic, 'ICJ Delivers Chagos Advisory Opinion, UK Loses Badly' (25 February 2019) www.ejiltalk.org/icj-delivers-chagos-advisory-opinion-uk-loses-badly/ accessed 26 March 2020; Stephen Allen, 'The Chagos Advisory Opinion and the Decolonization of Mauritius' (15 April 2019) www.asil.org/insights/volume/23/issue/2/chagos-advisory-opinion-and-decolonization-mauritius accessed 26 March 2020.

15 UNGA Resolution 73/295, Advisory opinion of the International Court of Justice on the legal consequences of the separation of the Chagos Archipelago from Mauritius in 1965 (24 May 2019). See Owen Bowcott and Julian Borger, 'UK Suffers Crushing Defeat in UN Vote on Chagos Islands', *Guardian* (London, 22 May 2019). The UK continues to reject the outcome of the advisory opinion: see Official Records A/73.PV.83 of the UNGA meeting (22 May 2019) 9–11. For a critique, see Thomas Burri, 'In the Wake of the ICJ's Opinion in *Chagos*: Britannia Waives the Rules' (Völkerrechtsblog, 9 July 2019) https://voelkerrechtsblog.org/in-the-wake-of-the-icjs-opinion-in-chagos-britannia-waives-the-rules/ accessed 26 March 2020.

16 Although there was a three-split vote, for the adoption of the 2017 UNGA resolution, the voting pattern of EU Member States was more in support of the UK: four Member States voted with the UK against the resolution (Bulgaria, Croatia, Hungary, Lithuania); 22 abstained (Austria, Belgium, Czech Republic, Denmark, Estonia, Finland, France, Germany, Greece, Ireland, Italy, Latvia, Luxembourg, Malta, Netherlands, Poland, Portugal, Romania, Slovakia, Slovenia, Spain, Sweden); only one voted in favour (Cyprus). Compare with the three-split vote for the 2019 UNGA resolution: only Hungary backed the UK by voting against; 19 Member States abstained (Belgium, Bulgaria, Croatia, Czech Republic, Denmark, Estonia, France, Germany, Italy, Latvia, Lithuania, Luxembourg, Malta, Netherlands, Poland, Portugal, Romania, Slovakia, Slovenia); seven EU Member States voted in favour (Austria, Cyprus, Finland, Greece, Ireland, Spain, Sweden).

17 Owen Bowcott, 'No British Judge on World Court for First Time in its 71-Year History', *Guardian* (London, 20 November 2017).

18 'Loss of ICJ Judge is a Failure of UK Diplomacy' (28 February 2018) www.parliament.uk/business/committees/committees-a-z/commons-select/foreign-affairs-committee/news-parliament-2017/icj-report-publication-17-19/ accessed 26 March 2020. Testimony before the parliamentary committee of the House of Commons denied that Brexit was an issue in the election. The Committee concluded:

> It is possible that this failure was not a one-off but might instead be an indication that the influence of the UK within the UN is at risk. Possible reasons suggested for this were: increased influence of Asian countries; a change in the standing of, and attitudes to, the UK itself; and changes in the relative influence of the Security Council and the General Assembly.

19 Richard Gowan, 'Separation Anxiety: European Influence at the UN after Brexit' (European Council on Foreign Relations, 10 May 2018) 10, www.ecfr.eu/publications/summary/separation_anxiety_european_influence_at_the_un_after_brexit accessed 26 March 2020.

20 Patrick Wintour, 'Thanks to Brexit, the British Voice Counts for Less at the UN', *Guardian* (London, 28 September 2018).

21 See, inter alia, Amelia Hadfield, 'Britain Against the World? Foreign and Security Policy in the "Age of Brexit"', in Benjamin Martill and Uta Staiger (eds), *Brexit and Beyond: Rethinking the Futures of Europe* (UCL Press 2018); Christopher Hill, 'Turning Back the Clock: The Illusion of a Global Political Role for Britain', in Benjamin Martill and Uta Staiger (eds), *Brexit and Beyond: Rethinking the Futures of Europe* (UCL Press 2018). See also, very outspoken, Denis MacShane, 'Brexit and the Decline of British Foreign Policy' (Strategic Europe, 28 July 2017), according to whom 'Brexit is the biggest influence-reducing move ever seen in Britain's history of international relations', https://carnegieeurope.eu/strategiceurope/72665 accessed 26 March 2020.

22 Gifkins, Jarvis and Ralph (n 3) 14.

23 Gifkins, Jarvis and Ralph (n 3) 1367.
24 Ibid.
25 Ralph, Gifkins and Jarvis (n 3) 15. The authors illustrate this point by the example of India's commitment to the UN peacekeeping mission in the DRC (MONUC), and how the Indian government lessened it in light of the tensions resulting from the UK's, the US' and France's interpretation of UNSC Resolution 1973 as authorizing the overthrow of the Gadaffi regime: ibid, 12–13. From this crisis the authors derive that

> [h]owever skilled diplomats are, they accrue more capital if the state they represent is willing to make material commitments (through development aid or peacekeeping personnel for instance), and they lose if the state is unwilling to make such commitment. It is also clear that diplomatic activism at the Council can be counterproductive if it is not sufficiently inclusive.

They conclude that

> [t]he lesson for the permanent members of the Council, especially those like the United Kingdom who rely more on the power of persuasion to discharge their special responsibility, is that the emerging powers will support robust human protection but not if they are taken for granted .... Without indicating a willingness to commit personnel to increasingly demanding mandates, the United Kingdom (and other permanent members) risks losing the support of those states (like India) that are willing to commit personnel, and by simplifying missions to keep troop contributing countries engaged with the Council, the United Kingdom risks not meeting its special responsibility to deliver mandates that protect civilians.

26 See the contribution by Ramses A Wessel, Chapter 14 in this volume.
27 See, inter alia, EEAS, 'Brexit: EU Keen to Ensure Closest Possible Cooperation with UK for Mutual Security and Defence', https://eeas.europa.eu/headquarters/headquarters-homepage/44590/brexit-eu-keen-ensure-closest-possible-cooperation-uk-mutual-security-and-defence_en accessed 26 March 2020. For the UK perspective, see the two papers published in 2017 covering internal and external security aspects and the future partnership: 'Security, Law Enforcement and Criminal Justice: A Future Partnership Paper' (18 September 2017) https://assets.publishing.service.gov.uk/government/uploads/system/uploads/attachment_data/file/645416/Security__law_enforcement_and_criminal_justice_-_a_future_partnership_paper.PDF accessed 26 March 2020; 'Foreign Policy, Defence and Development: A Future Partnership Paper' (12 September 2017), https://assets.publishing.service.gov.uk/government/uploads/system/uploads/attachment_data/file/643924/Foreign_policy__defence_and_development_paper.pdf accessed 26 March 2020. See also Susi Dennison (ed), 'Keeping Europe Safe after Brexit' (European Council on Foreign Relations Policy Brief, March 2018) www.ecfr.eu/page/-/keeping_europe_safe_after_brexit.pdf accessed 26 March 2020; Giovanni Faleg, 'The Implications of Brexit for the EU's Common Security and Defence Policy' (26 July 2016) www.ceps.eu/publications/implications-brexit-eu's-common-security-and-defence-policy accessed 26 March 2020; Luigi Lonardo, 'EU Common Foreign and Security Policy after Brexit: A Security and Defence Treaty for the "Deep and Special Partnership"' (DCU Brexit Institute, Working Paper, 27 April 2018).
28 Emmanuel Macron, 'Dear Europe, Brexit is a Lesson for All of Us: It's Time for Renewal', *Guardian* (London, 4 March 2019).
29 Simon Tisdall, 'Macron's Overblown Vision for Europe Shows How Much It Needs Britain', *Guardian* (London, 5 March 2019).
30 See, inter alia, James Black, Alexandra Hall, Kate Cox, Marta Kepe and Erik Silfversten, 'Defence and Security After Brexit: Understanding the Possible Implications of the UK's Decision to Leave the EU – Overview Report' (RAND Europe, 2017) 4, 12, www.rand.org/pubs/research_reports/RR1786z1.html accessed 26 March 2020. Rafael Sampson, 'Brexit and the CFSP: A Window of Opportunity?' https://is.muni.cz/th/ncmdp/Rafael_Sampson.pdf accessed 26 March 2020. For an analysis of the UK's possible relationship to CFSP post-Brexit, see, inter alia, Cornelia-Adriana Baciu, 'EU–UK Security Cooperation after Brexit: Towards a "Special Dialogue Framework"?' (16 April 2019) https://atlantic-community.org/eu-uk-security-cooperation-after-brexit-towards-a-special-dialogue-framework/ accessed 26 March 2020; Cornelia-Adriana Baciu and John Doyle (eds), *Peace, Security and Defence Cooperation in Post-Brexit Europe: Risks and Opportunities* (Springer 2019); Paul J Cardwell, 'The United Kingdom and the Common Foreign and Security Policy of the EU: From Pre-Brexit "Awkward Partner" to Post-Brexit "Future Partnership"?' 13 Croatian Yearbook of European Law and Policy 1; Federico Santopinto, 'CSDP after Brexit: The Way Forward' (Study for the European Parliament, May

2018); Ramses A Wessel, 'Friends with Benefits? Possibilities for the UK's Continued Participation in the EU's Foreign and Security Policy' (2019) 4 European Papers 427.

31 Jean C Juncker, 'Towards a Better Europe: A Europe that Protects, Empowers and Defends' (14 September 2016) https://ec.europa.eu/commission/presscorner/detail/en/SPEECH_16_3043 accessed 26 March 2020, pointing to the need for a single headquarters for CFSP operations, common military assets, an innovative European defence industry (for which Juncker announced the creation of a European Defence Fund) and making use of the possibilities which the Treaty of Lisbon foresees for permanent structured cooperation.

32 Rome Declaration of 25 March 2017, in which 'the leaders of 27 member states and of the European Council, the European Parliament and the European Commission' pledged to work towards

> a Union ready to take more responsibilities and to assist in creating a more competitive and integrated defence industry; a Union committed to strengthening its common security and defence, also in cooperation and complementarity with the North Atlantic Treaty Organisation, taking into account national circumstances and legal commitments.
>
> *(www.consilium.europa.eu/en/press/press-releases/2017/03/25/rome-declaration/pdf accessed 26 March 2020)*

33 Commission, 'Reflection Paper on the Future of European Defence' (7 June 2017) https://ec.europa.eu/commission/sites/beta-political/files/reflection-paper-defence_en.pdf accessed 26 March 2020.

34 See Council Decision (CFSP) 2017/2315 establishing permanent structured cooperation (PESCO) and determining the list of participating Member States [2017] OJ L331/57.

35 See Ursula von der Leyen, 'A Union that Strives for More: My Agenda for Europe. Political Guidelines for the Next European Commission 2019–2024' 19: 'We need further bold steps in the next five years towards a genuine European Defence Union. As part of the next long-term EU budget, I intend to strengthen the European Defence Fund to support research and capability development', www.europarl.europa.eu/resources/library/media/20190716RES57231/20190716RES57231.pdf accessed 26 March 2020.

36 See, inter alia, Jan Wouters and Anna-Luise Chané, 'Brussels Meets Westphalia: The European Union and the United Nations' in Piet Eeckhout and Manuel Lopez-Escudero (eds), *The European Union's External Action in Times of Crisis* (Hart Publishing 2016).

37 High Representative of the EU for Foreign Affairs and Security Policy, 'Shared Vision, Common Action: A Stronger Europe. A Global Strategy for the EU's Foreign and Security Policy' (June 2016) 8, 15.

38 See for the post-Lisbon practice, Thomas Mayr-Harting, 'Representing the European Union at the United Nations: The Security Council Dimension' in Nico Schrijver and Niels Blokker (eds), *Elected Members of the Security Council: Lame Ducks or Key Players?* (Brill Nijhoff 2019) 156–160. See on the pre-Lisbon practice J Verbeke, 'EU Coordination on UN Security Council Matters' in Jan Wouters, Frank Hoffmeister and Tom Ruys (eds), *The United Nations and the European Union* (TMC Asser Press 2006) 55.

39 Mayr-Harting (n 38) 161, indicating the most salient themes on which the EU presents positions.

40 See very recently, for example, the statement of the EU and its Member States at the UNSC open debate 'Silencing the Guns in Africa: Cooperation Between the United Nations and Regional Organizations', delivered by João Vale de Almeida, Head of the EU Delegation to the UN in New York, https://eeas.europa.eu/delegations/un-new-york/58861/eu-statement-united-nations-security-council-open-debate-silencing-guns-africa-cooperation_en accessed 26 March 2020.

41 See also Jan Wouters, 'Decision-Making Rules and Processes in International Organisations: The Case of the UN Security Council' (2016) 1 Security and Global Affairs 13–15.

42 High Representative of the EU for Foreign Affairs and Security Policy (n 36) 39.

43 For a discussion of the various positions of Member States regarding either the idea of an EU single seat or a German permanent seat on the UNSC, see, inter alia, Spyros Blavoukos and Dimitris Bourantonis, 'The EU's Performance in the United Nations Security Council' (2011) 33 Journal of European Integration 73; see also Alfonso Medinilla, Pauline Veron and Vera Mazzara, 'EU–UN Cooperation: Confronting Change in the Multilateral System' (ECDPM Discussion Paper, September 2019) 10, who remark that on this matter 'member states will act on the basis of their national interests first', https://ecdpm.org/wp-content/uploads/EU-UN-Cooperation-Confronting-Change-Multilateral-System-ECDPM-Discussion-Paper-260.pdf accessed 26 March 2020.

44 Verbeke (n 38) 55.

45 'Netherlands and Italy to Work in Concert on Security Council' (22 September 2016) www.government.nl/latest/news/2016/09/22/netherlands-and-italy-to-work-in-concert-on-security-council accessed 26 March 2020.
46 Angela Merkel, 'Rede zur 18: Jahreskonferenz des Rates für Nachhaltige Entwicklung' (Berlin, 4 June 2018) (author's translation).
47 See 'More Responsibility in the World', www.bundesregierung.de/breg-en/chancellor/more-responsibilityin-the-world-1141780 accessed 26 March 2020.
48 On Germany's longstanding campaign for a permanent seat in the UNSC for itself, for which it formed a coalition with Brazil, India and Japan (the 'G4'), see, inter alia, 'G4 Nations Bid for Permanent Security Council Seat' (22 September 2004) www.dw.com/en/g4-nations-bid-for-permanent-security-council-seat/a-1335522 accessed 26 March 2020; 'Brazil, Germany, Japan, India Call for UN Security Council Overhaul' (27 September 2018) https://agenciabrasil.ebc.com.br/en/internacional/noticia/2018-09/brazil-germany-japan-india-call-un-security-council-overhaul accessed 26 March 2020. See in recent years 'Joint Statement by Brazil, Germany, India and Japan', delivered by Ambassador Syed Akbaruddin, Permanent Representative of India to the United Nations, at the Informal Meeting of the General Assembly Second IGN Meeting (7–8 March 2017) www.pminewyork.org/adminpart/uploadpdf/89066statement.pdf accessed 26 March 2020; 'Joint G4 Statement by Brazil, Germany, India and Japan', delivered by HE Ambassador Yasuhisa Kawamura, Deputy Permanent Representative of Japan to the United Nations, at the Informal Meeting of the General Assembly, Second Intergovernmental Meeting on Security Council Reform (25 February 2019) www.un.emb-japan.go.jp/itpr_en/kawamura022519.html accessed 26 March 2020; and, most recently, 'Joint G4 Statement', delivered by Ambassador Syed Akbaruddin, Permanent Representative of India to the United Nations, Informal Meeting of the General Assembly on the Intergovernmental Negotiations on Security Council Reform (13 February 2020) www.pminewyork.gov.in/pdf/uploadpdf/statements__1903023260.pdf accessed 26 March 2020. See also, for the G4 campaign from an Indian perspective, Rajeesh Kumar, 'Waiting for Godot: India and United Nations Security Council Reform' (2017) 41 Strategic Analysis 546. For an early analysis of the *problématique*, see Klaus Dicke, 'Die Reform des Sicherheitsrates: Ein ständiger Sitz für Deutschland?' Bonn, Deutsche Gesellschaft für die Vereinten Nationen, Blaue Reihe 70 (1997) https://dgvn.de/fileadmin/publications/PDFs/Blaue_Reihe/Blaue_Reihe_70.pdf accessed 26 March 2020.
49 See also 'UN Security Council: Germany, France Share Presidency' (1 April 2019) www.dw.com/en/germany-pledges-hands-on-role-at-un-security-council/a-47226145 accessed 26 March 2020.
50 Edith Drieskens, 'Walking on Eggshells: Non-Permanent Members Searching for a EU Perspective at the UN Security Council' in Jan Wouters, Edith Drieskens and S Biscop (eds), *Belgium in the UN Security Council: Reflections on the 2007–2008 Membership* (Intersentia 2009) 182.
51 Verbeke (n 38) 55.
52 Drieskens (n 50) 182.
53 Mayr-Harting (n 38) 158.
54 PD (n 4).
55 But not completely: see, for example, para 99 on the conclusion of a framework participation agreement for enabling the UK to participate in future EU CSDP missions. The following sentence has been added in the 2019 version:

> Such an agreement would be without prejudice to the decision-making autonomy of the Union or the sovereignty of the United Kingdom, and the United Kingdom will maintain the right to determine how it would respond to any invitation or option to participate in operations or missions.

56 See the use of the plural in paras 92 and 97 of the Declaration.
57 For a verbatim record, see www.securitycouncilreport.org/atf/cf/%7B65BFCF9B-6D27-4E9C-8CD3-CF6E4FF96FF9%7D/s_pv_8482.pdf accessed 27 March 2020. See also 'Europe and UN Form Bulwark Against "Might Makes Right" Worldview, EU Foreign Affairs Chief Tells Security Council', *UN News* (12 March 2019) https://news.un.org/en/story/2019/03/1034531 accessed 27 March 2020. Mayr-Harting (n 38) 164, provides interesting insights on the practice of 'briefings' by the EU High Representative for Foreign Affairs and Security Policy to the UNSC:

> this allows the High Representative to address the Security Council under different conditions than those regulating the usual presentations by EU representatives to the Security Council. 'Briefings' give the High Representative the possibility to address the Council at the beginning of

> the meeting, normally following an introduction by the Secretary-General of the United Nations (who usually attends these sessions). The 15 Security Council then react to the presentation by the High Representative, and the relations between the UN and EU are the only topic of the meeting.

For a verbatim record of the session of 9 May 2017, see www.securitycouncilreport.org/atf/cf/%7B65BFCF9B-6D27-4E9C-8CD3-CF6E4FF96FF9%7D/s_pv_7935.pdf accessed 27 March 2020.

58 See www.securitycouncilreport.org/monthly-forecast/2020-02/eu-un-briefing-2.php accessed 27 March 2020. This session took place during Belgium's presidency of the Council, https://unric.org/en/belgium-puts-eu-un-cooperation-on-un-security-council-agenda/ accessed 27 March 2020.

59 Presidential Statement of 14 February 2014, https://undocs.org/S/PRST/2014/4 accessed 27 March 2020. Furthermore, the Statement commends the EU's 'involvement in international negotiations and mediation', the EU and its Member States' 'ongoing commitment to international peacekeeping, peacebuilding, humanitarian assistance, and financial as well as logistical support', 'the extensive co-operation between the European Union and the United Nations' and 'the European Union's role in supporting the United Nations operations in the areas of mutual concern'. The Statement concludes as follows: 'The Security Council welcomes the close cooperation between the United Nations and the European Union and encourages both organizations to further strengthen their institutional relations and strategic partnership, including through regular briefings by the European Union High Representative for Foreign Affairs and Security Policy to the Security Council.' According to Mayr-Harting, the Presidential Statement 'is undoubtedly one of the most comprehensive overall assessments of the EU's international action made at the UN in recent years' (Mayr-Harting (n 38) 163, fn 44).

60 See also the description of this practice with Mayr-Harting (n 38) 172. On the meeting of 18 May 2018, see www.whatsinblue.org/2018/05/un-security-council-and-eu-political-and-security-committee-informal-meeting.php accessed 27 March 2020; on the meeting of 24 May 2019, see www.whatsinblue.org/2019/05/informal-meeting-between-members-of-the-un-security-council-and-eu-political-and-security-committee-informal-meeting.php accessed 27 March 2020.

61 On the genesis of this practice, see Hugo Nunes da Silva, 'United in Adversity? The Europeanisation of EU Concertation Practices in a More Divided UN Security Council' (College of Europe EU Diplomacy Paper, 2019) 16–19.

62 These media stakeouts can nowadays be found on YouTube. See, for instance, for the EU Security Council Media Stakeout of 29 February on Syria, www.youtube.com/watch?v=onI0dhlK7wc accessed 27 March 2020; of 19 February 2020 on Ukraine, www.youtube.com/watch?v=yEHUnTXKink accessed 27 March 2020; of 13 February 2020 on Libya, www.youtube.com/watch?v=MXBlpJ2SHoQ accessed 27 March 2020; of 4 February 2020 on Myanmar, www.youtube.com/watch?v=lZ1l3DP4sxo accessed 27 March 2020.

63 European Union and UK on ballistic missiles in DPR Korea – Media Stakeout of 5 March 2020, www.youtube.com/watch?v=2wHZAi9uFTc accessed 27 March 2020.

64 On the practice of 'briefer of the month', which was already customary before the Treaty of Lisbon, see Mayr-Harting (n 38) 156–157.

65 This practice has already existed for a while: see Nicoletta Pirozzi, 'The EU's Contribution to the Effectiveness of the UN Security Council: Representation, Coordination and Outreach' (Istituto Affari Internazionali 2010) 3.

66 See Netherlands, Poland and Sweden, 'European cooperation in the United Nations Security Council – examples and lessons learned by the elected EU UNSC members in 2018' (7 December 2018); see also Esa Paasivirta and Thomas Ramopoulos, 'UN General Assembly, UN Security Council and UN Human Rights Council: The EU in State-Centred Multilateral Frameworks' in Ramses A Wessel and Jed Odermatt (eds), *Research Handbook on the European Union and International Organizations* (Edward Elgar Publishing 2019) 71–72, who mention in addition the practice in which the EU Delegation

> shares a briefing file with EU Member States that are members of the UNSC, where it gives a European perspective on the items in the agenda of the UNSC, recalling positions adopted by the Union previously thereon and further suggesting elements that can be reflected in statements.

67 Nunes da Silva (n 61) 15.

68 Council conclusions reinforcing the UN–EU strategic partnership on peace operations and crisis management: priorities 2019–2021 (18 September 2018) para 11.

69 See Pirozzi (n 65) 3.

70 Netherlands, Poland and Sweden (n 66).

71 Ibid. However, in the past, discussions on UNSC matters in CONUN and the PSC were 'often bypassed and the Member States ambassadors in New York are often recalcitrant to receive steering from their junior colleagues in the PSC': Daniele Marchesi, 'The EU Common Foreign and Security Policy in the UN Security Council: Between Representation and Coordination' (2010) 15 European Foreign Affairs Review 97, 101. On the limited role of the Brussels-based institutions and organs in the preparation of EU positions on issues discussed in the UNSC, see Paasivirta and Ramopoulos (n 66) 70.

72 It was a *présidence jumelée*, but not a co-presidency or common presidency: Eglantine Staunton, 'The UN Security Council in a Post-Brexit World: France and Germany Take the Lead' (12 March 2019) https://theconversation.com/the-un-security-council-in-a-post-brexit-world-france-and-germany-take-the-lead-113078 accessed 27 March 2020. See also, indicating the priorities of the twin presidency, 'Première in the United Nations Security Council' (28 March 2019) www.bundesregierung.de/breg-en/news/premi%C3%A8re-in-the-united-nations-security-council-1596308 accessed 27 March 2020.

73 Stéphanie Fillion, 'Security Council Presidency: Two Friends, France and Germany, Now Share an Office' (Passblue, 4 March 2019) www.passblue.com/2019/03/04/security-council-presidency-two-friends-france-and-germany-now-share-an-office/ accessed 27 March 2020.

74 Since Italian Foreign Minister Gianni de Michelis voiced the idea of an EU single seat during Italy's presidency in the autumn of 1990 there has been a lot of writings on this issue: see, inter alia, Spyros Blavoukas and Dimitris Bourantonis, 'The UN Security Council Reform Debate' in Knud Erik Joergensen and Katie Verlin Laatikainen (eds), *Routledge Handbook on the European Union and International Institutions* (Routledge 2013), 128; Spyros Blavoukas and Dimitris Bourantonis, 'The EU's Performance in the United Nations Security Council' (2011) 33 Journal of European Integration 731; Edith Drieskens, 'Curb Your Enthusiasm: Why an EU Perspective on UN Security Council Reform Does Not Imply an EU Seat' (2015) 1(1) Global Affairs 59; Christopher Hill, 'The European Powers in the Security Council: Differing Interests, Differing Arenas' in Katie Laatikainen and Karen Smith (eds), *Intersecting Multilateralisms: The European Union and the United Nations* (Palgrave Macmillan 2006) 49; Marco Pedrazzi, 'Italy's Approach to UN Security Council Reform' (2000) 35(3) International Spectator 49; F Paolo Fulci, 'Italy and the Reform of the UN Security Council' (1999) 34(2) International Spectator 7; Panos Tsakaloyannis and Dimitris Bourantonis, 'The European Union's Common Foreign and Security Policy and the Reform of the Security Council' (1997) 2 European Foreign Affairs Review 197.

75 Also Italy may need to be watched here. The proposal for giving the EU a permanent seat was strongly backed recently by Roberto Fico, the speaker for Italy's lower house of parliament: 'Italy Urges Permanent UN Security Council Seat for EU' *TCA Regional News* (18 December 2019).

76 For the English translation, see O Scholz, 'It is in Our Own Interest to Ensure that Europe is Strong, Sovereign and Fair' www.bundesfinanzministerium.de/Content/EN/Reden/2018/2018-11-28-Europe-speech-HU-Berlin.html;jsessionid=557785E76282F0B58A7FE433A12F852B.delivery2-master accessed 26 March 2020. For the original German version, see Olaf Scholz, 'Ein starkes, ein souveränes, ein gerechtes Europa liegt in unserem ureigenen Interesse' (Humboldt University, 28 November 2018) www.bundesfinanzministerium.de/Content/DE/Reden/2018/2018-11-28-Europarede-HU-Berlin.html;jsessionid=27DF052D7DEB59538926ED092E269A33 accessed 27 March 2020.

77 Cited in France24, 'Germany Calls for France to Give its UN Security Council Seat to the EU' (28 November 2011) www.france24.com/en/20181128-paris-france-german-proposal-un-eu-macron-merkel-security-council-nations accessed 27 March 2020.

78 See www.diplomatie.gouv.fr/en/french-foreign-policy/united-nations/news/events-2018/article/united-nations-q-a-excerpts-from-the-daily-press-briefing-29-11-18 accessed 27 March 2020. See also Pol Gradaigh, 'France Not Interested in Giving EU its UN Security Council Seat' *DPA International* (29 November 2018). However, see the arguments in favour of the EU succeeding France's permanent seat: Norman R Denny, 'A Union on the UN: Should France Keep its Security Council Permanent Seat?' (2010) 32(3) Harvard International Review 72.

79 Annegret Kramp-Karrenbauer, 'Europa jetzt richtig machen' *Welt am Sonntag* (10 March 2019) www.welt.de/politik/deutschland/article190037115/AKK-antwortet-Macron-Europa-richtig-machen.html accessed 27 March 2020, where she wrote: 'Die EU sollte künftig mit einem gemeinsamen ständigen Sitz im Sicherheitsrat der Vereinten Nationen vertreten sein.' The comments were badly received in France and viewed as election campaign language: see Hans Stark, 'Le traité d'Aix-la-Chapelle: promesse de convergence pour couple divisé' (Politique étrangère, 2019) 73, 81–82; Hajn-

alka Vincze, 'One Voice, But Whose Voice? Should France Cede its UN Security Council Seat to the EU?' (Center for the Study of America and the West at the Foreign Policy Research Institute, 20 March 2019) www.fpri.org/article/2019/03/one-voice-but-whose-voice-should-france-cede-its-un-security-council-seat-to-the-eu/ accessed 26 March 2020.

80 Article 5 of the Franco-German Treaty of Cooperation and Integration of 22 January 2019.

81 Of course, the problem remains that on a Council of 15, the EU is still somewhat overrepresented by having typically two to three elected members on the UNSC, next to France's permanent seat: see Nicoletta Pirozzi and Natalino Ronzitti, 'The European Union and the Reform of the UN Security Council: Toward a New Regionalism?' (Istituto Affari Internazionali Working Paper, 2012) 18.

82 See for an argument in favour of this approach, Peter Pindják, 'Time for the European Union to Reassert Itself in the UN Security Council' *Atlantic Council* (9 March 2020) www.atlanticcouncil.org/blogs/new-atlanticist/time-for-the-european-union-to-reassert-itself-in-the-un-security-council/ accessed 26 March 2020.

83 See, inter alia, Wouters and Chané (n 36); Edith Drieskens, 'Beyond Chapter VIII: Limits and Opportunities for Regional Representation at the UN Security Council' (2010) 7 International Organizations Law Review 149.

84 This was already observed in Marchesi (n 71) 112; and, in 1997, by Panos Tsakaloyannis and Dimitris Bourantonis, 'The European Union's Common Foreign and Security Policy and the Reform of the Security Council' (1997) 2 European Foreign Affairs Review 197, 200. See also the observation of Richard Gowan, at the occasion of the EU's divisions on the UN Global Compact on Migration in 2018:

> If the union cannot agree to a common stance on a non-binding thematic agreement, how on earth could it do so on the fast-moving crises that punctuate the council's agenda? Most realistic advocates of a stronger EU voice in multilateral affairs agree that the idea of an EU Security Council seat is a distraction.
>
> *(Richard Gowan, 'How Not to Save the World: EU Divisions at the UN' (22 January 2019) www.ecfr.eu/article/commentary_how_not_to_save_the_world_eu_divisions_at_the_un accessed 27 March 2020)*

85 In a Communication of 12 September 2018, 'A Stronger Global Actor: A More Efficient Decision-Making for EU Common Foreign and Security Policy' (COM(2018) 647 final), the Commission made the case for more qualified majority voting in the CFSP. Moreover, in her mission letter of 10 September 2019 to Josep Borrell, the new High Representative, Commission President-elect Ursula von der Leyen wrote:

> To be a global leader, the Union needs to take decisions in a faster and more efficient way. We must overcome unanimity constraints that hamper our foreign policy. When putting forward proposals, you should seek to use the clauses in the Treaties that allow certain decisions on the common foreign and security policy to be adopted by qualified majority voting.
>
> *(https://ec.europa.eu/commission/sites/beta-political/files/mission-letter-josep-borrell-2019_en.pdf accessed 27 March 2020)*

12
EU diplomacy after Brexit

Mauro Gatti

12.1 Introduction

The history of EU diplomacy is interwoven with UK–EU relations: the UK was the first state to establish a representation to the European Coal and Steel Community (ECSC) and the ECSC opened its first delegation abroad in the UK.[1] Brexit may mark another evolution of EU diplomacy, by affecting the EU's relations with third countries and creating new opportunities in the context of bilateral UK–EU relations.

The concept of 'EU diplomacy' is multifaceted. On the one hand, 'EU diplomacy' is the product of cooperation between the diplomatic missions of the Member States, which constitute an 'EU diplomatic network' of sorts. European diplomatic cooperation started early in the integration process, through regular meetings of Member States' diplomatic missions in third countries.[2] This practice is now codified in Art. 32 and 35 TEU, which stipulate that the diplomatic missions of the Member States must 'cooperate' to define and implement the Common Foreign and Security Policy (CFSP). On the other hand, the EU has a diplomacy of its own. Before the Lisbon Treaty, the European Commission created numerous delegations in third countries, which functioned as Community representatives de facto.[3] The representations of international organisations are functionally different from states' diplomatic missions. Commission delegations, in particular, were 'specialised missions', which protected the external interests of the internal market and the European nuclear industry.[4] States' diplomatic missions and the delegations of international organisations are different in terms of their status, too. The former enjoy full diplomatic privileges and immunities by virtue of international customary law, while the latter usually enjoy only functional immunities, on the basis of international agreements or domestic legislation.[5] Moreover, states' ambassadors take precedence in the order of the date of taking up their functions,[6] while the representatives of international organisations usually follow the representatives of states.

The European Commission never accepted the equation of its delegations with those of international organisations.[7] The European External Action Service (EEAS), which replaced the Commission in the management of what are now 'Union delegations',[8] expressly seeks 'equality with States'.[9] In terms of *legal status*, 'equality with states' is expressed mainly by the application of full diplomatic privileges and immunities to EU delegations, usually by virtue of international agreements.[10] Moreover, the EEAS insists that EU representatives be placed in the order of precedence according to the rules applicable to states.[11] This principle was accepted by several countries (e.g. the US),[12] while others maintain the EU's representative at the bottom of the state list (e.g. Colombia)[13] or do not include the EU's representative in the states' list at all (e.g. Brazil and UK).[14] The concept of 'equality with states' may be applied to the *functions* of EU delegations, too. The Union has more than 130 delegations in third countries,[15] which, unlike previous Commission delegations, can deal with virtually any policy issue, ranging from trade to security management.[16] Therefore, the functions of EU delegations, according to the EEAS, coincide with those of states' diplomatic missions, as recognised by the Vienna Convention on Diplomatic Relations (1961): representation, negotiation, information, promotion of friendly relations, and protection of the interests of the Union and its 'nationals'.[17] The delegations' ability to perform the latter function, however, has been put into question.[18]

While EU delegations are allegedly 'less' than national embassies in certain respects, they are also 'more' than states' missions, as they have an additional function: coordinating the diplomatic missions of EU Member States. Delegations thus link the first facet of EU diplomacy (the cooperation between the diplomatic missions of the Member States) and its second facet (the diplomacy of the Union *stricto sensu*).

This chapter suggests that Brexit may affect both facets of EU diplomacy. In the first place, Brexit may impact on the cooperation between the diplomatic missions of the Member States: as the UK has numerous diplomatic missions, its withdrawal reduces the size of the EU diplomatic network (section 12.2) and influences, albeit limitedly, the coordination of EU diplomacy (section 12.3). The reduced size of the EU diplomatic network might complicate consular protection of EU citizens in third countries, though this problem might be solved through the empowerment of EU delegations (sections 12.4 and 12.5). In fact, Brexit impacts the second facet of EU diplomacy (the diplomacy of the *Union*), too. The EU delegation in the UK will perform a key role in ensuring the implementation of the UK's Withdrawal Agreement (hereinafter: WA) and, consequently, might have unprecedented responsibilities concerning the protection of EU nationals in the UK. The EU delegation in the UK might thus come close to full functional 'equality with states' (section 12.6). It is concluded that Brexit constitutes a challenge for EU diplomacy but might also constitute an opportunity for the Union external representation (section 12.7).

For the sake of brevity, this contribution focuses on the activity of EU and Member States' diplomatic missions in the UK and other third countries and does not address either the position of EU delegations accredited to international organisations[19] or the role of representations accredited to the Union. Furthermore, the contribution does not address domestic aspects that incidentally affect EU diplomacy, such as the position of the British officials of the Union after Brexit.[20]

12.2 The downsizing of the EU diplomatic network

The most obvious consequences of Brexit in terms of EU diplomacy lie in the weakening of the network composed of the diplomatic missions of the Member States. The UK is relatively more influential than most EU Member States on the global stage and its withdrawal is unlikely to strengthen the diplomatic action of the EU. Moreover, the UK has a high number of diplomatic missions, which promote its action in numerous countries and contributed to the activity of the EU diplomatic network before Brexit.

The data collected by the EEAS in December 2019[21] show that, while the UK has embassies in 122 non-EU countries,[22] most Member States have much smaller networks (56 embassies as an average). Only three EU actors have more than 120 diplomatic missions in third countries: Germany (126), France (133), and the EU itself (133 delegations). Italy and Spain have 100 and 98 embassies, respectively, and all the other Member States have 80 missions or fewer. Sixteen Member States have fewer than 60 embassies and seven countries have fewer than 30 missions.

In 21 small and micro-states, neither the UK nor EU Member States have a diplomatic mission.[23] In the non-EU countries where the UK has an embassy, there is an average of about 12 diplomatic missions of EU Member States (13, if EU delegations are taken into account).

This might perhaps suggest that the EU diplomatic network remains robust after Brexit. However, the distribution of EU diplomatic missions in third countries is uneven. Among the countries hosting an embassy of the UK – i.e. where the EU diplomatic network was downsized because of Brexit – one may distinguish, for analytical purposes, five groups, which are affected differently by the UK's withdrawal.

The first group includes the countries where the UK has a diplomatic mission, but current EU Member States do not. This group includes only four small countries (Barbados, Belize, Guyana, and Solomon Islands) and, at any rate, an EU presence remains in two of those countries (Barbados and Guyana), which host EU delegations.

The second group is composed of countries hosting very few embassies of the current EU Member States (one to three). This group is composed of 19 third countries. These are mostly developing countries located primarily in Africa,[24] but also in Asia,[25] the Americas,[26] and Oceania.[27] In almost all these countries, the Union has a delegation.[28] France and Germany are the most represented Member States (14 and 13 embassies, respectively), whereas other Member States have limited representation (e.g. Italy has three embassies).

The third group is composed of countries with a wider, but below-average, EU diplomatic network (four to seven embassies of the Member States). This group includes 24 countries, prevalently small or mid-sized developing nations,[29] as well as North Korea. All these countries, except North Korea, host an EU delegation, too. In these countries the representation of EU Member States is relatively diverse: Germany has 24 embassies, France 22, Italy 16, Spain 15, and the Netherlands eight.

The fourth group includes countries hosting a below-average to average number of missions of EU Member States (8–12 embassies). This group is composed of 19 third countries, including 16 mid-sized developing countries,[30] a country from the EU 'neighbourhood' (Armenia), New Zealand, and Oman. Several Member states have embassies in these countries, for example, France (19 embassies), Germany (19), Italy (18), Netherlands (16), Spain (16), Sweden (11) Romania (nine), and Hungary (nine). The EU has a delegation in almost all these countries.[31]

The fifth group consists of countries with an above-average representation of EU Member States' embassies (13–27 missions) and is composed of 56 countries, including the biggest developing countries and most industrialised countries. The EU diplomatic network is strongest in China, India, Russia, and the US, where all the Member States have an embassy.

The above considerations suggest that Brexit, by reducing the size of the EU diplomatic network, is likely to weaken it, at least in quantitative terms, in numerous countries (see, in particular, the first, second, and third groups above). This may result in a reduced ability of the EU's diplomatic network to collect information and implement policies abroad, especially in small and medium-sized developing countries, where relatively few Member States have diplomatic missions. It may be hypothesised that the reduced size of the EU diplomatic network might increase the role of, and require greater contribution from, the Member States that have a high number of embassies in third countries (i.e. France, Germany, and, to a lesser extent, Italy and Spain). EU delegations that are present in almost every country where the UK has an embassy, might possibly contribute to strengthen the activity of the EU diplomatic network after Brexit, particularly in light of their coordinating role (see next section). For this purpose, however, the delegations would probably require additional human and financial resources, which are unlikely to be allocated in the short term, especially during the current economic crisis.

12.3 Coordination of the EU diplomatic network after Brexit

While Brexit reduces the size of the EU diplomatic network, it has limited and indirect impact on its coordination. European diplomatic cooperation originated in the practice and was codified in part with the Single European Act (SEA).[32] At present, EU primary law calls for 'cooperation' between the missions of the Member States (Art. 32, 35 TEU). Both primary and secondary law require EU delegations to act 'in close cooperation' with the missions of the Member States (Art. 221(2) TFEU) and 'support the Member States in their diplomatic relations'.[33] Neither primary nor secondary law expressly entrust the delegations with the responsibility to chair diplomatic meetings of Member States' diplomats, but they acquired this role in practice (though they do not chair consular meetings, see below, section 12.5).[34] Diplomatic meetings can be used for several purposes, such as the exchange of information or the preparation of joint reports for the Council.[35] Delegations may also deliver the Union position as well as the common position of the EU and its Member States (in respect of issues falling partly within the competence of the Union and partly within that of its Member States).[36] Such common positions may take the form of *démarches* (messages for third states) or 'local statements' (messages for the public).[37]

Brexit does not affect the EU's coordination in countries where EU delegations are present, but might impact on coordination arrangements in third states where the Union does not have a mission of its own. Although the EU has delegations in more than 130 countries, it does not have a permanent representation in several states, for budgetary or political reasons. For instance, the EU does not have delegations in either Iran or North Korea. Where the Union does not have a resident delegation, but one or more of the Member States have an embassy,[38] the EU's coordination and representation is ensured by the mission of the Member State exercising the Council presidency. If the Council presidency does not have a mission *in loco*, the responsibility to represent and coordinate the Union falls on the Member State which exercises the Council Presidency for the following six months. If the latter is not represented in the country either, the coordination is performed 'in rotation, for a period of six months', by another Member State represented in the country, following the order in which Member States are to exercise the Council Presidency.[39]

Since British missions are present in numerous third states (whereas several EU Member States are not, see above, section 12.2), UK missions often replaced the Council Presidency's embassies as EU representatives and coordinators. For instance, the countries that exercised the Council Presidency in 2015/2017 (Latvia, Luxembourg, the Netherlands, Slovakia and Malta) had between 11 and 79 embassies in third states.[40] Although the UK should have exercised the Council Presidency after Malta (second half of 2017), its embassies had responsibility of representation and coordination on behalf of the EU well before, because the aforementioned EU countries did not have embassies *in loco*. This occurred, for example, in Panama (first half of 2015), Turkmenistan (second half of 2015), and Mongolia (second half of 2016).[41]

The UK was expected to exercise the Council Presidency in 2017 but relinquished this opportunity because of the Brexit referendum. Therefore, the UK ceased coordinating European diplomacies long before its actual withdrawal and was replaced by other Member States as diplomatic coordinator in countries without either an EU delegation or a mission of the Council Presidency. For instance, French missions in third countries have exercised representation and coordination functions on behalf of the Union in more than 30 occasions since 2017.[42] Brexit thus increases the responsibility (and visibility) of Member States with a big diplomatic network, thereby confirming their centrality to EU diplomacy after Brexit, which was already mentioned above (see section 12.2). Such centrality is further emphasised by the effects of Brexit on the protection of EU nationals, as shown in the next section.

12.4 Consular protection in third states after Brexit: consular *démarches* ...

The reduced extension of the EU's diplomatic and consular network affects, not only the diplomatic relations of the Union, but also the protection of its 'nationals'. The protection of nationals (including natural and legal persons) is a crucial function of diplomatic missions: through this activity, the diplomatic mission acts as a 'reminder of our nationality'.[43]

Under international law, individuals should be protected by their state of nationality, at least in principle.[44] However, under Art. 23 TFEU and Art. 46 of the EU Charter of Fundamental Rights, every citizen of the Union, in the territory of a third country in which his/her state is not represented, is entitled to protection by the diplomatic or consular authorities of any other Member State, on the same conditions as the nationals of that state.[45]

Art. 23 TFEU and Art. 46 of the Charter arguably refer to both diplomatic and consular protection.[46] *Diplomatic protection* may be defined as the invocation, by a state, of the international responsibility of another state for an injury caused by an internationally wrongful act of that state to a natural or legal person that is a national of the former state.[47] Diplomatic protection may be performed through various means, including 'diplomatic action'.[48] This activity may partially overlap with *consular protection*, which may take the form of an action of diplomatic or consular agents before foreign authorities in favour of citizens who have been wronged (i.e. consular *démarche*).[49] Consular protection may also take a second form: the provision of assistance to the sending country's citizens (e.g. by providing emergency documents or money in case of emergencies).[50] While Art. 23 TFEU and Art. 46 of the Charter point at both diplomatic and consular protection, EU hard and soft law directly address only the consular protection of citizens. Therefore, this section and the next focus on the consular protection of EU citizens in third states after Brexit. Diplomatic protection is discussed in section 12.6, with respect to the activities of the EU delegation in the UK.

Consular protection in favour of nationals, as noted above, may be ensured through either (i) *démarches* (discussed in the remainder of this section) or (ii) the provision of assistance to the nationals (discussed in the next section). The first form of consular protection seems to constitute, according to the Council, a national competence, whose exercise is apparently unrestrained by Art. 23 TFEU. In fact, the action before foreign authorities in favour of EU citizens is addressed only by nonbinding EU instruments, which create general cooperation frameworks on consular issues and do not specifically address the protection of unrepresented Union citizens vis-à-vis third states. The Council Toolkit on Procedural Issues on Consular démarches (2016), in particular, suggests that, if the rights of an EU citizen are violated (e.g. in respect of prison conditions), the Council presidency and its missions *in loco* may conduct consultations with the other Member States and their missions. EU Member States may decide in the Council Working Party on Consular Affairs (presumably, by unanimity) to conduct a *démarche* to the authority of the receiving country.[51] The *démarche* is delivered on behalf of the 'EU Member States' by the Council Presidency.[52] If the *démarche* affects the CFSP (e.g. because it addresses the state of human rights in a third country), it is carried out, on behalf of both the Union and the Member States, by the mission of the Council Presidency 'together with the EU Delegation for the CFSP part'.[53]

Brexit does not prevent the delivering of *démarches* in favour of EU citizens: some EU Member States have a wide diplomatic and consular network and can still conduct *démarches* in favour of EU citizens (see above, section 12.2). It cannot be excluded, at any rate, that, given its relatively strong diplomacy and political weight, the UK might have contributed to the effectiveness of EU *démarches* in the past. For instance, EU diplomats reported that the UK led on lobbying activity in Cambodia in 2015 'due to lack of resource capacity in other MS Consular Sections'.[54]

To address this challenge, the Member States may consider relying on EU delegations, by systematically (but informally) empowering them to lead the consultations *in loco* and to deliver the EU *démarches*. This solution would convey an image of unity and would be especially useful in the countries where the Union has a close relationship with the host government, for example because the Union is a major donor. EU delegations might also ensure a better protection for EU citizens unrepresented by their state in a third country: perhaps, delegations are more likely to focus on the position of unrepresented citizens than the missions of other Member States. An extension of the delegations' role might be politically acceptable for the Member States, since it would not imply a conferral of additional powers to the Union: the delegation would informally deliver a *démarche* 'on behalf of the Member States of the EU'.[55]

12.5 ... and assistance to unrepresented EU citizens

The second aspect of consular protection – providing assistance to nationals – is regulated by Directive 2015/637 on Consular Protection and Directive 2019/997 on EU Emergency Travel Document, which implement Art. 23 TFEU and Art. 46 of the Charter.[56]

According to these Directives, EU Member States must provide assistance to unrepresented EU citizens[57] in third countries on the same conditions as to their own nationals, in respect of emergency situations (e.g. repatriation in case of natural disasters and wars) and other serious circumstances (e.g. loss of passport, illness, death, arrest, or the commission of a crime against EU citizens). The Directives are implemented, inter alia, through local cooperation among the missions of the Member States in third countries, which hold regular consular meetings. Consular meetings are chaired by a representative of a Member State.[58] In addition, a Member State may voluntarily assume the task of 'Lead State' in a third country and coordinate any support provided for unrepresented citizens in case of crises.[59]

Consular assistance remains, therefore, a responsibility of the *Member States*: EU delegations are required to merely 'support' Member States' missions in 'their role' of providing assistance.[60] Delegations also 'support' the chair of consular meetings and the 'Lead State'.[61] In practice, EU delegations occasionally do more than merely 'supporting', by directly providing assistance to EU citizens, notably in the context of emergencies. For instance, during the coronavirus crisis the EU delegation in Australia 'managed to secure seats on flights to Europe' and its vehicles 'picked up stranded European citizens unable to reach the gathering points'.[62] In any event, the tasks of delegations in this area remain limited and uncodified.

Brexit does not question EU citizens' ability to request consular assistance in third countries because there is at least one diplomatic mission of a Member State in almost every country where the UK has an embassy (see above, section 12.2), not to mention the consulates and honorary consulates of the remaining Member States.[63] However, Brexit might complicate the provision of consular protection, since it may generate greater workload for the missions of the remaining Member States. As noted above (section 12.2), there are several third countries hosting a few missions of EU Member States. For instance, in 19 countries where the UK has an embassy, there are only one to three missions of EU Member States. Brexit may result, therefore, in additional workload for the missions of some EU states (especially France and Germany). This problem might become particularly serious if some Member States decided to downsize their diplomatic and consular network because of the coronavirus-related economic crisis and, consequently, additional EU citizens found themselves 'unrepresented' in third countries.

The most practical solution lies, again, in extending EU delegations' mandate. The idea is not new.[64] During the drafting of the Decision establishing the EEAS, in particular, several Member States supported the idea of giving more responsibilities to the delegations in terms of consular protection, apparently because they intended to avoid an excessive workload of their diplomatic and consular services.[65] While consular protection, under international law, should be provided by the state of nationality, third states are generally content for assistance to be provided by other Member States.[66] Presumably, they would not object to the EU performing this function, either. Nonetheless, in 2011 the High Representative noted that 'a number of Member States' were 'clearly opposed to the EU taking on a greater role in this area' and the idea of involving delegations in consular assistance was eventually dropped.[67]

The UK has always been the most vocal opponent of the EU's involvement in consular protection at large, as it considered it to be 'best handled by Member States themselves'.[68] For years, UK authorities have stated that they would 'resist any actions that might undermine Member States' primacy' in this ambit.[69] The UK apparently opposed even an informal empowerment of delegations in practice. For instance, EU diplomats reported that in Nigeria in 2015 'clearly the UK was the MS that "quickly quashed" the suggestion that the EU del might lead on drafting a NV [*note-vérbale*] on detention notifications'.[70] After Brexit an empowerment of EU delegations in the area of consular protection – in respect of both the delivery of *démarches* and the assistance to EU citizens – is both timely and less unlikely.

Brexit might, therefore, constitute an opportunity for EU integration in respect of consular protection. It remains to be seen whether the remaining Member States will seize it. An incentive for the empowerment of EU delegations in the area of consular protection may come from the precedent that might be set by the new EU delegation in London, whose activity is likely to include the protection of EU nationals in the UK, as shown in the next section.

12.6 Protection of EU individuals in the UK

On 1 February 2020, the day after the UK's withdrawal from the Union, the EU closed the Commission representation in London and opened, in the same premises, an EU delegation. Since this delegation is very recent, it is impossible to reach definite conclusions about its activities. The legal framework of EU–UK relations, at any rate, provides some useful indications about its future tasks.

In principle, the EU delegation in the UK should be similar to the missions of the Union in other third states. The delegation is expected to be granted, like other delegations, 'privileges and immunities equivalent to those referred to in the Vienna Convention on Diplomatic Relations of 18 April 1961'.[71] The delegation in the UK will also perform the typical tasks of other EU delegations, i.e. diplomatic functions. The High Representative noted, at any rate, that

> in addition to the traditional responsibilities of an EU Delegation in a third country, such as EU diplomatic representation, EU coordination and reporting and promotion of the EU in the host country, the EU Delegation to the United Kingdom will have a key role in ensuring the implementation of the UK's Withdrawal Agreement.[72]

This additional task may arguably include the protection of EU 'nationals' in the UK.

As is well known, the Union and the UK concluded a WA, including a Protocol on Ireland/Northern Ireland (hereinafter: NI Protocol) and a Protocol relating to the Sovereign Base Areas in Cyprus, and a Protocol on Gibraltar.[73] The WA and its Protocols grant a specific status to the UK, which seems peculiar.[74] During the 'transition period', which started with the UK's withdrawal and is expected to last until the end of 2020, and may be extended once up to two years (December 2022),[75] the whole of 'Union law' is 'applicable to and in the United Kingdom',[76] though there are exceptions relating, for instance, to the UK's participation in EU institutions.[77] After the transition period, EU law ceases to bind the UK, at least in principle. Nonetheless, the WA and its Protocols make applicable to the UK several rules of EU law, notably in the areas of (a) freedom of movement of citizens and (b) freedom of movement of goods. Union citizens who exercised their right to reside in the UK or their right as frontier workers in the UK 'before the end of the transition period', as well as their family members, enjoy rights that are, to large extent, similar to the freedom of movement rights guaranteed by EU primary and secondary law (notably Directive 2004/38/EC).[78] These EU citizens enjoy their rights 'for their lifetime' (Art. 39 WA), assuming they apply for a residence permit and continue to reside in the UK.[79]

The WA also ensures freedom of movement of goods to a part of the UK, i.e. Northern Ireland. By virtue of the NI Protocol, most primary and secondary EU law rules on the movement of goods are applied in and to Northern Ireland after the end of the transition period (e.g. prohibition of customs duties, discriminatory taxation, and quantitative restrictions in respect of trade).[80] While Northern Ireland is formally 'part of the customs territory of the United Kingdom',[81] the NI Protocol requires the application in Northern Ireland, inter alia, of the EU's Customs Code.[82] Consequently, goods exported from Great Britain to Northern Ireland may be subject to custom duties and border checks.[83]

The EU rules applicable to the UK under the WA must be interpreted and applied in accordance with the methods and general principles of Union law (Art. 4(3) WA).[84] The UK is bound, in particular, to grant direct effect to the provisions contained or referred to in the WA which meet the conditions for direct effect under Union law (Art. 4(1) WA). Moreover, the UK should enable its judicial and administrative authorities, through 'domestic primary legislation', 'to disapply inconsistent or incompatible domestic provisions' (Art. 4(2) WA).

The WA is not entirely *sui generis*, since other agreements concluded by the Union make EU rules applicable to third countries. This is the case, for example, of the Agreement on the European Economic Area (EEA),[85] concluded by the EU, its Member States, and three members of the European Free Trade Area (EFTA), i.e. Iceland, Liechtenstein, and Norway. EFTA EEA states must ensure, to a large extent, free movement of persons and apply most EU internal market law.[86] Nonetheless, the WA has special features, that set it apart from other agreements concluded by the Union – and that suggest the specificity of the EU delegation in the UK.

In the first place, the WA contains relatively weak mechanisms for the enforcement of EU law and there is, consequently, a risk of misapplication of EU law in the UK. The application of the EEA agreement in EFTA states is subject to the control of the EFTA Surveillance Authority (whose functions are similar to the European Commission) and the EFTA Court, which interprets the EEA Agreement in light of the case law of the Court of Justice.[87] The WA, by contrast, is implemented by the British administration and judiciary. The Commission may bring infringement proceedings against the UK only for four years after the end of the transition period, and solely in respect of violations of EU law that occurred before the end of that period.[88] British courts may issue preliminary references for the Court of Justice regarding EU citizens' rights but only in cases which commenced at first instance within eight years from the end of the transition period.[89]

The application of the rules on free movement of goods in Northern Ireland constitutes a partial exception as the Court's jurisdiction in this area is not time-bound.[90] Nonetheless, the Union apparently expects the UK to misapply its law in Northern Ireland, to the extent that it requested – and obtained – that EU officials have a right to be present during any activities of

UK authorities relating to the implementation of provisions of Union law made applicable by the NI Protocol (e.g. the application of the customs code).[91]

The practice seems already to confirm the risks of misapplication of EU law, in respect of both goods and citizens. The UK government has put the NI Protocol into question, by publicly declaring that checks on trade between Great Britain and Northern Ireland are not necessary.[92] In addition, several commentators have alleged that EU citizens may face problems with evidence required for the residence application[93] and, more generally, may be affected by the 'hostile environment' for migration in the UK.[94]

The British judiciary might possibly sanction the misapplication of the WA by the UK administration, but this cannot be taken for granted. Moreover, the intervention of the judiciary might be insufficient or impossible. For instance, the WA requires the UK to disseminate information concerning the rights of EU citizens through national and local media.[95] However, concerns have been raised about the limited UK attempts at informing EU citizens.[96] A violation of the WA in this respect may hardly be sanctioned by a tribunal. In such circumstances, diplomatic initiatives might be necessary. It might be opportune, in particular, to exercise 'diplomatic protection' in favour of EU nationals, by invoking the responsibility of the UK for an injury caused to them by a violation of the WA.[97] Who should exercise such protection? To answer this question, one should take into account the second peculiar characteristic of the WA. This agreement was concluded in the EU-only form, whereas the EEA and other association agreements are concluded in the mixed form. Therefore, only the Union can exercise 'diplomatic protection' in the interest of Union nationals under the WA.

Diplomatic protection is traditionally exercised by states, not international organisations, but, as noted by the International Court of Justice, the principle underlying the rule of diplomatic protection 'leads to the recognition of this capacity as belonging to the Organization, when the Organization invokes, as the ground of its claim, a breach of an obligation towards itself'.[98] If the EU can undertake all the measures capable of assuring the correct application of the WA, it can also claim the injuries produced by it,[99] including the invocation of the responsibility of the UK in case of violation of EU nationals' rights. Diplomatic protection may be performed through 'diplomatic action or international judicial proceedings', as well as other means of peaceful settlement.[100] The WA includes dispute settlement procedures, such as consultations in the Joint UK–EU Committee (created by the WA) and arbitration.[101] These mechanisms, however, are cumbersome and are unlikely to be used on a regular basis to address individual cases. To solve disputes, the Union is likely to resort to 'diplomatic action', including the invocation of the UK international responsibility via *démarches* delivered by the EU delegation.[102]

It is worth noting that the UK cannot oppose the EU delegation's involvement in diplomatic protection: since the UK entered into an agreement with the Union, it must accept the Union's ability to claim, via its organs, the injuries caused to 'its' nationals by the violation of such agreement.

The EU delegation's ability to exercise diplomatic protection on behalf of the Union arguably implies the ability to protest before foreign authorities, i.e. the first form of consular protection presented above (see section 12.4). This form of consular protection is theoretically distinct from diplomatic protection, but these concepts tend to overlap in practice. For instance, the Union delegation may perform consular protection by delivering a *démarche* to the UK government, lamenting the violation of EU citizens' rights by the British administration. If an EU citizen exhausts domestic remedies in the UK, the EU delegation may also invoke the international responsibility of the UK for the injury caused to that citizen, thereby exercising diplomatic protection. It may be argued, therefore, that the EU delegation in the UK can exercise both consular and diplomatic protection in favour of EU nationals (including natural and legal persons).

The entrustment of consular and diplomatic protection functions on the EU delegation in the UK raises new questions in terms of institutional balance. Delivering a *démarche* constitutes an act of external representation of the Union and, as such, it can be performed by a Union delegation, which is entrusted with the EU's representation in third countries (Art. 221(1) TFEU). However, the ability to represent the Union does not necessarily coincide with the power to decide the Union position, as the Court of Justice noted in *Swiss Memorandum*.[103] Who decides whether the *démarche* should be delivered and what its content should be?

The delegation certainly needs to obtain the approval of the High Representative, as he/she has authority on EU delegations.[104] In addition, the approval of the Council might be required. A *démarche* arguably constitutes an act requiring 'an assessment to be made ... of the Union's interests in the context of its relations with a third country'.[105] The power to adopt it probably lies with the Council, which has policy-making and coordinating functions under Art. 16(1) TEU.[106] The Council (or a preparatory body) should arguably decide by qualified majority, since a WA-related *démarche* would concern areas such as free movement of citizens and goods, where qualified majority voting normally applies. It is possible that, on some occasions, the *démarche* might correspond to an established Union position. This would be the case, for instance, if several *démarches*, relating to different individuals, had similar content. If so, no approval by the Council would be necessary for the *démarche* to be delivered on behalf of the Union.[107]

If the EU delegation in the UK were effective in protecting EU nationals' rights, Union citizens might turn to it for protection when their rights are violated by UK authorities: the delegation may thus function as a 'reminder' of EU citizenship abroad.[108] A particularly close relationship between Union citizens in the UK and 'their' delegation would be logical, considering that they[109] benefit, by virtue of their *Union* citizenship, of rights defined in *Union* law, made applicable in the UK by virtue of an agreement concluded by the *Union* and potentially defended by a *Union* organ (the delegation).

There are, in any event, limits to the activity of the EU delegation in London. Since EU missions are generally not expected to exercise consular and diplomatic protection, one may wonder whether the Union delegation in the UK will have sufficient staff to perform such tasks in practice. Even if the EU delegation had enough resources, it would not have the power to completely replace the missions of EU members in terms of consular protection. The Union delegation may ensure the implementation of the WA – relating in particular to free movement of EU citizens and goods – but *démarches* falling within the scope of Member States' competences (e.g. regarding the treatment of EU citizens in UK prisons) should be delivered by the Member States' missions.[110] Moreover, the EU delegation in the UK is unlikely to provide consular assistance to EU citizens in situations such as arrest or loss of passport: under the current legal framework, EU citizens in all third countries, including the UK, must turn to their diplomatic and consular representation to obtain this form of assistance.[111]

12.7 Conclusion

Brexit constitutes both a challenge and an opportunity for EU diplomacy. Probably, the UK is not the global power some Brexiters imagine but remains a major regional power. Few Member States have a diplomatic network comparable to the UK. Brexit deprives the Union of political weight and representation abroad. It might also complicate access to consular protection for unrepresented EU citizens in third countries and indirectly increase the workload of other Member States' diplomatic and consular missions.

The remaining Member States might address these problems by coordinating their foreign policies and entrusting greater responsibilities to EU delegations, notably in terms of consular protection. Brexit might facilitate such an empowerment of EU delegations, since the UK opposed any development of Union delegations' ability to protect EU citizens.

The new EU delegation in the UK might set an important precedent in the area of consular and diplomatic protection. This delegation should ensure the implementation of the UK's WA and, consequently, might exercise diplomatic and consular protection in favour of EU nationals in the UK. If successful, this precedent might justify, from a political perspective, the empowerment of other delegations. It may also demonstrate that EU delegations can perform all diplomatic functions, like the diplomatic missions of sovereign states.

Brexit may thus facilitate the accomplishment of the long-term objective of the Union: 'equality with states' in the area of diplomacy. However, such a development is not inevitable. Probably, the UK is not the only Member State that opposes an expansion of the EU's role in the diplomatic and consular sphere.[112] Moreover, the Member States might be unwilling to provide EU delegations with the human and financial resources necessary to perform consular and diplomatic protection in practice. Considering the current political climate in Europe, further integration in a sector as sensitive as diplomacy cannot be taken for granted, with or without the UK.

Acknowledgements

I thank Giulia Evolvi and the editors for their comments. All errors are mine.

Notes

1 Luigi Boselli, 'Guide diplomatique pratique à l'usage des fonctionnaires en poste dans les délégations de la Commission de la C.E.' (European Commission 1992).
2 Foreign Ministers of the Member States, 'Report on European Political Cooperation' (13 October 1981).
3 See further David Spence, 'The European Commission's External Service' [2004] Public Policy and Administration 61.
4 Pierre Pescatore, *Les relations extérieures des communautés européennes : contribution à la doctrine de la personnalité des organisations internationales* (Collected Courses of the Hague Academy of International Law 1961) 192.
5 See further Michael Wood, 'Do International Organizations Enjoy Immunity under Customary Law?' in Niels Blokker and Nico Schrijver (eds), *Immunity of International Organizations* (Brill Nijhoff 2015) 37; Chittharanjan F Amerasinghe, *Principles of the Institutional Law of International Organizations* (Cambridge University Press 2005) 341–343. On EU immunities, see Ramses A Wessel, 'Immunities of the European Union' (2013) 10 International Organizations Law Review 395.
6 Vienna Convention on Diplomatic Relations, 18 April 1961, UN Treaty Series, vol 500, p 95, Art 16(1). For a partial exception, see Art 16(3).
7 Boselli (n 1) ch 2.
8 TFEU, Art 221.
9 EEAS, 'EU Delegations' Guide' (not published in open sources 2014), section 'Protocol: Diplomacy and Protocol', para 3.1.3.a.
10 See Graham Butler, 'The European Union and Diplomatic Law: An Emerging Actor in Twenty-First Century Diplomacy' in Paul Behrens (ed), *Diplomatic Law in a New Millennium* (Oxford University Press 2017) 319, 333.
11 EEAS (n 9), para 3.1.3.a.
12 US State Department, 'Diplomatic Corps Order of Precedence and Dates of Presentation of Credentials' (6 February 2020) https://web.archive.org/web/20200319171808/https:/www.state.gov/diplomatic-corps-order-of-precedence-and-dates-of-presentation-of-credentials accessed 1 April 2020; the EU delegation was temporarily 'downgraded' in 2018, see Nadja Hirsch, 'Question for written answer to the Commission' (14 January 2019) E-000154-19.
13 Colombian Ministry of Foreign Affairs, 'Orden de precedencia cuerpo diplomático acreditado en

Colombia' (10 March 2020) https://web.archive.org/web/20200319172234/www.cancilleria.gov.co/ministry/the_ministry/protocol/ceremonial/precedence accessed 1 April 2020.

14 Brazilian Ministry of External Relations, 'Orden de precedencia de los Jefes de Misión acreditados junto al Gobierno brasileño' https://web.archive.org/web/20200319172520/www.itamaraty.gov.br/es/cerimonial/10615-orden-de-precedencia-de-los-jefes-de-mision-acreditados-junto-al-gobierno-brasileno accessed 1 April 2020; UK Foreign and Commonwealth Office, 'Foreign Embassies in the UK' https://web.archive.org/web/20200322175723/www.gov.uk/government/publications/foreign-embassies-in-the-uk accessed 1 April 2020.

15 The Union has also several delegations accredited to international organisations, but the issue falls outside the scope of the present chapter.

16 See, for example, EU demarche to 3rd countries on the full implementation of UN Security Council resolutions on the Democratic People's Republic of Korea (DPRK), COREU URGENT CFSP/EAS/1421/17 (11 October 2017) https://web.archive.org/web/2019122 0085814/https://int.nyt.com/data/documenthelper/540-read-the-diplomatic-cables/27bc7c9cfe 024869481d/optimized/full.pdf accessed 1 April 2020.

17 EEAS (n 9), s 3.1.1.

18 Pia Kerres and Ramses A Wessel, *Apples and Oranges? Comparing the European Union Delegations to National Embassies* (CLEER 2015).

19 See further Juan Santos Vara, 'EU Representation to International Organisations: A Challenging Task for the EEAS' in Luis N González Alonso (ed), *Between Autonomy and Cooperation: Shaping the Institutional Profile of the European External Action Service* (CLEER 2014) 65.

20 Commission and EEAS, 'Note for the Attention of EEAS and Commission Staff of UK Nationality' (27 July 2018): 'staff with UK nationality only [can], in principle, no longer be employed in Delegations after the withdrawal of the United Kingdom'.

21 The following data are based on my elaboration of EEAS, 'Diplomatic Representation in Third Countries: 1st Semester 2020' EEAS (2019) 1354, 8–15.

22 UK High Commissions in Commonwealth countries are considered as 'embassies' for the purpose of the present analysis.

23 Antigua and Barbuda, Bahamas, Bhutan, Cook Islands, Dominica, Eswatini, Grenada, Kiribati, Lesotho, Liechtenstein, Maldives, Marshall Islands, Micronesia, Nauru, Niue, Palau, Saint Kitts and Nevis, Saint Vincent and Grenadines, Samoa, Tonga, Tuvalu.

24 Botswana, Eritrea, Gambia, Madagascar, Malawi, Mauritius, Seychelles, Sierra Leone, Somalia.

25 Bahrein, Brunei, Kyrgyzstan, Laos, Nepal, Tajikistan.

26 Haiti, Saint Lucia.

27 Papua New Guinea, Fiji.

28 With the exception of Bahrein, Brunei, Seychelles, and Saint Lucia.

29 Bangladesh, Bolivia, Cambodia, Cameroon, Costa Rica, Dominican Republic, Ecuador, El Salvador, Guatemala, Guinea, Honduras, Jamaica, Liberia, Mongolia, Namibia, Paraguay, Rwanda, South Sudan, Sri Lanka, Trinidad and Tobago, Turkmenistan, Yemen, and Zambia.

30 Afghanistan, Angola, Congo (Democratic Republic), Ghana, Mali, Mozambique, Myanmar, Panama, Senegal, Sudan, Tanzania, Uganda, Uruguay, Uzbekistan, Venezuela, Zimbabwe.

31 With the exception of Oman.

32 See Art 30(9) SEA.

33 Decision 2010/427, Art 5(10).

34 EEAS (n 9), 'Delegation Organisation: The Delegation', para 1.

35 See further Özlem Terzi, 'Coordination Between the EU Member States' Embassies and the EU Delegation in Turkey: A Case of European Diplomatic Representation' [2018] The Hague Journal of Diplomacy 97, 104–105; Heidi Maurer and Kristi Raik, 'Neither Fish nor Fowl: How EU Delegations Challenge the Institution of Diplomacy: The Cases of Moscow and Washington' (2018) 13 The Hague Journal of Diplomacy 57, 69; Federica Bicchi, 'The European Cooperation in the Southern Mediterranean: The Multilateralization of Bilateral Relations?' (2018) 13 The Hague Journal of Diplomacy 117.

36 Cf Court of Justice, judgment of 19 March 1996, C-25/94 *FAO* EU:C:1996:114, para 48; judgment of 27 March 2019, C-620/16 *OTIF* EU:C:2019:256, para 93. Alternatively, the delegation and the presidency may deliver the démarche jointly, see, for example, the Demarche by the European Union and its Member States on Norway's whaling activities, mentioned in the Summary record of Permanent Representatives Committee of 11 and 13 July 2018, Council doc 11441/18, para 82.

37 See, for example, European Union Delegation to Singapore, Joint Local Statement on the release of Singapore Prison Service's annual statistics on judicial executions in 2019 (21 February 2020) https://web.archive.org/web/20200402072539/https://eeas.europa.eu/delegations/singapore/74980/joint-local-statement-release-singapore-prison-services-annual-statistics-judicial-executions_en accessed 1 April 2020.
38 EEAS (n 21), 2.
39 Ibid.
40 EEAS, 'Diplomatic Representation in Third Countries: 2nd Semester' EEAS (2016) 849 (21 June 2016) 10–17.
41 Ibid, 9; EEAS, 'EU Diplomatic Representation in Third Countries: First Half of 2015' Ares (2014) 4229651, 10.
42 See, inter alia, EEAS, 'Diplomatic Representation in Third Countries: 1st Semester' EEAS (2016) 1756 (21 December 2016) 8; EEAS, 'Diplomatic Representation in Third Countries: 1st Semester' EEAS (2017) 1595 (18 December 2017) 7; EEAS, 'Diplomatic Representation in Third Countries: 2nd Semester 2019' EEAS (2019) 694 (26 June 2019) 7; EEAS (n 21) 7.
43 Rebecca Adler-Nissen, 'Symbolic Power in European Diplomacy: The Struggle Between National Foreign Services and the EU's External Action Service' (2013) 40 Review of International Studies 657, 670.
44 See International Law Commission, Draft Articles on Diplomatic Protection with commentaries, Yearbook of the International Law Commission, 2006, vol II, Part Two, comment to Art 1, para 3; International Court of Justice, 'Reparation for Injuries Suffered in the Service of the United Nations' I.C.J. Reports (1949), pp 174, 181.
45 See also Art 20 TFEU and Art 46 of the Charter of Fundamental Rights.
46 Art 46 of the Charter is indeed titled 'Diplomatic and Consular Protection'; similarly, Art 23 TFEU, in the German version, mentions 'diplomatic and consular protection' ('Diplomatischen und konsularischen Schutz').
47 International Law Commission (n 44) Art 1.
48 Permanent Court of International Justice, The Mavrommatis Palestine Concessions (30 August 1924) Series A – No 2, 12; International Law Commission (n 44), para 9.
49 Cf International Law Commission (n 44), comments to Art 1, paras 10–11.
50 This distinction may be inferred from the catalogue of the functions of consular missions, contained in the Vienna Convention on Consular Relations (24 April 1963) UN Treaty Series, vo1 596, p 261, at Art 5(a), (d) and (e). See, to this effect, Adolfo Maresca, *Le relazioni consolari* (Giuffrè 1966); Carlo Curti Gialdino, *Lineamenti di diritto diplomatico e consolare* (Giappichelli 2015) 405–406; Monica Guzman Zapater, 'La protecion consular como derecho derivado de la ciudadania' (2015) 28 Revista de derecho de la Unión Europea 259, 262–263, fn 14.
51 Council, 'Consular Démarches: Toolkit on Procedural Issues' Council document 8280/16 (26 April 2016) http://statewatch.org/news/2016/may/eu-council-consular-toolkit-8280-16.pdf accessed 1 April 2020.
52 Or, in the absence of diplomatic missions of the Presidency *in loco*, by another Member State or the EU delegation, see Council (n 51) 2–4, 6.
53 Alternatively, each state may deliver the *démarche* 'together with the EU Delegation' or the EU delegation may act alone on behalf of both the Union and its Member States, see Council (n 51).
54 Council 'Consular Cooperation Initiatives: Final Report' Council document 8347/16 (29 April 2016) Annex, 4.
55 Ibid, 6.
56 Council Directive 2015/637 on the coordination and cooperation measures to facilitate consular protection for unrepresented citizens of the Union in third countries and repealing Decision 95/553/EC [2015] OJ L106/1; Council Directive 2019/997 establishing an EU Emergency Travel Document and repealing Decision 96/409/CFSP [2019] OJ L163/1.
57 An EU citizen is unrepresented in a third country if his/her Member State has no embassy or consulate established there on a permanent basis, or if it has no embassy, consulate or honorary consul there which is effectively in a position to provide consular protection in a given case, see Art 6 Directive 2015/637 (n 56).
58 Ibid, Art 12.
59 Ibid, Art 13. See also European Union guidelines on the implementation of the consular Lead State concept [2008] OJ C317/6–8.

60 Council Decision 2010/427/EU establishing the organisation and functioning of the European External Action Service [2010] OJ L201/30, Art 5(10); see also Council Directive 2015/637 (n 56), arts 11–13.
61 Directive 2015/637 (n 56) arts 12, 13(3).
62 EEAS, 'Good Stories on Consular Support for EU Citizens Stranded Sbroad' https://web.archive.org/web/20200401033702/https://eeas.europa.eu/headquarters/headquarters-homepage/76203/good-stories-consular-support-eu-citizens-stranded-abroad_en accessed 1 April 2020.
63 For instance, Finland has a honorary consul in Belize, though it has no embassy there, see Finnish Foreign Ministry, Honorary Consulate of Finland, Belize City, https://web.archive.org/web/20200402132008/https://finlandabroad.fi/web/blz/honorary-consulates/-/asset_publisher/4sNllRsmWs2r/contactInfoOrganization/id/121067 accessed 1 April 2020. See further Dorina Baltag, 'EU External Representation Post-Lisbon: The Performance of EU Diplomacy in Belarus, Moldova and Ukraine' (2018) 13 The Hague Journal of Diplomacy 75, 82–83.
64 European Commission, Green Paper, Diplomatic and consular protection of Union citizens in third countries [2007] OJ C30/8; see also Madalina Moraru, 'An Analysis of the Consular Protection Directive: Are EU Citizens Now Better Protected in the World?' (2019) 56 Common Market Law Review 417, 426–428, 442; Elisa Baroncini, 'Le delegazioni dell'Unione Europea dopo il Trattato di Lisbona: struttura, status e funzioni' (2014) 6 Diritto comunitario e degli scambi internazionali 1.
65 See, for example, Louise van Schaik, 'The European External Action Service Fails to Impress the Dutch: Will it Bring Added Influence?' in European Policy Institutes Network, *Reviewing Member States' Commitment to the European External Action Service* (EPIN 2012) 19, 21–23.
66 European Scrutiny Committee, 'Sixteenth Report of Session 2006–07' (HC 41-xvi), Annex 1: UK response to the Commission's Green Paper on Diplomatic and consular protection of Union citizens in third countries, para 5.1, https://publications.parliament.uk/pa/cm200607/cmselect/cmeuleg/41-xvi/4105.htm accessed 1 April 2020.
67 High Representative, 'Report to the European Parliament, the Council and the Commission' (22 December 2011) www.eeas.europa.eu/archives/docs/images/top_stories/2011_eeas_report_cor.pdf accessed 1 April 2020.
68 Cited in UK European Scrutiny Committee, Diplomatic and consular protection of Union citizens in third countries, para 7.41, https://publications.parliament.uk/pa/cm201012/cmselect/cmeuleg/428-xlix/42810.htm accessed 1 April 2020.
69 Jim Murphy, UK Minister for Europe, cited in European Committee B, 'Diplomatic and Consular Protection' (House of Commons, 23 June 2008) https://publications.parliament.uk/pa/cm200708/cmgeneral/euro/080623/80623s01.htm accessed 1 April 2020.
70 Council (n 54) 17.
71 Decision of the High Representative of the Union for Foreign Affairs and Security Policy on the opening of a Delegation of the European Union to the United Kingdom of Great Britain and Northern Ireland (20 December 2018) ADMIN(2018) 41.
72 Statement by the High Representative on the opening of the EU Delegation in London (1 February 2020) https://ec.europa.eu/neighbourhood-enlargement/news_corner/news/united-kingdom-statement-high-representative-opening-eu-delegation-london_en accessed 1 April 2020.
73 Agreement on the withdrawal of the United Kingdom of Great Britain and Northern Ireland from the European Union and the European Atomic Energy Community [2020] OJ L29/7. Moreover, the UK and the EU have adopted a (nonbinding) Political Declaration, Political Declaration setting out the framework for the future relationship between the European Union and the United Kingdom [2020] OJ C34/12. On the implications of Brexit for Gibraltar and the Sovereign Base Areas in Cyprus, see Juan Santos Vara, Chapter 21, and Jed Odermatt, Chapter 22, in this handbook.
74 The UK and the EU are currently negotiating a 'Future Relationship' agreement, regarding cooperation issues not covered by the WA; as the content of this agreement is presently unknown, it is not taken into account in this analysis. See Council Decision 2020/266/EU authorising the opening of negotiations with the United Kingdom of Great Britain and Northern Ireland for a new partnership agreement [2020] OJ L58/53.
75 WA, Arts 126, 132.
76 See also WA, Arts 7, 128–129.
77 See, for example, WA, Art 128(2) and (3); see also WA, Art 128 (4), 129(7). On the transition period, see the contribution of Tobias Lock, Chapter 3, in this handbook.

78 See, in particular, WA, Art 10(1)(a), (c) and (e). On the notion of EU citizens and their family members, see Art 2 of Directive 2004/38 [2004] OJ L158/77.
79 See WA, Art 15(3); see further Michael Dougan, 'So Long, Farewell, Auf Wiedersehen, Goodbye: The UK's Withdrawal Package' [2020] Common Market Law Review, forthcoming.
80 NI Protocol, Art 5(5).
81 NI Protocol, Art 4(1); see also NI Protocol, Art 4(2)(3) and (4).
82 NI Protocol, Art 5(4) and Annex II to the Protocol.
83 See NI Protocol, Art 5(1) and (2).
84 To be sure, in the case of the WA, this interpretation is performed by national (UK) courts, not by an international tribunal (such as the EFTA Court).
85 [1994] OJ L1/3.
86 Peter Van Elsuwege and Merijn Chamon, *The Meaning of 'Association' Under EU Law: A Study on the Law and Practice of EU Association Agreements* (European Parliament 2019) 28; Luisa Lourenço, 'European Economic Area (EEA) and European Free Trade Association (EFTA)' in Ramses A Wessel and Jed Odermatt (eds), *Research Handbook on the European Union and International Organizations* (Edward Elgar 2019) 529.
87 EEA Agreement, Arts 6 and 119. See further EFTA Court, Joined cases E-9/07 and E-10/07 *L'Oréal*, paras 31, 37; Georges Baur, Carsten Zatschler, and Michael Sánchez Rydelski, *European Free Trade Association (EFTA) and the European Economic Area (EEA)* (Kluwer 2018) 183.
88 WA, Art 87.
89 WA, Art 158.
90 NI Protocol, Art 12(4) and (5).
91 NI Protocol, Art 12(2).
92 Lisa O' Carroll, 'Ireland UK Faces "Catastrophe" if Tories Continue with "No Checks in Irish Sea" Claim' *Guardian* (London, 4 March 2020).
93 Stijn Smismans, 'EU Citizens' Rights Post Brexit: Why Direct Effect Beyond the EU is Not Enough' (2018) 14 European Constitutional Law Review 443, 449.
94 Ibid, 444–445, 450; Dougan (n 79).
95 WA, art 18(1)(c).
96 Tanja Bueltmann, *Experiences and Impact of EU Settlement Scheme* (Northumbria University 2020) 12.
97 Cf International Court of Justice (n 44) 181–182.
98 Ibid, 182: 'only the party to whom an international obligation is due can bring a claim in respect of its breach'. In the *Odigitria* case, the Court of First Instance held that the Commission delegation in Guinea-Bissau was under a 'duty to provide diplomatic protection', under a bilateral agreement concluded by the Community, to the master of a vessel seized by a third country; judgment of 6 July 1995, *Odigitria v Council and Commission* T-572/93, EU:T:1995:131, paras 77 and 85. However, the Commission in that case was arguably required to provide consular assistance (not diplomatic protection), since it did not have to invoke the responsibility of Guinea-Bissau, but to request the fixing of a bank security.
99 Advocate General Jacobs in Case 162/96 *Racke v Hauptzollamt Mainz* EU:C:1997:582, para 50. See further Federico Forni, 'Diplomatic Protection in EU Law: What's New Under the Sun?' (2014) 9 The Hague Journal of Diplomacy 150, 166.
100 Permanent Court of International Justice (n 48); International Law Commission (n 44), para 9.
101 WA, Arts 167–181.
102 The EU has indeed delivered such *démarches* in practice; for instance, 'in August 2018, the EU made an official demarche to request Saudi Arabia to take appropriate actions against satellite and online piracy of TV programmes belonging also to EU right holders', Commission Staff Working Document, Report on the protection and enforcement of intellectual property rights in third countries (20 December 2019) SWD(2019) 452 final, 43.
103 Case 660/13 *Swiss Memorandum* EU:C:2016:616. See further on this case, Pieter Jan Kuijper, 'Recent Tendencies in the Separation of Powers in EU Foreign Relations: An Essay' in Eleftheria Neframi and Mauro Gatti (eds), *Constitutional Issues of EU External Relations Law* (Nomos 2018) 201, 222.
104 TFEU, Art 221(2).
105 *Swiss Memorandum* (n 103), para 39.
106 Ibid, paras 33 and 39.
107 See, by analogy, Council General Secretariat, Support of the European Union and its Member States for the demarche by New Zealand on the government of Japan concerning the resumption of whaling in the Southern Ocean (Council document 14908/15, 2 December 2015): 'The Commission would

like to recall that the joint demarche on Japanese scientific whaling reflects established Union positions, and therefore no approval by Council is necessary for the demarche to be conducted on behalf of the Union'.

108 Cf Adler-Nissen (n 43) 670.

109 That is, the EU citizens who exercised their right to reside in the UK or their right as frontier workers in the UK before the end of the transition period, see above.

110 Unless the Member States entrust this task to the EU delegation, see section 12.3.

111 The EU Emergency Travel Document is 'issued by a Member State', see Directive 2019/997 (n 56) Art 3.

112 See, for example, Moraru (n 64) 442.

13

Brexit and fisheries

International law issues, participation in RFMOs, reciprocal access and the future

Fernando Castillo de la Torre and Agnieszka Stobiecka-Kuik

13.1 Introduction

This chapter examines some legal issues arising from Brexit in the area of fisheries, an area which has been historically very influenced by external factors and international law. Analysis of the impact of Brexit must distinguish between the impact on bilateral relations (UK–EU), in particular in matters of reciprocal access to waters, and the impact on the relationships with third countries, in particular on the existing agreements concluded by the EU and the participation in Regional Fisheries Management Organisations (RFMOs).

Bearing in mind that this area develops in a very dynamic manner, the chapter focuses on the matters regarding what is covered by the Common Fisheries Policy (CFP). Admittedly, the transformational changes that Brexit will bring about in the fisheries sector also engage other aspects of EU law, such as trade (imports and exports of fishery products, with tariff but also non-tariff related issues) or internal market rules (employment of fishermen and women or investments in fisheries by nationals of other Member States).[1] We will refer to such aspects to the extent that, as we will see, future relations in the fisheries sector as regards access to waters and quotas sharing have been 'politically' linked to access to markets of fishery products.

First, we will briefly set the scene of the pre-Brexit legal situation, in order to better understand the changes, the challenges and the constraints. Second, we will explain the possible consequences of Brexit, in the absence of any agreement, and the alternative measures proposed or examined so far in order to mitigate the 'harder parts' of Brexit and, in some cases, to comply with possible underlying international obligations upon withdrawal. Even if a Withdrawal Agreement (WA) has now been concluded,[2] the examination of the situation which would have resulted in a 'no deal' scenario may still be interesting in case of absence of an agreement or arrangement covering fisheries after the end of the transition period. Third, we will examine the WA, both in its current form and, to the extent that it is relevant for this chapter, in the form adopted in the text agreed in November 2018.[3] Fourth, we will turn our attention more specifically to each category of international agreements, namely multilateral agreements, RFMOs and bilateral agreements, and, finally, we will briefly discuss the future agreement covering fisheries that the EU and the UK undertook to make best endeavours to conclude by 1 July 2020.

The basic principle of the new relationship is simple: since the withdrawal, the relationship between the EU and the UK is no longer governed by EU law, but by international law.

The UK's transformation into a third country, following its withdrawal from the EU, could bring about major changes in this regard that are difficult to evaluate as they will depend on the agreements the EU and UK reach on their future relations. However, the two parties will not be operating in a vacuum. The international law of the sea does provide for some reciprocal obligations which both the UK and the EU as coastal states will have to comply with.

A final preliminary point is needed in order to better understand the stakes in this sector. On the basis of the most recent figures, the landings by EU vessels of fish caught in UK waters amount to EUR 585 million, whereas the UK landings from EU waters amount to EUR 127 million. The UK imports from EU27 in 2015 amounted to EUR 1.31 billion and the UK exports to EU27 in 2015 amounted to EUR 1.34 billion. Yet, the UK is more dependent on that trade since most of the UK exports are directed to the EU market (almost 70 per cent), whereas the exports to the UK amount to less than 7 per cent of the EU27 exports.[4] All studies agree that the EU fishes in UK waters around seven or eight times as much as the UK vessels fish in the waters of other Member States.[5] That is why, as we will see, the EU has a clear interest in negotiations in this area, taking into account the wider context of the EU–UK future relationship, in particular the trade in fishery products.

13.2 Background

13.2.1 The Common Fisheries Policy

The principal aim of fisheries management under the CFP is to ensure sustainable long-term fishing yields for all stocks by 2015 where possible, and at the latest by 2020. This is referred to as maximum sustainable yield (MSY). Another increasingly important aim is to reduce unwanted catches and wasteful practices to the minimum or avoid them altogether, through the gradual introduction of a landing obligation, in principle by 2019. Lastly, the new CFP, as reflected in Regulation 1380/2013,[6] has overhauled its rules and management structure, with regionalisation and more extensive stakeholder consultation.

Fisheries management includes a combination of measures, such as rules on access to waters, fishing effort (to limit fishing capacity and vessel usage), technical measures (to regulate gear usage and where and when fishermen can fish), but also 'output' controls consisting of limiting the amount of fish from a particular fishery, in particular through fishing opportunities (total allowable catches, and quotas). As a general rule, fishing vessels registered in the EU fishing fleet register have equal access to all the EU waters and resources that are managed under the CFP. There are two temporary exceptions to this rule of equal access. Regulation 1380/2013 includes a Part VI on external policy, a reflection of the existence of an increasingly regulated environment at international level, and the establishment of sustainability as a strong internal but also external policy objective.

13.2.2 The international law of fisheries

The EU is a global player in the development of international fisheries law and in the development of multilateral fisheries governance. The United Nations Convention on the Law of the Sea (UNCLOS) was ratified by the EU in 1998,[7] and the United Nations Fish Stock Agreement (UNFSA) in 2003.[8] This latter agreement is particularly important for fisheries, as it is aimed at developing the fishery part of UNCLOS, in the understanding that the provisions of UNCLOS were not sufficient to address in particular the need for cooperative management of stocks straddling areas of national jurisdiction. Member States have also gradually ratified it.

International fisheries governance also includes a range of legal measures taken by the UN Food and Agriculture Organization (FAO), such as the Compliance Agreement (1993),[9] and the Port State Measures Agreement adopted in 2009.[10] Non-binding FAO guidelines include the Code of Conduct for Responsible Fisheries (1995) and related action plans on sharks, fishing capacity and seabirds, as well as an International Plan of Action to combat Illegal, Unreported and Unregulated (IUU) fishing (2001), and the Voluntary Guidelines on Flag State Performance (2014).[11]

13.2.3 RFMOs

UNFSA requires flag states to be members of an RFMO or cooperate with an RFMO, and to act within its rules, as a condition for allowing their vessels to engage in high seas fishing. The RFMOs are intergovernmental fisheries organisations that have the competence to establish fisheries conservation and management measures, such as catch and fishing effort limits, technical measures and control obligations. The organisations are open both to countries in the region (coastal states) and to countries that have an interest in the fisheries concerned.

There are now 18 RFMOs worldwide, as well as 20 fisheries advisory bodies (with more limited competences). Their mandates vary.[12] Although most shared or migratory stocks are now under management by one or more RFMOs, some gaps remain both in terms of species and area coverage. The main RFMO body generally decides by consensus of Members (or as in the case of some RFMOs, by majority voting), and the measures are subject to an *ex-post* objection procedure. The conservation and management measures so adopted are binding on RFMO Members (except for those who objected).

The exclusive competence of the Union on the conservation and management of fish resources[13] implies that international cooperation for the purpose of managing shared fishery resources is the responsibility of the Union and not of individual Member States.[14] The EU, represented by the Commission, plays an active role (mostly as a contracting party and therefore full member) in six tuna organisations and eleven non-tuna organisations.[15]

13.2.4 Bilateral fisheries agreements

Bilateral fisheries agreements define the rights of access of the EU fleet to fish resources in the Exclusive Economic Zone (EEZ) of third countries. A distinction is typically made between two types of agreements.

First, agreements involving financial compensation, concluded with third countries which share their surplus resources, in return for financial compensation borne by the EU budget and licence fees paid by the ship owners. The agreements with developing countries in West Africa and in the Indian and Pacific Oceans and the agreement with Greenland come under this category.[16] These types of agreements are known now as 'Sustainable Fisheries Partnership Agreements' (SFPA) after the 2013 reform of the CFP. The new CFP brought several principles into law: the agreements should be of mutual benefit to the Union and to the third country concerned; the standards for EU vessels fishing in EU waters should also apply to fishing outside EU waters; the agreements can target only surplus of the allowable catch, as referred to in UNCLOS. SFPAs also include an exclusivity clause, i.e. if the EU has a fisheries agreement with a third country, EU vessels cannot operate in the third country's waters outside the framework of this agreement, even when no protocol is in force.

Second, and more important for the Brexit debate, are reciprocal agreements, which concern an exchange of fishing possibilities between the EU and third countries and do not involve any financial contribution on the part of the EU, or any licence fee to be paid by the ship owners. This category includes the agreements with Norway, Iceland and the Faroe Islands, also known as the 'Northern agreements'. Many of the targeted stocks are shared, whereas different fishing fleets are not necessarily interested in the same stocks. These agreements concern EU fleets from eight Member States in particular. The management of these stocks has been sometimes challenging. The fisheries agreements with Norway and the Faroe Islands entered into force in 1981,[17] whereas the agreement with Iceland was signed in 1992 and came into force in 1993 (but is no longer in force). They were initially established for ten years, with subsequent tacit renewal for periods of six years (unless a notice of termination is given).

13.3 The situation in the absence of an international agreement ('no deal')

13.3.1 The obligations under international law

Following its withdrawal, the UK has sovereign control over the resources in its EEZ waters. Even if the UK and the EU could deny each other access, one element may nuance the impact of this new reality: the exercise of its sovereign rights in these waters must be done in accordance with the principles of public international law. As acknowledged in papers issued by UK authorities, the UK will continue to be bound by the requirements of UNCLOS and how they relate to the management of fisheries in any Brexit outcome. UNCLOS requires coastal states to give other states access to the surplus of the allowable catch in its EEZ and emphasises the need to minimise economic dislocation in states whose nationals have habitually fished in the zone. It also provides an obligation to cooperate with other coastal states on the management of shared stocks or stocks of associated species.

It will fall to the UK, taking into account the best scientific evidence available, to determine the allowable catch of the living resources in its EEZ.[18] However, it will have to do this with the objective of optimum utilisation, determined by its harvesting capacity. Moreover, where it does not have the capacity to exploit the entire allowable catch, other states will have access to the surplus, having particular regard to the need to minimise economic dislocation in those states whose nationals have habitually fished in the zone.[19] The question is to what extent the historic fishing shares over the last decades will be taken into account in the negotiations[20] to grant access to EU Member State fleets to resources in the UK waters and vice versa.

Moreover, there are obligations relating to the cooperation with coastal states with regard to common stocks. The UK and the EU have about 100 common stocks, i.e. fish stocks occurring in both the EEZ of the UK and in the EEZ of the EU. Under Article 63 of UNCLOS coastal states are obliged to 'seek to agree on measures necessary to coordinate and ensure the conservation and development of such stocks'. This means that consultations between the UK and the EU must take place to coordinate the establishment of the TAC (Total Allowable Catch). As far as the specific situation of straddling and highly migratory fish stocks are concerned, not only will the interests of the UK and EU come into play, but also those of the other Northeast Atlantic coastal states and of the competent regional fisheries management organisations, such as the North East Atlantic Fisheries Commission (NEAFC) and International Commission for the Conservation of Atlantic Tunas (ICCAT). In this regard, international law includes the obligation to cooperate, directly or through the appropriate organisations, with regard to these fish stocks.[21]

The 1964 London Fisheries Convention might have come into the debate at some point. However, to make sure that the UK was fully able to control UK waters after leaving the EU, the UK government gave notice on 3 July 2017 to withdraw from it (the notice will 'take effect' on 31 December 2020). This Convention provided that vessels from inter alia Denmark, France, Ireland, Belgium, Germany and the Netherlands had some access to the UK six to twelve nautical mile zone.[22] The Commission considered that such UK notice was irrelevant.[23] All twelve contracting parties had in the meantime become members of the EU. As a result of the entire replacement of the Convention by EU law between the UK and the EU Member States,[24] it had been terminated, in the sense of Article 59 of the Vienna Convention on the Law of Treaties. Yet, the applicability of the Convention in the past (and later the CFP) may have some importance when it comes to recognising some sort of 'historical rights' under UNCLOS. At least this is what states which had been traditionally fishing in those waters intend to claim.

13.3.2 Preparedness and contingency measures (on both sides)

Given the uncertainty as to the conclusion of the WA, for the event of a 'no deal' scenario, the Commission published in the course of 2018 and 2019 a number of communications with information on its ongoing 'preparedness' (unilateral informative measures in order to raise awareness and preparation for a non-orderly withdrawal) and 'contingency' (changes in EU law, normally applicable for a short period of time, to avoid short-term disruptions) work. It had identified in such communications priority areas where such measures could be necessary, given the significant impact a 'no deal' scenario would have for citizens and businesses. To the extent that comparable problems could arise in a situation of absence of a deal covering fisheries at the end of the transitional period provided for in the WA, it is of interest to give a brief account of such measures.

The Commission first set out the main consequences of Brexit for fisheries in a 'Notice to Stakeholders' issued on 9 April 2018, entitled 'Withdrawal of the United Kingdom and the EU Rules on Fisheries and Aquaculture'.[25] The Notice explains that as regards control and enforcement, in accordance with international law of the sea, fishing vessels wishing to engage in fishing activities in waters under the sovereignty or jurisdiction of a third country are required to obtain a fishing authorisation from that third country. In addition, fishing vessels performing fishing activities in third country waters are subject to applicable laws and regulations of the concerned coastal state and hence may undergo control and enforcement activities carried out by the authorities of the coastal state concerned. The flag state is responsible for diligently monitoring, including through authorisation schemes, the activities of vessels flying their flag when operating in third country waters, to ensure that such activities do not undermine the sustainability of the stocks in the coastal state's waters and are consistent with applicable conservation rules of the coastal state.

Against this background, access by Union vessels to third country waters under direct authorisations, granted by the third country authorities, fall under the authorisation procedure foreseen by Regulation (EU) 2017/2403 on the sustainable management of external fishing fleets.[26] As of the withdrawal date, these rules will apply to Union fishing vessels wishing to engage in fishing activities in waters of the UK. In turn, access by third country vessels to Union waters is subject to the authorisation procedure foreseen in Title III of Regulation (EU) 2017/2403.[27] As of the withdrawal date, these rules would apply to UK fishing vessels wishing to engage in fishing activities in Union waters. One of the conditions (not explicitly mentioned in the Notice) is typically to have an international agreement (or another type of legal coverage), between the third country and the EU. In the absence of any agreement or arrangement,[28] there is no legal basis for the Commission to issue licences to UK vessels.

The Notice also contains some information on access to ports of EU Member States, and on the import and export of fishery and aquaculture products, in particular on flag state notification and catch certification (in line with the IUU regime),[29] and on consumer information, labelling and marketing requirements.[30]

The UK government has also been issuing notices on this matter.[31] The UK is developing a new policy in the area, having adopted a Fisheries White Paper ('Sustainable fisheries for future generations') in July 2018 and by processing a number of pieces of legislation to fill the 'gap' left by the fact that EU fisheries law will not be applicable. A New Fisheries Bill is currently before the House of Lords, which would provide powers for the government to set and distribute fishing opportunities, and regulate foreign vessels' access to UK waters.[32]

Given the increased awareness of the uncertainty surrounding access by Union vessels to UK waters, as part of the ongoing contingency work, the co-legislators adopted, soon before the first Brexit date, two Regulations to help mitigate the significant impact that a 'no deal' Brexit would have on EU fisheries and ensure a coordinated EU-wide approach.[33] One Regulation amended the Regulation on the Sustainable Management of the External Fleets, to ensure that the EU was in a position to grant UK vessels access to EU waters until the end of 2019, on the condition that EU vessels were also granted reciprocal access to UK waters. The second Regulation would have allowed fishermen and operators from EU Members States to receive compensation under the European Maritime and Fisheries Fund for the temporary cessation of fishing activities. Taking into account the postponement of the Brexit date, similar contingency access measures were adopted in October 2019, for the year 2020.[34]

13.4 Fisheries in the Withdrawal Agreement

13.4.1 International negotiations and treaties during the transition period

13.4.1.1 The UK is bound by international agreements concluded by the Union

Article 129(1) WA provides that, during the transition period, the UK 'shall be bound by the obligations stemming from the international agreements concluded by the Union, by Member States acting on its behalf, or by the Union and its Member States acting jointly'.

The legal situation for the UK is well reflected in the recent Explanatory Memoranda of the government, for example concerning NEAFC:

> During the Implementation Period, the UK is to be treated as a Member State for the purposes of international agreements concluded by the EU. Pursuant to these, the UK would continue to be covered by the NEAFC Convention during the Implementation Period.[35]

Of course, whether or not this interpretation, whereby the UK is to be treated as a Member State even if it is not a Member State will remain uncontested by third countries remains to be seen. However, this is very much the common view of both the EU and UK, and communications to this effect have been sent to our international partners upon withdrawal.

13.4.1.2 Yet, its participation in decision-making processes in the area of external action becomes limited

Article 129(2) WA provides that during the transition period, representatives of the UK shall not participate in the work of any bodies set up by international agreements concluded by the Union, or by Member States acting on its behalf, or by the Union and its Member States acting jointly. There are two exceptions. First, where the UK participates in its own right. Second, if the Union exceptionally invites the UK to attend, as part of the Union's delegation, meetings or parts of meetings of such bodies, where the Union considers that the presence of the UK is necessary and in the interest of the Union, in particular for the effective implementation of those agreements during the transition period; such presence shall only be allowed where Member States' participation is permitted under the applicable agreements.

As regards the second exception, it is modelled on the exception foreseen in Article 128(5)(b) WA, but adapted to the specific context of international agreements. This exception applies only to meetings that take place before the end of the transition period. Attendance of the UK is only possible as part of the Union's delegation and where Member States' participation is allowed under the applicable agreements.

The rationale for this exception, unlike that provided for in Article 129(2)(a) WA, is not the UK's own interest but the interest of the Union, in particular in the effective implementation of international agreements, as part of Union law and by whose obligations the UK is bound, during the transition period. UK attendance can only take place exceptionally. Attendance can only take place upon invitation. It is therefore not for the UK or UK participant to decide whether or not the conditions of Article 129(2)(b) are met in a specific case. The representative of the EU should also, as appropriate, inform the other contracting party or parties to an international agreement, or the secretariat of the body set up through an international agreement, that any potential/possible invitations to the UK should be addressed to the responsible Union representative. Attendance must take place on a case-by-case basis. Permanent or semi-permanent observer status for the UK in bodies set up by international agreements cannot be granted. Both the 'necessity test' and the 'interest of the Union test' have to be fulfilled cumulatively. Both tests should be applied in particular with a view to the effective implementation of the international agreement. Both tests can in practice only lead to UK participation where UK-specific application/implementation measures in relation to the international agreement in question are at stake.

13.4.1.3 In particular, fishing opportunities

During the transition period the UK will continue to apply EU law (Art. 127(1)) and therefore the CFP. A specific issue arose during the negotiation, because a crucial element of the CFP, namely, the fishing opportunities, is fixed on an annual (or bi-annual) basis. The UK would not be sitting in the Institutions while decisions would be taken by the Council as regards its waters and resources every year.

According to Article 130 (entitled 'Specific arrangements relating to fishing opportunities'), during the transition period the UK will not be able to vote on fishing opportunities, as it will not be sitting in the Council, but it shall be consulted in respect of the fishing opportunities related to the UK.[36] The purpose of this provision is to give the UK the chance to provide its comments about fishing opportunities related to the UK during the annual decision-making process at Union level. It sets out specific arrangements concerning the fixing of fishing opportunities within the meaning of Article 43(3) TFEU, whereby the UK shall be consulted in respect of the fishing opportunities related to the UK for any period falling within the transition period, including in the context of the preparation of relevant international consultations and negotiations. Unlike the exceptions with regard to consultation of the UK in external action (see above in relation to Art. 129(5) WA), the exception set out in Article 130(1) and (2) WA is mandatory for the EU ('shall') and does not provide for discretion.

Overall, the UK share of quota will respect the relative stability key (Art. 130(4)). The UK will be provided with the opportunity to provide comments on the Annual Communication from the Commission on fishing opportunities, the scientific advice from the relevant scientific bodies and the proposals from the Commission for fishing opportunities for any period falling within the transition period (Art. 130(2)).

The setting of fishing opportunities for the first year after transition (and beyond) shall be conducted in the framework of the EU–UK agreement on fishing opportunities and sustainable management of resources that both parties must make best endeavours to conclude and ratify before 1 July 2020. The UK government has explained that the UK will be allowed to take part in the 2020 negotiations towards setting its own fishing opportunities in 2021.[37]

As some fishing opportunities derive from decisions adopted within RFMOs and bilateral bodies, Article 130(3) WA completes the picture of Article 129 and adds that

> notwithstanding point (b) of Article 129(2), with a view to allowing the United Kingdom to prepare its future membership in relevant international fora, the Union may exceptionally invite the United Kingdom to attend, as part of the Union's delegation, international consultations and negotiations referred to in paragraph 1 of this Article, to the extent allowed for Member States and permitted by the specific forum.

Article 130(3) is therefore *lex specialis* to Article 129(2)(b) WA. The purpose of this provision is to provide a specific legal basis for the Union to give the UK the opportunity to attend international fora, in which it could have taken part, if it were a Member State, considering that the consultations and negotiations will also concern fishing opportunities related to the UK during the transition period and the need for the UK to become familiar with such international consultations and negotiations of fishing opportunities with a view to preparing its future membership in the relevant fora. The decision to invite the UK to participate is a discretionary decision ('may') and is 'exceptional', as it derogates from the non-participation principle. Article 130(3) WA does not allow for the UK to attend internal meetings of the EU with its Member States that might arise during international consultations and negotiations, for example to prepare or to follow-up consultations and negotiations. Finally, the fishing opportunities have to concern the transition period.

13.4.1.4 The UK preparations to become a party to international instruments

The WA also contains provisions about the UK taking steps to accede to or negotiate certain international treaties. In accordance with the principle of sincere cooperation, Article 129(3) recalls that

> the United Kingdom shall refrain, during the transition period, from any action or initiative which is likely to be prejudicial to the Union's interests, in particular in the framework of any international organisation, agency, conference or forum of which the United Kingdom is a party in its own right.

However, specifically on the point of negotiating new agreements in the area of fisheries or becoming a party to existing agreements, paragraph 4 provides that

> during the transition period, the United Kingdom may negotiate, sign and ratify international agreements entered into in its own capacity in the areas of exclusive competence of the Union, provided those agreements do not enter into force or apply during the transition period, unless so authorised by the Union.

In other words, under the WA there is no need for ad hoc authorisation of each individual negotiation. This provision already contains an authorisation to take preparatory steps in an area of exclusive competence, in line with Article 2(1) TFEU.

13.4.2 The 'backstop': where fisheries tried to meet trade

The backstop included in the Protocol on Northern Ireland was quite important for fisheries during the negotiation. On this point the final text deviates from the first text.

In the text of November 2018, Article 6 of the Protocol set out that the free movement of fishery and aquaculture products would not be included in any backstop customs arrangements for the whole of the UK 'unless an agreement on access to waters and fishing opportunities is applicable between the Union and the United Kingdom' (Art. 6(1)). Because Northern Ireland would be part of the single customs territory, fish caught by vessels not registered in Northern Ireland would be subject to tariffs on import to Northern Ireland, and fish caught by Northern Irish fishermen could be subject to tariffs when being sold in Great Britain, unless an agreement between the UK and the EU on access to waters and fishing opportunities was reached. In other words, this Protocol made an explicit link between the future access to waters and trade in fisheries products.

Parts of these provisions, and in particular the link between trade and access to waters, were removed from the final text agreed. The prior Article 5 of the Protocol, referring to duties on landings from Northern Irish registered vessels, remained unchanged. The new Article 5(3) does take over parts of the previous text, by providing that the Joint Committee shall establish the conditions for exemption of customs duties for certain fishery and aquaculture products, brought into the customs territory of the Union by vessels flying the flag of the UK and having their port of registration in Northern Ireland. However, Article 6, now covering the protection of the UK internal market, does not refer to fisheries anymore.

13.5 The impact of Brexit on different categories of international agreements

13.5.1 Multilateral treaties

As regards multilateral treaties, and leaving aside RFMOs, the UK was already a contracting party to most of them (such as UNCLOS or UNFSA), as they cover areas beyond fisheries, and the impact of Brexit will be limited in these areas. They touch upon issues such as environment, for which the EU does not have exclusive competence (unless Art. 3(2) TFEU is applicable), or the delimitation of boundaries and sovereign rights, which are not considered to be among those for which the EU is competent either.[38] After the transition period, the UK will become responsible for the implementation of the entirety of such commitments.

A few weeks before the first date foreseen for Brexit, the UK introduced instruments to accede to two multilateral agreements which fall within the exclusive competence of the EU, namely the Agreement to Promote Compliance with International Conservation and Management Measures by Fishing Vessels on the High Seas[39] and the Agreement on Port State Measures to Prevent, Deter and Eliminate Illegal, Unreported and Unregulated Fishing.[40]

13.5.2 RFMOs

Participation in some RFMOs is crucial to ensure access. In general, there will be no automatic access for UK-registered vessels to fish in third country waters. The UK, once it is not part of the EU, will not be bound by the measures adopted by RFMOs. By not being a member, the possibility for UK vessels to fish in the areas covered by the RFMO will not be guaranteed. In case there is no agreement to this effect between the UK and the EU, British vessels would not be able to use the fishing opportunities allocated to the EU by the relevant RFMOs (and later internally allocated, in certain cases to British vessels). Under UNFSA, only those states which are members of the relevant RFMO or agree to apply its management measures may have access to the high seas fish stocks it manages. As explained by the UK Government, any fishing activity outside of UK waters will be considered Illegal, Unreported and Unregulated.'[41]

As we saw before, this has led to the WA containing certain provisions to safeguard the existing situation. Meanwhile, even before conclusion of the WA, the UK adopted a number of measures to ensure continuity of fishing in the event of a no-deal scenario. The UK government has made it clear that 'the UK will join all relevant regional fisheries management organisations (RFMOs) as quickly as possible after 1 January 2021', while recalling that 'the joining process may take up to 6 months so there may be a gap in the UK's membership. During this time, UK vessels may not be able to fish in international waters covered by RFMOs.'[42] On 8 February 2019, the UK government introduced various instruments to ensure continued UK membership of the following agreements: NEAFC, NASCO, NAFO, ICCAT and IOTC.[43] These RFMOs agreements have been concluded by the EU alone, in exercise of its exclusive competence. The UK government has made it clear that such accession would only commence once it has left the EU.[44]

These steps were taken before the WA was in force. Generally, the steps which the UK could take in view of possible participation in international agreements while still an EU member were at the time not fully settled between the EU and the UK. In principle, such unilateral moves, even of a preparatory nature, were contrary to EU obligations (exclusive competence), or at the very least to the principle of sincere cooperation.[45] At the same time, the EU side came to recognise that there may be good reasons for certain actions from the UK while still being a Member State, and the general line on the EU side was that for such preliminary actions, the UK should inform the Union beforehand,[46] and only act after having received a sort of *nihil obstat* from the Council, in the form of political conclusions.

In cases where some sort of decision of the main body of the RFMO is necessary to accept the UK as a member, an 'EU position' was needed, by way of a decision based on Article 218(9) TFEU, where conditions for its application were met. The Council adopted two such decisions relating to NEAFC[47] and NASCO.[48] Generally, in the absence of a WA, the UK would no longer be bound by EU positions and could seek new alliances with other states defending positions other than those advocated by the EU.[49] The activity of some of these RFMOs, such as NAFO or NEAFC, is key for the European fleet. The UK's exit should not affect the EU's presence in these organisations, but it could have consequences for the EU's relative weight within them. Yet, the EU has been generally favourable to approving such UK participation.

13.5.3 Bilateral relations

In the absence of a deal, in principle UK vessels would not be able to benefit from bilateral agreements, as they would not be considered 'EU vessels' in accordance with their terms. Whereas this may be of little significance in respect of certain agreements, such as SFPAs, it may have a significant impact on a few agreements. For example, the UK's withdrawal may have some influence on EU talks about sharing arrangements with Norway, given that, regarding quota exchanges, the resources in UK waters are significant. Yet here as well, other aspects may play a role such as for example Norwegian access to EU fisheries markets, where Norwegian products will be competing with UK ones. It is therefore not excluded that Brexit will have an enduring impact on the annual consultations between the EU and Norway, or could be used by EU counterparts to attempt to renegotiate certain deals. For the time being, the UK government has already signed continuity agreements with Norway (on 30 September 2019)[50] and with the Faroe Islands (on 15 October 2019)[51] to allow UK fishermen to continue accessing and catching fishing quotas in Norwegian and Faroese waters from 1 January 2021.

13.6 Conclusion: the future

A new fisheries deal, in whatever form it may finally take, is not only desirable, due to both parties' interest in maintaining fisheries activities, but also obligatory, due to the requirements of international law. Moreover, future dealings as regards the affected waters may have to involve also the other coastal states and those states with which the EU already has fisheries agreements that the UK will cease to be party to following its withdrawal from the EU. In any event, the content of the future EU–UK agreement must take into account the existing (bilateral and multilateral) agreements and the commitments undertaken in the framework of the NEAFC.

The Political Declaration setting out the Framework on the Future Relationship[52] includes a reference to a future agreement on access and quotas. It links any agreement on fisheries to the overall economic partnership: 'Within the context of the overall economic partnership, establishment of a new fisheries agreement on, inter alia, access to waters and quota share' (para. 73). It adds that

> the Parties will use their best endeavours to conclude and ratify their new fisheries agreement by 1 July 2020 in order for it to be in place in time to be used for determining fishing opportunities for the first year after the transition period.
>
> *(para. 74)*

The declaration also calls for 'cooperation bilaterally and internationally to ensure fishing at sustainable levels'. More fundamentally, reciprocal access and management of shared stock requires some degree of alignment as to the respective policies of the two sides: 'the Parties should cooperate on the development of measures for the conservation, rational management and regulation of fisheries, in a non-discriminatory manner'. This sentence reflects that the expectations are high in terms of the UK aligning with the basic principles of the CFP also in the future, while preserving some degree of autonomy which may allow for some minor policy differences. It is also stated that the UK and the EU 'will work closely with other coastal states and in international fora, including to manage shared stocks', a statement very much having in mind cooperation with Norway and in NEAFC.

On 25 February 2020, the Council adopted its negotiating directives.[53] They contain a section 12 on fisheries, setting out the aspirations and objectives of the EU, which are obviously high in this area. The final text should provide for 'a framework for the management of shared fish stocks, as well as the conditions on access to waters and resources and common technical and conservation measures'. It should secure continued responsible fisheries in line with the CFP, and 'should be underpinned by effective management and supervision, and dispute settlement and enforcement arrangements, including appropriate remedies' (para. 86). The EU objective is clearly 'to uphold Union fishing activities', in particular, the provisions 'should aim to avoid economic dislocation for Union fishermen that have been engaged in fishing activities in the United Kingdom waters' (para. 88). The directives give more precise indications of what such an approach should involve (para. 89). The link with the trade is stressed: 'the terms on access to waters and quota shares shall guide the conditions set out in regard of other aspects of the economic part of the envisaged partnership, in particular of access conditions under the free trade area' (para. 90). Nothing is specifically provided as regards relations with third countries.

Therefore, fisheries will play a central role in the overall EU–UK trade negotiations. The EU–UK fisheries relation is very intensive, and both will remain each other's most important partners in fisheries. Yet, both sides have set out very different positions on fisheries. First, the EU intends to make a direct link between reciprocal access and upholding shares and the trade agreement in fishery and aquaculture products, whereas the UK has been opposed to any such link.[54] Second, the UK wanted to negotiate access on an annual basis,[55] but the EU wants longer-term access to UK waters, under stable shares conditions. The EU will certainly insist that the principles set out in the CFP and multiannual plans for the Western Waters and the North Sea will be relevant for management of fisheries resources. In those long-term management plans there is typically a provision stating that in consultation with third countries the Union should attempt to ensure that joint stocks are managed in a sustainable manner consistent with the management plan. A challenge will be the large number of common stocks. Some consider hardly imaginable that during a few weeks at the end of the year agreement can be reached on the TAC of all those stocks (and the corresponding quotas for the parties) in the absence of agreement on principles and a stable framework, since they will concern not only shared stocks between the UK and EU, but also Norway and/or the Faroe Islands.

Some may argue that the importance of fisheries is disproportionate. Fisheries is a very small part of the UK economy, and a somewhat larger one, but still rather small, of the EU's. However, the economic activity from fisheries is concentrated in coastal areas, where it is important both socially and economically. More fundamentally, fisheries also featured prominently in the Brexit debate, in a somewhat symbolic way, perceived as linked to sovereignty (over waters). Yet, the UK fishing sector is varied and has different expectations from Brexit. Fishers are expecting greater fishing opportunities, but the processing sector and shellfish exporters have concerns about access to export markets and potential border delays. On the EU side, fisheries has been referred to as a red line issue by French ministers[56] and the link between reaching a deal on fisheries and other sectors which are a significant part of the UK economy, such as services, has also been highlighted by EU ministers and in the negotiating directives. Failure to find a solution for fisheries will impact the trade negotiations, and could have wide ranging consequences.

Acknowledgements

Opinions are purely personal and should not be attributed to the European Commission.

Notes

1 Changes in British law tightening the conditions for granting British registration to fishing vessels, to stop what was called at the time 'quota hopping', led to a series of significant judgments of the Court of Justice. On these topics generally, see certain sections of the EP Study: Sobrino Heredia, 'Research for PECH Committee – Common Fisheries Policy and BREXIT – Legal Framework for Governance' (2017) European Parliament, Policy Department for Structural and Cohesion Policies 19–23.

2 Agreement on the withdrawal of the United Kingdom of Great Britain and Northern Ireland from the European Union and the European Atomic Energy Community [2020] OJ L 29/7.

3 Agreement on the withdrawal of the United Kingdom of Great Britain and Northern Ireland from the European Union and the European Atomic Energy Community [2019] OJ C 144I/1.

4 Landings are 2011–2015 average and trade is extracted from EUMOFA.

5 On average, according to the UK government 'Sustainable Fisheries for Future Generations' (Fisheries White Paper July, 2018), between 2012 and 2016, UK vessels landed approximately 90,000 tonnes of

fish each year caught in other Member States' waters, and other Member States' vessels caught in the region of 760,000 tonnes of fish each year in UK waters. Other studies indicate different figures (Wageningen University and Research, 'European Consumers Pay the Price for Fish When Hard Brexit Occurs' (24 April 2018); Fishing for Leave, 'Flawed Fisheries Report Brings Serious Questions Over Economists Analyses' (27 April 2018); see also, B Le Gallic, S Mardle and S Metz, 'Research for PECH Committee – Common Fisheries Policy and Brexit – Trade and Economic Related Issues' (European Parliament Policy Department for Structural and Cohesion Policies, 2017)) but overall they all agree.

6 Regulation (EU) No 1380/2013 of the European Parliament and of the Council on the Common Fisheries Policy [2013] OJ L354/22.

7 The convention was approved on behalf of the now EU by Council Decision 98/392/EC concerning the conclusion by the European Community of the United Nations Convention of 10 December 1982 on the Law of the Sea and the Agreement of 28 July 1994 relating to the implementation of Part XI thereof [1998] OJ L179/1.

8 Council Decision 98/414/EC on the ratification by the European Community of the Agreement for the implementing of the provisions of the United Nations Convention on the Law of the Sea of 10 December 1982 relating to the conservation and management of straddling stocks and highly migratory fish stocks [1998] OJ L189/14.

9 Council Decision 96/428/EC on acceptance by the Community of the Agreement to promote compliance with international conservation and management measures by fishing vessels on the high seas [1996] OJ L177/24.

10 The FAO Agreement on Port State Measures to Prevent, Deter and Eliminate Illegal, Unreported and Unregulated Fishing (PSMA). It entered into force on 6 June 2006, www.fao.org/port-state-measures/background/parties-psma/en/ accessed 19 March 2020.

11 There are other multilateral agreements which do not strictly speaking relate to RFMOs. See, for a recent example, Council Decision (EU) 2018/1257 on the signing, on behalf of the European Union, of the Agreement to Prevent Unregulated High Seas Fisheries in the Central Arctic Ocean [2018] OJ L238/1.

12 Some of the RFMOs focus on particular highly migratory species, notably tuna, throughout vast geographical areas ('tuna RFMOs'). Others have broad mandates to manage all the fish stocks found in a specific area ('non-tuna RFMOs'). The International Whaling Commission and the North Atlantic Salmon Conservation Organization, have very specific mandates and deal with single species. Geographical cover can be limited to the high seas, or can include both the high seas and the EEZ of coastal states due to the biological unity of the stocks.

13 Pursuant to Article 3(1)(d) TFEU, the Union has exclusive competence for the conservation of marine biological resources under the CFP. Conversely, the other aspects of the CFP and environment fall, in accordance with Article 4(2)(d) and (e) TFEU, within the areas of shared competence of the Union.

14 While most RFMOs deal exclusively with fisheries management, certain RFMOs have also an environmental mandate beyond fisheries management. In these cases, the Union and Member States are members and have the right to intervene and decide on the basis of a declaration of competences that the Union presents typically prior to the meetings specifying whether each point of the agenda is for the Union or for Member States to decide upon. RFMOs covering shared competences are the Commission for the Conservation of Antarctic Marine Living Resources (CCAMLR) and the General Fisheries Commission for the Mediterranean (GFCM). In some cases, individual Member States are also members in their own right, in respect of overseas territories that are not part of the Union. Typical examples are Denmark on behalf of Greenland and the Faroe Islands, and France or UK on behalf of their overseas territories.

15 See https://ec.europa.eu/fisheries/cfp/international/rfmo accessed 19 March 2020. Obtaining full recognition of the role of the Union was not easily achieved, and it took a number of years and often amendments to the basic instruments to have such exclusivity clearly recognised by third parties. See Penas Lado, *The Common Fisheries Policy: The Quest for Sustainability* (Wiley 2016) ch 7. On RFMOs and the EU see also Paul Heckler, 'Regional Fisheries Management Organisations: Defining the EU and Member States Roles' in Ramses A Wessel and Jed Odermatt (eds), *Research Handbook on the European Union and International Organizations* (Edward Elgar 2019) 429.

16 See, for example, Fisheries Partnership Agreement between the European Community and the Islamic Republic of Mauritania OJ L 343 (8 December 2006) 1–60; Sustainable Fisheries Partnership Agreement between the European Union and the Republic of Seychelles OJ L 60 (28 February 2020) 5–44.

17 Council Regulation (EEC) No 2211/80 on the conclusion of the Agreement on fisheries between the European Economic Community and the Government of Denmark and the Home Government of the Faroe Islands. The Union has three fisheries agreements with Norway, namely the bilateral (Council Regulation (EEC) No 2214/80 on the conclusion of the Agreement on fisheries between the European Economic Community and the Kingdom of Norway [1980] OJ L226/47), the trilateral and the neighbouring agreements. The bilateral arrangement covers the North Sea and the Atlantic, the trilateral agreement covers Skagerrak and Kattegat (Denmark, Sweden and Norway) and the neighbourhood arrangement covers the Swedish fishery in Norwegian waters of the North Sea. The bilateral agreement between the EU and Norway is the Union's most important international fisheries agreement in terms of both the exchange of fishing opportunities and joint fisheries management measures. The quotas to be exchanged with Norway are negotiated annually, following consultations between the parties (typically in November) which result in non-binding Agreed Records. Such Records are later taken into account when the Council sets fishing opportunities every December for the following year. On the Norway agreement see, for details of yearly consultations, https://ec.europa.eu/fisheries/cfp/international/agreements/norway accessed 19 March 2020.

18 Art 61 UNCLOS.

19 Art 62 UNCLOS.

20 Art 70 UNCLOS.

21 Arts 63(1) and (2) and 64 UNCLOS; Arts 5 and 8 UNFSA.

22 The Convention related to fishing rights across the coastal waters of Western Europe, in particular the fishing rights in the North Sea, in the Skagerrak, in the Kattegat and on the European Atlantic coast. It gave right of full access to the fishing grounds between six and twelve nautical miles of the national coastline to the fishing industry of those contracting parties that had already been fishing there in the period 1953–1962.

23 As expressed on twitter by Michael Barnier on 2 July 2017: 'UK denunciation of London Convention = no change: EU law/Common Fisheries Policy had superseded it.'

24 In Case C-146/89 *Commission* v *United Kingdom* EU:C:1991:294, paras 40–44.

25 https://ec.europa.eu/info/sites/info/files/notice-to-stakeholders-brexit-fisheries-final.pdf accessed 19 March 2020.

26 Council Regulation (EU) 2017/2403 of the European Parliament and of the Council on the sustainable management of external fishing fleets [2017] OJ L 347/81. In this framework, provided that the EU and UK grant access to their respective waters and all criteria and conditions foreseen in Articles 4 to 7 of Regulation (EU) 2017/2403 are complied with, EU Member States may authorise their vessels to fish under such direct authorisations in accordance with the procedure set out in Arts 16 to 18 of Regulation (EU) 2017/2403.

27 Third country vessels may only engage in fishing activities in Union waters if in possession of an authorisation issued by the European Commission in accordance with Articles 32 to 34 of Regulation (EU) 2017/2403 and provided they comply with the other requirements in that Title, notably Art 38.

28 Art 62 UNCLOS. On this see also Joined Cases 103/12 and 165/12 *Parliament and Commission v Council* EU:C:2014:2400, paras 63–73.

29 Council Regulation (EC) No 1005/2008 establishing a Community system to prevent, deter and eliminate illegal, unreported and unregulated fishing [2008] OJ L 286/13.

30 Fishery and aquaculture products placed on the EU market are subject to specific market requirements set out in Regulation (EU) No 1379/2013 of the European Parliament and of the Council on the common organisation of the markets in fishery and aquaculture products [2013] OJ L354/1, which include the specific consumer information requirements (Chapter IV of Regulation (EU) No 1379/2013) and marketing standards on fishery and aquaculture products (Chapter III of Regulation (EU) No 1379/2013).

31 On 10 January 2019 it issued a notice on 'Commercial Fishing and Marketing of Seafood if There's No Brexit Deal' www.gov.uk/guidance/commercial-fishing-and-marketing-of-seafood-if-theres-no-brexit-deal accessed 19 March 2020, later superseded by one entitled 'Prepare Your Fisheries Business for Changes from 1 January 2021' www.gov.uk/guidance/the-fisheries-sector-and-preparing-for-eu-exit accessed 19 March 2020. The trade and market dimension of a no deal Brexit was highlighted in Notices to stakeholders on fisheries, which set out that the default scenario in case of a hard Brexit would be that the World Trade Organization (Most Favoured Nation) tariffs would apply. Imports of fish and fish products would be subject to the relevant documentary and SPS checks, and IUU rules.

This would entail an additional cost (and time delays) for the EU processing sector relying on imports from the UK. There are also several parliamentary studies and briefings on Brexit and Fisheries. See, inter alia, House of Commons, 'Fisheries and Brexit' (Briefing Paper, 30 October 2019) http://researchbriefings.files.parliament.uk/documents/CBP-8396/CBP-8396.pdf accessed 19 March 2020.

32 For 2017–2019, https://services.parliament.uk/bills/2017-19/fisheries.html, superseded by https://services.parliament.uk/bills/2019-21/fisheries.html accessed 19 March 2020. For an explanation, see Elena Ares, 'The Fisheries Bill 2017–19' (House of Commons Briefing Paper, 2019) http://researchbriefings.files.parliament.uk/documents/CBP-8442/CBP-8442.pdf accessed 19 March 2020.

33 Regulation (EU) 2019/498 of the European Parliament and of the Council amending Regulation (EU) 2017/2403 as regards fishing authorisations for Union fishing vessels in United Kingdom waters and fishing operations of United Kingdom fishing vessels in Union waters [2019] OJ L85I/25; Regulation (EU) 2019/497 of the European Parliament and of the Council amending Regulation (EU) No 508/2014 as regards certain rules relating to the European Maritime and Fisheries Fund following the withdrawal of the United Kingdom from the Union [2019] OJ L85I/22.

34 Regulation (EU) 2019/1797 of the European Parliament and of the Council amending Regulation (EU) 2017/2403 as regards fishing authorisations for Union fishing vessels in United Kingdom waters and fishing operations of United Kingdom fishing vessels in Union waters [2019] OJ L279I/7.

35 www.gov.uk/government/publications/ms-no52019-convention-on-future-multilateral-cooperation-in-north-east-atlantic-fisheries accessed 19 March 2020.

36 For the different versions of the text, and reactions thereto, during the negotiations, see House of Commons (n 31) 8–10.

37 UK Government, 'Explainer for the Agreement on the Withdrawal of the United Kingdom of Great Britain and Northern Ireland from the European Union' (14 November 2018).

38 Even if EU law may have an impact, see Case 146/89 *Commission v United Kingdom* EU:C:1991:294, on 'baselines'.

39 www.gov.uk/government/publications/ms-no82019-agreement-to-promote-compliance-with-international-conservation-and-management-measures-by-fishing-vessels-on-the-high-seas accessed 19 March 2020.

40 www.gov.uk/government/publications/ms-no102019-agreement-on-port-state-measures-to-prevent-deter-and-eliminate-illegal-unreported-and-unregulated-fishing accessed 19 March 2020.

41 www.gov.uk/guidance/the-fisheries-sector-and-preparing-for-eu-exit accessed 19 March 2020.

42 Ibid.

43 List of fisheries agreements, www.gov.uk/government/collections/miscellaneous-treaties-2013 accessed 19 March 2020. In detail, see [MS No 5/2019] Convention on Future Multilateral Cooperation in North-East Atlantic Fisheries; [MS No 6/2019] Agreement for the Establishment of the Indian Ocean Tuna Commission; [MS No 7/2019] Convention for the Conservation of Salmon in the North Atlantic Ocean; [MS No 9/2019] Convention for the Conservation of Atlantic Tunas; [MS No 11/2019] Convention on Cooperation in the Northwest Atlantic Fisheries.

44 The NEAFC Memorandum further explains that

> Taking account of this 90 day period, the UK has submitted its application for accession at this stage only as a contingency, to minimise the risk of a gap in coverage of the NEAFC Convention if the UK leaves the EU in a no-deal scenario. It is only in this scenario that the UK would proceed to deposit its instrument of accession by 30 March 2019.

45 For more on this, see: R A Wessel, 'Consequences of Brexit for International Agreements Concluded by the EU and its Member States' (2018) Common Market Law Review 101–132.

46 The Commission recalled, before the conclusion of the WA (see, for instance, the procedure followed for the negotiations of agreements on citizens' rights and other separation issues with EFTA states (ST-11942-2018-INIT-EN endorsed by the Council on 18 September 2018)), that where the UK intended to enter into negotiations with third countries in areas of Union competence, it had to inform the Union of its intentions so as to allow the Union to take a position whether to object or not to object to these negotiations. Accordingly, the Commission asked the UK to provide in a timely manner the Commission with information on all negotiations the UK was engaged in or intended to engage in before the withdrawal date in areas of Union competence. Although the situation varied from sector to sector, in the area of fisheries the UK had been informing the Commission of its intentions.

47 Council Decision (EU) 2019/510 on the position to be taken on behalf of the European Union in the framework of the Convention on future multilateral cooperation in the North-East Atlantic fisheries as

regards the application for accession to that Convention submitted by the United Kingdom [2019] OJ L85/22.

48 Council Decision (EU) 2019/937 on the position to be taken on behalf of the European Union in the framework of the Convention for the Conservation of Salmon in the North Atlantic Ocean as regards the application for accession to that Convention submitted by the United Kingdom [2019] OJ L149/61.

49 See Sobrino Heredia (n 1) 28, who mentions links with Canada in NAFO, or, in the context of CCAMLR, possible UK alliances with other countries which, like Australia or New Zealand, could be closer to its fishing concept, thereby weakening the EU's role in these organisations.

50 www.gov.uk/government/news/uk-fisheries-agreement-signed-with-norway accessed 19 March 2020.

51 www.gov.uk/government/news/uk-fisheries-agreement-signed-with-the-faroe-islands accessed 19 March 2020.

52 Political Declaration setting out the framework for the future relationship between the European Union and the United Kingdom OJ [2020] C34/12.

53 Council Directives 5870/20 for the negotiation of a new partnership with the United Kingdom of Great Britain and Northern Ireland.

54 Such a link is made, for example, in EU relations with Greenland. Protocol No 34 to the Treaties sets out the special arrangements applicable to Greenland fisheries today and links the free access of Greenlandic fishery products to the European market to the possibilities for access to its fishing zones that Greenland grants to the Union.

55 The 'Command Paper' states both that there should be 'annual negotiations on access to the parties' exclusive economic zones and fishing opportunities (total allowable catch and shares)', and that in negotiating fishing opportunities annually the UK 'will no longer accept the "relative stability mechanism", and will instead base them on "the principle of zonal attachment", which better reflects where the fish live, and is the basis for the EU's fisheries agreement with Norway' (UK Government, 'The Future Relationship with the EU: The UK's Approach to Negotiations' (27 February 2020), www.gov.uk/government/publications/our-approach-to-the-future-relationship-with-the-eu accessed 2 March 2020).

56 https://uk.ambafrance.org/Fisheries-an-absolute-red-line-in-Brexit-talks-Minister accessed 19 March 2020.

Part IV

Common foreign, security and defence policy after Brexit

14

Post-Brexit participation of the UK in EU foreign, security and defence policy

Ramses A. Wessel

14.1 Introduction

The United Kingdom has frequently indicated that Brexit should not lead to a complete detachment from the European Union's foreign, security and defence policy,[1] but that in this area EU membership should be replaced by a new security partnership, 'that is deeper than any other third country partnership and that reflects our shared interests, values, and the importance of a strong and prosperous Europe'.[2] In fact, given the – perceived – more intergovernmental nature of the Common Foreign and Security Policy (CFSP),[3] a continued participation in this policy area is often seen as easier to realise than participation in certain parts of the internal market.[4] This may have been the reason that in the view of the UK, the CFSP would not become part of a possible Comprehensive Free Trade Agreement and that the shape and form of the foreign security policy partnership was left open: 'Many policy areas – for example foreign policy or immigration policy – are for the UK Government to determine, within a framework of broader friendly dialogue and cooperation between the UK and the EU: they do not require an institutionalised relationship.'[5] The EU, on the other hand, aimed at including foreign and security policy issues in a comprehensive partnership with a unified governance structure,[6] and in the 'Draft text of the Agreement on the New Partnership with the United Kingdom' of March 2020, the 'Security Partnership' was indeed presented as one of the chapters.[7]

The wish to stay connected to CFSP may stand in stark contrast to the well-documented attempts by the UK to prevent any further integration in that area. The UK has a long history of blocking new initiatives to further integrate CFSP into the Union's legal order.[8] The somewhat peculiar situation of CFSP being the only policy area (apart from the European Neighbourhood Policy, ENP) in the Treaty on the European Union (TEU) rather than in the Treaty on the Functioning of the European Union (TFEU) was presented by the then British Foreign Minister Miliband in a victorious manner: 'Common foreign and security policy remains intergovernmental and in a separate treaty. Importantly ... the European Court of Justice's jurisdiction over substantive CFSP policy is clearly and expressly excluded.'[9]

Despite the fact that 'keeping CFSP intergovernmental' and 'keeping the Court out' has in the end not proven to be very successful,[10] the very perception of an intergovernmental CFSP renders it logical for the UK to continue participating, despite the fact that it has left the EU. With a view to the UK position paper on continued participation in CFSP, it has even been observed that 'in stressing the UK's contribution to the CFSP and ability to project its own priorities and set the debate ... the document seems as though it is a case for being part of the EU, rather than setting out a "new" arrangement.'[11] Indeed, many of these documents read as a plea for a full opt-in and CFSP is presented as one of the 'cherries' that can easily be picked without too much of an institutional hassle. In other words, the UK seems to be aiming at a relationship that would perhaps best be characterised as 'friends with benefits'.[12]

Indeed, EU foreign policy did not play a major role in the referendum campaign,[13] and, overall, the UK has always been quite supportive of the agreed CFSP policies and decisions.[14] It has been observed that the UK 'long ago recognized the fact that the EU is Britain's "point of departure" when it comes to foreign policy rather than the first thing that Britain bumps into'[15] and that 'it was generally strongly in the UK's interests to work through the EU in foreign policy'[16] if only to 'upload' its own policy preferences.[17] The latter quote is from a UK position paper, that deserves to be quoted more in length, as it clearly balances the advantages and disadvantages of UK involvement in CFSP:

> The key benefits included: increased impact from acting in concert with 27 other countries; greater influence with non-EU powers, derived from our position as a leading EU country; the international weight of the EU's single market, including its power to deliver commercially beneficial trade agreements; the reach and magnitude of EU financial instruments, such as for development and economic partnerships; the range and versatility of the EU's tools, as compared with other international organisations; and the EU's perceived political neutrality, which enables it to act in some cases where other countries or international organisations might not.
>
> Again according to the evidence, the comparative disadvantages of operating through the EU are: challenges in formulating strong, clear strategy; uneven leadership; institutional divisions, and a complexity of funding instruments, which can impede implementation of policy; and sometimes slow or ineffective decision-making, due to complicated internal relationships and differing interests. One commentator summarised it thus: 'The issue is not legal competence, but competence in general.' Some argued that the EU is at its most effective when the Member States, in particular the UK, France and Germany, are aligned and driving policy.[18]

Thus it might not have come as a surprise that the Political Declaration (PD) of November 2018 (slightly revised in October 2019) on the future EU–UK relationship foresees a 'security partnership', which 'should comprise law enforcement and judicial cooperation in criminal matters, foreign policy, security and defence, as well as thematic cooperation in areas of common interest'.[19] The PD continues by stating that 'To this end, the future relationship should provide for appropriate dialogue, consultation, coordination, exchange of information and cooperation mechanisms. It should also allow for secondment of experts where appropriate and in the Parties' mutual interest.'[20] And, 'The High Representative may, where appropriate, invite the United Kingdom to informal Ministerial meetings of the Member States of the Union.'[21] Where continued participation in the Common Security and Defence Policy (CSDP) is concerned, 'The future relationship should therefore enable the United Kingdom to participate on a case by case basis in CSDP missions and operations through a Framework Participation Agreement.'[22] In addition, continued collaboration is foreseen in projects of the European Defence Agency (EDA),[23] the European Defence Fund (EDF), the European Union Satellite Centre (EUSC) and in PESCO, the new permanent structured cooperation arrangements, to strengthen defence cooperation between the Member States.[24] Some of these elements returned in the Draft Agreement of March 2020,[25] which foresees a structured consultation on foreign policy, security and defence as well as close cooperation on sanctions and the exchange of information. It also allows for the participation of the UK in EU crisis management operations as well for involvement of the UK in the activities of the EDA. And, despite the fact that 'Brexit has thus far proved to be a trigger in favour of greater development in Security and Defence'[26] and allowed the EU to take steps that were previously more difficult, some continued involvement of a state with strong military potential and experience is also beneficial for the EU.

Despite these clear intentions, and despite the fact that some third state participation in CFSP and CSDP is indeed not uncommon (as we will see below) and may provide a framework for the discussion with the EU, the more far-reaching close cooperation in this area as envisaged by the UK raises a number of legal questions. After all, the Treaties have established cooperation between the Union and its Member States on foreign and security policy; no reference is made to any participation of third states in this policy area. Quite the opposite, perhaps, as the treaty provisions underline the need for consistency in many provisions[27] and impose a binding obligation of coherence in EU external relations on the Union, connecting the list of policy objectives in 21(2) TEU to each other and to the functioning of pertinent legal principles. CFSP is clearly connected to many other external policies of the Union, including sanctions, migration, trade, development, and environmental and energy policy. Moreover, through the case law of the Court of Justice the obligation of loyalty has become directly connected to the objective of 'ensur[ing] the coherence and consistency of the action and its [the Union's] international representation'.[28]

It will not be easy to uphold these rules and principles when participating third states are not equally bound by them. In that respect it should also be remembered that CFSP is a *Union* competence (e.g. Arts 24(1), 25 TEU, Art. 2(4) TFEU). In fact, throughout Title V TEU (on CFSP) it is made clear that *the Union* is in charge, loyally supported by the Member States (Art. 23(3) TEU). This also implies that for a well-functioning CFSP, the application of the Union principles is essential.[29]

While third state participation in CFSP and CSDP is far from unusual and scenarios for a post-Brexit participation of the UK in the Union's foreign, security and defence policy have been researched,[30] the present chapter will address a number of key legal questions related to the special position the UK has claimed in some of its position papers, that would lead to a new security partnership 'that is deeper than any other third country partnership'.[31] Section 14.2 will address the legal institutional possibilities and obstacles. Section 14.3 will analyse the relevant provisions in the Withdrawal Agreement (WA). This will be followed by an investigation into the options for third country participation in CFSP (section 14.4) and CSDP (section 14.5) on the basis of past experience. Section 14.6, finally, will be used to draw conclusions.

14.2 Legal institutional possibilities and obstacles

To start with the obvious: the term 'common' in Common Foreign, Security, and Defence Policy refers to the Union and its *Member States*. Article 26(2) TEU entails a general competence for the Council to 'frame the common foreign and security policy and take the decisions necessary for defining and implementing it on the basis of the general guidelines and strategic lines defined by the European Council'. The Council, in turn, 'shall consist of a representative of each Member State at ministerial level, who may commit the government of the Member State in question and cast its vote' (Art. 16(2) TEU). The CFSP provisions do not foresee the participation of non-EU states in the decision-making process. And, indeed, Article 28(2) TEU provides that the CFSP Decisions 'shall commit *the Member States* in the positions they adopt and in the conduct of their activity'.[32] In short, as also explained by the Comments on the Council's Rules of Procedure:

> It should be noted that it follows from the system of the Treaties, and from Article 16 TEU in particular, that the representation of the governments of the Member States of the Council is composed of nationals of the Member State concerned or, in any event, of a national of one of the Member States of the European Union. Therefore, the presence at a Council meeting of a national of a third State as a member of the delegation of a member of the Council should be ruled out, as it could be regarded by the other members of the Council as a factor which could affect the decision-making autonomy of the Council.[33]

This also prevents that – on the basis of Article 4 of the Council's Rules of Procedure – 'a member of the Council who is prevented from attending a meeting may arrange to be represented' by a UK representative. Any attempt to provide a formal role to the UK in CFSP decision-making would thus require a modification of the rules. This is not to say that all forms of participation of the UK in CFSP and CSDP are excluded (sections 14.4 and 14.5 will explore some practice of third country participation in CFSP). In institutional terms, several options have been discussed in the literature. First of all, the treaties are silent on the *presence* of third countries during the EU decision-making procedures. Yet, in the above interpretation offered by the Comments on the Rules of Procedure, the presence of third states during Council – and European Council – meetings seems excluded.[34] At the same time, the Rules provide some leeway to invite representatives of third countries to attend some of the Council's work. In view of the importance of this issue for a possible UK presence during Council meetings, the Comments on the Council's Rules of Procedure deserve to be quoted in length:

> Participation in Council meetings must not be confused with the *occasional presence of representatives of third States* or of international organisations, who are sometimes invited as observers to attend certain Council meetings or meetings of Council preparatory bodies concerning a specific item.
>
> Article 6(1) CRP provides that '... the deliberations of the Council shall be covered by the obligation of professional secrecy, except insofar as the Council decides otherwise'. Under this article, the Council may, whenever it considers it appropriate, decide by a simple majority to open its deliberations – or to disclose their content, inter alia by forwarding documents – to certain persons (or categories of persons).
>
> *The presence of observers* must be authorised by the Council for a specific item on the agenda. In this case, the Presidency must warn the Council members of this fact in advance. In respect of this item, the Council (or the relevant preparatory body) implicitly decides, by simple majority, to set aside the professional secrecy provided for in Article 6(1). The observer must leave the room once the deliberations on this item have ended, or when requested to leave by the Presidency. The third-party observer may be invited by the Council Presidency to state his or her views or inform the Council concerning the subject at issue.
>
> From a legal point of view, *the third party does not participate in the deliberations leading to the taking of a decision by the Council,* but simply provides the Council with information which it can draw upon before taking its decision.
>
> *The same rules apply to meetings of the Council's preparatory bodies.* The Presidency is responsible for organising the proceedings so as to preserve the Council's decision-making autonomy.[35]

With regard to the European Council, the regulatory provisions are (even) stricter as its Rules of Procedure provide that

> meetings in the margins of the European Council with representatives of third States … may be held in exceptional circumstances only, and with the prior agreement of the European Council, acting unanimously, on the initiative of the President of the European Council.[36]

Here, any presence of third countries during formal meetings seems to be fully excluded and even meetings 'in the margin' of the European Council are subject to strict conditions. However, despite the fact that for the UK being present at European Council meetings might be important politically, the influence of this institution on key foreign policy issues has been doubted.[37]

But, what about the lower organs? While the same rules apply to 'the Council's preparatory bodies', participation of third states in the Political and Security Committee (PSC) or in Working Parties has proven to be possible in practice, albeit not in Coreper (the Committee of Permanent Representatives; see further below). At the same time, the question is whether presence at informal Council meetings (e.g. so-called 'Gymnich meetings' organised by the rotating Presidency) is also to be excluded. The PD on the future relationship seems to leave this option open (see further below). In any case, unless anything else is arranged, participation of the UK in specific CSDP bodies, such as the European Institute for Security Studies, the European Defence Agency, and the European Satellite Centre will have to be phased out.[38]

While the above rules seem to underline that even on the basis of a special agreement an observer status of the UK at Council or Coreper meetings would be in conflict with primary law rules,[39] such a status could perhaps be foreseen for the UK in certain working parties.[40] However, the EU does not seem to be in favour of any form of 'half-member' status, let alone of voting rights for non-members.[41] While former High Representative Mogherini at the time seemed ready to explore these options,[42] the idea met with some critics among other officials, even where observer status in the PSC would be concerned.[43]

14.3 The Withdrawal Agreement

The WA – that was agreed upon between the EU and the UK in November 2018, was revised in October 2019, and entered into force on 1 February 2020 – does not devote too much text to CFSP, but basically extends the pre-Brexit situation during a transition period (until 31 December 2020). The general starting point is the following: 'Unless otherwise provided in this Agreement, Union law shall be applicable to and in the United Kingdom during the transition period' (Art. 127(1) WA). The UK's participation in CFSP is, however, made dependent on what will be agreed upon in the future relations agreement:

> In the event that the Union and the United Kingdom reach an agreement governing their future relationship in the areas of the Common Foreign and Security Policy and the Common Security and Defence Policy which becomes applicable during the transition period, Chapter 2 of Title V of the TEU [CFSP] and the acts adopted on the basis of those provisions shall cease to apply to the United Kingdom from the date of application of that agreement.[44]

It is interesting to note that, despite the general rule that nothing changes, the participation of the UK in the so-called PESCO in defence matters is excluded;[45] the UK can participate on an 'exceptional basis' only:

> [F]or the purposes of Article 42(6) and Article 46 TEU and of Protocol (No 10) on permanent structured cooperation established by Article 42 TEU, any references to Member

> States shall be understood as not including the United Kingdom. This shall not preclude the possibility for the United Kingdom to be invited to participate as a third country in individual projects under the conditions set out in Council Decision (CFSP) 2017/2315 on an exceptional basis, or in any other form of cooperation to the extent allowed and under the conditions set out by future Union acts adopted on the basis of Article 42(6) and Article 46 TEU.[46]

So, participation of the UK in PESCO as a third state will be possible 'on an exceptional basis'. In general, the possibility for third states to take part in PESCO projects was already foreseen in Article 9 of the PESCO Decision.[47] In anticipation of a specific Council Decision to that end, the Council furthermore recognised that

> a third State could, and would need to, provide substantial added value to the PESCO projects, contribute to strengthening PESCO and the CSDP and meet more demanding commitments, while fully respecting the principle of decision-making autonomy of the EU and its member states.[48]

In addition to the future possibility of the UK to participate in specific PESCO projects, the withdrawal agreement foresees the possibility to continue participation in some of the CSDP institutions and operations,[49] including financial contributions.[50] At the same time, the UK will remain bound by CFSP Decisions, unless it makes 'a formal declaration to the High Representative of the Union for Foreign Affairs and Security Policy, indicating that, for vital and stated reasons of national policy, in those exceptional cases it will not apply the decision'. Yet, even in that case, the rule continues to apply that it 'shall refrain from any action likely to conflict with or impede Union action based on that decision'.[51]

The situation after the transition period will thus depend on what can be agreed upon in the future relationship agreement. As we have seen, some hints may already be found in the PD that was adopted alongside the WA. The general plan seems to be to 'design flexible and scalable cooperation that would ensure that the United Kingdom can combine efforts with the Union to the greatest effect, including in times of crisis or when serious incidents occur'.[52] To that end the Declaration inter alia also foresees that the UK, upon invitation by the High Representative, join 'informal Ministerial meetings of the Member States of the Union'[53] and that it participate 'on a case-by-case basis in CSDP and operations through a Framework Participation Agreement'.[54] While the possibility to join informal meetings does as such not return in the Draft Agreement of March 2020, the possibility of UK participation in CSDP missions is regulated in a 'Protocol establishing a framework for the participation of the United Kingdom of Great Britain and Northern Ireland in European Union crisis management operations', that would be attached to the final Agreement.[55]

The latter will certainly also be beneficial to the EU. The UK is one of only two European states that have a nuclear capacity, it is one of the five spending 2 per cent of its GDP on defence and it is a permanent member of the UN Security Council.[56]

14.4 Third country participation in CFSP

The institutional obstacles discussed above should not prevent the UK from *any* form of participation in CFSP and CSDP. In fact, the participation of third states in these policies and actions has become common practice and also seems to contribute to the objective in Article 21 TEU that 'The Union shall seek to develop relations and build partnerships with third countries, and international, regional or global organisations which share [its] principles.' Some third states – Norway and Iceland in particular – take part in various theme specific Council working groups.[57] Candidate countries show that it is even possible to be an observer in the PSC.[58] However, the EU has no experience in giving observer rights that include the right to speak and agenda making to a non-EU member/non-candidate country in high-level formations such as the PSC, Coreper or the Foreign Affairs Council. Apart from the legal obstacles discussed above, granting such rights to the UK could also have political consequences. It has been observed that it could open the door to similar requests from other non-EU members such as Switzerland, Norway or Turkey (see also section 14.5). Moreover, it can possibly create political tensions in certain other EU Member States, like Sweden or Denmark, where Eurosceptic political parties could be tempted to push for 'half-member' status.[59]

In practice, third country participation in CFSP currently takes place on the basis of agreed frameworks for cooperation. Despite the fact that the future EU–UK foreign and security cooperation will most likely have a different basis (e.g. a Protocol attached to the overall cooperation Agreement), we will briefly mention some examples as they have been part of the debate on the possible scenarios. The first type of cooperation is formed by the EFTA/EEA (European Free Trade Association/European Economic Area) agreements.[60] While these agreements do not formally include cooperation on foreign and security policy, the EU has the habit of inviting EFTA/EEA countries to join EU statements and positions on foreign policy.[61] Furthermore, the EEA Council meets twice a year with representatives of the Commission and the European External Action Service (EEAS). Representatives of the European Council are present at those meetings as well as the representatives of the rotating Council presidency. During this EEA Council meeting, foreign policy is openly discussed while searching for consensus between the EU and the EEA nations.[62] The EU–Norway relationship serves as a good example of a continuous dialogue with the EU on numerous foreign policy issues.[63] This is done through a formal format that consists of two meetings per year between the Norwegian foreign ministers and the foreign minister of the EU. Additionally, there are several meetings where officials from Norway meet together with their counterparts from Iceland and Lichtenstein in CFSP working groups. So far Norwegian officials have participated in CFSP working groups that operate in policy areas that Norway has an interest in, such as the Balkans, Russia, anti-terrorism coordination and the Middle-East peace process. In the end, Norway is invited to sign EU foreign policy statements and thus to align its position to that of the EU.[64] Norway's policy is to join EU statements whenever possible.[65] It has been observed that 'Norway has thus been involved in essentially all of the core aspects of the EU CFSP'.[66] Apart from Norway (and Iceland) as active CFSP participants, Switzerland is worth mentioning as well. As a non-EEA EFTA member, Switzerland joins the EEA Council meetings and regularly joins EU foreign statements and participates in EU missions.[67]

Third country participation in CFSP is also possible on the basis of a Partnership and Cooperation Agreement (PCA). While some PCAs do not expressly refer to foreign policy cooperation (e.g. the one with the Philippines), the EU–Ukraine PCA did as it allowed Ukraine to join EU statements and positions as well as having high-level dialogues at ministerial level and regular meetings at senior official level.[68]

More comprehensive and in-depth cooperation is possible on the basis of an Association Agreement (AA). In the more recent AA between the EU and Ukraine, for example, Article 7 concerns cooperation on foreign and security policy and provides that:

> The Parties shall intensify their dialogue and cooperation and promote gradual convergence in the area of foreign and security policy, including the Common Security and

> Defence Policy (CSDP), and shall address in particular issues of conflict prevention and crisis management, regional stability, disarmament, non-proliferation, arms control and arms export control as well as enhanced mutually-beneficial dialogue in the field of space.[69]

Similar cooperation can be found in a number of Stabilisation and Association Agreements (SAAs).[70] Thus, in the EU–Serbia SAA Article 10 provides for 'an increasing convergence of positions of the Parties on international issues, including CFSP issues, also through the exchange of information as appropriate, and, in particular, on those issues likely to have substantial effects on the Parties' as well as 'common views on security and stability in Europe, including cooperation in the areas covered by the CFSP of the European Union'.[71] In general, candidate countries – which basically are almost all countries that have signed an SAA – are invited to join Gymnich meetings and participate as observers in the PSC.

More generally, the EU has gained experience with third country participation in CFSP through its ENP. As the agreements are all tailor-made, they do not all deal with foreign policy issues in the same manner. An example can be found in the EU–Georgia Action Plan, which – as 'Priority area 7' – mentions the goal to 'Enhance EU–Georgia cooperation on Common Foreign and Security Policy, including European Security and Defence Policy. Georgia may be invited, on a case by case basis, to align itself with EU positions on regional and international issues.'[72]

Similar notions may be found in so-called Framework Agreements. Thus, Article 3 of the 2017 Agreement with Australia provides for political dialogues and cooperation in the area of foreign policy,[73] as does the Strategic Partnership Agreement with Canada, that was negotiated alongside the Comprehensive Economic and Trade Agreement (CETA).[74]

These examples reveal the experience of the EU with the participation of third states in foreign and security policy. For the agreement that is currently under negotiation between the EU and the UK, examples can be drawn from the many existing agreements and arrangements.[75] In addition, ad hoc alignment with EU policies and actions remains possible. This will be particularly relevant in relation to (existing and new) sanctions.[76]

14.5 Third country participation in CSDP

Finally, apart from general CFSP cooperation, third country participation has proven to be possible in military and civilian missions in the context of the CSDP. Around 45 non-EU countries have contributed troops to CSDP missions and operations (approximately 30 if one detracts third countries that have since then become Member States). Four non-EU countries have participated in EU Battlegroups: Turkey, Norway, Ukraine and Macedonia.[77] This has included, for example, all NATO (North Atlantic Treaty Organization) members, and all EU candidate countries. The legal basis for such cooperation has been a treaty in the form of a Framework Participation Agreement (FPA) for more structural participation in CSDP missions, or a Participation Agreement for ad hoc participation in a mission. These agreements are concluded in the form of bilateral EU-only agreements on the basis of Articles 37 TEU and 218 TFEU.[78] Thus, for instance, the FPA with Turkey reveals the procedural rights of the participating country:

> The Republic of Turkey shall have the same rights and obligations in terms of day-to-day management of the operation as European Union Member States taking part in the operation, in accordance with the legal instruments referred to in Article 2(1) of this Agreement.[79]

This principle returns in all FPAs. Third countries are not involved in drafting the operations. They typically receive access to relevant documents once the participation has been accepted by the PSC. In practice, third countries are expected and required to accept the EU's schedule and procedures, and 'by nature, non-member states' participation in EU operations requires a certain degree of acceptance of EU practices, as well as a degree of subordination'.[80]

This latter point may be difficult for the UK to swallow, yet full participation in the preparation and formation of CSDP missions through, inter alia, the Civilian Committee, the EU Military Committee, the Politico-Military Group, the Civilian Planning and Conduct Capability, and the EU Military Staff will be difficult to realise. Apart from legal obstacles, other states that contribute extensively to CSDP missions – such as Turkey – are expected to demand equal treatment.[81] A possible starting point may be offered by the position of Norway. Norway has contributed assets and personnel to a large variety of CSDP missions and operations. This country currently has access to a regular dialogue with regards to EU foreign and security policy. Moreover, Norway's agreement allows the country to join CSDP missions and operations, as well as cooperation in the EDA.[82] Nevertheless, Norway struggles with similar decision-shaping problems.[83]

14.6 Conclusion

Despite the far-reaching ambitions of the UK to continue participating in the Common Foreign, Security and Defence Policy – and its desire to be 'friends with benefits' – legal questions arise as to the realisation of these ambitions.

The present contribution points to a number of restrictions in both EU primary and secondary law to allow the UK to maintain its participation in the key decision-making organs. This is not to say that all close cooperation will be excluded. The existing regimes with other third countries provide ample examples of a possible alignment of the UK with EU policies and the use by the EU of UK diplomacy and capabilities. In a political sense, however, the legal restrictions imply that, as one observer held: the 'UK would have to accept a foreign policy role as a "rule taker" rather than as a "rule maker", and as a follower rather than as a leader'.[84] This idea returned in the Draft text of the Agreement that was presented by the EU in March 2020, which not only provides that

> The United Kingdom shall associate itself with the relevant Decision by which the Council decides that the Union will conduct a crisis management operation, and with any other Decision by which the Council decides to extend a crisis management operation,

but even clearly underlines that 'The contribution of the United Kingdom to an EU crisis management operation shall be without prejudice to the decision-making autonomy of the Union.'[85]

Obviously, ongoing and future negotiations may lead to an unprecedented form of cooperation in this area, but given both some primary law restrictions and political positions taken by the EU,[86] any 'half member' status – with the UK participating in the institutional set-up and decision-making process – will probably have to be excluded (even) in the area of CFSP. Despite the obvious mutual benefits of a close cooperation on foreign and security policy, legal requirements of consistency also support the notion that CFSP cannot be the cherry to be picked. Over the years, the integration of CFSP and other external relations policies has become more intense and general Union principles largely apply to the CFSP regime. A renewed isolation of CFSP from other EU external relations policies would not only be a high price to pay, but would also violate key principles of Union law.

Acknowledgements

This contribution is based on an earlier (pre-Brexit) version that appeared as 'Friends with Benefits? Possibilities for the UK's Continued Participation in the EU's Foreign and Security Policy' (2019) 4 European Papers 427. Many thanks to my co-editors of this volume for their valuable suggestions. Credits are also due to Richard Haringsma, Eduard Hoek and Mikael Waelen for their valuable work on this topic in their Master's theses for the European Studies programme at the University of Twente. These theses are accessible here: https://essay.utwente.nl.

Notes

1 See already the remarks made by Prime Minister Cameron after the referendum; Charles Tannock, 'Brexit: The Security Dimension' (2016) www.charlestannock.com/brexit-security-dimension.pdf accessed 14 March 2020. The EU's negotiating guidelines for Brexit note that 'The EU stands ready to establish partnerships in areas unrelated to trade, in particular the fight against terrorism and international crime, as well as security, defence and foreign policy' European Council Article 50 Guidelines for Brexit Negotiations (Brussels, 29 April 2017) 7. See also UK Government 'Foreign Policy, Defence and Development: A Future Partnership Paper' (Position Paper, 2017) www.gov.uk/government/uploads/system/uploads/attachment_data/file/643924/Foreign_policy__defence_and_development_paper.pdf accessed 14 March 2020.

2 See the UK Government (n 1). See also the speech by PM Theresa May on 17 February 2018:

> Europe's security is our security. And that is why I have said – and I say again today – that the United Kingdom is unconditionally committed to maintaining it. The challenge for all of us today is finding the way to work together, through a deep and special partnership between the UK and the EU, to retain the co-operation that we have built and go further in meeting the evolving threats we face together.
>
> *(www.gov.uk/government/speeches/pm-speech-at-munich-security-conference-17-february-2018 accessed 14 March 2020)*

3 Elsewhere I have extensively dealt with the legal nature of CFSP; see recently for instance Ramses A Wessel, 'Integration and Constitutionalisation in EU Foreign and Security Policy' in Robert Schütze (ed), *Governance and Globalization: International and European Perspectives* (Cambridge University Press 2018) 339; or Ramses A Wessel, 'Resisting Legal Facts: Are CFSP Norms as Soft as They Seem?' (2015) 20 European Foreign Affairs Review 123.

4 Cf Crispin Blunt 'Post-Brexit EU–UK Cooperation on Foreign and Security Policy' (Chairman of House of Commons Foreign Affairs Committee Discussion Paper, 2017) 4:

> The CFSP and CSDP are already substantially intergovernmental in nature, respecting the autonomy of EU member states in foreign and defence policy. Therefore, it should be possible to conceive of mechanisms for a high degree of involvement of the UK, voluntarily and without a veto, in EU foreign, security and defence issues, respecting the autonomy of both the EU and UK.

And Ann Jacobs and Sophie Vanhoonacker, 'EU–UK Cooperation in CSDP After Brexit: Living Apart Together?' (Dahrendorf Forum Policy Brief, 2018): 'The intergovernmental character of CSDP cooperation and the relatively high scope for flexibility could be a further catalyst for a successful deal.'

5 UK Government, 'The Future Relationship with the EU: The UK's Approach to Negotiations' (Policy Paper, 2020).

6 Council Directives 5870/20 ADD 1 REV 3 for the negotiation of a new Partnership with the United Kingdom of Great Britain and Northern Ireland (Brussels, 25 February 2020):

> The aim of the negotiations is to establish a new partnership between the Union, and Euratom where relevant, and the United Kingdom that is comprehensive and covers the areas of interest outlined in the Political Declaration: trade and economic cooperation, law enforcement and judicial cooperation in criminal matters, foreign policy, security and defence and thematic areas of

cooperation. The envisaged partnership should form a coherent structure and be embedded in an overall governance framework.

7 See European Commission, Part Three Title II on Foreign Policy, Security and Defence in the 'Draft text of the Agreement on the New Partnership with the United Kingdom' (Brussels, 18 March 2020) https://ec.europa.eu/info/sites/info/files/200318-draft-agreement-forpolsec.pdf accessed 14 April 2020.

8 See for a comprehensive and very helpful analysis Paul James Cardwell, 'The United Kingdom and the Common Foreign and Security Policy of the EU: From Pre-Brexit "Awkward Partner" to Post-Brexit "Future Partnership"?' (2017) 13 Croatian Yearbook of European Law and Policy 1. Cf Daniel Seah, 'The CFSP as an Aspect of Conducting Foreign Relations by the United Kingdom: With Special Reference to the Treaty of Amity & Cooperation in Southeast Asia' [2015] International Review of Law 1; Anand Menon, 'Defence Policy and the Logic of "High Politics"' in Philipp Genschel and Markus Jachtenfuchs (eds), *Beyond the Regulatory Polity? The European Integration of Core State Power* (Oxford University Press 2013).

9 Secretary of State for Foreign and Commonwealth Affairs (David Miliband), HC Deb 20 February 2008, col 378.

10 Cf Ramses A Wessel (n 3); as well as Christoph Hillion and Ramses A Wessel, 'The Good, the Bad and the Ugly: Three Levels of Judicial Control over the CFSP' in Steven Blockmans and Panos Koutrakos (eds), *Research Handbook in EU Common Foreign and Security Policy* (Edward Elgar Publishing 2018) 65.

11 Cardwell (n 8) 18. Cf also Christophe Hillion, 'Norway and the Changing Common Foreign and Security Policy of the European Union' (NUPI Report, 2019) who concludes that the UK's 'technical note on consultation and cooperation on external security … ironically [displays] greater enthusiasm for the strengthening of the policy than at any point of its membership'. The 'technical note' can be found at www.gov.uk/government/publications/technical-note-on-consultation-and-cooperation-on-external-security accessed 14 March 2020.

12 Cf Ramses A Wessel 'Friends with Benefits? Possibilities for the UK's Continued Participation in the EU's Foreign and Security Policy' (2019) European Papers 427.

13 Kenneth A Armstrong, *Brexit Time: Leaving the EU – Why, How and When?* (Cambridge University Press 2017) 32; James Black, Alex Hall, Kate Cox, Marta Kepe and Erik Silfversten, *Defence and Security after Brexit* (RAND Europe 2017) 17.

14 Cardwell (n 8) 12. The quotes below were also found by Paul Cardwell.

15 David Allen, 'The United Kingdom: A Europeanized Government in a Non-Europeanized Polity' in Simon Bulmer and Christian Lequesne, *The Member States of the European Union* (Oxford University Press 2005) 138–139.

16 UK Government 'Review of the Balance of Competences between the United Kingdom and the European Union: Foreign Policy' (Report, 2013) 87, www.gov.uk/government/uploads/system/uploads/attachment_data/file/227437/2901086_Foreign_Policy_acc.pdf accessed 14 March 2020.

17 Hylke Dijkstra and Sophie Vanhoonacker, 'The Common Foreign and Security Policy' (2017) *Oxford Research Encyclopedia of Politics*.

18 UK Government (n 16) 7.

19 Political Declaration setting out the framework for the future relationship between the European Union and the United Kingdom, OJ [2020] C34/12, para 79.

20 Ibid, para 93.

21 Ibid, para 95.

22 Ibid, para 99. This echoes the objective of the UK to have 'a continued contribution to CSDP missions and operations, including UK personnel, expertise, assets, or use of established UK national command and control facilities'. See UK Government (n 1).

23 Continued participation of the UK in the EDA could take place on the basis of an administrative agreement, following the example by Norway that is allowed to participate in the agency's research and technology projects. See also Sarah Lain and Veerle Nouwens, 'The Consequences of Brexit for European Defence and Security' (Royal United Services Institute for Defence and Security Studies, Occasional Paper, 2017).

24 PD (n 19) paras 102, 104.

25 European Commission (n 7).

26 Scarlett McArdle, 'CSDP and the Development of the "Global EU": The Progress of EU Autonomy in the Shadow of Brexit' (2020) 4 Europe and the World: A Law Review 17.

27 Thus, Article 21(3) TEU provides:

> The Union shall respect the principles and pursue the objectives … in the development and implementation of the different areas of the Union's external action covered by this Title and by Part Five of the Treaty on the Functioning of the European Union, and of the external aspects of its other policies. The Union shall ensure consistency between the different areas of its external action and between these and its other policies. The Council and the Commission, assisted by the High Representative of the Union for Foreign Affairs and Security Policy, shall ensure that consistency and shall cooperate to that effect.

28 Case 266/03 *Commission v Luxembourg* EU:C:2005:34, para 60 and C-476/98 *Commission v Germany* EU:C:2002:631, para 66. See, more extensively, Ramses A Wessel and Joris Larik (eds), *EU External Relations Law: Text, Cases and Materials* (2nd edn, Hart Publishing 2020) chs 1–2.
29 Cf Ramses A Wessel, 'General Principles in CFSP Law' in Violeta Moreno-Lax, Päivi Neuvonen and Katja Ziegler (eds), *Research Handbook on General Principles of EU Law* (Edward Elgar Publishing 2020).
30 See for instance Richard G Whitman, 'The UK and EU Foreign, Security and Defence Policy after Brexit: Integrated, Associated or Detached?' (2017) 43 National Institute Economic Review 48; Malcolm Chalmers, 'UK Foreign and Security Policy after Brexit' (RUSI Briefing Paper, 2017) https://rusi.org/sites/default/files/201701_bp_uk_foreign_and_security_policy_after_brexit_v4.pdf accessed 14 March 2020.
31 See UK Government (n 1).
32 Emphasis added.
33 'Comments on the Council's Rules of Procedure' (2016) 16, www.consilium.europa.eu/media/29824/qc0415692enn.pdf accessed 14 March 2020.
34 While the Rules of Procedure of both the Council and the European Council do not address this issue expressly, these Rules imply that only representatives of Member States are present.
35 Comments (n 33) 39 emphasis added. See also European Parliament 'CSDP After Brexit: The Way Forward' (Directorate-General for External Policies, Policy Department Study, May 2018) www.europarl.europa.eu/RegData/etudes/STUD/2018/603852/EXPO_STU(2018)603852_EN.pdf accessed 14 March 2020.
36 Rules of Procedure of the European Council, art 4(2).
37 See Luigi Lonardo, 'The Relative Influence of the European Council in EU External Action' (2019) 36 Journal of Contemporary European Research 51:

> while it is true that the European Council is influential in the external relations of the EU, this might be the case only on non-critical issues. Instead, it fails to express an influential position when highly divisive topics are on the table, and there is no evidence of its influence.

38 Cf Agreement on the withdrawal of the United Kingdom of Great Britain and Northern Ireland from the European Union and the European Atomic Energy Community [2020] OJ L 29/7 (Withdrawal Agreement, WA) art 156 that deals with the budgetary questions during transition:

> Until 31 December 2020, the United Kingdom shall contribute to the financing of the European Defence Agency, the European Union Institute for Security Studies, and the European Union Satellite Centre, as well as to the costs of Common Security and Defence Policy operations.

39 Something, for instance, suggested by Richard G Whitman, 'The UK and EU Foreign and Security Policy: An Optional Extra' (2016) 87 Political Quarterly 254.
40 See also Jean Claude Piris, 'If the UK Votes to Leave: The Seven Alternatives to EU Membership' (Centre for European Reform, 2016) www.cer.eu/sites/default/files/pb_piris_brexit_12jan16.pdf. In an influential position paper, Blunt (n 4) has argued for far-reaching participation in for instance the PSC.
41 See also the Commission Foreign, Security and Defence Policy Slides (15 June 2018) in which the EU informally reacts to some of the UK's proposals, https://ec.europa.eu/commission/sites/beta-political/files/slides_on_foreign_security_defence_policy.pdf accessed 14 March 2020.
42 Remarks by Mogherini on EU–UK future partnership CFSP (2018) https://eeas.europa.eu/headquarters/headquarters-homepage/44528/remarks-hrvp-mogherini-eu-institute-security-studies-event-future-eu-foreign-security-and_en accessed 14 March 2020.
43 Jonathan Lis, 'Brexit's Toll on Foreign Policy: Losing Our Reputation Day After Day' *Politics* (London, 17 July 2017).

44 WA, art 127(2).
45 See extensively on PESCO, Steven Blockmans, 'The EU's Modular Approach to Defence Integration: An Inclusive, Ambitious and Legally Binding PESCO?' (2018) 55 Common Market Law Review 1785.
46 WA, art 17(7a).
47 Council Decision (CFSP) 2017/2315 establishing permanent structured cooperation (PESCO) and determining the list of participating Member States [2017] OJ L 331/57.
48 Council Conclusions 10048/19 (Luxembourg, 17 June 2019).
49 Yet, art 129(7) WA provides a number of limitations:

> During the transition period, the United Kingdom shall not provide commanders of civilian operations, heads of mission, operation commanders or force commanders for missions or operations conducted under Articles 42, 43 and 44 TEU, nor shall it provide the operational headquarters for such missions or operations, or serve as framework nation for Union battlegroups. During the transition period, the United Kingdom shall not provide the head of any operational actions under Article 28 TEU.

50 WA, art 157:

> Until 31 December 2020, the United Kingdom shall contribute to the financing of the European Defence Agency, the European Union Institute for Security Studies, and the European Union Satellite Centre, as well as to the costs of Common Security and Defence Policy operations, on the basis of the contribution keys set out in point (a) of Article 14(9) of Council Decision (EU) 2016/13531, in Article 10(3) of Council Decision 2014/75/CFSP2, in Article 10(3) of Council Decision 2014/401/CFSP3 and in the second subparagraph of Article 41(2) of the Treaty on European Union, respectively, and in accordance with Article 5 of this Agreement.

51 WA, art 129. See on the legal implications of this rule Wessel (n 3).
52 PD, art 92.
53 PD, art 97.
54 PD, art 101.
55 European Commission (n 7).
56 Cf Luigi Lonardo, 'EU Common Foreign and Security Policy after Brexit: A Security and Defence Treaty for the "Deep and Special Partnership"' (DCU Brexit Institute Working Paper, 2018) 5.
57 Pernille Rieker, 'Outsidership and the European Neighbourhood Policy: The Case of Norway' (2017) 3 Global Affairs 1; Hillion (n 11).
58 Lis (n 43).
59 Piris (n 40). The possibility of voting rights for the UK was also excluded by the HR/VP in answering questions by reporters: 'Remarks' (n 42) as well as by the European Parliament in Resolution 2018/2573(RSP) on the framework for EU–UK cooperation (Strasbourg, 14 March 2018).
60 See on the EEA in relation to Brexit: Christophe Hillion, 'Brexit Means Br(EEA)xit: The UK Withdrawal from the EU and its Implications for the EEA' (2018) 55 Common Market Law Review 135.
61 See also Kateryna Zarembo, 'Ukraine in EU Security: An Undervalued Partner' (FRIDE Policy Brief 2011) 88; as well as Norwegian Ministry of Foreign Affairs 'Cooperation on Foreign and Security Policy' (2018) www.regjeringen.no/en/topics/european-policy/Norways-relations-with-Europe/eu_fusp/id684931/ accessed 20 March 2020; Atli Isleifsson, 'Brothers without Arms: Explaining Iceland's Participation in European Union CSDP Operations' (Lund University Master's Thesis in European Affairs, Department of Political Science 2014); and European Commission, 'Screening Report Iceland' (2011) https://ec.europa.eu/neighbourhood-enlargement/sites/near/files/pdf/iceland/key-documents/screening_report_31_is_internet_en.pdf accessed 20 March 2020.
62 See, for instance, Council of the EEA Conclusions EEE 1605/1/16 (Brussels, 15 November 2016).
63 See Hillion (n 11).
64 Pernille Rieker, 'Norway and the ESDP: Explaining Norwegian Participation in the EU's Security Policy' (2006) 15 European Security 281; and Helene Sjursen, 'Norway and the EUs Foreign and Security Policy' in Erik Oddvar Eriksen and John Erik Fossum (eds), *The European Union's Non-Members: Independence under hegemony?* (Routledge 2015).
65 Norwegian Ministry of Foreign Affairs (n 61).
66 Hillion (n 11) 5.

67 Cf Council conclusions on EU relations with the Swiss Confederation (28 February 2017) www.consilium.europa.eu/en/press/press-releases/2017/02/28/conclusions-eu-swiss-confederation/ accessed 14 March 2020.
68 Partnership and Cooperation Agreement between the European Communities and their Member States, and Ukraine (Section II) [1994] OJ L 49/3.
69 Association Agreement between the European Union and its Member States, of the one part, and Ukraine, of the other part [2016] OJ L 161/03.
70 Cf Dragan Đukanovi , 'The Process of Institutionalization of the EU's CFSP in the Western Balkan Countries during the Ukraine Crisis' (2015) 21 Croatian International Relations Review 81.
71 Stabilisation and Association Agreement between the European Communities and their Member States, of the one part, and the Republic of Serbia, of the other part [2008] OJ L 278.
72 EU–Georgia Action Plan (2006) https://library.euneighbours.eu/content/eu-georgia-action-plan accessed 14 March 2020. See more extensively the contribution by Adam Łazowski in this volume.
73 2017 Framework Agreement between the European Union and its Member States, of the one part, and Australia, of the other part. See Joint Proposal for a Council Decision on the conclusion of the Framework Agreement between the European Union and its Member States, of the one part, and Australia, of the other part JOIN/2016/051 final – 2016/0367 (NLE).
74 2016 Strategic Partnership Agreement between the European Union and its Member States, of the one part, and Canada, of the other part [2016] OJ L 329.
75 In that respect, the PD indeed foresees a 'Political Dialogue on Common Foreign and Security Policy (CFSP) and Common Security and Defence Policy (CSDP) as well as sectoral dialogues' (art 97).
76 It has been observed that the 'European Union Withdrawal Bill 2017–19' will copy existing EU sanctions measures into UK law and may also provide a legal basis for new sanctions regimes. See Lonardo (n 56) 9. See more extensively on this topic, the contribution by Sara Poli Chapter 15, this volume.
77 See Anne Bakker, Margriet Drent and Dick Zandee, 'European Defence: How to Engage the UK after Brexit?' (Clingendael Report, July 2017) 11. This report also provides a good overview of the current and past participation of the UK in CSDP missions.
78 Ibid. See also Lonardo (n 56) 10.
79 Turkey's FPA (annex II, Section 2, Article 6 (5)).
80 Thierry Tardy, 'CSDP: Getting Third States on Board' (European Union Institute for Security Studies Brief, 2014) 6.
81 See also the European Parliament (n 35) 19: '[S]hould London be granted too many privileges, many other countries would go back on the attack to call for similar rights.'
82 Fraser Cameron, 'After Brexit: Prospects for UK–EU Cooperation on Foreign and Security Policy' (European Policy Centre Policy Brief, 2017) http://aei.pitt.edu/92359/ accessed 14 March 2020.
83 Nicole Koenig, 'Towards Norway Plus? EU–UK Defence Cooperation Post-Brexit' (Jacques Delors Institut Berlin Policy Paper, 2018) www.delorscentre.eu/en/publications/detail/publication/towards-norway-plus-eu-uk-defence-cooperation-post-brexit accessed 14 March 2020.
84 Cardwell (n 8) 21. Cf also the monograph by the late Simon Duke, *Will Brexit Damage our Security and Defence? The Impact on the UK and EU* (Palgrave Macmillan 2019).
85 'Protocol establishing a framework for the participation of the United Kingdom of Great Britain and Northern Ireland in European Union crisis management operations' in European Commission (n 7), art 2.
86 The position of the European Parliament has also been quite clear in this respect (n 59):

> The European Parliament notes that, on common foreign and security policy, the UK as a third country will not be able to participate in the EU's decision-making process and that EU common positions and actions can only be adopted by EU Member States; points out, however, that this does not exclude consultation mechanisms that would allow the UK to align with EU foreign policy positions.

15

UK sanctions policy after Brexit

From dependence to autonomy?

Sara Poli

15.1 Introduction

In the post-Brexit era, there is a general expectation that the cooperation between the UK and the EU in the area of the Common Foreign and Security Policy ('CFSP') and, in particular, in the adoption of restrictive measures[1] against third countries[2] or non-state entities[3] will be intense. We can say that during the tight negotiations that led to the endorsement of the Withdrawal Agreement ('WA') by the European Council in November 2018 (and later to its modification in October 2019),[4] the discussion on the future relations in the field of the CFSP was probably one of the less controversial issues. This may be due to the nature of the EU competence in this area, which has distinctive intergovernmental features with respect to the rest of EU law. The most important procedural and institutional specificities of the CFSP are the application of the unanimity rule in the adoption of CFSP Decisions and the limited jurisdiction of the Court of Justice. The impact of the EU's activity in this field on Member States' sovereignty is reduced. It is therefore unsurprising that the wish to regain sovereignty is less pressing for the UK in the area of CFSP than in all other areas where the EU integrationist model applies fully.[5] The EU's action in setting sanctions was not perceived as a meaningful threat to the exercise of the UK's sovereignty. On the contrary, once the UK Prime Minister triggered Art. 50 TEU, not a single occasion was missed to emphasise that there was a common interest in close cooperation in this area post exit day.[6]

In order to appreciate how the UK sanctions policy will be shaped in the future, the next section will examine the provisions of the WA that specifically apply to the field of restrictive measures during the implementation period.[7] In the third section, the way the UK legal order was adapted to incorporate the 'EU sanctions *acquis*' will be briefly explained. The most important elements of the Sanction Act and Money Laundering Act (SAMLA) will be highlighted. This is the domestic legislation that regulates the power of UK ministers to continue to implement UN and EU-derived sanctions. In the fourth section, we will dwell on how the UK may shape its sanctions in the future, after the expiry of the implementation period. It will be shown how in the post-Brexit era the UK will be able to set out its own autonomous restrictive measures and decide the terms of its obligation to apply UN-related sanctions. At the time of writing, the negotiation of the security partnership between the EU and UK has not started yet. Therefore, it is not clear how the bilateral relations in foreign affairs will develop. Yet, it is possible to identify in which areas there may be convergence or divergence between the EU and the UK's sanctions policies in the near future. Finally, section 15.5 will identify some reasons of concerns for due process rights and for the protection of the right to an effective judicial protection that arise out of the SAMLA; the implications of the regained sovereignty for the addressees of sanctions will also be assessed.

15.2 The UK's obligations under the withdrawal agreement in the field of CFSP during the implementation period

The WA provides for the principle of continuity in the application of EU law during the transition period.[8] In the field of the CFSP this means that Decisions adopted under title V chapter II of the TEU, setting up sanctions of EU or UN origin, will continue to bind the UK. In the Protocol on the UK and Northern Ireland there is a specific provision dealing with custom duties and movements of goods: Art. 5 (4) of the Protocol refers to provisions of Union law, listed in Annex II, that apply 'to and in the United Kingdom with respect of Northern Ireland'.[9] Annex II makes a list of EU law provisions, including 'Restrictive measures in force based on Article 215 TFEU, insofar as they relate to trade in goods between the Union and third countries.' This means that all EU measures imposing trade restrictions for foreign policy objectives will have to be respected by the UK and Northern Ireland as long as the Protocol is in force.

As we shall see in the next section, the UK has copied the EU 'sanctions *acquis*' into its legal order. In principle, since Union law will remain applicable during the transition period, this means that the changes to restrictive measures, enacted *after* 1 February 2020, will have to be reflected in UK domestic legislation. Yet, there will be no representation of this country in the Council or in any other EU bodies involved in the adoption of restrictive measures; therefore, the UK will not be able to influence the EU decision-making process. The EU institutions may decide to consult the UK, when there is a need for coordination and to the extent that this is in the EU's interest.[10] This may happen for example in the context of the UN Security Council (UNSC) when a decision has to be taken on sanctions. Yet, this does not guarantee that the UK will actually be systematically consulted; a decision to this effect is taken on a case by-case-basis. This loss of decision-making power is probably considered tolerable for the UK since it is time-limited and lasts until the end of the transition period.

It may be wondered whether the UK's implementation of the EU-derived sanctions, especially those decided after 1 February 2020, is likely to be problematic, considering that this country will not be able to participate in the Council's foreign affairs meetings. In reality, there seems to be no reason for the UK not to apply Decisions setting up sanctions, considering that in practice it has often favoured the enactment of restrictive measures and, to the author's knowledge, has never precluded their adoption in recent times. In legal terms, the UK has to ensure that the obligations resulting from the WA are respected[11] and, more specifically, under the provisions of this agreement related to EU external action, it is bound by the principle of sincere cooperation; it must refrain

> from any action or initiative which is likely to be prejudicial to the Union's interests, in particular in the framework of any international organisation, agency, conference or forum of which the United Kingdom is a party in its own right.[12]

In the context of sanctions, this provision implies that the obligation to respect the principle of sincere cooperation also covers the UN, which is at the origin of selected sanction regimes[13] that are part of the EU sanctions *acquis*. Should the UK breach a CFSP Decision setting up a restrictive measure after exit day, it would violate the mentioned principle.

In addition, the WA provides the UK with a special right in the field of CFSP. The UK may refuse to apply a CFSP decision for 'vital and stated reasons of national policy'.[14] This provision echoes the Luxembourg compromise which survives in the Lisbon Treaty and is also applicable to the field of CFSP.[15] Therefore, in case the UK wishes not to be bound by a restrictive measure it would merely need to invoke Art. 129(6) of the WA. In all likelihood, the right not to apply CFSP measures remains symbolic as far as sanctions are concerned: indeed, as was mentioned, it is difficult to identify situations in which the EU would be willing to sanction a third country where the UK would opt for not following the EU in its own national interests. In the unlikely event that the UK decided to distance itself from an EU sanctions policy, this could only happen in relation to the institution of EU autonomous restrictive measures,[16] but not with respect to UN-derived measures. Indeed, the UK is bound to apply the latter sanctions under the UN Charter.

A further noteworthy aspect of EU–UK cooperation during the transition period is that in a case where a UK court has doubts on the validity of CFSP decisions instituting sanctions, it is possible to refer to the Court of Justice in the framework of a preliminary ruling,[17] as it has happened in the context of the Rosneft case.[18]

Finally, it should be mentioned that, under Art. 127(2) of the WA, the EU and the UK may negotiate and conclude an agreement governing their future relationship in the areas of the CFSP and the Common Security and Defence Policy before the end of the transition period. Such a Treaty, which would be an EU-only agreement, could enter into force before 31 December 2020 (or at a later date if the end of the transition is postponed under the circumstances defined by Art. 132 (1)). In this case, chapter II of Title V of the TEU and the acts adopted on the basis of those provisions, including restrictive measures, would cease to be in force in the UK, as of the date of the conclusion of the agreement.[19] This would mean that the UK would regain full autonomy in creating sanctions regimes before the expiry of the transition period. Given the limited temporal extension of the implementation period (between 1 February and 31 December 2020) and the prohibition for a UK minister to ask for an extension of the implementation period in the Joint Committee set up by the WA,[20] it may be difficult for the parties to conclude an agreement in this area before the end of the transition. Yet, it might not be impossible given the uncontentious nature of the cooperation and the relatively simple concluding procedure of an agreement in the field of security (with no need for ratification by all Member States).

15.3 The adaptation of the UK legal order to EU sanctions law

In order to incorporate EU law into the domestic legal order, in preparation for the transition period and exit day (which was set to be on 29 March 2019), the UK had to enact a Statute, the European Union (Withdrawal) Act (hereafter 'EUWA') in 2017, that repealed the European Communities Act of 1972,[21] which had implemented the UK's accession agreement. The EUWA defined how the EU *acquis* could be transformed into domestic legislation. The idea was that the Act was to convert EU law as it applied the last day that the UK was a member of the EU 'wherever practical and sensible'.[22] The ultimate goal was to ensure that acts of EU origin would be applied as much as possible in continuity with the pre-exit era, thus providing legal certainty to the UK citizens and firms. The EUWA lays down basic principles and leaves it to the Ministers of the Crown to incorporate 'direct EU legislation',[23] in so far as it has 'effect in EU law immediately before exit day'. CFSP Decisions setting up restrictive measures, both of UN and EU origin, are based on Art. 29 of the TEU. Therefore, they do not fall within this category of legislation, which includes only three types of acts: Regulations, Decisions under

Art. 288 TFEU and 'EU tertiary legislation'.[24] Thus, the EUWA only makes it possible to incorporate Regulations under Art. 215(2) of the TFEU, giving effect to CFSP Decisions instituting economic sanctions, but not CFSP Decisions (adopted under Art. 29 TEU). In addition, the Statute had the effect of freezing the EU sanctions within the UK legal order but did not provide for the possibility to substantially amend the EU-derived legislation.[25] This is why the SAMLA was adopted.[26] The new Statute entered into force in May 2018; it is a broad legislative framework that creates a regulation-making power[27] for the government[28] in the field of sanctions: 'appropriate ministers' are empowered to enact specific sector-related Statutes and to decide how the UK will shape its sanctions policy. The new legislation ensures that the UK has an autonomous basis to implement UN[29] and EU sanctions. The government's strategy was to gradually incorporate the EU-derived sanctions so that, even in a no-deal scenario, the UK would have been able to continue to apply sanctions adopted while being part of the EU. The SAMLA also amends other pieces of legislation, taking the exit from the EU as an opportunity to reform the Counter Terrorism Act of 2008 and the money laundering regulations,[30] which are UK autonomous sanction mechanisms, in order to continue 'to align the UK with international standards'.[31]

It should be noted that the new Statute also empowers the receding country to create new sanctions regimes independently from the UN and the EU, thus making it possible to repatriate the sanctioning power in this area. Under domestic law, sanctions may be imposed having in mind the national interest only and with the advantage that neither the target, nor the typology of sanctions, needs to be agreed with the EU Member States. More precisely, the Secretary of State or the Treasury are empowered to adopt sanctions[32] as a national security and foreign policy tool, in addition to other broadly formulated purposes.[33]

A wide range of sanctions is available under the SAMLA. These are immigration sanctions, that is to say, travel bans (s. 4) but also financial (s. 3), trade (s. 5) and aircraft and shipping sanctions (ss. 6 and 7). Therefore, ships and aircrafts may be targeted in addition to designated persons and persons connected with a prescribed country.

Between 2017 and early 2019 and on the basis of the mentioned primary legislation, the UK has adopted secondary legislation in the form of regulations for each of the UN-derived[34] and autonomous sanctions regimes.[35]

Yet, the UK regulations are likely to become outdated quite rapidly after the start of the implementation period. Indeed, the Council frequently amends the texts of the CFSP decisions to change both the scope *ratione personae* and *ratione materiae* of the sanctions. Thus, the UK will have to adapt to these kinds of changes, without being able to influence the decision-making process. The SAMLA makes it possible for the ministers to exercise 'temporary powers in relation to EU lists' so as, for example, to update the list of designated persons each time that there are changes resulting from an EU autonomous decision or a UNSC resolution.[36] Such powers can be exercised for a limited time which is assumed to expire at the end of the transition period or even before it in case the EU and the UK manage to conclude an agreement in the area of the CFSP, as envisaged by the WA.

15.4 Parallel sanctions by default for the UK or an autonomous sanctions policy?

It is now appropriate to consider how the UK will shape its sanctions policy after the end of the transition period. Although the UK will regain sovereignty in imposing sanctions, this does not mean that it will have a very different policy from that of the EU on the substantive aspects of the sanctions regimes. As the House of Lords recognises, 'While the Sanctions and Anti-Money

Laundering Bill would allow the UK to implement unilateral sanctions regimes, sanctions are most effective when imposed in concert with international partners.'[37] It may be expected that the UK will establish parallel sanctions to those of the EU, as other third European countries do, including Switzerland, Norway, the Western Balkans countries, Ukraine, Moldova and Georgia.[38] This is true for economic sanctions whose effectiveness would be jeopardised if the concerned European country decided to act unilaterally. It is likely that there will be close coordination between the parties in devising restrictive measures since there are no legal or political obstacles to the development of a 'frictionless' and intense cooperation between the parties in this area. Such a model of cooperation was also favoured by the European Parliament which 'did not exclude consultation mechanisms that would allow the UK to align with EU foreign policy positions, joint actions, notably on human rights, or multilateral cooperation, especially in the frameworks of the UN, OSCE and Council of Europe'.[39] According to some scholars, the UK will have to remain mindful of EU sanctions policy considering that these sanctions will apply to EU nationals and companies incorporated in the EU.[40] The wish that the UK remain aligned to EU sanctions in the post-Brexit era was also expressed by the House of Lords.[41]

Actually, it is difficult to imagine that the EU will impose sanctions against a third country and the UK will not follow the move. It is also unlikely that there will be a disconnection between the UK and EU sanctions policy vis-à-vis Iran. The decision made by Trump to unilaterally withdraw from the Joint Comprehensive Plan of Action (JCPOA) was not replicated by the UK who has reconfirmed commitment to the full and effective implementation of the nuclear deal with Iran in the framework of the Joint Commission that oversees the implementation of the deal in June 2018.[42] The UK has also participated in the decision-making that led to the reactivation of the so-called 'blocking Regulation' of 1996. The latter was aimed at blocking the extraterritorial effects of sanctions adopted by the US against Cuba. In 2018 that piece of legislation was amended so as to prohibit persons and companies from complying with the secondary sanctions enacted by the former country with respect to Iran.[43]

A further hint suggesting that the UK is likely to align to sanctions imposed by the EU is that the UK has not used its national competence to adopt sanctions as long as the EU was empowered to do so and actually exercised its powers. The fact that the EU has competence in the field of CFSP does not mean that Member States are compelled to act together to adopt restrictive measures. The UK has contributed to shaping EU sanctions policy rather than acting on its own when it comes to sanctions against third country regimes. So far there has been no need for the UK to adopt independent measures from those of the EU. This is confirmed by the new thematic sanctions regime, created by the EU and aimed at countering the proliferation of chemical weapons. One of the reasons that led to its creation was the Salisbury chemical attack which was carried out with a 'military-grade nerve agent of a type developed by Russia', according to a statement adopted by G7 Foreign Ministries countries.[44] The adoption of the new sanctions regime in 2019[45] was favoured by the UK.

Having said that the UK and the EU will closely cooperate in adopting sanctions, let us now turn to the mechanisms enabling the Parties to work together. The Political Declaration, setting out the framework for the future relationship between the EU and the UK,[46] contains a section dedicated to sanctions. Paragraph 97 of this text provides that the High Representative may, where appropriate, invite the UK to informal ministerial meetings of the Member States of the Union. Certainly, should the UK be consulted on a regular basis on the setting up of sanctions and on their management, this would be quite exceptional treatment; indeed, this is a right that is not available to European countries such as Switzerland or Norway, which often align to EU sanctions after their adoption,[47] although there have been cases in which Norway was invited to participate in informal meetings.[48] Yet, the UK's expertise on sanctions may prove so valuable that a special institutional arrangement[49] providing a 'meaningful right' of participation to the EU sanctions policy may be truly in the interests of the EU.

It should be noted that although the Political Declaration creates the basis for intense cooperation through consultation between the Parties on all aspects of sanctions,[50] it does not envisage alignment of the UK to the EU sanctions policy as the general rule. Although there could well be situations in which the EU and UK foreign policy objectives are aligned, this is not the default situation. Paragraph 98 states that in the cases where these objectives converge, 'An intensified exchange of information at appropriate stages of the policy cycle of this sanctions regime will take place, with the possibility of adopting sanctions that are mutually reinforcing.' But the general rule seems to be that the parties pursue 'independent sanctions policies driven by their respective foreign policies', as suggested by paragraph 97. At the same time, the negotiating Directives of the Council for the conclusion of a new partnership with the UK envisages the UK's role as a rule-taker. It is worth quoting these directives in full:

> To enable the alignment of the United Kingdom with the Union sanction policy, when and where foreign policy objectives are shared, the envisaged partnership should facilitate dialogue and mutual exchange of information between the Union and the United Kingdom at appropriate stages of the policy cycle of their respective sanction regimes.[51]

At the expiry of the implementation period, it is likely that there will be some differences between the sanction policies of the EU bloc and that of the UK, especially as far as individual restrictive measures are concerned. For example, the latter may wish to add the name of a person to the list of addressees of sanctions decided by the former. The UK will be able to make this choice and the decision is likely to be made more rapidly than at EU level where the group of EU Member States need to decide unanimously. It should be noted that the UK sanctions policy has already given signs of diversifying from that of the EU. Shortly after the EU suspended most of the sanctions against Zimbabwe for humanitarian reasons, the UK announced that, after the end of the transition period, it will re-list one of the persons who has benefited from the EU decision: Ms Grace Mugabe.[52]

There are also other opportunities of differentiation for future UK sanctions policy. The 2018 SAMLA provides that sanctions regulations can be adopted, inter alia, to 'further a foreign policy objective'.[53] The Secretary of State may enact sanctions regulations to establish new restrictive measures for this purpose. The UK government was particularly interested in enacting sanctions that targeted the perpetrators of human rights abuses or cyber attacks. While a regime in the latter area was set up by the EU in 2017,[54] at the moment there are no Magnitsky-style sanctions[55] in the EU, unlike in the US and Canada. The European Parliament favours the creation of this regime; its position was disclosed at the killing of Mr Kashoggi, the Saudi Arabian dissident journalist, who was suppressed by nationals of Saudi Arabia in Turkey.[56] The UK foreign affairs minister made a joint declaration with his German and French counterparts on 14 October 2018 condemning the extra-judicial killing by Saudi Arabia agents. However, no sanctions were adopted by the UK. The House of Commons has criticised the government for its failure to make clear whether the UK will act unilaterally in this area.[57]

Recently, the High Representative of the Union, Mr Borrell, announced in his first meeting of the Council of Foreign Affairs (9 December 2019) that a study will be commissioned to decide about these types of sanctions. Certainly, the EU has competence to act against countries or persons engaging in human rights abuses vis-à-vis human rights defenders or other public figures, given that one of the objectives of its external action is to consolidate and support human rights.[58] So long as the EU has not acted, Member States are free to adopt unilateral sanctions and some of them have already taken the lead.[59] In principle, this means that the UK could do the same even during the implementation period, given that the SAMLA offers the legal basis for the UK to adopt its own regime.[60] Would the principle of sincere cooperation, as defined in the WA, mean the UK had to wait until the EU has not taken a definitive decision on the creation of the concerned sanctions regime? Probably the answer is positive, although the UK would not be alone in breaching this principle: indeed, as mentioned above, even some current Member States have already enacted unilateral Magnitsky-style sanctions.

Finally, the UK may wish to enact the so-called 'immigration sanctions' which consist in refusing the entry to designated persons for reasons of foreign policy. In contrast with economic sanctions which need to be applied in the widest number of states as possible for them to be effective, travel bans can be enacted independently of the EU. This implies that the UK government may be free both to impose entry restrictions against selected persons that the EU was not willing to adopt or to expand the number of persons included in the list of a CFSP Decision instituting such bans.

15.5 The SAMLA and the right to effective judicial protection

It may be wondered whether the SAMLA sets out rules that are broadly similar in terms of due process standards to those applicable in the EU. This is particularly important given that the UK will not be bound by the European Charter of Fundamental Rights anymore, as a result of s. 5(4) of the EUWA, although it will remain obliged to respect the European Convention of Human Rights and Fundamental Freedoms. In the EU, the Council has to comply with the Charter when adopting sanctions and has issued guidelines to inform the public and potential addressees of sanctions on how the EU sanctions policy is managed and how listing decisions are made.[61] The Council's restrictive measures can be challenged before the General Court and on appeal before the Court of Justice, under Art. 275 (2) TFEU. Numerous annulment actions have been examined since the pre-Lisbon era.[62] It can be said that the judiciary has contributed to strengthening the due process rights of the addressees of sanctions, which is an essential aspect of a Union based on the rule of law. The Council has a duty to motivate its decisions to freeze assets and to list a natural or legal person or other non-state entities and groups only when they fulfil the designation criteria and the Council has evidence that they do.[63] A failure to gather information substantiating the restrictive measure may also lead, in special circumstances, to the award of damages to the addresses of sanctions.[64] The Council's listing decisions may be annulled not only if they are not motivated but also for manifest error of assessment in including the name of a natural or legal person in the list of persons subject to restrictive measures. While the Council does not frequently de-list persons targeted by sanctions to execute a ruling of the Court of Justice, it should be said that the right to an effective judicial review is strong in the EU.[65] In the most recent case law, involving Ukrainian applicants, the Court annulled the listing since the Council had failed to verify whether the Ukrainian judicial decisions, on which the challenged restrictive measures were based, had respected the right of defence and the right to effective judicial protection of the addressee of the sanction.[66] Will the UK be able to respect the same standards of protection of due process rights and the right to an effective judicial protection as in the EU? The SAMLA's practice will tell.

It should also be noted that the position of natural and legal persons or other non-state entities, targeted by the UK, will get worse in terms of access to justice after the end of the transition period. Indeed, the addresses of individual sanctions will no longer be able to challenge them before the Court of Justice in the context of the preliminary ruling procedure raised by UK courts.[67] Therefore, the addressees of UK sanctions will have to rely on the remedies laid down by the provisions of the SAMLA and possibly by the European Convention on Human Rights. This implies that the Strasbourg Court will have more cases to hear involving persons targeted by the UK. It will be interesting to see how the EU institutions, including the Court of Justice, would react in a case where a UK listing decision, which was made in parallel to the EU, was to be found in breach of one of the rights protected by the European Convention of Human Rights.[68] This situation raises potential risks for the autonomy of the Court of Justice in reviewing restrictive measures.

Turning again the attention to the SAMLA, we can say that it raises a number of concerns which will be briefly identified. The first is related to the evidentiary burden that is necessary in order for the UK Secretary of State to include the name of a person in a list of individuals who are subject to assets freeing orders or travel bans. This aspect is not strictly related to the right to judicial protection; yet, it is a relevant index of the directions that the UK sanctions policy may take. 'An appropriate minister' may designate a person merely when he 'has reasonable grounds to suspect that that person is involved directly or indirectly in an activity that justifies the adoption of sanctions'. This test has lowered the standard of the TAFA,[69] thus making it easier to target persons. Actually, the UK Regulations that introduced UN and EU derived sanctions adopts this test. However, the Court of Justice sets a higher threshold to list a non-state entity.[70] In *Kadi*, the notorious judgement concerning sanctions in the field of counter terrorism, the Court stated that there has to be a sufficiently solid factual basis to substantiate the reasons for listing.[71] In the context of third countries sanctions, the listing decision is subject to a test which is more restrictive than that of the UK. This is shown by *Anbouba*[72] in which the Court had to decide whether the Council's decision to list a Syrian businessman, associated with the country's regime, was justified. The Court held that

> the Council discharges the burden of proof borne by it when it presents to the Courts of the European Union a set of indicia sufficiently specific, precise and consistent to establish that there is a sufficient link between the person subject to a measure freezing his funds and the regime being combated.[73]

A second element of concern is related to the review process of designations of persons, under the EU autonomous sanctions regimes. When a person's name is included in a list of a sanction regulation, the review of this decision is made every three years.[74] This may be considered a very long period if compared with that of EU autonomous sanctions which are usually revised every year. It should be added that in the SAMLA persons may be designated by description, that is to say, with no need to specify their names.[75]

A further important reason for preoccupation has to do more with the right to an effective judicial protection: under the SAMLA, it is not possible to *directly* challenge designations in Courts. A request to revoke the designation must be submitted to the minister who made it and the latter does not have an obligation to answer; he may decide to 'take no action with respect to the request'.[76] If a negative decision is made by the minister, the designated person will be able to challenge it before the courts. Yet, this form of administrative review[77] is not satisfying since the addressees cannot challenge the decision to insert the name in the list directly before a Court, as happens in the EU legal order.

It should be noted that when a legal or natural person is targeted by the UK, in order to implement a UN Security Council resolution, they do not even have a right to challenge this decision before a court.[78] Indeed, a request to be de-listed must be made to the Secretary of State and he/she will use 'its best endeavours' to secure that the person's name is removed from the relevant UN list.[79] There are no time limits for a decision to be made by the Secretary of State and the minister may also refuse to make such a request to the UN bodies. Such a decision is subject to review before a court. However, even if the minister asks for the de-listing of the name, the decision in itself rests with the UN Security Council or the subsidiary organs of that body.[80] In addition, in the UN context, it is not possible to challenge the decisions made by the UN Security Council before a judicial body. By contrast, in case an application for annulment of a listing decision of UN origin is made before the Court of Justice, the latter has the power to review its legality and could, in principle, annul it even if the CFSP Decision implements a UNSC resolution.

15.6 Conclusions

For the UK, withdrawal from the EU Treaties has implied a loss of decision-making power to institute sanctions in the EU. Since this former Member State has greatly influenced the adoption of sanctions and has been an important source of information in the area of counterterrorism,[81] its exit is also detrimental to the EU. The UK's contribution to European sanctions policy has been described by a civil servant of the Council service as remarkable both for the substance and the quality of improvements in the sanctions process. He added that a 'very valuable input, as regards quality, could be lost, unless other ways are found of preserving it'. He also mentioned that there might be fewer listings after the UK left.[82]

It is not yet clear what directions UK sanctions policy will take in the post-Brexit era and this lack of strategy became the object of criticism by the House of Commons in 2018.[83] Certainly, the UK in the post-Brexit era has the power to adopt its own sanctions and also the capacity and the resources to do this; however, its economic sanctions are effective only if the EU and its Member States follow a similar policy. The most likely scenario is that the UK will opt for alignment with EU sanctions.[84] Indeed, even if the UK has gained formal autonomy from the organisation in shaping its sanctions policy, it is more dependent on the EU than in the past. Indeed, in its new status of third country, it will be more difficult for the UK to convince EU Member States to adopt sanctions, if the latter are reluctant to do so. Yet, in case the Council does not manage to create a new sanctions regime, it is also possible that the UK will take the lead in creating new sanctions regimes.

Notes

1 The word 'restrictive measures' and 'sanctions' are used interchangeably. Restrictive measures are adopted on the basis of CFSP decisions founded on art 29 TEU. For recent studies in this area see, Christina Eckes, 'The Law and Practice of EU Sanctions' in Steven Blockmans and Panos Koutrakos (eds), *Research Handbook on the EU's Common Foreign and Security Policy* (Routledge 2018); Sara Poli, *Le misure restrittive autonome dell'Unione europea* (Editoriale Scientifica 2019).
2 Such as arms or trade embargos.
3 Such as legal or natural persons or other non-state entities and groups, including terrorists and terrorist organisations.
4 Agreement on the withdrawal of the United Kingdom of Great Britain and Northern Ireland from the European Union and the European Atomic Energy Community [2020] OJ L 29/7.
5 Yet, see for a different view the contribution by Ramses A Wessel, Chapter 14 in this volume.
6 See for details Luigi Lonardo, 'EU Common Foreign and Security Policy after Brexit: A Security and Defence Treaty for the "Deep and Special Partnership"' (DCU Brexit Institute Working Paper, 2018) 2.
7 The contribution by Szép and Van Elsuwege focuses more on the lessons learned from other third state alignments to EU sanctions, Chapter 16 in this volume.
8 WA, art 127(1).

9 Ibid.
10 WA, art 129(5) states: 'Without prejudice to Article 127(2), whenever there is a need for coordination, the United Kingdom may be consulted, on a case-by-case basis.'
11 WA, art 5:

> The Union and the United Kingdom shall, in full mutual respect and good faith, assist each other in carrying out tasks which flow from this Agreement. They shall take all appropriate measures, whether general or particular, to ensure fulfilment of the obligations arising from this Agreement and shall refrain from any measures which could jeopardise the attainment of the objectives of this Agreement. This Article is without prejudice to the application of Union law pursuant to this Agreement, in particular the principle of sincere cooperation.

12 Ibid, art 129(3).
13 More precisely, under c 1 the SAMLA is designed to enable sanctions to be made for the purposes of compliance with UN obligations or other international obligations or for the purposes of furthering the prevention of terrorism or for the purposes of national security or international peace and security or for the purposes of furthering foreign policy objectives. The Statute further aims at making

> provisions for the purposes of the detection, investigation and prevention of money laundering and terrorist financing and for the purposes of implementing Standards published by the Financial Action Task Force relating to combating threats to the integrity of the international financial sanctions.

Regime sanctions of UN origin are: Somalia, Al-Qaida, ISIL/1267, Iraq, Liberia, Lebanon, Democratic Republic of Congo, Democratic Republic of Korea, Libya, Afghanistan, Guinea-Bissau, Central Africa Republic, Yemen, South Sudan, Sudan. Eritrea sanctions were revoked in 2019.
14 WA, art 129(6).
15 TEU, art 31(2), para 2.
16 In contrast, the UK will not refuse to apply a CFSP act giving effect to a UN sanction since the obligation to implement a UNSC resolution setting up sanctions, results from the UN Treaty, which the UK is bound to respect under international law. In addition, the UK is a country with a right to veto within the UNSC and therefore it could prevent the adoption of a UN sanction if it were against the decision to sanction a certain third country.
17 WA, art 86(2).
18 Case C-72/15 P *PJSC Rosneft Oil Company* EU:C:2017:236. In this case the Court of Justice interpreted art 24 TEU and 275 TFEU setting out the conditions for judicial review of selected CFSP Decisions. The competence to rule on the validity of these measures, in the context of preliminary rulings, was acknowledged by the Court. It is not yet clear whether the Court has also the competence to interpret them. Therefore, UK courts could not use art 267 TFEU to ask for an interpretation of these measures.
19 WA, art 127(2).
20 WA, art 164.
21 EUWA, s 1. For a comment see P Craig, 'Brexit and the UK Constitution' in Jeffrey Jowell and Colm O'Cinneide (eds), *The Changing Constitution* (Oxford University Press 2019) 95.
22 Department for Exiting the European Union, 'Legislating for the United Kingdom's Withdrawal from the European Union' Cm 9446 (March 2017) 7, https://assets.publishing.service.gov.uk/government/uploads/system/uploads/attachment_data/file/604516/Great_repeal_bill_white_paper_accessible.pdf accessed 3 March 2020.
23 EUWA, s 3(1)a. This provision defines as direct EU legislation, EU Regulations, EU Decisions and EU tertiary legislation. The meaning of each of these acts is specified in s 20.
24 See for the definition EUWA s 20.
25 See the Explanatory Notes to the Sanctions and Anti-Money Laundering Bill [HL] as introduced in the House of Lords on 18 October 2017 (HL Bill 69), para 13, www.legislation.gov.uk/ukpga/2018/13/pdfs/ukpgaen_20180013_en.pdf accessed 10 March 2020.
26 See Sanctions and Anti-Money Laundering Act 2018, www.legislation.gov.uk/ukpga/2018/13/contents/enacted accessed 11 March 2020.
27 SAMLA c 1.
28 The attribution of broad powers to the ministers was criticised by the House of Lords during the legislative process. Ben Smith, 'The Sanctions and Anti-Money Laundering Bill 2017–19' (House of Commons Briefing Paper, 15 February 2018) 5–8.

29 See (n 13).
30 In order to counter terrorism the UK may implement UN and EU sanctions and adopt its own sanctions as specified in three Statutes: Terrorist Asset-Freezing Act 2010 (TAFA 2010), Counter Terrorism Act 2008 (CTA 2008) and the Anti-Terrorism, Crime and Security Act 2001 (ATCSA 2001). The SAMLA covers anti-terrorism sanctions since part 1 of the TAFA was repealed (see para 59).
31 See Explanatory Notes to the Sanctions and Anti-Money Laundering Bill (n 25), s 1.
32 SAMLA covers sanctions regimes and anti-money laundering and counter-terrorist financing sanctions.
33 The purposes of the sanctions are widely defined in c 1, subsections 1 and 2. See also Explanatory Notes (n 25) points 22 to 24. These are:

> a. complying with a United Nations obligation; b. complying with any other international obligations (which could include obligations from UK membership of other international organisations, for example the Organisation for Security and Co-operation in Europe (OSCE), as well as other international treaties or agreements); i. further the prevention of terrorism both in the UK and elsewhere; ii. are in the interests of national security; iii. are in the interests international peace and security; or iv. further a foreign policy objective: to implement UNSC resolutions or to comply with obligations of other organizations.

34 The texts of the Regulations enacting UN sanctions against third countries or to counter terrorism may be found at www.legislation.gov.uk/ accessed 11 March 2020.
35 These are Regulations concerning the following sanctions regimes: Venezuela (reg 135 of 2019), Democratic Republic of Congo (reg 433 of 2019), Iran (nuclear sanction regime enacted by reg 461 of 2019), Iran (human rights sanctions enacted by reg 134 of 2019) Guinea Bissau (reg 554 of 2019), Belarus (reg 600 of 2019), Zimbabwe (reg 604 of 2019), Syria (reg 792 of 2019), Russia (reg 855 of 2019), Burundi (reg 1142 of 2019), Guinea (reg 1145 of 2019), Turkey (reg 1512 of 2019), Burma (reg 539 of 2018), Mali (reg 972 of 2017). Thematic sanctions such as those for cyber attacks were enacted through reg 856 of 2019 and that for chemical weapons through reg 618 of 2019. Finally, counter-terrorism sanctions were adopted through reg 577 of 2019 and the ISIL (Da'esh) and Al-Qaida sanctions were laid down in reg 466.
36 SAMLA c 34.
37 European Union Committee, 'Brexit: Sanctions Policy' (2017–19 HL, 50) 39.
38 See for more details the contribution by Peter Van Elsuwege and Viktor Szép, Chapter 16 in this volume.
39 European Parliament Resolution 2018/2573 on the framework of the future EU–UK relationship (Brussels, 14 March 2018) para 21.
40 Richard Gordon, Michael Smyth and Tom Cornell, *Sanctions Law* (Hart Publishing 2019) 167.
41 European Union Committee, 'The Legality of EU Sanctions' (2016–17 HL, 102) 30, https://publications.parliament.uk/pa/ld201617/ldselect/ldeucom/102/102.pdf accessed 10 March 2020.
42 See 'Joint Comprehensive Plan of Action' (Joint Commission Statement, 6 July 2018) https://eeas.europa.eu/headquarters/headquarters-homepage/48076/statement-joint-commission-joint-comprehensive-plan-action_en accessed 12 March 2020.
43 Commission delegated Regulation (EU) 2018/1100 of 6 June 2018 amending the Annex to Council Regulation (EC) No 2271/96 protecting against the effects of extra-territorial application of legislation adopted by a third country, and actions based thereon or resulting therefrom, OJ 2018, LI 199/1.
44 www.g7.utoronto.ca/foreign/180416-salisbury.html accessed 10 March 2020.
45 Council Decision (CFSP) 2018/1544 concerning restrictive measures against the proliferation and use of chemical weapons [2018] OJ L 259/25 and Council Regulation (EU) 2018/1542 concerning restrictive measures against the proliferation and use of chemical weapons [2018] OJ L 259/12.
46 Political Declaration setting out the framework for the future relationship between the European Union and the United Kingdom [2020] OJ C34/12.
47 Erica Moret and Fabrice Pothier, 'Sanctions after Brexit' (2018) 60 Global Politics and Strategy 190. See also the contribution by Ramses A Wessel, Chapter 14 in this volume.
48 Cristophe Hillion, 'Norway and the Changing Common Foreign and Security Policy of the European Union' (NUPI Report, 2019) 23.
49 On the legal and political obstacles to formally involve the UK in the Council or European Council, see Ramses Wessel, 'Friends with Benefits? Possibilities for the UK's Continued Participation in the EU's Foreign and Security Policy' (2019) European Papers 432–434.

50 This should include the exchange of information on listings and their justification, development, implementation and enforcement, as well as technical support, and dialogue on future designations and regimes.
51 Council Directive 5870/20 for the negotiation of a new partnership with the United Kingdom of Great Britain and Northern Ireland, para 133.
52 www.telegraph.co.uk/business/2020/02/22/britain-prepares-reimpose-sanctions-grace-mugabe-brexit/ accessed 12 March 2020.
53 SAMLA c 23 c) iv).
54 Council Decision (CFSP) 2019/797 concerning restrictive measures against cyber-attacks threatening the Union or its Member States [2019] OJ L 129/I/3 and Council Regulation (EU) 2019/796 of 17 May 2019 concerning restrictive measures against cyber-attacks threatening the Union or its Member States [2019] OJ L 129 I/1.
55 See 'Global Magnitsky Human Rights Accountability Act' of 23 December 2016, ss 1261–1265, Subtitle F, Public Law 114–328, of the FY17 National Defense Authorization Act. For comments with respect to the position of the UK see, Ben Smith and Joanna Dawson, 'The Magnitsky Legislation' (House of Commons Briefing Paper, 6 July 2018).
56 European Parliament Resolution P8_TA(2018)0434 on the killing of journalist Jamal Khashoggi in the Saudi consulate in Istanbul, para 11.
57 House of Commons Foreign Affairs Committee, 'Fragmented and Incoherent: The UK's Sanctions Policy' https://publications.parliament.uk/pa/cm201719/cmselect/cmfaff/1703/170302.htm accessed 12 March 2020.
58 TEU, art 21 (2) b).
59 These are Estonia, Latvia and Lithuania, as reported by the House of Commons Foreign Affairs Committee (n 57) 8. The US and Canada adopted financial sanctions against a group of Saudi Arabians who were supposed to be involved in the killing of the journalist. In the EU only France and Germany decided to adopt sanctions vis-à-vis 17 persons coming from the concerned country. No decision was taken at the EU level, although the brutal killing was firmly criticised by High Representative Mogherini. See 'Speech by High Representative/Vice-President Federica Mogherini at the European Parliament Plenary Session on the Killing of the Saudi Journalist Jamal Khashoggi in the Saudi Consulate in Istanbul' at the plenary session of the European Parliament (23 October 2018).
60 See SAMLA c 1(2) and also the comments made by Aline Doussin, 'The UK Sanctions Bill: A Practical Overview of the Post-Brexit UK Sanctions Regime' (2018) 24 International Trade Law and Regulation 47.
61 See http://data.consilium.europa.eu/doc/document/ST-10254-2015-INIT/en/pdf accessed 12 March 2020.
62 Compare the contribution by Szép and Van Elsuwege in this volume and Sara Poli (n 1).
63 The most clear example is provided by case C-416/18 P *Mykola Yanovych Azarov v Council* EU:C:2019:602.
64 See Case T-384/11, *Safa Nicu Sepahan Co v Council* EU:T:2014:986 and the comments by Charlotte Beaucillon, 'Opening Up the Horizon: The ECJ's New Take on Country Sanctions' (2018) 55 Common Market Law Review 413–414.
65 See for more details Sara Poli, 'Judicial Protection and Its Limits in the Case Law Concerning Individual Restrictive Measures in the European Union' in Eleftheria Neframi and Mauro Gatti (eds), *Constitutional Issues of EU External Relations Law* (Nomos 2018) 287–306.
66 See, for example, Case T-244/16 and T-285/17 *Viktor Fedorovych Yanukovych v Council* EU:T:2019:502 and Case T-248/18 *Sergej Arbuzov v Council* EU:T:2019:511.
67 The possibility to use art 267 of the TFEU to challenge the validity of CFSP Decisions was recognised for the first time in the Rosneft judgement in Case C-72/15 P (n 18), raised by a UK court.
68 For a case involving sanctions of UN origin see the judgement *Al-Dulimi and Montana management inc. v Switzerland* App no 5809/08 (ECtHR, 21 June 2016). In this judgement Switzerland was found to breach art 6(1) ECHR since in 2008 the Swiss Federal court refused to examine the merit of the action brought by a number of former officials of the Iraqi government against the confiscation of their properties, enacted by Switzerland to implement a UNSC Resolution of 2003.
69 The test in TAFA (n 30) was that of 'reasonable belief' and the listing by the UK of terrorists has been rare since 2010, when the date this Statute came into force. Gordon *et al.* (n 40) 67.
70 *Contra*, see Smith (n 28) 19.
71 Joined Cases 584/10, 593/10 and 595/10 *European Commission and Others v Yassin Abdullah Kadi* EU:C:2013:518, para 119.

72 Case 605/13 P *Anbouba v Council* EU:C:2015:248.
73 Ibid, para 51.
74 SAMLA c 24, para 4.
75 This happens with respect to persons who belong to a group (i.e. a terrorist organisation) and it is not possible for the government to know all the names of all the members of this group. See SAMLA c 11. See Smith (n 28) 45–46.
76 SAMLA c 23, paras 1–3.
77 There is a specific Regulation making provision for the procedure applicable to request a review, variation or revocation of a designation or ship specification. See Reg Sanction review procedure Regulations 1219 of 2018.
78 Gordon *et al.* (n 40) 203.
79 SAMLA c 25, para 2. The same regime applies to the request of delisting of ships designated by the UNSC.
80 SAMLA c 25, para 5.
81 Catherine Flaesch-Mougain and Isabelle Bosse Platière, 'Brexit et action extérieure de l'Union européenne' (2016) 52 Revue trimestrielle de droit européen 783.
82 European Union Committee (n 41) 25.
83 House of Commons Foreign Affairs Committee (n 57) 21.
84 See the contribution by Szép and Van Elsuwege, Chapter 16 in this volume.

16
EU sanctions policy and the alignment of third countries
Relevant experiences for the UK?

Viktor Szép and Peter Van Elsuwege

16.1 Introduction

Sanctions, also known as 'restrictive measures', are key instruments of the EU's Common Foreign and Security Policy (CFSP).[1] They are used as foreign policy instruments aimed at increasing the cost of non-compliance with essential principles of international law, democracy and human rights. Moreover, they may directly target individuals, i.e. natural and legal persons, as a result of their links with a particular political regime or terrorist organisation. In the past decades, the legal and political framework of the EU's sanctions policy significantly developed, not least as a result of the Lisbon Treaty which abolished the old pillar structure and expanded the jurisdiction of the Court of Justice of the EU (CJEU) in relation to the judicial review of restrictive measures.[2]

At present, the EU has adopted sanctions against 35 countries and issued three thematic sanctions regimes regarding chemical weapons, cyber-attacks and terrorism, making it the world's second-most active user of restrictive measures after the United States (US).[3] It is widely recognised that the United Kingdom (UK) was one of the driving forces behind the EU's active sanctions policy.[4] For instance, with respect to countries such as Russia and Iran, the UK actively promoted the collective imposition of restrictive measures within the framework of the CFSP.[5] Hence, EU membership has helped the UK to achieve its foreign policy and national security goals.[6]

Taking into account that the effectiveness of sanctions inter alia depends upon the existence of a broad international coalition,[7] it is evident that Brexit creates a challenge for both the UK and the EU. For the UK, taking back control of national sovereignty may undermine the strength of the unilaterally adopted measures. For the EU, the strength of its sanctions policy may also be affected by the absence of a key international player such as the UK. Hence, a certain alignment of the EU's and the UK's sanctions policies after Brexit seems to be in the interest of both parties. It is, therefore, no coincidence that the political declaration setting out the framework for future EU–UK relations devotes a separate section on sanctions.[8] While stressing the existence of 'independent sanctions policies driven by their respective foreign policies', the parties also explicitly recognise 'sanctions as a multilateral foreign policy tool and the benefits of close consultation and cooperation'.[9] The document further provides that:

> Consultation on sanctions should include the exchange of information on listings and their justification, development, implementation and enforcement, as well as technical support, and dialogue on future designations and regimes. Where foreign policy objectives that underpin a specific future sanction regime are aligned between the Parties, intensified exchange of information at appropriate stages of the policy cycle of this sanctions regime will take place, with the possibility of adopting sanctions that are mutually reinforcing.

Hence, there is a clear commitment to closely align the sanctions policies of the EU and the UK after Brexit. The key question, of course, is how such an alignment may materialise in practice? For this purpose, the current contribution will analyse the alignment experience of other third countries in order to draw certain lessons for the post-Brexit sanctions regime between the EU and the UK. After a brief overview of the legal framework of the UK's sanctions policy under the withdrawal agreement (section 16.2), the alignment practice of other European non-EU Member States is studied (16.3) before reflecting upon possible models for the EU–UK relationship (16.4).

16.2 The UK's sanctions policy after Brexit: implications of the withdrawal agreement

Whereas the UK formally left the EU on 1 February 2020, the direct implications for the UK's sanctions policy are fairly limited. Until the end of the transition period, EU law remains applicable to and in the UK. In other words, EU sanctions continue to apply in the UK during the transition period. This period is foreseen to apply until 31 December 2020 but may be extended for up to one or two years.[10] Significantly, the withdrawal agreement also explicitly provides that a specific agreement governing the relationship between the EU and the UK in the areas of CFSP and Common Security and Defence Policy (CSDP) may enter into force during the transition period.[11] In such a scenario, EU law in relation to those areas will cease to apply to the UK from the date of application of that agreement.[12]

Hence, until the introduction of a new legal regime, the UK's sanctions policy remains determined by EU law. There is a certain flexibility in the sense that the UK may make a formal declaration to the High Representative of the Union for Foreign Affairs and Security Policy, indicating that it will not apply a CFSP decision in exceptional cases related to vital and stated reasons of national security.[13] In general, however, the UK's status as a former EU Member State will continue to affect its sanctions policy.

At the EU level, the division of competences largely determines the sanctions policy.[14] Restrictive measures falling within EU competences (e.g. export bans) are adopted by qualified majority in the form of a Council Regulation on the basis of Article 215 TFEU, which is preconditioned on a unanimously adopted CFSP Council Decision.[15] Arms embargoes and travel bans are unanimously adopted in the form of a CFSP Council Decision on the basis of Article 29 TEU and are directly implemented by the Member States. As can be revealed from the case law of the CJEU, Member States cannot advance their particular foreign or security policy interests at the expense of their EU law obligations.[16]

Taking into account that about two-thirds of the UK's sanctions regimes derive from the EU,[17] Brexit implies 'a seismic shift' in how the UK adopts, imposes and implements economic and financial sanctions. For this purpose, new domestic legislation has been adopted in the form of the Sanctions and Anti-Money Laundering Act 2018 (SAMLA).[18] The SAMLA ensures the rolling over of EU sanctions regimes and provides the legal basis for the adoption of autonomous UK sanctions in the future. However, as observed by the European Union Committee of the House of Lords, 'the principal interests and threats facing the UK and the EU-27 will not change fundamentally when the UK leaves the EU'.[19] For this reason, and taking into account that 'sanctions are more effective when they are applied on a multilateral basis', a certain alignment between the EU and UK sanctions after Brexit seems very logical.[20] The key question, of course, is what this 'alignment' entails in practice and how it can be organised from a legal point of view. Some inspiration may be drawn from the alignment experience of other third countries.

16.3 The practice of alignment of non-EU countries with EU sanctions regimes: a possible way forward after Brexit?

16.3.1 The sanctions alignment practices of non-EU countries

While cooperation in foreign and security policy is one of the primary objectives of both the UK and the EU, its concrete form remains rather obscure. The political declaration on the future post-Brexit relationship between the EU and the UK only refers generally to 'the benefits of close consultation and cooperation', including the exchange of information on sanctions regimes, 'with the possibility of adopting sanctions that are mutually reinforcing'.[21] One possible way to move forward is to unilaterally align with the EU sanctions regimes. In practice, European neighbourhood countries – including European Economic Area (EEA) states, candidate and potential candidate states and Eastern Partnership (EaP) countries – are invited by the High Representative of the Union for Foreign Affairs and Security Policy to join EU sanctions once a decision has been made by the Member States. In general, third countries are not legally obliged to join EU sanctions regimes. However, most of them accept the invitations either because they would like to join the EU or they share the EU's values and objectives.

With the aim to explore the possible scenarios for the UK after Brexit, we have collected both statistical data on the alignment rates of third countries as well as explored the legal and political framework under which they operate their foreign policy cooperation with the EU. As far as the statistical data are concerned, our study covers 15 non-EU states' sanctions policy alignment.[22] We have collected 229 press releases published by the High Representative of the Union for Foreign Affairs and Security Policy containing information whether neighbouring states have accepted the invitations to join EU sanctions regimes within a period between May 2010 and April 2019.[23]

Generally, candidate states implement the larger number of EU sanctions regimes because CFSP declarations form part of the *acquis*.[24] Without implementing CFSP declarations and decisions, including restrictive measures, they would not be able to join the EU. Hence, this explains the rather high alignment rates of EU candidate countries. However, as will be explained further, there are significant exceptions such as Serbia or Turkey. The next group of states are the European Free Trade Association (EFTA) countries whose practice shows a similar pattern. They have fewer incentives to join EU sanctions regimes – and have no legal obligation to do so – but they implement around 90 per cent of the measures because they generally share the same foreign and security policy priorities. The alignment of EaP countries varies between 0.01 per cent and 66.8 per cent, which can be connected to their varying bilateral relations with the EU (see Figure 16.1).

In addition to the strong willingness of third countries to join, the mechanisms of alignment also have significance for the possible post-Brexit model of the UK. The following subsections examine selective case studies of non-EU countries with the intention of showing how these countries decide on alignment with the EU sanctions mechanism, how (legally) formalised these procedures are and whether there are any institutional specificities in the applied mechanisms.

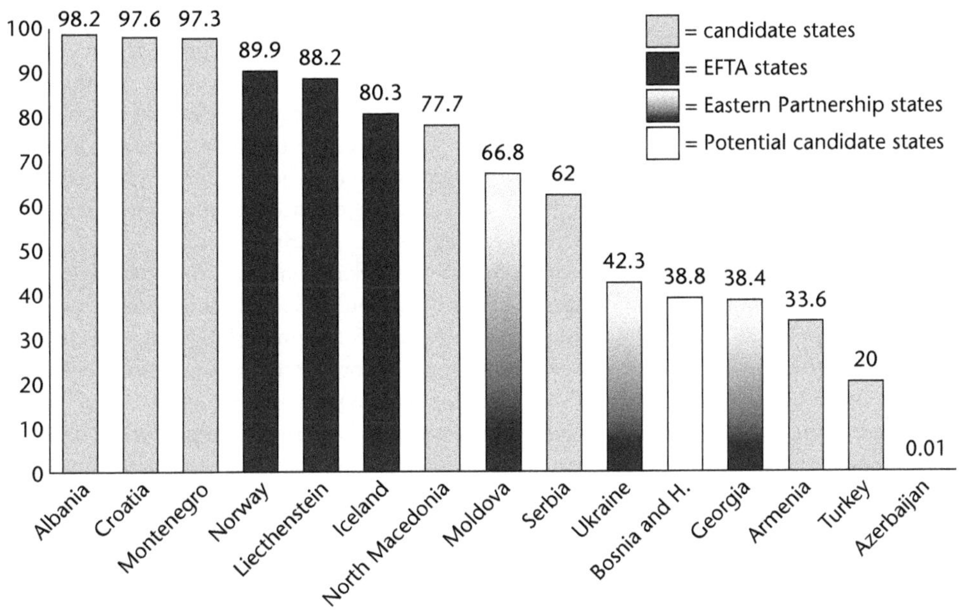

Figure 16.1 Alignment of third countries with EU sanctions regimes between May 2010 and April 2019 (data available regarding Croatia until its accession, July 2013). Author's elaboration.

16.3.2 Candidate and potential candidate countries

Enlargement is often seen as a catalyst for legislative approximation. This can also be seen in the alignment with CFSP declarations, including sanctions. As the EU document on the guidelines on implementation of sanctions states, 'candidate countries should be systematically invited to align themselves with the measures imposed by the EU'.[25] For example, *Croatia*, before becoming a full member of the EU, aligned itself with all sanctions.[26] However, *Turkey*'s foreign policy alignment with CFSP declarations shows different patterns from other candidates. Its behaviour can be partly explained by its protracted accession process and its more sceptical attitude towards European integration over the years. Already in 2004, the European Commission reported that

> Turkey aligns itself with significantly fewer EU declarations than the other candidate countries … Turkey is sometimes hesitant to align itself to EU positions on issues touching its vital foreign policy and security interests. This is in marked difference to the conduct of all other candidate, associated and SAP countries.[27]

However, Turkey's foreign policy alignment was welcomed between the period of 2003 and 2014.[28] The alignment rate between 2007 and 2014 was over 70 per cent for Turkey.[29] Since 2011, however, Turkey has shown increasing reluctance towards alignment which manifested in a decreasing number of common actions. In 2014, Turkey even rebuffed criticism on waning foreign policy alignment. The country complained about the fact that it is kept out of the decision-making procedures despite making important contributions to EU defence.[30] The

2014 country report on Turkey highlighted that 'alignment with EU declarations and Council decisions significantly declined compared to previous years'.[31] In 2018, Turkey aligned itself only with ten out of 64 EU declarations and Council decisions representing an alignment rate of only 16 per cent.[32] Along with Serbia, which had an alignment rate of around 52 per cent according to the Commission's 2018 progress report, Turkey was one of the European countries that did not join EU-led sanctions against Russia which sparked debates on the need for alignment by candidate countries.[33] On several occasions, Serbian Prime Minister Vučić, criticised the asymmetric nature of the EU enlargement process and underlined that he did not feel any responsibility for sanctions that were adopted by the EU without having consulted Serbia.[34]

The low alignment rates of Turkey and Serbia are remarkable taking into account that the progressive harmonisation with CFSP statements and decisions is part of these countries' commitment to accept the EU *acquis* as part of their preparations for membership. A specific negotiating chapter of the pre-accession negotiations is devoted to foreign security and defence policy. Moreover, the political dialogue established under the Stabilisation and Association Agreement (SAA) between the EU and Serbia also aims at an increasing convergence of positions on CFSP issues.[35] Hence, a more pro-active approach regarding the candidate countries' alignment with the EU's sanctions policy may be expected in anticipation of their envisaged EU membership. In this respect, it is noteworthy that the 2019 Commission monitoring report on Serbia explicitly defined the improvement of this country's alignment with EU declarations and Council decisions on CFSP matters – including restrictive measures – as one of the priorities to be tackled.[36]

16.3.3 EEA countries and Switzerland

The agreement on the EEA[37] does not cover foreign and security policy issues, however the final act includes a declaration regarding the establishment of a political dialogue between the EU and the EEA Member States.[38] The declaration affirms the objective of the contracting parties to strengthen their political dialogue on foreign policy and to develop closer relations in spheres of mutual interest. For achieving these objectives, the political dialogue can be performed, for example, within informal exchanges of view at ministerial level at meetings of the EEA Council or consultations at conferences and in international organisations. Moreover, the contracting parties are committed to making full use of existing diplomatic channels, in particular the diplomatic representations in the capital of the country holding the EU Presidency, in Brussels and in the capitals of the EFTA countries. Even though the declaration is a non-binding instrument, it provides a voluntary and informal framework for cooperation between the EU and EFTA member states. The current practice of the EEA countries illustrates that the informal mechanism fosters the foreign policy dialogue involving cooperation also in sanctions policy alignment. The EEA members are showing a high degree of acceptance of the EU autonomous sanctions on third countries varying between 88.9 per cent and 80.3 per cent in the observed period. Norway's alignment model in particular contains certain interesting policy, institutional and legal characteristics.

Historically, Norway has not often used economic sanctions, unless the restrictive measures were based on resolutions of the UN Security Council. Nevertheless, in 1985, the Norwegian government concluded an informal arrangement with the member states of the European Communities to establish an information exchange mechanism relating to activities falling within the scope of the European Political Cooperation (EPC). This mechanism has been formalised within the 'political dialogues' under the EEA that can take place at several levels. For instance, Norway can consult at the level of experts or political directors. Moreover, Norway is invited to several

CFSP-related working groups in order to join declarations, including sanctions regimes. Norwegian sanctions policy has changed direction in the 2000s and Norway increasingly joins EU sanctions, even autonomous sanctions, where there has not been any resolution by the UN Security Council. Today, alignment with EU sanctions has become the rule rather than the exception. From a legal point of view, Norway's policy is well anchored in constitutional law and the procedure is formalised in the Sanctions Act of 2001 (*Sanksjonslova*).[39] Under the Sanctions Act, EU restrictive measures and other international non-military measures with which Norway has aligned itself[40] are adopted through government regulations and also their quick and efficient implementation is ensured.[41]

Norway's high degree of alignment (89.9 per cent) with the EU sanctions regimes indicates that the government decides nearly automatically to join EU restrictive measures. However, in certain cases, when specific concerns or national interest were at stake, the rapid implementation of the government was criticised. The EU sanctions against Russia have been a striking example. Unlike most of the previous EU sanctions regimes, where the targeted countries were not only geographically but also in political terms far from Norway's focus (Myanmar, Iran etc.), the case of Russia concerned Norway's interest more deeply. Even though the Norwegian government acted quickly in terms of alignment, the EU sanctions also generated immediate implications for Norwegian companies, especially operating in the oil industry, which were present on the Russian market[42] and, therefore, not surprisingly, criticism against the alignment was formulated.[43] There is a growing awareness that engaging with the EU in CFSP matters, notably with respect to restrictive sanctions, comes at a cost whereas there are relatively limited channels to influence the EU's policy. In contrast to the sophisticated institutional mechanisms established under the EEA Agreement, there is no comprehensive framework or strategic platform for cooperation in relation to the CFSP. The discussions concerning the UK's further alignment with the CFSP (see further at section 16.4) may change this situation in the future. At least, the evolution of the UK's relations with the EU are followed carefully in Norway and may provide a platform for a revision of the current arrangement.[44]

In comparison to Norway, which is an EEA member state and a model partner in terms of alignment with EU sanctions, the situation of Switzerland is significantly different. The bilateral relations between Switzerland and the EU are governed by sectoral agreements signed in 1999 and 2004 (Bilaterals I and II), but, unlike the EEA, these agreements are not significant in terms of foreign policy cooperation. This may be related to the tradition of Swiss neutrality and its long-term reluctance vis-à-vis the implementation of international sanctions which manifested itself, among others, in its absence from the UN until 2002. It was only in the beginning of the 1990s when Switzerland re-conceptualised its permanent neutrality by declaring that the implementation of sanctions under Chapter VII of the UN Charter was not incompatible with its neutral position.[45] The Federal Supreme Court affirmed in the case of the sanctions imposed against Croatia in the 1990s that the non-implementation of UN Security Council resolutions would be in opposition with universal *ordre public* despite not being a member of the organisation. A report issued in 1993 by the Federal Council also confirmed that the implementation of non-military sanctions could be considered compatible with its neutrality. It was also reaffirmed that the country would implement international sanctions other than the UN on a case-by-case basis and by taking into account Swiss interests.[46] For example, Switzerland adopted the first EU sanctions against Yugoslavia in 1998 and it also implemented EU sanctions against Myanmar (Burma) in 2000. Nevertheless, the country always put emphasis on the voluntary and autonomous nature of its actions concerning the implementation of international sanctions.

Initially, Switzerland used pre-existing legislation (e.g. *Loi sur le materiel de guerre*[47] or *Loi sur le contrôle des biens à des fins civiles et militaires*[48]) for the purpose of implementing arms embargos on a case-by-case basis. If the country ought to implement sanctions other than arms embargos, the Federal Council had to enact executive orders directly based on the Federal Constitution. These executive orders were based on Article 102 (paragraphs 8 and 9) of the previous Federal Constitution. With the entry into force of the new Constitution on 1 January 2000, however, executive orders were based directly on new Article 184. For various reasons, new framework legislation was adopted in 2002, called the Federal Act on the Implementation of International Sanctions (EmbA, *Loi fédérale sur l'application de sanctions internationales, LEmb*).[49] This new legislation, entered into force in 2003, provides a legal basis for the implementation of non-military international sanctions. It allows implementation of sanctions adopted by the UN, Organisation for Security and Co-operation in Europe (OSCE) and the most important trading partners (Art. 1 EmbA), in particular the EU. Clearly, however, the new legislation could not be seen as an automatic obligation of Switzerland to taking part in international sanctions. The Federal Council remains competent to decide on a case-by-case basis to implement non-military international sanctions.[50] A report published in 2012 still emphasised in relation to EU sanctions that, before implementing them, the Federal Council will always examine the general interest of the country and judge them on a case-by-case basis.[51] With the new legislation, however, executive orders issued by the Federal Council are directly based on the EmbA. About half of the EU's autonomous sanctions are implemented by Switzerland.[52]

16.3.4 Eastern Partnership countries

The EaP, formally launched in 2009 as a specific policy framework for the EU's eastern neighbours (Armenia, Azerbaijan, Belarus, Georgia, Moldova, Ukraine), aims to develop close political, legal and economic relations with the countries concerned. Within this context, a new generation of Association Agreements (AA) has been concluded with Ukraine, Moldova and Georgia and a less far-reaching Comprehensive and Enhanced Partnership Agreement (CEPA) with Armenia. With Azerbaijan, an old Partnership and Cooperation Agreement (PCA) is still in place in anticipation of a new bilateral agreement. Belarus is a special case in the sense that there is no bilateral framework agreement in force and the country is itself the subject of sanctions.

The divergent bilateral legal relations also imply different commitments in terms of alignment with the EU's sanctions regime. The most far-reaching commitments can be found in the AAs. They all refer to the objective of political cooperation and *convergence* on foreign and security matters.[53] In contrast, the CEPA with Armenia only includes a more general political dialogue clause without including any reference to the objective of convergence.[54] As argued by Guillaume Van der Loo, the notion of convergence 'stands for a *rapprochement* in the area of CFSP and CSDP that goes beyond mere cooperation' requiring, amongst others, a more systematic alignment to CFSP decisions.[55] It is, therefore, no coincidence that the alignment figures of the associated EaP countries are higher than for non-associated EaP countries.

However, the references to convergence do not imply that the associated EaP countries align their foreign policy with every single EU position. The statistical information regarding the third countries' alignment with EU sanctions, be it partially covering the period before the formal entry into force of the AAs, reveals alignment rates ranging from 66.8 per cent (Moldova) to 38.4 per cent (Georgia) with Ukraine in the middle (42.3 per cent).[56] In addition, reference can be made to the Commission implementation reports which look more generally at the level of alignment with all EU CFSP declarations. The reports on Ukraine reveal an upward trend from 37 per cent in 2012,[57] to 47 per cent in 2013[58] and 73 per cent in 2014.[59] Somewhat surprisingly, the latest figures reveal a somewhat different picture: between January 2018 and 23

October 2018, Ukraine aligned with 26 out of 58 CFSP declarations it had been invited to support.[60] However, the European Commission does not provide any particular comments about the reasons for non-alignment but bluntly observes that 'Ukraine has continued to cooperate with the EU on regional and international issues.'[61] Moldova's record of foreign policy alignment shows that country's fluctuating willingness to adopt most CFSP declarations. Moldova aligned itself with 77 per cent of CFSP Declarations in 2011,[62] 90 per cent in 2012, 88 per cent in 2013[63] and 63 per cent in 2014.[64] The latest available report reveals that Moldova aligned itself with 34 out of 49 EU declarations in 2017 (69 per cent) which is comparable to the year before (71 per cent).[65] Finally, as far as Georgia is concerned, the alignment rate has been around 50 to 55 per cent in recent years.[66] Hence, the ambitious objectives of foreign policy alignment and convergence under the new generation of AAs has so far not resulted in a remarkable increase of alignment rates.

16.3.5 Different approaches to sanctions alignment

As the above case studies show, the alignment of third countries with EU sanctions is determined predominantly by their own foreign policy priorities and, specifically, by their relationship to the EU. The countries' methods, practices and institutions can be explained and grouped in several models. Broadly speaking, three major approaches can be considered. First, the most autonomous model, a sort of '*á la carte* alignment' is implemented by Switzerland. The Swiss approach is determined predominantly by its neutral status, however it is also significant that EU–Swiss relations established by bilateral treaties do not intend to conduct substantial cooperation or dialogue in the area of foreign and security policy. Consequently, within this *á la carte* approach, Switzerland decides autonomously on a case-by-case basis to implement international and EU non-military sanctions. Second, Norway's '*self-constraint*' in sanctions policy and the routine alignment show a method which enables the quick and efficient implementation of sanctions regimes introduced by the EU. The difference between this approach and the *á la carte* alignment lies in the stronger cohesion between the EEA countries and the EU as well as in the institutionalised mechanisms (e.g. dialogues) established in foreign policy fields. Therefore, Norway still has control over its own sanctions policy but sees an opportunity in cooperating with the EU in this area. Finally, the *coordinated alignment* to EU sanctions represents the least autonomous approach of third states including candidates, potential candidates and, to a lesser extent, the associated EaP countries. This model gives the EU an important tool for involving third states and influencing their sanctions policy, which might make the EU's sanctions regime stronger and more efficient. This influence is based on clauses in bilateral agreements devoted to political cooperation and convergence in the area of CFSP. Even though the third countries formally remain autonomous in their sanctions policy, due to a (soft) conditionality, they are slightly pressured to implement the EU sanctions mechanism. This is most obvious with respect to the candidate countries which are supposed to implement the entire EU *acquis*, including the area of CFSP, upon accession to the EU. Nevertheless, as the examples of Turkey and Serbia reveal, the actual alignment rates are in practice lower than what may be expected.

16.4 Future cooperation in sanctions policy between the EU and the UK

The Sanctions and Anti-Money Laundering Act 2018 provides the legal foundation for the UK's post-Brexit sanctions policy.[67] This new act gives power to an appropriate minister (Secretary of State or the Treasury) to adopt regulations imposing sanctions and differentiates between five types of sanctions: financial sanctions, immigration sanctions, trade sanctions, aircraft sanctions and shipping sanctions. In addition to these standard instruments, the bill also provides competence to impose other sanction measures not defined here, if it is appropriate for the purposes of compliance with a UN obligation.[68] In line with the consultation, the new sanctions Act stresses the importance of flexibility and includes detailed procedural provisions to suspend the sanctions, grant licences and apply exceptions. As commentators observed, the new domestic legal framework signals the potential for a more flexible approach when compared with the standard exceptions and licensing grounds contained in current underlying legislation of the EU.[69]

In a report entitled 'Fragmented and Incoherent: The UK's Sanctions Policy', the House of Commons Committee on Foreign Affairs heavily criticised the government's approach since the adoption of the SAMLA. In particular, it found that the government's activity on sanctions focused too much on ensuring the continuation of existing EU sanctions under UK law, without a clear strategy for the future.[70] In view of the Committee:

> The UK cannot afford the risk of allowing its sanctions policy be dictated by the decisions of others. Instead, the UK must seize the opportunity to become a global leader in sanctions policy and must aim to set the international gold standard for strategy, design and implementation.[71]

In its response, the government confirmed the priority to transfer existing sanction regimes into domestic law in order to avoid an implementation gap at the time of Brexit. At the same time, it also revealed its ambitions for the future development of the UK's sanctions policy. Whereas 'the UK will continue to seek opportunities for international cooperation, as sanctions are most effective when multiple countries act together', it is noteworthy that the option of structured alignment with the EU sanctions regime was not explicitly mentioned. Rather, the UK perceives itself as a leading actor and envisages to 'use its permanent seat on the UN Security Council and its relationships with the US and other allies to coordinate the imposition, implementation and lifting of sanctions at a global level'.[72]

With respect to future relations with the EU, it is only announced that:

> The UK wants a supportive and constructive relationship, as constitutional equals, and as friends and partners to face the challenges that lie ahead. Whilst the UK will exercise the power to impose sanctions independently, this will not prevent the UK from being able to co-operate with the EU. The outcome will be that Britain enjoys both freedom of manoeuvre and the option of working alongside the EU on sanctions where our objectives align.[73]

In other words, the UK seeks a model of co-operation rather than structural alignment with the EU's sanctions regimes. In this respect, the EU is not regarded as an exclusive or special partner for the development of the UK's own sanctions policy. Rather, the EU is conceived as one of the relevant actors on a par with the US, Australia and Canada. This is a crucial difference in comparison to the position of other neighbouring countries, which all – to a varying extent as identified above – look at the EU as the main source of inspiration. At best, the UK's interest may be compared to the Swiss approach of '*à la carte* alignment'. The fundamental difference, of course, is that Switzerland, as a neutral country, does not take initiatives with respect to the introduction of sanctions, whereas the UK regards itself as a 'global moral anchor' and as an initiator of sanctions for which it will seek the support of like-minded countries.[74] As far as sanctions are concerned, the UK may thus be considered as a 'norm-shaper' rather than a 'norm-taker'.

From this perspective, it is noteworthy that the Council's negotiating directives for a new partnership with the UK envisage 'the alignment of the United Kingdom with the Union sanction policy'.[75] The use of the word 'alignment' rather than 'co-operation', which is the term used in official UK documents, already reveals a different approach.

Whereas both the EU and the UK agree on the need of convergence in relation to foreign policy issues, in particular with respect to the adoption and implementation of sanctions, the concrete views and expectations on the future relationship differ. On the one hand, the EU stressed on several occasions that a non-EU Member State cannot have the same rights as EU Member States implying that any participation in the EU decision-making process is excluded and, at best, a model of voluntary alignment and close consultation *à la* Norway is feasible. From a UK perspective, the model of voluntary alignment is not very attractive since the third countries cannot actively negotiate the content of the sanctions regimes and are essentially recipients rather than brokers of EU sanctions legislation.[76] It, therefore, proposes an 'unprecedented partnership', involving the establishment of a separate UK–EU political forum for the discussion and coordination of sanctions policies.[77]

Arguably, a compromise between both visions may be included in a future framework agreement between the EU and the UK, which could take the form of an AA.[78] The common institutional framework established under the legal formula of association allows for a dense political dialogue and permanent consultation, with the only limit that associated countries cannot take part in the actual EU decision-making process.[79] Accordingly, the new agreement is supposed to create the necessary institutional structures for dialogue and mutual exchange of information between the EU and the UK at appropriate stages of the policy cycle of their respective sanction regimes.[80] In contrast to the situation of other third countries, this will most likely be a more open format for consultation and cooperation rather than a one-way alignment with the EU's sanctions regime.

A first test case for EU–UK sanctions cooperation in the post-Brexit period concerns the UK's interest in developing a new human rights sanctions regime, also known as 'Magnitsky sanctions', named after Sergei Magnitsky who died in a Moscow prison after investigating tax fraud in Russia. The US already introduced the so-called 'Magnitsky Act' in 2012 as a legal basis for instituting travel bans and asset freezes to human rights violators. Whereas the initial version of the Act aimed to address the Russian individuals involved in Magnitsky's case, the scope of the Act was later amended to include individuals of any nationality involved in human rights violations.[81]

Within the EU, the three Baltic states and the UK already introduced a Magnitsky-type of legislation and, on several occasions, the European Parliament called for an EU-wide sanctions regime in response to gross human rights violations.[82] In December 2019, High Representative Borell announced his intention to develop this initiative, which will require the approval of all EU Member States.[83] The key question is to what extent Brexit will affect this process, taking into account that the UK has always been one of the key promoters of such an EU-wide approach. In any event, the introduction of an autonomous UK human rights sanctions regime is considered to be a key priority for the UK after Brexit.[84] Already before Brexit, the requirement of such as an approach was heavily discussed in the UK parliament and with the addition of a 'Magnitsky clause' to the Sanctions and Anti-Money Laundering Act 2018, the UK is clearly moving in this direction.[85]

16.5 Concluding remarks

Despite the clear interest of both the UK and the EU to continue a close security partnership after Brexit,[86] there is a clear risk of divergence in relation to their respective sanctions policies.

On the one hand, an autonomous British sanctions policy can be developed on the basis of the new Sanctions and Anti-Money Laundering Act 2018. On the other hand, the UK is no longer represented at the EU decision-making table, which implies that it can no longer play its traditional role as honest-broker in the pursuit of unanimity, which is required for the adoption of EU-wide sanctions. Moreover, the alignment of the EU and UK sanctions regimes poses significant legal and political challenges. Apart from divergent interests in imposing or maintaining restrictive measures against certain countries and/or individuals, the role of courts should also not be underestimated. Under Article 275 TFEU, restrictive measures against national or legal persons can be challenged before the CJEU but, after Brexit, this no longer affects the UK's sanctions thus implying an increased risk of divergence in practice.[87] Hence, it appears the alignment of EU and UK sanctions will not come automatically and requires some kind of new institutional arrangement.[88]

Several scenarios for a post-Brexit arrangement in the area of foreign policy cooperation, including the alignment of sanctions policies, may be distinguished.[89] The most far-reaching model implies a form of integration without membership. This would give the UK a particular role at the decision-shaping phase of EU sanctions implying the granting of a special status in and access to the Foreign Affairs Council and the Political and Security Committee. Whereas such a new model would certainly fit the UK's ambition to develop an unprecedented form of foreign policy cooperation, it is difficult to reconcile with the EU's views on strategic autonomy and the status of the UK as a third country after Brexit.[90] Hence, the establishment of a structural consultation mechanism as part of a broader political dialogue but separate from the EU's internal structures seems to be an alternative model which follows more closely the EU's established practice. This would imply a more institutionalised version of the EEA/Norway model of association. Third, in the absence of such formalised arrangements, the UK may proceed along the lines of the US, which implies that the alignment of sanctions regimes is largely based upon informal contacts with Member States and the European External Action Service. Whereas such a scenario is not to be excluded, it largely appears to be a fall-back option. A more structured form of cooperation and alignment, with respect to each other's autonomy and sovereignty, would be more in line with both the increasing significance of the CFSP as an integrated but specific EU policy and the UK's desire to take back control of its own foreign policy. In any event, Brexit has put the debate about the institutionalisation of CFSP cooperation and sanctions alignment with third countries on the agenda. As a result, developments with the UK as a new third country may have some spillover effects for the EU's relations with other neighbouring countries.

Notes

1 See, for example, Martin Russel, 'EU Sanctions: A Key Foreign and Security Policy Instrument' (European Parliamentary Research Service, May 2019) www.europarl.europa.eu/RegData/etudes/BRIE/2018/621870/EPRS_BRI(2018)621870_EN.pdf accessed 10 June 2019.

2 Christina Eckes, 'The Law and Practice of EU Sanctions' in Steven Blockmans and Panos Koutrakos (eds), *Research Handbook on the EU's Common Foreign and Security Policy* (Edward Elgar Publishing 2018).

3 For an overview, see EU sanctions map at www.sanctionsmap.eu accessed 10 June 2019.

4 It is estimated that more than half of existing EU sanctions designations are based on UK evidence and intelligence. See HM Government, 'Framework for the UK–EU Security Partnership' (9 May 2018) 32, www.gov.uk/government/publications/framework-for-the-uk-eu-security-partnership accessed 14 February 2019.

5 See Richard M Nephew and David Mortlock, 'Brexit's Implications for UK and European Sanctions Policy' (Centre on Global Energy Policy Reports, October 2016) https://academiccommons.columbia.

edu/doi/10.7916/D8J1053R accessed 20 March 2019; Tom Keatinge, 'Brexit and the UK's Sanctions Policy: From Leader to Follower' (RUSI Newsbrief, April 2017) https://rusi.org/publication/newsbrief/brexit-and-uk%E2%80%99s-sanctions-policy-leader-follower accessed 20 March 2019.
6 European Union Committee, 'Brexit: Sanctions Policy' (2017–19 HL, 50) 21.
7 Anthonius De Vries, Clara Portela and Borja Guijarro-Usobiaga, 'Improving the Effectiveness of Sanctions: A Checklist for the EU' (CEPS Special Report, 6 November 2014) www.ceps.eu/publications/improving-effectiveness-sanctions-checklist-eu accessed 25 March 2019.
8 On the UK sanctions policy after Brexit, see Sara Poli's Chapter 15 in this handbook.
9 Political declaration setting out the framework for the future relationship between the European Union and the United Kingdom OJ (2020) C34/12 (PD).
10 Agreement on the withdrawal of the United Kingdom of Great Britain and Northern Ireland from the European Union and the European Atomic Energy Community [2020] OJ L 29/7, arts 127, 132 (WA).
11 On the post-Brexit participation of the UK in CFSP and CSDP after Brexit, see Ramses A Wessel's Chapter 14 in this volume.
12 WA, art 127, para 2.
13 WA, art 129, para 6.
14 Piet Eeckhout, *EU External Relations Law* (Oxford University Press 2011) 501–511.
15 Council of the EU, 'Sanctions Guidelines: Update', doc 5664/18 (4 May 2018).
16 See Case C-120/94 *Commission of the European Communities v Hellenic Republic* EU:C:1995:109, Opinion AG Jacobs; Case C-124/95 *The Queen, ex parte Centro-Com Srl v HM Treasury and Bank of England* EU:C:1997:8, paras 23–30. See also Viktor Szép, 'Foreign Policy without Unilateral Alternatives: EU Member State Interests and the Imposition of Economic Sanctions' in Márton Varju (ed), *Between Compliance and Particularism: Member State Interests and European Union Law* (Springer 2019).
17 Other sanctions derive from the UN and the OSCE. For an overview, see House of Lords, European Union Committee, 'Brexit: Sanctions Policy' (8th Report of Session 2017–19) https://publications.parliament.uk/pa/ld201719/ldselect/ldeucom/50/5003.htm accessed 20 August 2019.
18 Sanctions and Anti-Money Laundering Act 2018 (SAMLA) https://services.parliament.uk/bills/2017-19/sanctionsandantimoneylaundering.html accessed 20 August 2019.
19 European Union Committee (n 6) 2.
20 Ibid.
21 PD (n 9).
22 Only the countries which are officially and publicly invited to align themselves with the EU's sanctions policy are included in the study. This explains why Switzerland is not in Figure 16.1. Also, for Kosovo, there are no relevant statistics since it was not publicly invited in the period under scrutiny.
23 All press releases can be found on the website of the EEAS, https://eeas.europa.eu/headquarters/headquarters-homepage_en accessed 20 August 2019. This instrument has been used since this is the only channel through which the invitation for third country alignment with EU sanctions is made public. See European Union Committee (n 6) 23.
24 Within EU accession negotiations, a specific chapter is devoted to foreign, security and defence policy. See https://ec.europa.eu/neighbourhood-enlargement/policy/conditions-membership/chapters-of-the-acquis_en accessed 20 August 2019.
25 'Guidelines on implementation and evaluation of restrictive measures (sanctions) in the framework of the EU Common Foreign and Security Policy' http://data.consilium.europa.eu/doc/document/ST-11205-2012-INIT/en/pdf accessed 28 May 2017, 21.
26 Paul James Cardwell, 'The Legalisation of European Union Foreign Policy and the Use of Sanctions' in Kenneth Armstrong (ed), *Cambridge Yearbook of European Legal Studies* (Cambridge University Press 2015).
27 'Regular Report on Turkey's Progress Towards Accession' https://ec.europa.eu/neighbourhood-enlargement/sites/near/files/archives/pdf/key_documents/2004/rr_tr_2004_en.pdf accessed 3 June 2017, 154–155.
28 Knud Erik Jørgensen, 'Foreign and Security Policy: A Case of the Politics of Alignment' in Aylin Güney and Ali Tekin (eds), *The Europeanization of Turkish Public Policies: A Scorecard* (Routledge 2016).
29 Cardwell (n 26).
30 Tulay Karadeniz, 'Turkey Rebuffs EU Criticism on Waning Foreign Policy Alignment' *EUObserver* (London, 9 December 2014).

31 'Turkey Progress Report' https://ec.europa.eu/neighbourhood-enlargement/sites/near/files/pdf/key_documents/2014/20141008-turkey-progress-report_en.pdf accessed 28 May 2019, 75.
32 'Turkey 2018 Progress Report' https://ec.europa.eu/neighbourhood-enlargement/countries/detailed-country-information/turkey_en accessed 28 May 2019, 96.
33 Elin Hellquist, 'Either With Us Or Against Us? Third-Country Alignment with EU Sanctions Against Russia/Ukraine' (2016) Cambridge Review of International Affairs 29.
34 Tatia Dolidze, 'EU Sanctions Policy Towards Russia: The Sanctioner-Sanctionee's Game of Thrones' (CEPS Working Document 502, January 2015) www.ceps.eu/ceps-publications/eu-sanctions-policy-towards-russia-sanctioner-sanctionees-game-thrones/ accessed 28 May 2019.
35 SAA with Serbia, art 10 (2) b). It is noteworthy that the more recently concluded SAA with Kosovo is even more specific and explicitly refers to convergence with CFSP measures 'in particular restrictive measures taken by the EU against third countries, natural or legal persons or non-State entities'. See SAA with Kosovo, art 11 (2) c).
36 Commission Staff Working Document 'Serbia 2019 Report' SWD (2019) 219 final, 91–92.
37 Agreement on the European Economic Area [1994] OJ No L001.
38 Declaration by the Governments of the Member States of the EC and the EFTA States on Political Dialogue, EEA Agreement – Final Act, 16, www.efta.int/media/documents/legal-texts/eea/the-eea-agreement/Final%20Act/FinalAct.pdf accessed 27 July 2017.
39 Act of 27 April 2001 No 14 relating to the implementation of international, non-military measures involving the suspension of or restrictions on economic and other relations with third countries or movements, Section 1, https://lovdata.no/dokument/NL/lov/2001-04-27-14 accessed 10 July 2019.
40 Sanctions that are adopted by the UN Security Council are implemented by regulations under the Act of 7 June 1968 No 4 relating to the implementation of mandatory decisions of the United Nations Security Council, see https://lovdata.no/dokument/NL/lov/1968-06-07-4 accessed 10 July 2019.
41 The Sanctions Act establishes also criminal law consequences for intentional breach of the regulations implementing sanctions, see s 3 of the act.
42 'Norway to Sign Up to EU Sanctions Against Russia' *Reuters* (London, 30 July 2014) www.reuters.com/article/ukraine-crisis-sanctions-norway-idUSL6N0Q54OY20140730 accessed 15 July 2019.
43 Nina Berglund, 'Norway Won't Lift Russian Sanctions' News in English (Oslo, 20 April 2017) www.newsinenglish.no/2017/04/20/norway-wont-lift-russian-sanctions/ accessed 15 July 2019.
44 Christophe Hillion, 'Norway and the Changing Common Foreign and Security Policy of the European Union' (Norwegian Institute of International Affairs Report, January 2019) www.nupi.no/Publikasjoner/CRIStin-Pub/Norway-and-the-changing-Common-Foreign-and-Security-Policy-of-the-European-Union accessed 10 July 2019.
45 Mathias Charles Krafft, Daniel Thürer and Julie Antoinette Stadelhofer, 'Switzerland' in Vera Gowlland-Debbas (ed), *National Implementation of United Nations Sanctions: A Comparative Study* (Martinus Nijhoff Publishers 2004).
46 'Rapport sur la politique extérieure de la Suisse dans les années 90' www.amtsdruckschriften.bar.admin.ch/viewOrigDoc.do?id=10107650 accessed 14 April 2017, 169.
47 'Loi fédérale sur le matériel de guerre' www.admin.ch/opc/fr/classified-compilation/19960753/index.html accessed 15 April 2017.
48 'Loi fédérale sur le contrôle des biens utilisables à des fins civiles et militaires, des biens militaires spécifiques et des biens stratégiques' www.admin.ch/opc/fr/classified-compilation/19960740/index.html accessed 15 April 2017.
49 'Loi fédérale sur l'application de sanctions internationales 2003' www.admin.ch/opc/fr/classified-compilation/20000358/index.html accessed 15 April 2017.
50 Message concernant la loi fédérale sur l'application de sanctions internationales du 20 décembre 2000 (2000) www.admin.ch/opc/fr/federal-gazette/2001/1341.pdf accessed 20 April 2017, 1360, 1364.
51 Rapport sur la politique économique extérieure 2012. Messages concernant des accord économiques inernationaux et Rapport sur les mesures tarifaires prises en 2012, www.seco.admin.ch/dam/seco/fr/dokumente/Publikationen_Dienstleistungen/Publikationen_Formulare/Aussenwirtschaft/berichte_aussenwirschaftspolitik/aussenwirtschaftsbericht_2012.pdf.download.pdf/Rapport%20sur%20la%20politique%20%C3%A9conomique%20ext%C3%A9rieure%202012.pdf accessed 22 April 2017, 1255.
52 Sanctions de la Suisse' www.seco.admin.ch/seco/fr/home/Aussenwirtschaftspolitik_Wirtschaftliche_Zusammenarbeit/Wirtschaftsbeziehungen/exportkontrollen-und-sanktionen/sanktionen-embargos/sanktionsmassnahmen.html accessed 17 April 2017.
53 See, for example, Association Agreement with Ukraine, Preamble, arts 4, 7.

54 On the difference between association agreements and non-association agreements, see Peter Van Elsuwege and Merijn Chamon, 'The Meaning of Association under EU Law: A Study on the Law and Practice of EU Association Agreements' www.europarl.europa.eu/thinktank/en/document.html?reference=IPOL_STU%282019%29608861 accessed 20 November 2019.
55 Guillaume Van der Loo, *The EU-Ukraine Association Agreement and Deep and Comprehensive Free Trade Area: A New Legal Instrument for EU Integration without Membership* (Brill Nijhoff 2016), 192.
56 See Figure 16.1.
57 'Implementation of the European Neighbourhood Policy in Ukraine Progress in 2012 and Recommendations for Action' http://eur-lex.europa.eu/legal-content/EN/TXT/PDF/?uri=CELEX:52013SC0084&from=en accessed 20 May 2017.
58 'Implementation of the European Neighbourhood Policy in Ukraine Progress in 2013 and Recommendations for Action' http://eeas.europa.eu/archives/docs/enp/pdf/2014/country-reports/ukraine_en.pdf accessed 20 May 2017.
59 'Implementation of the European Neighbourhood Policy in Ukraine Progress in 2014 and Recommendations for Action' http://eeas.europa.eu/archives/docs/enp/pdf/2015/ukraine-enp-report-2015_en.pdf accessed 20 May 2017.
60 'Association Implementation Report on Ukraine' https://eeas.europa.eu/headquarters/headquarters-homepage/53485/association-implementation-report-ukraine_en accessed 20 May 2019, 6.
61 Ibid.
62 'Implementation of the European Neighbourhood Policy in the Republic of Moldova Progress in 2011 and Recommendations for Action' https://publications.europa.eu/en/publication-detail/-/publication/04d6ef91-b0ac-48fe-82ab-8c593c397131/language-en accessed 22 May 2017.
63 'Implementation of the European Neighbourhood Policy in the Republic of Moldova Progress in 2013 and Recommendations for Action' http://eur-lex.europa.eu/legal-content/EN/TXT/PDF/?uri=CELEX:52014SC0093&from=en accessed 22 May 2017.
64 'Implementation of the European Neighbourhood Policy in the Republic of Moldova Progress in 2014 and Recommendations for Actions' http://eeas.europa.eu/archives/docs/enp/pdf/2015/repulic-of-moldova-enp-report-2015_en.pdf accessed 22 May 2017.
65 'Association Implementation Report on Moldova' https://eeas.europa.eu/diplomatic-network/eastern-partnership/42497/2018-association-implementation-report-moldova_en accessed 1 June 2019, 5.
66 'Association Implementation Report on Georgia' https://eeas.europa.eu/sites/eeas/files/2019_association_implementation_report_georgia_en.pdf accessed 10 July 2019, 5.
67 SAMLA (n 18).
68 Details of such sanctions shall be laid down in secondary legislation. The draft also proposes specific powers to supplement the UK's existing anti-money laundering regime. See Sanctions and Anti-Money Laundering HL Bill (2017–19) ch 3.
69 David Harris and Jason Hungerford, 'New UK Sanctions Bill Following Post-Brexit Consultation' (Norton Rose Fulbright, November 2017) www.nortonrosefulbright.com/knowledge/publications/149040/new-uk-sanctions-bill-following-post-brexit-consultation accessed 10 September 2019.
70 Foreign Affairs Committee, 'Fragmented and Incoherent: The UK's Sanctions Policy' (HC 2017–19, 1703-I) para 49.
71 Ibid, para 51.
72 Foreign Affairs Committee, 'Fragmented and Incoherent: The UK's Sanctions Policy – Government's Response to the Seventeenth Report' (HC 2017–19, 2642-I) para 6.
73 Ibid.
74 Ibid, 4–5.
75 Council 5870/20 ADD 1 REV 3 Directives for the negotiation of a new partnership with the United Kingdom of Great Britain and Northern Ireland (Brussels, 25 February 2020), para 133.
76 European Union Committee (n 6) 24.
77 Ibid.
78 PD, para 120 (n 9).
79 See Van Elsuwege and Chamon (n 54).
80 See also European Commission, 'Recommendation for a Council Decision authorising the opening of negotiations for a new partnership with the United Kingdom of Great Britain and Northern Ireland' COM (2020) 35 final, para 128.

81 This amendment was adopted in 2016, implying a reference to the 'Global Magnitsky Act', see www.state.gov/global-magnitsky-act/ accessed 14 February 2020.
82 For an overview, see Clara Portela, 'Targeted Sanctions Against Individuals on Grounds of Grave Human Rights Violations: Impact, Trends and Prospects at EU Level' www.europarl.europa.eu/RegData/etudes/STUD/2018/603869/EXPO_STU(2018)603869_EN.pdf accessed April 2018.
83 Alexandra Brzozowski, 'EU Ministers Break Ground on European "Magnitsky Act"' *Euractiv* (Brussels, 10 December 2019) www.euractiv.com/section/justice-home-affairs/news/eu-ministers-break-ground-on-european-magnitsky-act/ accessed 14 February 2020.
84 See Letter from Minister of State, Foreign and Commonwealth Office, to the Chair of the Committee, 'Legal position regarding the introduction of autonomous UK human rights sanctions', annex to House of Commons Foreign Affairs Committee (n 72) https://publications.parliament.uk/pa/cm201719/cmselect/cmfaff/2642/2642.pdf accessed 14 February 2020.
85 Ben Smith and Joanna Dawson, 'Magnitsky Legislation' (House of Commons Briefing Paper, 16 July 2018) http://researchbriefings.files.parliament.uk/documents/CBP-8374/CBP-8374.pdf accessed 25 February 2020.
86 See more extensively the contribution by Wessel, Chapter 14 in this volume.
87 Carmen-Cristina Cîrlig and Laura Puccio, 'The Future Partnership between the European Union and the United Kingdom: Negotiating a Framework for Relations after Brexit' (European Parliamentary Research Service September, 2018) 85.
88 See also Erica Moret and Fabrice Pothier, 'Sanctions after Brexit' (2018) 60 Survival 179.
89 See also Richard Whitman who argues that the UK may become an integrated, associated or detached partner of the EU post-Brexit. See Richard G Whitman, 'The UK and EU Foreign, Security and Defence Policy after Brexit: Integrated, Associated or Detached?' (2017) 238 National Institute Economic Review 43.
90 For instance, in her speech at the EU Institute for Security Studies, Federica Mogherini explicitly stated that 'Britain will not be a "half-member" or a member "ad honorem" … either you are a member or you are not'. See Speeches by Michel Barnier and Federica Mogherini at the EU Institute for Security Studies Conference (14 May 2018) https://eeas.europa.eu/headquarters/headquarters-homepage/44486/brexit-mogherini-and-barnier-discuss-eu-foreign-and-security-policy-post-brexit-live-1700_id accessed 25 February 2020.

17

EU crisis management operations and international responsibility post-Brexit

Scarlett McArdle

17.1 Introduction

Questions of international responsibility and, in particular, where such responsibility for wrongful acts should lie, have long been raised in relation to the European Union.[1] This has been all the more true for its actions in the area of crisis management.[2] With crisis management operations depending upon the 'borrowing' of personnel from Member States in order to operationalise these wide ranging activities, they are prime for the question of whether responsibility lies with the EU or the Member States. In spite of the fact that the Lisbon Treaty definitively addressed the question of legal personality[3] and, therefore, the capacity of the EU to incur responsibility for wrongs it commits externally, and crisis management being a Union competence,[4] this has not addressed the full picture of where responsibility lies.

There are first of all difficulties within the basic legal principles of responsibility, primarily in terms of the principle of attribution and clarity of where actions will be traced in order to establish responsibility for wrongs. The principle of attribution causes fundamental issues in terms of crisis management. With the relevant principle of attribution being the determination of where 'effective control' lies, this can be complex. Crisis management operations depend upon the borrowing of personnel, from both Member States and third States, and these personnel retain very strong links with their home state. While the EU has developed significantly in terms of clearer internal command structures, the determination of command and control over specific actions depends on individual factual circumstances.[5] It can, therefore, first of all, be difficult to establish, and, second of all, differ between and even within operations. Such an uncertain principle leads to lack of clarity as to where responsibility lies. This is only compounded by the interpretation of this principle as requiring a high level of control that is often not feasible to definitively establish within institutional frameworks.

The departure of the UK from the EU raises further questions in this regard. Indications are that the UK will continue to engage with crisis management, with both sides agreed from the outset on the need for continued cooperation in the area of security and defence.[6] From early on, the UK expressed a clear desire that Brexit would not mean a complete removal of the UK from the overall area of Common Foreign and Security Policy (CFSP) generally, but rather that a new partnership should be developed that is 'deeper than any other third country partnership and that reflects our shared interests, values, and the importance of a strong and prosperous Europe'.[7] It is this call for a highly developed and distinct approach of the UK that further complicates the area of responsibility for actions arising from crisis management operations.

While little has currently been firmly established, the Political Declaration did manage to set out an initial framework for the future relationship between the UK and the EU. In order to allow for UK participation in EU Common Security and Defence Policy (CSDP), the declaration mentions 'close cooperation in Union-led crisis management missions, both civilian and military' and participation 'on a case-by-case basis in CSDP missions and operations through a Framework Participation Agreement (FPA)'.[8] The specific nature of this FPA remains uncertain, however, while the UK is seeking something that mirrors, and *goes beyond*, existing third state relationships, the EU has developed red lines that appear to be fundamentally opposed to this. The EU is clear that any post-Brexit security and defence partnership should (i) not prejudice the EU's decision-making autonomy, (ii) reflect a balance of rights and obligations, and (iii) not grant benefits equivalent to a Member State.[9] They overall have been clear that any relationship should 'not disrupt [the] EU's relationships with [other] third countries'.[10] There are clearly difficulties here to address. The current indications within the Political Declaration are that there may be some compromises that enable a distinct agreement to be developed. This may not be to the level of engagement that the UK is seeking but it would be further than any current third state has gone. Should an agreement arise that does allow such a distinct and potentially complex relationship then that gives rise to difficulties in terms of clarity of command and control and, through this, questions of international responsibility that go further than any previous difficulties in questions between the EU and its Member States or, indeed, involving third states.

It is this issue that forms the basis of the current contribution. The argument is made that the weaknesses in the principle of attribution would be fundamentally exacerbated by the new and distinct relationship between the EU and the UK. This will be done by a brief examination of the issues surrounding attribution and responsibility pre-Brexit between the EU and its Member States and also the EU and third states, before considering the difficulties of applying attribution beyond this to a post-Brexit agreement. The chapter will then finally consider some of the practical difficulties of the adjudication of responsibility. This has long been a problem internationally with limited judicial fora before which institutional frameworks can be questioned and a difficulty of immunity from prosecution.[11] The question of judicial fora is one that has become further exacerbated in the EU context with the stringent approach to autonomy taken by the Court of Justice of the European Union (CJEU) in terms of seeking to maintain its own jurisdictional monopoly.[12] This is even more complicated in the post-Brexit environment with the ongoing statements from the UK that it is seeking to break away from the jurisdiction of the CJEU and the ongoing commitment by the CJEU to be the sole body responsible for the interpretation and application of EU law. These are not reconcilable positions and it is argued that the likely outcome will be a failure to resolve disputes.

17.2 Crisis management and the complexity of applying the principles of international responsibility

With around 45 countries having previously contributed to crisis management operations as non-Member States and few operations existing without some third state involvement, the involvement of third states is certainly not new or unusual.[13] The different ways in which third states have participated in CSDP missions has been addressed elsewhere in this book.[14]

Responsibility exists in order to ensure consequences for wrongs; it is, therefore, a highly important part of the international legal system.[15] Its application to the EU as an external actor has long been discussed,[16] particularly in terms of its actions in the area of crisis management. This is an area which is prime for potential breaches, due to the wide-ranging nature of the activities concerned.[17] With the primary difficulty being in the determination of where command and control for actions and, through this, responsibility for wrongs lies, an unprecedented and complex relationship in crisis management post-Brexit only further complicates this area.

With the key principles of responsibility emerging initially in relation to the state and then being expanded and mapped on international organisations,[18] their ability to fully apply beyond the state generally, and in relation to EU crisis management operations specifically, has been much debated.[19] This problem becomes particularly pronounced with the principle of attribution and seeking to determine where actions lie. Responsibility arises for an internationally wrongful act, which is constituted by a breach of international law that is attributable to the responsible actor.[20] While the concept of linking a wrong with an actor, which is the role of attribution, is a logical step within a legal system made up of collective actors, its role and construction has been subject to much criticism.[21]

17.2.1 Crisis management and effective control: foundational problems

The attribution of actions between the EU and its Member States has been questioned numerous times. Attribution is first of all established for the actions of organs and agents of an international organisation.[22] This will not generally be relevant for crisis management operations, with personnel not amounting to organs or agents. Furthermore, there has been case law before the CJEU establishing that operations as a whole are not organs or agents, but 'missions' and 'of limited duration'.[23] The more relevant provision will be Article 7 of the Articles on the Responsibility of International Organisations (ARIO), which attributes the actions of organs or agents that have been 'loaned' to an institution, to that institution if it exercises 'effective control' over the organ or agent. The difficulty with this article, both generally and in this specific context, lies first of all with the lack of definition of the test.[24] The second problem is the nature of the test. As a result of the lack of definition, a great deal of 'borrowing' has been had from the interpretation of the test developed within the law of state responsibility, which requires a significant level of control.[25] There should be consideration of the actions in question, rather than simply looking at the institutional relationships, but this can be a complicated determination.[26] These difficulties can be seen from the limited case law in the area, which has not only been subject to critique but has also demonstrated shifting approaches to effective control in practice.[27]

Moreover, this high level of control can be difficult to determine within institutional frameworks. The 'transparent' nature of institutions as legal persons who are dependent upon other legal persons for their actions can make it difficult to establish where an action lies: with the institution or with its Member States who often act to operationalise its actions.[28] Overall, the test of effective control has been criticised as inappropriate when faced with institutional frameworks.[29] When considering the EU and effective control, more specifically, some internal institutional progress has been made in terms of the development of a clearer command and control structure. Even this, however, would not definitively establish actions of personnel within a crisis management operation as being those of the EU. A crucial aspect to effective control is that its determination is in relation to the particular factual circumstances of each case.

While the recognition that there needs to be a consideration of specific factual conduct is positive, it does not do anything to address the fact that the nature of this principle fundamentally fails to consider the frequent nature of actions in this area. Effective control seeks to navigate between numerous different actors, at a minimum between a state and an international organisation. In the context being considered here, it is often the case that action will involve a number of different actors and seeking to determine which actor has complete control over these actions is simply not realistic.

The difficulty with EU crisis management has traditionally been discussed in terms of the division of responsibility between the EU and Member States contributing personnel; when are personnel under the control of the EU and when are they under the control of their home state? When considering the relationship just between the EU and its Member States, this is something that has evolved over time. Some have argued that personnel in CSDP operations exist as de facto organs as the EU exercises effective control.[30] With these operations now being governed by a significantly developed international governance framework, the argument made by some is that effective control can be applied *mutatis mutandis* to these missions.[31]

To an extent, there is a central EU structure that governs operations. Decisions on crisis management operations are made by the Council after it has been advised by the Political and Security Committee.[32] Within the realms of either military or civilian operations, there are EU bodies that plan and oversee these missions. In military operations an increased role has been developed for the EU Military Committee (EUMC) and EU Military Staff (EUMS) and more recently came the development of the Committee on Civilian Aspects of Crisis Management (CIVCOM) and the Civilian Planning and Conduct Capabilities Unit (CPCC).[33] Within the overall planning structures, therefore, there has been a clear move towards making these more definitively 'European' and to demonstrate that control is exercised at the EU level. However, control cannot just be considered at the high overall planning level. Rather, it must also be considered at the operational level. These operations remain staffed by individuals 'loaned' from states, whether they are Member States or third states. While they act under the auspices of the EU in terms of these operations, they do so while remaining significantly under the authority of their home state. With effective control being required to such a high standard, it is questionable whether this system would be sufficient to definitively establish control at the EU level; with Member States retaining control definitely in disciplinary and criminal matters, this could be enough to consider an issue with effective control. It is difficult to determine, as a rule, that responsibility could be clearly established as a rule in crisis management operations. Ultimately, in relation to any determination of control and attribution, there needs to be consideration of the factual circumstances on a case by case basis to determine where control specifically lies in the circumstances of that wrong. Although it is necessary to have an approach that recognises factual circumstances may differ and that each individual case needs to be considered, however, this is also problematic in definitively establishing, within the context of a wrong, what exactly has happened and, through this, where control lies. The difficulty, however, is in continued flexibility of the concept of effective control as well as the fluid nature of these operations.

The question as to how this may arise and work in practice also remains. There exist examples of actions of personnel acting under the auspices of EU operations being attributed to their home state. One such case can be seen before the Cologne Administrative Court, which attributed the transfer of piracy suspects to Kenya by German personnel in Operation Atalanta to Germany and not to the EU.[34] The primary focus was that the decision-making, initiation, and implementation of the transfer of suspects had been made by German authorities and this was irrespective of the command systems being exercised by the EU during the mission. Overall, significant control had been retained by the German authorities and the level of effective control by the EU was not met. This shows that control can shift easily within an operation and effective control simply does not respond, with clarity, to the type of action being seen here. A further argument can be made that national measures do remain subject to judicial review and, while CJEU jurisdiction remains limited in the area of CFSP and CSDP, this allows for a determination of responsibility and could open up some of the possibilities of shared responsibility.

17.2.2 Crisis management, effective control, and third states

The above difficulties are those that exist even in the most straightforward of circumstances within the basic relationship between the EU and its own Member States. There exist further difficulties when considering the involvement of third states here. While some aspects are common between Member States and third states, the latter do pose some specific challenges. On the face of it, there is some clarity that attempts to draw little distinction between Member States and third states, with Framework Partnership Agreements (FPAs) attempting to incorporate third state personnel into EU command structures.

When considering, first of all, actions of personnel on the ground, standard provisions within FPAs grant third countries 'the same rights and obligations in terms of day-to-day management of the operation as the Member States of the European Union taking part in the operation'.[35] From this it may appear that little should differ between these two groups of states, if the operational aspects should be common between the two categories. The more specific question of control, however, can become more complex. Standard FPA provisions first of all state that national authorities are expected to 'transfer the Operational control' of their forces and personnel to the EU Operation Commander.[36] This must also be read together, however, with the provision that 'without prejudice to the agreement on status of forces/mission', the third state 'shall exercise jurisdiction over its personnel participating in the EU crisis management operation'.[37] This can also be taken together with a provision identified as common to some FPAs that 'the contributing state reserves the ultimate right to stop its personnel from undertaking activities and/or to remove them from the operation'.[38] While there is recognition within crisis management operations that home Member States will retain some link with their personnel, this does go further and suggests a stronger link. With Member States, there is retention of jurisdiction of their personnel, but there is also the obligation to work in cooperation with the EU and for the benefit of the operation.[39] This obligation simply does not exist with third states.

The difficulty of this relationship can then pose further challenges when faced with effective control. The question of control becomes less clear with this due to the different chains of command and the various possibilities for command to shift and change within the context of an operation. While it must, again, be noted that control is something that is determined and understood in the particular factual circumstances, the attempt at drawing personnel under the command structures of the EU is not entirely clear. When considering the FPA with Turkey, for example, Article 6 on chain of command shows the interaction at play. While operational command of personnel is transferred to the EU Operations Commander, full command of personnel is retained by national authorities.[40] The Head of Mission is named as exercising command and control of the operation but this has to be viewed together with command being retained by national authorities. Furthermore, disciplinary control is stated as lying with the Head of Mission, but also being possible by Turkish authorities, 'where required'.[41]

While all of this is fairly standard, when envisaging a situation where control is being assessed, it is not so straightforward as to consider the formal command structures that exist and utilising them to track responsibility. Rather, it is entirely feasible that control may shift within an operation. As seen above, this has happened in the context of the EU and its own Member States, and the German case is not the only example of this.[42] When considering third states and the greater retention of control by home states, this is all the more likely to occur.

There is a further difficulty to consider, which is the exclusion of third states from the formal processes both establishing and ending operations. Issues of responsibility can arise on the ground but they can also begin in terms of determining the nature of an operation. As stated above, the processes surrounding the decision-making of an operation do not involve third states. It may not always be so straightforward as to detach operations on the ground from the formal decision-making processes. Further questions may arise as to actions that implement decisions, especially if these actions are carried out involving discussions from a home state. There were, for example, a number of discussions surrounding the initial mandate of EUNAVFOR Med, a military operation in the Mediterranean aiming to prevent loss of life at sea following significant numbers seeking to travel across the sea to seek refuge in Europe.[43] The third strand of the operation gave rise to a number of concerns in the literature,[44] namely the 'taking of operational measures against vessels and related assets suspected of being used for human smuggling or trafficking inside the coastal states territory, with the necessary legal framework established by UNSCR and following coastal state consent'.[45] This was determined as part of the remit of the operation and, while the EU consistently stated that the operation would be carried out in accordance with international law, the term 'operational measures' is a rather wide one. The determination as to what may be appropriate may come down to a decision on the ground and, if questionable actions were carried out by third state personnel in discussion with their home state, the question could arise as to where control for this lay. Detaching these two elements of decision-making and action can become complex and further demonstrates one of the difficult aspects of requiring determination of a high level of control on a factual and case-by-case basis.

Even with formal determinations that third states exist within the governance command and control structures of the EU, this does not provide a simple answer to the question of wrongs committed and where control lies. Effective control is not established by virtue of formal structures but rather by considering the control in the particular case at hand. The circumstances of each individual case must be addressed. While effective control remains so flexible and unclear in its application, this will continue to be an issue.

17.2.3 Crisis management, effective control, and the UK

Much of what arises generally in relation to third states will also cause difficulties for the UK–EU relationship and some of the questions surrounding responsibility will only be capable of being addressed fully once further detail is known about the specific arrangements. There will likely be further difficulties, however, arising from the extra elements to the relationship that the UK is seeking to have. As mentioned above the FPA that the UK is seeking may not go to the lengths of engagement in institutions that the UK has sought, but the Political Declaration does indicate a development further than that sought with even the currently most significant contributors. Overall the UK will contribute on a case-by-case basis but there exists the possibility of an invitation to the UK to informally participate in ministerial meetings on an occasional basis, as appropriate. There is also mention of increased dialogue, flexible consultation, and close cooperation. While there may not be the possibility of involvement in formal decision-making, the UK may gain earlier access in the planning process and a possibility of UK staff being seconded to designated Operations Headquarters in military operations, as proportionate to the level of its contribution.[46] In taking the UK further than has previously been seen in relation to other FPAs, they potentially complicate the systems of command and, in doing so, raise further questions with attribution and, through this, responsibility. Overall, these distinctions can be categorised as (i) enabling a greater knowledge from the UK in terms of EU planning, and the possibility of, at least, informal influence over the decision-making processes, and (ii) a more significant role for UK staff compared to some third states, particularly in terms of the role of UK staff within Operations Headquarters. Each of these distinct roles for the UK can have some influence, to a greater or lesser extent, in terms of definitively establishing a high level of control.

The first strand of these, with increased knowledge and potential informal influence of the UK, poses the lesser challenge. The first strand of these, with increased knowledge and potential informal influence of the UK, poses the lesser challenge in terms of the willingness for dialogue and flexible consultation, as well as gaining earlier access in the planning process It is entirely possible that this may prove beneficial in enabling greater planning to be done on the role of different forces and how they collaborate and engage with one another. When considering levels of control, either in the midst of planning or during the course of an operation, this dialogue and access seems like it would exist outside the understood systems of control. These processes would not form a part of the existing EU mechanisms and internal structures, but rather would exist alongside them. With multiple systems of dialogue existing alongside one another, this can cause a degree of complexity in determining the boundaries of a decision. This becomes all the more difficult when faced with the potential informal influence of the UK over the decision-making processes. Informal influence within the decision-making processes is much harder to track and trace compared to formal decision-making. It is difficult to envisage responsibility as a consequence of informal decision-making. Although some discussions may be had in this regard in terms of legal obligations being traced as a result of informal decision-making, the focus here remains on effective control. In developing a secondary strand of actor alongside the formal processes, questions of influence and control can then give rise to complexity about where a particular action lies. This is likely to be a lesser issue but should be recognised.

The second consideration of the potential secondment of UK staff within Operations Headquarters gives rise to the most significant number of questions in terms of control. The UK has sought to develop a highly involved role, but from other statements made by the UK in the negotiations it is also apparent that it is keen to maintain a significant degree of internal control.[47] The UK has continually stated its desire to be outside the control of EU internal mechanisms, in particular the Court of Justice and the jurisdiction of new EU laws.[48] The engagement of personnel of a third state in the Operations Headquarters places them at the core of an operation, enabling influence at this very core. This may then cause further questions in terms of control. In the event of a wrong occurring during the course of an operation, this could raise questions that go further than the standard questions of effective control. The engagement of UK personnel here enables the engagement of a third state within the core of the institutional command structure that has been developed by the EU. The question of the command structure, while not definitive as mentioned above, does give an initial indication of control. Even this foundation could be called into question here. The engagement of the UK, with the potential retention of control by national authorities, can then question the very basis of control structures. With effective control generally requiring such a high level in order to determine whether control is established, enabling actors to influence or potentially have control at this core causes further uncertainty.

Overall, effective control is a difficult test to engage with. Its lack of definition, the ongoing lack of clarity in the case law, and also the continuing approach that it should result in a high level of control, all combine to leave a great deal of uncertainty as to the application of this area of law. In an area where wrongs can occur, a great deal more clarity is needed as to who can be claimed against in the circumstances of a wrong occurring. There also arises a further weakness within this area, which Brexit will only prove a further challenge to. Even should the principles of responsibility themselves be addressed sufficiently, currently there remains a significant challenge in terms of anyone actually bringing a claim in this regard; there are a substantial lack of available judicial avenues before which claims can be brought.

17.3 Crisis management and the adjudication of international responsibility

The difficulties with international responsibility are not limited to the principles themselves. There is further, a more practical, difficulty that will become ever more complex following Brexit and that is the question of the adjudication of international responsibility. The question of where and how cases concerning wrongs committed in the context of crisis management operations occur is already a complex one. When we consider the potential future relationship between the EU and the UK, as a former Member State but still more involved partner in this area, and the legal complexity concerned, this could create a further layer of difficulty in addressing this question.

There already exist questions regarding the judicial fora before which cases could be brought. While the CJEU may be highly developed, its potential role in CFSP, and through this in addressing crisis management operations, remains restricted.[49] Ultimately, the most likely circumstance that would see the Court accepting jurisdiction would be where wrongs occur within the context of a crisis management operation that could also be connected to other areas of EU competence. This would be complex but not impossible. It is also worth contemplating that the options for complainants to petition the court and make an argument that a wrong has been committed remain highly restrictive.[50] Furthermore, the question of dispute settlement outside the EU legal order is highly complex with the CJEU closely guarding its role as the adjudicator of matters of EU law. Case law has continually shown the CJEU being reluctant to accept external dispute settlement mechanisms, as they may infringe on the jurisdictional autonomy of the CJEU.[51] This has continued to show the practical challenge of questioning the actions of the EU; not only are there issues within the EU judicial framework but there are significant restrictions in enabling actions to be heard externally.

This issue can also be seen directly in the attempt to address dispute settlement within the Withdrawal Agreement. Somewhat of a compromise is reached with the interpretation of Union law remaining the domain of the CJEU, but there also being the creation of a system outside both the UK and the EU in the establishment of the Joint Committee.[52] The Joint Committee will have responsibility for implementation and application of the Agreement and will be made up of representatives of both the EU and the UK.[53] While this is a sensible approach in negotiation terms, it remains to be seen how the specific role of the Joint Committee will be seen. While its remit as apart from the CJEU has been quite carefully developed, it is difficult to see how they can have entirely distinct roles. Perhaps in some ways the difficulties of this can be aligned with those seen in *Opinion 2/13*.[54] Whereas in *Opinion 2/13* there was a need to consider the regulation of the integration of two legal orders in the EU and the European Convention on Human Rights, the Withdrawal Agreement is addressing the same concept but from the opposite position; it is considering the disintegration and the regulation of that. The potential consequences should not be underestimated here and an aspect that has, at points, seemed logical and carefully thought out could result in some difficult legal questions as to when its remit becomes engaged and the dividing line between the Joint Committee and the CJEU.

While that question is a significant one, it is limited in its reference to security and defence where potential adjudication of disputes is one that has ongoing discussions and difficulties. The question of international legal responsibility, where responsibility is determined for a breach of an international obligation which is attributed to the wrongful actor, has long been discussed generally in relation to the EU but also specifically in the field of security and defence. These discussions have predominantly focused upon determining the division of action between the

EU and its Member States, which has enough complexity in its considerations when contemplating that the core concept of attribution largely seeks to determine an individual actor for an individual act.

The UK has consistently stated that it will not continue to accept the direct jurisdiction of the CJEU.[55] While this is a clear position, it remains highly problematic when faced with the EU's longstanding position that protecting the autonomy of its legal order requires CJEU oversight.[56] The fine balance between these two positions can be seen in the agreement reached within the Withdrawal Agreement on the Joint Committee and the role of the CJEU:

> Where a dispute submitted to arbitration in accordance with this Title raises a question of interpretation of a concept of Union law, a question of interpretation of a provision of Union law referred to in this Agreement or a question of whether the United Kingdom has complied with its obligations under Article 89(2), the arbitration panel shall not decide on any such question. In such case, it shall request the Court of Justice of the European Union to give a ruling on the question. The Court of Justice of the European Union shall have jurisdiction to give such a ruling which shall be binding on the arbitration panel.[57]

There is a clear determination that disputes concerning EU law will continue to fall under the remit of the CJEU. While this is a logical approach in line with the EU's position on protecting and upholding the autonomy of its own legal order, it may not always be so straightforward to determine the significance of the involvement of EU law. This involves an inevitable interaction of normative frameworks. This position presupposes clarity in the dividing lines between the different legal orders when the position may be further complex than this.

Some have questioned whether the answer to this may lie in the development of a further court, perhaps akin to the European Free Trade Ares (EFTA) Court.[58] The difficulty with this is that it continues to fall foul of the two fundamentally opposing positions outlined above; it continues to maintain a close relationship with the CJEU while being distinct and outside this arrangement. Furthermore, if this were to be developed solely in relation to trade, it would largely have little relevance for crisis management. Any development of a further judicial framework would need to be agreed to with a degree of compromise from both sides which is currently difficult to envisage.

17.4 Conclusion

The question of international responsibility has continued to pose a challenge when faced with institutional actors such as the EU. The principles have weaknesses at their very core, in particular in terms of the concept of effective control that is so central to the principle of attribution. This caused a longstanding question with the EU and its crisis management operations, and the challenge of Brexit only further complicates this. With the likely future relationship in the area of crisis management being a newly distinct one, even if not to the level of that desired by the UK, this creates a newly complex legal framework.

As further legal strands and developments are added to this, first in the guise of third states and then more recently with Brexit, this complicates the legal framework even further. With the complication of the legal framework through the involvement of a partner which is a former EU Member State that has also participated – and will continue to participate – in ongoing missions, the determination of control becomes harder to establish. This is most particularly difficult when considering the flexible and uncertain nature of control; an uncertain test is being applied to an unclear legal framework in which the extent to which the UK participated in ways that are similar to EU Member States will be crucial. It also becomes more concerning that, even should some agreement be formally reached regarding the determination of control, that there remain few avenues before which claims of responsibility could be made. Even if the problems within the principles were to be fully addressed, this would not address the issue of enabling claims of responsibility to be made, and redress to be gained, following breaches of international law. With this being the primary role of responsibility and Brexit now raising the potential for difficulties further, the gaps in terms of principles and in terms of access to redress seem to only be widening.

Notes

1 Albrecht Conze, *Die völkerrechtliche Haftung der Europäischen Gemeinschaft* (Nomos, 1987); Christian Pitschas, *Die völkerrechtliche Verantwortlichkeit der Europäischen Gemeinschaft und ihrer Mitgliedstaaten* (Duncker & Humblot 2001); Malcolm Evans and Panos Koutrakos (eds) *The International Responsibility of the European Union: European and International Perspectives* (Hart 2013).

2 Aurel Sari and Ramses Wessel, 'International Responsibility for EU Military Operations: Finding the EU's Place in the Global Accountability Regime' in Bart Van Vooren, Steven Blockmans and Jan Wouters (eds), *The Legal Dimension of Global Governance: What Role for the EU?* (Oxford University Press 2013) 126; Marten Zwanenburg, 'Toward a More Mature ESDP: Responsibility for Violations of International Humanitarian Law by EU Crisis Management Missions' in Steven Blockmans (ed), *The European Union and Crisis Management Policy and Legal* Aspects (TMC Asser Press, 2008) 395.

3 Art 47 TEU.

4 Arts 24(1), 25 TEU. Art 2(4) TFEU; for a more detailed discussion of the legal framework in this area, see the contribution by Wessel, Chapter 14 in this volume.

5 No definition is given in the articles or commentaries but in a 2004 report, the International Law Commission (ILC) described 'effective control' as 'the factual control that is exercised over the specific conduct taken by the organ or agent placed at the receiving organization's disposal': International Law Commission, *Report of the International Law Commission*, UN GAOR, 56th sess, Supp No 10, UN Doc A/59/10 (6 August 2004) 111 para 3.

6 European Council, 'Conclusions: Negotiating Guidelines for Brexit', EUCO XT 20004/17, 7; HM Government, 'Foreign Policy, Defence and Development: A Position Paper' https://assets.publishing.service.gov.uk/government/uploads/system/uploads/attachment_data/file/643924/Foreign_policy__defence_and_development_paper.pdf accessed 13 April 2019.

7 See UK Government, 'Foreign Policy, Defence and Development: A Future Partnership Paper' (Policy Paper, 2017). See also the speech by PM Theresa May on 17 February 2018:

> Europe's security is our security. And that is why I have said – and I say again today – that the United Kingdom is unconditionally committed to maintaining it. The challenge for all of us today is finding the way to work together, through a deep and special partnership between the UK and the EU, to retain the co-operation that we have built and go further in meeting the evolving threats we face together.
>
> *(www.gov.uk/government/speeches/pm-speech-at-munich-security-conference-17-february-2018 accessed 14 March 2020)*

8 Political Declaration setting out the framework for the future relationship between the European Union and the United Kingdom, OJ [2020] C34/12, para 92.

9 European Commission – Task Force for the Preparation and Conduct of the Negotiations with the United Kingdom under Article 50 TEU, 'Foreign, Security and Defence Policy' [slides] (Brussels, June 2018) https://ec.europa.eu/commission/sites/beta-political/files/slides_on_foreign_security_defence_policy.pdf accessed 14 March 2020.

10 European Commission (n 9).

11 August Reinisch, 'The Immunity of International Organizations and the Jurisdiction of their Administrative Tribunals' (2008) 7 Chinese Journal of International Law 285.

12 See Opinion 2/13 [2014] EU:C:2014:2454 and Opinion 1/17 (CETA) EU:C:2019:72; Daniel Halberstam, 'It's the Autonomy, Stupid! A Modest Defense of Opinion 2/13 on EU Accession to the ECHR, and the Way Forward' (2015) German Law Journal 105.

13 Thierry Tardy, 'CSDP: Getting Third States on Board' (European Union Institute for Security Studies Brief, 2014) 6.
14 See, in particular, the contribution by Wessel in this volume.
15 Paul Reuter, 'Trois observations sur la codification de la responsabilité international des États pour fait illicite' in *Le Droit international au service de la paix, de la justice et du développementa Mélange Michel Virally* (Pedone 1991) 390; reproduced in Paul Reuter, *Le développement de l'ordre juridique internationala Écrits de droit international* (Economica 1995) 574; cited in A Pellet, 'The Definition of Responsibility in International Law' in James Crawford, Alain Pellet and Simon Olleson (eds) *The Law of International Responsibility* (Oxford University Press 2010) 3.
16 Pellet (n 15) 3; Frank Hoffmeister, 'Litigating Against the European Union and Its Member States: Who Responds Under the ILC's Draft Articles on International Responsibility of International Organizations' (2010) 21 European Journal of International Law 723; Evans and Koutrakos (n 1); Sari and Wessel (n 2) 126.
17 Art 42(1) TEU states that

> The common security and defence policy shall be an integral part of the common foreign and security policy. It shall provide the Union with an operational capacity drawing on civilian and military assets. The Union may use them on missions outside the Union for peace-keeping, conflict prevention and strengthening international security in accordance with the principles of the United Nations Charter.

18 Articles on Responsibility of States for Internationally Wrongful Acts, with commentaries 2001, Yearbook of the International Law Commission 2001, 2001, vol II, Part Two. United Nations General Assembly Resolution A/RES/56/83, adopted by the General Assembly on 12 December 2001 (ASR); Articles on the Responsibility of International Organizations, with Commentaries 2011, Yearbook of the International Law Commission, 2011, vol II, Part Two; United Nations General Assembly Resolution 66/100 of 9 December 2011 (ARIO).
19 Evans and Koutrakos (n 1); Sari and Wessel (n 2) 126.
20 ASR arts 1–2 (n 18); ARIO arts 3–4 (n 18).
21 Bérénice Boutin, 'Responsibility of the Netherlands for the Acts of Dutchbat in *Nuhanović* and *Mustafić*: The Continuous Quest for a Tangible Meaning for "Effective Control"' in the Context of Peacekeeping' (2012) 25 Leiden Journal of International Law 521; Aurel Sari, 'Autonomy, Attribution and Accountability: Reflections on the *Behrami* Case' in Richard Collins and Nigel White (eds), *International Organizations and the Idea of Autonomy: Institutional Independence in the International Legal Order* (Routledge 2011) 257; Christian Tomuschat, 'Attribution of International Responsibility: Direction and Control' in Evans and Koutrakos (n 1) 7.
22 ARIO art 6 (n 18).
23 Case T-271/10 *H v Council and Commission* Order of the General Court of 22 July 2010, para 19.
24 See (n 5).
25 In particular, *Military and Paramilitary Activities in and against Nicaragua (Nicaragua v United States of America)* Merits, ICJ Reports 1986, 14; *Application of the Convention on the Prevention and Punishment of the Crime of Genocide* Judgment, ICJ Reports 2007, 15 (ICJ Reports).
26 Commentary to art 7 ARIO, para 4 (n 18); Paolo Palchetti, 'Attributing the Conduct of Dutchbat in Srebrenica: The 2014 Judgment of the District Court in the Mothers of Srebrenica Case' (2015) 62 Netherlands International Law Review 279, 281.
27 See *Behrami and Behrami v France* and *Saramati v France, Germany and Norway* Decision (Grand Chamber) of 2 May 2007 on the admissibility of applications No 71412/01 and No 78166/01 (2007) 45 EHRR SE10; *Al Jedda v the United Kingdom* Application no 27021/08, Judgment, 7 July 2011; *Netherlands (Ministry of Defence and Ministry of Foreign Affairs) v Nuhanovic* Final appeal judgment, ECLI/NL/HR/2013/BZ9225, ILDC 2061 (NL 2013), 12/03324, 6 September 2013, Supreme Court.
28 For a discussion of the nature of international organisations, see Catherine Brölmann, *The Institutional Veil in Public International Law: International Organisations and the Law of Treaties* (Hart 2007).
29 Nigel D White, 'Institutional Responsibility or Private Military and Security Companies' in Francesco Francioni and Natalino Ronzitti (eds), *War by Contract: Human Rights, Humanitarian Law and Private Contractors* (Oxford University Press 2011) 381, 383.
30 See Sari and Wessel (n 2).
31 Ramses Wessel and Leonard Den Hertog, 'EU Foreign, Security and Defence Policy: A Competence: Responsibility Gap' in Evans and Koutrakos (n 1) 351.

32 TEU, art 42(2); TEU, art 38; European External Action Service, 'Common Security and Defence Policy (CSDP) Structure, Instruments, Agencies' https://eeas.europa.eu/topics/common-security-and-defence-policy-csdp/5392/csdp-structure-instruments-and-agencies_en accessed 13 April 2019.
33 Ibid.
34 VG Köln Urteil vom 11 November 2011 Az 25 K 4280/09 openjur 2012 83059, https://openjur.de/u/451905.html (available in German and accessed 14 April 2020); Oberverwaltungsgericht Nordrhein-Westfalen, Urteil vom 18 September 2014, available in German at https://openjur.de/u/733280.html accessed 14 April; Frederick Naert, 'European Union Common Security and Defence Policy Operations' in André Nollkaemper and Ilias Plakokefalos (eds), *The Practice of Shared Responsibility in International Law* (Cambridge University Press 2017) 697–698.
35 See, for example, Council Decision 2006/482/CFSP concerning the conclusion of the Agreement between the European Union and the Republic of Turkey establishing a framework for the participation of the Republic of Turkey in the European Union crisis management operations [2006] OJ L 189, art 6(5).
36 Ibid, art 6(3).
37 Ibid, art 3(3).
38 European Union Committee, 'Brexit: Common Security and Defence Policy Missions and Operations' (HL 2017–19, 132) ch 4.
39 Art 4(3) and the principle of sincere cooperation; art 28(2) TEU also provides that the CFSP Decisions 'shall commit the Member States in the positions they adopt and in the conduct of their activity'.
40 EU–Turkey FPA (n 35) art 6(2) and (3).
41 Ibid, art 6(4) and (5).
42 For further discussion and an example of Greece and the difficulties of control within Operation Atalanta see Efthymios Papastavridis, 'Piracy' in André Nollkaemper and Ilias Plakokefalos (eds), *The Practice of Shared Responsibility in International Law* (Cambridge University Press 2017) 329–331.
43 EUNAVFOR Med operation SOPHIA, https://eeas.europa.eu/csdp-missions-operations/eunav formed-operation-sophia_en accessed 16 July 2018; and European External Action Service (EEAS), 'EUNAVFOR Med operation Sophia: Mission' (16 January 2018) https://eeas.europa.eu/sites/eeas/files/january_2018_-_factsheet_on_eunavfor_med_mission_english.pdf accessed 16 July 2018.
44 Paul Strauch, 'When Stopping the Smuggler Means Repelling the Refugee: International Human Rights Law and the European Union's Operation to Combat Smuggling in Libya's Territorial Sea' (2017) 126 Yale Law Journal 2421.
45 EUNAVFOR Med operation SOPHIA (n 43); EEAS (n 43).
46 Political Declaration (n 8) para 103.
47 HM Government, 'The United Kingdom's Exit From, and New Relationship With, the European Union' (White Paper, 2017); Theresa May, Speech: 'The Government's Negotiating Objectives for Leaving the EU' (17 January 2017) www.gov.uk/government/speeches/the-governments-negotiating-objectives-for-exiting-the-eu-pm-speech accessed 14 April 2020.
48 Ibid.
49 With questions of jurisdiction and the Court of Justice, see Christoph Hillion and Ramses A Wessel, 'The Good, the Bad and the Ugly: Three Levels of Judicial Control over the CFSP' in Steven Blockmans and Panos Koutrakos (eds), *Research Handbook in EU Common Foreign and Security Policy* (Edward Elgar Publishing 2018) 65; Paul J Cardwell 'On "Ring-Fencing" the Common Foreign and Security Policy in the Legal Order of the European Union' (2013) 64 Northern Ireland Legal Quarterly 443.
50 TFEU art 263.
51 Opinion 2/13 (n 12).
52 Agreement on the withdrawal of the United Kingdom of Great Britain and Northern Ireland from the European Union and the European Atomic Energy Community [2020] OJ L 29/7 (WA) art 164.
53 Ibid.
54 Opinion 2/13 (n 12).
55 Prime Minister's Office, 'Prime Minister's Letter to Donald Tusk Triggering Article 50' www.gov.uk/government/publications/prime-ministers-letter-to-donald-tusk-triggering-article-50/prime-ministers-letter-to-donald-tusk-triggering-article-50 accessed 13 April 2019.
56 Opinion 2/13 (n 12).
57 WA, art 174 (n 52).
58 House of Lords European Union Committee, 'Dispute resolution and enforcement after Brexit' (HL 2017–19, 130) 13; Jed Odermatt, 'How to Resolve Disputes Arising from Brexit: Comparing International Models' (2018) 15 International Organisations Law Review 295, 313–314.

Part V

Brexit and specific international arrangements

18
Brexit and EU agencies
Opting-in from the outside?

Andrea Ott

18.1 Introduction

The post-Brexit landscape and future EU–UK future relations are still nebulous as the ink on the final UK Withdrawal Agreement (WA) begins to dry.[1] It might come as a surprise, but EU agencies and the UK's future role in them have been a focal point of the UK's political statements and policy papers since the UK decided to leave the Union. Already in March 2018 at her Mansion House speech, the former British prime minister Theresa May proposed an 'associated membership to EU agencies'. She framed it the following way:

> We will also want to explore with the EU, the terms on which the UK could remain part of EU agencies such as those that are critical for the chemicals, medicines and aerospace industries: the European Medicines Agency, the European Chemicals Agency, and the European Aviation Safety Agency. We would, of course, accept that this would mean abiding by the rules of those agencies and making an appropriate financial contribution, ... associate membership of these agencies is the only way to meet our objective of ensuring that these products only need to undergo one series of approvals, in one country. Second, these agencies have a critical role in setting and enforcing relevant rules. And if we were able to negotiate associate membership we would be able to ensure that we could continue to provide our technical expertise. Third, associate membership could permit UK firms to resolve certain challenges related to the agencies through UK courts rather than the ECJ.[2]

The UK's strategy paper of July 2018 took up these ideas, addressing future UK participation in the internal market related agencies and the law-enforcement 'key agencies' (European Police Office (Europol) and Eurojust).[3] The UK House of Commons committee spoke of a 'move beyond third country status' and securing a 'third country plus' agreement, which recognises 'the weight and the important value' of the UK's contribution to Eurojust and other EU justice and home affairs agencies.[4] In addition, multiple references to EU agencies found their way into the revised Political Declaration annexed to the WA.[5] Hence, both parties 'explore the possibility of cooperation of United Kingdom authorities with Union agencies such as the European Medicines Agency (EMA), the European Chemicals Agency (ECHA), and the European Aviation Safety Agency (EASA)' or 'work together to identify the terms for the UK's cooperation via Europol and Eurojust'.[6]

This contribution aims to analyse the current framework of and conditions for third country participation in EU agencies, in order to define the precise conditions for a 'third country plus agreement' or 'associated membership' in EU agencies. One central premise is that third countries' participation in EU policies determines the framework of participation in EU agencies and not the other way around. The higher the stakes of the third country in an EU policy, the more rights can be included for the third country in the EU agencies. For example, Switzerland and Norway participate in the Schengen regime[7] and therefore have some voting rights in the Management Board of Frontex.[8]

The future framework between the EU and the UK thus determines the form of their future participation in this area. This framework could be agreed in a broader association agreement or a free trade agreement with additional sectoral agreements. The revised Political Declaration provides some first indications of the direction, but also showcases two decisive changes in comparison to its earlier version. One concerns the internal market agencies and deleting the sentence that the UK will 'consider aligning with Union rules in relevant areas'. The second revision relates to an explicit reference to the Court of Justice of the European Union (CJEU). This reference has been deleted in the section on the security partnership.[9] The WA covers EU agencies, just like any other institution, to address legal uncertainties in the transition phase and when the UK applies EU law without membership.[10] Consequently, the UK has lost its voting rights and is reduced to an observer status in EU agencies during the transitional period.[11]

Obviously, a dividing line remains between EU members and non-EU members. Third countries cannot gain equal rights in EU institutions or contribute to the EU's autonomous decision-making.[12] So any form of privileged status in EU agencies cannot amount to the same status as assigned to EU Member States. Also, misunderstandings can arise from different types of participation foreseen for third countries. The Political Declaration refers to a privileged third country status for the UK regarding the European Maritime Safety Agency[13] and an administrative arrangement[14] to be concluded concerning a future collaboration with the European Defence Agency (EDA).

This contribution will first briefly analyse what functions EU agencies fulfil in the EU institutional system. It will then assess possibilities for cooperation by first analysing whether a general EU policy approach exists towards third country participation and, second, by carving out the gradual differences of involvement and the possible routes for future UK participation.

18.2 EU agencies in the EU's institutional landscape

EU agencies are part of the EU administration and are an institutional tool to implement policies or programmes. Article 13 TEU addresses the main institutions involved in policy-making, but no general norm in primary law is devoted to the role of EU agencies. Only three agencies are mentioned specifically in relation to the policies they contribute to. This concerns the EDA in Articles 42 and 45 TEU, whereas Article 85 TFEU addresses Eurojust and Article 88 TFEU Europol. Other Treaty provisions only refer to agencies in relation to other institutions or institutional actors such as the Ombudsman (Art. 228 TFEU), the Court of Auditors (Art. 287 TFEU) and the legal review of agencies' acts by the Court of Justice (Art. 263 TFEU).

The proliferation of agencies is a phenomenon of EU law and politics since the 1970s and there is currently no EU policy area that is not supported by an EU agency.[15] Agencies can be defined as independent permanent bodies established by EU secondary law with their own legal personality and entrusted with mainly technical, scientific and managerial tasks.[16] They exist separately from EU institutions and, therefore, also have a certain degree of administrative and financial autonomy. While the institutional balance enshrined in Article 13(2) TEU is not directly applicable, EU agencies implementing EU policies are bound by the implications of the institutional balance and limits of the delegation of powers highlighted by the *Meroni* judgment[17] and further defined by the *Romano* and *ESMA* cases.[18] The delegating authority under primary law cannot confer more power than it possesses under the Treaty,[19] the delegation of powers cannot be presumed but must be expressly provided,[20] and the delegation of discretionary powers to a body which is not established by primary law is excluded. Finally, this body, to which the powers have been delegated, is prevented from executing real regulatory powers[21] and may implement only clearly defined executive powers that need to be supervised by the delegating authority.[22] This reasoning has been considered a doctrine to which EU institutions have adhered to until today[23] and it is understood that it is reinforced by Article 290 TFEU. Nevertheless, practice teaches us that agencies have developed over time and have even been installed with quasi-legislative powers as the new generations of agencies in the form of EASA, EMA or ECHA demonstrate.[24] Consequently, a further categorisation allows agencies to be split-up into non-decision-making agencies, operational agencies and decision-making agencies.[25]

The creation of EU agencies has allowed the European Commission greater room to concentrate on its core tasks and policy priorities, as more specific and technical administrative tasks were delegated to the agencies. Agencies are supposed to provide the expertise that the regulator needs but would not have otherwise, thereby increasing public acceptance of their decisions. The rationale behind the creation of many agencies is three-fold: they support the Commission but also the Council in the execution of administrative tasks; they are often created as a response to contested and highly politicised issues;[26] and they have a networking function. The latter implies that they can bring together experts from different EU Member States, either through the composition of an agency's internal organs or by establishing cooperation between national authorities. Thereby, agencies are used to establish uniformity in national administrations. The characterisation of EU agencies as 'in-betweeners', between the EU institutions, has been used to highlight the role situated between the Commission and its Member States.[27]

There are currently 45 decentralised agencies, mostly created by the European Parliament (EP) and the Council or, depending on their legal basis, by acts of the Council only. Furthermore, there are three agencies in the field of the Common Foreign and Security Policy (CFSP) which have been created by the Council. These are the EDA, the European Union Institute for Security Studies (EUISS) and the European Union Satellite Centre (SatCen). The attempts to streamline the structures of agencies have not been successful until now but a joint statement on decentralised agencies by the Council, the Commission and the EP from 2012 highlights characteristic structural elements, such as that the agency is independent and is steered by a management board consisting of representatives of Member States, the Commission and possibly the EP.[28] Agencies are spread all over the EU Member States. With regard to Brexit, the decision to leave the Union had immediate consequences for UK-located EU agencies, the EMA and the European Banking Authority (EBA). Following a decision by the EU27, they were relocated to Amsterdam (EMA) and Paris (EBA) in November 2017.

18.3 The EU's policy and legal framework enabling third country participation in EU agencies

The extent to which third countries participate in EU policies and programmes determines the possibilities and depth of their participation in agencies. The EU initially employed no consistent policy towards third country participation in EU policies and programmes. Decisions followed a differentiation between third European countries and depended on the legal and policy framework linking the third country to the EU. The former European Commission President Romano Prodi's 2002 remark on 'sharing everything but institutions'[29] with neighbouring states was directed at the European Neighbourhood countries (ENP) without an EU accession perspective. Prodi further explained it as 'an aim to extend to this neighbouring region a set of principles, values and standards which define the very essence of the European Union'.[30] However, these aims remained less ambitious in practice and became narrowed down to EU programmes and policies. A Commission communication mapped this out as a gradual and selective process.[31] Some of these ideas only found more detailed reflection in the comprehensive and deep trade agreements (DCTFA) with the three ENP countries, Ukraine, Moldova and Georgia recently.[32] Next to the ENP countries, accession candidates profit from a more systematic approach towards their participation in agencies. In December 1997 and 2003, the European Council explicitly stated into the direction of EU candidate countries that:

> 19. Some Community programmes (e.g. education, training and research) will be open to applicant States and this will enable them to familiarize themselves with the Union's policies and working methods. Such participation will have to be determined case-by-case, with each applicant State making a steadily increasing financial contribution of its own.
> 20. The applicant States should be allowed to take part, as observers and for the points which concern them, in the management committees responsible for monitoring the programmes to which they contribute financially, under specific arrangements adapted to the case in question. The Community agencies in which applicant countries will be able to participate will be determined on a case-by-case basis.[33]

Agency participation serves the purpose of familiarising candidate countries with the EU and its programmes.[34] Candidate countries are given an observer status and this is implemented between the EU and Turkey, for instance, in a 2002 framework agreement on the participation of Turkey in Union programmes.[35] The approach to the nearer neighbourhood countries has also progressed, as indicated above. The DCFTAs, the new generation of association agreements with Ukraine, Moldova and Georgia, explain that this association aims for political association and economic integration between the Parties 'based on common values and close links, including by increasing participation in EU policies, programmes and agencies'.[36] All of these DCFTAs include a provision on the participation in EU agencies and programmes. Thus, Article 450 of the Ukrainian Association agreement stipulates that Ukraine can

> participate in EU agencies relevant to the implementation of this agreement and other EU agencies, where their establishing regulations permit, and as laid down by these establishing regulations. Ukraine shall enter into separate agreements with the EU to enable its participation in each such agency and to set the amount of its financial contribution.[37]

From these rules, some general pre-conditions for agency participation by third European states can be deduced.

1 Participation in an agency must be relevant for an underlying association agreement's purpose and aims[38] and
2 the EU agencies' founding regulations allow for third country participation.
3 Another international agreement has to be concluded to establish the concrete conditions of participation between the Union and the third country.[39]

However, until now, only certain association agreements qualify for such third country privileged participation. These are the DCFTAs with the ENP countries, the accession association of the Western Balkan states and Turkey, the European Economic Area (EEA) agreement with Norway, Iceland and Liechtenstein and the Swiss bilaterals with the EU. These either qualify because they enable participation in the EU internal market and Schengen or have the underlying aim of familiarising the European states with EU agencies, programmes and policies. Furthermore, for ENP and accession candidates, the respective agencies are selected on the basis of case-by-case arrangements.

The purpose and aim of agency participation is organised for the following three different country groups: the EEA members (Norway, Iceland and Liechtenstein) and Switzerland concerning their Schengen participation in the European Border and Coast Guard Agency (Frontex), the EU's law enforcement agency (Europol) and the EEA countries for the internal market agencies and their internal market participation; Switzerland regarding agencies relevant for the sectoral market-access agreements;[40] and a case-by-case participation in selected agencies by ENP and accession countries due to content of the association and familiarising them with EU programmes and agencies. Especially, Schengen participation demonstrates a blurring of lines between members and non-members. The UK (until the end of the transition period),[41] Ireland and Denmark enjoy specific legal regimes when it comes to the Area of Freedom, Security and Justice (AFSJ). The UK and Ireland operate on the basis of a complex opt-in and opt-out regime,[42] while Denmark opts-in to this *acquis* under international law. This has implications for the AFSJ agencies Eurojust, Europol and Frontex and the past participation of the UK. Thus, Norway, as a non-member, is involved in Frontex with voting rights and the UK was only included as an observer without voting rights.[43] Also the Danish opt-out from the AFSJ necessitated a separate EU–Denmark international agreement to accommodate the participation in Europol.[44]

For this contribution, participation in EU agencies by third European countries is categorised into four groups: (1) *sui generis* membership by EU Member State Denmark due to its international law opt-out in Europol, Eurojust and EASO, (2) the Schengen third states' semi-membership by Norway, Iceland and Switzerland with limited voting rights in Frontex, (3) the EEA (Norway, Iceland and Liechtenstein) countries' membership in internal market agencies without voting rights and (4) the observer status and international cooperation for EEA, accession and ENP countries.[45] These categories are distinguished by the intensity of the third countries' policy participation and the necessity to integrate them related to the effective functioning of the EU policies.

18.4 Third European countries in EU agencies: four participation categories

As explained above, third country participation requires an underlying association agreement and the EU agencies' founding regulations have to allow for such third country participation. A closer look at the agencies' founding acts reveals that two forms of international participation have to be distinguished. In the first form, the founding regulations have a specific norm covering the involvement of third countries in agencies. In this case, third country participation in an agency concerns a more integrative form of cooperation which allows third countries to participate in the agency's action and its management structures.[46] An EU analytic paper in 2010 explained that a majority of agencies' founding regulations foresee participation of third countries in agencies[47] or the cooperation between the agency and a third country (while 15 are also open to cooperation with international organisations as well). The second form includes rules on international cooperation and allows agencies to organise international relations with third countries and international organisations.[48] Frontex, EASA or European Food Safety Agency (EFSA) cooperate with third states' authorities, international programmes and organisations through working arrangements.[49] And this is not limited to the European continent but extends to cooperation globally.

The example of the EBA reveals that third countries have concluded an international agreement and 'are applying Union law in the areas of competence of the agency'.[50] The European Agency for the Cooperation of Energy Regulators (ACER) requires these countries to have concluded an agreement with the EU whereby they have adopted and are applying Union law in the field of energy and if relevant in the fields of environment and competition. Some agencies' founding regulations are rather detailed, as the Fundamental Rights Agency (FRA) demonstrates, which also refers explicitly to the integration of candidates in its preamble.[51] This is specified in more detail in Article 28 of the Founding Regulation:

1. The Agency shall be open to the participation of candidate countries as observers.
2. The participation and the respective modalities shall be determined by a decision of the relevant Association Council, taking into account the specific status of each country. The decision shall indicate in particular the nature, extent and manner in which these countries will participate in the Agency's work, within the framework set in Articles 4 and 5, including provisions relating to participation in initiatives undertaken by the Agency, to the financial contribution and to staff. The decision shall be in line with this regulation and with the Staff Regulations of Officials of the European Communities and the Conditions of Employment of Other Servants of the European Communities. The decision shall provide that the participating country may appoint an independent person fulfilling the qualifications for persons referred to in Article 12(1)(a) *as observer to the Management Board without right to vote.* Upon the decision of the Association Council the Agency may deal with fundamental rights issues within the scope of Article 3(1) in the respective country, to the extent necessary for the gradual alignment to Community law of the country concerned.
3. The Council, acting unanimously on a proposal by the Commission, may decide to invite a country with which a Stabilisation and Association Agreement has been concluded by the European Community to participate in the Agency as an observer. In that case, paragraph 2 shall apply accordingly.[52]

Some literature sources categorise third countries in EU agencies along the lines of full membership, observers or a cooperation framework.[53] This is useful but can also be misleading. The participation has to be understood against the backdrop of EU policies to which the agencies contribute and the extent to which third countries align to policies (internal market, Schengen, enlargement) to which EU agencies contribute.[54] Also, no third country enjoys full membership of EU agencies equalling EU Member States. Exceptionally, we witness a semi-membership under clearly circumscribed circumstances with voting rights in the management board. However, the majority of third countries enjoy an observer status only, without voting rights in the management board or committees of agencies.

18.4.1 Sui generis *participation: Denmark's international law and the UK's (former) EU law opt-in into Europol and Eurojust*

This category is not the classical third country participation, but it demonstrates an important example of the current arrangements involving EU agencies in the AFSJ. The bits and pieces integration,[55] or differentiated approach, visible in this policy neglects the classical divide between EU members and non-members and could form an inspiration for the UK. The Danish arrangement in Europol comes closest to a third country arrangement because EU Member State Denmark participates in these agencies only under international law and not under EU law.[56] The attempt to revise the Danish opt-out for the AFSJ into an opt-in failed with the Danish referendum in December 2015.[57] This had consequences for the Danish participation in Europol. Europol evolved from an international organisation with a separate international legal personality established under the Europol Convention into an intergovernmental agency pre-Lisbon,[58] finally achieving its delayed 'Lisbonisation' in May 2016 under the Europol regulation.[59] A tailor-made solution for the ongoing Danish participation in Europol was necessary and was found in the international agreement between Denmark and Europol just two days before Europol lost its treaty-making capacity.[60] The arrangement in the form of the international agreement and administrative arrangement (Art. 17 of the Agreement) gives Danish police no direct search access to Europol's databases. Instead, Danish police officers will be posted at Europol headquarters in The Hague and have indirect access to data. They have acquired an observer status (without voting rights) in Europol's management board.[61] The Danish side accepted judicial remedies against the European Data Protection Supervisor, liability under EU law and jurisdiction of the CJEU. In the same vein, in October 2019, Eurojust concluded an international agreement with Denmark on criminal justice cooperation.[62]

The Danish participation under international law demonstrates a keen interest by the AFSJ outsiders to participate in AFSJ agencies. Despite the UK's decision to leave the Union, the UK made use of its right to opt-in to the Europol Regulation in May 2017.[63] The WA extends the body of EU law (the 'acquis'), including EU agencies such as Europol, to the UK during the transition period. Article 127(5) WA provides that the UK continues to have a right to opt-in to the Justice and Home Affairs (JHA) measures which amend, build upon or replace an existing measure that the UK has adopted in relation to the Schengen *acquis* or the AFSJ. However, the UK has no right to opt-in to any new JHA measures adopted under the AFSJ during the time of application of the WA. The EU may invite the UK to cooperate in relation to new measures adopted in this area. The WA, however, also states that the UK does not retain its involvement in 'decision-making and governance of the bodies, offices and agencies of the Union'.[64]

This reflects the general principle outlined above that a dividing line between members and non-EU members prevails. The former director of Europol, Rob Wainwright, stressed the important role of the UK in Europol as

> the lead Member State in several important projects that coordinate the activities of many Member States, Europol, and others, in the field of modern slavery, for example … and in combating certain forms of large-scale fraud and cocaine-trafficking. The UK is in the driving seat in coordinating highly complex, large-scale multinational operations.[65]

This justifies the question of whether the UK could qualify for a Danish deal regarding Europol and Eurojust, a deal that secured Denmark a better position than any other third country partner, and make it a unique type of cooperation partner.[66] This can be, however, denied by the conditions with which Denmark has to comply to get this special status and especially the fact that the agreement stresses Denmark's special position as an EU Member State. In addition, the preamble of the agreements emphasises the Danish participation in Schengen and the Nordic passport union.[67]

Instead, the UK's position is more comparable to the non-EU members Norway, Iceland and Liechtenstein, whose positions are influenced by the participation in EU policies such as the internal market or Schengen. Yet, it appears that the UK's lack of commitment to participate in Schengen could have implications on the extent to which the EU can and will facilitate access to Europol. At least it is clear that the tailor-made solution for Denmark will not be copied in the UK.

18.4.2 Schengen states' functional semi-membership in Frontex

A unique status exists for the EEA states (Norway, Iceland and Liechtenstein)[68] and Switzerland, which have agreed to apply the Schengen rules. The Frontex Regulation preamble covers this situation. In the case of Norway and Iceland, arrangements have been agreed for their participation in Frontex, including provisions on financial contributions and staff.[69] The same has also been agreed with Switzerland and Liechtenstein.[70] In all of these cases, it is ensured that these countries are represented on the Frontex Management Board and have voting rights 'as regards decisions on specific activities to be carried out at its external borders' and

> as regards decisions on specific activities under Article 3 (joint operations and pilot projects at external borders), Article 7 (management of technical equipment), Article 8 (support for Member States in the circumstances requiring increased technical and operational assistance at external borders) and Article 9(1), first sentence (joint return operations) to be carried out with human resources and/or equipment made available by Switzerland.[71]

Functional membership in Frontex is necessary for the EEA countries and Switzerland, which are associated to the Schengen *acquis*. For this reason, Switzerland and Liechtenstein concluded an international agreement with the EU in 2010, explaining the detailed conditions of participation. Both countries have voting rights in the Management Board for 'decisions on specific activities to be carried out at its external borders' and 'specific activities', joint operations and pilot projects, to be carried out with human resources and equipment from these countries. In return, these countries commit to a financial contribution, accept the legal status and liability rules and the jurisdiction of the CJEU in line with Article 19(2), (4) of the Frontex founding Regulation 2007/2004.[72] During its membership, the UK already attempted to participate in Frontex when Frontex was established according to Regulation 2007/2004.[73] However, this was denied by the Court as it was a measure developing the provisions of the Schengen *acquis* in which the UK did not participate.[74] The UK, however, has attended Frontex Management Board meetings as an observer in the past, but without the right to vote. The UK also participated in operations, although this had to be authorised on a case-by-case basis by an absolute majority of the Frontex Management Board.[75] One notable example of this was the deployment of the HMS *Bulwark* as part of Operation Triton in the summer of 2015, during which it rescued over 4,747 people. That year, the UK participated in at least six separate Frontex operations, and organised a Joint Return Operation to Albania. This cooperation is also supported by exchanges of border surveillance data. Article 19 of Regulation 1052/2013, which established the Eurosur surveillance system, also empowers Member States (but not Frontex directly) to conclude bilateral or multilateral agreements with the UK and Ireland, allowing them to share certain limited sets of data and information. However, as the UK is not interested in applying the Schengen *acquis*, it will not be able to profit from a similar privileged status as applied to Schengen third states.

18.4.3 Members without voting rights in internal market related agencies (EEA countries)

Most of the country groups mentioned above, EEA, ENP countries and candidate countries, qualify to be observers only. This observer status provides them with access to the know-how of the agencies, but does not endow them with any – to use the EEA terminology – decision-*making*, but rather leaves them with decision-*shaping* influence.[76] However, the EEA countries applying EEA relevant *acquis* have to be distinguished from this group. They form a separate subcategory to ensure the proper application of the internal market *acquis* and the involvement of EU agencies in it. Internal market relevant agencies provide the EEA countries with a separate status as 'members without voting rights' which distinguishes them from other observers, such as those from accession candidates and ENP countries. EASA stipulates in Article 1 of its rules of procedure of the management board that

> the term 'member' or 'members' means a representative of a Member State of the European Union and a representative of the European Commission, being 'member with voting right' as well as a representative from Liechtenstein, Iceland, Norway and Switzerland, being 'member without voting right'.[77]

The EFSA's Advisory Forum comprises representatives of the national food safety authorities of the 27 EU Member States, Iceland and Norway. Each national authority is responsible for risk assessment of the food chain at the national level, although the exact roles may vary by country. Observers from Switzerland and the EU candidate countries also attend Advisory Forum meetings. ECHA foresees in its rules of procedures that the Management Board may also include one observer of each EEA–EFTA Member State appointed by the corresponding authorities for a maximum term of four years as soon as the EEA Joint Committee decides on participation of EEA/EFTA states in the work of the ECHA.[78] EMA does not cover third country participation in its founding regulation but the authorisation of medicine is of EEA relevance and Iceland and Norway are national competent authorities responsible for the authorisation of medicines available in the EU that do not pass though the centralised procedure. This member status without voting rights reflects the existence of an internal market between the EU/EEA countries. The UK does not strive for such complete integration in all four freedoms and the EU will also prevent a piecemeal approach towards individual freedoms to secure the integrity of the internal market.[79]

18.4.4 Observers and international cooperation of third European countries

Finally, for agencies outside the field of the Schengen *acquis*, the EEA, accession candidates and ENP countries are assigned observer status which is agreed upon on a case-by-case basis. Article 5 of the management board of EASA details the admission of observers/representatives of third countries:

> 1. The attendance as observers or experts and of persons whose opinion might be of interest shall be agreed by the Board on a case by case basis. The organisation of, and attendance at, hearings on specific matters shall be decided in the same manner.
> 2. Any State which has been accepted as a candidate for membership of the European Union shall be entitled to appoint a representative to attend the Board's meetings as observer when the accession negotiations have been finalised.

3. Representatives of European third countries having entered into agreements with the Community in accordance with Article 66 of the Basic Regulation, shall be entitled to attend the Board's meetings under the terms and conditions specified in such agreements.
4. Representatives of European third countries not covered by paragraphs 2 or 3 may be invited to attend the Board's meetings as observers provided such countries have concluded appropriate arrangements in accordance with Article 27 of the Basic Regulation.[80]

As highlighted above, such an observer status is again linked to policy frameworks of the ENP, accession candidates and the EEA. This can be provided on a case-by-case basis to the UK but requires a solid policy framework justifying such cooperation.

Most of the EU agencies' founding regulations enable international cooperation with third countries and international organisations within the existing mandate of the respective agency. The agencies will conclude working arrangements with the competent authorities of third countries and with international organisations.[81] European countries with an accession perspective have an observer status in the European Environmental Agency or EASA but countries outside the policy framework of ENP, accession or Association Agreements, such as Russia or Japan, will not participate as observers. The Russian aviation authorities, nevertheless, concluded a working arrangement with EASA. These arrangements facilitate technical cooperation, as, for instance, on the exchange of information on aircraft safety, but stop short of regulatory cooperation and standardisation.[82] For EFSA this international cooperation is defined as support for the EU in its international commitments; scientific cooperation with international organisations with responsibility for providing scientific advice or setting international standards, in the area of food and feed safety, animal health and welfare as well as plant health; and bilateral scientific cooperation with third country risk assessment organisations.[83] Hence, agencies have a supporting role in EU external relations with third countries and cannot independently set up regulatory cooperation and information exchange. Their action needs to fall into their legal mandate and requires either the approval from the Commission or the Council.[84]

Hence, all European neighbours of the Union fall into the three groups mentioned above. Nevertheless, EU agencies (e.g. EASA, EMA, ECHA and EFSA) cooperate with strategic partner authorities from Russia, the US, Japan or Canada. The UK could fall into such a category but it would be a far cry from all the advantages the UK enjoyed when fully participating in most of the EU agencies pre-Brexit.

18.5 Conclusions: reconciling the UK's vision and wishes with the EU's existing framework of participation

As highlighted above, the EU attaches conditions to third country agency participation, and this participation is clearly linked to participation in EU policies, especially the core policies such as Schengen and the internal market. The UK will have to fit into the EU's benchmarks set for extending EU policies to third countries, namely that a balance between rights and obligations exist, the autonomy of the Union's decision-making is guaranteed and that the third country does not interfere with the EU's understanding of the integrity of the EU's internal market or other EU policies.[85]

From the outset, the UK's focus is its transition into a third country with regard to the law enforcement agencies in particular. Reasons can be found in the importance of these types of agencies for the future security of both sides, the role the UK has played in these agencies in the past, but also of a flexible 'bits and pieces' nature from which the UK profited pre-Brexit. The UK's participation was characterised as a flexible opt-in and opt-out mechanism in the AFSJ policies, which came close to a third country status. In the past, the UK could opt-in to certain pieces, such as the European Arrest Warrant and Europol and this construction was only blocked for Frontex when the CJEU argued that Frontex formed a development of the Schengen *acquis* in which the UK did not participate.[86] This situation cannot improve and can only become a more static opt-in through an international agreement with all its legal and logical limits to achieve alignment in related AFSJ legislation, participation in agencies and information exchange. A qualitative difference between Denmark as an EU Member State and the UK is apparent and blocks a tailor-made Danish solution. Furthermore, the EU will insist on conditionality and safeguards in any sectoral policy agreements or association agreement. These conditions concern the autonomy of the EU's decision-making, the jurisdiction of the EU court, human rights and data protection and the evolution of the *acquis* with effective suspension or termination clauses. This chapter has revealed that this will seriously limit the UK's options to opt-in from the outside.

Notes

1 Agreement on the withdrawal of the United Kingdom of Great Britain and Northern Ireland from the European Union and the European Atomic Energy Community [2020] OJ L 29/7 (WA).
2 Former UK prime minister Theresa May speech on our future economic partnership with the European Union (2 March 2018) www.gov.uk/government/speeches/pm-speech-on-our-future-economic-partnership-with-the-european-union accessed 1 May 2020.
3 HM Government, 'The Future Relationship Between the UK and the EU' (Policy Paper, July 2018), 8, 10, https://assets.publishing.service.gov.uk/government/uploads/system/uploads/attachment_data/file/786626/The_Future_Relationship_between_the_United_Kingdom_and_the_European_Union_120319.pdf accessed 1 May 2020. See HM Government, 'Technical Note on Security, Law Enforcement and Criminal Justice' (Policy Paper, May 2018) www.gov.uk/government/publications/technical-note-on-security-law-enforcement-and-criminal-justice accessed 1 May 2020.
4 UK participation in the EU Agency for Criminal Justice Cooperation (Eurojust): post-adoption opt-in, 23 January 2019, House of Commons, Commons Select Committee, https://publications.parliament.uk/pa/cm201719/cmselect/cmeuleg/301-li/30110.htm, accessed on 5 May 2020.
5 To be precise, under the regulatory aspects for goods, air and maritime transport, security partnership, defence capabilities development and illegal migration, see Political Declaration setting out the framework for the future relationship between the European Union and the United Kingdom OJ [2020] C34/12, 1–16 (PD).
6 Ibid.
7 Council Decision 1999/437/EC on certain arrangements for the application of the Agreement concluded by the Council of the European Union and the Republic of Iceland and the Kingdom of Norway concerning the association of those two States with the implementation, application and development of the Schengen acquis OJ [1999] L 176, 31–33.
8 Art 63 (3) European Borders and Coast Guard Regulation 2019/1896 OJ 2019 L245/1.
9 PD (n 5) para 129: 'The Parties recognise the value in facilitating operational cooperation between the United Kingdom's and Member States' law enforcement and judicial authorities, and will therefore work together to identify the terms for the United Kingdom's cooperation via Europol and Eurojust.'
10 WA Preamble:

> Considering that it is in the interest of both the Union and the United Kingdom to determine a transition or implementation period during which – notwithstanding all consequences of the United Kingdom's withdrawal from the Union as regards the United Kingdom's participation in the institutions, bodies, offices and agencies of the Union, in particular the end, on the date of entry into force of this Agreement, of the mandates of all members of institutions, bodies and agencies of the Union nominated, appointed or elected in relation to the United Kingdom's

membership of the Union – Union law, including international agreements, should be applicable to and in the United Kingdom, and, as a general rule, with the same effect as regards the Member States, in order to avoid disruption in the period during which the agreement(s) on the future relationship will be negotiated.

11 Art 7 WA with the exceptions under Art 128 (5) WA.
12 See case involving Switzerland where Switzerland could not claim to be treated – comparable as a Member State – in regard to the bilateral on transport as a privileged applicant in the Art 263 TFEU procedure: Case T-319/05 *Switzerland v. Commission* EU:T:2010:367. And see generally the case law of the ECJ on the autonomy of the EU legal order: Opinion 1/17 (CETA) EU:C:2019:341.
13 PD (n 5) para 63.
14 PD (n 5) para 102.
15 See the overview with Paul Craig, *EU Administrative Law* (2nd edn, Oxford University Press 2012) 145–146.
16 Merijn Chamon, *EU Agencies* (Oxford University Press 2016) 9.
17 Case 9–56 *Meroni v. High Authority* EU:C:1958:7.
18 Case 98/90 *Romano* EU:C:1981:104: 'an administrative commission, may not be empowered by the Council to adopt acts "having the force of law"'; C-270/12 *UK v. EP/Council (ESMA)* EU:C:2014:18.
19 Paul Craig (n 15) 160; Stefan Griller and Andreas Orator, 'Meroni revisited: Empowering European Agencies Between Efficiency and Legitimacy' (New Modes of Governance Project 2007) 5, www.eu-newgov.org/database/DELIV/D04D40_WP_Meroni_Revisited.pdf accessed 1 May 2020.
20 Takis Tridimas, 'Financial Supervision and Agency Power: Reflections on ESMA' in Niamh Nic Shuibhne and Laurence W Gormley (eds), *From Single Market to Economic Union: Essays in Memory of John A. Usher* (Oxford University Press 2012) 61.
21 See on this Robert Schütze, 'Constitutional Limits to Delegated Powers' in Antonis Antoniadis, Robert Schütze and Eleanor Spaventa (eds), *The European Union and Global Emergencies* (Hart Publishing 2011) 60; and Eduardo Chiti, 'An Important Part of the EU's Institutional Machinery: Features, Problems and Perspectives of European Agencies' (2009) 46 Common Market Law Review 1395, 1404, 1420.
22 Tridimas (n 20) 61.
23 C-409/13 *Council v. Commission* EU:C:2015:217; see generally Merijn Chamon, 'EU Agencies Between Meroni and Romano or the Devil and the Deep Blue Sea' (2011) 48 Common Market Law Review 1055.
24 See, for instance, further Paul Craig, *EU Administrative Law* (3rd edn, Oxford University Press 2018) 160.
25 Chamon (n 16) 24–44.
26 This is particularly visible in the case of EFSA which was created in the aftermath of the BSE crisis. The financial crisis led to the creation of the three European Supervisory Authorities (ESAs) and, in the recent so-called migration crisis, the existing agencies Frontex and Europol were strengthened.
27 See further Ellen Vos, 'EU Agencies on the Move: Challenges Ahead' (SIEPS, 2018) http://sieps.se/en/publications/2018/eu-agencies-on-the-move-challenges-ahead/ accessed 1 May 2020.
28 'Joint Statement on Decentralized Agencies' https://europa.eu/european-union/sites/europaeu/files/docs/body/joint_statement_and_common_approach_2012_en.pdf accessed 1 May 2020. See generally, Ellen Vos, 'EU Agencies, Common Approach and Parliamentary Scrutiny' (European Parliamentary Research Service Study, 2018) www.europarl.europa.eu/RegData/etudes/STUD/2018/627131/EPRS_STU(2018)627131_EN.pdf accessed 1 May 2020.
29 Romano Prodi, 'A Wider Europe: A Proximity Policy as the Key for Stability' (Sixth ECSA–World Conference Jean Monnet Project, Brussels 5–6 December 2002).
30 Ibid.
31 Communication from the Commission to the Council and the EP on the general approach to enable ENP partner countries to participate in Community agencies and Community programmes COM(2006) 724.
32 See for instance Art 1 (2) a), Art 450–452 of the Association Agreement with Ukraine [2014] L 161/3.
33 Luxembourg European Council 12 and 13 December 1997 Presidency conclusions; Commission Communication to the Council, Participation of candidate countries in Community programmes, agencies and committees COM(99) 710 final.

34 Commission Communication to the Council, 'Participation of candidate countries in Community programmes, agencies and committees' COM(99) 710 final. See further F Coman-Kund, 'Assessing the Role of EU Agencies in the Enlargement Process: The Case of the European Aviation Safety Agency' (2012) 8 Croatian Yearbook of European Law and Policy 338.

35 Agreement between the European Community and the Republic of Turkey concerning the participation of the Republic of Turkey in the European Environment Agency and the European Environment Information and Observation Network [2001] OJ L213/112–119; Agreement between the European Community and the Republic of Turkey on the participation of the Republic of Turkey in the work of the European Monitoring Centre for Drugs and Drug Addiction [2007] OJ L323/24–33. Croatia received an observer status in the Fundamental Rights Agency (FRA) according to the EU–Croatia SAA Council Decision 1/2010.

36 For instance, Association Agreement (AA) with Georgia and Art 1 of the AA.

37 AA with Moldova: participation in Union agencies and programmes Article 140

> The Republic of Moldova shall be allowed to participate in all agencies of the Union open to the participation of the Republic of Moldova in accordance with the relevant provisions establishing those agencies. The Republic of Moldova shall enter into separate agreements with the EU to enable its participation in each such agency, including the amount of financial contribution.

AA with Georgia: participation in European Union agencies and programmes Article 380

> Georgia shall be allowed to participate in all agencies of the Union open to the participation of Georgia in accordance with the relevant provisions establishing those agencies. Georgia shall enter into separate agreements with the EU to enable its participation in each such agency including the amount of its financial contribution.

38 And in the EU's neighbourhood (so the EU's accession candidates, ENP, EFTA countries).

39 Due to the two pillar structure between the EU and EFTA countries concerning the EEA, for the EEA countries the participation in an EU agency will be organised through a Decision of the EEA Joint Committee.

40 So for EASA, Decision No 2/2019 of the Joint European Union/Switzerland Air Transport Committee set up under the Agreement Between the European Community and the Swiss Confederation on Air Transport of 10 December 2019 replacing the Annex to the Agreement between the European Community and the Swiss Confederation on Air Transport OJ L 3 (7 January 2020) 1–23.

41 Though it remains a 'frozen' status and new opt-ins are disabled according to Art 127 (5) WA.

42 See Paula García Andrade's contribution, Chapter 8 in this volume.

43 See, for instance, Decision of the Management Board of 24 March 2006 on the Frontex framework decision on practical arrangements for UK participation in Frontex operational activities.

44 See generally, Koen Lenaerts and Piet Van Nuffel, *European Union Law* (Sweet & Maxwell 2011) paras 10–028 to 10–029. Agreement on Operational and Strategic Cooperation between the Kingdom of Denmark and Europol.

45 See other attempts of categorisation: Nicolai von Ondarza and Camille Borrett, 'What the Agencies' Existing Third Country Relations Can Teach Us About the Future EU–UK Relationship' www.swp-berlin.org/fileadmin/contents/products/arbeitspapiere/Brexit_and_EU_agencies.pdf accessed 1 May 2020, or Marja-Liisa Öberg, 'Third Countries in EU Agencies: Participation and Influence' in Herwig C H Hofmann, Ellen Vos and Merijn Chamon (eds), *The External Dimension of EU Agencies and Bodies* (Edgar Elgar Publishing 2019) 204.

46 See also Öberg (n 45) 206.

47 Twenty-one were mentioned at the time and among them Frontex, EMA, EFSA, FRA, ECHA, EASA, EBA, EASO (European Asylum Support Office). See further https://europa.eu/european-union/sites/europaeu/files/docs/body/fiche_18_sent_to_ep_cons_2011-03-16_en.pdf accessed 1 May 2020.

48 See on the details Florin Coman-Kund, *European Union Agencies as Global Actors: A Legal Study of the European Aviation Safety Agency, Frontex and Europol* (Routledge 2018) and Andrea Ott, Ellen Vos and Florin Coman-Kund, CLEER Working Paper 2013/7; Andrea Ott, 'EU Regulatory Agencies in EU External Relations: Trapped in a Legal Minefield Between European and International Law' (2008) 13 European Foreign Affairs Review 4, 515–540.

49 Ibid.

50 Art 75 EBA regulation. Art 49 EFSA: have concluded agreements with the EC by virtue of which they have adopted and apply Community legislation in the field covered by the Regulation.

51 'The Agency should be open to the participation of candidate countries.'
52 Emphasis added.
53 Marko Milenkovic 'European Union Agencies and Third Countries: Increasing Opportunities Within Differentiated Integration' *Blogactiv* (Brussels, 26 January 2018); see also Nicolai von Ondarza and Camille Borrett 'Brexit and EU Agencies: What the Agencies' Existing Third Country Relations can Teach Us About the Future EU–UK Relationship' (SWP Working Paper, April 2018) www.swp-berlin.org/fileadmin/contents/products/arbeitspapiere/Brexit_and_EU_agencies.pdf accessed 1 May 2020.
54 See also in this regard, Öberg (n 45) 204–221.
55 See generally Deidre Curtin, 'Brexit and the EU area of Freedom, Security and Justice: Bespoke Bits and Pieces' (CSF-SSSUP Working Paper, 2017) www.csfederalismo.it/images/csf_sssp/csf-sssp_curtin_brexit_eu_area_freedomsecurity_5_2017.pdf accessed 1 May 2020, with reference to her own piece, Deidre Curtin, 'The Constitutional Structure of the Union: A Europe of Bits and Pieces' (1993) 30 Common Market Law Review 17.
56 This is reflected in the preamble of the Frontex Regulation:

> In accordance with Articles 1 and 2 of Protocol No 22 on the position of Denmark annexed to the TEU and to the TFEU, Denmark is not taking part in the adoption of this Regulation and is not bound by it, or subject to its application. Given that this Regulation builds upon the Schengen acquis, Denmark shall, in accordance with Article 4 of that Protocol, decide within a period of six months after the Council has decided on this Regulation whether it will implement it in its national law.

57 Declaration to minimise the negative effects of the Danish departure from Europol, following the referendum in Denmark on 3 December 2015, by the President of the European Commission, Jean-Claude Juncker, the President of the European Council, Donald Tusk and the Prime Minister of Denmark, Lars Løkke Rasmussen (15 December 2016).
58 Council Decision establishing the European Police Office (Europol) [2009] OJ L 121/37; see further, Andrea Ott, 'EU Regulatory Agencies in EU External Relations: Trapped in a Legal Minefield Between European and International Law' (EFAREV 2008) 516.
59 Regulation (EU) 2016/794 of 11 May 2016 on the European Union Agency for Law Enforcement Cooperation (Europol) and replacing and repealing Council Decisions 2009/371/JHA, 2009/934/JHA, 2009/935/JHA, 2009/936/JHA and 2009/968/JHA, OJ 2016 L 135/53.
60 Agreement on Operational and Strategic Cooperation between the Kingdom of Denmark and the European Police Office (29 April 2017).
61 Ibid, Art 8.
62 www.eurojust.europa.eu/doclibrary/Eurojust-framework/agreements/Agreement%20on%20criminal%20justice%20cooperation%20between%20Eurojust%20and%20the%20Kingdom%20of%20Denmark%20(2019)/Eurojust-Denmark-2019-10-07_EN.pdf accessed 1 May 2020.
63 See http://data.consilium.europa.eu/doc/document/ST-15753-2016-INIT/en/pdf accessed 1 May 2020.
64 Art 7 and 127 WA.
65 House of Lords European Union Committee 18th Report of Session 2017–19, 'Brexit: The Proposed UK–EU Security Treaty' (11 July 2018) https://publicatios.parliament.uk/pa/ld201719/ldselect/ldeucom/164/16408.htm#footnote-109 accessed 8 May 2020.
66 See on this 'Cooperation between Europol and Denmark, state of play after 6 months of the full implementation of the agreement' (30 April 2018).
67 Paras 5 and 6 in the preamble of the Agreement. See also on this Deidre Curtin, 'The UK and the AFSJ: Bespoke Bits and Pieces' in Federico Fabbrini (ed), *The Law and Politics of Brexit* (Oxford University Press 2017) 198.
68 The participation of EFTA countries in agencies' activities is governed by Art 82 of the EEA Agreement and Protocol 31.
69 Arrangement between the European Community and the Republic of Iceland and the Kingdom of Norway on the modalities of the participation by those States in the European Agency for the Management of Operational Cooperation at the External Borders of the Member States of the European Union [2007] OJ L 188, 19–23.
70 Arrangement between the European Community, of the one part, and the Swiss Confederation and the Principality of Liechtenstein, of the other part, on the modalities of the participation by those States

in the European Agency for the Management of Operational Cooperation at the External Borders of the Member States of the European Union [2010] OJ L 243, 4–15.

71 Ibid, Art 1 of the arrangement.

72 Art 6 of the Arrangement with Norway and Iceland. Such as limited voting rights of representatives of the Swiss Confederation and the Principality of Liechtenstein on the Frontex Management Board, financial contributions of both countries to the Frontex budget, protection and confidentiality of data, the legal status of Frontex in both countries, the liability of Frontex, the recognition by both countries of the jurisdiction of the European Court of Justice over Frontex, privileges and immunities of Frontex and its staff, and access of nationals of both countries to be engaged under contract by Frontex.

73 The former founding Frontex Regulation [2004] OJ L 349, 1–11.

74 Case C-77/05 *UK v Council* EU:C:2007:803.

75 House of Lords, 'Leaving the European Union: Frontex and UK Border Security Cooperation Within Europe' (24 April 2017) http://researchbriefings.files.parliament.uk/documents/LIF-2017-0039/LIF-2017-0039.pdf accessed 1 May 2020.

76 EASA – seven observers from Albania, Bosnia and Herzegovina, Croatia, Former Yugoslav Republic of Macedonia (FYROM), Montenegro, Serbia, UN Mission in Kosovo, and four observers from EASA's Advisory Council; ECHA – two observers from Norway and Iceland; EMCDDA – six observers from Scientific Committee, United Nations Office on Drugs and Crime (UNODC), Council of Europe, World Health Organization (WHO), Turkey and Reitox National Focal Points (spokesperson); EMA – three observers from: Norway, Iceland and Liechtenstein; European Training Foundation (ETF) – one observer each from Croatia, FYROM and Turkey; European Global Navigation Satellite Systems Agency (GSA) – two observers from Secretary-General/High Representative and European Space Agency (ESA).

77 Art 5 EASA Rules of procedures.

78 ECHA Rules of Procedure, https://echa.europa.eu/documents/10162/13608/mb_02_2007_final_rules_of_procedure_en.pdf/77282306-205c-4e66-9a2d-453f10e5dc17 accessed 1 May 2020.

79 See on this, European Council (Article 50) negotiating guidelines (Brussels, 29 April 2017); Speech by Michel Barnier at the Centre for European Reform on 'The Future of the EU' (20 November 2017); European Parliament Resolution of 13 December 2017 on the state of play of negotiations with the United Kingdom (2017/2964(RSP)).

80 www.easa.europa.eu/sites/default/files/dfu/EASA%20MB%20Decision%2006-2011%20Adopting%20the%20MB%20Rules%20of%20Procedure%20SIGNED.pdf accessed 1 May 2020.

81 See for instance Art 42 of the Regulation 2019/1149 founding the European Labour Authority [2019] OJ L 189/21–56. Florin Coman-Kund 'The International Dimension of the EU Agencies: Framing a Growing Legal-Institutional Phenomenon' (2018) 23 European Foreign Affairs Review 97; Ott *et al.* (n 48).

82 Coman-Kund (n 81) 113.

83 International Scientific Cooperation European Food Safety Authority (June 2014) www.efsa.europa.eu/sites/default/files/corporate_publications/files/iscmap1416.pdf, accessed 9 May 2020.

84 On the different forms of approval Ott *et al.* (n 48).

85 See further, for instance, Peter Van Elsuwege, 'Exporting the Internal Market Beyond the EU's Borders' in Fabian Amtenbrink, Gareth Davies, Dimitry Kochenov and Justin Lindeboom (eds), *The Internal Market and the Future of European Integration: Essays in Honour of Laurence W. Gormley* (Cambridge University Press 2019) 637–650.

86 Case C-71/05 *UK v Council* EU:C:2007:419.

19

Disentangling the UK from EU environmental agreements after Brexit

The challenges posed by mixed agreements and soft law

Teresa Fajardo

19.1 Introduction

For the United Kingdom, disentangling[1] itself from international environmental agreements that were negotiated and ratified by the European Union (EU) and its Member States will pose many challenges arising from the particularities of this field of international law. Mixed agreements and *soft law* are the main instruments of the EU's external action in the field of environmental protection.[2] They made it possible for the EU to protect the environment by supporting green multilateralism in international conferences and organisations, in particular, those of the United Nations family. They have also been incorporated into EU legislation, thus strengthening their legal nature and paving their way to national orders and overcoming national positions regarding international law. After Brexit, the UK will have to determine the way in which it will be bound both by international environmental agreements and soft law, taking into account the general requirements that have been agreed upon in the Agreement on the withdrawal of the United Kingdom of Great Britain and Northern Ireland from the European Union and the European Atomic Energy Community (Withdrawal Agreement; WA)[3] and the Political Declaration setting out the framework for the future relationship between the European Union and the United Kingdom[4] (Political Declaration). International environmental agreements and soft law also play an important role in the first Draft legal agreement for the future EU–UK Partnership presented by the EU as they serve to set out the bases for a common level playing field for the protection of the environment.[5]

In a Brexit perspective, international environmental law is a particularly sensitive field of international law because it had a seminal effect in both the EU and the domestic legal orders. Its importance dates back as far as the United Nations' Stockholm Conference on the Human Environment[6] that generated awareness about environmental problems and triggered the adoption by the European Economic Community (EEC) and its Member States of the first Programme of Action on the Environment in 1973.[7] This moment was a challenge for both the EEC and its Member States because the integration process that began with the approximation of national legislations had to accept that in the case of environmental protection, domestic environmental legislation was in its early stages or did not even exist at all. The seminal effect of international environmental law in the EEC legislation was thereafter of tantamount importance. Ever since, the UK legal order has incorporated EU environmental legislation that had transposed international environmental agreements, not hindered by any adverse consequences of its usual dualist approach towards international law instruments.[8] Since after Brexit and the transition period, international environmental law will no longer reach the UK legal order through EU law, the UK dualist approach to international law will again determine the way in which it will be bound both by international agreements and international soft law in this field. Thus, the UK will have to decide whether to transpose into its legal order international environmental agreements before ratifying them,[9] assuming a task that was the EU's responsibility before. Therefore, during the transition period and afterwards, the domestic measures and the EU regulations will be subject to a rolling over exercise that will change the references to 'the European Union' into 'the United Kingdom'.[10] However, as pointed out by Macrory and Newbigin, this process of rolling over is not guaranteed to have effect in the case of soft law of European and international origin.[11]

On many occasions, soft law declarations and accords in the field of environmental protection have received a legislative response from the EU. Hundreds of political statements, guidelines, declarations of principles and memoranda of understanding made their way into EU legislation and policies. Thus, the Rio Declaration on Environment and Development and its principles[12] and the Sustainable Development Goals[13] have been integrated in EU policies and strategies as an overarching framework for policy development and law-making process. The UK, when disentangling itself from the EU's external action and its green diplomacy, will have to take a position of its own on these relevant but non-binding instruments of green multilateralism, especially on those that were adopted in international bodies where Member States spoke on behalf of or alongside the EU.

In addition to its activities to protect the global environment, the EU has become a green normative power and a champion of multilateralism because it is through EU environmental law that international environmental agreements have reached their highest levels of compliance, thanks to the implementation by EU Member States.[14] However, after Brexit, even if the UK decides (and is allowed) to remain a party to these international environmental agreements or to enter into them in its own right, they 'do not offer comparable levels of protection to that afforded by the EU's regulatory and enforcement frameworks'.[15] The perils of lower levels of protection will be among the most important issues on the agenda of negotiations of future agreements. Notwithstanding the UK's efforts to minimise future regulatory engagements with the EU,[16] international environmental agreements and soft law may serve to establish common standards of environmental protection and a level playing field that will facilitate access to the single market.

The purpose of this chapter is to examine international environmental law, including soft law, as case studies of a broader analysis of the impact of Brexit on the status of the UK as a party to multilateral environmental agreements. Thus, the second section examines the legal implications of the UK's disentangling from multilateral environmental agreements (MEAs hereafter) by distinguishing three categories of agreements: EU-only international environmental agreements, UK-only agreements (but negotiated and ratified on behalf of the EU) and mixed agreements. The third section explores the UK's position towards the environmental soft law that EU external action contributed to bring about. This environmental soft law will serve to find a common understanding on environmental principles as shown by the Draft agreement for the future EU–UK Partnership that differs from the UK's approach to negotiations.[17] The final remarks consider the EU's possibilities to lead as a green normative power and champion of multilateralism with or without the UK as an ally.

19.2 Disengaging from multilateral environmental agreements

Most international environmental agreements create a legal regime starting from a nuclear framework convention that is further developed through protocols and non-binding accords. This is, for instance, the case for the Framework Conventions on Climate Change and Biological Diversity and its protocols. The UK's process of disengaging from the EU legal order that incorporates the more than 40 environmental agreements[18] that have been ratified by the UK and the EU,[19] will be a challenge from the point of view of both UK constitutional law and international law. In any case, the disengagement from all those treaties will have some common features, as well as particularities, depending on the sectors and formulae used to ratify and to comply with them.

Most MEAs do not regulate relations between states but establish an environmental protection regime and foresee its enforcement and implementation through the adoption of national legislation, shaping the way states exercise their sovereign competences in the field of the environment. Moreover, MEAs develop embryonic institutional systems based on a Conference of the Parties (CoP) and organs for control and promotion of compliance. The EU's transposition and compliance mechanisms have achieved further regulatory development of most MEAs that often contain provisions with different intensities of normativity. The EU institutions endorse and bring forward the tasks of controlling and promoting compliance with environmental obligations, under the control attributed to the Court of Justice of the European Union (CJEU). In the post-Brexit scenario, this system is to continue as a source of 'the interpretation of those EU rules to which the UK had agreed to adhere as a matter of international law' during the transition period, but not beyond it.[20]

Faced with this complex regulatory and institutional scenario, the British Government simply assumed that the continuity of environmental agreements was guaranteed and that no legal problems could arise from soft law instruments. Thus, in its statements throughout the process of disentangling from the EU legal order, it disregarded the complexity of the legal and political aspects related to the UK's relationships with the EU and its Member States, as well as those concerning relations with third parties. The United Kingdom of Environmental Law Association (UKELA), after completing the mapping of international agreements, criticised this view:

> These statements are ambiguous because they do not recognise that although the Government's intention to honour its international commitments after Brexit is uncontroversial, it will not be a simple task for the Government to withdraw the UK from the EU whilst remaining bound by all of these agreements, or preserving the implementation of these international commitments. … [A]s noted in the House of Lords Energy and Environment Sub-Committee report on Brexit: Environment and Climate Change: 'Those international agreements that have been implemented through EU law … present a distinct challenge'.[21]

UKELA distinguished three different categories of agreements[22] according to competences and responsibilities assumed and the possible ways of disengaging from the EU while remaining bound by them: EU-only international environmental agreements, UK-only agreements (but negotiated and ratified on behalf of the EU) and mixed agreements. These categories were included in Article 129(1) of the WA[23] establishing that 'during the transition period, the United Kingdom shall be bound by the obligations stemming from the international agreements concluded by the Union, by Member States acting on its behalf, or by the Union and its Member

States acting jointly'. This Article 129(1) was closed with a mere footnote that says 'The Union will notify the other parties to these agreements that during the transition period the United Kingdom is to be treated as a Member State for the purposes of these agreements', but nothing else was clarified regarding the UK's future status. Thus, this classification also serves to highlight some of the problems derived from the legal transition initiated by Brexit such as the need to counteract the effects of the dualist approach towards international law characteristics of the UK legal system and the future relations with third countries and the EU.

19.2.1 EU-only international environmental agreements

As far as the first category is concerned, agreements to which the EU became a party by virtue of its exclusive competence on the matter, it needs to be clarified whether and when the UK will start the process of joining these. Some authors fear that 'unless the UK ratifies these agreements itself, the backstop they provide will be lost'.[24] Thus, during the transition period, the UK, according to Article 129(4) WA,

> may negotiate, sign and ratify international agreements entered into in its own capacity in the areas of exclusive competence of the Union, provided those agreements do not enter into force or apply during the transition period, unless so authorised by the Union.

On the other hand, fear that 'the UK will lose the "backstop" they provide in terms of obligations, rights and minimum standards'[25] is overestimated considering that most obligations of these treaties are already part and parcel of UK legislation, regardless of the EU's seminal role. Unless a most unlikely clean slate effect is foreseen by the UK Government of Prime Minister Boris Johnson and is subsequently accepted by the UK Parliament, the legislation originated in the EU must be given new labels in order to guarantee compliance with international standards, or new UK legislation must be adopted in order to incorporate it. This 'rolling over' exercise will have to consider that in most cases international treaties have grown teeth through EU legislation before it moulded national legal orders. EU-only international environmental agreements are not so numerous[26] and the UK has already started to join some of them,[27] while others will require new negotiations for accession and ratification since they have been stalled for some decades, relying on EU legislation.[28] The UK will also have to join the compliance mechanisms and committees of these treaties, which in any case are 'softer' compared to the Union's strict control mechanisms.[29]

19.2.2 UK-only agreements concluded on behalf of the EU

The second category covers the UK-only agreements that were concluded on behalf of the EU.[30] From an internal perspective, these agreements have been enforced through EU legislation as in the case of the Convention on International Trade in Endangered Species of wild flora and fauna (CITES) that the EU could only join in 2015. Rolling over the EU legislation that transposed them will be the solution to avoid any infringement of international agreements that would be derived automatically from the impact of a great repeal bill. In all these cases, rolling over legislative efforts is an exercise in deleting the word 'EU' from the UK legislation and replacing it with 'UK'. In the case of the directly applicable EU regulations, the exercise might imply just a longer period of adoption but with a similar consequence: erasing the traces of the EU origin and keeping the rest. But more will be required, since environmental legislation faces the challenge of its implementation and compliance, and this sometimes necessitates a cooperative approach. As CITES shows, the synergies achieved by the EU Member States through the implementation of EU regulations and more recently with the adoption of the EU Action Plan to fight wildlife trafficking, and the plans adopted by each Member State, are put at risk. Transnational cooperation made a difference in terms of fighting environmental crime. If cooperation channels are not maintained, Brexit can jeopardise the progress that was made earlier. CITES legislation includes both the EU Wildlife Trade regulations and the UK regulations that contain enforcement powers, sanctions and fees relating to its implementation. This exercise of rolling over the EU legislation has already been undertaken in the case of CITES but has hit the wall of the status of membership and collaboration in the EU institutions, agencies and networks in the post-Brexit era, particularly in the case of EUROPOL, EUROJUST, the European Network of Prosecutors for the Environment (ENPE) or the EU Forum of Judges for the Environment (EUFJE). The updated WA did not maintain the previous ambition of continuing to be part of EU agencies and programmes since the amendments to do so were also defeated.[31] Likewise, the UK's new 'Approach on Negotiations' of February 2020 states that 'the UK is not seeking membership of EUROPOL', only cooperation on similar terms to the 'dedicated third country arrangements' that EUROPOL has with the US and other non-EU countries.[32] From now on, the UK will have to face a transnational problem that could be better solved by sharing the information of the EU-TWIX database or the collaboration with the EU Member States' law enforcement agencies.

19.2.3 Environmental mixed agreements

With regard to the third category as provided for in Article 129(1) of the WA, the so-called mixed agreements, there is a dual internal and external dimension. However, the lack of a procedural legal basis dedicated to these agreements in the EU treaties explains the lack of a formal reaction after Brexit, despite the anticipated costs. The internal dimension raises the question of the UK's compliance with environmental mixed agreements in post-Brexit times considering the effects that its dualist approach to international law can cause. Some problems concern their invocation by individuals, a theoretical question that was already analysed by Schermers many years ago:

> Let us assume, for example, that both the United Kingdom and the Community are parties to a mixed agreement. Under domestic law the British citizen cannot invoke the agreement in court, but under Community law he can. Under domestic law British courts never apply treaties, but under Community law they should do so. Does that lead to unacceptable consequences? In theory it does not, as the treaty obligations invoked under Community law are either not the same ones as those invoked under domestic law or they do not apply to the same facts.[33]

However, this does not mean that British citizens will lose the protection they have enjoyed so far, since most mixed agreements have been implemented through EU environmental legislation in their entirety and are part and parcel of the UK legal order in the same way as for the other categories covered by Article 129(1) WA. The reason for this is that most of the environmental mixed agreements started their life as substantive mixed agreements, as neither the EU nor its Member States had the competence to negotiate them alone, but most of them subsequently became so-called false mixed agreements once the EU had pre-empted the competence through the adoption of common rules. Thus, after Brexit, UK domestic compliance with these mixed agreements is so far guaranteed by the environmental legislation originating in the EU.

By contrast, the external dimension of environmental mixed agreements requires taking into account their effects towards third countries as well as the EU and the Member States, even though the UK Government has expressed its willingness to comply with them in several important public declarations by relevant authorities.[34] So, in the House of Lords Report on Environment and Climate Change, the former Minister, Dr Coffey, concurred: 'It is my understanding that as the UK is already a party in its own right, it absolutely will stick to the commitments, and is obliged to, once we leave.'[35] Other authors also believe 'that after withdrawing from the European Union, the United Kingdom will assume all the competences previously resting with the European Union and would be therefore bound automatically by all mixed agreements'.[36]

However, the status of the UK as a full party to those agreements is not so clear, since the EU and its Member States will have to agree to recognise the UK as a third party.[37] To establish that this has been done as a consequence of the WA and that it is covered under the Political Declaration does not hold as a legal assumption. The principle *pacta sunt servanda* as well as the rules of the Vienna Convention on the Law of the Treaties should be honoured to their full extent.[38] Another possible scenario would be for Member States to take the opportunity to introduce reservations – where permitted by the treaty – and interpretative declarations in respect of the UK and its territories, as will be discussed in other chapters of this volume. This was the case with Spain that incorporated a clause of territoriality with respect to Gibraltar in the Paris Agreement on climate change.[39] In the case of Gibraltar as well, the implementation of environmental mixed agreements such as the Bern Convention that was developed through the Habitat and the Bird Directives will represent an exceptional challenge. Since some of the UK and the Spanish marine areas of protection overlap,[40] the transition negotiations will expose the different levels of environmental protection that will result from abandoning the Natura 2000 Network and the EU enforcement mechanisms. The UK's international commitments to protect nature will be limited to those derived from its participation in the Emerald Network of the Bern Convention.[41]

Adaptation of mixed environmental agreements should also be necessary where the specific formula used to sign them requires adjustment as in the case of the Paris Agreement on climate change, the obligations of which were accepted by the EU and its Member States as a bloc. Thus, the UK's effort will require recalibration 'as it disentangles its "Nationally Determined Contribution" (NDC) from the EU's'. But, the recalibration of the UK effort, as Born says, 'does not affect the architecture of the Paris Agreement'.[42]

Other questions that will have to be addressed in future negotiations are those related to the environmental clauses incorporated in the legal instruments of the European Neighbourhood Policy and the Development Cooperation Policy, which are all concluded as mixed agreements. These environmental clauses are the expression of EU environmental conditionality, which makes cooperation and granting of aid to third countries dependent on accession and compliance with multilateral environmental treaties. The presence of the UK in these agreements, or a minor cooperation through funding them, is certainly not guaranteed in the future, since the British Government has an agenda of its own, possibly leaving EU environmental conditionality behind. The proposal made by Theresa May seems forgotten. She presented the formula of *cooperative accords* as the tools to channel:

> [C]ollective endeavours to better understand and improve people's lives within and beyond Europe's borders – establishing cooperative accords for science and innovation, culture and education, development and international action, defence research and development, and space, so that the UK and the EU can continue to work together in these areas, including through EU programmes, with the UK making an appropriate financial contribution.[43]

19.3 On *soft law*

Given the background of the author,[44] this contribution approaches the phenomenon of *soft law* from an international law perspective. In international law, soft law flows from the lack of consensus on sensitive areas that hinders the adoption of international binding instruments. Instead, soft law proposes a horizon of legal expectations that, in the case of environmental protection, states may or may not consider to incorporate into their public policies and legislation. The varying intensity of this emerging normativity determines future follow-ups as well as the prospects of compliance of a *pactum de contrahendo*[45] that the EU and its Member States have often honoured when adopting binding instruments and environmental policies. It is inside the realm of EU law where this *pactum de contrahendo* has been fleshed out on the many occasions where it led to legal instruments, subject to enforcement mechanisms. Environmental soft law also serves to align the EU and its Member States' goals with those of green multilateralism as promoted by UN institutions. In the perspective of Brexit, the Political Declaration setting out the framework for the future relationship between the EU and the UK is somehow a *pactum de contrahendo* that will have to be honoured by both the UK and the EU and its Member States.

Regarding international environmental soft law, international resolutions and recommendations, memoranda of understanding or accords have become part of EU legislation[46] or have been developed through their own guidelines. In this latter case, some of the international soft law instruments that became EU soft law might be repealed or ignored after Brexit. On the other hand, UK soft law can become the tool to comply with international obligations, as in the case of the Ramsar Convention on Wetlands of international importance. However, as Macrory and Newbigin fear, 'these non-legislative means of implementation can easily be changed without Parliamentary scrutiny, and if they become more common practice post-Brexit could seriously weaken the effective implementation of international obligations within the domestic context'.[47]

The discussion on the competence to participate on the adoption of soft law in international organisations is becoming more important since it can further develop in a legal sense.[48] However, it was not controversial in the case of the EU's support to the most relevant United Nations Conferences and global strategies, as the importance of the Sustainable Development Goals for the future cooperation of the UK and the EU has been recognised in the Political Declaration. These soft law instruments that incorporate the environmental principles that were codified in the EU Treaties might play a crucial role in the sensitive task of establishing mutual understanding on the levels of protection to be incorporated in future agreements and the principles informing them.

The principle of non-regression is one of the important issues at stake in the first Draft legal agreement for the future EU–UK Partnership presented by the EU. This principle serves to define the level playing field[49] that should be accepted by both the EU and the UK in future agreements, even though this principle was not incorporated in the WA. Despite the UK's commitment included in the first proposal of the EU (Withdrawal Agreement) Bill 2018[50] to adopt a non-regression principle that would guarantee high standards of environmental protection, the last version of the EU (Withdrawal Agreement) Act 2019 supressed any reference to environmental principles and the amendments to reintroduce it were rejected.[51] The Political Declaration that refers to shared values does not have the legal nature to amend this misstep,[52] but the Draft legal agreement for the future EU–UK Partnership has reintroduced it in its Article 2.30 on non-regression of the level of protection in Section 6 on Environment and Health, which proposes in its first paragraph that:

> 1. A Party shall not adopt or maintain any measure that weakens or reduces the level of environmental protection provided by the Party's law and practices and by the enforcement thereof, below the level provided by the common standards applicable and targets agreed within the Union and the United Kingdom at the end of the transition period, and by their enforcement.

In its fourth paragraph this Article 2.30 also reintroduces the environmental principles '[r]eflecting their common principles at the end of the transition period and their commitment to the 1992 Rio Declaration on Environment and Development, in giving effect to the obligations set out in this Section'. Thus,

> the Parties shall respect the following principles in their respective environmental law and practices:
>
> (a) the precautionary principle;
> (b) the principle that preventive action should be taken;
> (c) the principle that environmental damage should as a priority be rectified at source; and
> (d) the 'polluter pays' principle.

In this new proposal for the negotiations, however, the European institutions have renounced invoking the principle of a high level of protection that is also enshrined among the other principles of Article 191(2) TFEU. Article 2.30(4) also refers to the 1992 Rio Declaration – which is a soft law instrument of tantamount importance for international environmental law since some of its principles are now customary law – in order to serve as one of the bases of the 'level playing field' together with the 'common principles at the end of the transition period', which now represents the status quo for environmental protection.[53]

With a very distant position, the British government has adopted its new 'Approach to Negotiations', which does not address environmental protection in a specific section,[54] but as an element of the foreseen Comprehensive Free Trade Agreement (CFTA) where it is subordinated to other issues. Thus, the first paragraph of its Chapter 27 on Trade and Environment says:

> The Agreement should include reciprocal commitments not to weaken or reduce the level of protection afforded by environmental laws in order to encourage trade or investment. In line with precedent, such as CETA, the Agreement should recognise the right of each party to set its environmental priorities and adopt or modify its environmental laws. The Agreement should also include commitments from both parties to continue to implement effectively the multilateral environmental agreements to which they are party. The Agreement should establish cooperation provisions between the parties on environmental issues.[55]

The British Government's approach has reduced the international environmental agreements to a mere reference in the CFTA, out of sync with the main purpose. However, just as in the case of Theresa May's proposal, it has assumed that the continuity of multilateral environmental agreements is guaranteed based on a general principle of cooperation.

19.4 Final remarks

It is difficult to understand how politicians have dismissed the perils of Brexit and how it hardens all future relations in a world where cooperation is needed more than ever, especially when it comes to the protection of the environment. The EU's external action to protect the environment has revealed that its objectives could only be effectively achieved by ignoring borders that cannot stop climate change, biodiversity loss, pollution, desertification and other disasters, such as the coronavirus pandemic that threaten the planet and our lives. On its own, the environment is a sector of external action that, as former DG Environment Director Falkenberg said many years ago, leads the EU to face the risks of becoming irrelevant as an external actor due to the fact that it is no longer a main part of environmental problems such as climate change and therefore it does not have leeway to be part of the solutions. This is now another reality that the UK will have to face alone. Adding efforts and responsibilities is what has made the EU and its Member States reliable and dependable partners in green multilateralism and in the under-resourced green governance of the United Nations architecture. The UK Government has lost sight of this scenario where cooperative action is needed to make a difference.

Despite the commitments assumed in the WA and the Political Declaration, setting out a *pactum de contrahendo* between the EU and the UK, in the field of environmental agreements too many synergies and collaborations are being put at risk. The damage that Brexit will cause goes beyond sovereignty and politics in the frail framework of green multilateralism. Continuity, coherence and consistency are the pillars of diplomacy and international relations. In these fields, divorcés pay a high price for unresolved mistrust. With Brexit, loss of opportunities will have to be considered on both sides of the rupture for many reasons affecting the UK and the EU in their now-divided external actions for environmental protection. It will also require the UK to assume those managerial and unattractive tasks left to the EU green diplomacy and to start negotiating environmental agreements as one more third state party among those who by themselves do not make a difference.

On the EU side of the rupture, the exit of the UK will reveal either that some of the obstacles to the consolidation of the EU as a green normative power and champion of green multilateralism have disappeared or that, on the contrary, the Union has lost part of the diplomatic power that the UK helped to build up and that has been beneficial to both for so many years. Thus, Brexit also serves to revisit the disputes between the European institutions in which the UK was among the ranks of the resistance against losing competences through the monopoly of representation invested in the European Commission by the Lisbon Treaty. Now, in the post-Brexit situation, it has to be considered whether new possibilities will be open to those Member States claiming mixed agreements as a recast procedure for the exercise of shared external competences and representation. The only certainty is that the doubt surrounding the renegotiation of environmental agreements and soft law will be an exciting and most demanding case study during the transition period and beyond.

Acknowledgements

This research has been made possible thanks to the financing of the I+D+i Project A-SEJ-299-UGR18 of the FEDER Operational Programme 2018, 'The Redefinition of the External Action of the European Union after Brexit' (EU-External) directed by Diego Liñán Nogueras and Pablo Martín Rodríguez.

Notes

1 In his work on the UK's disentangling from the EU legal order, Odermatt explored the 'external' dimension of the process, that is, international law issues that arise concerning international treaties entered into by the EU and the UK and the 'internal' dimension, examining how international law

might play a role in disentangling the UK from the EU legal order. He also discussed the future agreements between the UK and the EU, and how international law may provide some models for the UK's future relationship with the EU. Jed Odermatt, 'Brexit and International Law: Disentangling Legal Orders' (2017) 31 Emory International Law Review 1051.

2 For an overview of this legal sector see Elisa Morgera (ed), *The External Environmental Policy of the European Union: EU and International Law Perspectives* (Cambridge University Press 2012); Teresa Fajardo, 'La Política Exterior de la Unión Europea en materia de Medio ambiente' in José María Beneyto Pérez (ed), *IX Vol. Tratado de Derecho y Políticas de la Unión Europea, Acción Exterior de la Unión Europea* (Thomson-Reuters Aranzadi, 2017).

3 See the European Union (Withdrawal Agreement) Act 2020 and the Council Decision (EU) 2020/135 on the conclusion of the Agreement on the withdrawal of the United Kingdom of Great Britain and Northern Ireland from the European Union and the European Atomic Energy Community [2020] OJ 29/1.

4 See Political Declaration setting out the framework for the future relationship between the European Union and the United Kingdom [2020] OJ C 34/01 (Political Declaration).

5 This document was transmitted to the UK on 18 March 2020, following consultation with the European Parliament and Council. It says on the website that presents it that 'It translates into a legal text the negotiating directives approved by the General Affairs Council on 25 February 2020, in line with the political declaration agreed between the EU and the UK in October 2019' https://ec.europa.eu/info/publications/draft-text-agreement-new-partnership-united-kingdom accessed 2 April 2020.

6 This was the first United Nations conference addressing the protection of the environment, www.un-documents.net/unchedec.htm accessed 2 April 2020.

7 It was set out in the Declaration of the Council of the European Communities and of the representatives of the Governments of the Member States Meeting in the Council of 22 November 1973 (Official Journal No C 112 of 20 December 1973).

8 See Henry G Schermers, 'The Internal Effect of Community Treaty-Making' in David O'Keeffe and Henry G Schermers, *Essays in European Law and Integration* (Kluwer 1982).

9 See Foreign and Commonwealth Office, Treaties and Memoranda of Understanding (MoUs): Guidance on Practice and Procedures (2014) 6, https://assets.publishing.service.gov.uk/government/uploads/system/uploads/attachment_data/file/293976/Treaties_and_MoU_Guidance.pdf accessed 10 March 2020.

10 See on this rolling-over exercise also the contribution by Adam Łazowski, Chapter 9 in this volume.

11 See Richard Macrory and Joe Newbigin, 'Brexit and International Environmental Law' (Centre for International Governance Innovation Paper, December 2017) 6–7.

12 Regarding its role, Boyle and Freestone said 'Rio Declaration is overtly intended to initiate new law for the international community of States; for this reason many of its provisions are formulated in normative and obligatory terms, although the declaration is formally non-binding'. Alan E Boyle and David Freestone (eds) *International Law and Sustainable Development: Past Achievements and Future Challenges* (Oxford University Press 1999).

13 See the Resolution of the General Assembly, 'Transforming our World: The 2030 Agenda for Sustainable Development' A/RES/70/1.

14 Thus, in the last UK Environmental Implementation Review (EIR), it is said that

> [t]he EU is committed to strengthening environmental law and its implementation globally. … The EIR is one of the tools to ensure that the Member States set a good example by respecting European Union environmental policies and laws and international agreements.

See Commission, 'The EU Environmental Implementation Review 2019 Country Report: United Kingdom' SWD (2019) 118 final.

15 See Charlotte Burns, Viviane Gravey and Andy Jordan, 'UK Environmental Policy Post-Brexit: A Risk Analysis' (Report commissioned by Friends of the Earth, England, Wales and Northern Ireland, 2018) 5.

16 Blake considers

> Of particular concern is the EU's 'level playing field' demand, laid out in the (albeit non-binding) Political Declaration for a future trading relationship. This would effectively prevent the UK from achieving regulatory autonomy or from pursuing an independent trade policy.

David Blake, 'How Bright are the Prospects for UK Trade and Prosperity Post-Brexit?' (City Research on Line, University of London, 2018) https://openaccess.city.ac.uk/id/eprint/19673/ accessed 1 February 2020.

17 See UK Government, 'The Future Relationship with the EU: The UK's Approach to Negotiations' (27 February 2020) www.gov.uk/government/publications/our-approach-to-the-future-relationship-with-the-eu accessed 1 April 2020.

18 See the list of the 40 agreements plus protocols in UK Government, 'Annex 3 The UK's International Agreements to Protect or Improve the Environment' (Policy Paper: A Green Future: Our 25 Year Plan to Improve the Environment, 2018) www.gov.uk/government/publications/25-year-environment-plan accessed 10 March 2020.

19 See UK Environmental Law Association, 'Brexit and Environmental Law: The UK and International Environmental Law After Brexit' (UKELA Report, 2017) www.ukela.org/common/Uploaded%20files/brexit%20docs/international%20env%20law%202017.pdf accessed 5 March 2020.

20 See the proposal of European Union (Withdrawal Agreement) Bill (July 2018) para 118, www.gov.uk/government/publications accessed 10 March 2020.

21 See UKELA (n 19) 6, citing European Union Committee, 'Brexit: Environment and Climate Change' (HL 2016–2017, 109). This report gathers the opinion of academia and practitioners:

> Prof Macrory, Abi Bunker, Head of Policy and Advocacy at the RSPB, and The Wildlife Trusts all argued for close parliamentary scrutiny of any changes to legislation adopted through the Great Repeal Bill, in order to maintain standards and avoid a 'race to the bottom'. In this context, we note Prime Minister Theresa May's statement on 17 January 2017 that 'it will be for the British Parliament to decide on any changes to that law [converted from the EU *acquis* into British law] after full scrutiny and proper Parliamentary debate'.
>
> *(HL 2016–2017, 109, 18, para 46)*

22 Ibid.

23 Presented to Parliament pursuant to Section 1 of the European Union (Withdrawal) Act (No. 2) 2019 and Section 13 of the European Union (Withdrawal) Act 2018, 19 October 2019. This Article 129 was not changed by the final EU (Withdrawal) Act, 23 January 2020, https://assets.publishing.service.gov.uk/government/uploads/system/uploads/attachment_data/file/840655/Agreement_on_the_withdrawal_of_the_United_Kingdom_of_Great_Britain_and_Northern_Ireland_from_the_European_Union_and_the_European_Atomic_Energy_Community.pdf accessed 5 February 2020.

24 See Burns *et al.* (n 15) 18 and UKELA (n 19) 6.

25 Ibid.

26 See the list of conventions of the UKELA Report (n 19).

27 The Minamata Convention on Mercury appears in the UKELA Report (n 19) among these EU-only conventions but the UK finally ratified it in 2018 and always considered it a mixed agreement.

28 As will be the case for the Food and Agriculture Organization Agreement on Port State Measures to Prevent, Deter and Eliminate Illegal, Unreported and Unregulated Fishing 2009 that will require negotiations for accession and to comply with the domestic procedures and the Convention on the Protection and use of Transboundary Watercourses and International Lakes in which the UK has been a signatory since 1992 but not a party.

29 In the case of the Convention for the Conservation of Atlantic Tunas 1966 ('ICCAT'), the UK ceased to be a Party to the Convention as of 1 January 1998 except in respect of its overseas territories. Now it will have to join the convention again and its Conservation and Management Measures Compliance Committee.

30 Until 2015 when the EU became a party to the CITES on 8 July 2015, see Council Decision (EU) 2015/451 [2015] OJ L 75/01.

31 Charley Coleman and Nicola Newson, 'European Union (Withdrawal Agreement) Bill: Briefing for Lords Stages' (House of Lords Briefing, 2020) 1.

32 See UK Government (n 17).

33 Schermers (n 8) 174.

34 The UKELA Report (n 19) gathers the speech of the Prime Minister, Theresa May, on the intention to preserve compliance with international law after the UK withdraws that was afterwards seconded and repeated by the Secretary of State for Exiting the European Union, the Secretary of State for the Environment, Food and Rural Affairs.

35 HL 2016–2017, 109, 14, para 48.

36 Ibid. The consulted experts, Professors Macrory and Lee also concluded that the UK would still be bound by mixed agreements.
37 See Stefano Fella, 'UK Adoption of the EU's External Agreements After Brexit' (House of Commons Briefing Paper, 2018).
38 See Odermatt (n 1); Ramses A Wessel, 'Consequences of Brexit for International Agreements Concluded by the EU and its Member States' (2018) 55 Common Market Law Review 1119.
39 The Spanish Declaration says

> In the case where this Agreement is ratified by the United Kingdom and its application extended to the territory of Gibraltar, Spain wishes to make the following declaration:
>
> 1 Gibraltar is a non-autonomous territory whose international relations come under the responsibility of the United Kingdom and which is subject to a decolonisation process in accordance with the relevant decisions and resolutions of the General Assembly of the United Nations.
> 2 The authorities of Gibraltar have a local character and exercise exclusively internal competences which have their origin and their foundation in the distribution and attribution of competences performed by the United Kingdom in compliance with its internal legislation, in its capacity as sovereign State on which the mentioned non-autonomous territory depends.
> 3 As a result, the eventual participation of authorities of Gibraltar in the application of this Agreement will be understood as carried out exclusively as part of the internal competences of Gibraltar and cannot be considered to modify in any way what was established in the two previous paragraphs.
> 4 The application of this Agreement to Gibraltar cannot be interpreted as an recognition of any rights or situations regarding areas not covered by article 10 of the Treaty of Utrecht of 13 July 1713, concluded between the Crowns of Spain and of the United Kingdom.
>
> *(United Nations Treaty Collection, https://treaties.un.org/pages/ViewDetails.aspx?src=TREATY&mtdsg_no=XXVII-7-d&chapter=27#EndDec accessed 10 April 2020)*

40 See Jesús Verdú Baeza 'Espacios marinos protegidos en el área del Estrecho de Gibraltar: Incidencia del Brexit' (2019) 10(2) Revista Catalana de Dret Ambiental 1.
41 As Jackson has remarked 'After the Brexit vote in the UK, it remains an open question whether the UK's Natura 2000 sites might become (or perhaps remain) part of the Emerald Network', Andrew L R Jackson, *Conserving Europe's Wildlife Law and Policy of the Natura 2000 Network of Protected Areas* (Routledge Research in International Environmental Law 2018).
42 Camilla Born, 'Brexit and the Paris Agreement' *Briefing Paper E3G* (June 2016).
43 Proposal of the Prime Minister, 10.
44 See Teresa Fajardo, *Soft Law*, Oxford Bibliographies (Oxford University Press 2014).
45 Owada defines

> A *pactum de contrahendo* or *pactum de negotiando* [as] a binding legal instrument under international law by which contracting parties assume legal obligations to conclude or negotiate future agreements. Despite this seemingly straightforward explanation, however, distinguishing a legally binding *pactum de contrahendo* or *pactum de negotiando* from non-binding political declaration[s] or statements of intent (Non-Binding Agreements) can be difficult in practice.

Hisashi Owada, '*Pactum of contrahendo, pactum of negotiando*', Max Planck Encyclopedia of Public International Law (OPIL, 2020) https://opil.ouplaw.com/view/10.1093/law:epil/9780199231690/law-9780199231690-e1451 accessed 10 April 2020.

46 It happened with the Copenhagen Accord in 2009 when the Union had to accept its failure to reach a binding agreement and committed itself to go beyond what was only a soft law instrument. See Declaration of the EU and its Member States, 'Expression of Willingness to be Associated with the Copenhagen Accord and Submission of the Quantified of the Economy-Wide Emissions Reduction Targets for 2020', https://unfccc.int/files/meetings/cop_15/copenhagen_accord/application/pdf/europeanunioncphaccord_app.1.pdf accessed 10 March 2020. The EU considered the Copenhagen Accord

> as a first step towards a new legally binding global climate change agreement, as if it were not the sad evidence of its failure as a normative power. Leading by example of virtuous compliance again, the EU notified in time its emission reduction targets, assuming a unilateral commitment to reduce its overall emissions by 20% of 1990 levels and a conditional offer to increase this cut to

> 30% provided that other major emitters agree to take on their fair share of a global reduction effort.

Teresa Fajardo 'Revisiting the External Dimension of the Environmental Policy of the European Union: Some Challenges Ahead' (2010) 7 Journal for European Environmental & Planning Law 365.

47 Macrory and Newbigin (n 11) 7.

48 See Theodore Konstadinides, 'In the Union of Wine: Loose Ends in the Relationship between the European Union and the Member States in the Field of External Representation' (2015) 21 European Public Law 683; Ramses A Wessel, 'Normative Transformations in EU External Relations: The Phenomenon of "Soft" International Agreements' (2020) West European Politics.

49 Draft legal agreement (n 4) ch 2.

50 Ibid, para 42. This principle of non-regression had been incorporated as inspiring the legal process of adaptation and rolling over of the EU legislation as a limit that will guarantee that UK citizens will not suffer any regression in the standards of environmental protection that they have enjoyed while being an EU citizen. See Martin Nesbit and David Baldock, 'Non-Regression and Environmental Legislation in the Future EU–UK Relationship' (IEEP, 2018).

51 Coleman and Newson (n 31).

52 Political Declaration, para 2, 3:

> 2. The Union and United Kingdom are determined to work together to safeguard the rules-based international order, the rule of law and promotion of democracy, and high standards of free and fair trade and workers' rights, consumer and environmental protection, and cooperation against internal and external threats to their values and interests. 3. In that spirit, this declaration establishes the parameters of an ambitious, broad, deep and flexible partnership across trade and economic cooperation with a comprehensive and balanced Free Trade Agreement at its core, law enforcement and criminal justice, foreign policy, security and defence and wider areas of cooperation. Where the Parties consider it to be in their mutual interest during the negotiations, the future relationship may encompass areas of cooperation beyond those described in this political declaration. This relationship will be rooted in the values and interests that the Union and the United Kingdom share. These arise from their geography, history and ideals anchored in their common European heritage. The Union and the United Kingdom agree that prosperity and security are enhanced by embracing free and fair trade, defending individual rights and the rule of law, protecting workers, consumers and the environment, and standing together against threats to rights and values from without or within.

53 The European Commission Recommendation for the negotiations of a new partnership with the UK foresees

> The envisaged partnership should ensure that the common level of environmental protection provided by laws, regulations and practices is not reduced below the level provided by the common standards applicable within the Union and the United Kingdom at the end of the transition period in relation to at least the following areas: access to environmental information; public participation and access to justice in environmental matters; environmental impact assessment and strategic environmental assessment; industrial emissions; air emissions and air quality targets and ceilings; nature and biodiversity conservation; waste management; the protection and preservation of the aquatic environment; the protection and preservation of the marine environment; the prevention, reduction and elimination of risks to human health or the environment arising from the production, use, release and disposal of chemical substances; and climate change. This should take into account the fact that the Union and the United Kingdom share a common biosphere in respect of cross-border pollution. The envisaged partnership should lay down minimum commitments reflecting standards, including targets, in place at the end of the transition period in those areas, where relevant. The envisaged partnership should ensure the Parties respect the precautionary principle and the principles that preventive action should be taken, that environmental damage should as a priority be rectified at source and that the polluter should pay.

European Commission, Recommendation for a Council Decision authorising the opening of negotiations for a new partnership with the United Kingdom of Great Britain and Northern Ireland, COM(2020) 35 final (3 February 2020). See also the Council, Supplementary directives for the negotiation of an agreement with the United Kingdom of Great Britain and Northern Ireland setting out the arrangements for its withdrawal from the European Union, XT 21004/18, ADD1 REV2, BXT 5 (29 January 2018).

54 It says

> The parameters for that future relationship are set out in the UK/EU Political Declaration of 17 October. As that Declaration makes clear, a Comprehensive Free Trade Agreement (CFTA) should be at its core. This Agreement should be on the lines of the FTAs already agreed by the EU in recent years with Canada and with other friendly countries, and this paper sets out the structure and the policy content of such a CFTA in some detail. The CFTA should be supplemented by a range of other international agreements covering, principally, fisheries, law enforcement and judicial cooperation in criminal matters, transport, and energy, and once again this paper sets out the content of such agreements in detail. All these agreements should have their own appropriate and precedented governance arrangements, with no role for the Court of Justice.

UK Government, 'The Future Relationship with the EU: The UK's Approach to Negotiations' (27 February 2020) www.gov.uk/government/publications/our-approach-to-the-future-relationship-with-the-eu accessed 1 April 2020.

55 Ibid.

20 The future of judicial cooperation in criminal matters between the EU and the UK

Chloé Brière

20.1 Introduction

Since the referendum in June 2016 and the preparation for the United Kingdom's (UK) withdrawal from the European Union (EU), numerous uncertainties have arisen. Some of them have been resolved over time, as political deals and last-minute negotiations served to solve outstanding issues. This was notably the case regarding the negotiations of the modalities under which the UK would withdraw from the EU on 31 January 2020, almost one year after the initial date of withdrawal fixed on 31 March 2019, on the basis of a revised withdrawal agreement finalised in October 2019. The uncertainty has now moved on to new issues with the beginning of the second step of negotiations, equally – if not more complex – regarding the future relationship between the UK and the EU. This process, which is supposed to be carried out in a short 11-month period, is particularly challenging. It must combine the answer to the intention of the UK to 'take back control', while preserving certain forms of cooperation elaborated and improved over its 47 years of EU membership and respecting the integrity and the coherence of the EU legal order.

This contribution addresses the possibility of reaching balanced solutions for the UK's withdrawal and future relations between the EU and the UK in one specific area of cooperation, namely judicial cooperation in criminal matters. On the basis of its external competences, the EU has developed a vast array of forms of cooperation, with varying intensities and modalities, depending among other factors, on the third country's geographical proximity, its participation in the Schengen area or its past experiences of cooperation with the EU in this field.[1] The UK's withdrawal does not therefore occur in a legal vacuum, and both its withdrawal and its future relations with the EU in criminal matters insert themselves among existing forms of cooperation. While the negotiations in the course of 2020 will shape the modalities of future EU–UK cooperation, the present chapter seeks to analyse whether it can be done in a manner that is consistent with the existing 'models' of cooperation with external partners.

Before starting to analyse these issues, it is worth recalling what the external dimension of judicial cooperation in criminal matters is. Internally, such cooperation has been developed progressively by the EU and the Member States since the 1990s, and today results in a complex set of instruments, sometimes compared to an ecosystem.[2] Aiming at combating crime, they participate in enabling national judicial authorities to conduct cross-border criminal proceedings, in a manner respecting procedural safeguards and fundamental rights. Among the instruments that form part of this ecosystem, the most known are probably the European Arrest

Warrant (EAW),[3] which provides for the surrender of suspects and convicted criminals, and the European Investigation Order (EIO),[4] which organises the collection of evidence in a different Member State. Of relevance are also Framework Decisions on the transfer of prisoners[5] or on the recognition of probation measures and alternative sanctions.[6] These instruments, often based on the principle of mutual recognition, offer mechanisms of cooperation including time limits for the execution of the requests, and pre-defined grounds of refusal, supporting smoother and faster cooperation. The EU's activities also entail the creation of a European Judicial Network[7] facilitating direct exchanges between judicial authorities, and the possibility of relying on the assistance of the EU Judicial Cooperation Agency, Eurojust,[8] in cases involving more than two Member States. Judicial authorities in EU Member States thus benefit from an unprecedented level of cross-border cooperation in criminal matters. They can also rely on traditional instruments of mutual legal assistance and extradition, which constitute the main basis for cooperation with third countries, albeit with more rigid and lengthy procedures. To further facilitate external judicial cooperation, the EU has developed various mechanisms involving third countries and international organisations active in combating crime. These forms of cooperation are sometimes based on existing multilateral instruments, such as conventions and protocols elaborated in the Council of Europe,[9] or within the United Nations,[10] or on specific instruments concluded by the EU with specific countries. In such cases, various possibilities exist ranging from ad hoc mechanisms, very close to EU standards, concluded for instance with countries participating in the Schengen area, such as Norway or Iceland;[11] to more classic international law mechanisms applicable with more distant partners, such as the agreements on extradition and mutual legal assistance concluded with the United States of America (USA)[12] or Japan.[13] Eurojust, also supports external judicial cooperation, notably via the conclusion of cooperation agreements.[14]

To determine the impact of Brexit and the definition of a future EU–UK relationship on existing external judicial cooperation in criminal matters, the chapter will be structured as follows. It will start with a brief reminder of the previous position of the UK towards the development of judicial cooperation in criminal matters within the EU (section 20.2). It will then move on to the regime applicable during the transition period, in order to analyse whether it impacts external cooperation in criminal matters (20.3). The contribution will then move to the analysis of the possible options regarding the future EU–UK relationship (20.4) and to identifying issues in which EU external relations law offers guidance (20.5).

20.2 The role of the UK in the development of judicial cooperation within the EU

The role of the UK in this field is inextricably linked to its attitude towards increased cooperation between EU Member States in criminal justice, a field very close to the powers of the States to ensure and preserve national security, and also very much reflecting the diversity of national judicial traditions. The UK's approach can be characterised as follows: the country has been both reserved about certain developments, and played an essential role for the success of others.

At first, the UK may have appeared as a State with a certain reluctance towards the development of EU instruments supporting judicial cooperation in criminal matters. With the entry into force of the Lisbon Treaty, the country extended the specific opt-out regime that applied previously to measures regarding visa, asylum and immigration. By virtue of this opt-out, provided for in Protocol 21,[15] the UK, together with Ireland, was not bound by measures adopted in the framework of the Area of Freedom, Security and Justice (AFSJ), nor by international agreements concluded in this field, or by judgments of the Court of Justice of the EU (CJEU). This opt-out regime was accompanied with a discretionary opt-in,[16] which offered the possibility to participate in new EU instruments whenever the UK considered it relevant, or when these new instruments amended a measure in which the UK previously agreed to participate. The UK used its capacity to join in a very strategic way. It sometimes indicated its decision to opt in from the moment the Commission presented its proposal and then took part in the negotiations, like for the Directive on the EIO. In contrast, on other occasions, it opted in after the text was adopted, like for the Eurojust Regulation,[17] or it excluded its participation, like for most of the Directives on procedural rights.[18] This specific regime allowed for the UK's participation *à la carte*, and inserted variable geometry in the EU area of criminal justice, whose negative consequences were pinpointed by those considering it as coherent and consistent system with weights and counterweights.[19]

In addition to this opt-out/opt-in regime, the UK also obtained a specific transitional regime concerning the 130 EU criminal justice instruments adopted before the entry into force of the Lisbon Treaty. Under Article 10 of Protocol 36, the Lisbon Treaty foresaw a specific legal regime for these instruments. From 2009 to 2014, their previous regime would continue to apply, with the optional jurisdiction of the CJEU and the impossibility for the Commission to launch infringement proceedings. As from December 2014, the instruments still in force would be subject to the ordinary EU law regime, with the full jurisdictions of the CJEU and the availability of infringement proceedings. The UK was the only Member State that obtained the possibility to withdraw from these instruments before the end of the transition period and to notify its intention to participate again in these instruments. In July 2013, the UK's authorities exercised that possibility and notified their intention to seek to opt back into 35 instruments.[20] After internal parliamentary debate, negotiations with the Commission and the Member States, and amendments to national legislation, the EU institutions adopted in December 2014 two decisions authorising the UK to take part in these 35 measures.[21] In practice, this meant that the UK triggered its opt-out from the 130 acts of the ex-third pillar *acquis*, to re-join only 35 of them.[22] No complex calculation is required to realise that it meant that certain key EU instruments, such as the Framework Decision on conflicts of jurisdiction,[23] stopped applying to the UK. This episode had already raised many comments and concerns, and it has been referred to in more recent debates about Brexit. Some commentators stressed then a feeling of déjà vu, as in 2014 already, words like 'taking back control' or 'clawing back competences' were heard.[24]

Last but not least, the UK did not take part in the abolition of internal border controls in force within the Schengen area.[25] By virtue of a separate Protocol to the Treaties,[26] it had the right to carry out checks on persons to verify their right to enter its territory and to determine whether or not to grant persons permission to enter. The UK did nevertheless have the possibility of participating in some measures of the Schengen *acquis*, notably those on judicial cooperation, and to request to take part in measures building on the Schengen *acquis*.[27] Twice the Council denied the UK the possibility of participating in specific measures, namely the 2004 Frontex Regulation[28] and the Regulation on the Visa Information System.[29] In both cases, denials led to proceedings before the CJEU, which gave the Court the occasion to highlight the need of maintaining the coherence of the Schengen *acquis*.[30]

Yet, the UK was also a driving force in the development of judicial cooperation in criminal matters. The principle of mutual recognition was first put forward by Home Secretary Jack Straw at the Cardiff European Council in 1998.[31] The idea was presented as a way to forestall attempts for supranational European integration in criminal matters and to ensure a 'lighter-touch' integration whereby cooperation between national authorities would be encouraged without modifying national laws.[32] The principle of mutual recognition was later proclaimed in the Tampere European Council conclusions of 1999.[33] It has since then been considered the cornerstone for judicial cooperation in criminal matters, and it constitutes the basis of many instruments of judicial cooperation. The UK also strongly supported and used very frequently certain EU criminal law instruments, such as the EAW. As an illustration, from 2004 to 2016, the UK surrendered almost 10,000 individuals to other EU Member States and more than 1,400 requested persons were returned to the UK.[34] Furthermore, the UK had significant weight in the development of Eurojust. Two out of five of the Presidents of Eurojust came from the UK (Aled Williams and Eurojust's inaugural president Mike Kennedy).[35] The UK also regularly participates in Eurojust's activities. In 2017, British authorities organised 34 and participated in 48 coordination meetings (ranked second behind Germany which organised 33 and participated in 61 meetings).[36] British authorities were also the authorities most involved in Joint Investigation Teams (72 in 2018, the second country being Romania with 56 JITs).[37]

The UK has thus played a contrasted but essential role in the development of judicial cooperation in criminal matters. The specific regimes it obtained did not prevent it from becoming a key partner, with whom EU Member States developed strong and well-established cooperation. As a consequence, the perspective of not being able to rely on certain EU instruments is raising serious concerns among practitioners.[38] Such concerns were already voiced in 2013 when the UK was discussing the list of measures it would 're-opt-back-in', but they are even stronger nowadays. This explains why the future of judicial cooperation between the EU and the UK has been and remains one of the many issues discussed in the withdrawal negotiations and beyond.

20.3 The legal regime applicable until the end of the transition period

As from 1 February 2020, the legal regime governing judicial cooperation in criminal matters between the UK and the 27 EU Member States has changed. Organised by the final version of the Withdrawal Agreement (WA),[39] this regime is unique, and only applies to the UK, a third country which is a former EU Member State. The text allows for the preservation of most of the cooperation mechanisms for the duration of the transition period, which may be extended beyond December 2020 (Article 132). Nevertheless, in accordance with the European Union (Withdrawal) Act,[40] the possibility of requesting an extension is at the moment foreclosed.[41]

The general provisions of the WA have an impact on the UK's participation in the work of Eurojust. As from 1 February, as EU law remains applicable until the end of the transition period, the UK remains an active participant in the activities of Eurojust, but it no longer participates in its management body (Article 7). The UK also retains until the end of the transition period its access to the networks, information systems and databases established under EU law (Article 8), which covers the Case Management System used by Eurojust.

In the field of judicial cooperation in criminal matters *stricto sensu*, the UK's withdrawal has a limited impact, provided that the requests for cooperation are made before the end of the transition period.[42] The WA preserves the continuity of ongoing judicial cooperation proceedings, by providing that 12 instruments, such as the Framework Decision on the EAW,[43] the Framework Decision on the European Criminal Records Information System[44] or the Directive in the EIO[45] continue to apply (Article 62(1)). As the UK had previously tailored its participation in pre- and post-Lisbon EU criminal law instruments, this does not cause a major disruption. It is furthermore in line with the case law of the CJEU, which had the occasion in 2018 to stress that the UK's withdrawal from the EU does not bar the execution of EAWs as long as there is no concrete evidence to suggest that the persons concerned will be deprived of the opportunity to assert his/her fundamental rights before the UK's courts and tribunals.[46] The

British authorities also retain the possibility of continuing their participation in joint investigation teams (Article 62(2)), and to share and request information from Eurojust (Article 62(3)).

The main change probably concerns the UK's participation in new EU criminal law measures, as the country retains only the possibility to opt in for proposals amending, replacing or building upon measures in which the UK previously opted in. Regarding new proposals, the UK may only be invited to cooperate with the EU Member States under the modalities foreseen for third countries (Article 127(5)), which marks the change in the status of the UK as a third country, with whom cooperation starts to form part of the external dimension of judicial cooperation in criminal matters.

Another element marks such change of status, as three Member States – namely Germany, Austria and Slovenia – declared that, during the transition period, their national executing judicial authorities may refuse to surrender its nationals to the UK pursuant to an EAW (Article 185).[47] This is due to reasons related to fundamental principles of their national law, in particular constitutional limits regarding the extradition of their nationals outside the EU. In Germany for instance, Article 16(2) of the Fundamental Law limits the extradition of nationals to situations in which the request comes from an EU Member State and/or an international court. Even though Germany, Austria and Slovenia are not the EU Member States sending the highest numbers of EAWs to the UK, these notifications are important. In cases involving nationals of these countries,[48] surrender is now barred, and other instruments, relating notably to the transfer of criminal proceedings,[49] must be applied, with additional costs and difficulties. They thus mark a first decrease in the intensity of judicial cooperation in criminal matters between the UK and the EU.

In conclusion, the WA preserves, as it does in other policy areas, in large part, existing judicial cooperation in criminal matters between the UK and the 27 EU Member States. A clear gap can nonetheless be identified: the end of the UK's participation in the European Judicial Network,[50] composed of contact points that act as active intermediaries to ease judicial cooperation, liaising either with a judicial authority of their own State or with the contact points of other Member States. Despite the usefulness of this network, as of February 2020, the UK is now considered a third country and the tools developed by the network are no longer available to practitioners. Nevertheless, the WA avoided a 'cliff-edge scenario' and ensured continuous cooperation, while the future relationship between the UK and the EU is being negotiated.

20.4 Lessons learned from existing EU external cooperation

Judicial cooperation in criminal matters counts among the fields in which both the EU and the UK share a mutual interest in maintaining close cooperation. This was already mentioned in the negotiating guidelines adopted by the European Council in March 2018,[51] and it was taken on in the Political Declaration.[52] The EU–UK future partnership 'will provide for comprehensive, close, balanced and reciprocal law enforcement and judicial cooperation in criminal matters' (para. 80), which should notably be

> underpinned by long-standing commitments to the fundamental rights of individuals, including continued adherence and giving effect to the European Convention on Human Rights (ECHR), and adequate protection of personal data, … and to the transnational *ne bis in idem* principle and procedural rights.
>
> *(para. 81)*

In order to achieve such an ambitious level of cooperation and to give shape to this future EU–UK relationship, precedents of cooperation with third countries have been referred to as potential sources of inspiration.[53] While the UK government had in the past indicated its preference for special treatment,[54] the EU has remained silent on that particular point.[55] They nevertheless became a potential parameter for framing the negotiations, so the next paragraphs will analyse the forms of cooperation developed in two key aspects of judicial cooperation, namely extradition and mutual legal assistance (MLA).

20.4.1 Options available for extradition and mutual legal assistance

The first option to be discussed concerns geographically distant third countries such as Australia, Japan or the USA, with whom the EU has developed looser forms of cooperation. The USA is the partner with whom the EU concluded its first international criminal justice agreements:[56] an agreement on extradition[57] and an agreement on MLA,[58] which contain traditional modalities of cooperation. For extradition, dual criminality requirement applies[59] and requests are transmitted through diplomatic channels.[60] The agreement is furthermore complemented by bilateral agreements concluded by the USA and each EU Member State. For MLA, traditional mechanisms also apply, with for instance requests being transferred via central authorities.[61] These agreements were later complemented by a specific agreement, known as the Umbrella Agreement,[62] which provides additional standards for the protection of personal data,[63] and the two parties initiated in 2019 discussions on exchange of electronic evidence.[64] Cooperation with the USA presents specificities linked to the importance of transatlantic cooperation in security matters and counter-terrorism, yet recent developments illustrate the importance of complying with some standards, in particular data protection standards,[65] and the CJEU has had opportunity to interpret these agreements.[66]

The EU has also been engaged in cooperation with Japan, with whom it signed in 2010 its first agreement on MLA.[67] Resulting from ten years of negotiations, the text is the first that is not complemented by bilateral agreements concluded by Member States, and it is considered a more ambitious agreement.[68] It still organises the transmission of requests through central authorities but provides a list of grounds for refusal of assistance, including notably situations in which the request concerns political offences, or the person has already been finally convicted or acquitted for the same facts (Article 11(1)). Dual criminality requirement may be waived, except when coercive measures in obtaining the evidence are required (Article 11(2)).[69]

A last and weaker form of cooperation can be found in the partnerships the EU developed with Australia and Canada, which remain very basic. As an example, the EU–Australia Framework Agreement[70] contains limited provisions on judicial cooperation in criminal matters, referring to the possibility of enhancing such cooperation on the basis of relevant international instruments, such as Conventions signed within the United Nations of the Council of Europe, and with the cooperation between relevant Australian authorities and Eurojust (Article 32(3)). These options can be disregarded – at least for the time being – as potential sources of inspiration for future EU–UK cooperation, especially in light of forms of cooperation developed with countries geographically closer to the EU.

The second option to be discussed is countries geographically close to the EU which do not participate in the Schengen area and with whom free movement of persons does not apply. Here we can for instance refer to the countries of the Western Balkans participating in the Stabilisation and Association Process. Judicial cooperation is developed on various bases: association agreements including programmatic provisions on judicial cooperation in criminal matters, regional instruments involving third countries and EU Member States, and/or bilateral instruments concluded by EU Member States. Most importantly, in its cooperation with these countries, the EU can rely on the conventions elaborated within the Council of Europe. The

European Convention of Human Rights (ECHR) is of fundamental importance, as its States parties are subject to the jurisdiction of the European Court of Human Rights (ECtHR), which can through its case law develop a level of protection of fundamental rights recognised as adequate by the EU, especially concerning procedural guarantees in criminal proceedings.[71]

In addition, specific judicial cooperation instruments are relevant: the 1959 European Convention on Mutual Assistance in Criminal Matters[72] and its two additional protocols[73] on the one hand, and the 1957 European Convention on Extradition,[74] and its four additional protocols[75] on the other hand. Although they do not fully replicate the advanced forms of cooperation elaborated within the EU, they remain very important instruments for allowing cooperation in criminal matters with non-EU countries. The 2001 Additional Protocol amends the European Convention on Mutual Assistance and introduced new provisions on the temporary transfer of detained persons, on hearing by video and audio conference, and provided for direct exchanges of requests between judicial (or administrative) authorities, and the spontaneous exchange of information. In other terms, it introduced within the legal framework of the Council of Europe forms of cooperation that are possible between EU Member States, on the basis of the 2000 EU Convention on Mutual Assistance in Criminal Matters,[76] without nevertheless reaching the same intensity of cooperation as under the EIO.

Similarly, the 1957 European Convention on Extradition fails to offer a level of cooperation as advanced as the EAW. Under the Convention, the principle of dual criminality applies and there is no exception foreseen to it. Extradition shall be granted in respect of offences punishable under the laws of the requesting and requested Parties by deprivation of liberty or under a detention order for a maximum period of at least one year or by a more severe penalty (Article 2). The Convention does not apply to political offences (Article 3) and each Contracting State has the right to refuse extradition, including on the basis of a series of grounds for refusal (e.g. risk of violation of the principle of *ne bis in idem* – Article 9, etc.). Some of these features may prevent the execution of an extradition request or cause substantial delays, notably due to the involvement of central authorities and the political dimension in cross-border cooperation.

Last but not least, the EU has also elaborated specific forms of judicial cooperation in criminal matters with third countries which are part of the Schengen area and which accept free movement of persons. These countries, such as Norway, Iceland or Switzerland, are in a particular position. They participate in the Schengen *acquis* on judicial cooperation in criminal matters.[77] In addition, Iceland and Norway have concluded with the EU two specific agreements, which allow them to benefit from the closest forms of cooperation a non-EU Member State has obtained. First, a specific Convention on surrender procedures,[78] provides for a regime close to the EAW. Although it foresees the possibility of reintroducing double criminality requirements, a higher number of grounds of refusals[79] or the possibility for States to refuse the extradition of nationals,[80] this agreement allows for smoother extradition procedures. Its entry into force was however complicated: signed in 2006, it only entered into force on 1 November 2019. The two countries also benefit from another Treaty through which certain provisions of the EU Convention on Mutual Assistance in Criminal Matters applies to their cooperation with EU Member States.[81] This offers them an advantage as certain provisions of that Convention were borrowed for their insertion in the EIO Directive.[82] However, such forms of advanced cooperation come with additional guarantees. Both texts also provide for specific political dispute settlement systems, under which the termination of the agreements may be decided.[83] They also contain a 'judicial review provision' under which parties keep under constant review the development of the case law of the CJEU and the case of the competent national courts, and regularly exchange such case law.[84]

20.4.2 Cooperation with Eurojust

Cooperation with Eurojust is in a way easier to envisage, as the agency has, like its sister agency for police cooperation, Europol, long experience of cooperating with third countries.[85] The evolution of its legal framework, namely the adoption of the Eurojust Regulation in 2018,[86] has modernised the legal framework regulating its external cooperation, without fundamentally changing its modalities.[87]

The most advanced form of cooperation is the posting of Eurojust's liaison magistrates to third countries (Article 53), whose tasks shall include 'any activity designed to encourage and accelerate all forms of judicial cooperation in criminal matters'. These magistrates would act for all EU Member States, which has important symbolic value and facilitates even further judicial cooperation with third countries, but this provision has not been used in practice yet.[88]

Cooperation can also take the form of cooperation agreements. They constitute one of the bases for the exchange of strategic and operational data with third countries. Under the Regulation, such transfer of data can take place on the basis of an adequacy decision of the Commission adopted in accordance with Directive 2016/680/EU;[89] an international agreement concluded between the EU and that third country pursuant to Article 218 TFEU;[90] or a cooperation agreement signed under the previous regime (Article 45 (1)). These cooperation agreements also permit the posting of Liaison Prosecutors at Eurojust, who have access to Eurojust's operational tools and can initiate cases requiring coordinated cross-border prosecutions. As of 2020, Eurojust has concluded 12 cooperation agreements[91] and six liaison prosecutors have been appointed.[92] The countries with whom cooperation is the most advanced are those cooperating with the EU in the field of security on the basis of other instruments, among which we can find Schengen-associated countries, countries participating to the pre-accession process and the USA.

Finally, Eurojust can still assist third countries with judicial cooperation even in the absence of a cooperation agreement. The agency can coordinate, with the consent of the Member States concerned, the execution of requests for judicial cooperation issued by a third country where these requests require execution in at least two Member States as part of the same investigation (Article 54). The agency can also intervene to assist in a case involving one Member State and a third country when there is an essential interest in providing such assistance in a specific case (Article 3(5)). This type of ad hoc cooperation is facilitated by Eurojust's network of 52 contact points, helping prosecutors to identify and contact the competent authorities in third countries.[93]

The discussions reveal that the external dimension of judicial cooperation in criminal matters has reached a certain maturity, marked by a diversity of cooperation mechanisms, not only within the EU, but also beyond. These precedents of cooperation result in a picture of concentric circles – the closer ties the third country has with the EU, the stronger cooperation is. These considerations are not necessarily limited strictly by geography, as illustrated by the close relationship developed with the USA. Yet the forms of cooperation that resemble the most the mechanisms provided under EU law were developed with countries with a particularly close relationship to the EU, being part of the Schengen area and accepting free movement of persons. They also become particularly relevant in the elaboration of the content of the future relationship between the EU and the UK in criminal matters. The question remains whether they will be a strict framework within which such cooperation will be developed; or whether new tailored-made forms of cooperation will be designed.

20.5 Possibilities envisaged by both parties

Defining the future of cooperation in criminal matters is an integral part of the negotiations on the future relations between the EU and the UK. EU criminal law instruments established unique mechanisms and actors supporting, facilitating and accelerating cooperation in this field. Whereas the WA maintained the application of key instruments, the form and substance of future cooperation mechanisms remains to be negotiated and approved by both parties. The release of their respective positions in the matter thus deserves close attention.

In conformity with the procedure applicable for the conclusion of international agreements, the European Commission presented on 3 February 2020 a proposal for a negotiating mandate, which was adopted on 25 February 2020 by the Council after amendments by the Member States.[94] Their adoption was closely followed by the British government releasing on 27 February 2020 its own approach to the negotiations.[95] Both documents are essential, as they contain indications regarding the substance of future judicial cooperation in criminal matters.

From the EU's perspective, the future agreement should provide for the UK's cooperation with Eurojust in line with arrangements for the cooperation with third countries (para. 122). On extradition, the EU supports effective arrangements based on streamlined procedures subject to judicial control and time limits to surrender persons, with the possibilities to waive double criminality for certain offences, to determine their applicability to political offences and own nationals, and to allow asking for additional guarantees (para. 123). The European Convention on Extradition may be a possibility to develop such arrangements, even though it may reintroduce politicisation of the procedure, with the necessity to obtain authorisation from central authorities and ministries, where the EAW system relies upon direct contacts between independent judicial authorities. The European Convention on Mutual Assistance is also mentioned, as it allows States parties to regulate their mutual relations on the basis of a special system (Article 26(4)), including by imposing time limits and providing standard forms (para. 124), and by facilitating the exchange of information on criminal records (para. 125).

The UK seems to share this reference to existing forms of cooperation with third countries. Its approach to the negotiations refers to Eurojust's cooperation with the USA as a precedent (paras 49–50), and to arrangements delivering fast and effective MLA, building on and improving the European Conventions (para. 52). This may be reinforced by the fact that these two Conventions were envisaged as fall-back options in case of a no-deal Brexit,[96] a possibility that may be reactivated in 2021. However, disparities may arise on future arrangements on extradition. The UK's approach is more specific and calls for a fast-track extradition agreement based on the Surrender Agreement with Norway and Iceland (para. 51).

The EU might not be ready to accept such an option, considering that this agreement was negotiated with countries participating in the Schengen area and accepting free movement of persons. In that respect, previous EU texts pinpointed among the negotiation's parameters the risk of upsetting relations with other countries,[97] which might become concrete should Iceland and Norway react negatively to the UK obtaining a similar extradition regime even though it does not participate in the Schengen area. Further tensions might arise regarding the procedural safeguards applicable in criminal proceedings. Both parties stress the importance of fundamental rights and procedural safeguards in their future judicial cooperation. However, the EU's position refers to the provision for its automatic termination if the UK denounced the ECHR, and its automatic suspension if the UK abrogates the Human Rights Act,[98] the domestic legislation giving further effect to rights and freedoms guaranteed under the ECHR (para. 118). The UK's approach supports the insertion of provisions on fundamental rights protection and suspension and termination mechanism, but it marks its preference for not specifying the way such protection would be ensured, nor the reasons for invoking the suspension or termination of the agreement (paras 31–33).

These respective positions, which may evolve during the negotiations, allow us to identify already some potentially sticky points, and the law of EU external relations may be relevant as it would potentially shape (or be modified by) their future cooperation.

20.6 Guidance from EU external relations law

As the negotiations take place, and whereas an important uncertainty remains concerning the form and content of the future relationship, EU external relations law can be of guidance. An essential question resides in the scope and nature of the competence at the disposal of the EU for the conclusion of the agreement, and whether the Member States will have to be involved. The EU treaties no longer include a provision allowing the EU to conclude agreements in the field of judicial cooperation in criminal matters.[99] The EU's current external competence could thus be implicit, and be derived from the possibilities provided for in Article 216 TFEU. On MLA, the existence of two internal instruments, the EU Convention and the EIO, may support the argument that the provisions on the matter would be an exclusive competence of the EU. However, on extradition, such reasoning may not apply. The agreement with Norway and Iceland was a mixed agreement, as evidenced by the insertion of provisions on their provisional application, pending domestic constitutional procedures in some Member States.[100] The sensitivity of extradition of States' own nationals may also support a mixed agreement, and national constitutional courts will most probably pay close attention to these provisions. In practice, although the agreement may enter provisionally into force, the necessity to obtain its ratification by each Member State might delay its full entry into force. Furthermore, some States might express reservations about certain provisions, such as those on extradition, excluding their implementation in cases involving their own nationals. These elements might lead to 'variable geometry' and differentiation in future cooperation in criminal matters between the EU and the UK.[101]

The duty of consistency in the EU's external relations may also be relevant. It could be interpreted as preventing the elaboration of a specific UK-tailored cooperation, especially in light of its status as a country not participating in the Schengen area. If interpreted strictly, this principle may prevent the possibility of replicating the surrender agreement with Norway and Iceland for the future extradition regime between the EU and the UK. Nevertheless, the EU Negotiating Directives themselves sometimes depart from such duty, granting a preferential treatment to the UK. It is for instance the case when considering the arrangements on exchange of information on criminal records. The EU seems to support future arrangements approximating those enabled by EU law, in so far as technically and legally possible and considered necessary (para. 125), when this possibility has never been agreed with any third country, not even the Schengen associates.[102] The duty of consistency may further become a bargaining tool, notably to refuse the insertion of suspension and termination mechanisms referring explicitly to the ECHR, which was also never previously agreed with any third country.[103] Their insertion in the future agreement already appeared as one of the points of divergence after the first round of negotiations.[104]

Other EU constitutional law particularly relevant in the field of external relations may also be mobilised in the course of the negotiations and beyond. As the agreement envisaged at present is an association agreement, it would be concluded in accordance with the procedure provided for in Article 218 TFEU. The consent of the European Parliament will be required, and this institution has paid in the past close attention to the protection of fundamental rights. This may lead to a strict scrutiny of the provisions ensuring the continuous respect for fundamental rights. The European Parliament may even, like it did for the EU–Canada PNR agreement,[105] request an Opinion to the CJEU to verify the conformity of the envisaged agreement with EU law, and in particular the EU Charter of Fundamental Rights.

Last but not least, should the negotiations progress too slowly or fail, the UK and EU Member States may be inclined to negotiate separate agreements outside the EU legal framework, either ad hoc multilateral agreements, or bilateral agreements. There are precedents where third countries seek to negotiate bilateral agreements in criminal matters when negotiations with the EU are too long or complicated.[106] In such a situation, the duty of sincere cooperation, binding on the EU Member States, becomes relevant. This duty may restrain the Member States' freedom to conclude bilateral agreements, even in areas of shared competences and even more so when an EU negotiating mandate has been agreed.[107]

In conclusion, the UK's withdrawal from the EU and the negotiations of new cooperation mechanisms in criminal matters offer an opportunity to take stock of the external dimension of this field and to test the application of fundamental principles of EU external relations law therein. Most importantly it will also be a field in which the dynamics of the broader negotiations on the future relations between the EU and the UK will materialise. Would the future agreement be part of a general association agreement governed by a single institutional framework, as the EU suggested?[108] Or be a separate instrument with its own governance mechanism, as advocated by the UK's government?[109] Would precedents of cooperation with third countries be taken as reference points? Or would the strong shared interest in pursuing close collaboration prevail and lead to specific arrangements? These questions are not specific to cooperation in criminal matters, and in this field, like in others, political and practical considerations may overcome legal principles and constraints.

Notes

1 On the consequences of the UK's withdrawal from the EU for external action in the AFSJ, see Paula García Andrade's Chapter 8 in this Handbook.
2 Speech by Michel Barnier at the European Union Agency for Fundamental Rights (19 June 2018) SPEECH/18/4213.
3 Council Framework Decision 2002/584/JHA on the European arrest warrant and the surrender procedures between Member States [2002] OJ L190/1.
4 Directive 2014/41/EU of the European Parliament and the Council regarding the European Investigation Order in criminal matters [2014] OJ L130/1.
5 Council Framework Decision 2008/909/JHA on the application of the principle of mutual recognition to judgments in criminal matters imposing custodial sentences or measures involving deprivation of liberty for the purpose of their enforcement in the European Union [2008] OJ L327/27.
6 Council Framework Decision 2008/947/JHA on the application of the principle of mutual recognition to judgments and probation decisions with a view to the supervision of probation measures and alternative sanctions [2008] OJ L337/102.
7 Council Decision 2008/976/JHA on the European Judicial Network [2008] OJ L348/130.
8 Regulation (EU) 2018/1727 on the European Union Agency for Criminal Justice Cooperation (Eurojust) [2018] OJ L295/138 (Eurojust Regulation).
9 European Convention on Mutual Assistance in Criminal Matters [1959] ETS 30, and European Convention on Extradition [1957] ETS 24.
10 Convention against Transnational Organised Crime [2000] UNTS 2225.
11 Council Decision 2006/697/EC on the signing of the Agreement between the European Union and

the Republic of Iceland and the Kingdom of Norway on the surrender procedure between the Member States of the European Union and Iceland and Norway [2006] OJ L292/1. Referred to as the Surrender Agreement with Norway and Iceland.

12 Agreement between the EU and the USA on extradition [2003] OJ L181/27, and Agreement between the EU and the USA on mutual legal assistance [2003] OJ L181/34.

13 Agreement between the European Union and Japan on mutual legal assistance in criminal matters [2010] OJ L39/20.

14 www.eurojust.europa.eu/about/Partners/Pages/third-states.aspx accessed 23 February 2020.

15 Protocol 21 on the position of the UK and Ireland in respect of the Area of Freedom, Security and Justice [2008] OJ C115/295; replacing Protocol 4 attached to the Treaty of Amsterdam (Protocol 21).

16 They may express their wish within three months after a proposal or an initiative has been presented to the Council (Protocol 21, art 3 (1)), or any time after the adoption of a measure (Protocol 21, art 4).

17 The Regulation was adopted in November 2018, and the UK decided to opt-in in March 2019.

18 Out of the six procedural rights directives, the UK government has decided not to opt-in in four of them (Directive 2013/48/EU on the right of access to a lawyer; Directive 2016/343/EU on the presumption of innocence; Directive 2016/1919/EU on legal aid for suspects and accused persons; and Directive 2016/800/EU on procedural safeguards for children). See British Institute for International and Comparative Law, 'FAQ: EU Criminal Justice Rights in the UK' www.biicl.org/documents/1712_faq_eu_criminal_justice_rights_in_the_uk.pdf?showdocument=1 accessed 23 February 2020.

19 See for instance Anne Weyembergh, Inés Armada and Chloé Brière, 'Critical Assessment of the Existing European Arrest Warrant Framework Decision' (Research paper for the European Parliament, 2014) 63. See also Anne Weyembergh, 'Consequences of Brexit for European Union Criminal Law' (2017) 8 New Journal of European Criminal Law 289.

20 Council Document 12750/13 (Brussels, 26 July 2013). The list of measures is available here in Vaughne Miller, 'In Brief: The 2014 Bloc Opt-Out and Selective Opt-Back-Ins' (House of Commons Briefing, 2013) www.parliament.uk/briefing-papers/SN06684/in-brief-the-2014-bloc-optout-and-selective-optbackins accessed 23 February 2020. Some of these instruments included some provisions of the Schengen *acquis*, to which the UK was already part in accordance with two Council Decisions (2000/365/EC and 2004/926/EC).

21 Council Decision 2014/857/EU concerning the notification of the UK of its wish to take part in some of the provisions of the Schengen acquis which are contained in acts of the Union in the field of police cooperation and judicial cooperation in criminal matters and amending decisions 2000/365/EC and 2004/926/EC [2014] OJ L345/1. Commission Decision 2014/856/EU concerning the notification of the UK of its wish to take part in some of the provisions of the Schengen acquis which are contained in acts of the Union in the field of police cooperation and judicial cooperation in criminal matters adopted before the entry into force of the Treaty of Lisbon and which are not part of the Schengen acquis [2014] OJ L345/6.

22 Thérèse Blanchet, 'The Brexit Impact on Criminal Justice Cooperation in Ireland' (Association for Criminal Justice Research and Development 20th Conference Report, 2017) 7.

23 Council Framework Decision 2009/948/JHA on prevention and settlement of conflicts of exercise of jurisdiction in criminal proceedings [2009] OJ L328/42.

24 Blanchet (n 22) 7.

25 For example, the Convention Implementing the Schengen Area [2000] OJ L239/19, and its chapters on mutual assistance in criminal matters, the application of the *ne bis in idem* principle, extradition and transfer of the enforcement of criminal judgments.

26 Protocol 3 attached to the Treaty of Amsterdam, now Protocol 20 attached to the Treaty of Lisbon.

27 Article 4 Protocol 19 on the Schengen acquis integrated into the framework of the EU attached to the Treaty of Lisbon [2008] OJ C115/290.

28 Council Regulation (EC) No 2007/2004 establishing a European Agency for the management of operational cooperation at the external borders of the Member States of the European Union [2004] OJ L 349/1.

29 Regulation (EC) No 767/2008 concerning the Visa Information System (VIS) and the exchange of data between Member States on short-stay visas [2008] OJ L 218/60.
30 Case 482/08 *United Kingdom vs Council (Visa Information System)* EU:C:2010:631, paras 47–48. See also Case 77/05 *United Kingdom vs Council (Frontex)* EU:C:2007:803, paras 61–62.
31 Valsamis Mitsilegas, 'European Criminal Law after Brexit' (2017) 28 Criminal Law Forum 247.
32 Ibid.
33 European Council Presidency Conclusions (Tampere, 15 and 16 October 1999).
34 Sergio Carrera, Valsamis Mitsilegas, Marco Stefan and Fabio Giuffrida, 'Criminal Justice and Police Cooperation between the EU and the UK after Brexit: Towards a Principled and Trust-Based Partnership' (CEPS and QMUL Task Force Report, 2018) 56.
35 Mitsilegas (n 31) 240.
36 Eurojust, 'Annual Report' (2017) 17.
37 Eurojust, 'Annual Report' (2018) 41.
38 For an illustration of such concerns, see the oral evidence provided by Deputy Assistant Commissioner Richard Martin, National Police Chiefs' Council to the House of Lords, Select Committee on the European Union, 3 March 2020, https://committees.parliament.uk/download/file/?url=%2Foralevidence%2F137%2Fdocuments%2F1344&slug=ceuefev1criminaljusticemitsilegasmartin030320docx accessed on 25 March 2020.
39 A previous version which was never ratified was agreed upon in 2019 (see Withdrawal Agreement [2019] OJ C66I/1), and the current version is Agreement on the withdrawal of the United Kingdom of Great Britain and Northern Ireland from the European Union and the European Atomic Energy Community [2020] OJ L29/7.
40 European Union (Withdrawal Agreement) Act 2020, s 33. See also Explanatory Notes, para 322.
41 See, for example, amendment NC12 to the Coronavirus Bill providing for a repeal of the above-mentioned provision, https://publications.parliament.uk/pa/bills/cbill/58-01/0122/amend/coronavirus_daily_cwh_0320.8-14.html accessed 23 March 2020.
42 Confirmations of receipt or arrest may be requested within ten days after the end of the transition period, where the competent authority has a doubt on whether a request has been made before the end of the transition period (Article 64 WA).
43 (n 3).
44 Council Decision 2009/316/JHA on the establishment of the European Criminal Records Information System in application of Article 11 of Framework Decision 2009/315/JHA [2009] OJ L93/33.
45 (n 4).
46 Case 327/18 PPU *Minister for Justice and Equality v RO* EU:C:2018:733.
47 Declaration by the European Union made in accordance with the third paragraph of Article 185 of the Agreement on the Withdrawal of the United Kingdom of Great Britain and Northern Ireland from the European Union and the European Atomic Energy Community [2020] OJ L29/188.
48 These notifications do not apply however to EAWs issued against EU citizens or third country nationals, who may still be executed by these countries.
49 In the absence of an EU law instrument, the matter is covered by the European Convention on the Transfer of Proceedings in Criminal Matters (1972) ETS 73, but only Austria ratified it, Slovenia signed it and Germany did neither.
50 Council Decision 2008/976/JHA on the European Judicial Network [2008] OJ L348/130.
51 European Council (Art 50) Guidelines (Brussels, 23 March 2018) EUCO XT 20001/18.
52 Political declaration setting out the framework for the future relationship between the European Union and the United Kingdom [2020] OJ C34/12.
53 See, for example, Task Force For Relations with the UK, 'Law Enforcement and Judicial Cooperation in Criminal Matters' (Internal EU27 preparatory discussions on the future relationship, 16 January 2020) 13, para 36; or UK Government, 'Security, Law Enforcement and Criminal Justice: A Future Partnership Paper' (Policy Paper, 18 September 2017) 13, para 3.
54 UK Department on Exiting the EU, 'The Future Relationship between the United Kingdom and the European Union' (Policy Paper, 12 July 2018) 57, para 6 b).
55 Task Force Article 50, 'Police & Judicial Cooperation in Criminal Matters' (Internal EU27 preparatory discussions on the framework for the future relationship, 29 January 2018) 7–8.

56 For a detailed analysis of these agreements see Valsamis Mitsilegas, 'The New EU–USA Cooperation on Extradition, Mutual Legal Assistance and the Exchange of Police Data' (2003) 8 European Foreign Affairs Review 515.
57 Agreement on extradition between the EU and the USA [2003] OJ L181/27.
58 Agreement on mutual legal assistance between the EU and the USA [2003] OJ L181/34.
59 Art 4 defines extraditable offences as offences 'punishable under the laws of the requesting and requested States by deprivation of liberty for a maximum period of more than one year or by a more severe penalty'.
60 Art 6 – directly between the Ministries of Justice.
61 Art 4 (3)a).
62 Agreement between the USA and the EU on the protection of personal information relating to the prevention, investigation, detection, and prosecution of criminal offences [2016] OJ L336/3.
63 These rules include notably clear limitations on data use, right to access to personal data and to rectification, notification in the case of data security breaches, and judicial redress and enforceability of rights.
64 See, for example, Council Report 13713/19 on the second round of negotiations in view of an agreement between the EU and the USA on cross-border access to electronic evidence for judicial cooperation in criminal matters (2019).
65 The Commission has notably issued two adequacy decisions, the latter limited to the framework provided by the EU–USA Privacy Shield (Commission Implementing Decision (EU) 2016/1250 on the adequacy of the protection provided by the EU–USA Privacy Shield [2016] OJ L207/1) and the former being annulled by the ECJ in Case 362/14 *Digital Rights Ireland* EU:C:2015:650.
66 For example, Case 191/16 *Romano Pisciotti* EU:C:2018:222.
67 Agreement between the EU and Japan on mutual legal assistance in criminal matters [2010] OJ L39/20.
68 See among others Anne Weyembergh and Irene Wieczorek, 'The Curious Case of the EU–Japan Mutual Legal Assistance Agreement', forthcoming.
69 For two Member States, Austria and Hungary, dual criminality requirement always applies.
70 Framework Agreement between the EU and its Member States and Australia [2017] OJ L237/7.
71 'Police Arrest and Assistance of a Lawyer' or 'Right Not to be Tried or Punished Twice' (ECtHR Factsheets) www.echr.coe.int/Documents/FS_Police_arrest_ENG.pdf www.echr.coe.int/Documents/FS_Non_bis_in_idem_ENG.pdf accessed 27 February 2020.
72 (n 9).
73 First Additional Protocol (1978) ETS 99; Second Additional Protocol (2001) ETS 182.
74 European Convention on Extradition (1957) ETS 24.
75 First Additional Protocol (1975) ETS 86; Second Additional Protocol (1978) ETS 98; Third Additional Protocol (2010) ETS 209; Fourth Additional Protocol (2012) ETS 212.
76 Convention on mutual assistance in criminal matters between the Member States of the EU [2000] OJ L197/3.
77 Agreement concluded by the Council of the European Union, the Republic of Iceland and the Kingdom of Norway on the association of these two states to the implementation, to application and to the development of the acquis de Schengen [1999] OJ L176/36; and Agreement between the European Union, the European Community and the Swiss Confederation on the Swiss Confederation's association with the implementation, application and development of the Schengen acquis [2008] OJ L53/52.
78 Agreement between the European Union and the Republic of Iceland and the Kingdom of Norway on the surrender procedure between the Member States of the European Union and Iceland and Norway [2006] OJ L292/1.
79 On the differences with the EAW, see Carrera *et al.* (n 34) 66–70.
80 Council document 11808/19, Notifications and declarations attached to the agreement.
81 Agreement between the European Union and the Republic of Iceland and the Kingdom of Norway on the application of certain provisions of the Convention on Mutual Assistance in Criminal Matters between the Member States of the European Union and the 2001 Protocol thereto [2004] OJ L26/3.

82 As an example, Alessandra Grio, 'The Defendant's Rights in the Hearing by Videoconference' in Stefano Ruggieri (ed), *Transnational Evidence and Multicultural Inquiries in Europe?* (Springer 2014) 119–126.
83 Agreement on the surrender procedure, Article 38 and Agreement on MLA, Article 4.
84 Agreement on the surrender procedure, Article 37, and Agreement on MLA, Article 2.
85 See the contribution by Andrea Ott, Chapter 18 in this volume.
86 Eurojust Regulation (n 8).
87 Chloé Brière, 'Cooperation of Europol and Eurojust with External Partners in the Fight Against Crime: A Legal Appraisal' in Merijn Chamon, Ellen Vos and Herwig Hofmann (eds), *The External Dimension of EU Agencies and Bodies* (Edward Elgar 2019) 59–77.
88 Laura Surano, 'L'action extérieure d'Eurojust' in Marianne Dony (ed), *La dimension externe de l'espace de liberté, de sécurité et de justice au lendemain de Lisbonne et de Stockholm: un bilan à mi-parcours* (Editions de l'université de Bruxelles 2012) 216.
89 Directive (EU) 2016/680 on the protection of natural persons with regard to the processing of personal data by competent authorities for the purposes of the prevention, investigation, detection or prosecution of criminal offences or the execution of criminal penalties, and on the free movement of such data [2016] OJ L119/89.
90 See www.eurojust.europa.eu/about/Partners/Pages/third-states.aspx accessed 3 March 2020.
91 With the following countries: Albania, Georgia, Iceland, Liechtenstein, Moldova, Montenegro, North Macedonia, Norway, Serbia, Switzerland, Ukraine and the USA.
92 Liaison prosecutors from Montenegro, Norway, North Macedonia, Switzerland, Ukraine and the USA.
93 See www.eurojust.europa.eu/about/Partners/Pages/third-states.aspx accessed 3 March 2020.
94 Annex to Council Decision, Directives for the negotiations of a new partnership with the UK (Brussels, 25 February 2020) 5870/20 ADD1 REV3.
95 HM Government, 'The Future Relationship with the EU: The UK's Approach to Negotiations' (London, February 2020) CP 211.
96 See the Law Enforcement and Security (Amendment) (EU Exit) Regulations 2019, No 742, Part 14, and its explanatory memorandum, paras 2.3, 2.9 and 2.10.
97 Task Force Article 50 (n 55).
98 Human Rights Act (1998) c 42.
99 Ex-art 38 TEU. On this explicit legal basis, see Claudio Matera, 'The External Dimension of the Area of Freedom, Security and Justice' in Ramses A Wessel and Joris Larik (eds), *EU External Relations Law* (Hart Publishing 2020) 401–436.
100 Ramses Wessel, 'Cross-Pillar Mixity: Combining Competences in the Conclusion of EU International Agreements' in Christophe Hillion and Panos Koutrakos (eds), *Mixed Agreements Revisited: The EU and its Member States in the World* (Hart Publishing 2010) 41.
101 See, for example, Dominik Brodowski, 'Judicial Cooperation between the EU and Non-Member States' (2011) 2 New Journal of European Criminal Law 33–34.
102 Steve Peers, 'Justice and Home Affairs in the Future UK/EU Relationship: Analysis of the Negotiation Positions' http://eulawanalysis.blogspot.com/2020/02/justice-and-home-affairs-in-future-ukeu.html accessed 7 March 2020.
103 See, for example, UK's approach, para 33. In the Surrender Agreement with Norway and Iceland, there is only a general reference to the ECHR in the preamble (para 11), and a provision that the agreement does not affect the protection of fundamental rights (art 1 (3)).
104 Remarks by Michel Barnier after the first EU–UK negotiation round (5 March 2020) SPEECH/20/402.
105 Opinion 1/15 *EU-Canada PNR Agreement* EU:C:2017:592.
106 See, for example, the US interest in such bilateral agreements on the exchange of e-evidence in case the negotiations with the EU take too long, mentioned by Didier Reynders before the LIBE Committee (20 January 2020).
107 On possible restrictions in ASFJ fields, see JHA Council, 'Conclusions on Readmission Agreements and the Consequences of the Entry into Force of the Amsterdam Treaty' (Council Doc 8654/99, 27–28 May 1999), and on the obligations binding on Member States, see, for example, Case 266/03 *Commission v. Luxembourg* EU:C:2005:341, para. 60, both discussed in Marise Cremona, 'Defending

the Community Interest: The Duties of Cooperation and Compliance' in Marise Cremona and Bruno de Witte (eds), *EU Foreign Relations Law: Constitutional Fundamentals* (Hart Publishing 2008) 160–164.

108 EU Directives (n 95) para 147.

109 HM Government (n 96) para 30.

Part VI

Contested and external effects of Brexit

21

The implications of the Withdrawal Agreement for Gibraltar

Is Spain taking back control?

Juan Santos Vara

21.1 Introduction

As a result of Brexit, the relations between Spain and Gibraltar are governed by the Withdrawal Agreement (WA) and the future agreements that will be concluded between the EU and the UK. The relations between Spain and Gibraltar have become international relations that will not be determined by EU law. The WA includes a Protocol on Gibraltar addressing the specific issues that the withdrawal of the UK from the EU creates in respect of Gibraltar.[1] From the beginning of the negotiations between the UK and the EU, it was clearly understood that the withdrawal of the UK from the EU would have major implications for Gibraltar.[2] Gibraltar is the last remaining colony in Europe still pending decolonization. The sovereignty over Gibraltar was ceded by Spain under the 1713 Treaty of Utrecht. However, the implications of the withdrawal did not play a major role in the referendum campaign. It is understandable that the great majority of the population of Gibraltar voted in favour of remaining in the EU.[3] It was also perceived that losing the umbrella of the EU would allow Spain to get important concessions from the UK with respect to Gibraltar for the first time in history. When the UK joined the former European Communities, Gibraltar was considered a territory for whose external relations the UK was responsible (Art. 335(3) TFEU).[4] Although Gibraltar is not an integral part of the UK, Spain had to accept the favourable legal regime achieved by Gibraltar when it joined the EU that was believed to be detrimental to the Spanish interests.[5] Even though is not an integral part of the UK, EU law applied to Gibraltar, including the four freedoms of the internal market, with a few exceptions. Now, after Brexit, the EU will have to decide how it will engage with Gibraltar, a territory that has been included in the United Nations list of 'Non-Self-Governing Territories' for many decades. In 1963, Gibraltar was included in the list of territories subject to decolonization. In 1968, the General Assembly (GA) expressly requested the UK, as the administering power, to put an end to the colonial situation of Gibraltar before 1 October 1969. The GA pointed out also that maintaining this colonial status of Gibraltar would be contrary to the purposes and principles of the Charter.[6] Since the 1960s, the GA has been calling every year on the British and Spanish Governments to reach a definitive solution to the status of Gibraltar on the basis of international law and the relevant UN resolutions. Brexit will also have an impact on the UK relationship with other territories of contested or limited sovereignty that are not dependent on the UK.[7]

The UK Government has always argued during the negotiation process with the EU that Brexit will allow it to regain its sovereignty. The core message of the Leave campaign was about 'taking back control' or asserting sovereignty. It was even argued that Brexit day would be a kind of 'UK independence day'.[8] Paradoxically, the withdrawal of the UK may be detrimental to British sovereignty in practice in relation to Gibraltar. The questions directly affecting this issue could not be addressed in the Brexit negotiations, since the dispute over the sovereignty of Gibraltar must be resolved bilaterally between the UK and Spain, as pointed out before.[9] As regards the future relations between the EU and the UK, Spain was conferred a veto power in respect of Gibraltar. The European Council guidelines adopted on 29 April 2017 stated that 'after the United Kingdom leaves the Union, no agreement between the EU and the United Kingdom may apply to the territory of Gibraltar without the agreement between the Kingdom of Spain and the United Kingdom'.[10] It is surprising that the UK Government had not mentioned the future of Gibraltar in the Article 50 notification letter of the UK's intention to withdraw from the EU, sent to the President of the European Council on 29 March 2017 because Gibraltar is not an integral part of the UK.

Much of the discussion during the Brexit negotiations focused on the status of Northern Ireland during and after the transition period. The political relevance and sensitive nature of the border between the Republic of Ireland and Northern Ireland led to a blockage of the negotiations on several occasions. Yet, there are also territorial borders between the UK and two other EU Member States in the UK's Sovereign Bases Areas (SBA) in Cyprus and Gibraltar. The solutions reached for Northern Ireland and SBA in Cyprus are completely different from the case of Gibraltar in the WA. While the SBA remain part of the EU customs territory and certain areas of the EU *acquis* and Northern Ireland will remain aligned to a limited set of EU rules, notably related to goods, and the Union's Customs Code will apply to all goods entering Northern Ireland, Gibraltar will not be linked to the EU after the transition period, unless otherwise agreed.[11]

The Protocol on Gibraltar, as well as the Protocol on Ireland/Northern Ireland and the Protocol on the SBA in Cyprus, form an integral part of the WA (Art. 182 WA). The Protocol on Gibraltar aims to adequately address any potential negative effect on the withdrawal of the UK from the EU on the close social and economic relations between Gibraltar and the surrounding Spanish territory known as 'Campo de Gibraltar'. The Protocol creates a new framework of cooperation between Spain and Gibraltar. Spain has not tried to obtain concessions over the sovereignty of the territory during the negotiations of the WA, but has focused its diplomatic efforts on addressing key issues of concern for Spain.

The aim of this chapter is to explore the implications of the WA and, in particular, of the Protocol on Gibraltar for the future of the British colony. Brexit will have important implications for different policy areas and territories and there will be a need to find practical solutions to develop the future relationship between the EU and the UK, as well as to assess the implications for various areas of contested sovereignty. First, the status of Gibraltar in international and EU law will be examined. In order to understand the demands of Spain in respect of Gibraltar during the negotiation process of the WA, it should be clarified that Gibraltar is a territory that has not yet completed its decolonization process (section 21.2). Second, the implications of the Protocol on Gibraltar and the Memoranda of Understanding (MoUs) agreed between Spain and the UK will be analysed paying particular attention to their legal value (section 21.3). Fourth, the interpretation of Article 184 of the WA gave rise to an intensive political debate in Spain in the last weeks of November 2018. It is important to examine whether the concerns raised by Spain found a satisfactory solution (section 21.4). Finally, the debate that took place as regards the Commission's proposal to modify the visa Regulation to grant UK citizens visa-free travel to the EU clearly shows that Gibraltar is able to contaminate the political debate over more substantial implications of Brexit (section 21.5).

21.2 The status of Gibraltar in international law and EU law

The UN Special Committee on Decolonization has included Gibraltar in the UN list of 'Non-Self-Governing Territories' that are still subject to decolonization since the 1960s. The UN has always stated that, in the process of decolonization of Gibraltar, the principle of self-determination is not applicable but rather that of restitution of Spanish territorial integrity.[12] From a Spanish perspective, the colonial status of Gibraltar encroaches upon the territorial integrity of Spain. The long-standing dispute over the sovereignty of Gibraltar has to be resolved through bilateral negotiations between Spain and the UK. The UN GA has always considered that the question of Gibraltar has to be settled through negotiations, taking into account the interests of the population of the colony. In the Lisbon Declaration of 1980 and the Brussels Declaration of 1984, the governments of Spain and the UK undertook to resolve the dispute in a spirit of friendship and in accordance with the pertinent UN resolutions. In 2004, the UK and Spanish Foreign Ministers and the Chief Minister of Gibraltar established a new trilateral (or tripartite) Forum for Dialogue, with Gibraltar participating on an equal basis with the UK and Spain. These trilateral talks collapsed in 2011, following the election of the Partido Popular Spanish Government, which demanded the renewal of bilateral negotiations with the UK over Gibraltar's sovereignty. The peculiar status of Gibraltar in international law has necessarily had an impact on the Brexit negotiations and has guided Spanish diplomatic efforts on this issue.[13]

In the run-up to the Brexit referendum, Spain's then Foreign Minister, José Manuel García-Margallo, had repeatedly called for joint-sovereignty proposals to be immediately revived, should the UK vote to leave the EU, arguing that Brexit offered an excellent opportunity to settle the dispute over sovereignty. After the Brexit referendum, Mr García-Margallo presented such proposals at the fourth Committee of the UN General Assembly in October 2016 as the only avenue for Gibraltar to maintain free trade and free movement with the EU after Brexit.[14] The Spanish Government proposed exercising joint sovereignty over Gibraltar as regards defence, foreign relations, border control and asylum and immigration.[15] However, the current Spanish Government, led by Pedro Sánchez since June 2018, adopted a more pragmatic approach and focused its efforts during the Brexit negotiations on resolving practical issues and not on claiming Spanish sovereignty over Gibraltar.

As a result of the Act of Accession of Denmark, Ireland and the United Kingdom of 1973, Gibraltar has enjoyed a special status in the EU.[16] It provided for certain derogations in relation to Gibraltar, including exclusion from the Common Agricultural and Fisheries Policies, and from the customs union (including VAT and common commercial policies).[17] When Spain joined the EU in 1986, it had to accept the favourable legal regime achieved by Gibraltar that was clearly detrimental to Spanish interests. As explained before, the fact that Gibraltar is just a British colony did not lead to the non-application of EU law, including the four freedoms of the internal market. However, the Act of Accession of Spain acknowledged that the Spanish accession did not have any effect on the respective legal positions of the UK and Spain with regard to the sovereignty of Gibraltar. The Court of Justice of the EU (CJEU) has recognized in several cases that Gibraltar does not form part of the territory of the UK and is a colony for whose external relations the UK is responsible.[18] The sovereignty dispute is outside the reach of EU law.[19] However, the CJEU has also been called to rule on the infringements of EU law by the UK as regards Gibraltar on several occasions.[20]

21.3 The implications of the Protocol on Gibraltar and the Memoranda of Understanding agreed between Spain and UK

The preamble to the Protocol on Gibraltar recalls that the law of the EU and of Euratom ceases in its entirety to apply to Gibraltar from the date of entry into force of the WA, so since 31 January 2020. Unlike the Protocol on Northern Ireland, no modifications were introduced in the final version of the WA agreed in October 2020 with respect to Gibraltar.[21] The Protocol on Gibraltar includes only six articles that refer to citizens' rights, air transport law, fiscal matters and protection of financial interests, environment protection and fishing, cooperation in police and customs matters and the tasks of the Specialized Committee on the implementation of the Protocol on Gibraltar established by the WA. The Protocol also creates three Spanish–British committees that will be tasked with addressing issues of concern as regards the rights of cross-border workers (Art. 1), certain environmental protection matters and fishing (Art. 4) and with monitoring and coordination between the relevant competent authorities in police and customs matters (Art. 5). These bilateral committees will report to the Special Committee on Gibraltar established by the institutional provisions of the WA, which is in charge of monitoring the implementation and application of the Protocol.[22] As it has already been pointed out 'although the Protocol is expressed in legally binding terms, most of the obligations it imposes are extremely vague, which will make it difficult to verify non-compliance'.[23] With the exception of Article 1 on citizens' rights, the rest of the provisions of the Protocol will only be applicable during the transition period.[24]

Even though Spain is not a contracting party to the WA or the Protocol, the obligations arising from it are mainly addressed to Spain and the UK since both states are obliged to cooperate on the issues included in the Protocol. The Protocol is to be implemented in accordance with the respective constitutional orders of Spain and the UK, which means that in the case of the UK the Government of Gibraltar is trusted with the implementation. The preamble to the Protocol also refers to the MoUs concluded between Spain and the UK in relation to citizens' rights, tobacco and other products, cooperation on environmental matters and cooperation in police and customs matters, as well as a bilateral agreement in relation to taxation and the protection of financial interests.

The MoUs signed in November 2018 between Spain and the UK are aimed at reducing inequality between the Rock and 'Campo de Gibraltar'. While Gibraltar has reached a high standard of living, the surrounding area of Spain suffers a very high level of unemployment. The Protocol on Gibraltar forms a package with the four bilateral MoUs signed between Spain and the UK in respect of Gibraltar.[25] In the last decades, Spain has been trying to obtain concessions from the UK in the same issues addressed by these instruments, but it has never been successful. The MoUs only came into effect when the WA entered into force and will cease to have effect at the end of the transition period, unless the UK and Spain agree to extend their application. The four MoUs also explicitly state in their preambles that they 'do not imply any modification of the respective legal positions of the Kingdom of Spain or of the United Kingdom with regard to sovereignty and jurisdiction in relation to Gibraltar'. Therefore, Spain cannot use the content of these instruments or any activity or measure taken in their application to claim sovereignty or co-sovereignty of the colony.

As regards citizens' rights, Spain and the UK are called to cooperate 'with a view to preparing and underpinning the effective implementation of Part Two of the Withdrawal Agreement on citizens' rights', in particular to frontier workers residing in Gibraltar or in Spain.[26] The MoU on Citizens' Rights establishes the basis for administrative cooperation between the competent authorities for the implementation of the withdrawal of the UK in relation to people living in the Gibraltar area and, in particular, frontier workers. Thousands of Spanish nationals from the surrounding area of Gibraltar travel every day to the Rock to work there. The MoU on Citizens limits itself to stating that Spanish citizens living or with interests in the Rock, and Gibraltarians in Spain, will not be discriminated against and 'all social benefits will be extended to workers on both sides, under current and future arrangements'. As it has been stated, 'the ultimate goal is to safeguard the interests of Spanish frontier workers in Gibraltar, avoiding major disruption to their daily lives, and to forestall negative effects on socio-economic development in the region'.[27]

The main controversies between Spain and the UK as regards Gibraltar are reflected in the Protocol. First, it is stated that EU law on air transport which did not apply to the Gibraltar airport before the date of entry into force of the WA will not be applicable afterwards. However, the Protocol establishes the possibility that in case Spain and the UK reach an agreement on the use of Gibraltar airport to make EU law applicable to Gibraltar during the transition period. However, it does not seem a feasible scenario. Second, in respect of tobacco, the Protocol requires the UK to ensure that certain international conventions on tobacco control are extended to Gibraltar by 30 June 2020 and also to ensure that there is a system of traceability and security measures for tobacco products in Gibraltar which is equivalent to EU law by 30 June 2020.[28] What is even more important for Spain, the Government of Gibraltar has committed to ensure that, by 30 June 2020, the average retail price differential of tobacco products will be no more than 32 per cent greater than in Spain for the equivalent tobacco products.[29] Gibraltar represents the biggest entry point for illegal tobacco products into Spain. It is ironic that after many years without any specific agreement on this issue, the Government of Gibraltar declares in the context of the Brexit negotiations that it is 'concerned about the health consequences of smoking and the existence of an illicit trade in tobacco in the area around Gibraltar'.[30]

Third, on the environment protection and fishing and cooperation in police and customs matters, the Protocol establishes also the basis for administrative cooperation between the competent authorities. It foresees the establishment of a Technical and Coordination Committee to improve cooperation and the exchange of information on air quality, water quality, waste management, the assessment of environmental impact for projects with a significant transboundary effect, the protection of marine habitats, the wider marine environment and bunkering activities.[31] The MoU on environmental cooperation is very important for Spain since Gibraltar has resorted in the last years to illegal activities such as placing cement and other materials in the Bay of Algeciras to expel Spanish fishermen from fishing activities in the area. The MoU on environmental cooperation 'marks an important step forward as regards the current state of cross-border cooperation between Spain and the UK in relation to Gibraltar'.[32] There has been no formal cooperation on cross-border environmental issues since 2011 when Spain withdrew from the tripartite Forum for Dialogue (Spain, UK and Gibraltar). In addition, the MoU on Cooperation in Police and Customs Matters aims to reach 'close cooperation for the correct application of criminal and customs laws in order to prevent and combat criminal offences and infringements of the criminal and customs laws applicable in Gibraltar and in the surrounding area'.[33] During the transition period European legislation remains fully applicable to the police cooperation between Spain and Gibraltar as it was applied before Brexit.[34]

Fourth, as regards fiscal matters and protection of financial interests, the Protocol establishes the basis for administrative cooperation between the competent authorities for achieving full transparency in tax matters, and in respect of protecting financial interests. The UK also commits to international standards in this area being complied with in Gibraltar, in particular the standards of the G20 and Organisation for Economic Co-operation and Development (OECD) on transparency and harmful tax practices. It is worth mentioning that the UK accepted to negotiate with Spain, for the first time in history, an international agreement aiming to reduce the unfair competition from Gibraltar, where many businesses choose to register because of the lower taxes even though their activities take place in Spain.[35] As a result of Brexit, an agreement was signed between Spain and the UK in March 2019 aiming to improve cooperation in the field of taxation.[36] The taxation agreement aims to assure a high level of cooperation from the Gibraltar competent tax authorities with Spain. It is important to point out that the Agreement is the first international treaty signed by the UK and Spain with respect to Gibraltar since the Treaty of Utrecht in 1713. It is an agreement that commits Gibraltar to aligning with EU law on matters related to transparency, administrative cooperation, harmful tax practices and money laundering after Brexit.[37] Brexit by itself will not allow Spain to assert its sovereignty in relation to Gibraltar, but it has given Spain an excellent opportunity to 'take back control' over many issues of serious concern to Spain and, in particular, the fight against fraud and tax evasion. The taxation agreement was conceived to be applicable even in the case of Brexit not having taken place.

The British Government and the Gibraltar Government have also developed a document called 'Concordat' concerning the implementation of the Gibraltar Protocol and related MoUs. It seems that the British Government wishes to reassure Gibraltar that Brexit will not change the internal constitutional arrangements. The Concordat states that 'the implementation of the Protocol will fully respect the constitutional arrangements in place in respect of Gibraltar and in particular the Constitution of Gibraltar of 2006'.[38] For this reason, the Gibraltar authorities will be vested with the powers of implementation in relevant areas covered by the Protocol even though the UK is responsible in international law for compliance with the Protocol. Since the Government of Gibraltar is worried about its future relationship with Spain after Brexit, the Concordat states that the British Government shares the objective 'to secure a future relationship for Gibraltar which appropriately reflects its particular geographic, socio-economic and constitutional characteristics and needs'.

It is very important to analyse the legal effects of the MoUs signed between Spain and the UK in respect of Gibraltar. The relevance of non-binding agreements in international law is far from new.[39] States and international organizations establish relations with other subjects of international law not only by concluding international agreements, but also in the form of non-binding instruments, which are often formally designated as MoUs, joint declarations, joint actions, joint codes of conduct or similar terms. Even if such instruments are not legally binding, they set out the framework for cooperation in several fields. The increasing use of non-binding agreements is explained by the flexibility that they infuse in EU external relations.[40] In addition, non-binding agreements may be more suitable to the political sensitivity of the subject of the agreements or to its changing nature.[41]

As regards the legal value of the MoUs signed between the UK and Spain, it must be recalled that international law follows a non-formalist approach to determine the legal effects of international instruments. In practice, attention should be paid to the intention of the parties and not only to the denomination of the instrument.[42] Both the text and context of the MoUs on Gibraltar clearly support the view that Spain and the UK intended the instruments not to be legally binding. The use of terms that are common in non-binding instruments such as 'will' or 'may', the procedure followed for their conclusion and the lack of official publication of the texts confirm that no legal obligations arise from them between the relevant states. On the contrary, the Protocol on Gibraltar states clearly that Spain and the UK intended to conclude an international treaty on taxation and the protection of financial interests from the beginning of the Brexit negotiations. In conclusion, the Brexit negotiations have allowed Spain to reach an agreement with the UK on practical issues which have caused serious concerns in Spain in the last decades, such as the smuggling of tobacco products, environmental problems and unfair fiscal competition from Gibraltar.

21.4 Gibraltar and the territorial application of the Withdrawal Agreement

Article 3(1) b of the WA makes clear that any reference in the Agreement to the UK is, when the context so requires, to be understood as referring also to Gibraltar 'to the extent that Union law was applicable to it before the date of entry into force of this Agreement'. However, Article 184 of the WA devoted to the negotiations on the future relationship between the EU and the UK states that both parties will use 'their best endeavors, in good faith and in full respect of their respective legal orders, to take the necessary steps to negotiate expeditiously the agreements governing their future relationship'. Since this provision does not refer to the need to get consent from the Spanish Government to apply any future agreement to Gibraltar, it was interpreted by Spain as disregarding the European Council guidelines of 29 April 2017 which established that after the UK left the Union, no agreement between the EU and the UK could apply to the territory of Gibraltar without the consent of Spain.[43] The Spanish Prime Minister, Pedro Sánchez, even expressed his reluctance to support the WA at the extraordinary meeting of the European Council to be held on 25 November 2018, unless a solution was found to this sensitive issue. Sánchez said that he would not attend the meeting of the European Council if acceptable guarantees on Gibraltar were not put in place before the summit. Even though the WA could have been approved by qualified majority in the Council, the lack of support of one Member State to the WA would have clearly weakened the political consensus needed to deal with the implications of Brexit.

The concern of Spain as regards the territorial application of the WA in respect of Gibraltar led to the adoption of two joint interpretative declarations by the European Council and the Commission and a letter sent to the Spanish Prime Minister by the President of the European Council and the European Commission, one day before the extraordinary meeting of the European Council of November 2018. In addition, on 24 November 2018, the British Permanent Representative sent a letter to the Secretary-General of the Council of the EU on the interpretation of Article 184 of the WA. Under these conditions, the European Council endorsed the WA by consensus and invited the Commission, the European Parliament and the Council to take the necessary steps to ensure that the agreement entered into force on 30 March 2019, as it was originally planned.[44]

According to the interpretative Declaration on Article 184 of the WA, this provision

> imposes no obligations regarding the territorial scope of such agreements. Therefore, there is no obligation or presumption, on the basis of this provision, for such agreements to have the same territorial scope as the one provided for in Article 3 of the Withdrawal Agreement.

This interpretation is confirmed by the letter sent by the British Permanent Representative to the Secretary-General of the Council. Also, the European Council and the Commission took note of the declaration sent by the UK in relation to the interpretative declaration.

It is very common for states and international organizations to resort to interpretative declarations which are normally attached to their expression of consent to be bound by multilateral treaties. According to the International Law Commission, an interpretative declaration is 'a unilateral statement, however phrased or named, made by a State or an international organization, whereby that State or that organization purports to specify or clarify the meaning or scope of a treaty or of certain of its provisions'.[45] In the case of the EU, it is also very common to resort to interpretative interpretations not only with the occasion of the adoption of new Treaties, but also in the daily practice of the institutions, in particular in the case of the European Council when national interests come into conflict.[46]

As it was pointed out before, the interpretation of Article 184 of the WA gave rise in Spain to an intensive political debate in the last weeks of November 2018. While some political parties considered that the concerns of Spain found a satisfactory solution, others held that the interpretative declarations are not legally binding. As a result of this debate, the legal value of the interpretative declarations adopted by the European Council and the Commission was seriously questioned. However, this issue is well settled in international law and, in particular, in the two Vienna Conventions on the Law of Treaties of 1969 and 1986. According to Article 31(1) of the Vienna Convention of 1969, 'a treaty shall be interpreted in good faith in accordance with the ordinary meaning to be given to the terms of the treaty in their context and in the light of its object and purpose'. It seems clear that the interpretative declarations adopted by the parties have to be taken into account when determining the context. The context for the purpose of the interpretation of a treaty includes 'any instrument which was made by one or more parties in connection with the conclusion of the treaty and accepted by the other parties as an instrument related to the treaty'.[47] Accordingly, the Interpretative Declaration on Article 184 of the WA is clearly linked to the WA and forms part of its context.[48] The interpretation of Article 184 of the WA was also confirmed by the letter sent by the British Permanent Representative to the Secretary-General of the Council.[49] As it has been held, 'had the clarifications contained in the declaration been included instead in a provision of the Withdrawal Agreement ..., they would have had the same interpretative value that should be recognized here'.[50]

The implications arising from the second interpretative declaration included in the minutes of the European Council meeting of 25 November 2018 complement the effects of the first declaration (Declaration of the European Council (Art. 50) and the European Commission on the territorial scope of the future agreements). The European Council and the Commission held that

> after the United Kingdom leaves the Union, Gibraltar will not be included in the territorial scope of the agreements to be concluded between the Union and the United Kingdom. However, this does not preclude the possibility to have separate agreements between the Union and the United Kingdom in respect of Gibraltar.

The second declaration issued by the European Council and the Commission is an additional guarantee confirming the content of the European Council Guidelines adopted in April 2017. It is clearly stated that any separate agreement between the EU and the UK on Gibraltar will always require a prior agreement of Spain. As it was pointed out before, the terms of the Declaration on the territorial scope of the future agreements were confirmed in the letter of 24 November 2018 sent by the Presidents of the European Council and the European Commission to the Spanish Prime Minister.

The territorial scope of the future partnership between the UK and the EU is also recalled in the Council Decision authorizing the opening of negotiations for a new partnership with the UK of 25 February 2020.[51] Therefore, the EU is fully respectful of the territorial integrity of its Member States as guaranteed by Article 4(2) of the TEU, and the application of any future agreement between the EU and the UK will require a prior agreement of Spain. As it has been argued, whether these separate future agreements are mixed agreements or whether they are configured as EU-only agreements they will require the consent of Spain in respect of Gibraltar.[52]

The Protocol on Gibraltar and the four MoUs signed between Spain and the UK on 29 November 2018 represent the first substantial agreement reached over issues that have created serious frictions between both parties in the last decades. Brexit has allowed for the first time in history to establish a framework that will address the most sensitive areas of concern for the relations between Spain and Gibraltar. Spain has tried on several occasions in the past to obtain concessions from the UK and Gibraltar through several rounds of negotiations, but the results have always been fruitless.

21.5 The debate on the amendment of the visa regulation

As part of the Contingency Action Plan for a withdrawal without an agreement between the UK and the EU, the Commission proposed to grant UK citizens visa-free travel to the EU.[53] UK citizens coming to the Schengen area for a short stay (90 days in any 180 days) would be granted visa-free travel. If the UK had withdrawn from the EU without an agreement, the visa-free travel mechanism would have been applied automatically. The visa exemption will also be applicable after the transition period. Obviously, the visa-free mechanism is based on the expectation that the UK will grant full visa reciprocity to the nationals of all Member States. In the event that the UK introduces a visa requirement for nationals of at least one Member State in the future, the existing reciprocity mechanism would not apply anymore.

A footnote was included in Article 2 of the Regulation on visa-free travel after Brexit, at the request of Spain, qualifying Gibraltar as 'a colony of the British Crown'. The text also states that 'there is a controversy between Spain and the United Kingdom concerning the sovereignty over Gibraltar, a territory for which a solution has to be reached in light of the relevant resolutions and decisions of the General Assembly of the United Nations'.[54] The reference to Gibraltar as 'a colony of the British Crown' led to a very critical reaction by the British Government, arguing that it is not a colony because it is 'a full part of the UK family and has a mature and modern constitutional relationship with the UK. This will not change due to our exit from the EU.'[55] Spain's original demand was to state that Gibraltar forms part of the UN list of non-self-governing territories pending decolonization. Since French Polynesia and New Caledonia are also included in the UN list, France was very reluctant to support the Spanish position. The final compromise reached between Spain and France was to qualify Gibraltar as 'a colony of the British Crown'. The LIBE Committee opposed the inclusion of the footnote that qualified Gibraltar as a colony. A group of MEPs were not willing to accept the terminology proposed by the Council because of its colonial connotations. Ironically, the Rapporteur of the dossier was the British MEP Claude Moraes.

21.6 Conclusions

The purpose of the Protocol on Gibraltar is focused on ensuring an orderly withdrawal from the EU in relation to Gibraltar and addressing any potential negative effects on the close social and economic relations between Gibraltar and the surrounding area of Spain. However, with the exception of Article 1 on citizens' rights, the rest of the provisions of the Protocol will only be applicable during the transition period. There are no precedents that could be a reference for the situation that Gibraltar faces. Brexit has led to the non-applicability of Article 355(3) TEU. However, breaking up the relations between Gibraltar and the EU would have very negative consequences, both for Gibraltar and for the Spanish population of 'Campo de Gibraltar'. The Political Declaration setting out the framework on the future relationship does not include any reference to Gibraltar.[56] The future relationship between Gibraltar and the EU will be governed by the agreements that will be negotiated between the EU and the UK.

The Protocol on Gibraltar and the MoUs agreed between Spain and the UK in November 2018 refer to issues that have been detrimental to the Spanish interests in the last decades, such as the smuggling of tobacco products, environmental problems and unfair fiscal competition from Gibraltar. Even though the MoUs are not legally binding instruments, they have allowed Spain to get important concessions from the UK in the most sensitive areas for Spain. Therefore, the Brexit negotiations have allowed Spain to gain leverage in the dispute while postponing a direct push for sovereignty. For the first time since Spain joined the EU, it has managed to get a more balanced relationship with the UK with respect to Gibraltar. Gibraltar faces potentially significant economic consequences as a result of Brexit. The extent to which these consequences will be realized depends to a large extent on the outcome of the negotiations between the UK and the EU, and on the reaction of Spain. The agreement or agreements on the future UK–EU relationship could nevertheless include specific bilateral arrangements agreed between Spain and Gibraltar, for example, in relation to local border traffic management.

As regards the interpretation of Article 184 of the WA, the European Council and the Commission fully understood the sensitivity of this issue for Spain and found a satisfactory solution underlining the solidarity of the EU with Spain on this matter. The adoption of two interpretative declarations by the European Council and the Commission (one on Art. 184 of the WA and another on the territorial scope of the future agreements) gave solid clarifications as regards the interpretation of Article 184 WA. There is no doubt that Spain could use its veto power in the future with respect to any future agreement between the EU and the UK that is applicable to Gibraltar.

Probably, Spain will not seek to involve the sovereignty dispute in the negotiations of the future Comprehensive Free Trade Agreement and in other areas of cooperation outlined in the Political Declaration (law enforcement and judicial cooperation in criminal matters, foreign policy, security and defence and thematic areas of cooperation).[57] Despite the clear interest of both the UK and Spain to continue a close relationship between the British colony and 'Campo de Gibraltar', the debate on the amendment of the visa Regulation which aims to grant visa-free travel to British citizens shows clearly that Gibraltar has the potential to contaminate the discussion on more substantial implications of Brexit and, in particular, the future comprehensive partnership that will be negotiated between the UK and the EU. Failure to find solutions to the issues that concern Spain in respect of Gibraltar will have an impact on the negotiations between the EU and UK. It is understandable that Spain is seeking to use the Brexit negotiations to gain leverage in the dispute with the UK and to take back a certain degree of control. Spain is pushing for the inclusion of a similar footnote in all future EU legislation adopted as regards Brexit. However, the support of other EU Member States cannot always be taken for granted. Arguably, a compromise between both countries may be included in a future framework agreement between the EU and the UK, following the precedent of the Protocol on Gibraltar.

Acknowledgements

This contribution has been written within the framework of the research project EUMABEXT, funded by the Spanish Government (RTI2018-099097-B-I00).The author would like to thank Ramses A. Wessel and Polly R. Polak for their comments on an earlier draft of this chapter.

Notes

1 Agreement on the withdrawal of the United Kingdom of Great Britain and Northern Ireland from the European Union and the European Atomic Energy Community [2020] OJ L 29/7, arts 127, 132 (WA).

2 See European Union Committee, 'Brexit: Gibraltar' (HL 2016–17, 116); Magdalena Martín Martínez and José Martín y Pérez de Nanclares (eds), *El Brexit y Gibraltar* (Colección Escuela Diplomática 2017).
3 Ibid.
4 Ibid.
5 On the legal regime of Gibraltar in the EU, see Cristina Izquierdo Sans and Antonio Remiro Brotons, *Gibraltar en la Comunidad Europea: consecuencias sobre el contencioso hispano-británico y el proceso de construcción europea* (Universidad Autónoma de Madrid 1996).
6 Resolution 2429 [XXIII] of 18 December 1968.
7 On the implications of Brexit for other territories of contested sovereignty, see Jed Odermatt's Chapter 22 in this volume.
8 Jon Stone, 'EU Referendum: Boris Johnson Says Thursday Could Become Britain's "Independence Day"' *Independent* (London, 21 June 2016).
9 The Union has a duty to uphold respect for the constitutional identity of its Member States and for the essential functions of each state, especially those aimed at preserving its territorial integrity (Art 4.2 TEU).
10 European Council Article 50 Guidelines for Brexit Negotiations (Brussels, 29 April 2017), para 24. This guideline has been recalled in the Council supplementary negotiating directives of 29 January 2018 and in the European Council guidelines of 14 March 2018, para 24.
11 See Protocol on the Sovereign Base Areas of the United Kingdom of Great Britain and Northern Ireland in Cyprus and Protocol on Ireland/Northern Ireland in the WA (n 1).
12 See Resolutions 1514 [XV] of 14 December 1960, 2070 [XX] of 16 December 1965, 2353 [XXII] of 19 December 1967, 2429 [XXIII] of 18 December 1968. See Paz Andrés Sáenz de Santa María, 'Brexit y Gibraltar: la perspectiva de Naciones Unidas', in Martínez and Martín y Pérez de Nanclares (n 2).
13 The dispute between the UK and Spain over the sovereignty of Gibraltar goes beyond the purpose of this chapter. It has rightly stated that Brexit offers Spain 'a golden opportunity to resume these negotiations and to seek a definitive resolution to a colonial dispute that has gone on for far too long' (José Martín y Pérez de Nanclares, 'Brexit and Gibraltar: The Spanish Proposal for Joint Sovereignty' (2016) 20 Spanish Yearbook of International Law 305). In other words,

> Brexit has created a new legal playing field, in Europe and beyond, with new rules. But it also offers a historic moment for Spain to redefine its relationship with Gibraltar, providing opportunities for new formulas to be considered, seeking new ways forward and a solution to this age-old dispute.
>
> *(Alejandro del Valle Gálvez, 'Gibraltar, "year zero": Brexit, Cosovereignty and New Opportunities for Spain' (Real Instituto Elcano, 2016) 1)*

14 The Spanish Permanent Representative to the United Nations, on 4 October 2016, presented the proposal for co-sovereignty in the following terms:

> I would like to announce today, before this Commission, that Spain has formally invited the United Kingdom to open negotiations enabling us to reach an agreement so that the provisions of the EU Treaties may continue to apply to Gibraltar. With EU law as it stands, the only possibility for this to be the case once the United Kingdom has left the EU is for there to be a political tie between Gibraltar and Spain – which will continue to be an EU member. We would like to reach an agreement with United Kingdom on a joint sovereignty system which would enable Gibraltar to stay in the EU, and based on the recognition of as broad a self-government as possible – which is compatible with Spain's constitutional system – and on an advantageous personal status for Gibraltarians, which could include dual nationality.
>
> *(A/C/.4/71/SR.3, 2–3)*

15 See Martín y Pérez de Nanclares (n 13).
16 See Izquierdo Sans and Remiro Brotons (n 5).
17 Art 28 of the 1973 Act of Accession by Denmark, the UK and Ireland. It was the only British Overseas Territory included in the EU. Since 2004, Gibraltar has also participated in elections to the European Parliament as part of the South West England region, following a successful challenge against its disenfranchisement at the European Court of Human Rights (*Matthews v United Kingdom* (1999) 28 EHRR 361 (ECHR)).
18 See Case 30/01 *Commission v. United Kingdom* EU:C:2003:489, para 47. See also Case 145/04 *Spain v. United Kingdom* EU:C:2006:543, paras 14–15; Case 349/03 *Commission v. United Kingdom* EU:C:2005:488, para 41.

19 See art 4(2) TEU. See also Case 298/89 *Government of Gibraltar v. Council* EU:C:1993:267, para 22.
20 See Case 6/04 *Commission v. United Kingdom* EU:C:2005:626; Case 349/03 (n 18). The most recent cases are Case 591/15 *Gibraltar Betting & Gaming* EU:C:2017:449 and Case 192/16 *Fisher* (C-192/16) EU:C:2017:762. In the last case, British courts asked the Court of Justice to determine whether the relations between the UK and Gibraltar are purely internal situations that are not subject to the freedoms of the internal market or are intra-Community fully subject to the application of the four freedoms.
21 The original text of the WA was adopted on 14 November 2018 and endorsed by the European Council on 25 November 2018, https://ec.europa.eu/commission/publications/agreement-withdrawal-united-kingdom-great-britain-and-northern-ireland-european-union-and-european-atomic-energy-community_nl accessed 14 March 2020.
22 WA, arts 164–165.
23 Carmen Martínez Capdevila, 'Thoughts on the Legal Value of the Instruments Concerning Gibraltar Adopted in Relation to the EU–UK Withdrawal Agreement' (2018) 22 Spanish Yearbook of International Law 1.
24 See Attorney General, 'EU Exit Legal Position on the Withdrawal Agreement' (December 2018) 28.
25 Council Decision on the signing, on behalf of the European Union and of the European Atomic Energy Community, of the Agreement on the withdrawal of the United Kingdom of Great Britain and Northern Ireland from the European Union and the European Atomic Energy Community COM(2018) 833 final (5 December 2018).
26 WA Protocol on Gibraltar, art 1.
27 Inmaculada González Garcia and Miguel Acosta Sánchez, 'The Consequences of Brexit for Gibraltar' (2018–2019) 3 Cuadernos de Gibraltar–Gibraltar Reports 12.
28 WA Protocol on Gibraltar, art 3.
29 See Memorandum of Understanding on Tobacco and other Products, 1.
30 Ibid.
31 Memorandum of Understanding on Cooperation on Environmental Matters.
32 González Garcia and Acosta Sánchez (n 27) 16.
33 Memorandum of Understanding on Cooperation in Police and Customs Matters, 1.
34 See Protocol 21 to the Treaty of the European Union.
35 See Jesús A Cañas, 'Gibraltar da el visto bueno al tratado para excluirlo de la lista de paraísos fiscales' *El País* (Madrid, 4 March 2019).
36 International Agreement on Taxation and the Protection of Financial Interests Between the United Kingdom of Great Britain and Northern Ireland and the Kingdom of Spain regarding Gibraltar London and Madrid (4 March 2019) https://assets.publishing.service.gov.uk/government/uploads/system/uploads/attachment_data/file/786284/CS_Spain_1.2019_Tax_Gib.pdf accessed 22 March 2020.
37 See UK Parliament, 'International Agreement on Taxation and the Protection of Financial Interests Between the United Kingdom of Great Britain and Northern Ireland and the Kingdom of Spain regarding Gibraltar' https://publications.parliament.uk/pa/ld201719/ldselect/ldeucom/342/34204.htm accessed 22 March 2020.
38 Concordat Concerning the Implementation of the Gibraltar Protocol to the Withdrawal Agreement and Related Memoranda of Understanding, p 2, www.gov.uk/government/publications/eu-exit-negotiations-gibraltar-memoranda-of-understanding accessed 22 March 2020.
39 See, for example, George Abi-Saab, 'Eloge du "droit assourdi": Quelques réflexions sur le rôle de la soft law en droit international contemporain' in *Nouveaux itinéraires en droit: Hommage à François Rigaux* (Bruylant 1993) 62ff; Jean D'Aspremont, 'Softness in International Law: A Self-Serving Quest for New Legal Materials' (2008) 19 European Journal of International Law 1075; José Antonio Pastor Ridruejo, 'Le droit international à la veille du vingt et unième siècle: normes, faits et valeurs. Cours général de droit international public' (1998) 274 Collected Courses of the Hague Academy of International Law 51.
40 See Jean Pierre Cassarino, 'Informalizing EU Readmission Policy' in Florian Trauner y Ariadna Ripoll Servent (ed), *The Routledge Handbook of Justice and Home Affairs Research* (Routledge 2018); Ricardo Gosalbo Bono y Frederit Naert, 'The Reluctant (Lisbon) Treaty and Its Implementation in the Practice of the Council' in Piet Eeckhout and Manuel López Escudero (eds), *The European Union's External Action in Times of Crisis* (Hart Publishing 2016); Juan Santos Vara, 'Soft International Agreements on Migration Cooperation with Third Countries: A Challenge to Democratic and Judicial Controls in the EU' in Juan Santos Vara and Sergio Carrera (eds), *Constitutionalising the External Dimensions of EU Migration Policies in Times of Crisis: Legality, Rule of Law and Fundamental Rights Reconsidered* (Edward

Elgar Publishing 2019); Ramses Wessel, *Normative Transformations in EU External Relations: The Phenomenon of 'Soft' International Agreements* (West European Politics 2020).

41 Paula García Andrade, 'The Role of the European Parliament in the Adoption of Non-Legally Binding Agreements with Third Countries' in Juan Santos Vara and Soledad R. Sánchez-Tabernero (eds), *The Democratization of EU International Relations Through EU Law* (Routledge 2018) 116.

42 See *Aegean Sea Continental Shelf Case (Greece v. Turkey), Jurisdiction of the Court* ICJ Reports (1978) 39; *Delimitation and Territorial Questions between Qatar and Bahrein, Jurisdiction and Admissibility* ICJ Reports (1994) 112, para 23.

43 European Council Article 50 Guidelines (n 10), para 24.

44 Special (Art. 50) meeting of the European Council (Brussels, 25 November 2018).

45 Report of the International Law Commission Sixty-third session (26 April to 3 June and 4 July to 12 August 2011), A/66/10/Add.1.

46 See Martínez Capdevila (n 23). According to the rules of procedure of the European Council, the minutes of each meeting that have to be drawn up afterwards include 'the statements made by the European Council and those whose entry has been requested by a member of the European Council'. See 'Comments on the Council's Rules of Procedure' (2016) 16, www.consilium.europa.eu/media/29824/qc0415692enn.pdf accessed 20 March 2020.

47 Vienna Convention, art 31(2)b.

48 See Spanish Ministry of Foreign Affairs, Cooperation and European Union, Comunicado 171, 'Valor jurídico de las declaraciones en relación a Gibraltar (Brexit) www.exteriores.gob.es/Portal/es/SalaDePrensa/Comunicados/Paginas/2018_COMUNICADOS/20181127_COMU171.aspx accessed 23 March 2020.

49 The letter states that

> her Majesty's Government notes that the sole purpose of Article 184 of the Withdrawal Agreement is to create best endeavors obligations for the Union and the United Kingdom to negotiate agreements governing their future relationship; that it imposes no obligations regarding the territorial scope of such agreements; and that there is therefore no obligation or presumption, on the basis of this provision, for such agreements to have the same territorial scope as the one provide for in Article 3 of the Withdrawal Agreement.

50 Martínez Capdevila (n 23) 5.

51 Council of the EU, Annex to Council Decision authorising the opening of negotiations with the United Kingdom of Great Britain and Northern Ireland for a new partnership agreement (Brussels, 25 February 2020).

52 Martínez Capdevila (n 23).

53 Proposal for a Regulation of the European Parliament and of the Council amending Council Regulation (EC) No 539/2001 listing the third countries whose nationals must be in possession of visas when crossing the external borders and those whose nationals are exempt from that requirement, as regards the withdrawal of the United Kingdom from the Union COM(2018) 745 final.

54 Art 2, Regulation (EU) 2019/592 amending Regulation (EU) 2018/1806 listing the third countries whose nationals must be in possession of visas when crossing the external borders and those whose nationals are exempt from that requirement, as regards the withdrawal of the United Kingdom from the Union [2018] OJ L 103/1.

55 Alex Barker, 'Gibraltar Dubbed "Crown Colony" in EU No-Deal Brexit Law' *Financial Times* (London, 31 January 2019); Daniel Boffey, 'Brexit: Visa-Free Travel Plans Spark Gibraltar "Colony" Row' *Guardian* (London, 1 February 2019). The UK lamented 'that our approaches to Spain to develop more helpful and appropriate language had not been reciprocated'.

56 Political Declaration setting out the framework for the future relationship between the European Union and the United Kingdom [2020] OJ C34/12.

57 Ibid.

22
Brexit and international legal sovereignty

Jed Odermatt

22.1 Introduction

The purpose of this volume is to analyse 'the implications of Brexit for the EU and UK external relations'.[1] One of the implications of the United Kingdom's withdrawal from the European Union is that the UK will have an autonomous foreign policy, and much of the focus of this debate has been on the shape of the UK's trade and economic relations after Brexit. Yet the UK will also have to decide whether, and to what extent, it will align itself with and support the foreign policy of the EU in a number of other areas.[2] In some areas of mutual concern, such as climate change, sustainable development, financial stability and the fight against terrorism, the EU and UK policies and interests will likely align.[3] Another area of the UK's foreign policy that will be affected by Brexit is its relationship with areas of contested or limited sovereignty. In recent years, the EU has faced legal questions regarding its relationship with various 'contested territories'. Outside the EU, the UK will also face questions about how it will engage with such territories. The UK's relationship with these territories uncovers certain understandings of sovereignty. In much of the Brexit debate, the issue of sovereignty mostly concerned the UK's internal sovereignty, and its freedom to decide its own laws within the EU. This chapter focuses on the issue of international legal sovereignty. It discusses how Brexit also shows how the UK projects a certain understanding of sovereignty, one which has been shaped in part by its history as a colonial power.

The following section introduces various conceptions of 'sovereignty' in international law and international relations. There has been discussion about how Brexit may have the effect of 'bringing back' the UK's domestic, or Westphalian, sovereignty (the absence of external rule). There has been less discussion of the dimension of international legal sovereignty (juridical equality between states). Some explanations of Brexit tend to emphasize how a British conception of sovereignty – one that focuses on domestic or Parliamentary sovereignty – challenges a continental European understanding of sovereignty, one which is much more open to shared sovereignty and multiple layers of authority. The Brexit process, one which has focused on issues of domestic sovereignty, also reveals questions about the UK's conceptions of, and approach to, international legal sovereignty.

The chapter then turns to a number of cases of where issues of sovereignty arise through the process of Brexit. The cases selected show how the UK's (and EU's) relationship with these entities may be affected through Brexit, and what this says about conceptions of sovereignty in the UK. It examines the cases where the EU has existing legal relationships – Palestine, Cyprus (Sovereign Base Areas and Northern Cyprus), and Western Sahara – and explores the issues of international legal sovereignty related to each of these. In each of these relationships, there are EU agreements relating to those territories, or there has been litigation in the EU that touches upon their international legal status. Of course, these are not the only relationships that give rise to issues of sovereignty in the context of Brexit. During the negotiation of the EU–UK Withdrawal Agreement,[4] negotiations on the so-called 'backstop' in Northern Ireland exposed a historical tension from the UK's colonial past. The future of the UK's overseas territories after Brexit, in particular Gibraltar, reveals similar issues related to international legal sovereignty.[5]

22.1.1 Brexit and conceptions of sovereignty

Debates about the UK's membership of the EU – both before and after the Brexit referendum – employed the language of sovereignty.[6] Some commentators have suggested that the real reason for the UK vote to leave the EU was essentially about sovereignty: 'In the minds of some of the most passionate Brexiters, the economic case for leaving the EU is less important than the prospect of the UK asserting its *sovereignty*.'[7] The language of the Leave campaign also demonstrates this, invoking the imagery of the UK under the yoke of foreign rule from Brussels, and arguing that exiting the Union would be the UK's 'independence day'.[8] The Leave campaign's core message, about 'taking back control', was essentially a message about regaining perceived *legal* independence, that is, that the UK would once again be in control of its own laws and courts, without 'foreign' interference. One Leave campaigner put it bluntly: 'Brexit means sovereignty'.[9]

The EU project has always been a certain experiment in sovereignty. The practice of states joining and establishing international organizations is a form of limiting state sovereignty, a process by which states 'transfer' certain sovereign powers to an international institution.[10] Philpott describes how '[t]he European Union does not replace states, but rather "pools" their sovereignty into a common "supranational" institution in which they no longer make decisions independently'.[11] EU Member States have chosen to exercise their sovereignty in association with other Member States, and by so doing have voluntarily restricted their ability to create and define laws independently. Yet these Member States have remained fully sovereign in terms of international legal sovereignty, and the EU itself is not considered to possess international legal sovereignty.

Different conceptions of sovereignty are revealed; a zero-sum game where sovereignty is lost to an international institution, and a conception of sovereignty as being shared, pooled, or exercised in association with other states and at various levels. Brexit has been framed as the outcome of a much longer historical trend, a clash between these two different conceptions of sovereignty. Heuser, for instance, traces the historical tension in Europe between the 'sovereigntist, independentist stance embodied in the 2016 Brexit referendum vote' and its antithesis, 'a universal empire or monarchy'.[12] Heuser shows how the British distrust for a 'greater Europe' and its insistence on a particular understanding of state sovereignty are part of this tension in international relations. Whether or not EU membership did compromise British sovereignty, the idea that the UK was under a form of foreign control had a strong emotional resonance. It was argued that through EU membership, the British voters 'somehow felt that British sovereignty was manipulated, bruised, or perhaps even surrendered unnecessarily'.[13] This contradiction is shown in a 2017 UK Government White Paper that says '[w]hilst Parliament has remained sovereign throughout our membership of the EU, it has not always felt like that'.[14] Part of the problem in this debate is that the term 'sovereignty' has been used to mean a number of different things. Gordon argues that much of the confusion stems from these different conceptions of sovereignty:

> There is much confusion about how exactly sovereignty is (or should have been) applicable in these various debates. In no small part this is due to the conflation of different understandings of sovereignty. Of particular importance has been a failure to appreciate the distinction between internal and external ideas of sovereignty: the domestic concept of parliamentary sovereignty as a fundamental principle of UK constitutional law, and the national sovereignty of the UK as a state engaged in supranational and international systems and relationships.[15]

Discussing the 'Brexit fiasco', John Agnew also argues '[t]he entangled meanings given to the words sovereignty and territory represent the root of the problem'.[16] Indeed, the different conceptions of sovereignty have been discussed in international law and international relations literature. Bartleson, for example, argues that the disagreement about the meaning of sovereignty in international law is 'less on divergent accounts of the world, and more on the ontological status implicitly accorded to concepts by these authors'.[17]

A useful typology of sovereignty was offered by Stephen Krasner, who distinguishes between various elements of the idea. Krasner defines international legal sovereignty as 'the practices associated with mutual recognition, usually between territorial entities that have formal juridical independence'.[18] International legal sovereignty is contrasted with the other ways that sovereignty is used: Westphalian sovereignty, domestic sovereignty, and interdependence sovereignty. Domestic or internal sovereignty, for example, is defined as 'the formal organization of political authority within the state and the ability of public authorities to exercise effective control within the borders of their own polity'.[19] These elements of sovereignty are interrelated. Krasner gives the example of sovereignty in the context of the EU

> [t]he exercise of one kind of sovereignty – for instance, international legal sovereignty – can undermine another kind of sovereignty, such as Westphalian sovereignty, if the rules of a state enter into an agreement that recognizes external authority structures, as has been the case for the members of the European Union.[20]

Joining the EU was thus a 'voluntary compromise of Westphalian sovereignty'[21] but also an *exercise* of the UK's international legal sovereignty.

International legal sovereignty has become an organizing principle of the international system. Jackson argues 'in the contemporary world, sovereignty has been primarily linked with the idea that states are autonomous and independent from each other'.[22] Sovereignty is 'both an idea of *supreme* authority in the state, and an idea of political and legal *independence* of geographically separate states'.[23] It concerns the relationship between the state and its citizens, but is also an idea that that organizes a system of multiple, independent, sovereign states.[24] It connotes both supremacy within a territory, but also legal independence on the international plane. The British parliament is sovereign, but only has the authority to make laws with respect to the UK; international legal sovereignty implies that it does not have the authority to control other states and vice versa.

22.1.2 International legal sovereignty

Discussions of sovereignty in the UK context often turn on the 'Westphalian' idea of sovereignty, of ultimate control within a territory. Yet the UK's conception of sovereignty has also been shaped by this international dimension, and by its history as a colonial power. Membership of the EU was not only considered an affront to the British conception of internal (parliamentary) sovereignty, but it also challenged a certain notion of British exceptionalism. The idea of the UK turning into (or returning to) a 'global Britain' or to re-engage with the Commonwealth, appear to stem from this mind-set. Discussing the various 'revolutions in sovereignty' Philpott argues that the revolution of colonial independence, where this Westphalian ideal spread globally, is the most recent of the historical shifts that have impacted sovereignty.[25] It is no longer legitimate for one state to exercise control over a foreign people. In the case of colonialization, colonial territories may have exercised a degree of *internal* authority, but the colonies did not possess international legal sovereignty until they became juridically independent, sovereign states.

It is not just Brexit, but also the legacies of the UK's colonial past, that give rise to questions of international legal sovereignty. The recent Advisory Opinion of the International Court of Justice (ICJ) on *Legal Consequences of the Separation of the Chagos Archipelago from Mauritius in 1965*,[26] demonstrates how the process of decolonization remains incomplete. The ICJ found that continued British administration of the islands was 'a wrongful act', and that the UK has an obligation to return the islands to Mauritius. While the process of decolonization has now mostly taken place, there remain territories that do not possess full legal independence, that is, international legal sovereignty. The UN Special Committee on Decolonization, for example, lists seventeen 'Non-Self-Governing Territories' that are still subject to the process of decolonization, ten of which have the UK as an administrating power. This includes Gibraltar, (discussed in the previous chapter), the only territory which comprised part of the EU, giving rise to another set of legal questions.[27]

This chapter explores the potential impact of Brexit on the UK's relationship with a number of territories – Palestine, Cyprus (SBAs and Northern Cyprus) and Western Sahara – and the issues associated with international legal sovereignty that arise. At first glance, each of these territories is unique, and does not fall within any existing legal or political category. Yet for each of these cases, the UK's withdrawal from the EU exposes a number of legal and political questions related to international legal sovereignty.[28] Moreover, in each of these cases, there has been significant involvement of the EU, through, for example, the EU's international agreements with those territories, or through judgments of the Court of Justice of the European Union (CJEU), which have touched upon the legal status of the territory. The chapter deals with these heterogeneous entities to demonstrate the myriad sovereignty issues that arise as a result of Brexit, for the UK, the EU and the entities themselves.

22.2 The UK and areas of contested sovereignty

22.2.1 Palestine

Since 2012, the State of Palestine has been a 'Non-member Observer State' in the United Nations. However, it does not enjoy universal recognition by other states and its territorial borders remain subject to dispute. For example, the International Criminal Court (ICC) recently requested the submission of *amicus curiae* observations on the ICC's territorial jurisdiction in Palestine,[29] showing how its territory remains contested. The UK does not recognize Palestine as a state. In 2011, the UK abstained in the vote on United Nations General Assembly Resolution 67/19, which granted the State of Palestine the status of 'non-member observer state'. While the UK does not officially recognize Palestine, it has established relations with the Palestinian Authority. The UK also has significant historical ties with Palestine as the UK was a former administrator of the Mandate of Palestine. Indeed, some of the ongoing issues regarding its legal status and territorial borders can be traced to the decisions of the British administration of Palestine following the First World War.

While the UK does not recognize the State of Palestine, as an EU Member State it was bound by a trade agreement between the EU and Palestinian Authority. On 18 February 2019, the UK and the Palestinian Authority signed a 'trade continuity agreement'[30] to continue this relationship after the UK leaves the EU. The UK–Palestinian Authority Political, Trade and Partnership Agreement[31] seeks to maintain the effects of the existing EC–PLO Association Agreement,[32] and will come into force at the end of the implementation period. Rather than establish a new trade agreement, this interim agreement merely replaces, in relations between the UK and Palestine, the EC–PLO Association Agreement. The Explanatory Memorandum to the new agreement stipulates that '[n]othing in the UK–Palestinian Authority Interim Agreement should be interpreted as recognition by the UK of Palestine as a State'. Moreover, since the UK does not recognize the state of Palestine, the agreement shall not be considered a 'treaty' for the purposes of the Constitutional Reform and Governance Act 2010.[33] The UK–Palestinian Authority Agreement is therefore not subject to the same parliamentary review and scrutiny process as other agreements, as it is concluded between the UK and the Palestinian Authority rather than a state or international organization.[34]

The UK Department for International Trade (DIT) points to the importance of this agreement, stating that '[t]he agreement demonstrates the UK's commitment to strengthening bilateral cooperation, promoting Palestinian economic growth, and maintaining the UK's strong commitment to a 2-state solution'.[35] Yet the agreement does nothing more than continue the existing trading arrangements; it reproduces the EU–PLO agreement, but with required changes, such as replacing references to the 'European Union' and 'Member States' with the UK. Since there is very little trade between Palestine and the UK, the economic impact of this agreement on the UK and Palestine is likely to be minimal.

The more significant aspect of the agreement in terms of international legal sovereignty relates to the agreement's territorial application. Article 4 of the UK–Palestine agreement sets out that:

> For the avoidance of doubt in relation to incorporated Article 73, this Agreement shall apply, to the extent that and under the conditions which the amended EU–Palestinian Authority Interim Association Agreement applied to the United Kingdom and the territories for whose international relations the United Kingdom is responsible immediately before the amended EU–Palestinian Authority Interim Association Agreement ceased to apply to the United Kingdom.[36]

The UK–Palestinian Authority Agreement deals with two issues of territorial application. First, it will apply to the UK and the 'territories for whose international relations the United Kingdom is responsible'. This is different from the EU–PLO agreement, which defines its territorial application as 'to the territories in which the Treaty establishing the European Community is applied'. The Lord's European Union Committee pointed to this possible discrepancy, requesting DIT to clarify to which territories – especially the Crown Dependencies and British Overseas Territories – the agreement applies.[37]

The second question relates to the territorial application in Palestine. As the EU–PLO Agreement, the EU-Palestinian Authority agreement applies to the territories of West Bank and Gaza. This, of course, gives rise to difficulties in the context of the territory of Palestine. One of the legal questions that has arisen in this context is whether products produced within the Israeli settlements in the Occupied Palestinian Territories could benefit from preferential tariff treatment under EU–Israel agreement. This issue has been addressed in the UK's interim agreement with Israel, which sets out that '[p]roducts produced in the Israeli settlements located within the territories brought under Israeli administration since June 1967 are not entitled to benefit from preferential tariff treatment'.[38]

International law issues related to Palestine have been subject to adjudication before the CJEU. In *Brita*,[39] the CJEU decided whether goods produced in Israeli settlements in the West Bank could fall within the scope of the EC–Israel Association Agreement. The CJEU found that it could not, based on international law. It found that if it were to interpret the EC–Israel Association Agreement so that the Israeli customs authorities enjoy competence in respect of products originating in the West Bank, this would be tantamount to imposing on the Palestinian customs authorities an obligation to refrain from exercising the competence conferred upon them by virtue of the EC–PLO Protocol. One of the effects of the judgment was to underline the position of the EU that 'products obtained in locations which have been placed under Israeli administration since 1967 do not qualify for the preferential treatment provided for under that agreement'.[40] A question that arises in relation to Brexit is whether the UK will continue to uphold this legal position of the CJEU in the application of the UK's agreements with Israel and the Palestinian Authority.

In its 2019 judgment in *Organisation juive européenne*,[41] the CJEU addressed the question whether EU law requires products originating from occupied territories to be labelled as originating in 'Israeli settlements'. The dispute was technically about consumer protection; however, the Court found that consumers' purchasing decisions may be informed by the issue of whether foodstuffs originated in settlements established in violation of international law.[42] Thus, legal questions regarding the occupied territories not only arise from disputes regarding trade agreements, but also in the application of law in fields such as consumer protection. Again, after the implementation period, the UK will no longer be bound by judgments of the CJEU and its interpretation of EU agreements. However, similar issues may continue to arise before courts in the UK.

22.2.2 Cyprus

The island of Cyprus also gives rise to questions related to international legal sovereignty. The Republic of Cyprus is an EU Member State and is recognized as having international legal sovereignty over the entire island of Cyprus. However, it is not able to exercise full domestic sovereignty over the island's territory in practice, as the north remains occupied and controlled by the 'Turkish Republic of Northern Cyprus'. The island is also the location of two British Overseas Territories.

As with Palestine, the legal status of these territories is shaped in part by the history of the British Empire. Cyprus was a former British protectorate (1878–1914) and in 1914 was unilaterally annexed into the British Empire. In 1925, Cyprus had the status of Crown Colony, until it achieved independence as the Republic of Cyprus in 1960. Cyprus became an EU Member State on 1 May 2004, although at the time of accession the dispute with Northern Cyprus had not been resolved. Cyprus continues to have close political and economic links with the UK. Along with Malta, it is the only other EU Member State that is part of the Commonwealth. The UK is a significant trading partner for Cyprus, and tourism from the UK has been of particular importance. Cyprus is one of the EU Member States that will be significantly affected by Brexit.

22.2.2.1 Sovereign Base Areas

Under the 1960 Treaty of Establishment, when Cyprus became independent, the UK retained two SBAs, of Akrotiri and Dhekelia. These are British Overseas Territories administered by the

UK Ministry of Defence, rather than the Foreign and Commonwealth Office. The SBAs therefore do not constitute a part of the sovereign territory of Cyprus. These are not considered territories that remain subject to colonization, and Cyprus does not claim sovereignty over the territories. While there has been focus on how Brexit may impact the UK's territorial border with Ireland and the status of Gibraltar, the effects on Akrotiri and Dhekelia, in which thousands of EU citizens reside (around 15 000 citizens of Cyprus), has not received the same level of attention. Yet as with Ireland and Gibraltar, the effect of Brexit is to establish a land border between an EU Member State (Cyprus) and a former Member State (UK).

The SBAs have never been a part of the territory of the EU. Article 355 (5) (b) TFEU sets out that the EU Treaties 'shall not apply to the United Kingdom Sovereign Base Areas of Akrotiri and Dhekelia in Cyprus'. Article 355 TFEU adds an important exception, however: 'except to the extent necessary to ensure the implementation of the arrangements set out in the Protocol on the Sovereign Base Areas of the United Kingdom of Great Britain and Northern Ireland in Cyprus'. This refers to Protocol No. 3 on the SBAs that is part of the Act of Accession of Cyprus.[43] The protocol recognizes the need to apply certain parts of Union law with respect to the SBAs. They include the SBAs in the Union's customs territory with a view to preventing custom posts or other barriers at the border. This means that Union law applied in the SBAs to the extent necessary to ensure the implementation of the arrangements set out in Protocol No. 3. This is covered by a complex system in which certain areas of EU law are applied in relation to freedom of movement, customs, VAT, excise and food safety. The SBAs, while not part of the EU or the Single Market, therefore remained part of the EU's Customs Territory. One problem posed by Brexit was that, once the UK left the EU, goods would no longer be able to flow freely between the SBAs and Cyprus, as Cyprus would be required to apply customs and regulatory controls at the border. Another important issue is the protection of the interests of Cypriots who live and work in the SBAs. Protocol 3 to the Act of Accession seeks to ensure that those who are living and working in the SBAs are treated the same, to the extent possible, as those who reside and work in the Republic of Cyprus.

The status of Akrotiri and Dhekelia is addressed in the Protocol on SBAs in Cyprus, which is an integral part of the EU–UK Withdrawal Agreement. Unlike the Withdrawal Agreement, which was negotiated bilaterally between the UK and the Union, the Protocol was negotiated by representatives of the European Commission, Cyprus and the UK. The Protocol seeks to preserve, as far as possible, the status quo in the relationship between the SBAs and Cyprus. This means that they will remain part of the Union's custom territory and certain areas of EU *acquis* (areas stipulated in Protocol 3) will apply on the territories.[44] The EU–UK Withdrawal Agreement establishes a Committee on issues related to the implementation of the Protocol relating to the SBAs in Cyprus.[45] This Committee is given the responsibility to facilitate the implementation and application of the Protocol and to discuss issues giving rise to any difficulty raised by the EU or the UK. With the exception of security and military affairs, the Protocol confers responsibility on the Republic of Cyprus to implement and enforce Union law.[46]

22.2.2.2 Northern Cyprus

The Turkish Republic of Northern Cyprus (TRNC) has exercised de facto control over the northern part of Cyprus since the invasion of the island by Turkey in 1974. This invasion and subsequent occupation have been internationally condemned as illegal. In 1964, the UN Security Council demanded 'an immediate end to foreign military intervention in the Republic of Cyprus'.[47] UN Security Council Resolution 541 states that Northern Cyprus' declaration of statehood is invalid and calls upon states not to recognize any Cypriot state other than the

Republic of Cyprus.[48] TRNC stands out in this regard as being subject to numerous UN Security Council Resolutions calling upon states to not recognize the territory.[49] Thus, while the Republic of Cyprus has international legal sovereignty with respect to the entire island (except for the SBAs) it exercises de facto control over only a part of the island. To recognize this reality, Protocol 10 to the Act of Accession sets out that the EU *acquis* is suspended in relation to the territory of Northern Cyprus. Northern Cyprus is thus considered to be part of the EU, although the application of EU law is suspended there. Goods originating in Northern Cyprus are allowed to enter the EU customs territory without tariffs, but are still subject to checks on food safety etc.

The CJEU has also dealt with cases that touch upon the status of Northern Cyprus. In *Anastasiou*[50] the Court dealt with legal questions that arose from the UK's policy towards Northern Cyprus. Under the EC–Cyprus Association Agreement,[51] imports of citrus fruit and potatoes from the Republic of Cyprus had to be accompanied by certificates issued by the customs authorities of Cyprus as evidence of the originating status of the products. The UK did not accept origin and phytosanitary certificates that had been issued by the authorities of TRNC. However, it did accept the import of goods originating in the north in the name of the 'Republic of Cyprus' or 'Cyprus Customs Authorities', even though these were not issued by the authorities of the Republic of Cyprus. Exporters in the Republic of Cyprus argued that such practice violated the EC–Cyprus Agreement and its Protocol. The High Court (Queen's Bench division) in the UK referred the questions on the interpretation of EU law to the Court of Justice. The UK argued that its policy sought to prevent discrimination and benefit the entire population of Cyprus, while at the same time pursuing a policy of non-recognition towards Northern Cyprus.

The Commission argued that such policy was also in conformity with international law, in particular the ICJ's 1971 *Namibia*[52] advisory opinion. The Commission argued that this set out a principle according to which a policy of non-recognition of a state should not deprive the population of the non-recognized state certain benefits granted by a treaty. The Court found, however, that the obligations under the agreement and protocol were clear, precise, and unconditional, and the situation in Cyprus did not necessitate a departure from the obligations related to rules of origin. Moreover, the acceptance of movement certificates that had not been issued by the Republic of Cyprus would constitute denial of the very object and purpose of the system. The Court also rejected the argument based on the *Namibia* opinion, reasoning that the legal and factual situations in Cyprus and Namibia were not comparable, and no analogy could be drawn for the purposes of interpreting the agreement.

As with *Brita* discussed above, *Anastasiou* is an example of how the application of a trade agreement can give rise to sensitive legal questions related to international legal sovereignty. The dispute arises from the UK's policy of non-recognition of the territory. It sought a pragmatic solution to the problem caused by the difficulty or impossibility of producers in the north of Cyprus to obtain certificates from the Republic of Cyprus. Some commentary from international lawyers[53] argued that the Court's approach was based on a misconception of what a policy of non-recognition implies. Talmon argues, for instance, that co-operation with the authorities of an unrecognised entity does not imply recognition of that entity, and that such cooperation can have the effect of ameliorating the harsher consequences of the non-recognition policy on the affected population. The case demonstrates how issues of foreign policy, such as non-recognition, can come before EU and domestic courts in the form of disputes arising from its economic relations.[54]

Brexit is unlikely to have an impact, however, on the trade or other relations between the UK and Northern Cyprus. It is more likely that it will lead to practical issues for British citizens living in the north of the island. The British High Commission in Nicosia advised Britons living in the north on some of the legal and practical issues that may arise from Brexit, such as on the recognition of drivers' licences and immigration controls. The High Commissioner notes that 'the local residency rules and procedures for Britons in the north should remain the same there before and after Brexit'.[55]

22.2.3 Western Sahara

Western Sahara is one of the seventeen territories considered by the UN Committee on Decolonization to be 'non-self governing'.[56] Its international status remains contested, and is sometimes described as a 'disputed' territory. According to the UK Government, the status of Western Sahara is 'undetermined'.[57] While Moroccan sovereignty of the territory is not internationally recognized, Western Sahara does not enjoy universal recognition as a state.[58] A number of states have also since withdrawn recognition or suspended diplomatic relations. The United Nations Security Council (UNSC) has on a number of occasions emphasized that people of Western Sahara, the Saharwi people, have the right to self-determination, but the outcome of its status is subject to continuing negotiations under the auspices of the United Nations.[59] The UK supports the political process under which this right to self-determination is to be expressed.[60] As a permanent member of the UN Security Council, it has continually voted in favour of extending the mandate of the United Nations Mission for the Referendum in Western Sahara (MINURSO).[61]

The EU's relationship with Western Sahara has been the subject of considerable criticism in recent years. In particular, it has been argued that the EU's international agreements with Morocco do not comply with international law since they have been applied with respect to the territory of Western Sahara. This issue made its way to the CJEU, which was asked to decide whether these agreements violated international law binding on the Union. The cases of *Front Polisario*[62] and *Western Sahara Campaign UK*,[63] both involved legal challenges to the validity of international agreements between the EU and Morocco, on the basis that they applied to the territory of Western Sahara in violation of international law.

Western Sahara Campaign UK originated as a request for a preliminary ruling from the courts of England and Wales (High Court of Justice (England & Wales), Queen's Bench Division). It involved a challenge to the validity of agreements in force between the EU and Morocco. The EU law dimension of the case is significant. The referring court noted that, had the case not included an EU law dimension, the court would unlikely have had the power to review the legality of the agreement: '[t]here is little doubt that if the present challenge was solely based on common law rules, a domestic court might dismiss a claim that depends on an assessment of the legality of actions of a foreign sovereign'.[64] This is based on the 'act of state doctrine' in English law. This doctrine is not absolute, however, and it 'may be disapplied on grounds of public policy where there is a violation of international law or a grave infringement of fundamental human rights'.[65] However, the referring court opined that the exceptions did not apply in these circumstances. It was thus EU law, specifically Article 3(5) Treaty on European Union (which commits the Union to respect international law) that allowed a challenge of the acts in question. Once the UK is no longer bound by EU law, it may become difficult for parties to challenge the legality of agreements on the basis that they violate international law.

As with Palestine and Israel discussed above, the UK's trade relations with Morocco will continue with an interim agreement. These agreements tend to offer only a technical reproduction of the existing agreements covered by the EU, with the purpose of providing continuity in the UK's trading relationship. The Agreement establishing an Association between the

United Kingdom of Great Britain and Northern Ireland and the Kingdom of Morocco[66] thus seeks to replace, for the UK, the Association Agreement between the EU and the Kingdom of Morocco. The EU–Morocco Association Agreement now applies to goods that originate in the territory of Western Sahara. This been replicated in the UK–Morocco Agreement.[67] The House of Lords EU Select Committee has pointed to some issues with this agreement regarding its application to Western Sahara. An open letter expresses concern 'that the UK is seeking to roll-over the EU–Morocco Association Agreement into UK legislation without due attention to the ongoing Moroccan occupation of Western Sahara'.[68] The Lords Committee has brought the UK–Morocco Agreement to the attention of the House, stating in particular that 'the inclusion of Western Sahara in the UK Agreement raises an important question of policy about how the UK should balance its commitment to Western Sahara's "undetermined" status with its pursuit of a trade agreement with Morocco'.[69] The agreement should be scrutinized to determine whether it is in conformity with the UK's international obligations as well as the CJEU's judgments related to Western Sahara. As with the CJEU jurisprudence dealing with the EU's relationship with Palestine and Northern Cyprus, the UK will no longer be bound by the cases dealing with Western Sahara upon the end of the implementation period.

22.3 Conclusion

Debates about Brexit have almost exclusively focused on the internal, Westphalian, aspect of sovereignty and the extent to which the UK will regain 'control' over its laws and courts. This chapter has analysed some of the implications of Brexit for issues of international legal sovereignty. For the most part, the UK's legal and political position towards these territories will remain the same. Outside the EU, the UK can decide how to regulate its relations with entities such as the State of Palestine, Northern Cyprus, and Western Sahara, but to date it has mostly sought to continue the status quo *ante*. As the UK seeks to preserve these arrangements, for instance by seeking to roll over EU trade agreements (Palestine, Western Sahara) and other legal arrangements (Cyprus) to the context of the UK's bilateral relations, sovereignty issues emerge. The UK will have to decide whether to align its foreign policy in relation to such territories with that of the EU, especially in relation to the jurisprudence of the CJEU.

A more complicated picture emerges in relation to the legal disputes that arise regarding the UK's relationships with those territories. UK courts will no longer be bound by the interpretations of the CJEU, and may develop a different approach towards these territories. Moreover, outside the EU, litigants may have fewer legal avenues to challenge these decisions. Whereas the CJEU has dealt with legal issues related to these territories in recent years, UK courts may be more reluctant to review issues of foreign policy.

As the UK seeks to define its new relationship with the EU and the rest of the world, the issue of sovereignty will remain a key issue. In these debates, sovereignty is viewed in terms of the UK's domestic sovereignty, and its ability to define its own laws. Yet this contribution shows how issues related to international legal sovereignty also arise from the Brexit process, especially in relation to the territories discussed in this chapter. Although EU membership never jeopardized the UK's international legal sovereignty, the Brexit process reveals how issues of international legal sovereignty remain when the UK seeks to define its relationship with these territories. This process also reveals how the UK's history as a colonial power has also shaped its conception of sovereignty. The territories discussed in this chapter may not be strategically or economically important to the UK or the EU, and they have not featured in debates about the UK's foreign policy after Brexit. Yet these relationships show how the issue of sovereignty, and the confusion caused by the different conceptions, will persist after Brexit.

Notes

1 See Introduction to this volume.
2 On the implications of Brexit for Common Foreign and Security Policy (CFSP), see Ramses A Wessel's Chapter 14 in this volume.
3 See Annex to the 'Recommendation for a Council Decision authorising the opening of negotiations for a new partnership with the United Kingdom of Great Britain and Northern Ireland' (Brussels, 3 February 2020) COM(2020) 35.
4 Agreement on the withdrawal of the United Kingdom of Great Britain and Northern Ireland from the European Union and the European Atomic Energy Community [2019] OJ C 384I (Withdrawal Agreement, WA).
5 On the implications of Brexit for Gibraltar, see Juan Santos Vara's Chapter 21 in this volume.
6 See Vernon Bogdanor, 'Europe and the Sovereignty of the People' (2016) 87 Political Quarterly 348.
7 David Allen Green, 'No-Deal Brexit and the Sovereignty Myth' *Financial Times* (London, 2 August 2018).
8 Jon Stone, 'EU Referendum: Boris Johnson Says Thursday Could Become Britain's "Independence Day"' *Independent* (London, 21 June 2016).
9 Daniel Hannan, 'Brexit Means Sovereignty' *Spectator* (London, 4 August 2016). Hannan understands sovereignty in this context as 'the ultimate right to determine laws'.
10 See Dan Sarooshi, *International Organizations and their Exercise of Sovereign Powers* (Oxford University Press 2005).
11 Daniel Philpott, *Revolutions in Sovereignty: How Ideas Shaped Modern International Relations* (Princeton University Press 2001) 39.
12 Beatrice Heuser, *Brexit in History: Sovereignty or a European Union?* (Hurst 2019) 3.
13 Morad Eghbal and Karen O'Rourke, 'Post-Brexit: A Continuum for State Sovereignty. UK's Challenge to Balance Legitimacy, Capital, Development and Human Needs' (2016) 23 ILSA Journal of International & Comparative Law, 6.
14 Department for Exiting the European Union, 'The United Kingdom's exit from, and new partnership with, the European Union' (Policy Paper, 15 May 2017) www.gov.uk/government/publications/the-united-kingdoms-exit-from-and-new-partnership-with-the-european-union-white-paper/the-united-kingdoms-exit-from-and-new-partnership-with-the-european-union-2 accessed 3 March 2020.
15 Michael Gordon, 'The UK's Sovereignty Situation: Brexit, Bewilderment and Beyond …' (2016) 27 King's Law Journal 33.
16 John Agnew, 'Taking Back Control? The Myth of Territorial Sovereignty and the Brexit Fiasco' (2019) 8(2) *Territory, Politics, Governance* 259–272.
17 Jens Bartelson, 'The Concept of Sovereignty Revisited' (2006)17 European Journal of International Law 463.
18 Stephen D Krasner, *Sovereignty: Organized Hypocrisy* (Princeton University Press, 1999) 4.
19 Ibid.
20 Ibid.
21 Ibid, 238.
22 Robert Jackson, *Sovereignty: The Evolution of an Idea* (Polity Press 2007) 1.
23 Ibid.
24 Ibid.
25 Philpott (n 11).
26 Advisory Opinion of 25 February 2019.
27 TFEU, art 355(3): 'The provisions of the Treaties shall apply to the European territories for whose external relations a Member State is responsible.'
28 On issues of 'contested sovereignty' and the EU, see Dimitris Bouris and Dimitris Papadimitriou, 'The EU and Contested Statehood in its Near Abroad: Europeanisation, Actorness and State-building' (2020) 25 Geopolitics 273.
29 International Criminal Court, Pre-Trial Chamber I, 'Order Setting the Procedure and the Schedule for the Submission of Observations' ICC-01/18-14 (28 January 2020).
30 Department for International Trade, 'UK and Palestinian Authority sign trade continuity agreement' (Press Release, 18 February 2019) www.gov.uk/government/news/uk-and-palestinian-authority-sign-trade-continuity-agreement accessed 3 March 2020.

31 Interim Political, Trade and Partnership Agreement between the United Kingdom of Great Britain and Northern Ireland, of the one part, and the Palestine Liberation Organization (PLO) for the benefit of the Palestinian Authority of the West Bank and the Gaza Strip, of the other part (Ramallah, 18 February 2019) (UK–Palestinian Authority Agreement, not in force) https://assets.publishing.service.gov.uk/government/uploads/system/uploads/attachment_data/file/781389/MS_14.2019_IPTP_PLO.pdf accessed 3 March 2020.

32 Euro-Mediterranean Interim Association Agreement on trade and cooperation between the European Community, of the one part, and the Palestine Liberation Organization (PLO) for the benefit of the Palestinian Authority of the West Bank and the Gaza Strip, of the other part [1997] OJ L 187.

33 European Union Committee, 'Scrutiny of International Agreements' (2017–19 HL 321) para 56.

34 Constitutional Reform and Governance Act 2010, s 25. The Act defines a 'treaty' as a written agreement '(a) between States or between States and international organisations, and (b) binding under international law'.

35 Department for International Trade (n 30).

36 UK–Palestinian Authority Agreement, art 4.

37 European Union Committee (n 33) paras 70–71.

38 Trade and Partnership Agreement between the Government of the United Kingdom of Great Britain and Northern Ireland and the Government of the State of Israel (Tel Aviv, 18 February 2019) (not in force) www.gov.uk/government/publications/cs-israel-no12019-ukisrael-trade-and-partnership-agreement accessed 9 March 2020.

39 Case 386/08 *Brita v Hauptzollamt Hamburg Hafen* EU:C:2010:91.

40 Ibid, para 64.

41 Case 363/18 *Organisation juive européenne* EU:C:2019:954.

42 Ibid, para 55.

43 Act concerning the conditions of accession of the Czech Republic, the Republic of Estonia, the Republic of Cyprus, the Republic of Latvia, the Republic of Lithuania, the Republic of Hungary, the Republic of Malta, the Republic of Poland, the Republic of Slovenia and the Slovak Republic and the adjustments to the Treaties on which the European Union is founded – Protocol No 3 on the sovereign base areas of the United Kingdom of Great Britain and Northern Ireland in Cyprus [2003] OJ L 236 (Protocol No 3).

44 Ibid, art 2(1):

> The Sovereign Base Areas, taking into account the Treaty of Establishment, shall be part of the customs territory of the Union. For this purpose, the provisions of Union law on customs and the common commercial policy, including provisions of Union law providing for customs controls of specific goods or for specific purposes, shall apply to and in the Sovereign Base Areas.

45 WA, art 165(1)(d).

46 Protocol No 3, art 2(10): 'The Republic of Cyprus shall be responsible for the implementation and enforcement in the Sovereign Base Areas of the provisions of Union law referred to in paragraph 7'.

47 UN Security Council Resolution 353, 20 July 1974.

48 UN Security Council Resolution 541, 18 November 1983.

49 Ibid; UN Security Council Resolution 550, 11 May 1984.

50 Judgment in *Anastasiou* C-432/92 EU:C:1994:277.

51 Agreement of 19 December 1972 establishing an Association between the European Economic Community and the Republic of Cyprus, annexed to Council Regulation (EEC) No 1246/73 of 14 May 1973.

52 *Legal Consequences for States of the continued presence of South Africa in Namibia (South-West Africa) notwithstanding Security Council Resolution 276(1970)*, Advisory Opinion, ICJ Rep [1971] p 16.

53 See S Talmon, 'The Cyprus Question Before the European Court of Justice' (2001) 12 European Journal of International Law 4, 727–750; C Greenwood and V Lowe, 'Unrecognised States and the European Court' (1995) Cambridge Law Journal 4–6.

54 Marise Cremona, 'Case C-432/92, R. v. Minister of Agriculture, Fisheries and Food, ex parte S.P. Anastasiou (Pissouri) Ltd. and others, Judgment of 5 July 1994' (1996) Common Market Law Review 1, 125–135.

55 See British High Commission in Cyprus, Open letter to Britons resident in the north of Cyprus, 29 March 2019.

56 See United Nations Special Committee on Decolonization, List of Non-Self-Governing Territories, www.un.org/en/decolonization/nonselfgovterritories.shtml accessed 9 March 2020.
57 'Western Sahara and the UK' www.gov.uk/world/western-sahara/news accessed 3 March 2020.
58 One list of recognitions puts the current number at eighty-four. See www.usc.es/en/institutos/ceso/RASD_Reconocimientos.html accessed 3 March 2020.
59 ICJ, *Western Sahara*, Advisory Opinion of 16 October, paras 70, 162.
60 Foreign and Commonwealth Office, Statement by David Clay, UK Deputy Political Coordinator at the United Nations, at the Security Council Briefing on Western Sahara (1 November 2018) www.gov.uk/government/speeches/path-to-providing-self-determination-for-the-people-of-western-sahara accessed 3 March 2020.
61 UN Security Council Resolution 2440, 31 October 2018.
62 Case 104/16 P *Council v Front Polisario* EU:C:2016:973.
63 Case 266/16 *Western Sahara Campaign UK* EU:C:2018:118.
64 *Western Sahara Campaign UK, R (on the application of) v HM Revenue and Customs* [2015] EWHC 2898, para 7.
65 See *Belhaj & Anor v Straw & Ors* [2014] EWCA Civ 1394, para 81.
66 Agreement establishing an Association between the United Kingdom of Great Britain and Northern Ireland and the Kingdom of Morocco (London, 26 October 2019) (not in force) https://assets.publishing.service.gov.uk/government/uploads/system/uploads/attachment_data/file/854581/CS_Morocco_2.2019_UK_Morocco_Agreement_establishing_an_Association.pdf accessed 9 March 2020.
67 Agreement establishing an Association between the United Kingdom of Great Britain and Northern Ireland and the Kingdom of Morocco, annex E, para 2: 'Products originating in Western Sahara subject to controls by customs authorities of Morocco shall benefit from the same trade preferences as those granted by the United Kingdom to products covered by this Agreement.'
68 Trade Justice Movement, 'Civil Society Organisations Raise Concerns about UK–Morocco Association Agreement' (23 January 2020) www.tjm.org.uk/blog/2020/civil-society-organisations-raise-concerns-about-uk-morocco-association-agreement accessed 3 March 2020.
69 European Union Committee, 'Scrutiny of International Agreements' (2019–21 HL 14) para 20.

23
The cross-channel reach of EU law in the UK post-Brexit

Elaine Fahey

23.1 Introduction

The 'reach' of EU law, how it is forced upon or foisted upon or voluntarily accepted by third countries, partners, associations or regions is a vast multi-disciplinary theory. It is explained through the success of the EU as a 'soft power' and good global actor, evolving to promote its values and norms initially through its trade policy, immortalised in the early work of Ian Manners' 'Normative Power Europe'.[1] It emphasises the soft 'behind the scenes' diplomacy of a large trading bloc and its immense soft power. But it does not help with the legal detail. The reach of EU law is not necessarily an institutionalised phenomenon, arguably lacks clear-cut subjects or objectives and probably has weak institutional underpinnings at best. The reach of EU law has been increasingly shown to have little to do with third country parties or trade models but is rather an independent phenomenon traced in a variety of literature across disciplines where EU law is used by parties, entities or jurisdictions without being legally required to so do.[2] It never takes place from such a level of alignment as the UK will begin from. There is in reality some likelihood of the impossibility of the removal of EU law from the UK legal order given the reach of EU law in certain fields. Brexit will certainly become an important case study of the reach of EU law and a high level of regulatory alignment – *as a starting point.*

While post-Brexit there will likely be inevitable global reach of EU law in the UK, the metrics will in all likelihood be highly contestable. The UK is likely to become a highly esoteric study of the global reach of EU law and will thereby necessitate detailed cross-sectoral understandings. Brexit has exposed an important debate as to the gap between the reach of EU law and how much 'reach' partners need to expect, comply with or develop, because it has revealed an interesting question as to how much the EU clearly communicates or advocates the transfer of its rules to a partner country. On the one hand, a former Member State is in a different position from regular third-party countries to be negotiated with. The UK Government has regularly repeated the mantra in negotiations that Canada or Japan are not asked to follow EU law – 'so why should we?' On the other hand, it appears that the extent to which the EU requires alignment or exports its rules to its trade partners is sectorally contested but also more broadly under-explored.

The relationship between globalisation and rule-transfer in the agenda of 'Global Britain', with Britain's distinctive history as an Imperialist power and a longstanding process of disengagement of its former colonies therefrom, makes these questions all the more interesting. The significant agenda of deregulation to complete with the UK, to exit the European Convention on Human Rights (ECHR) and to diverge as an entity from the EU has been a vibrant agenda of the Brexit negotiations. The future relationship is mired in the additional complexity of new age tariff and tech wars across the Atlantic and the erosion of trust and value in international organisations.[3] The global dimension to Brexit and its place in the EU's Global Strategy going forward thus remains highly uncertain and contentious, however much there is an EU 'business as usual' mantra.[4] It is worth bearing in mind how British actors have regularly used the EU to promote policy norms globally and have shaped common EU norms.[5] This background context to these issues renders the reach of law an extraordinarily rich and thorny question. Yet there are also important contestations within global governance as to the movement of rules, worthy of exploration, which conventionally overlook the EU. This will assume much more significance going forward as the UK evolves as a third country qua former Member State.

The chapter aims to provide a 'bird's eye' scientific approach to the overall issue of reach and EU law in the UK going forward. The chapter is not fixated upon an outcome at the time of writing and explores the longer-term trends on the application of EU rules outside trade agreements, the exportation of EU rules in trade agreements and the interpretation of EU rules post-exit in UK law. This chapter considers reach from a variety of disciplines – from global governance, law, international relations (IR), political economy – varying from the legal to the political and beyond legal scholarship and also reaching into the domestic legal order – i.e. the domestic understanding thereof in national law. The chapter subsequently considers: global governance perspectives (section 23.2), law and IR (23.3), political economy (23.4), EU law 'within' international agreements (23.5), followed by domestic UK provisions on EU law post-exit (23.6).

23.2 Global governance perspectives: on rule-taking and rule-making

The reality of contemporary globalisation where there are limited rule-makers and multiple rule-takers is a tricky question of global power. Brexit is significant for the tangential role played in its discussions and negotiations on the place of global governance and globalisation, and the concrete meaning of 'Global Britain'. The lexicon or vocabulary of 'rule-makers' and 'rule-takers' comprises a vast multidisciplinary literature depicting the development of global power and standard-setting.[6] It is arguably a rather crude distinction between the regulatory giants globally and the 'rest'. It is a literature which in contemporary times is mainly focused upon Brazil, China, India and Mexico, working within the global legal order as a system of rules evolved from the so-called post-'Washington Consensus' to markets and the regulatory state. Some of the most significant case studies which are non-legal fixate upon very specific regions (e.g. developing countries) and a select number of sectors (e.g. space, financial services, international trade and investment).[7] It is notable that much of this literature is not legal in its focus but rather centred on power and government. Global governance literature is atypically not interested in the mechanisms or procedures of law. Much of the literature focuses upon the size of China and its emerging role in the global legal order as it seeks to establish its own place.[8] However, notably such developments as the Belt and Road Initiative (BRI) are seen to take place without the need for law, treaties or courts.[9] This feeds into the mode of analyses thus central to depicting rule-makers and takers. It is striking also that the EU is *not* historically part of this literature and emphasises its recent origins as a literature. A 'rule-taker' is considered universally to be an adverse state of affairs where the power dynamic puts the rule-taker at a position of less influence, authority and significance than the 'rule-maker', a point only tacitly raised to date in most UK debates.[10] However, there is a certain over-simplification of such debates to portray a state of affairs as a binary 'either' or 'e-ither'.

Early on in the Brexit negotiations, Empire 2.0 or a significant revival of the Commonwealth as a rule-making organisation, was mooted with a view to the UK become a global rule-maker with the capacity to take on the EU. It is in discrete sectors, such as financial services, that the

UK is portrayed as a potential rule-maker.[11] In particular, the UK Government appears to advance global rule-making aspirations in sectors where the EU has yet to advance its agenda or where it is highly contested, for example, Artificial Intelligence.[12] One important example of rule-taking as a starting point for UK law is data. Data rules relating to digital technology also increasingly constitutes a complex set of policies where the EU's regulatory forces are extensive. The advent of the EU as a global data actor has generated significant debates on the force and reach of the EU's General Data Protection Regulation (GDPR), its adequacy processes, the place of digital trade in its new generation trade agreements, etc.[13] One of the most early and detailed legal exchanges taking place at the time of writing in the EU–UK trade negotiations relates to data adequacy.[14] This is in response to universal views of business, industry and parliament that EU data standards were high and worth aspiring to and too difficult to emulate as a rule-maker or liable to cause unnecessary regulatory replication. There, the UK has already sought to show extensively how it has essentially equivalent laws to the EU and has sufficiently high standards of data flows, protections, institutions and other GDPR related factors to show 'adequacy'. Data is a good example of where it has placed the language of 'rule-taking' more centrally in debates where the EU's impact upon its partners is subject to new levels of analysis. Brexit is likely to intensify such sectoral debates but also pose challenges as to understanding the dynamics of rule-making and taking in such bifurcatory terms.

23.3 Law and EU IR: on the taking and receiving of EU law internationally

23.3.1 'Reach' and EU law

The global reach of EU law nowadays denotes a variety of situations where the EU acts as a 'rule-exporter' to many countries, organisations and associations and gives its rules or compels others to take them, setting high standards or cohesive standards for a block of half a billion consumers, traders and enterprises and so on. It is of much significance that the UK will begin with the highest level of EU law 'reach'. Research indicates that market-based views on moving *away* from this position will be extremely difficult, if not impossible.

The reach of EU law is charted in literature over several decades and is distinctively developed often by US and Swiss-based authors as much as from EU-based authors/scholars across a range of disciplines rendering it a rich field of global thought.[15] Its development by authors *outside* the EU in its analysis often of third countries also has the advantage of bringing added global value as 'external thought' or 'thinking' to current debates. Thus the global reach of EU law through rule-transfer denotes how the EU has adopted rules and standards governing half a billion citizens, traders, business, companies and markets, across a range of subject areas, that other polities, markets and businesses have in turn adopted voluntarily or have been compelled to do so out of sheer necessity.

The reach of EU law encompasses the perceived 'spillover' effect of EU regulatory standards on US rules in the realm of, inter alia, genetically modified foods, data privacy standards and chemical safety rules (the so-called 'Brussels effect');[16] the extent to which EU legal rules are actually transplanted in the US, for example, the transposition of EU environmental standards in California, Boston and Maine ('From Brussels with Love');[17] the incorporation of EU vehicle emissions standards into Chinese and Japanese law;[18] EU makeup standards in Malaysia and innovative transfers of policies from the EU to the US in socio-economic fields of law.[19] It arguably also spans the internationalisation of EU law and Europeanisation of international law as a phenomenon in non-economic fields of law, as much as technical and administrative procedures and standards in, for example, environmental and food law.[20]

The size and scale of the EU, as a market and as a polity, governing half a billion people and businesses, has thus generated forms of 'rule-transfer'.[21] Some draw a distinction between the EU's transfer of legal rules and governance practices externally, for example, the EU's uploading of its governance to the UN Convention on Disabilities.[22] Additionally, there is a body of *non-legal* scholarship describing the diffusion of values specifically from the EU to the US legal order across legal fields, notably in data protection and data privacy, not understood as rule-transfer but clearly linked thereto.[23] Moreover, from areas as diverse as the internal market,[24] EU refugee law,[25] data protection,[26] EU environmental law, EU banking and financial services and taxation law,[27] fundamental rights, to EU competition law,[28] it is now perceived as a commonplace occurrence of EU law that it has global reach through novel forms of extra-territoriality. It is also understood to be commonplace that international lobbyists have set up business in Brussels, often in US law firms' European offices located there, to engage in lobbying and try to influence from the 'inside'.[29] Increasingly, the EU has a broad understanding of international civil society which it must engage with in third countries, for example, in trade agreements. The degree to which the UK will become immersed or affected by this remains unworkable at the time of writing but is probably reasonable to assume its likely integration into the span of EU law in these facets is beyond dispute.

23.3.2 'Reach' and its methodology

As Cremona and Scott outline, there is a significant challenge in formulating EU global action and its effects.[30] This is particularly the case with respect to some of the most complex topics of global governance such as migration, data, the environment and financial services, where the EU seeks to have global effects and lead global change despite, among other things, asymmetric competence or weak institutional formulations.[31] The movement of EU rules beyond borders is not ultimately well understood as an interdisciplinary ideal.[32] It seems likely that some of these key topics of global governance where the EU faces contestation in regulating with global effects but still exercises significant global effects, i.e. data, the environment and financial services will become challenging for the UK to resist their reach. Yet how will the depth of reach be understood?

One of the most controversial aspects of EU law remains its tendency to provoke convergence with entities not seeking, wanting or striving for the active components of convergence. Litigation as to territory often shows the 'worst' side of the global reach of EU law or projected convergence.[33] It is precisely the active component of the movement of rules here as an idea that attracts the most controversy. Naturally, the Court of Justice of the European Union (CJEU) has downplayed any understanding of extra-territoriality in this context. Yet, territory and global reach constitute one of the murkiest dimensions of the reach of EU law.[34] In the EU's manifold new trade negotiations, the place of the reach of EU law is never openly advertised or advanced. There is much misconception also concerning the scientific contours of convergence and what is envisaged and proposed with third country partners and contrasted with what is agreed as an outcome.[35] The methodology of depicting the global dimension of EU law has never been more topical but it is also important to note how so many scholars can also be at cross-purposes with one another highlighting the methodological challenges of the span of EU law.[36] How forceful should one suggest EU successes or failures are has a large bearing upon the outcome normatively. Is the EU a good global actor in migration in the same way as climate change? It is arguably hard to put forward such a thesis. Is the EU a weak or strong global data actor? Arguably that depends upon the situation or condition.[37] As the external dimension of EU law evolves and possibly EU IR law can be considered to have achieved many successes, the means thereof often are highly contestable. It remains to be seen which aspects of EU law are of most significance post-Brexit.

The many metrics of 'reach' will likely assume greater salience in UK debates on policy going forward. It seems also likely that dispute will emerge as to key areas of contestability such as data, environment and financial services which will explain better the contours of this reach.

The chapter next turns to non-legal dimensions of the reach of EU rules in political economy scholarship.

23.4 Political economy: the reach of EU rules in trade agreements with third parties

23.4.1 Overview

The Brexit debate will be centred in the future at some point on measuring how much acceptance of and alignment with EU law *has* taken place and will continue to take place. There is a vast literature on this which is explored here. The EU shifted its focus in trade in recent times to preferential trade agreements and addressing regulatory barriers to trade and it has evolved into a significant global trade actor. In particular, it has sought to pursue regulatory convergence since 2006 in its Global Europe Communication, seeking 'regulatory convergence wherever possible'.[38] Some draw distinctions between regulatory coordination, convergence and harmonisation but it is not watertight and some equate harmonisation with the adoption of EU rules.[39] As the Organisation for Economic Co-operation and Development (OECD) states, just as the distinction between convergence and harmonisation can be blurred, so too can the distinction between convergence and equivalence, where the former will require the latter.[40] Also, as Young states, regulatory coordination is politically and administratively more complicated than traditional trade liberalisation. Changes to regulations may require legislature to change domestic laws or regulators to adopt new rules. For these reasons, international regulatory coordination is very complex and rare.[41] This complexity opens up the possibilities for actors such as the EU, which it has readily sought to exploit. Thus, the idea that EU law promotes alignment or convergence is in itself not at all remarkable given some of the core strengths of EU law and its single market and related rules. Yet it is much more nuanced than mere exportation.

The EU's product standards are considered to be particularly high and strict,[42] and the Commission has in the past emphasised encouraging others to adopt EU standards so as to liberalise trade with its partners.[43] The EU also has developed robust rules governing financial services and has engaged actively in international cooperation as to these.[44] The EU's competition regulation and governance framework is recognised as one of the world's most sophisticated, and the EU has been particularly active in promoting international competition cooperation and international networks.[45] The EU has some of the most stringent protections of personal data globally[46] and has prompted others to follow suit and significant other countries are exploring their adoption, for example, China and the US.[47] The EU has also sought to promote a deeper social agenda by promoting both environmental and labour standards through trade agreements.[48] The EU has been regarded as the most strict global environmental regulator.[49] As a result it is perhaps not surprising that in these areas the EU can reasonably be expected to be trying to export and for which its power resources should be considerable.[50]

23.4.2 On alignment and the EU's third party agreements

The most detailed studies of alignment of third countries with EU law arguably come from the subject of political economy. Political economy scholars have recently attempted to show how EU 'next generation' trade agreements do not amount to rule-taking with EU law, instead they tend to promote 'alignment'.[51] Young has demonstrated that there is a 'common, if rather casual, assumption' that the EU exports its regulations through preferential trade agreements (PTAs).[52] Considering four early 'new generation' PTAs – those with Canada, Central America, Singapore and South Korea – and the Commission's opening position in the Transatlantic Trade and Investment Partnership negotiations, Young argues that the EU constantly does *not* end up exporting its rules to its partners.[53] Instead, he has sought to show how across a spectrum of regulatory issues there has been very limited regulatory coordination with third country partners. Moreover, where it has occurred, it has focused on establishing the equivalence of different rules or on convergence based on international, not European, standards. Indeed, he has shown that while a substantial strand of the EU-as-a-global-actor literature is concerned with the extent to which the EU seeks to promote its values and norms through trade policy consensus, it is, however, heavily influenced by PTAs with countries with particularly close economic and political relations with the EU – countries in its 'neighbourhood' and the African, Caribbean and Pacific (ACP) countries and should not be so easily assumed to exist with countries less economically and politically connected to the EU. Young's work is extremely significant for it shows the nuances that are required to investigate reach, depth and breadth. It goes without saying that the need for sectoral studies is critical – yet many are a pre-requisite?

Others argue that much more nuance needs to be imbedded into how the EU exports its rules, while viewing the dynamic of power advantage more selectively. For example, EU rules have created important 'first-mover' advantage in the absence of comprehensive rules of the partner, for example as occurred in privacy.[54] As Wolfe states, the key outcome of Young's work on whether the EU exports its regulations through PTAs is debateable in certain fields.[55] And so Wolfe would contend that the 'Brussels effect' trumps Young's nuancing of exportation. He contends that the regulatory power of EU law is much easier to accept economically, politically and legally as it is more obvious as a phenomenon in fields such as digital trade and data protection, given the high standards and force of the EU's GDPR and incentivisation of higher standards globally. As Wolfe thus states pithily, Young's work may be the rule – but Bradford may also prove an important exception in key fields.[56] These are significant debates in political economy as to the reach of EU rules which look only set to continue, not dissipate. These studies are significant attempts to evaluate regulatory transfer. They will become of even more significance post-Brexit, where metrics of the reach of EU law may become highly politicised and sensitive in certain sectors.

The chapter next turns to the *formal* place of EU law within and beyond international agreements.

23.5 EU human rights law 'in' international agreements: non-regression clauses, essential elements and conditionality in EU FTAs

23.5.1 Overview

The EU has a complex past when it comes to formal clauses in its trade agreements which arguably form the broader legal-political metric of the reach of EU law encompassing its rules, values and standards as to human rights. The exit of the UK from the ECHR and the 'reform' of UK human rights law has long been on the agenda of the UK Conservative Party.[57] Post-Brexit, these issues may assume a heightened salience with the UK in the event of complex divergences emerging. Many such clauses in trade agreements state that it is inappropriate for partners to weaken standards, for example to attract trade or investment.[58] As Bartels states, the EU's byzantine and historically lax approach to 'regression' clauses in trade agreements and their enforcement is a thorny challenge of the international dimension of Brexit.[59] Non-regression clauses can be defined as clauses placing barometers on regulatory levels but there is dispute about its precise meaning. It has arisen in the context of Brexit and an EU demand for regulatory alignment in the form of a level playing field regulatory and governance framework, to prevent the UK's regulatory race to the bottom and undercut the EU. Others interpret a request for a non-regression clause as a means to prevent more comparative advantage from a close 'competitor'.[60] Some might say that the EU's post-Lisbon free trade agreements (FTAs) with partners such as Japan or Canada set regression standards *internationally* rather than with reference to EU law.[61] Also, the link in post-Lisbon political framework agreements between Economic Partnership Agreements (EPAs) and Strategic Partnership Agreements (SPAs) is a key feature of the EU's deeper trade agenda.[62] If no political framework agreement exists, an essential elements clause included in FTAs and references to human rights norms and the commitments of parties to these also feature in the preamble of most EU agreements. Such a clause is usually complemented by provisions on cooperation and dialogue on human rights. Serious breaches of the essential elements clauses may trigger the suspension in whole or part of the overall framework agreement and all the linked agreements, including the trade agreement (non-execution clause). Since 1995, the EU has a systematic policy of including human rights clauses in all future international trade agreements, encompassing a vast range of EU partners. The core of the human rights clause is an essential elements clause which is given operate effect via a non-execution clause whereby a failure to fulfil an obligation under the agreement entitles the other party to take appropriate measures. They have been applied to cases involving gross human rights violations and military coups but have the potential to cover a range of matters.

Since 2008, the EU has introduced labour and environmental provisions in its trade agreements in sustainable development chapters requiring the parties to 'strive' for high levels of protection or 'ensure high levels of protection' (e.g. Cariform). There is also an obligation not to encourage trade or foreign investment to enhance or maintain a competitive advantage by lowering levels of protection. The EU agreements provide for varying degrees of civil society involvement in monitoring these provisions.[63] For example, in early 2020, after a rigorous multi-level evaluation, the European Commission withdrew part of the tariff preferences granted to Cambodia under the EU's 'Everything But Arms' (EBA) trade scheme due to the serious and systematic violations of the human rights principles enshrined in the International Covenant on Civil and Political Rights.[64]

There are significant variances here that are of note. It is difficult to extrapolate more from this than the fact that the reach of EU law within international agreements is immense but also highly variable and multi-level.[65]

The chapter briefly looks next at two of the EU's latest and most developed FTAs, with Canada and Japan, and their linkage clauses as to essential elements and non-regression and their likely application and salience for the UK post-Brexit.

23.5.2.1 The EU–CETA SPA linkage

The EU–Canada Economic and Trade Agreement (CETA) has been hailed as the gold standard for trade agreements and considered as a World Trade Organization (WTO) plus agreement ready to address the new economy and behind the border aspects of economic interactions.[66] The former European Commissioner for Trade Cecilia Malmström vociferously emphasised the need for Canada to accept EU law standards in media postings throughout the negotiations and thereafter.[67] The relationship between the EPA and SPA in the EU–Canada relationship is thus of much note. A major research project studying the implementation of CETA in Canada affords interesting insights on the concept of acquisition of EU rules.[68] The EU–Canada SPA was signed in 2016.[69] It makes provision in its essential elements clause in Article 28.3: 'for a situation to constitute a "particularly serious and substantial violation"' of Article 2(1) the 'gravity and nature would have to be of an exceptional sort such as a coup d'État or grave crimes that threaten the peace, security and well-being of the international community'. It is linked to the EU–Canada (CETA) agreement whereby it states that 'a particularly serious and substantial violation of human rights or non-proliferation, as defined in paragraph 3, could also serve as grounds for the termination of the EU-Canada Comprehensive Economic and Trade Agreement (CETA)'. This serves as a high-water mark of EU linkages of an EPA and SPA as to fundamental rights with a developed country partner.

23.5.2.2 EU–Japan EPA and SPA linkage

By contrast, the EU and Japan agreed an EPA in 2018. The SPA (together with the EPA) was signed at the Tokyo summit on 17 July 2018.[70] The SPA represents a framework strengthening the overall partnership, by promoting political and sectoral cooperation and joint actions in more than 40 areas of common interest. The EU–Japan SPA and EPA are legally independent and separate. There are no legal 'linkage provisions' as SPA Article 43 (8) underscores. The SPA represents here institutionalised political/policy dialogue and secures the long-term mutual commitments, regardless of domestic politics. The SPA has not enhanced coercive power on either side – SPA matters will be handled through diplomatic negotiations, rather than legal threats. SPA and EPA legal linkage is practically none, apart from extreme and unlikely cases of serious violation of essential elements. Should that case arise, EPA termination remains legally possible, but politically impossible. Japan is an interesting case where the death penalty still exists, and where women's rights and labour rights vary greatly from the EU, unlike Canada, in very significant fundamental rights areas of EU law. Yet the lack of a linkage clause here between the documents does not reflect these realities.

The sliding scale of understanding the depth of these clauses and their variability is important for the future of UK–EU relations. They put important complications upon the question of how much EU law the EU exports and how much political pressure the EU exudes to accept EU standards, even if not precisely the EU's rules. This development is quite important in so far as it exposes a schism between partners and non-partners and the institutionalised dimensions of EU IR. There can be no 'correct answer' to the question of what these clauses actually mean as an overall policy given their considerable variability. Rather, the reach of EU rules, values and standards appears as a sliding scale with considerable bilateral variability, even with highly developed countries. It remains to be seen the extent to which these specific clauses evolve in the post-Brexit landscape and whether stricter or more general versions apply. They form the basis for potentially significant disputes to be resolved with the UK or form important political tools even if not legally capable of being satisfied. The diversity of approach with leading developed economies is of much concern and will not strengthen the EU case to act against the UK should such issues arise.

The UK and EU exchanged negotiation objectives and select texts in early 2020 and a draft UK–EU treaty text circulated by the EU in March 2020, although detailed relevant provisions were still not in existence at the time of writing. Nonetheless, the development of UK secession from the Council of Europe is far from a remote possibility. It remains to be seen how the final tests of the EU–UK treaty develop but, irrespective of the outcome, the existing precedents for essential elements and related clauses are highly problematic.

The EU's variable approach makes it a complex assessment to make as to the reach of EU law and the future of such clauses post-Brexit.

The chapter next turns to the UK internal laws applicable to Brexit and its withdrawal from the corpus of EU law.

23.6 The UK's view of the reach of EU law

23.6.1 The (UK) EU Withdrawal Act 2018

The UK Parliament commonly enacts *circa* 35–40 primary statutes per annum, and approximately 2,000 statutory instruments. Approximately 20,000–25,000 EU measures became part of UK law pursuant to the European Union (Withdrawal) Act 2018 (EUWA). The EUWA received Royal Assent on 26 June 2018. It represents an extraordinary and vast legislative exercise and its interpretation will add a new chapter to understanding rule-making, rule-taking, exportation of rules and the reach of EU law. EUWA has the intention still to repeal the European Communities Act 1972 and make other provision in connection with the withdrawal of the UK from the EU. EUWA purported to freeze EU law in time in the UK and preserve it, in some form of legal gymnastics exercise. Its attempt to freeze the content of an evolving subject, would have grounded UK law in subjects, fields and disciplines which may readily alter or change, raising many rule of law concerns.[71]

Post-exit EU case law raises many thorny issues on a practical level as to the reach of EU law. Many thousands of EU laws will be retained pursuant to sections 2–4 of the EUWA. These rules will continue to exist in the EU and will be interpreted by the EU courts. While the logic of exit from the EU demands that we should not be bound by such post-exit CJEU rulings, hence section 6(1), such rulings may be uncontroversial and helpful for section 6(2) gave the UK courts discretion to take cognisance of CJEU rulings, and acts done by other EU entities, that might affect retained law. After significant controversies as to when courts would find it appropriate to have regard to CJEU jurisprudence, the text was amended as to the interpretation of retained EU law, section 6.6 thus provided that pre-Brexit judgments of the CJEU would continue to be binding on UK courts and only the UK Supreme Court could depart from those judgments. Section 6(3)–(6) stated: 'a court or tribunal may have regard to anything done on or after exit day by the European Court, another EU entity or the EU so far as it is relevant to any matter before the court or tribunal'. The key distinguishing criterion here was relevance and it gave discretion to the UK courts to draw upon such case law. While authorisation to the judiciary may appear unnecessary and indeed pointless, as Craig states, there are practical reasons for such wording in so far as

> the UK will be retaining the self-same provisions in UK law, and therefore it is more likely that UK courts might derive assistance from EU case law. This is more especially so where the UK commits to a regime of 'equivalence' with EU regulations, which will be jeopardised if UK law departs to any significant degree from the interpretation afforded to the EU rules.[72]

23.6.2 European Union (Withdrawal Agreement) Act 2020: post-exit CJEU case law

However, a significant amendment to the EUWA was made by the European Union (Withdrawal Agreement) Act 2020 in Part 4 thereof in section 26. In a new clause on 'interpretation of retained EU law and relevant separation agreement law' the Act dramatically widens the possibilities of courts in the UK departing from CJEU case law. It is alleged to blur the distinction between the independent judiciary and executive by giving powers to adopt secondary legislation to do several things.[73] It widens the list of courts and tribunals not bound by retained EU caws law; it regulates the extent to which or circumstances in which a Court or tribunal is not to be bound by retained by EU case law; and it sets out the test which would apply in deciding whether to depart from any retained EU case law including considerations relevant to any court applying the test for when to depart from such case law. However, the section also provides a list of the judiciary as to which a minister must consult. The Act of 2020 tries to put clearer water between those following EU law and those not and shows that it is an incredibly complex task 'to fend off' the forces of EU law. The retrospective time-freeze approach adopted in UK law could become a highly artificial exercise and with little substantive legal rationale.[74]

23.7 Conclusions

Brexit is likely to become a highly unique instance of the global reach of EU law, *starting* from levels of alignment that are unprecedented in the global legal order. Recent empirical work from political economy scholars suggests that global reach or the Brussels Effect does not happen with partners and is misunderstood as to its institutional format. Clearly, the EU advocates more than rule-transfer to prospective and current partners. Brexit constitutes a microcosm of such developments.

The reach of EU law is not a precise science or art but its reach can be documented in many ways. It differs vastly across subject fields and disciplines. A sharply variable range of methodologies is applied across disciplinary boundaries to understand how EU law has global reach. Brexit is an extraordinarily complex tale anyway never mind to isolate precisely how the reach of rules applies. Brexit may amount to the most significant form of global reach ever – but it is likely to be contested, for example, politically, legally and/or socially. The capacity of EU negotiators and EU institutions to communicate the effects of the reach of EU law upon prospective partners or, alternatively, to communicate clearly alignment criteria is a significant future research agenda, never mind with a former Member State integrated in EU law to the highest level. Still, degrees of regulatory alignment appear as the main hallmark of EU negotiations worthy of exploration. Part of the methodological challenges of the global reach of EU law or the Brussels effect is its temporal measurement and how it is understood. It is an outcomes-based idea, beyond Europeanisation and by definition probably is only accurately understood as a fait accompli.

The impossibility of the repeal of EU standards and rules is a likely outcome of globalisation, not Brexit, where many international standards increasingly replicate EU standards, and EU standards and rules are obligated to incorporate, replicate and help improve international standards carefully.[75] The UK also faces the veritable impossibility of repeal of many EU rules and standards unlike any other third country where so many businesses, associations, trade bodies etc., have EU rules inbuilt into their systems, organisations and practices. There is a significant danger that the reach of EU law is grossly underestimated and how it could become a punitive dimension of future political discourse. The UK Act as a 'repeal' mechanism was quickly overshadowed by the need for legal certainty and stability through the incorporation of EU law. Domestic efforts in legislation to temper the contours of interpretative powers are mostly political acts for domestic consumption and little regard appears to be had for the cognitive dissonance arising from retaining vast quantities of EU law that will become outdated, and maintaining an awkward legal and political hold over this situation.

It is striking that the reach of EU law outside trade agreements, or required alignment with EU law with third country partners in trade agreements, is not framed clearly by the EU. The

EU has seldom been depicted in emerging literature. It is also worth stating that so-called essential elements clauses commonly found in EU trade agreements or SPAs alongside new generation framework agreements do not 'pin' the conduct of the third country to comply with all EU law or even sectorally. Brexit has exposed many of these under-explored nuances in the search for clarity on what a withdrawing former Member State can and should expect in negotiations. There are likely no easy solutions but it seems abundantly clear that there will be significant reach of EU law across the Channel post-Brexit, even if not mediated through the language of rule-taking.

Notes

1 Ian Manners, 'Normative Power Europe: A Contradiction in Terms?' (2002) 40 Journal of Common Market Studies 235.
2 Anu Bradford, *The Brussels Effect: How the European Union Rules the World* (Oxford University Press 2020).
3 Karen Smith, 'The European Union in an Illiberal World' (2017) 116 Current History 83.
4 Joris Larik, 'The EU's Global Strategy, Brexit and "America First"' (2018) 23 European Foreign Affairs Review 343.
5 Sebastian Steingass, 'Too Effective for Europe: The UK Norm Advocacy and the Case of EU International Cooperation' (2019) 58 Journal of Common Markey Studies 384.
6 See for an overview Anna Triandafyllidou, *Global Governance from Regional Perspectives* (Oxford University Press 2017); Scott Kennedy (ed) *From Rule Takers to Rule Makers: The Growing Role of Chinese in Global Governance* (Indiana University Research 2012).
7 Charles Lees, 'Rule Makers and Rule Takers: On Volkspartei Adaptation and Strategy' (2010) 19 German Politics 89; David Skidmore, *The Unilateralist Temptation in American Foreign Policy* (Routledge 2011); Jenny Clegg, 'China at the Global Summit Table: Rule-Taker, Deal-Wrecker or Bridge-Builder?' (2011) 17 Contemporary Politics 447; Henry Gao, 'China's Ascent in Global Trade Governance: From Rule Taker to Rule Shaker, and Maybe Rule Maker?' in Carolyn Deere-Birkbeck (ed), *Making Global Trade Governance Work For Development* (Cambridge University Press 2011) 153, 162, 167–172; Lazslo Bruszt and Gerald A McDermott, 'Integrating Rule-Takers: Transnational Integration Regimes Shaping Institutional Change in Emerging Market Democracies' (2012) 19 Review of International Political Economy 742; José Célio Silveira Andrade and José Antônio Puppim de Oliveira, 'The Role of the Private Sector in Global Climate and Energy Governance' (2015) 130 Journal of Business Ethics 375; Daniel S Hamilton, 'Rule-Makers or Rule-Takers? An American Perspective on Transatlantic Trade and Investment Partnership' (2016) 21 European Foreign Affairs Review 365; Kenneth W Abbott, David Levi-Faur and Duncan Snidal, 'Theorizing Regulatory Intermediaries: The RIT Model' (2017) 670 Annals of the American Academy of Political and Social Science 14; Jonathan Bonnitcha, 'International Investment Arbitration in Myanmar: Bounded Rationality, But Not as We Know It' (2017) 18 Journal of World Investment & Trade 974; Sufian Jusoh, Muhammad Faliq Abd Razak and Mohamad Azim Mazlan, 'Malaysia and Investor–State Dispute Settlement: Learning From Experience' (2017) 18 Journal of World Investment & Trade 890; Romesh Weeramantry, 'International Investment Law and Practice in the Kingdom of Cambodia: An Evolving "Rule-Taker"?' (2017) 18 Journal of World Investment & Trade 942; Duncan Robinson, 'From Rule-Maker to Rule-Taker' *Financial Times* (London, 30 March 2017).
8 For example Gao (n 7); Pak K Lee, Gerald Chan and Lai Ha Chan, 'China in Darfur: Humanitarian Rule-Maker or Rule-Taker?' (2012) 38 Review of International Studies 423; Su-Yan Pan, 'China's Approach to the International Market for Higher Education Students: Strategies and Implications' (2013) 35 Journal of Higher Education Policy and Management 249; Scott Kennedy (ed), *From Rule Takers to Rule Makers: The Growing Role of Chinese in Global Governance* (Indiana University Research 2012); Leïla Choukroune, 'China and the WTO Dispute Settlement System' (2012/1) China Perspectives 49.
9 For example, Markus Brunnermeier, Rush Doshi and Harold James, 'Beijing's Bismarckian Ghosts: How Great Powers Compete Economically' (2018) 41 Washington Quarterly 161; Julien Chaisse and Mitsuo Matsushita, 'China's "Belt and Road" Initiative: Mapping the World Trade Normative and Strategic Implications' (2018) 52 Journal of World Trade 1, 163–185; Heng Wang, 'China's Approach

to the Belt and Road Initiative: Scope, Character and Sustainability' (2019) 22 Journal of International Economic Law 29.

10 Ibid.

11 Anne Deighton, 'Norwegians Cannot See the UK as a Rule-taker' *Financial Times* (London, 19 December 2018); Jon Rees, 'City Observers, Lobbyists: UK Cannot Become a Financial Rule-Taker after Brexit' *SNL European Financials Daily* (Charlottesville, 24 July 2018); Simon Wolfson 'Brexit Britain should be a Rule-Taker on Goods, but not Services' *Financial Times* (London, 3 June 2018).

12 *The Economist*, 'Britain's Regulatory-Divergence Dilemma' (1 February 2020) www.economist.com/britain/2020/02/01/britains-regulatory-divergence-dilemma accessed 1 April 2020; UK Government, 'AI Sector Deal' www.gov.uk/government/publications/artificial-intelligence-sector-deal/ai-sector-deal accessed 21 May 2019.

13 For example, Gráinne De Burca, 'Introduction to the Symposium on the GDPR and International Law' (2020) 114 AJIL Unbound 1; Robert Wolfe, 'Learning about Digital Trade: Privacy and E-Commerce in CETA and TPP' (2019) 18 World Trade Review 63; Bradford (n 2).

14 UK Government, 'Explanatory Framework for Adequacy Discussions' (12 March 2020) www.gov.uk/government/publications/explanatory-framework-for-adequacy-discussions accessed 1 April 2020.

15 Joanne Scott, 'From Brussels with Love: The Transatlantic Travels of European Law and the Chemistry of Regulatory Attraction' (2009) 57 American Journal of Comparative Law 897; Anu Bradford, 'The Brussels Effect' (2012) 107 Northwestern University Law Review 1; Anu Bradford, 'The Brussels Effect: The Rise of a Regulatory Superstate in Europe' (Chicago's Best Ideas Lecture, 2012) https://chicagounbound.uchicago.edu/chicagos_best_ideas/26 accessed 1 April 2020; Alasdair Young, 'The European Union as a Global Regulator? Context and Comparison' (2015) 22 Journal of European Public Policy 1233; Anu Bradford, 'Exporting Standards: The Externalization of the EU's Regulatory Power via Markets' (2015) 42 International Review of Law and Economics 158. See also Elaine Fahey, *The Global Reach of EU Law* (Routledge 2016); Bradford (n 2).

16 Young (n 15); Bradford, 'Exporting Standards' (n 15).

17 Scott (n 15).

18 Mathieu Rousselin, 'But Why Would They Do That? European External Governance and the Domestic Preferences of Rule Importers' (2012) 8 Journal of Contemporary European Research 470.

19 For example, Katerina Linos, *The Democratic Foundations of Policy Diffusion: How Health, Family, and Employment Laws Spread Across Countries* (Oxford University Press 2013).

20 Joana Mendes, 'EU Law and Global Regulatory Regimes: Hollowing Out Procedural Standards?' (2012) 10 International Journal of Constitutional Law 988.

21 Sandra Lavenex and Frank Schimmelfennig, 'EU Rules Beyond Borders: Theorizing External Governance in European Politics' (2009) 16 Journal of European Public Policy 791.

22 Grainne De Búrca, 'The European Union in Negotiation of the UN Disability Convention' (2010) 35 European Law Review 174.

23 Gregory Shaffer, 'Globalisation and Social Protection: The Impact of EU and International Rules in the Ratcheting Up of US Data Privacy Standards' (2000) 25 Yale Journal of International Law 1; David Bach and Abraham L Newman, 'Self-Regulatory Trajectories in the Shadow of Public Power: Resolving Digital Dilemmas in Europe and the United States' (2004) 17 Governance 387; Mark A Pollack and Gregory C Shaffer, *When Cooperation Fails: The International Law and Politics of Genetically Modified Foods* (Oxford University Press 2009).

24 Piet Eeckhout, *The European Internal Market and International Trade: A Legal Analysis* (Oxford University Press 1994); Marise Cremona, 'The European Union as a Global Actor: Roles, Models and Identity' (2004) 41 Common Market Law Review 553.

25 Hélène Lambert, Jane McAdam and Maryellen Fullerton (eds), *The Global Reach of European Refugee Law* (Cambridge University Press 2013).

26 Cedric Ryngaert 'Symposium Issue on Extraterritoriality and EU Data Protection' (2015) 5 International Data Privacy Law 221.

27 Suzanne Kingston, 'Territoriality in EU (Taxation) Law: A Sacred Principle, or Dépassé?' in Joaschim Englisch (ed), *International Tax Law and New Challenges from Constitutional and Legal Pluralism* (IBFD 2015).

28 See Florian Wagner-von Papp, 'Competition Law, Extra-Territoriality and Bilateral Agreements' in Ariel Ezrachi (ed), *Research Handbook on International Competition Law* (Edward Elgar 2012).

29 For example, Emilia Korkea-Aho, '"Mr Smith Goes to Brussels": Third Country Lobbying and the Making of EU Law and Policy' (2016) 18 Cambridge Yearbook of European Legal Studies 45.

30 Marise Cremona and Joanne Scott (eds), *EU Law Beyond EU Borders: The Extraterritorial Reach of EU Law* (Oxford University Press 2019).
31 See 'Introduction' in Bradford (n 2).
32 Karina Shyrokykh and Davilė Rimkutė, 'EU Rules Beyond its Borders: The Policy-Specific Effects of Transgovernmental Networks and EU Agencies in the European Neighbourhood' (2019) 57 Journal of Common Market Studies 749.
33 See Case 266/16 *Western Sahara Campaign UK v Commissioners for Her Majesty's Revenue and Customs and Secretary of State for Environment, Food and Rural Affairs* EU:C:2018:118 or Case 363/18 *Organisation Juivre Europeenne Vignoble Psagot Ltd v Ministre de l'Economie et des Finances* EU:C:2019:954.
34 See Joanne Scott, 'The New EU Extra-Territoriality' (2014) 51 Common Market Law Review 1343.
35 See Young (n 15).
36 See cf Cremona and Scott (n 30).
37 De Burca (n 13); Elaine Fahey, 'The Global Dimension of the EU's AFSJ: On Internal Transparency and External Practice' (NYU Jean Monnet Paper, 2018).
38 Communication from the Commission to the Council, The European Parliament, The European Economic and Social Committee and the Committee of The Regions, 'Global Europe: Competing in the World' (Brussels, 2006) (COM 567 final).
39 Stephen Woolcock, '2014 EU Policy on Preferential Trade Agreements in the 2000s' (2014) 20 European Law Journal 718.
40 OECD, *International Regulatory Co-operation: Addressing Global Challenges* (OECD Publishing 2013) 55.
41 Ibid, 54.
42 Bradford, 'Exporting Standards' (n 15).
43 COM 567 final (n 38) 5, 9.
44 Elliott Posner, 'Financial Transformation in the European Union' in Sophie Meunier and Kathleen R McNamara (eds), *Making History: European Integration and Institutional Change at Fifty* (Oxford University Press 2007); cf David Howarth and Lucia Quaglia, 'Brexit and the Battle for Financial Services' (2018) 25 Journal of European Public Policy 1118.
45 Sophie Meunier and Kalypso Nicolaïdis, 'The European Union as a Conflicted Trade Power' (2006) 13 Journal of European Public Policy 906.
46 Graham Greenleaf, 'The Influence of European Data Privacy Standards Outside Europe: Implications for Globalization of Convention 108' (2012) 2 International Data Privacy Law 68, 68–70.
47 Wei Sheng, 'One Year after GDPR, China Strengthens its Data Protection Laws' (Technode, 19 June 2019).
48 Meunier and Nicolaïdis (n 45).
49 David Vogel, *The Politics of Precaution: Regulating Health, Safety, and Environmental Risks in Europe and the United States* (Princeton University Press 2012) 4–5.
50 Alasdair R Young, 'Liberalizing Trade, not Exporting Rules: The Limits to Regulatory Co-ordination in the EU's "New Generation" Preferential Trade Agreements' (2015) 22 Journal of European Public Policy 1253.
51 Ibid. See also Young (n 15).
52 Ibid, 1253.
53 That is, the EU's implemented PTAs with Central America (EU–CA) and South Korea (KOREU); its signed agreements with Canada (the Comprehensive Economic and Trade Agreement [CETA]) and Singapore (EU–S); and its position in the Transatlantic Trade and Investment Partnership (TTIP) negotiations with the United States.
54 Abraham L Newman and Elliott Posner, 'International Interdependence and Regulatory Power: Authority, Mobility, and Markets' (2011) 17 European Journal of International Relations 589.
55 Wolfe (n 13) 77–78.
56 Ibid, 78.
57 *Financial Times*, 'Data Case Defeat Increases Tory Pressure to Quit ECHR' (13 February 2020) www.ft.com/content/7daf254e-4e5c-11ea-95a0-43d18ec715f5 accessed 1 April 2020; *Guardian*, 'UK must Leave European Convention on Human Rights, says Theresa May' (25 April 2016) www.theguardian.com/politics/2016/apr/25/uk-must-leave-european-convention-on-human-rights-theresa-may-eu-referendum accessed 1 April 2020.
58 Lorand Bartels, 'Social Issues in Regional Trade Agreements: Labour, Environment and Human Rights' in Simon Lester, Bryan Mercurio and Lorand Bartels (eds), *Bilateral and Regional Trade Agreements* (Cambridge University Press 2015).

59 Ibid.
60 Daniel Boffey, 'EU will Seek "Non-Regression" Clause to Tie UK to Environmental Standards' *Guardian* (London, 10 April 2018).
61 Bartels (n 58).
62 European Parliament 'Human Rights in EU Trade Agreements: The Human Rights Clause and its Application' (EPRS Briefing July, 2019) www.europarl.europa.eu/RegData/etudes/BRIE/2019/637975/EPRS_BRI(2019)637975_EN.pdf accessed 1 April 2020.
63 At p 381.
64 The Commission's decision followed in-depth engagement with the Cambodian government and stakeholders. In particular, during the last 12 months, the Commission and the European External Action Service conducted fact-finding missions to Cambodia and held several meetings with the Cambodian authorities at both technical and political levels.
65 Katharina L Meissner and Lachlan McKenzie, 'The Paradox of Human Rights Conditionality in EU Trade Policy: When Strategic Interests Drive Policy Outcomes' (2019) 26 Journal of European Public Policy 1273.
66 Comprehensive Economic and Trade Agreement (CETA) between Canada, of the one part, and the European Union and its Member States, of the other part [2017] OJ L 11, 23–1079. Elaine Fahey, 'CETA and Global Governance Law' (2017) 2 European Papers 293–302; Robert Finbow, 'Implementing CETA: A Preliminary Report' (EU–Canada Network Policy Brief, 2019) https://carleton.ca/caneunet/wp-content/uploads/Robert-Finbow-Implementing-CETA-A-Preliminary-Report-Policy-Brief-August-2019.pdf accessed 1 April 2020.
67 Fahey (n 66).
68 Finbow (n 66).
69 Strategic Partnership Agreement (SPA) between the European Union and its Member States, of the One Part, and Canada, of the other Part [2016] OJ L 329, 45.
70 Agreement between the European Union and Japan for an Economic Partnership [2018] OJ L 330, 3–899; Council Decision (EU) 2018/1197 on the signing, on behalf of the European Union, and provisional application of the Strategic Partnership Agreement between the European Union and its Member States, of the one part, and Japan, of the other part [2018] OJ L 216, 1–3; Strategic Partnership Agreement between the European Union and its Member States, of the one part, and Japan, of the other part [2018] OJ L 216, 4–22.
71 See All Party Parliamentary Group on the Rule of Law 'Rule of Law Questions for the Repeal Bill' (APPG Meeting Report, 4 July 2017) www.biicl.org/documents/1700_2017-07-11_-_appg_report_4_july_2017_-_repeal_bill.pdf?showdocument=1 accessed 1 April 2020; Ian Forrester, 'European Union Law in the UK after Brexit' (2018) 23 Judicial Review 45; Mark C Elliott and Stephen Tierney, 'Political Pragmatism and Constitutional Principle: The European Union (Withdrawal) Act 2018' (21 September 2018) forthcoming in Public Law; University of Cambridge Faculty of Law Research Paper No 58/2018, https://ssrn.com/abstract=3252985 accessed 1 April 2020; Martin Brenncke, 'Statutory Interpretation and the Role of the Courts after Brexit' (2019) 25 European Public Law 637; Sionaidh Douglas-Scott, 'The Constitutional Implications of the EU (Withdrawal) Act 2018: A Critical Appraisal' (Queen Mary School of Law Legal Studies Research Paper, 2019) https://ssrn.com/abstract=3316710 accessed 1 April 2020; UK Parliament 'The Status of Retained EU Law' (30 July 2018) https://researchbriefings.parliament.uk/ResearchBriefing/Summary/CBP-8375 accessed 1 April 2020. Law that has been retained pursuant to ss 3 and 4 EUWA can be modified by primary legislation. It can also be modified by subordinate legislation, if it is made under a power which permits such modification by virtue of Henry VIII clauses, which enable subordinate legislation to override primary legislation; any other provision made by or under the EUWA; any provision made by or under an Act of Parliament passed before, and in the same session as, the EUWA; or any provision made on, or after, the passing of the EUWA by or under primary legislation. Paul Craig, 'European Union (Withdrawal) Bill: Legal Status of EU Retained Law' (UK Constitutional Law Association, 2018) https://ukconstitutionallaw.org/ accessed 1 April 2020. Stephen Laws, 'Giving "Deemed" Domestic Law Status to Retained EU Law' (UK Constitutional Law Association, 2018) https://ukconstitutionallaw.org/ accessed 1 April 2020; Paul Craig, 'Constitutional Principle, the Rule of Law and Political Reality: The European Union (Withdrawal) Act 2018' (2019) 82 Modern Law Review 319; Steve Peers, 'The Withdrawal Agreement Act: Implementing the Brexit Withdrawal Agreement in the UK (EU Law Analysis, 2020) http://eulawanalysis.blogspot.com/2020/02/the-withdrawal-agreement-act.html accessed 1 April 2020.

72 Craig, 'Constitutional Principle' (n 71).
73 Ibid.
74 Eric Maurice, 'European Law will Apply "For Years" in the UK, says EU Judge' *EU Observers* (Brussels, 25 July 2017); Elaine Fahey, 'Brexit and the Global Reach of EU Law' (2017) 20 Irish Journal of European Law 16.
75 Fahey (n 74).

Index

Page numbers in *italics* denote figures.

For Product Safety Concerns and Information please contact our EU representative GPSR@taylorandfrancis.com
Taylor & Francis Verlag GmbH, Kaufingerstraße 24, 80331 München, Germany

www.ingramcontent.com/pod-product-compliance
Ingram Content Group UK Ltd.
Pitfield, Milton Keynes, MK11 3LW, UK
UKHW050232200926
475702UK00020B/2986
9780367610326